NEW YORK REVIEW BOOKS
CLASSICS

THE JOURNAL

HENRY DAVID THOREAU (1817–1862) was born and
lived the greater part of his life in Concord, Massachusetts.
He studied at Harvard, where he became a disciple of
Emerson, and after graduating in 1837 returned to Concord
to teach school with his brother. In Concord, he became
acquainted with the members of the Transcendentalist Club
and grew especially close to Emerson, for whom he worked
as a handyman. Thoreau also began to write for *The Dial*
and other magazines, and in 1839 he made the boat trip that
became the subject of his first book, *A Week on the Concord
and Merrimack Rivers* (1849). On July 4, 1845, he moved into
the hut he'd constructed on Walden Pond, where he remained
until September 6, 1847—a sojourn that inspired his great
work *Walden*, published in 1854. In the 1850s, Thoreau
became increasingly active in the abolitionist cause, meeting
John Brown at Emerson's house in 1857 and, after the attack
on Harpers Ferry, writing passionately in Brown's defense.
Short trips to Maine and Cape Cod resulted in two post-
humously published books (*The Maine Woods* and *Cape
Cod*), and a visit to New York led to a meeting with Walt
Whitman. Suffering from tuberculosis, Thoreau traveled
to the Great Lakes for the sake of his health, but finding
no improvement and realizing that he was going to die,
returned home to Concord to put his papers in order and

to write his final essays, drawing as always on the Journal, the work that was the source of all his other works and the defining undertaking of his adult life.

DAMION SEARLS is the author of *Everything You Say Is True*, a travelogue, and *What We Were Doing and Where We Were Going*, stories. He is also an award-winning translator from German, French, Norwegian, and Dutch, most recently of Rainer Maria Rilke's *The Inner Sky: Poems, Notes, Dreams* and Marcel Proust's *On Reading*. He has produced an experimental edition of Herman Melville's *Moby-Dick*, called *; or The Whale*, and his translation of the Dutch writer Nescio's stories is forthcoming from NYRB Classics.

JOHN R. STILGOE is the author of many books and the Robert and Lois Orchard Professor in the History of Landscape at Harvard University.

THE JOURNAL

1837–1861

HENRY DAVID THOREAU

Edited by
DAMION SEARLS

Preface by
JOHN R. STILGOE

NEW YORK REVIEW BOOKS

nyrb

New York

THIS IS A NEW YORK REVIEW BOOK
PUBLISHED BY THE NEW YORK REVIEW OF BOOKS
435 Hudson Street, New York, NY 10014
www.nyrb.com

The editor would like to thank the city of Lisbon, Portugal, and Het beschrijf's writers residency in Vollezele, Belgium, for support during the making of this book.

Library of Congress Cataloging-in-Publication Data
Thoreau, Henry David, 1817–1862.
 [Journal]
 The journal, 1837–1861 / by Henry David Thoreau ; preface by John R. Stilgoe ; edited by Damion Searls.
     p. cm. — (New York Review Books classics)
  ISBN 978-1-59017-321-3 (alk. paper)
 1. Thoreau, Henry David, 1817–1862—Diaries. 2. Authors, American
—19th century—Diaries. I. Searls, Damion. II. Title.
 PS3053.A2 2009
 818'.303—dc22

                              2009009758

ISBN 978-1-59017-321-3

Printed in the United States of America on acid-free paper.
10 9 8 7 6 5 4 3 2 1

CONTENTS

PREFACE

"To Pine Hill for chestnuts." And on the way an Irish-immigrant woman and her son, bent double under loads of firewood, Old World in appearance but doing "the squaw's part in many respects," encounter the solitary walker. Another day, "To owl's nest. The young owls are gone." Period. Fledglings flown. But the day after, a question recorded. "What if we feel a yearning to which no breast answers? I walk alone." Then some thoughts about frivolity, society, and personal shallowness. On the last day of one September, a musing about the color of leaves: "The white ash has got its autumnal mulberry hue." But then something more. "It is with leaves as with fruits and woods, and animals and men; when they are mature their different characters appear." And the next day, something else, down by the railroad track. "Just put a fugitive slave, who has taken the name of Henry Williams, into the cars for Canada."

Here find the private musings of a solitary seer, the odd man of Concord. "Hornets, hyenas, and baboons are not so great a curse to a country as men of a similar character," Thoreau decided one early-autumn day. But then again, he knew he had circumscribed his life, focused his energy within the town bounds of Concord, walking the edges as a surveyor, pacing the whole as a self-appointed visionary. "It is a charmed circle which I have drawn around my abode, having walked not with God but with the devil. I am too well aware when I have crossed this line."

What line? He knew the town boundary lines, knew enough to look beyond, to see "such near hills as Nobscot and Nashoba," the far-off glimmerings of others in the sunlight. He knew the paths and byways and shortcuts and railroad rights-of-way and the rivers along which he rowed and skated and swam. He knew the line dividing his private goals from "the mean and narrow-minded men" he scorned, as when one of sixty asked about buying a bearing orchard when he might have planted fruit trees thirty years earlier. Arrogant, supercilious, observant, but often doubting himself, he wrote for himself, averring that "most New England biographies and journals—John Adams's not excepted—affect me like opening of the tombs." And the tombs he meant lay in the Concord graveyard, not Luxor.

Winter prompted him to ponder journalizing. He moved about the house, from one sunny window to another. "My Journal is that of me which would else spill over and run to waste," but then again, maybe not. Another winter day, another vision of the book. "To set down such choice experiences that my own writings may inspire me and at last I may make wholes of parts." Journalizing is not journalism but "a distinct profession" rescuing details and truths from oblivion. "Contemplation of the unfinished picture may suggest its harmonious completion," every thought "a nest egg" a long time from hatching. "Thoughts accidentally thrown together become a frame in which more may be developed and exhibited. Perhaps this is the main value of a habit of writing, of keeping a journal,—that so we remember our best hours and stimulate ourselves." And in another January, years later, something similar but not the same: "In keeping a journal of one's walks and thoughts it seems to be worth the while to record those phenomena which are most interesting to us at the time." Indeed. "Such is the weather." The weather. That which shapes the Concord-circumscribed world, the affairs of just farmers and vagrants, the turn of seasons, the color of everything, the fall of light and shadow: the weather. Here is much about weather, including weather beyond the windowpane but not beyond the manuscript book, and in all weather, much of the footprints of Henry David Thoreau, the man who "thus *tracks himself*" in journal pages, he who worried at how much "is out of my line."

Faces bothered him. "In the evening went to a party. It is a bad place to go to,—thirty or forty persons, mostly young women, in a small room, warm and noisy." Women loud, women pretty. All jumbled, lost in the clacking roar. "I rarely look people in their faces," he concluded, before recording a far more pleasant encounter with an old farmer in the woods, farmer and journal writer eating crackers and cheese together. But then, a few months later, faces and looking again. "When a man asks me a question, I look him in the face. If I do not see any inquiry there, I cannot answer it." And will not. "His face expressed no more curiosity or relationship to me than a custard pudding." From parties and public encounters and most other "machinery of modern society," from what the Journal records as autumn melancholy, Thoreau fled to the woods, to solitude. "The society of young women is the most unprofitable I have ever tried. They are so light and flighty that you can never be sure whether they are there or not there." Like the owls, they are very often gone. Faces float in the pages that follow: they swirl like leaves in the slow-flowing Concord. They float faster in the rain. "Here is a rainy day, which keeps me in the house." Here is a Thoreau raw, colliding, recording, not the polished author of a book about life on the edge of Walden Pond.

"A man hangs out innumerable signs by which we may know him." Here stand signs, not all clear. "Bathing is an undescribed luxury. To feel the wind blow on your body, the water flow on you and lave you, is a rare physical enjoyment this hot day." He swam, then stood at the confluence of cold brook and warm pond. "When I thrust my arm down where it was only two feet deep, my arm was in the warm water of the pond, but my hand in the cold water of the brook." Another July, years later. "I find the water considerably colder at the bottom while I stand up to my chin, but the sandy bottom much warmer to my feet than the water. The heat passes *through* the water without being absorbed by it much." Sensory experience produces the joy and even ecstasy for which he notes, once, the Journal exists. He smelled pennyroyal while walking along a hillside, backtracked, sniffed, and found a tiny, solitary plant, trodden. He examined guns. Precisely. "Looked at a Sharp's rifle, a Colt's revolver, a Maynard's, and a Thurber's revolver." Some have smoother actions than others. "The last fires fastest (by a steady pull), but not so smartly." Not as nice in the hand, dry-fired or not. A warm day in December, "true Indian summer," and "the walker perspires" and enjoys the perspiration: a November years later brings weather "finger-cold" and air "so bracing and whole-some" it makes him cast stones on the first ice. And by that November, the journal writer eats differently, once avoiding meat, tea, coffee, "etc., etc.," because "it appeared more beautiful to live low and fare hard." But change swept his palate and diet and table. "I find myself somewhat less particular," and "grown more coarse and indifferent," more a gourmand and less the hoer and eater of beans.

"All this you will see, and much more, if you are prepared to see it,—if you *look* for it," he notes of a November rainy day when he walked out to Poplar Hill, what he asserts might be any hill. Look acutely, descry the "bright-red tops or crescents of the scarlet oaks," and delight. "Otherwise, regular and universal as this phenome-non is, you will think for threescore years and ten that all the wood is at this season sere and brown." So appears not the sign but the sign painter, the word colorist, the practical, frost-nipped-hands philosopher. "Objects are concealed from our view not so much because they are out of the course of our visual ray as because there is no intention of the mind and eye toward them." So emerges one core of the Journal. "We do not realize how far and widely, or how near and narrowly, we are to look. The greater part of the phenom-ena of nature are for this reason concealed to us all our lives." Jour-nal becomes prism. "The actual objects which one person will see from a particular hilltop are just as different from those which an-other will see as the persons are different." Transcendentalism slogs through mud, over hobble ice, uphill, outdoors, in bad weather. Transcendentalism grates, scrapes, works. "The scarlet oak must, in a sense, be in your eye when you go forth." The mind is its own paint pot, its own discovery, its own creator of serendipitous find-ing of rare plants and the disguised slave catcher lurking near the railroad depot.

"The colors are now: light blue above (where is my cyanometer? Saussure invented one, and Humboldt used it in his travels); landscape russet and greenish, spotted with fawn-colored plowed lands, with green pine and gray or reddish oak woods intermixed, and dark-blue or slate-color water here and there." So one May 1st apparition, recorded, and enlivened by "a strong, invigorating scent" up from the fresh meadows. But Thoreau knew the limits of words, even the limits of the well-disciplined eye. "We are armed with language adequate to describe each leaf in the field, or at least to distinguish it from each other, but not to describe a human character." But the pages following at least sketch Thoreau, making a hazy-mirror self-portrait, including such long, involved, despairing passages as that beginning "I once set fire to the woods." Here find the color of Thoreau, then the color illuminated and shaded by the circumscribed landscape and society of Concord and by the telegraph tapping out the weather in New York and Portland, the telegraph line not out of his line, not in the end.

"I would fain make two reports in my Journal, first the incidents and observations of to-day; and by to-morrow I review the same and record what was omitted before, which will often be the most significant and poetic part." So he wrote after decades of keeping the Journal, still musing on what he experienced, what he recorded, and what the record became, aging like winter apples. "The men and things of to-day are wont to lie fairer and truer in to-morrow's memory." Journal-writing conjures hyper-reality, then, enduring sharpness of shape that slices deeply time and again. "Often I can give the truest and most interesting account of any adventure I have had after years have elapsed, for then I am not confused, only the most significant facts surviving in my memory." What follows here is not the memory of Thoreau but his memory mine, his private store of promptings, his paint-pot personal notes, and his record of making and writing that record. "I now begin to pluck wild apples," interrupts one September entry. And here follows his harvest.

—John R. Stilgoe

INTRODUCTION

In 1837, David Henry Thoreau was twenty years old. He would soon begin to call himself Henry David but he never changed his name legally or officially, and throughout his life many people in Concord continued to call him "David Henry," Thoreau stubbornly correcting them. He graduated from Harvard College, where Ralph Waldo Emerson delivered his stirring Phi Beta Kappa address, "The American Scholar," on August 31; whether Thoreau attended the lecture is not known but he surely read and absorbed it, having already checked Emerson's manifesto *Nature* out of the library in April and in June, and the two men became close when Thoreau returned to his family home in Concord in the fall. Thoreau would live with his family for the rest of his life except for a short stay in New York, a couple of years helping out at the Emersons' while Ralph Waldo was away on lecture tours, and the two years, two months, and two days that he lived in a cabin he built for himself on Emerson's woodlot at Walden Pond. Perhaps more important than anything else that happened to him in 1837, Thoreau began to keep a journal: "'What are you doing now?' he asked. 'Do you keep a journal?' So I make my first entry to-day." The "he" in this first entry is undoubtedly Emerson.

Thoreau's journal started out as a notebook among others, for quotations, mini-essays, and poetry. He often tore out pages to use as drafts for his books, lectures, and essays, and for other reasons, so the first dozen years of the journal—chronologically more than half—survive only in fragments, sometimes secondhand (for example, from his first two volumes of 546 and 396 pages, neither of which survives, Thoreau selected a limited number of entries and recopied them in 1841, calling them "Gleanings—Or What Time Has Not Reaped Of My Journal"). He spent the 1840s honing his craft as a writer and published his first book, *A Week on the Concord and Merrimack Rivers*, in 1849, but the book was a commercial disaster, plunging him into debt (some practical consequences of this failure are described in the memorable entry of October 28, 1853; see p. 232). As a result, he redirected his ideas of authorship, of writerly vocation, and of the meaning of publication. Around 1850, he began to keep journal entries regularly and date them consistently; instead of tearing out pages, he preserved the volumes intact, making marginal list marks and copying the passages he wanted into other notebooks, drawing vertical lines through copied text. No longer a grab bag, the journal became the Journal: an investigation of dailyness, seasons, and the relationship between self and nature—a hybrid and incompletable book but a book in its own right nonetheless, with an ecology all its own.

This Journal is not literally what Thoreau wrote each day: he often wrote up entries days later, from notes, and as the cross-referencing footnotes show, he would also go back years later and make further additions and connections. Instead, the Journal is a record of what he and Nature did on a given day, and how those doings affected each other. In the course of his life Thoreau may have discovered a species of bream, perfected the technology of manufacturing pencils, and anticipated modern techniques of cranberry farming, but his most lasting discoveries were about the interactions of different systems: how the seasons affect water levels, how animals propagate seeds, how one growth of forest trees succeeds the previous one, how the lake affects the shore or the river the riverbanks, and, most centrally, how the life he led shaped Henry David Thoreau and vice versa. Emerson had four children, was a beloved lecturer, and connected well with other people, and he wrote about Self-Reliance; Thoreau never married, is not known to have had any lovers, and was naturally prickly, defensive, and off-putting, and the deepest and most passionate intelligence in his writing concerns connection and relation—Concord is not only the subject of a pun in the first line of *Walden,* it is Thoreau's main subject. (Then again, this dichotomy of character is too neat: Emerson, for instance, left his sick wife, Lidian, and their young children in Thoreau's care to go to Europe in 1847, writing coldly to Lidian, "I foresee plainly that the trick of solitariness never can leave me," while Thoreau wrote to Emerson, "Lidian and I make very good housekeepers. She is a very dear sister to me.... [Young Eddy Emerson] very seriously asked me, the other day, 'Mr. Thoreau, will you be my father?'" The extent to which one's attention outward and attention inward intermingle is always a deeper mystery than it may seem.) Thoreau writes with surprising perceptiveness and empathy about others—poor Irish laborers, escaped slaves he helped send north to Canada, fellow villagers—and in a deeper sense his writing, especially *Walden*, speaks to readers with extraordinary intimacy, making claims upon us that some of us enjoy and others reject. I think of Thoreau's cabin, along with Proust's cork-lined room, as the two iconic sites of literary communion, of burrowing into the heart of the reader by looking inward in solitude. (Proust too started off as a follower of Emerson's, and at one point planned to translate *Walden* into French; when he read excerpts in another translation, he praised them by saying: "It is as though one were reading them inside oneself, so much do they arise from the depths of our intimate experience.")

Thus the purpose of Thoreau's Journal was not simply to gather as many details and facts as possible but to provide his connecting, analogizing intelligence with more to connect—more to, as he would say, "turn into poetry." Readers, or at least critics, of Thoreau were slow to pick up on this synthesizing quality. Although long recognized as an important quarry for biographical information, a testing ground for Thoreau's other works, and a storehouse of some of the finest nature writing in the English language, the Journal was not often considered as a literary work of its own until the 1980s. There have been many editions of selected bits of the Journal, but it is a book ill served by selections because it is above all a book of rhythms: the long ebb and flow of the year and the quicker rhythms of Thoreau's roving from topic to topic. The present book—the largest one-volume edition yet published—is conceived as an abridgment, not a selection: it aims to preserve the feel of the Journal as a whole.

Some books are ill-served by abridgments, too, and admittedly much of what is most essential to this one is lost: its scope, its daily-ness. There is simply no way to streamline experiencing the fact that Thoreau wrote a longish essay about the events of the day, day after day, month after 80- or 100- or 120-page month. His life, as Hans Richter once said about Kurt Schwitters's, was more full of incident each day than the entire Trojan War, and any abridgment of, say, June 23, 1852, from nine pages down to one or two will lose a lot. That said, the premise and prerequisite of this edition is that much else essential about the Journal survives abridgment.

Since my primary goal has been to preserve the feel of the Journal as a book in its own right, I avoided surrounding the text with thumbnail biographies or explanatory notes—this edition can simply be read; supplementary information is easily available elsewhere; the volume is already long enough. Nor did I divide the Journal into calendar years or months, because it is not primarily an annal or chronicle. Some pauses to catch one's breath are useful, though, so there are chapter breaks, which I placed in the least extrinsic way possible by having them correspond to the physical volumes of Thoreau's handwritten original. (The sixteenth surviving hand-written volume, when he began his full-fledged journal practice, was labeled "III" by Thoreau; the previous one was labeled "II" and there is none surviving labeled "I." Throughout part two of the present edition, beginning with chapter III—that is, throughout the Journal proper—the chapter numbers and occasional chapter titles are how Thoreau labeled each of his physical notebooks.)

The early, notebooky years of the Journal are different in character than the rest, and I have abridged them drastically. Still, the differences have been rather overstated by writers on Thoreau. The same associative mind is at work, only with such a thin seedbed of facts to work from and explore the connections among that the results are necessarily more affected and "literary." It is only when Thoreau's experience, and the Journal itself, had snowballed to a large enough scope that he could use it fully:

Perhaps this is the main value of a habit of writing, of keeping a journal.... Having by chance recorded a few disconnected thoughts and then brought them into juxtaposition, they suggest a whole new field in which it was possible to labor and to think. Thought begat thought. (January 22, 1852)

The later years of the Journal, in turn, have often been dismissed as too facty, too scientific and not literary or philosophical enough. This, I think, is flatly not true. Thoreau is as concerned as ever to make the facts interesting, to see them in relation to himself and others. His notes are simply more detailed and specific than yours or mine would be, his patience irritating to those who do not share it, like the Concord farmer who saw him spend a whole day watching the bullfrogs (see the note on p. 493). But it is precisely because of Thoreau's patience that the animals came to him. The ideas too.

Seasons mattered deeply to Thoreau and I have tried to preserve the balance between the seasons, from his long summer walks to his heavier reading in the snowed-in winters. Months mattered to him too: his first book was organized as a week, and his second, *Walden*, as a year; the massive project Thoreau was building toward in the last years of his life, which he sometimes called his "Kalendar" (after John Evelyn), would have covered just about everything in the ecosystem—the "economy," in Thoreau's term—of Concord. I made sure to include one set of months less abridged than the rest, a representative Thoreau calendar with an extra March to fetch the year around:

March 1853 (pp. 178–193)
April 1856 (pp. 374–384)
May 1852 (pp. 131–142)
June 1851 (pp. 49–58)
July 1852 (pp. 149–162)
August 1854 (pp. 272–281)
September 1851 (pp. 71–84)

October 1857 (pp. 456–474)
November 1858 (pp. 519–531)
December 1856 (pp. 416–429)
January 1855 (pp. 293–307)
February 1860 (pp. 595–609)
March 1859 (pp. 544–559)

These 180 pages constitute a sort of book within the book and might fruitfully be read on their own. They are still abridged—those thirteen months in full would be twice the length of the book in your hands—but they let you see, in somewhat fuller form, what April meant to Thoreau, or July, or glorious October. Finally, of course, days are at the heart of any journal. Many readers, myself included, like to read a day's entry on the anniversary of that day, which is a good way to flip and browse in this book. However, I could rarely keep a day's entire entry, typically eight or ten or fifteen pages long. Whenever I did, I indicated it by putting the date in capital letters, thus any entry with an uncapitalized date is less than Thoreau's full entry, even long entries like August 30, 1856 (six pages here; twelve pages in full).

Across the arc of the Journal as a whole, I reflected Thoreau's changing interests; for the years when he was preoccupied with, say, turtles, I kept a lot of entries about turtles, and I always tried to keep enough texture to show, for example, his depression and reduced writing in 1855, after *Walden* was published. This is part of what I mean by trying to produce an abridgment of the whole, not just a selection of "the good bits." There are plenty of good bits here, of course, but the point is that they are not as good when torn out of context. To take one example, "The bluebird carries the sky on his back" (April 3, 1852, p. 121) is a great line: the bluebird comes with the spring and thus can said to bring it as much as vice versa; Thoreau reverses apparent cause and effect to emphasize interconnection, in a powerful visual rhyme that captures too how eagerly he welcomed the spring after the burden of hard New England winters. Of the four major one-volume selections from the Journal before the present edition, two keep only this one line from April 3, 1852; two omit the day altogether. I chose to keep another paragraph—with its sunlight and landscape full of light, the reflections from the grass, and Thoreau's locating himself "on the *back* of the hill"—because some alchemy of these details is what produced the poetic insight.

To abridge nine-tenths of the letter while preserving the spirit, I have had to cut not only entries but paragraphs and sentences within entries, sometimes even parts of sentences, splicing the remainders together. A few of these cuts are to make the text more readable: I omit Latin names from some of his lists of sightings, since this edition conveys his use of botanical terminology well enough; I tend to skip obscure allusions rather than footnoting them; Thoreau's cross-references often take the now-archaic form "*vide* 19th *inst.*," and I avoided replacing "*vide*" with "see" but saw no reason to keep "*inst.*"; and so on. The overwhelming majority of cuts, however, are solely for space, not to change the tone. For instance, Thoreau mentions the time and destination of his walks almost every day; I kept only enough to convey the rest. I abbreviated some of his longer lists, and indicated in brackets the scope of what was omitted. I condensed the thirty-nine pages on John Brown (October 19–22, 1859) into a few of the most powerful lines, then kept Thoreau's references to Brown in later entries, to suggest the depth of his engagement. The entry of September 6, 1858, is fourteen paragraphs long, and I kept half of one, with four sentences cut from the middle and the following phrase in brackets omitted: "It is much larger than what I saw before; is still abundantly in flower; four and a half feet high, [leaves, perhaps arundinaceous, eighteen inches long; panicle, nine inches long]." In all these cases and throughout the rest of the book, the goal of my editorial interventions was to let Thoreau's Journal speak for itself as much as possible, so rather than call attention to them with ellipses and give the book a patchwork appearance, I let them do their work in silence. (The interested reader can always check an entry against Thoreau's original; see the "About the Text and Suggested Reading" section for bibliographical information.)

Perhaps it would be helpful to look at one example in greater detail. The entry of May 23, 1853, four and a half pages long, is trimmed to a page in this edition (p. 200). I cut his dateline ("P.M.—To Ministerial Swamp") and a first general paragraph ("The poet must bring to Nature the smooth mirror in which she is to be reflected.... No genius will excuse him from importing the ivory which is to be his material"), matters which are conveyed elsewhere in this edition, and also the beginning of the day's details: "That small veronica (*V. arvensis*) by Mrs. Hosmer's is the same with that on the Cliffs; there is also the smooth or *V. serpyllifolia* by her path at the brook. This is the fifth windy day. A May wind—a washing wind. Do we not always have after the early thunder-showers a May storm?" and a few sentences more. I kept the sentence about lupines after the passage on "the *flavor* of my thoughts," to indicate the presence of concrete facts and avoid too much sententiousness, but cut the rest of the paragraph: "White-weed will open perhaps to-morrow or next day. For some time dandelions and mouse-ear have been seen gone to seed—autumnal sights. I have not yet seen a white oak (and put with it swamp white and chestnut) fairly in bloom." Another omitted half page follows, on dor-bugs, geum, and a fragrance "as if the vales were vast saucers full of strawberries, as if our walks were on the rim of such a saucer"; in my second paragraph I removed the sentence in brackets below, not for any fault of its own but only because the rest could survive without it:

> White clover. I see the light purple of the rhodora enlivening the edges of swamps—another color the sun wears. [It is a beautiful shrub seen afar, and makes a great show from the abundance of its bloom unconcealed by leaves, rising above the andromeda.] Is it not the most showy *high-colored* flower or shrub? Flowers are the different colors of the sunlight.

Finally, my last paragraph—the third-to-last paragraph of Thoreau's full entry—omits the sentences in brackets below:

> An abundance of pure white fringed polygalas, very delicate, by the path at Harrington's mud-hole. Thus many flowers have their nun sisters, dressed in white. At Loring's Wood heard and saw a tanager. That contrast of a *red* bird with the green pines and the blue sky! Even when I have heard his

note and look for him and find the bloody fellow, sitting on a dead twig of a pine, I am always startled. (They seem to love the darkest and thickest pines.) That incredible red, with the green and blue, as if these were the trinity we wanted. Yet with his hoarse note he pays for his color. I am transported; these are not the woods I ordinarily walk in. [He sunk Concord in his thought.] How he enhances the wildness and wealth of the woods! This and the emperor moth make the tropical phenomena of our zone. [There is warmth in the pewee's strain, but this bird's colors and his note tell of Brazil.]

The nuns in white after "the different colors of the sunlight" earlier, the trinity and vaguely Christlike "bloody" tanager, the "wildness and wealth of the woods," and finding tropical phenomena even in New England were what I felt needed to be preserved in this paragraph. Now all this attention to what is not included makes the present edition seem like a poor thing indeed—as of course it is, compared to the 7,000-page whole—but my hope is that the reader coming across page 200 in this book will not feel the lack.

Like any journal, Thoreau's is repetitive, which suggests natural places to shorten the text but these are precisely what need to be kept in order to preserve the feel of a journal, Thoreau's in particular. I trimmed many of Thoreau's repetitions but kept them whenever possible, because they are important to Thoreau and because they are beautiful. Sometimes he repeats himself because he is drafting, revising, constructing sentences solid enough to outlast the centuries. Sometimes he repeats himself because he is struck yet again by the sound of the crickets or the look of the moonlight or the misery of November. Such repeated reports, I imagine, pleased him, as someone who valued habit and character so highly. Sometimes, I suspect, he copied his own words because he liked to copy: no one's commonplace books could run to a million words— those are just the ones that survive, in addition to a two-million-word Journal, and enormous quantities of other writing—without a sheer love of sitting with pen in hand, a printed book and a blank page both open before him. Thoreau was a *writer*, and a re-writer. *Walden* went through seven drafts longhand.

Finally, I should say that this abridgment does not claim to be objective. I chose passages for inclusion not necessarily because of their importance to Thoreau's biography, or to cultural or natural history, but because I liked them: the book is shaped by my personal proclivities as much as by anything else—a preference for berrying over fishing, owls over muskrats, ice over sunsets, to name a few at random. Thoreau himself always insisted that this personal approach is the most truthful, the *only* truthful way to respond to the world:

> The reason why naturalists make so little account of color is because it is so insignificant to them; they do not understand it. But the lover of flowers or animals makes very much of color. To a fancier of cats it is not indifferent whether one be black or gray, for the color expresses *character*. (October 1861)

> There is no such thing as pure *objective* observation. Your observation, to be interesting, i.e. to be significant, must be *subjective*. The sum of what the writer of whatever class has to report is simply some human experience....The man of most science is the man most alive. (May 6, 1854)

In trying to preserve the character of Thoreau's book, then, I have not tried to repress the fact that I fancy it—it was less important to me to be objective than to be engaged and alive to what the book was doing to me as I read it. That's how Thoreau read too:

> I read of the Amazon that its current, indeed, is strong, but the wind always blows up the stream. This sounds too good to be true. (July 23, 1860)

You can see him, deep in his final illness, picturing himself on the river, feel him living what he reads.

For now, enough explanations. "As to criticism, man has never to make allowance to man; there is naught to excuse, naught to bear in mind. All the past is here present to be tried; let it approve itself if it can" (November 5, 1839). This abridgment is "a record of my discoveries," as Thoreau called his Journal, and it aims to be capacious enough for readers to make discoveries of their own.

—DAMION SEARLS

ABOUT THE TEXT AND
SUGGESTED READING

EDITIONS OF THE JOURNAL

The Journal of Henry David Thoreau, 14 vols., edited by Bradford Torrey and Francis H. Allen, was first published in 1906 and is currently in print in a two-volume edition from Dover Books, photoreduced but easily readable; it was also reprinted by Peregrine Smith Books in 1984 with volume introductions by Walter Harding and including a lost volume first published by Perry Miller as *Consciousness in Concord* in 1958. Any of these editions is highly recommended for the reader who wants 6,000 more great pages where this book came from. Although flawed and incomplete in certain ways, as later editors have often discussed, the 1906 edition provided more than enough material and its editors' free correction of spelling, capitalization, and so on was suitable for this abridgment, so the 1906/1984 edition was my main source text. I have simplified it occasionally, for example by either using Torrey and Allen's bracketed interpolations without the brackets or by omitting them altogether.

The material from Thoreau's 1861 trip to Minnesota (pp. 659–664) is taken from *The First and Last Journeys of Thoreau*, 2 vols., edited by F. B. Sanborn (Boston: Bibliophile Society, 1905).

The definitive scholarly edition of the Journal is being published in sixteen volumes by Princeton University Press in their series The Writings of Henry D. Thoreau. To date, seven volumes are in print, each costing around $100; the material not yet in book form is available online at www.library.ucsb.edu/thoreau/writings_journals.html. This edition is the only reliable one for scholars, and it contains a substantial amount of early material that was found or reconstructed since the 1906 edition. However, the text is scrupulously unmodernized—for example, leaving Thoreau's casual original punctuation untouched—so it was less suitable for the present edition. A few proper names omitted from the 1906 edition, out of consideration for people who were still alive or their families, were supplied from the Princeton Journal, and one rather dirty drawing suppressed in 1906 (p. 414) was restored from the Morgan Library's copy of Thoreau's Journal. My thanks to Elizabeth Witherell, editor of The Writings of Henry D. Thoreau, for her assistance.

A Year in Thoreau's Journal: 1851, edited and with an excellent introduction by H. Daniel Peck (Penguin Classics, 1993), presents a full, unabridged year of the Princeton Journal text in accessible form.

The four one-volume selections mentioned in my introduction are Odell Shepard, *The Heart of Thoreau's Journals* (1927, 1954; Dover, 1961); Laurence Stapleton, *H. D. Thoreau: A Writer's Journal,* with a very good introduction (Dover, 1960); Carl Bode, *The Selected Journals of Henry David Thoreau* (Signet, 1967); and Jeffrey S. Cramer, *I to Myself: An Annotated Selection from the Journal of Henry D. Thoreau* (Yale University Press, 2007), the largest of the four, with plentiful annotations but with roughly half the text of the present edition and at times, in my view, privileging historical information over the Journal itself. Walter Harding's *Selections from the Journals* (Dover, 1995) is fifty-five pages long. There are many other thematic selections available, on mountains, on cats and dogs, and so forth; several blogs are devoted to Thoreau's Journal as well.

OTHER WRITINGS BY THOREAU

Walden is his masterpiece. *Wild Fruits*, edited by Bradley P. Dean and first published by W. W. Norton in 2000, is a reconstruction of Thoreau's unfinished late work drawn largely from the Journal: a wonderful book and the best indication we are ever likely to have of where Thoreau's writing was going at the end of his life. *The Maine Woods* is his best straightforward travel writing.

Of the essays, my favorite is "Wild Apples": a powerful late essay and proof of Thoreau's undiminished powers, of how he continued to integrate facts of nature with facts of the spirit. It is contained in *Wild Fruits* but dispersed between the main text and appendices; it is better read in any of the collections of Thoreau's essays in which it appears. Essays covering the same ground as parts of the Journal include "Autumnal Tints," "Huckleberries," "Slavery in Massachusetts," and the three essays on John Brown.

Among the many online sources, www.library.ucsb.edu/thoreau is the most reliable.

BIOGRAPHIES

Robert Sullivan's recent *The Thoreau You Don't Know* (HarperCollins, 2009) is a lively and very good introduction to Thoreau and his times, especially useful for anyone who comes to Thoreau with the impression that he was basically a cranky, unpleasant person. Walter Harding, *The Days of Henry Thoreau* (1965, 1982; Princeton University Press, 1992), is the best chronicle of the historical facts; Robert D. Richardson, Jr., *Henry Thoreau: A Life of the Mind* (University of California Press, 1986), is the best source for Thoreau's reading and thought and the intellectual context of the Journal.

CHRONOLOGY

1817   David Henry Thoreau is born on July 12, in Concord, Massachusetts. Siblings: Helen (b. 1812), John (b. 1815), and Sophia (b. 1819).

1835   Catches the tuberculosis he will suffer from throughout his life,
and which will eventually lead to his death

1836   Teaches school with Orestes Brownson, the most politically radical Transcendentalist: a tough, pro-labor reformer who advocated
destroying banks and abolishing inherited wealth. Emerson's *Nature* published.

1837   Graduates Harvard College and returns to Concord during the
Panic of 1837, a major nationwide economic downturn whose
effects would last for years, with bank failures and record fore-
closures and unemployment. Gets a job teaching but resigns after
being told to use corporal punishment on his students. Begins
his lifelong involvement in the family pencil and graphite business; his improvements make Thoreau Pencils the highest quality
in America. Hawthorne's *Twice-Told Tales* published. October 22:
Begins his Journal.

1838   Opens a private school, later with his brother, John. Henry teaches
Latin, Greek, French, and sciences; the school emphasizes reason-
ing and field trips over rote memorization.

1839   Henry and John both fall in love with seventeen-year-old Ellen
Sewall. On August 31, Henry and John leave for a two-week trip
on the Concord and Merrimack rivers. John proposes to Sewall
and is accepted, but her mother convinces her to break the engagement; Henry then proposes by letter and is rejected. "I never
felt so badly sending a letter in my life," Ellen later says.

1840–41   Publishes his first essays and translations; the peak of his efforts writing poetry.

1842   John cuts himself with a razor on January 1, develops lockjaw, and dies in Henry's arms on January 11. Henry suffers psychosomatic symptoms of lockjaw so severe that his family fears for his life. He recovers, then Emerson's young son Waldo, whom Thoreau had helped raise, also dies. John's death is probably the great loss of Henry's life. Hawthorne, thirteen years older than Henry, moves to Concord and they become friends.

1843   After publishing two well-received nature essays, moves to Staten Island for seven months, where he tutors Emerson's nephew and tries to make it as a writer in New York; homesick, often ill, and unable to find regular literary employment, moves back to Concord.

1844   Accidentally starts a fire that burns down much of the Concord woods.

1845   On July 4, moves into a cabin he has built on Emerson's land near Walden Pond, where he would stay for two years, two months, and two days. Remains in close contact with family and friends.

1846   Spends a night in jail for not paying his taxes, the centerpiece of his most influential essay, "Resistance to Civil Government" or "Civil Disobedience" (1849).

1849   Henry's sister Helen dies of tuberculosis. *A Week on the Concord and Merrimack Rivers*, expanded and reconceived as a book to honor John's memory, is published; Emerson had encouraged Thoreau to agree to pay the costs, but then gives it a lukewarm review. The book is a commercial failure; Thoreau begins regular work as a surveyor to pay off his debts.

1850   Around this time, reconceives of the project of his Journal. Hawthorne's *The Scarlet Letter* published.

1851   Is enraged by passage of Fugitive Slave Act and becomes increasingly involved in the Underground Railroad. Hawthorne's *The House of the Seven Gables* and Melville's *Moby-Dick* published.

1852   Hawthorne's *The Blithedale Romance* and Stowe's *Uncle Tom's Cabin* published.

1854   *Walden* published, a modest success that leads to increased work as a lecturer, and widespread admirers.

1855   First edition of Whitman's *Leaves of Grass* published.

1856   A long trip to survey in Perth Amboy, New Jersey; meets Whitman, who gives him an inscribed copy of *Leaves of Grass*.

1859   Father dies; Henry takes over the family business. John Brown's raid on Harpers Ferry: Thoreau had heard him speak and given money, now delivers a fiery speech to large audiences in Concord, Worcester, and Boston; organizes and speaks at a memorial in Concord on the day of Brown's execution, December 2; and helps a fugitive member of Brown's group escape to Canada.

1860   Reads Darwin's *Origins of Species*, some of whose ideas he had been arriving at independently. Catches a cold (probably the flu from Bronson Alcott on November 29, and spends the evening of December 3 staying up late arguing about John Brown instead of resting), which develops into bronchitis and his final illness.

1861   Illness continues to worsen; travels to Minnesota in the summer in a last attempt to improve his health (the dry climate was thought to be good for lung problems). Back in Concord, unable to go outdoors much of the time, spends his last months cross-referencing the Journal, compiling over 750 pages of enormous lists and charts of a wide range of seasonal phenomena, and pulling together his last essays, the books *The Maine Woods* and *Cape Cod,* and the work that would eventually be published as *Faith in a Seed* and *Wild Fruits.*

1862   When asked if he has made his peace with God, replies, "I was not aware we had quarreled." Dies on May 6, age forty-four; last words are "moose" and "Indian."

PERSONS OFTEN MENTIONED IN THE JOURNAL

R.W.E. or E.	Ralph Waldo Emerson, Thoreau's mentor, patron, and friend
Emerson	Usually refers not to Ralph Waldo but to George B. Emerson, author of *Report on the Trees and Shrubs of Massachusetts*
Gray	Asa Gray, author of the popular *Manual of the Botany of the Northern United States*
W.E.C. or C.	(William) Ellery Channing, Thoreau's most frequent companion on walks and other excursions
Sophia	Henry's sister, who shared many of his interests: frequent companion on walks and excursions by boat, antislavery activist, botanist, and later editor of Henry's papers

The identity of other individuals is either given in a short note in the text or should be clear from context. Bracketed footnotes and bracketed italicized text in the body are mine; other footnotes and bracketed notes in the text are Thoreau's.

Part One
GLEANINGS

By all means use sometimes to be alone.
Salute thyself: see what thy soul doth wear.
Dare to look in thy chest; for 't is thine own:
And tumble up and down what thou find'st there.
    Who cannot rest till he good fellows find,
    He breaks up house, turns out of doors his mind.
                    HERBERT, *The Church Porch.*

Friends and companions, get you gone!
'T is my desire to be alone;
Ne'er well, but when my thoughts and I
Do domineer in privacy.
                    BURTON, *Anatomy of Melancholy.*

Two Paradises are in one,
To live in Paradise alone.
                    MARVELL, *The Garden.*

I.

GLEANINGS—OR WHAT TIME HAS NOT REAPED OF MY JOURNAL

Oct. 22 [1837]. "What are you doing now?" he asked. "Do you keep a journal?" So I make my first entry to-day.

SOLITUDE

To be alone I find it necessary to escape the present,—I avoid myself. How could I be alone in the Roman emperor's chamber of mirrors? I seek a garret. The spiders must not be disturbed, nor the floor swept, nor the lumber arranged.

The Germans say, "Es ist alles wahr wodurch du besser wirst."

THE MOULD OUR DEEDS LEAVE

Oct. 24. Every part of nature teaches that the passing away of one life is the making room for another. The oak dies down to the ground, leaving within its rind a rich virgin mould, which will impart a vigorous life to an infant forest. The pine leaves a sandy and sterile soil, the harder woods a strong and fruitful mould.

So this constant abrasion and decay makes the soil of my future growth. As I live now so shall I reap. If I grow pines and birches, my virgin mould will not sustain the oak; but pines and birches, or, perchance, weeds and brambles, will constitute my second growth.

DUCKS AT GOOSE POND

Oct. 29. Two ducks, of the summer or wood species, which were merrily dabbling in their favorite basin, struck up a retreat on my approach, and seemed disposed to take French leave, paddling off with swan-like majesty. They are first-rate swimmers, beating me at a round pace, and—what was to me a new trait in the duck character—dove every minute or two and swam several feet under water, in order to escape our attention. Just before immersion they seemed to give each other a significant nod, and then, as if by a common understanding, 't was heels up and head down in the shaking of a duck's wing. When they reappeared, it was amusing to observe with what a self-satisfied, darn-it-how-he-nicks-'em air they paddled off to repeat the experiment.

THE ARROWHEAD

A curious incident happened some four or six weeks ago which I think it worth the while to record. John and I had been searching for Indian relics, and been successful enough to find two arrowheads and a pestle, when, of a Sunday evening, with our heads full of the past and its remains, we strolled to the mouth of Swamp Bridge Brook. As we neared the brow of the hill forming the bank of the river, inspired by my theme, I broke forth into an extravagant eulogy on those savage times, using most violent gesticulations by way of illustration. "There on Nawshawtuct," said I, "was their lodge, the rendezvous of the tribe, and yonder, on Clamshell Hill, their feasting ground. This was, no doubt, a favorite haunt; here on this brow was an eligible lookout post. How often have they stood on this very spot, at this very hour, when the sun was sinking behind yonder woods and gilding with his last rays the waters of the Musketaquid, and pondered the day's success and the morrow's prospects, or communed with the spirit of their fathers gone before them to the land of shades!

"Here," I exclaimed, "stood Tahatawan; and there" (to complete the period) "is Tahatawan's arrowhead."

We instantly proceeded to sit down on the spot I had pointed to, and I, to carry out the joke, to lay bare an ordinary stone which my whim had selected, when lo! the first I laid hands on, the grubbing stone that was to be, proved a most perfect arrowhead, as sharp as if just from the hands of the Indian fabricator!!!

HOAR FROST AND GREEN RIVER

Nov. 28. Every tree, fence, and spire of grass that could raise its head above the snow was this morning covered with a dense hoar frost. The trees looked like airy creatures of darkness caught napping. On this side they were huddled together, their gray hairs streaming, in a secluded valley which the sun had not yet penetrated, and on that they went hurrying off in Indian file by hedgerows and watercourses, while the shrubs and grasses, like elves and fairies of the night, sought to hide their diminished heads in the snow.

The branches and taller grasses were covered with a wonderful ice-foliage, answering leaf for leaf to their summer dress. The centre, diverging, and even more minute fibres were perfectly distinct and the edges regularly indented.

These leaves were on the side of the twig or stubble opposite to the sun (when it was not bent toward the east), meeting it for the most part at right angles, and there were others standing out at all possible angles upon these, and upon one another.

It struck me that these ghost leaves and the green ones whose forms they assume were the creatures of the same law. It could not be in obedience to two several laws that the vegetable juices swelled gradually into the perfect leaf on the one hand, and the crystalline particles trooped to their standard in the same admirable order on the other.

The river, viewed from the bank above, appeared of a yellowish-green color, but on a nearer approach this phenomenon vanished; and yet the landscape was covered with snow.

HEAVEN ON EARTH

Jan. 6. As a child looks forward to the coming of the summer, so could we contemplate with quiet joy the circle of the seasons returning without fail eternally. As the spring came round during so many years of the gods, we could go out to admire and adorn anew our Eden, and yet never tire.

WHAT TO DO

March 5. But what does all this scribbling amount to? What is now scribbled in the heat of the moment one can contemplate with somewhat of satisfaction, but alas! to-morrow—aye, to-night—it is stale, flat, and unprofitable,—in fine, is not, only its shell remains, like some red parboiled lobster-shell which, kicked aside never so often, still stares at you in the path.

What may a man do and not be ashamed of it? He may not do nothing surely, for straightway he is dubbed Dolittle—aye! christens himself first—and reasonably, for he was first to duck. But let him do something, is he the less a Dolittle? Is it actually something done, or not rather something undone?

COMPOSITION

March 7. We should not endeavor coolly to analyze our thoughts, but, keeping the pen even and parallel with the current, make an accurate transcript of them. Impulse is, after all, the best linguist, and for his logic, if not conformable to Aristotle, it cannot fail to be most convincing. The nearer we approach to a complete but simple transcript of our thought the more tolerable will be the piece, for we can endure to consider ourselves in a state of passivity or in involuntary action, but rarely our efforts, and least of all our rare efforts.

THE LOSS OF A TOOTH

Aug. 27. Verily I am the creature of circumstances. Here I have swallowed an indispensable tooth, and so am no whole man, but a lame and halting piece of manhood. I am conscious of no gap in my soul, but it would seem that, now the entrance to the oracle has been enlarged, the more rare and commonplace the responses that issue from it. I have felt cheap, and hardly dared hold up my head among men, ever since this accident happened. Nothing can I do as well and freely as before; nothing do I undertake but I am hindered and balked by this circumstance. Virtue and Truth go undefended, and Falsehood and Affectation are thrown in my teeth,—though I am toothless. But let the lame man shake his leg, and match himself with the fleetest in the race. So shall he do what is in him to do. But let him who has lost a tooth open his mouth wide and gabble, lisp, and sputter never so resolutely.

RIVERS

Sept. 5. For the first time it occurred to me this afternoon what a piece of wonder a river is,—a huge volume of matter ceaselessly rolling through the fields and meadows of this substantial earth, making haste from the high places, by stable dwellings of men and Egyptian Pyramids, to its restless reservoir. One would think that, by a very natural impulse, the dwellers upon the headwaters of the Mississippi and Amazon would follow in the trail of their waters to see the end of the matter.

THE DREAM VALLEY

Jan. 20, 1839. The prospect of our river valley from Tahatawan Cliff appeared to me again in my dreams.

DRIFTING

[April.] Drifting in a sultry day on the sluggish waters of the pond, I almost cease to live and begin to be. A boatman stretched on the deck of his craft and dallying with the noon would be as apt an emblem of eternity for me as the serpent with his tail in his mouth. I am never so prone to lose my identity. I am dissolved in the haze.

July 25. There is no remedy for love but to love more.

The hardest material obeys the same law with the most fluid. Trees are but rivers of sap and woody fibre flowing from the atmosphere and emptying into the earth by their trunks, as their roots flow upward to the surface. And in the heavens there are rivers of stars and milky ways. There are rivers of rock on the surface and rivers of ore in the bowels of the earth. And thoughts flow and circulate, and seasons lapse as tributaries of the current year.

The future reader of history will associate this generation with the red man in his thoughts, and give it credit for some sympathy with that race. Our history will have some copper tints and reflections, at least, and be read as through an Indian-summer haze; but such were not our associations. But the Indian is absolutely forgotten but by some persevering poets.

The white man has commenced a new era. What do our anniversaries commemorate but white men's exploits? For Indian deeds there must be an Indian memory; the white man will remember his own only. We have forgotten their hostility as well as friendship.

For the Indian there is no safety but in the plow. If he would not be pushed into the Pacific, he must seize hold of a plow-tail and let go his bow and arrow, his fish-spear and rifle. This the only Christianity that will save him.

His fate says sternly to him, "Forsake the hunter's life and enter into the agricultural, the second, state of man. Root yourselves a little deeper in the soil, if you would continue to be the occupants of the country."

But I confess I have no little sympathy with the Indians and hunter men. They seem to me a distinct and equally respectable people, born to wander and to hunt, and not to be inoculated with the twilight civilization of the white man.

Father Le Jeune, a French missionary, affirmed "that the Indians were superior in intellect to the French peasantry of that time," and advised "that laborers should be sent from France in order to work for the Indians."

The Indian, perchance, has not made up his mind to some things which the white man has consented to; he has not, in all respects, stooped so low; and hence, though he too loves food and warmth, he draws his tattered blanket about him and follows his fathers, rather than barter his birthright. He dies, and no doubt his Genius judges well for him. But he is not worsted in the fight; he is not destroyed. He only migrates beyond the Pacific to more spacious and happier hunting-grounds.

ÆSCHYLUS

Nov. 5. We are accustomed to say that the common sense of this age belonged to the seer of the last,—as if time gave him any vantage ground. But not so: I see not but Genius must ever take an equal start, and all the generations of men are virtually at a standstill for it to come and consider of them. Common sense is not so familiar with any truth but Genius will represent it in a strange light to it. Let the seer bring down his broad eye to the most stale and trivial fact, and he will make you believe it a new planet in the sky.

As to criticism, man has never to make allowance to man; there is naught to excuse, naught to bear in mind.

All the past is here present to be tried; let it approve itself if it can.

POETRY

Jan. 26. No definition of poetry is adequate unless it be poetry itself. The poet does not need to see how meadows are something else than earth, grass, and water, but how they are thus much. He does not need discover that potato blows are as beautiful as violets, as the farmer thinks, but only how good potato blows are.

The poem is drawn out from under the feet of the poet, his whole weight has rested on this ground.

Its eccentric and unexplored orbit embraces the system.

Feb. 14. Beauty lives by rhymes. Double a deformity is a beauty. Draw this blunt quill over the paper, and fold it once transversely to the line, pressing it suddenly before the ink dries, and a delicately shaded and regular figure is the result, which art cannot surpass. [*A sheet with specimens is slipped into the Journal.*]

A very meagre natural history suffices to make me a child. Only their names and genealogy make me love fishes. I would know even the number of their fin-rays, and how many scales compose the lateral line. I fancy I am amphibious and swim in all the brooks and pools in the neighborhood, with the perch and bream, or doze under the pads of our river amid the winding aisles and corridors formed by their stems, with the stately pickerel. I am the wiser in respect to all knowledges, and the better qualified for all fortunes, for knowing that there is a minnow in the brook. Methinks I have need even of his sympathy, and to be his fellow in a degree. I do like him sometimes when he balances himself for an hour over the yellow floor of his basin.

April 8. How shall I help myself? By withdrawing into the garret, and associating with spiders and mice, determining to meet myself face to face sooner or later. Completely silent and attentive I will be this hour, and the next, and forever. The most positive life that history notices has been a constant retiring out of life, a wiping one's hands of it, seeing how mean it is, and having nothing to do with it.

June 22. What a man knows, that he does.

When we are shocked at vice we express a lingering sympathy with it. Dry rot, rust, and mildew shock no man, for none is subject to them.

June 26. The best poetry has never been written, for when it might have been, the poet forgot it, and when it was too late remembered it; or when it might have been, the poet remembered it, and when it was too late forgot it.

The highest condition of art is artlessness.

Truth is always paradoxical.

He will get to the goal first who stands stillest.

There is one let better than any help, and that is,—*Let-alone.*

By sufferance you may escape suffering.

He who resists not at all will never surrender.

When a dog runs at you, whistle for him.

Say, Not so, and you will outcircle the philosophers.

Stand outside the wall, and no harm can reach you. The danger is that you be walled in with it.

June 27. I am living this 27th of June, 1840, a dull, cloudy day and no sun shining. The clink of the smith's hammer sounds feebly over the roofs, and the wind is sighing gently, as if dreaming of cheerfuler days. The farmer is plowing in yonder field, craftsmen are busy in the shops, the trader stands behind the counter, and all works go steadily forward. But I will have nothing to do; I will tell fortune that I play no game with her, and she may reach me in my Asia of serenity and indolence if she can.

July 6. Let the daily tide leave some deposit on these pages, as it leaves sand and shells on the shore. So much increase of *terra firma*. This may be a calendar of the ebbs and flows of the soul; and on these sheets as a beach, the waves may cast up pearls and seaweed.

Aug. 7. A wave of happiness flows over us like sunshine over a field.

Aug. 13. A man should be collected and earnest in his bearing—moving like one and not several, like an arrow with a feather for its rudder—and not like a handful of feathers bound to a rod—or a disorderly equipage which does not move unanimously. Addison says somewhat to the purpose—"I lay it down therefore for a rule, that the whole man is to move together;"—otherwise, he says, a man "is hopping instead of walking, he is not in his entire and proper motion."

A worm is as good a traveller as a grasshopper or cricket; with all their activity they do not hop away from drought nor forward to summer. No hopping animal migrates.

Sept. 21. In the old Chinese book which the French call "L'Invariable Milieu" occurs this sentence—"L'ordre établi par le ciel s'appelle *nature*; ce qui est conforme à la nature s'appelle *loi*; l'établissement de la loi s'appelle *instruction*."

God's order is nature—man's order is law—and the establishment of law is the subject of instruction.

Some of these old distinctions imply a certain grandeur and completeness in the view, far better than any modern acuteness and accuracy—They are a thought which darted through the universe and solved all its problems.

Oct. 11. Every idea was long ago done into nature as the translators say—There is walking in the feet—mechanics in the hand—climbing in the loose flesh of the palms—boxing in the knuckles &c, &c.

Oct. 15. Men see God in the ripple but not in miles of still water. Of all the two-thousand miles that the St. Lawrence flows—pilgrims go only to Niagara.

Nov. 11th I obtained a levelling instrument and circumferentor combined, and have since ascertained the height of the cliff-hill—and surveyed other objects.

Height of Cliff Hill above the River

Progress		Position	Elevation.
1st rise	12.10		12.10
2d	12.91		25.01
3d	12.63		37.64
	11.49		49.13
	12.80		61.93
	12.50		74.43
	13.26	Bars in wall	87.69
	12.41		100.10
	12.40		112.50
	13.20	Near split Rock	149.68
	12.47	Stone in path	162.15
	12.31		174.46
	11.44	Stone by bars	185.90
	13.26	Stone in path near rock on right.	199.16
	12.64	Two birches by wall	211.80
	12.		223.80
	7.29	Top of Rock in Woods	231.09

Dec. 2. I should wither and dry up if it were not for lakes and rivers. I am conscious that my body derives its genesis from their waters, as much as the muskrat or the herbage on their brink. The thought

of Walden in the woods yonder makes me supple jointed and limber for the duties of the day. Sometimes I thirst for it.

There it lies all the year reflecting the sky—and from its surface there seems to go up a pillar of ether, which bridges over the space between earth and heaven.

Water seems a middle element between earth and air. The most fluid in which man can float.

Across the surface of every lake there sweeps a hushed music.

Dec. 18. I find Gibbon to have been less a man and more of a student than I had anticipated. His Roman History, by his own confession, was undertaken from no higher motive than the love of fame. In his religious views he did not differ nobly from mankind, but rather apologized and conformed. He was ambitious and vain.

I hear him smack his lips at the prospect of a pipe of wine to be sent from England to Lausanne. There is not recorded of him, that I know, a single reckless and heroic action, which would have been worth a thousand histories. That would have been to Rise and Stand. I think of him only as the laborious ambitious student who wrote the Decline & Fall, during those 56 years—which after all it does not concern me to read.

Jan. 2. The shrub oaks rustling in the thin cold breeze are a simmering crackling fire. They have more heat than the pines. Green is a cold color.

The richness of the outline of the wood against the sky is in proportion to the number of distinct interstices through which the light straggles to us.

Every needle of the white pine trembles distinctly in the breeze, which on the sunny side gives the whole tree a shimmering seething aspect.

I stopped short in the path today to admire how the trees grow up without forethought regardless of the time and circumstances. They do not wait as men do—now is the golden age of the sapling—Earth, air, sun, and rain, are occasion enough—.

Jan. 10. A perfectly healthy sentence is extremely rare. Sometimes I read one which was written while the world went round, while grass grew and water ran.

Jan. 22. I hear it complained of some modern books of genius, that they are irregular, and have no flow, but we should consider that the flow of thought is more like a tidal wave than a prone river, and is the effect of a celestial influence, or sort of ground swell, it may be, and not of any declivity in its channel, each wave rising higher than the former, and partially subsiding back on it. But the river flows, because it runs down hill, and descends faster, as it flows more rapidly. The one obeys the earthly attraction, the other the heavenly attraction. The one runs smoothly because it gravitates toward the earth alone, the other irregularly because it gravitates toward the heavens as well.

Though I should front an object for a lifetime I should only see what it concerned me to see.

Jan. 26. I had a dream last night which had reference to an act in my life in which I had been most disinterested and true to my highest instinct but completely failed in realizing my hopes; and now, after so many months, in the stillness of sleep, complete justice was rendered me. It was a divine remuneration. In my waking hours I could not have conceived of such retribution; the presumption of desert would have damned the whole. But now I was permitted to be not so much a subject as a partner to that retribution. It was the award of divine justice, which will at length be and is even now accomplished.

Good writing as well as good acting will be obedience to conscience. There must not be a particle of will or whim mixed with it.

If we can listen, we shall hear. By reverently listening to the inner voice, we may reinstate ourselves on the pinnacle of humanity.

Jan. 29. Of all strange and unaccountable things this journalizing is the strangest. It will allow nothing to be predicated of it; its good is not good, nor its bad bad. If I make a huge effort to expose my innermost and richest wares to light, my counter seems cluttered with the meanest homemade stuffs; but after months or years I may discover the wealth of India, and whatever rarity is brought overland from Cathay, in that confused heap, and what perhaps seemed a festoon of dried apple or pumpkin will prove a string of Brazilian diamonds, or pearls from Coromandel.

Feb. 2. For our aspirations there is no expression as yet, but if we obey steadily, by another year we shall have learned the language of last year's aspirations.

Feb. 3. We are constantly invited to be what we are; as to something worthy and noble. I never waited but for myself to come round; none ever detained me, but I lagged or tagged after myself.

Feb. 4. Thursday. When you are once comfortably seated at a public meeting, there is something unmanly in the sitting on tiptoe and *qui vive* attitude,—the involuntarily rising into your throat, as if gravity had ceased to operate,—when a lady approaches, with quite godlike presumption, to elicit the miracle of a seat where none is.

Such a state of unrest becomes only a fluttered virtue. No, be true to your instincts, and sit; wait till you can be genuinely polite, if it be till doomsday, and not lose your chance everlastingly by a cowardly yielding to young etiquette. By your look say unto them, The lines have fallen to me in pleasant places, and I will fill that station God has assigned me.

If a stranger enter with sufficient determination into a crowded assembly, as if commissioned by the gods to find a seat there, as the falling stone by a divine impulse seeks a resting-place, each one will rise without thinking to offer his place. When presumptuous womanhood demands to surrender my position, I bide my time,— though it be with misgiving,—and yield to no mortal shove, but expect a divine impulse. Produce your warrant, and I will retire; for not now can I give you a clear seat, but must leave part of my manhood behind and wander a diminished man, who at length will not have length and breadth enough to fill any seat at all.

Feb. 6. Saturday. When I select one here and another there, and strive to join sundered thoughts, I make but a partial heap after all. Nature strews her nuts and flowers broadcast, and never collects them into heaps. A man does not tell us all he has thought upon truth or beauty at a sitting, but, from his last thought on the subject, wanders through a varied scenery of upland, meadow, and woodland to his next. Sometimes a single and casual thought rises naturally and inevitably with a queenly majesty and escort, like the stars in the east. Fate has surely enshrined it in this hour and circumstances for some purpose. What she has joined together, let not man put asunder. Shall I transplant the primrose by the river's brim, to set it beside its sister on the mountain? *This* was the soil it grew in, *this* the hour it bloomed in. If sun, wind, and rain came *here* to cherish and expand it, shall not we come here to pluck it? Shall we require it to grow in a conservatory for our convenience?

Feb. 7. Sunday. Without greatcoat or drawers I have advanced thus far into the snow-banks of the winter, without thought and with impunity. When I meet my neighbors in muffs and furs and tippets, they look as if they had retreated into the interior fastnesses from some foe invisible to me. They remind me that this is the season of winter, in which it becomes a man to be cold. For feeling, I am a piece of clean wood of this shape, which will do service till it rots, and though the cold has its physical effect on me, it is a kindly one, for it "finds its acquaintance there." May not the body defend itself against cold by its very nakedness, and its elements be so simple and single that they cannot congeal? I call it a protestant warmth. My limbs do not tire as formerly, but I use myself as any other piece of nature, and from mere indifference and thoughtlessness may break the timber.

Feb. 8. All we have experienced is so much gone within us, and there lies. It is the company we keep. One day, in health or sickness, it will come out and be remembered. Neither body nor soul forgets anything. The twig always remembers the wind that shook it, and the stone the cuff it received. Ask the old tree and the sand.

My Journal is that of me which would else spill over and run to waste, gleanings from the field which in action I reap. I must not live for it, but in it for the gods. As if it were not kept shut in my desk, but were as public a leaf as any in nature. It is papyrus by the riverside; it is vellum in the pastures; it is parchment on the hills.

It is always a chance scrawl, and commemorates some accident,—as great as earthquake or eclipse. Upland and lowland, forest and field have been ransacked.

Feb. 9. I have been breaking silence these twenty-three years and have hardly made a rent in it. Silence has no end; speech is but the beginning of it. My friend thinks I *keep* silence, who am only choked with letting it out so fast. Does he forget that new mines of secrecy are constantly opening in me?

Feb. 10. I asked a man to-day if he would rent me some land, and he said he had four acres as good soil "as any outdoors." It was a true poet's account of it. He and I, and all the world, went outdoors to breathe the free air and stretch ourselves. For the world is but outdoors,—and we duck behind a panel.

Feb. 13. My neighbor says that his hill-farm is poor stuff and "only fit to hold the world together." He deserves that God should give him better for so brave a treating of his gifts, instead of humbly putting up therewith. It is a sort of stay, or gore, or gusset, and he will not be blinded by modesty or gratitude, but sees it for what it is; knowing his neighbor's fertile land, he calls his by its right name. But perhaps my farmer forgets that his lean soil has sharpened his wits. This is a crop it was good for.

Feb. 14. Sunday. I am confined to the house by bronchitis, and so seek to content myself with that quiet and serene life there is in a warm corner by the fireside, and see the sky through the chimney-top. Sickness should not be allowed to extend further than the body. We need only to retreat further within us to preserve uninterrupted the continuity of serene hours to the end of our lives.

As soon as I find my chest is not of tempered steel, and heart of adamant, I bid good-by to these and look out a new nature. I will be liable to no accidents.

Feb. 26. Friday. My prickles or smoothness are as much a quality of your hand as of myself. I cannot tell you what I am, more than a ray of the summer's sun. What I am I am, and say not. Being is the great explainer.

Feb. 28. Nothing goes by luck in composition. It allows of no tricks. The best you can write will be the best you are. Every sentence is the result of a long probation. The author's character is read from title-page to end. And so of the rest of our actions; it runs as straight as a ruled line through them all, no matter how many curvets about it. Our whole life is taxed for the least thing well done; it is its net result. How we eat, drink, sleep, and use our desultory hours, now in these indifferent days, with no eye to observe and no occasion to excite us, determines our authority and capacity for the time to come.

March 13. Saturday. Very few men can speak of Nature with any truth. They confer no favor; they do not speak a good word for her. Most cry better than they speak. You can get more nature out of them by pinching than by addressing them. It is naturalness, and not simply good nature, that interests. I like better the surliness with which the woodchopper speaks of his woods, handling them as indifferently as his axe, than the mealy-mouthed enthusiasm of the lover of nature. Better that the primrose by the river's brim be a yellow primrose and nothing more, than the victim of his bouquet or herbarium, to shine with the flickering dull light of his imagination.

How alone must our life be lived! We dwell on the seashore, and none between us and the sea.

March 27. Saturday. Magnanimity, though it look expensive for a short course, is always economy in the long run. Be generous in your poverty, if you would be rich. To make up a great action there are no subordinate mean ones. If a man charges you eight hundred pay him eight hundred and fifty, and it will leave a clean edge to the sum. It will be like nature, overflowing and rounded like the bank of a river, not close and precise like a drain or ditch.

April 4. Sunday. The rattling of the tea-kettle below stairs reminds me of the cow-bells I used to hear when berrying in the Great Fields many years ago, sounding distant and deep amid the birches. That cheap piece of tinkling brass which the farmer hangs about his cow's neck has been more to me than the tons of metal which are swung in the belfry.

April 7. Wednesday. My life will wait for nobody, but is being matured still irresistibly while I go about the streets and chaffer with this man and that to secure it a living. It will cut its own channel, like the mountain stream, which by the longest ridges and by level prairies is not kept from the sea finally. So flows a man's life, and will reach the sea water, if not by an earthy channel, yet in dew and rain, overleaping all barriers, with rainbows to announce its victory. It can wind as cunningly and unerringly as water that seeks its level; and shall I complain if the gods make it meander?

Sept. 4. Saturday. I think I could write a poem to be called "Concord." For argument I should have the River, the Woods, the Ponds, the Hills, the Fields, the Swamps and Meadows, the Streets and Buildings, and the Villagers. Then Morning, Noon, and Evening, Spring,

Summer, Autumn, and Winter, Night, Indian Summer, and the Mountains in the Horizon.

A book should be so true as to be intimate and familiar to all men, as the sun to their faces,—such a word as is occasionally uttered to a companion in the woods in summer, and both are silent.

Dec. 15. I seem to see somewhat more of my own kith and kin in the lichens on the rocks than in any books. It does seem as if mine were a peculiarly wild nature, which so yearns toward all wildness. I know of no redeeming qualities in me but a sincere love for some things, and when I am reproved I have to fall back on to this ground. This is my argument in reserve for all cases. My love is invulnerable. Meet me on that ground, and you will find me strong. When I am condemned, and condemn myself utterly, I think straightway, "But I rely on my love for some things." Therein I am whole and entire. Therein I am God-propped.

Dec. 23. Concord.—A forest is in all mythologies a sacred place, as the oaks among the Druids and the grove of Egeria; and even in more familiar and common life a celebrated wood is spoken of with respect, as "Barnsdale Wood" and "Sherwood." Had Robin Hood no Sherwood to resort to, it would be difficult to invest his story with the charms it has got. It is always the tale that is untold, the deeds done and the life lived in the unexplored secrecy of the wood, that charm us and make us children again,—to read his ballads, and hear of the greenwood tree.

Dec. 24. Friday. I want to go soon and live away by the pond, where I shall hear only the wind whispering among the reeds. It will be success if I shall have left myself behind. But my friends ask what I will do when I get there. Will it not be employment enough to watch the progress of the seasons?

Dec. 25. I don't want to feel as if my life were a sojourn any longer. That philosophy cannot be true which so paints it. It is time now that I begin to live.

Jan. 5. Wednesday. I find that whatever hindrances may occur I write just about the same amount of truth in my Journal; for the record is more concentrated, and usually it is some very real and earnest life, after all, that interrupts. All flourishes are omitted. If I saw wood from morning to night, though I grieve that I could not observe the train of my thoughts during that time, yet, in the evening, the few scrannel lines which describe my day's occupations will make the creaking of the saw more musical than my freest fancies could have been. I find incessant labor with the hands, which engrosses the attention also, the best method to remove palaver out of one's style. One will not dance at his work who has wood to cut and cord before the night falls in the short days of winter; but every stroke will be husbanded, and ring soberly through the wood; and so will his lines ring and tell on the ear, when at evening he settles the accounts of the day. I have often been astonished at the force and precision of style to which busy laboring men, unpracticed in writing, easily attain when they are required to make the effort. It seems as if their sincerity and plainness were the main thing to be taught in schools,—and yet not in the schools, but in the fields, in actual service, I should say. The scholar not unfrequently envies the propriety and emphasis with which the farmer calls to his team, and confesses that if that lingo were written it would surpass his labored sentences.

Who is not tired of the weak and flowing periods of the politician and scholar, and resorts not even to the Farmer's Almanac, to read the simple account of the month's labor, to restore his tone again? I want to see a sentence run clear through to the end, as deep and fertile as a well-drawn furrow which shows that the plow was pressed down to the beam. If our scholars would lead more earnest lives, we should not witness those lame conclusions to their ill-sown discourses, but their sentences would pass over the ground like loaded rollers, and not mere hollow and wooden ones, to press in the seed and make it germinate.

Jan. 8. What offends me most in my compositions is the moral element in them. The repentant say never a brave word. Their resolves should be mumbled in silence. Strictly speaking, morality is not healthy. Those undeserved joys which come uncalled and make us more pleased than grateful are they that sing.

[*Thoreau's brother John died of lockjaw in Thoreau's arms on Jan. 11, 1842. Thoreau developed psychosomatic symptoms so severe that his family feared for his life, but he recovered.*]

Feb. 21. I must confess there is nothing so strange to me as my own body. I love any other piece of nature, almost, better.

I was always conscious of sounds in nature which my ears could never hear,—that I caught but the prelude to a strain. She always retreats as I advance. Away behind and behind is she and her meaning. Will not this faith and expectation make to itself ears at length? I never saw to the end, nor heard to the end; but the best part was unseen and unheard.

I am like a feather floating in the atmosphere; on every side is depth unfathomable.

I feel as if years had been crowded into the last month, and yet the regularity of what we call time has been so far preserved as that I [*Two lines missing from the manuscript*] will be welcome in the present. I have lived ill for the most part because too near myself. I have tripped myself up, so that there was no progress for my own narrowness. I cannot walk conveniently and pleasantly but when I hold myself far off in the horizon. And the soul dilutes the body and makes it passable. My soul and body have tottered along together of late, tripping and hindering one another like unpracticed Siamese twins. They two should walk as one, that no obstacle may be nearer than the firmament.

There must be some narrowness in the soul that compels one to have secrets.

Feb. 23. I am glad that it was so because it could be.

March 1. Whatever I learn from any circumstances, that especially I needed to know. Events come out of God, and our characters determine them and constrain fate, as much as they determine the words and tone of a friend to us. Hence are they always acceptable as experience, and we do not see how we could have done without them.

March 11. My life, my life! why will you linger? Are the years short and the months of no account? How often has long delay quenched my aspirations! Can God afford that I should forget him? Is he so indifferent to my career? Can heaven be postponed with no more ado?

Our doubts are so musical that they persuade themselves.

March 17. Thursday. I have been making pencils all day, and then at evening walked to see an old schoolmate who is going to help make the Welland Canal navigable for ships round Niagara. He cannot see any such motives and modes of living as I; professes not to look beyond the securing of certain "creature comforts." And so we go silently different ways, with all serenity, I in the still moonlight through the village this fair evening to write these thoughts in my journal, and he, forsooth, to mature his schemes to ends as good, maybe, but different. So are we two made, while the same stars shine quietly over us. If I or he be wrong, Nature yet consents placidly. She bites her lip and smiles to see how her children will agree. So does the Welland Canal get built, and other conveniences, while I live. Well and good, I must confess. Fast sailing ships are hence not detained.

March 19. Saturday. When I walk in the fields of Concord and meditate on the destiny of this prosperous slip of the Saxon family, the unexhausted energies of this new country, I forget that this which is now Concord was once Musketaquid, and that the *American race* has had its destiny also. I find it good to remember the eternity behind me as well as the eternity before. Wherever I go, I tread in the tracks of the Indian. I pick up the bolt which he has but just dropped at my feet. And if I consider destiny I am on his trail.

Nature has her russet hues as well as green. Indeed, our eye splits on every object, and we can as well take one path as the other. If I consider its history, it is old; if its destiny, it is new. I may see a part of an object, or the whole. I will not be imposed on and think Nature is old because the season is advanced. I will study the botany of the mosses and fungi on the decayed wood, and remember that decayed wood is not old, but has just begun to be what it is.

March 20. How simple is the natural connection of events. We complain greatly of the want of flow and sequence in books, but if the journalist only move himself from Boston to New York, and speak as before, there is link enough. Is not my life riveted together? Has not it sequence? Do not my breathings follow each other naturally?

II.
1842–1847

March 27. Cliffs.—Two little hawks have just come out to play, like butterflies rising one above the other in endless alternation far below me. They swoop from side to side in the broad basin of the tree-tops, with wider and wider surges, as if swung by an invisible pendulum. They stoop down on this side and scale up on that.

Suddenly I look up and see a new bird, probably an eagle, quite above me, laboring with the wind not more than forty rods off. It was the largest bird of the falcon kind I ever saw. I was never so impressed by any flight. She sailed the air, and fell back from time to time like a ship on her beam ends, holding her talons up as if ready for the arrows. I never allowed before for the grotesque attitudes of our national bird.

The eagle must have an educated eye.

See what a life the gods have given us, set round with pain and pleasure. It is too strange for sorrow; it is too strange for joy. One while it looks as shallow, though as intricate, as a Cretan labyrinth, and again it is a pathless depth. Say not that Nature is trivial, for to-morrow she will be radiant with beauty. I am as old—as old as the Alleghanies. I was going to say Wachusett, but it excites a youthful feeling, as I were but too happy to be so young.

March 28. If I cannot chop wood in the yard, can I not chop wood in my journal? Can I not give vent to that appetite so? I wish to relieve myself of superfluous energy.

March 31. Thursday. I cannot forget the majesty of that bird at the Cliff. It was no sloop or smaller craft hove in sight, but a ship of the line, worthy to struggle with the elements. It was a great presence, as of the master of river and forest. His eye would not have quailed before the owner of the soil; none could challenge his rights. And then his retreat, sailing so steadily away, was a kind of advance. How is it that man always feels like an interloper in nature, as if he had intruded on the domains of bird and beast?

The really efficient laborer will be found not to crowd his day with work, but will saunter to his task surrounded by a wide halo of ease and leisure. There will be a wide margin for relaxation to his day. He is only earnest to secure the kernels of time, and does not exaggerate the value of the husk. Why should the hen set all day? She can lay but one egg, and besides she will not have picked up materials for a new one. Those who work much do not work hard.

I know of no rule which holds so true as that we are always paid for our suspicion by finding what we suspect. There can be no fairer recompense than this. Our suspicions exercise a demoniacal power over the subject of them. By some obscure law of influence, when we are perhaps unconsciously the subject of another's suspicion, we feel a strong impulse, even when it is contrary to our nature, to do that which he expects but reprobates.

These arrowheads are of every color and of various forms and materials, though commonly made of a stone which has a conchoidal fracture. Many small ones are found, of white quartz, which are mere equilateral triangles, with one side slightly convex. These were probably small shot for birds and squirrels.

It is a matter of wonder how the Indians made even those rude implements without iron or steel tools to work with. It is doubtful whether one of our mechanics, with all the aids of Yankee ingenuity, could soon learn to copy one of the thousands under our feet. It is well known the art of making flints with a cold chisel, as practiced in Austria, requires long practice and knack in the operator, but the arrowhead is of much more irregular form, and, like the flint, such is the nature of the stone, must be struck out by a succession of skillful blows.

An Indian to whom I once exhibited some, but to whom they were objects of as much curiosity as to myself, suggested that, as white men have but one blacksmith, so Indians had one arrowhead-maker for many families. But there are the marks of too many forges—unless they were like travelling cobblers—to allow of this.

All parts of nature belong to one head, as the curls of a maiden's hair. How beautifully flow the seasons as one year, and all streams as one ocean!

It is hard to know rocks. They are crude and inaccessible to our nature. We have not enough of the stony element in us.

It is the saddest thought of all, that what we are to others, that we are much more to ourselves,—avaricious, mean, irascible, affected, —we are the victims of these faults. If our pride offends our humble neighbor, much more does it offend ourselves, though our lives are never so private and solitary.

How many young finny contemporaries of various character and destiny, form and habits, we have even in this water! And it will not be forgotten by some memory that we *were* contemporaries. It is of *some* import. We shall be some time friends, I trust, and know each other better. Distrust is too prevalent now. We are so much alike! have so many faculties in common! I have not yet met with the philosopher who could, in a quite conclusive, undoubtful way, show me *the*, and, if not *the*, then how *any*, difference between man and a fish. We are so much alike! How much could a really tolerant, patient, humane, and truly great and natural man make of them, if he should try? For they are to be understood, surely, as all things else, by no other method than that of sympathy. It is easy to say what they are not to us, *i.e.*, what we are not to them; but what we might and ought to be is another affair.

The bream is the familiar and homely sparrow, which makes her nest everywhere, and is early and late.

The pickerel is the hawk, a fish of prey, hovering over the finny broods.

The pout is the owl, which steals so noiselessly about at evening with its clumsy body.

The shiner is the summer yellowbird, or goldfinch, of the river.

The sucker is the sluggish bittern, or stake-driver.

The minnow is the hummingbird.

The trout is the partridge woodpecker.

The perch is the robin.

July 5, 1845. Saturday. Walden.—Yesterday I came here to live. My house makes me think of some mountain houses I have seen, which seemed to have a fresher auroral atmosphere about them, as I fancy of the halls of Olympus. I lodged at the house of a saw-miller last summer, on the Caatskill Mountains, high up as Pine Orchard, in the blueberry and raspberry region, where the quiet and cleanliness and coolness seemed to be all one,—which had their ambrosial character. He was the miller of the Kaaterskill Falls. They were a clean and wholesome family, inside and out, like their house. The latter was not plastered, only lathed, and the inner doors were not hung. The house seemed high-placed, airy, and perfumed, fit to entertain a travelling god. It was so high, indeed, that all the music, the broken strains, the waifs and accompaniments of tunes, that swept over the ridge of the Caatskills, passed through its aisles. Could not man be man in such an abode? And would he ever find out this grovelling life? It was the very light and atmosphere in which the works of Grecian art were composed, and in which they rest.

July 6. I wish to meet the facts of life—the vital facts, which are the phenomena or actuality the gods meant to show us—face to face, and so I came down here. Life! who knows what it is, what it does? If I am not quite right here, I am less wrong than before; and now let us see what they will have.

July 14. What sweet and tender, the most innocent and divinely encouraging society there is in every natural object, and so in universal nature, even for the poor misanthrope and most melancholy man! There can be no really black melan-choly to him who lives in the midst of nature and has still his senses. While I enjoy the sweet friendship of the seasons I trust that nothing can make life a burden to me. This rain which is now watering my beans and keeping me in the house waters me too. I needed it as much. And what if most are not hoed! Those who send the rain, whom I chiefly respect, will pardon me.

Sometimes, when I compare myself with other men, methinks I am favored by the gods. They seem to whisper joy to me beyond my deserts, and that I do have a solid warrant and surety at their hands, which my fellows do not. I do not flatter myself, but if it were possible *they* flatter me. I am especially guided and guarded.

Twenty-three years since, when I was five years old, I was brought from Boston to this pond, away in the country,—which was then but another name for the extended world for me,—one of the most ancient scenes stamped on the tablets of my memory, the oriental Asiatic valley of my world, whence so many races and inventions have gone forth in recent times. That woodland vision for a long time made the drapery of my dreams. That sweet solitude my spirit seemed so early to require that I might have room to entertain my thronging guests, and that speaking silence that my ears might distinguish the significant sounds. Somehow or other it at once gave the preference to this recess among the pines, where almost sunshine and shadow were the only inhabitants that varied the scene, over that tumultuous and varied city, as if it had found its proper nursery.

Left house on account of plastering, Wednesday, November 12th, at night; returned Saturday, December 6th.

The wisdom of some of those Greek fables is remarkable. The god

Apollo (Wisdom, Wit, Poetry) condemned to serve, keep the sheep of *King* Admetus. So is poetry allied to the state.

Reading suggested by Hallam's History of Literature.
    1. "Abelard and Heloise."
    2. Look at Luigi Pulci. His "Morgante Maggiore," published in 1481, "was to the poetical romances of chivalry what Don Quixote was to their brethren in prose."
    3. Leonardo da Vinci. The most remarkable of his writings still in manuscript. For his universality of genius, "the first name of the fifteenth century."
    4. Read Boiardo's "Orlando Innamorato," published between 1491 and 1500, for its influence on Ariosto and its intrinsic merits. Its sounding names repeated by Milton in "Paradise Regained."
    [Etc.]

It was a bright thought, that of man's to have bells; no doubt the birds hear them with pleasure.

All matter, indeed, is capable of entertaining thought.

Part Two
THE JOURNAL

III.

Sunday, May 12, 1850, visited an ancient garrison-house now occupied by Fred. Ayer, who said it was built one hundred and fifty or one hundred and sixty years ago by one Emerson, and that several oxen were killed by lightning while it was building. There was also a pear tree nearly as old as the house. It was built of larger and thicker and harder brick than are used nowadays, and on the whole looked more durable and still likely to stand a hundred years. The hard burnt blue-black ends of some of the bricks were so arranged as to checker the outside. He said it was considered the handsomest house in Haverhill when it was built, and people used to come up from town some two miles to see it. He thought that they were the original doors which we saw. There were but few windows, and most of them were about two feet and a half long and a foot or more wide, only to fire out of. The oven originally projected outside. There were two large fireplaces. I walked into one, by stooping slightly, and looked up at the sky. Ayer said jokingly that some said they were so made to shoot wild geese as they flew over. The chains and hooks were suspended from a wooden bar high in the chimney. The timbers were of immense size.

In all my rambles I have seen no landscape which can make me forget Fair Haven. I still sit on its Cliff in a new spring day, and look over the awakening woods and the river, and hear the new birds sing, with the same delight as ever. It is as sweet a mystery to me as ever, what this world is. Fair Haven Lake in the south, with its pine-covered island and its meadows, the hickories putting out fresh young yellowish leaves, and the oaks light-grayish ones, while the oven-bird thrums his sawyer-like strain, and the chewink rustles through the dry leaves or repeats his jingle on a tree-top, and the wood thrush, the genius of the wood, whistles for the first time his clear and thrilling strain,—it sounds as it did the first time I heard it. The sight of these budding woods intoxicates me,—this diet drink.

The strong-colored pine, the grass of trees, in the midst of which other trees are but as weeds or flowers,—a little exotic.

Humboldt says, "It is still undetermined where life is most abundant: whether on the earth or in the fathomless depths of the ocean."

As I walked, I was intoxicated with the slight spicy odor of the hickory buds and the bruised bark of the black birch, and, in the fall, the pennyroyal.

The river is higher than it has been at this season for many years.

When the far mountains are invisible, the near ones look the higher.

To-day, May 31st, a red and white cow, being uneasy, broke out of the steam-mill pasture and crossed the bridge and broke into Elijah Wood's grounds. When he endeavored to drive her out by the bars, she boldly took to the water, wading first through the meadows full of ditches, and swam across the river, about forty rods wide at this time, and landed in her own pasture again. She was a buffalo crossing her Mississippi. This exploit conferred some dignity on the herd in my eyes, already dignified, and reflectedly on the river, which I looked on as a kind of Bosphorus.

I love to see the domestic animals reassert their native rights,—any evidence that they have not lost their original wild habits and vigor.

The year has many seasons more than are recognized in the almanac. There is that time about the first of June, the beginning of summer, when the buttercups blossom in the now luxuriant grass and I am first reminded of mowing and of the dairy. Every one will have observed different epochs. There is the time when they begin to drive cows to pasture,—about the 20th of May,—observed by the farmer, but a little arbitrary year by year. Cows spend their winters in barns and cow-yards, their summers in pastures. In summer, therefore, they may low with emphasis, "To-morrow to fresh woods and pastures new." I sometimes see a neighbor or two united with their boys and hired men to drive their cattle to some far-off country pasture, fifty or sixty miles distant in New Hampshire, early in the morning, with their sticks and dogs. It is a memorable time with the farmers' boys, and frequently their first journey from home. The herdsman in some mountain pasture is expecting them. And then in the fall, when they go up to drive them back, they speculate as to whether Janet or Brindle will know them. I heard such a boy exclaim on such an occasion, when the calf of the spring returned a heifer, as he stroked her side, "She knows me, father; she knows me." Driven up to be the cattle on a thousand hills.

I once set fire to the woods. Having set out, one April day, to go to the sources of Concord River in a boat with a single companion, meaning to camp on the bank at night or seek a lodging in some neighboring country inn or farmhouse, we took fishing tackle with us that we might fitly procure our food from the stream, Indian-like. At the shoemaker's near the river, we obtained a match, which we had forgotten. Though it was thus early in the spring, the river was low, for there had not been much rain, and we succeeded in catching a mess of fish sufficient for our dinner before we had left the town, and by the shores of Fair Haven Pond we proceeded to cook them. The earth was uncommonly dry, and our fire, kindled far from the woods in a sunny recess in the hillside on the east of the pond, suddenly caught the dry grass of the previous year which grew about the stump on which it was kindled. We sprang to extinguish it at first with our hands and feet, and then we fought it with a board obtained from the boat, but in a few minutes it was beyond our reach; being on the side of a hill, it spread rapidly upward, through the long, dry, wiry grass interspersed with bushes.

"Well, where will this end?" asked my companion. I saw that it might be bounded by Well Meadow Brook on one side, but would, perchance, go to the village side of the brook. "It will go to town," I answered. While my companion took the boat back down the river, I set out through the woods to inform the owners and to raise the town. The fire had already spread a dozen rods on every side and went leaping and crackling wildly and irreclaimably toward the wood. That way went the flames with wild delight, and we felt that we had no control over the demonic creature to which we had given birth. We had kindled many fires in the woods before, burning a clear space in the grass, without ever kindling such a fire as this.

As I ran toward the town through the woods, I could see the smoke over the woods behind me marking the spot and the progress of the flames. The first farmer whom I met driving a team, after leaving the woods, inquired the cause of the smoke. I told him. "Well," said he, "it is none of my stuff," and drove along. The next I met was the owner in his field, with whom I returned at once to the woods, running all the way. I had already run two miles. When at length we got into the neighborhood of the flames, we met a carpenter who had been hewing timber, an infirm man who had been driven off by the fire, fleeing with his axe. The farmer returned to hasten more assistance. I, who was spent with running, remained. What could I do alone against a front of flame half a mile wide?

I walked slowly through the wood to Fair Haven Cliff, climbed to the highest rock, and sat down upon it to observe the progress of the flames, which were rapidly approaching me, now about a mile distant from the spot where the fire was kindled. Presently I heard the sound of the distant bell giving the alarm, and I knew that the town was on its way to the scene. Hitherto I had felt like a guilty person,—nothing but shame and regret. But now I settled the matter with myself shortly. I said to myself: "Who are these men who are said to be the owners of these woods, and how am I related to them? I have set fire to the forest, but I have done no wrong therein, and now it is as if the lightning had done it. These flames are but consuming their natural food." (It has never troubled me from that day to this more than if the lightning had done it. The trivial fishing was all that disturbed me and disturbs me still.) So shortly I settled it with myself and stood to watch the approaching flames. It was a glorious spectacle and I was the only one there to enjoy it. The fire now reached the base of the cliff and then rushed up its sides. The squirrels ran before it in blind haste, and three pigeons dashed into the midst of the smoke. The flames flashed up the pines to their tops, as if they were powder.

When I found I was about to be surrounded by the fire, I retreated and joined the forces now arriving from the town. It took us several hours to surround the flames with our hoes and shovels and by back fires subdue them. In the midst of all I saw the farmer whom I first met, who had turned indifferently away saying it was none of his stuff, striving earnestly to save his corded wood, his stuff, which the fire had already seized and which it after all consumed.

It burned over a hundred acres or more and destroyed much young wood. When I returned home late in the day, with others of my townsmen, I could not help noticing that the crowd who were so ready to condemn the individual who had kindled the fire did not sympathize with the owners of the wood, but were in fact highly elate and as it were thankful for the opportunity which had afforded them so much sport; and it was only half a dozen owners, so called, though not all of them, who looked sour or grieved, and I felt that I had a deeper interest in the woods, knew them better and should feel their loss more, than any or all of them. The farmer whom I had first conducted to the woods was obliged to ask me the shortest way back, through his own lot. Why, then, should the half-dozen owners and the individuals who set the fire alone feel sorrow for the loss of the wood, while the rest of the town have their spirits raised? Some of the owners, however, bore their loss like men, but other some declared behind my back that I was a "damned rascal;" and a flibbertigibbet or two, who crowed like the old cock, shouted some reminiscences of "burnt woods" from safe recesses for some years after. I have had nothing to say to any of them. The locomotive engine has since burned over nearly all the same ground and more, and in some measure blotted out the memory of the previous fire. For a long time after I had learned this lesson I marvelled that while matches and tinder were contemporaries the world was not consumed; why the houses that have hearths were not burned before another day; if the flames were not as hungry now as when I waked them. I at once ceased to regard the owners and my own fault,—if fault there was any in the matter,—and attended to the phenomenon before me, determined to make the most of it. To be sure, I felt a little ashamed when I reflected on what a trivial occasion this had happened, that at the time I was no better employed than my townsmen.

That night I watched the fire, where some stumps still flamed at midnight in the midst of the blackened waste, wandering through the woods by myself; and far in the night I threaded my way to the spot where the fire had taken, and discovered the now broiled fish,—which had been dressed,—scattered over the burnt grass.

This has been a cool day, though the first of summer. The prospect of the meadows from Lee's Hill was very fine. I observe that the shadows of the trees are very distinct and heavy in such a day, falling on the fresh grass. They are as obvious as the trees themselves by mid-afternoon. Commonly we do not make much account of the distinct shadows of objects in the landscape.

To-day, June 4th, I have been tending a burning in the woods.

You must burn against the wind always, and burn slowly. When the fire breaks over the hoed line, a little system and perseverance will accomplish more toward quelling it than any man would believe. When a fire breaks out in the woods, and a man fights it too near and on the side, in the heat of the moment, without the systematic coöperation of others, he is disposed to think it a desperate case, and that this relentless fiend will run through the forest till it is glutted with food; but let the company rest from their labors a moment, and then proceed more deliberately and systematically, giving the fire a wider berth, and the company will be astonished to find how soon and easily they will subdue it. The woods themselves furnish one of the best weapons with which to contend with the fires that destroy them,—a pitch pine bough. It is the best instrument to thrash it with. There are few men who do not love better to give advice than to give assistance.

However large the fire, let a few men go to work deliberately but perseveringly to rake away the leaves and hoe off the surface of the ground at a convenient distance from the fire, while others follow with pine boughs to thrash it with when it reaches the line, and they will finally get round it and subdue it, and will be astonished at their own success.

As I was fighting the fire to-day, in the midst of the roaring and crackling,—for the fire seems to snort like a wild horse,—I heard from time to time the dying strain, the last sigh, the fine, clear, shrill scream of agony, as it were, of the trees breathing their last, probably the heated air or the steam escaping from some chink. At first I thought it was some bird, or a dying squirrel's note of anguish, or steam escaping from the tree. You sometimes hear it on a small scale in the log on the hearth.

Here it is the 8th of June, and the grass is growing apace.

Not till June can the grass be said to be waving in the fields. When the frogs dream, and the grass waves, and the buttercups toss their heads, and the heat disposes to bathe in the ponds and streams, then is summer begun.

June 21. A fire is without doubt an advantage on the whole. It sweeps and ventilates the forest floor, and makes it clear and clean. It is nature's besom. By destroying the punier underwood it gives prominence to the larger and sturdier trees, and makes a wood in which you can go and come. I have often remarked with how much more comfort and pleasure I could walk in woods through which a fire had run the previous year. It will clean the forest floor like a broom perfectly smooth and clear,—no twigs left to crackle underfoot, the dead and rotten wood removed,—and thus in the course of two or three years new huckleberry fields are created for the town,—for birds and men.

When the lightning burns the forest its Director makes no apology to man, and I was but His agent. Perhaps we owe to this accident partly some of the noblest natural parks. It is inspiriting to walk amid the fresh green sprouts of grass and shrubbery pushing upward through the charred surface with more vigorous growth.

Getting into Patchogue late one night in an oyster-boat, there was a drunken Dutchman aboard whose wit reminded me of Shakespeare. We were detained three hours waiting for the tide, and two of the fishermen took an extra dram at the beach house. Then they stretched themselves on the seaweed by the shore in the sun to sleep off the effects. One was an inconceivably broad-faced young Dutchman,—but oh! of such a peculiar breadth and heavy look, I should not know whether to call it more ridiculous or sublime. You would say that he had humbled himself so much that he was beginning to be exalted. An indescribable mynheerish stupidity. I was less disgusted by their filthiness and vulgarity, because I was compelled to look on them as animals, as swine in their sty. For the whole voyage they lay flat on their backs on the bottom of the boat, in the bilge-water and wet with each bailing, half insensible and wallowing in their vomit. But ever and anon, when aroused by the rude kicks or curses of the skipper, the Dutchman, who never lost his wit nor equanimity, though snoring and rolling in the vomit produced by his debauch, blurted forth some happy repartee like an illuminated swine. It was the earthiest, slimiest wit I ever heard. The countenance was one of a million. It was unmistakable Dutch. In the midst of a million faces of other races it could not be mistaken. It told of Amsterdam. I kept racking my brains to conceive how he could have been born in America, how lonely he must feel, what he did for fellowship.

There was a cross-eyed fellow used to help me survey,—he was my stake-driver,—and all he said was, at every stake he drove, "There, I should n't like to undertake to pull *that* up with my teeth."

It sticks in my *crop*. That's a good phrase. Many things stick there.

IV.

Sept. 19. The trees on the bank of the river have white furrows worn about them, marking the height of the freshets, at what levels the water has stood.

Water is so much more fine and sensitive an element than earth. A single boatman passing up or down unavoidably shakes the whole of a wide river, and disturbs its every reflection.

The air is an element which our voices shake still further than our oars the water.

My companion said he would drink when the boat got under the bridge, because the water would be cooler in the shade, though the stream quickly passes through the piers from shade to sun again. It is something beautiful, the act of drinking, the stooping to imbibe some of this widespread element, in obedience to instinct, without whim. We do not so simply drink in other influences.

It is pleasant to have been to a place by the way a river went.

The forms of trees and groves change with every stroke of the oar.

There is a good echo from that wood to one standing on the side of Fair Haven. It was particularly good to-day. The woodland lungs seemed particularly sound to-day; they echoed your shout with a fuller and rounder voice than it was given in, seeming to *mouth* it. You had to choose the right key or pitch, else the woods would not echo it with any spirit, and so with eloquence. Of what significance is any sound if Nature does not echo it?

I used to strike with a paddle on the side of my boat on Walden

Pond, filling the surrounding woods with circling and dilating sound, awaking the woods, "stirring them up," as a keeper of a menagerie his lions and tigers, a growl from all. All melody is a sweet echo. We wake the echo of the place we are in, its slumbering music.

I should think that savages would have made a god of echo.

I will call that Echo Wood.

There was a sawmill once on Nut Meadow Brook, near Jennie's Road. These little brooks have their history. They once turned sawmills. They even used their *influence* to destroy the primitive forests which grew on their banks, and now, for their reward, the sun is let in to dry them up and narrow their channels. Their crime rebounds against themselves.

What does education often do? It makes a straight-cut ditch of a free, meandering brook.

Nov. 11. Now is the time for wild apples. I pluck them as a wild fruit native to this quarter of the earth, fruit of old trees that have been dying ever since I was a boy and are not yet dead. From the appearance of the tree you would expect nothing but lichens to drop from it, but underneath your faith is rewarded by finding the ground strewn with spirited fruit. Frequented only by the woodpecker, deserted now by the farmer, who has not faith enough to look under the boughs. Food for walkers. Sometimes apples red inside, perfused with a beautiful blush, faery food, too beautiful to eat,—apple of the evening sky, of the Hesperides.

This afternoon I heard a single cricket singing, chirruping, in a bank, the only one I have heard for a long time, like a squirrel or a little bird, clear and shrill,—as I fancied, like an evening robin, singing in this evening of the year. A very fine and poetical strain for such a little singer. I had never before heard the cricket so like a bird. It is a remarkable note. The earth-song.

That delicate, waving, feathery dry grass which I saw yesterday is to be remembered with the autumn. The dry grasses are not dead for me. A beautiful form has as much life at one season as another.

The autumnal (?) dandelion is still bright.

I saw an old bone in the woods covered with lichens, which looked like the bone of an old settler, which yet some little animal had recently gnawed, and I plainly saw the marks of its teeth, so indefatigable is Nature to strip the flesh from bones and return it to dust again. No little rambling beast can go by some dry and ancient bone but he must turn aside and try his teeth upon it. An old bone is knocked about till it becomes dust; Nature has no mercy on it. It was quite too ancient to suggest disagreeable associations. It was like a piece of dry pine root. It survives like the memory of a man. With time all that was personal and offensive wears off.

Nov. 16. I found three good arrowheads to-day behind Dennis's. The season for them began some time ago, as soon as the farmers had sown their winter rye, but the spring, after the melting of the snow, is still better.

In literature it is only the wild that attracts us. Dullness is only another name for tameness. It is the untamed, uncivilized, free, and wild thinking in Hamlet, in the Iliad, and in all the scriptures and mythologies that delights us,—not learned in the schools, not refined and polished by art. A truly good book is something as wildly natural and primitive, mysterious and marvellous, ambrosial and fertile, as a fungus or a lichen. Suppose the muskrat or beaver were to turn his views to literature, what fresh views of nature would he present! The fault of our books and other deeds is that they are too humane, I want something speaking in some measure to the condition of muskrats and skunk-cabbage as well as of men,—not merely to a pining and complaining coterie of philanthropists.

I discover again about these times that cranberries are good to eat in small quantities as you are crossing the meadows.

What shall we do with a man who is afraid of the woods, their solitude and darkness? What salvation is there for him? God is silent and mysterious.

Some of our richest days are those in which no sun shines outwardly, but so much the more a sun shines inwardly. I love nature, I love the landscape, because it is so sincere. It never cheats me. It never jests. It is cheerfully, musically earnest. I lie and relie on the earth.

Land where the wood has been cut off and is just beginning to come up again is called sprout land.

The partridge-berry leaves checker the ground on the side of moist hillsides in the woods. Are *they* not properly called *checker*-berries?

My Journal should be the record of my love. I would write in it only of the things I love, my affection for any aspect of the world, what I love to think of. I have no more distinctness or pointedness in my yearnings than an expanding bud, which does indeed point to flower and fruit, to summer and autumn, but is aware of the warm sun and spring influence only. I feel ripe for something, yet do nothing, can't discover what that thing is. I feel fertile merely. It is seedtime with me. I have lain fallow long enough.

Notwithstanding a sense of unworthiness which possesses me, not without reason, notwithstanding that I regard myself as a good deal of a scamp, yet for the most part the spirit of the universe is unaccountably kind to me, and I enjoy perhaps an unusual share of happiness. Yet I question sometimes if there is not some settlement to come.

Nov. 26. Went to-night to see the Indians, who are still living in tents.

Their spear very serviceable. The inner, pointed part, of a hemlock knot; the side spring pieces, of hickory. Spear salmon, pickerel, trout, chub, etc.; also by birch-bark light at night, using the other end of spear as pole.

Their sled, *jeborgon* or *jebongon* (?), one foot wide, four or five long, of thin wood turned up in front; draw by a strong rope of basswood bark.

Canoe of moose-hide. One hide will hold three or four. Can be taken apart and put together very quickly. Can take out cross-bars and bring the sides together. A very convenient boat to carry and cross streams with. They say they did not make birch canoes till they had edge tools. The birches the lightest. They think our birches the same, only second growth.

Their *kee-nong-gun*, or cradle, has a hoop to prevent the child being hurt when it falls. Can't eat dirt; can be hung up out of way of snakes.

Aboak-henjo, a birch-bark vessel for water. Can boil meat in it with hot stones; takes a long time. Also a vessel of birch bark, shaped like a pan. Both ornamented by scratching the bark, which is wrong side out. Very neatly made. Valued our kettles much.

Did not know use of eye in axe. Put a string through it and wore it round neck. Cut toes.

Did not like gun. Killed one moose; scared all the rest.

A drizzling and misty day this has been, melting the snow. The mist, divided into a thousand ghostly forms, was blowing across Walden. Mr. Emerson's Cliff Hill, seen from the railroad through the mist, looked like a dark, heavy, frowning New Hampshire mountain. I do not understand fully why hills look so much larger at such a time, unless, being the most distant we see and in the horizon, we suppose them farther off and so magnify them. I think there can be no looming about it.

Nov. 28. Thursday. Cold drizzling and misty rains, which have melted the little snow. The farmers are beginning to pick up their dead wood. Within a day or two the walker finds gloves to be comfortable, and begins to think of an outside coat and of boots.

It is remarkable, but nevertheless true, as far as my observation goes, that women, to whom we commonly concede a somewhat finer and more sibylline nature, yield a more implicit obedience even to their animal instincts than men. The nature in them is stronger, the reason weaker. There are, for instance, many young and middle-aged men among my acquaintance—shoemakers, carpenters, farmers, and others—who have scruples about using animal food, but comparatively few girls or women. The latter, even the most refined, are the most intolerant of such reforms. It is, perchance, a part of woman's conformity and easy nature. Her savior must not be too strong, stern, and intellectual.

V.

Dec. 23. Here is an old-fashioned snow-storm. There is not much passing on railroads. The engineer says it is three feet deep above. Walden is frozen, one third of it, though I thought it was all frozen as I stood on the shore on one side only.

I can discern a faint foot or sled path sooner when the ground is covered with snow than when it is bare. The depression caused by the feet or the wheels is more obvious; perhaps the light and shade betray it, but I think it is mainly because the grass and weeds rise above it on each side and leave it blank, and a blank space of snow contrasts more strongly with the woods or grass than bare or beaten ground.

Even the surface of the snow is wont to be in waves like billows of the ocean.

Dec. 24. In walking across the Great Meadows to-day on the snow-crust, I noticed that the fine, dry snow which was blown over the surface of the frozen field, when I looked westward over it or toward the sun, looked precisely like steam curling up from its surface, as sometimes from a wet roof when the sun comes out after a rain.

Saw a shrike pecking to pieces a small bird, apparently a snow-bird. At length he took him up in his bill, almost half as big as himself, and flew slowly off with his prey dangling from his beak. I find that I had not associated such actions with my idea of birds. It was not birdlike.

Feb. 12. Wednesday. A beautiful day, with but little snow or ice on the ground. Though the air is sharp, as the earth is half bare the hens have strayed to some distance from the barns. The hens, standing around their lord and pluming themselves and still fretting a little, strive to fetch the year about.

I find that it is an excellent walk for variety and novelty and wildness, to keep round the edge of the meadow,—the ice not being strong enough to bear and transparent as water,—on the bare ground or snow, just between the highest water mark and the present water line,—a narrow, meandering walk, rich in unexpected views and objects. The line of rubbish which marks the higher tides—withered flags and reeds and twigs and cranberries—is to my eyes a very agreeable and significant line, which Nature traces along the edge of the meadows. It is a strongly marked, enduring natural line, which in summer reminds me that the water has once stood over where I walk. Sometimes the grooved trees tell the same tale. The wrecks of the meadow, which fill a thousand coves, and tell a thousand tales to those who can read them. Our prairial, mediterranean shore.

It is only necessary that man should start a fence that Nature should carry it on and complete it. The farmer cannot plow quite up to the rails or wall which he himself has placed, and hence it often becomes a hedgerow and sometimes a coppice.

There is something more than association at the bottom of the excitement which the roar of a cataract produces. It is allied to the circulation in our veins. We have a waterfall which corresponds even to Niagara somewhere within us.

How, when a man purchases a thing, he is determined to get and get hold of it, using how many expletives and how long a string of synonymous or similar terms signifying possession, in the legal process! What's mine's my own. An old deed of a small piece of swamp land, which I have lately surveyed at the risk of being mired past recovery, says that "the said Spaulding his Heirs and Assigns, shall and may from this (?) time, and at all times forever hereafter, by force and virtue of these presents, lawfully, peaceably and quietly have, hold, use, occupy, possess and enjoy the said swamp," etc.

May 21. Wednesday. Yesterday I made out the black and the white ashes. A double male white ash in Miles's Swamp, and two black ashes with sessile leaflets. A female white ash near railroad, in Stow's land. The white ashes by Mr. Prichard's have no blossoms, at least as yet.

If I am right, the *black* ash is improperly so called, from the color of its bark being lighter than the white.

The leaves of my new pine on Merriam's or Pine Hill are of intermediate length between those of the yellow pine and the Norway pine. I can find no cone to distinguish the tree by; but, as the leaves are *semicylindrical* and not *hollowed* I think it must be the red or Norway Pine, though it does not look very red, and is *spruce!* answering perhaps to the description of the yellow pine, which is sometimes called spruce pine.

I have heard now within a few days that peculiar dreaming sound of the frogs which belongs to the summer,—their midsummer night's dream.

I think that we are not commonly aware that man is our contemporary,—that in this strange, outlandish world, so barren, so prosaic, fit not to live in but merely to pass through, that even here so divine a creature as man does actually live. Man, the crowning fact, the god we know. While the earth supports so rare an inhabitant, there is somewhat to cheer us. I think that the standing miracle to man is man. Behind the paling yonder, come rain or shine, hope or doubt, there dwells a man, an actual being who can sympathize with our sublimest thoughts.

The frog had eyed the heavens from his marsh, until his mind was filled with visions, and he saw more than belongs to this fenny earth. He mistrusted that he was become a dreamer and visionary. Leaping across the swamp to his fellow, what was his joy and consolation to find that he too had seen the same sights in the heavens, he too had dreamed the same dreams!

From nature we turn astonished to this *near* but supernatural fact.

May 25. A fine, freshening air, a little hazy, that bathes and washes everything, saving the day from extreme heat. Walked to the hills south of Wayland by the road by Deacon Farrar's. First vista just beyond Merron's (?), looking west down a valley, with a verdant-columned elm at the extremity of the vale and the blue hills and horizon beyond. These are the resting-places in a walk. We love to see any part of the earth tinged with blue, cerulean, the color of the sky, the celestial color.

There we found the celandine in blossom. The *Pyrus arbutifolia*, variety *melanocarpa*. Gray makes also the variety *erythrocarpa*. Is this the late red choke-berry of the swamps? and is the former the earlier black one of the swamps?

The marsh-marigold, *Caltha palustris*, improperly called cowslip.

The *Cratœgus coccinea* (?), or scarlet-fruited thorn (?).

Thyme-leaved veronica, little bluish-white, streak-petalled flower by road sides. *Silene Pennsylvanica*.

What is the orange-yellow aster-like flower of the meadows now in blossom with a sweet-smelling stem when bruised?[*]

What the delicate pinkish and yellowish flower with hoary-green stem and leaves, of rocky hills.[†]

Now, at 8.30 o'clock P.M., I hear the dreaming of the frogs. So it seems to me, and so significantly passes my life away. It is like the dreaming of frogs in a summer evening.

June 3. I observed the grass waving to-day for the first time,—the swift Camilla on it. It might have been noticed before.

Clover has blossomed.

June 7. My practicalness is not to be trusted to the last. To be sure, I go upon my legs for the most part, but, being hard-pushed and dogged by a superficial common sense which is bound to near objects

---

[*] Golden senecio.

[†] Corydalis.

by beaten paths, I am off the handle, as the phrase is,—I begin to be transcendental and show where my heart is. I am like those guinea-fowl which Charles Darwin saw at the Cape de Verd Islands. He says, "They avoided us like partridges on a rainy day in September, running with their heads cocked up; and if pursued, they readily took to the wing."

It is a certain faeryland where we live. I wonder that I ever get five miles on my way, the walk is so crowded with events and phenomena. How many questions there are which I have not put to the inhabitants!

But how far can you carry *your* practicalness? How far does your knowledge really extend? When I have read in deeds only a hundred years old the words "to enjoy and possess, he and his assigns, *forever*," I have seen how short-sighted is the sense which conducts from day to day. When I read the epitaphs of those who died a century ago, they seem deader even than they expected. A day seems proportionally a long part of your "forever and a day."

One of those gentle, straight-down rainy days, when the rain begins by spotting the cultivated fields as if shaken from a pepper-box; a fishing day, when I see one neighbor after another, having donned his oil-cloth suit, walking or riding past with a fish-pole, having struck work,—a day and an employment to make philosophers of them all.

June 8. Sunday. In F.A. Michaux's, *i.e.* the younger Michaux's, "Voyage à l'ouest des Monts Alléghanys, 1802," printed at Paris, 1808:—

The current of the Ohio is so swift in the spring that it is not necessary to row. Indeed rowing would do more harm than good, since it would tend to turn the ark out of the current on to some isle or sand-bar, where it would be entangled amid floating trees. This has determined the form of the bateaux, which are not the best calculated for swiftness but to obey the current. They are from fifteen to fifty feet long by ten to twelve and fifteen, with square ends, and roof of boards like a house at one end. The sides are about four and a half feet above the water. "I was alone on the shore of the Monongahela, when I perceived, for the first time, in the distance, five or six of these bateaux which were descending this river. I could not conceive what those great square boxes were, which, abandoned to the current, presented alternately their ends, their sides, and even (or also (?), *et même*) their angles. As they came nearer, I heard a confused noise but without distinguishing anything, on account of the elevation of the sides. It was only on ascending the bank of the river that I perceived, in these bateaux, many families carrying with them their horses, cows, poultry, dismounted carts (*charrettes*), plows, harnesses, beds, agricultural implements, in short all that constitute the movables of a household (*ménage*) and the carrying on (*exploitation*) of a farm." But he was obliged to paddle his log canoe "*sans cesse*" because of the sluggishness of the current of the Ohio in April, 1802.

After travelling more than three thousand miles in North America, he says that no part is to be compared for the "*force végétative des forêts*" to the region of the Ohio between Wheeling and Marietta. Thirty-six miles above the last place he measured a plane tree on the bank of the Ohio which, at four feet from the ground, was forty-seven in circumference. Tulip and plane trees, his father had said, attained the greatest diameter of North American trees.

Gathered the first strawberries to-day.

June 11. Wednesday. Last night a beautiful summer night, not too warm, moon not quite full, after two or three rainy days. Walked to Fair Haven by railroad, returning by Potter's pasture and Sudbury road. I feared at first that there would be too much white light, like the pale remains of daylight, and not a yellow, gloomy, dreamier light; that it would be like a candlelight by day; but when I got away from the town and deeper into the night, it was better. I hear whip-poor-wills, and see a few fireflies in the meadow.

New beings have usurped the air we breathe, rounding Nature, filling her crevices with sound. To sleep where you may hear the whip-poor-will in your dreams!

The woodland paths are never seen to such advantage as in a

moonlight night, so embowered, still opening before you almost against expectation as you walk; you are so completely in the woods, and yet your feet meet no obstacles. It is as if it were not a path, but an open, winding passage through the bushes, which your feet find.

Ah, that life that I have known! How hard it is to remember what is most memorable! We remember how we itched, not how our hearts beat. I can sometimes recall to mind the quality, the immortality, of my youthful life, but in memory is the only relation to it.

I hear the night-warbler breaking out as in his dreams, made so from the first for some mysterious reason.

Our spiritual side takes a more distinct form, like our shadow which we see accompanying us.

I do not know but I feel less vigor at night; my legs will not carry me so far; as if the night were less favorable to muscular exertion,— weakened us, somewhat as darkness turns plants pale. But perhaps my experience is to be referred to being already exhausted by the day, and I have never tried the experiment fairly. Yet sometimes after a hard day's work I have found myself unexpectedly vigorous.

Only the Hunter's and Harvest moons are famous, but I think that each full moon deserves to be and has its own character well marked. One might be called the Midsummer-Night Moon.

By night no flowers, at least no variety of colors. The pinks are no longer pink; they only shine faintly, reflecting more light. Instead of flowers underfoot, stars overhead.

My shadow has the distinctness of a second person, a certain black companion bordering on the imp, and I ask, "Who is this?" which I see dodging behind me as I am about to sit down on a rock.

No one, to my knowledge, has observed the minute differences in the seasons. Hardly two nights are alike. The rocks do not feel warm to-night, for the air is warmest; nor does the sand particularly. A book of the seasons, each page of which should be written in its own season and out-of-doors, or in its own locality wherever it may be.

When you get into the road, though far from the town, and feel the sand under your feet, it is as if you had reached your own gravel walk. You no longer hear the whip-poor-will, nor regard your shadow, for here you expect a fellow-traveller. You catch yourself walking merely. The road leads your steps and thoughts alike to the town. You see only the path, and your thoughts wander from the objects which are presented to your senses. You are no longer in place. It is like conformity,—walking in the ways of men.

In Charles Darwin's "Voyage of a Naturalist round the World," commenced in 1831:—

Hail in Buenos Ayres as large as small apples; killed thirteen deer, beside ostriches, which last also it blinded, etc., etc. Dr. Malcomson told him of hail in India, in 1831, which "much injured the cattle." Stones flat, one ten inches in circumference; passed through windows, making round holes.

I would like to read Azara's Voyage.

Horses first landed at the La Plata in 1535. Now these, with cattle and sheep, have altered the whole aspect of the country,—vegetation, etc. "The wild pig in some parts probably replaces the peccari; packs of wild dogs may be heard howling on the wooded banks of the less frequented streams; and the common cat, altered into a large and fierce animal, inhabits rocky hills."

The great table-land of southern Mexico makes the division between North and South America with reference to the migration of animals.

Tree ferns in Van Diemen's Land (lat. 45°) six feet in circumference.

JUNE 13. Walked to Walden last night (moon not quite full) by railroad and upland wood-path, returning by Wayland road. Last full moon the elms had not leaved out,—cast no heavy shadows,—and their outlines were less striking and rich in the streets at night.

I noticed night before night before last from Fair Haven how valuable was some water by moonlight, like the river and Fair Haven Pond, though far away, reflecting the light with a faint glimmering sheen, as in the spring of the year. The water shines with an inward light like a heaven on earth. The silent depth and serenity and majesty of water! Strange that men should distinguish gold and diamonds, when these precious elements are so common. I saw a distant river by moonlight, making no noise, yet flowing, as by day, still to the sea, like melted silver reflecting the moonlight. Far away it lay encircling the earth. How far away it may look in the night, and even from a low hill how miles away down in the valley! As far off as paradise and the delectable country! There is a certain glory attends on water by night. By it the heavens are related to the earth, undistinguishable from a sky beneath you. And I forgot to say that after I reached the road by Potter's bars,—or further, by Potter's Brook,—I saw the moon suddenly reflected full from a pool. A puddle from which you may see the moon reflected, and the earth dissolved under your feet. The magical moon with attendant stars suddenly looking up with mild lustre from a window in the dark earth.

I observed also the same night a halo about my shadow in the moonlight, which I referred to the accidentally lighter color of the surrounding surface; I transferred my shadow to the darkest patches of grass, and saw the halo there equally. It serves to make the outlines of the shadow more distinct.

But now for last night. A few fireflies in the meadow. Do they shine, though invisibly, by day? Is their candle lighted by day? It is not nightfall till the whip-poor-wills begin to sing.

As I entered the Deep Cut, I was affected by beholding the first faint reflection of genuine and unmixed moonlight on the eastern sand-bank while the horizon, yet red with day, was tingeing the western side. What an interval between those two lights! The light of the moon,—in what age of the world does that fall upon the earth? The moonlight was as the earliest and dewy morning light, and the daylight tinge reminded me much more of the night. There were the old and new dynasties opposed, contrasted, and an interval between, which time could not span. Then is night, when the daylight yields to the nightlight. It suggested an interval, a distance not recognized in history. Nations have flourished in that light.

When I had climbed the sand-bank on the left, I felt the warmer current or stratum of air on my cheek, like a blast from a furnace.

The white stems of the pines, which reflected the weak light, standing thick and close together while their lower branches were gone, reminded me that the pines are only larger grasses which rise to a chaffy head, and we the insects that crawl between them. They are particularly grass-like.

How long do the gales retain the heat of the sun? I find them retreated high up the sides of hills, especially on open fields or cleared places. Does, perchance, any of this pregnant air survive the dews of night? Can any of it be found remembering the sun of yesterday even in the morning hours. Does, perchance, some puff, some blast, survive the night on elevated clearings surrounded by the forest?

The bullfrog belongs to summer. The different frogs mark the seasons pretty well,—the peeping hyla, the dreaming frog,* and the bullfrog. I believe that all may be heard at last occasionally together.

I heard partridges drumming to-night as late as 9 o'clock. What singularly space penetrating and filling sound! Why am I never nearer to its source?

We do not commonly live our life out and full; we do not fill all our pores with our blood; we do not inspire and expire fully and entirely enough, so that the wave, the comber, of each inspiration shall break upon our extremest shores, rolling till it meets the sand which bounds us, and the sound of the surf come back to us. Might not a bellows assist us to breathe? That our breathing should create a wind in a calm day! We live but a fraction of our life. Why do we not let on the flood, raise the gates, and set all our wheels in motion? He that hath ears to hear, let him hear. Employ your senses.

The newspapers tell us of news not to be named even with that in its own kind which an observing man can pick up in a solitary walk, as if it gained some importance and dignity by its publicness. Do we need to be advertised each day that such is still the routine of life?

The tree-toad's, too, is a summer sound.

I hear, just as the night sets in, faint notes from time to time from some sparrow (?) falling asleep,—a vesper hymn,—and later,

---

*Toad

in the woods, the chuckling, rattling sound of some unseen bird on the near trees. The nighthawk booms wide awake.

By moonlight we see not distinctly even the surface of the earth, but our daylight experience supplies us with confidence.

As I approached the pond down Hubbard's Path, after coming out of the woods into a warmer air, I saw the shimmering of the moon on its surface, and, in the near, now flooded cove, the water-bugs, darting, circling about, made streaks or curves of light. The moon's inverted pyramid of shimmering light commenced about twenty rods off, like so much micaceous sand. But I was startled to see midway in the dark water a bright flamelike, more than phosphorescent light crowning the crests of the wavelets, which at first I mistook for fireflies, and thought even of cucullos.* It had the appearance of a pure, smokeless flame a half-dozen inches long, issuing from the water and bending flickeringly along its surface. I thought of St. Elmo's lights and the like. But, coming near to the shore of the pond itself, these flames increased, and I saw that even this was so many broken reflections of the moon's disk, though one would have said they were of an intenser light than the moon herself; from contrast with the surrounding water they were. Standing up close to the shore and nearer the rippled surface, I saw the reflections of the moon sliding down the watery concave like so many lustrous burnished coins poured from a bag with inexhaustible lavishness, and the lambent flames on the surface were much multiplied, seeming to slide along a few inches with each wave before they were extinguished; and I saw how farther and farther off they gradually merged in the general sheen, which, in fact, was made up of a myriad little mirrors reflecting the disk of the moon with equal brightness to an eye rightly placed. The pyramid or sheaf of light which we see springing from near where we stand only, in fact, is the outline of that portion of the shimmering surface which an eye takes in. To myriad eyes suitably placed, the whole surface of the pond would be seen to shimmer, or rather it would be seen, as the waves turned up their mirrors, to be covered with those bright

---

*["Cocuyo," a West Indian firefly.]

flame-like reflections of the moon's disk, like a myriad candles everywhere issuing from the waves; *i.e.* if there were as many eyes as angles presented by the waves, the whole surface would appear as bright as the moon; and these reflections are dispersed in all directions into the atmosphere, flooding it with light. No wonder that water reveals itself so far by night; even further in many states of the atmosphere than by day. I thought at first it some unusual phosphorescence. In some positions these flames were star-like points, brighter than the brightest stars. Suddenly a flame would show itself in a near and dark space, precisely like some inflammable gas on the surface,—as if an inflammable gas made its way up from the bottom.

I heard my old musical, simple-noted owl. The sound of the *dreaming* frogs prevails over the others. Occasionally a bullfrog near me made an obscene noise, a sound like an eructation, near me. I think they must be imbodied eructations. They suggest flatulency.

The pond is higher than ever, so as to hinder fishermen, and I could hardly get to the true shore here on account of the bushes. I pushed out in a boat a little and heard the chopping of the waves under its bow. And on the bottom I saw the moving reflections of the shining waves, faint streaks of light revealing the shadows of the waves or the opaqueness of the water.

As I climbed the hill again toward my old bean-field, I listened to the ancient, familiar, immortal, dear cricket sound under all others, hearing at first some distinct chirps; but when these ceased I was aware of the general earth-song, which my hearing had not heard, amid which these were only taller flowers in a bed, and I wondered if behind or beneath this there was not some other chant yet more universal. Why do we not hear when this begins in the spring? and when it ceases in the fall? Or is it too gradual?

After I have got into the road I have no thought to record all the way home,—the walk is comparatively barren. The leafy elm sprays seem to droop more by night (??).

June 15. Sunday. Darwin still:— [*3 pages of notes*]
Saw the first wild rose to-day on the west side of the railroad

causeway. The whiteweed has suddenly appeared, and the clover gives whole fields a rich and florid appearance,—the rich red and the sweet-scented white. The fields are blushing with the red species as the western sky at evening. The blue-eyed grass, well named, looks up to heaven. And the yarrow, with its persistent dry stalks and heads, is now ready to blossom again. The dry stems and heads of last year's tansy stand high above the new green leaves.

After walking by night several times I now walk by day, but I am not aware of any crowning advantage in it. I see small objects better, but it does not enlighten me any. The day is more trivial.

June 29. There is a great deal of white clover this year. In many fields where there has been no clover seed sown for many years at least, it is more abundant than the red, and the heads are nearly as large. Also pastures which are close cropped, and where I think there was little or no clover last year, are spotted white with a humbler growth. As this is the season for the swarming of bees, and this clover is very attractive to them, it is probably the more difficult to secure them; at any rate it is the more important to secure their services now that they can make honey so fast. It is an interesting inquiry why this year is so favorable to the growth of clover!

The panicled cornel, a low shrub, in blossom by wallsides now.

I thought that one peculiarity of my "Week" was its *hypæthral* character, to use an epithet applied to those Egyptian temples which are open to the heavens above, *under the ether.* I thought that it had little of the atmosphere of the house about it, but might wholly have been written, as in fact it was to a considerable extent, out-of-doors. It was only at a late period in writing it, as it happened, that I used any phrases implying that I lived in a house or led a *domestic* life. I trust it does not smell of the study and library, even of the poet's attic, as of the fields and woods; that it is a hypæthral or unroofed book, lying open under the ether and permeated by it, open to all weathers, not easy to be kept on a shelf.

The potatoes are beginning to blossom.

July 2. A traveller! I love his title. A traveller is to be reverenced as such. His profession is the best symbol of our life. Going from —— toward ——; it is the history of every one of us.

It takes but little distance to make the hills and even the meadows look blue to-day. That principle which gives the air an azure color is more abundant.

To-day the milkweed is blossoming. Some of the raspberries are ripe, the most innocent and simple of fruits, the purest and most ethereal. Cherries are ripe. Strawberries in the gardens have passed their prime.

July 6. There is some advantage in being the humblest, cheapest, least dignified man in the village, so that the very stable boys shall damn you. Methinks I enjoy that advantage to an unusual extent. There is many a coarsely well-meaning fellow, who knows only the skin of me, who addresses me familiarly by my Christian name. I get the whole good of him and lose nothing myself.

The red clover heads are now turned black. It is but a short time that their rich bloom lasts. The white is black or withering also. Whiteweed still looks white in the fields. Blue-eyed grass is now rarely seen. The grass in the fields and meadows is not so fresh and fair as it was a fortnight ago. It is dryer and riper and ready for the mowers. Now June is past. June is the month for grass and flowers. Now grass is turning to hay, and flowers to fruits. Already I gather ripe blueberries on the hills. The red-topped grass is in its prime, tingeing the fields with red.

VI.

July 14. Passing over the Great Fields (where I have been surveying a road) this forenoon, where were some early turnips, the county commissioners plucked and pared them with their knives and ate them. I, too, tried hard to chew a mouthful of raw turnip and realize the life of cows and oxen, for it might be a useful habit in extremities. These things occur as the seasons revolve. These are things which travellers will do.

July 16. Wednesday. Methinks my present experience is nothing; my past experience is all in all. I think that no experience which I have to-day comes up to, or is comparable with, the experiences of my boyhood. And not only this is true, but as far back as I can remember I have unconsciously referred to the experiences of a previous state of existence. My life was ecstasy. In youth, before I lost any of my senses, I can remember that I was all alive, and inhabited my body with inexpressible satisfaction; both its weariness and its refreshment were sweet to me. I can remember how I was astonished. I looked in books for some recognition of a kindred experience, but, strange to say, I found none. With all your science can you tell how it is, and whence it is, that light comes into the soul?

Berries are just beginning to ripen, and children are planning expeditions after them. They are important as introducing children to the fields and woods, and as wild fruits of which much account is made. During the berry season the schools have a vacation, and many little fingers are busy picking these small fruits. It is ever a pastime, not a drudgery. I remember how glad I was when I was kept from school a half a day to pick huckleberries on a neighboring hill all by myself to make a pudding for the family dinner. Ah, they got nothing but the pudding, but I got invaluable experience beside! A half a day of liberty like that was like the promise of life eternal. It was emancipation in New England. O, what a day was there, my countrymen!

Now, at 4 P.M., I hear the pewee in the woods, and the cuckoo reminds me of some silence among the birds I had not noticed. The vireo (red-eyed?) sings like a robin at even, incessantly,—for I have now turned into Conant's woods. The oven-bird helps fill some pauses. The poison sumach shows its green berries, now unconscious of guilt. The heart-leaved loosestrife (*Lysimachia ciliata*) is seen in low open woods. The breeze displays the white under sides of the oak leaves and gives a fresh and flowing look to the woods. The river is a dark-blue winding stripe amid the green of the meadow. What is the color of the world? Green mixed with yellowish and reddish for hills and ripe grass, and darker green for trees and forests; blue spotted with dark and white for sky and clouds, and dark blue for water. Beyond the old house I hear the squirrel chirp in the wall like a sparrow; so Nature merges her creations into one. I am refreshed by the view of Nobscot and the southwestern vales, from Conantum, seething with the blue element. Here comes a small bird with a ricochet flight and a faint twittering note like a messenger from Elysium. The rush sparrow jingles her small change, pure silver, on the counter of the pasture. From far I see the rye stacked up. A few dead trees impart the effect of wildness to the landscape, though it is a feature rare in an old settled country.

Green apples are now so large as to remind me of coddling and the autumn again. The season of fruits is arrived. The dog's-bane has a pretty, delicate bell-like flower. The Jersey tea abounds. I see the marks of the scythes in the fields, showing the breadth of each swath the mowers cut. Filberts are formed, and you may get the berry stains out of your hands with their husks, if you have any. Nightshade is in blossom. Came through the pine plains behind James Baker's, where late was open pasture. These are among our pleasantest woods,—open, level, with blackberry vines interspersed and flowers, as lady's-slippers, earlier, and pinks on the outskirts. Each tree has room enough. And now I hear the wood thrush from the shade, who loves these pine woods as well as I.

July 18. I might have added to the list of July 16th the *Aralia hispida*, bristling aralia; the heart-leaved loosestrife (*Lysimachia ciliata*); also the upright loosestrife (*L. racemosa*), with a rounded terminal raceme; the tufted vetch (*Vicia cracca*). Sweet-gale fruit now green.

July 19. Here I am thirty-four years old, and yet my life is almost wholly unexpanded. How much is in the germ! There is such an interval between my ideal and the actual in many instances that I may say I am unborn. There is the instinct for society, but no society. Life is not long enough for one success. Within another thirty-four years that miracle can hardly take place. Methinks my seasons revolve more slowly than those of nature; I am differently timed. I am contented. This rapid revolution of nature, even of nature in me, why should it hurry me? Let a man step to the music which he hears, however measured. Is it important that I should mature as soon as an apple tree? aye, as soon as an oak? May not my life in nature, in proportion as it is supernatural, be only the spring and infantile portion of my spirit's life? Shall I turn my spring to summer? May I not sacrifice a hasty and petty completeness here to entireness there? If my curve is large, why bend it to a smaller circle? My spirit's unfolding observes not the pace of nature. The society which I was made for is not here.

July 22. The season of morning fogs has arrived. I think it is connected with dog-days. Perhaps it is owing to the greater contrast between the night and the day, the nights being nearly as cold, while the days are warmer?

I bathe me in the river. I lie down where it is shallow, amid the weeds over its sandy bottom; but it seems shrunken and parched; I find it difficult to get *wet* through. I would fain be the channel of a mountain brook. I bathe, and in a few hours I bathe again, not remembering that I was wetted before. When I come to the river, I take off my clothes and carry them over, then bathe and wash off the mud and continue my walk. I would fain take rivers in my walks endwise.

July 23. 8 A.M.—A comfortable breeze blowing. Methinks I can write better in the afternoon, for the novelty of it, if I should go abroad this morning. My genius makes distinctions which my understanding cannot, and which my senses do not report. If I should reverse the usual,—go forth and saunter in the fields all the forenoon, then sit down in my chamber in the afternoon, which it is so unusual for me to do,—it would be like a new season to me, and the novelty of it inspire me. The wind has fairly blown me outdoors; the elements were so lively and active, and I so sympathized with them, that I could not sit while the wind went by. Is the literary man to live always or chiefly sitting in a chamber through which nature enters by a window only? What is the use of the summer?

The mind is subject to moods, as the shadows of clouds pass over the earth. Pay not too much heed to them. Let not the traveller stop for them. They consist with the fairest weather. By the mood of my mind, I suddenly felt dissuaded from continuing my walk, but I observed at the same instant that the shadow of a cloud was passing over the spot on which I stood, though it was of small extent, which, if it had no connection with my mood, at any rate suggested how transient and little to be regarded that mood was. I kept on, and in a moment the sun shone on my walk within and without.

The button-bush in blossom. The tobacco-pipe in damp woods. Certain localities only a few rods square in the fields and on the hills, sometimes the other side of a wall, attract me as if they had been the scene of pleasure in another state of existence.

But this habit of close observation,—in Humboldt, Darwin, and others. Is it to be kept up long, this science? Do not tread on the heels of your experience. Be impressed without making a minute of it. Poetry puts an interval between the impression and the expression,—waits till the seed germinates naturally.

July 25. Friday. Started for Clark's Island at 7 A.M.

At 9 A.M. took the Hingham boat and was landed at Hull. There was a pleasure party on board, apparently boys and girls belonging to the South End, going to Hingham. There was a large proportion of ill-dressed and ill-mannered boys of Irish extraction. A sad sight to behold! Little boys of twelve years, prematurely old, sucking cigars! I felt that if I were their mothers I should whip them and send them to bed. Such children should be dealt with as for stealing or impurity. What right have parents to beget, to bring up, and attempt to *educate* children in a city? I thought of infanticide among the Orientals with complacency. I seemed to hear infant voices lisp, "Give us a fair chance, parents." There is no such squalidness in the country.

July 29. Tuesday. A northeast wind with rain, but the sea is the wilder for it. In the afternoon I sailed to Plymouth, three miles, notwithstanding the drizzling rain, or "drisk," as Uncle Ned called it. We passed round the head of Plymouth beach, which is three miles long. I did not know till afterward that I had landed where the Pilgrims did and passed over the Rock on Hedge's Wharf. Returning, we had more wind and tacking to do.

This sailing on salt water was something new to me. The boat is such a living creature, even this clumsy one sailing within five points of the wind. The sailboat is an admirable invention, by which you compel the wind to transport you even against itself. It is easier to guide than a horse; the slightest pressure on the tiller suffices. I think the inventor must have been greatly surprised, as well as delighted, at the success of his experiment. It is so contrary to expectation, as if the elements were disposed to favor you. This deep, unfordable sea! but this wind ever blowing over it to transport you! At 10 P.M. it was perfectly fair and bright starlight.

July 31. At 11 A.M. set sail to Plymouth.

Mr. Thomas Russell, who cannot be seventy, at whose house on Leyden Street I took tea and spent the evening, told me that he remembered to have seen Ebenezer Cobb, a native of Plymouth, who died in Kingston in 1801, aged one hundred and seven, who remembered to have had personal knowledge of Peregrine White, saw him an old man riding on horseback (he lived to be eighty-three). White was born at Cape Cod Harbor before the Pilgrims got to Plymouth. Pilgrim Hall. They used to crack off pieces of the Forefathers' Rock for visitors with a cold chisel, till the town forbade it. The stone remaining at wharf is about seven feet square.

LEFT Plymouth at 9 A.M., August 1st.

I could make a list of things ill-managed. We Yankees do not deserve our fame. *Viz.*: Why have we not a decent pocket-map of the State of Massachusetts? There is the large map. Why is it not cut into half a dozen sheets and folded into a small cover for the pocket? Are there no travellers to use it? Well, to tell the truth, there are but few, and that's the reason why. Men go by railroad, and State maps hanging in bar-rooms are small enough. The State has been admirably surveyed at a great cost, and yet Dearborn's Pocket-Map is the best one we have!

Aug. 4. As my eye rested on the blossom of the meadow-sweet in a hedge, I heard the note of an autumnal cricket, and was penetrated with the sense of autumn. Was it sound? or was it form? or was it scent? or was it flavor? It is now the royal month of August.

Aug. 5. Ah, what a poor, dry compilation is the "Annual of Scientific Discovery!" I trust that observations are made during the year which are not chronicled there,—that some mortal may have caught a glimpse of Nature in some corner of the earth during the year 1851. One sentence of perennial poetry would make me forget, would atone for, volumes of mere science. The astronomer is as blind to the significant phenomena, or the significance of phenomena, as the wood-sawyer who wears glasses to defend his eyes from sawdust. The question is not what you look at, but what you see.

Aug. 8. 7.30 P.M.—To Conantum.

The moon has not yet quite filled her horns.

Might not this be called the Invalid's Moon, on account of the warmth of the nights? The principal employment of the farmers now seems to be getting their meadow-hay and cradling some oats, etc.

Aug. 17. For a day or two it has been quite cool, a coolness that was felt even when sitting by an open window in a thin coat on the west side of the house in the morning, and you naturally sought the sun at that hour. The coolness concentrated your thought, however. As I could not command a sunny window, I went abroad on the morning of the 15th and lay in the sun in the fields in my thin coat, though it was rather cool even there. I feel as if this coolness would do me good. If it only makes my life more pensive! Why should pensiveness be akin to sadness? There is a certain fertile sadness which I would not avoid, but rather earnestly seek. It is positively joyful to me. It saves my life from being trivial. My life flows with a deeper current, no longer as a shallow and brawling stream, parched and shrunken by the summer heats. My heart leaps into my mouth at the sound of the wind in the woods. I, whose life was but yesterday so desultory and shallow, suddenly recover my spirits, my spirituality, through my hearing. For joy I could embrace the earth; I shall delight to be buried in it. And then to think of those I love among men, who will know that I love them though I tell them not! I sometimes feel as if I were rewarded merely for expecting better hours. I did not despair of worthier moods, and now I have occasion to be grateful for the flood of life that is flowing over me. I am not so poor: I can smell the ripening apples; the very rills are deep; the autumnal flowers, the *Trichostema dichotomum*,—not only its bright blue flower above the sand, but its strong wormwood scent which belongs to the season,—feed my spirit, endear the earth to me, make me value myself and rejoice; the quivering of pigeons' wings reminds me of the tough fibre of the air which they rend. I thank you, God. I do not deserve anything, I am unworthy of the least regard; and yet I am made to rejoice. I am impure and worthless, and yet the world is gilded for my delight and holidays are prepared for me, and my path is strewn with flowers. It seems to me that I am more rewarded for my expectations than for anything I do or can do. And why should I speak to my friends? for how rarely is it that I am I; and are they, then, they? We will meet, then, far away. Ah, the very brooks seem fuller of reflections than they were! Ah, such provoking sibylline sentences they are! The shallowest is all at once unfathomable. How can that depth be fathomed where a man may see himself reflected? The rill I stopped to drink at I drink in more than I expected. Nut Meadow Brook where it crosses the road beyond Jenny Dugan's that was. I do not drink in vain. I mark that brook as if I had swallowed a water snake that would live in my stomach. I have swallowed something worth the while. The day is not what it was before I stooped to drink. Ah, I shall hear from that draught! It is not in vain that I have drunk. I have drunk an arrowhead. If flows from where all fountains rise.

How many ova have I swallowed? Who knows what will be hatched within me? There were some seeds of thought, methinks, floating in that water, which are expanding in me. The man must not drink of the running streams, the living waters, who is not prepared to have all nature reborn in him,—to suckle monsters. The snake in my stomach lifts his head to my mouth at the sound of running water. When was it that I swallowed a snake? I have got rid of the snake in my stomach. I drank of stagnant waters once. That accounts for it. I caught him by the throat and drew him out, and had a well day after all. Is there not such a thing as getting rid of the snake which you have swallowed when young, when thoughtless you stooped and drank at stagnant waters, which has worried you in your waking hours and in your sleep ever since, and appropriated the life that was yours? Will he not ascend into your mouth at the sound of running water? Then catch him boldly by the head and draw him out, though you may think his tail be curled about your vitals.

Aug. 19. Clematis Virginiana; calamint; *Lycopus Europeus*, water horehound.

This is a world where there are flowers.

P.M.—To Marlborough Road *via* Clamshell Hill, Jenny Dugan's, Round Pond, Canoe Birch Road (Deacon Dakin's), and White Pond.

The poet must be continually watching the moods of his mind, as the astronomer watches the aspects of the heavens. What might we not expect from a long life faithfully spent in this wise? The humblest observer would see some stars shoot. A faithful description as by a disinterested person of the thoughts which visited a certain mind in threescore years and ten, as when one reports the number and character of the vehicles which pass a particular point. As travellers go round the world and report natural objects and phenomena, so faithfully let another stay at home and report the phenomena of his own life,—catalogue stars, those thoughts whose orbits are as rarely calculated as comets. It matters not whether they visit my mind or yours,—only that it come from heaven. A meteorological journal of the mind. You shall observe what occurs in your latitude, I in mine.

The grass in the high pastures is almost as dry as hay. The seasons do not cease a moment to revolve, and therefore Nature rests no longer at her culminating point than at any other. If you are not out at the right instant, the summer may go by and you not see it. How much of the year is spring and fall! how little can be called summer! The grass is no sooner grown than it begins to wither.

I do not like to hear the name of particular States given to birds and flowers which are found in all equally,—an Maryland yellow-throat, etc., etc. The *Canadenses* and *Virginicas* may be suffered to pass for the most part, for there is historical as well as natural reason at least for them. Canada is the peculiar country of some and the northern limit of many more plants. And Virginia, which was originally the name for all the Atlantic shore, has some right to stand for the South.

I fear that the character of my knowledge is from year to year becoming more distinct and scientific; that, in exchange for views as wide as heaven's cope, I am being narrowed down to the field of the microscope. I see details, not wholes nor the shadow of the whole. I count some parts, and say, "I know." The cricket's chirp now fills the air in dry fields near pine woods.

Aug. 20. The *Rhexia Virginica* is a showy flower at present.

How copious and precise the botanical language to describe the leaves, as well as the other parts of a plant! Botany is worth studying if only for the precision of its terms,—to learn the value of words and of system. It is wonderful how much pains has been taken to describe a flower's leaf, compared for instance with the care that is taken in describing a psychological fact. Suppose as much ingenuity (perhaps it would be needless) in making a language to express the sentiments! We are armed with language adequate to describe each leaf in the field, or at least to distinguish it from each other, but not to describe a human character.

VII.

Aug. 22. It is the fault of some excellent writers—De Quincey's first impressions on seeing London suggest it to me—that they express themselves with too great fullness and detail. They give the most faithful, natural, and lifelike account of their sensations, mental and physical, but they lack moderation and sententiousness. They do not affect us by an ineffectual earnestness and a reserve of meaning, like a stutterer; they say all they mean. Their sentences are not concentrated and nutty. Sentences which suggest far more than they say, which have an atmosphere about them, which do not merely report an old, but make a new, impression; sentences which suggest as many things and are as durable as a Roman aqueduct; to frame these, that is the *art* of writing. Sentences which are expensive, towards which so many volumes, so much life, went; which lie like boulders on the page, up and down or across; which contain the seed of other sentences, not mere repetition, but creation. If De Quincey had suggested each of his pages in a sentence and passed on, it would have been far more excellent writing.

Aug. 28. The pretty little blue flower in the Heywood Brook, Class V, Order 1. Corolla about one sixth of an inch in diameter, with five rounded segments; stamens and pistil shorter than corolla; calyx with five acute segments and acute sinuses; leaves not opposite, lanceolate, spatulate, blunt, somewhat hairy on upper side with a midrib only, sessile; flowers in a loose raceme on rather long pedicels. Whole plant decumbent, curving upward. Wet ground. Said to be like the forget-me-not.

Raphanus Raphanistrum, or wild radish, in meadows.

Evening.—A new moon visible in the east.

I omit the unusual—the hurricanes and earthquakes—and describe the common. This has the greatest charm and is the true theme of poetry. You may have the extraordinary for your province, if you will let me have the ordinary. Give me the obscure life, the cottage of the poor and humble, the workdays of the world, the barren fields, the smallest share of all things but poetic perception. Give me but the eyes to see the things which you possess.

Aug. 29. The air is filled with mist, yet a transparent mist, a principle in it you might call *flavor*, which ripens fruits. This haziness seems to confine and concentrate the sunlight, as if you lived in a halo. It is August.

Aug. 31. One of these drooping clusters of potato balls would be as good a symbol, emblem, of the year's fertility as anything,—better surely than a bunch of grapes. Fruit of the strong soil, containing potash (?). The vintage is come; the olive is ripe.

Why not for my coat-of-arms, for device, a drooping cluster of potato balls,—in a *potato* field?

What right has a New England poet to sing of wine, who never saw a vineyard, who obtains his liquor from the grocer. A Yankee singing in praise of wine! It is not sour grapes in this case, it is sweet grapes; the more inaccessible they are the sweeter they are. It seemed to me that the year had nothing so much to brag of as these potato balls. Do they not concern New-Englanders a thousand times more than all her grapes?

Sept. 1. Is not disease the rule of existence? There is not a lily pad floating on the river but has been riddled by insects. Almost every shrub and tree has its gall, often-times esteemed its chief ornament and hardly to be distinguished from the fruit. If misery loves company, misery has company enough. Now, at midsummer, find me a perfect leaf or fruit.

Sept. 2. What affinity is it brings the goldfinch to the sunflower—both yellow—to pick its seeds? Whatever things I perceive with my entire man, those let me record, and it will be poetry.

In a day or two the first message will be conveyed or transmitted over the magnetic telegraph through this town, as a thought traverses space, and no citizen of the town shall be aware of it. The atmosphere is full of telegraphs equally unobserved. We are not confined to Morse's or House's or Bain's line.

Raise some sunflowers to attract the goldfinches, to feed them as well as your hens.

I now begin to pluck wild apples.

Old Cato says well, "*Patremfamilias vendacem, non emacem, esse oportet.*" These Latin terminations express better than any English that I know the greediness, as it were, and tenacity of purpose with which the husbandman and householder is required to be a seller and not a buyer,—with mastiff-like tenacity,—these *lipped* words, which, like the lips of moose and browsing creatures, gather in the herbage and twigs with a certain greed. This termination *cious* adds force to a word, like the lips of browsing creatures, which greedily collect what the jaw holds; as in the word "tenacious" the first half represents the kind of jaw which holds, the last the lips which collect. It can only be pronounced by a certain opening and protruding of the lips; so "avaricious." These words express the sense of their simple roots with the addition, as it were, of a certain lip greediness. Hence "capacious" and "capacity," "emacity." When these expressive words are used, the hearer gets something to chew upon. What is *luscious* is especially enjoyed by the lips. To be edacious and voracious is to be not nibbling and swallowing merely, but eating and swallowing while the lips are greedily collecting more food.

There is a reptile in the throat of the greedy man always thirsting and famishing. It is not his own natural hunger and thirst which he satisfies.

A fire in the sitting-room to-day. Walk in the afternoon by Walden road and railroad to Minn's place, and round it to railroad and home. Carried umbrellas, it mizzling. As in the night, now in the rain, I smell the fragrance of the woods. The prunella leaves have turned a delicate claret or lake color by the roadside. I am interested in these revolutions as much as in those of kingdoms. Is there not tragedy enough in the autumn? Walden seems to be going down at last.

Sept. 3. Why was there never a poem on the cricket? Its creak seems to me to be one of the most prominent and obvious facts in the world, and the least heeded.

2 P.M.—To Hubbard's Swimming-Place and Grove in rain.

As I went under the new telegraph-wire, I heard it vibrating like a harp high overhead. It was as the sound of a far-off glorious life, a supernal life, which came down to us, and vibrated the lattice-work of this life of ours.

The ivy leaves are turning red. Fall dandelions stand thick in the meadows.

How much the Roman must have been indebted to his agriculture, dealing with the earth, its clods and stubble, its dust and mire. Their farmer consuls were their glory, and they well knew the farm to be the nursery of soldiers. Read Cato to see what kind of legs the Romans stood on.

Walk often in drizzly weather, for then the small weeds (especially if they stand on bare ground), covered with rain-drops like beads, appear more beautiful than ever,—the hypericums, for instance. They are equally beautiful when covered with dew, fresh and adorned, almost spirited away, in a robe of dewdrops.

Identified spotted spurge (*Euphorbia maculata*), apparently out of blossom. Shepherd's-purse and chickweed.

As for walking, the inhabitants of large English towns are confined almost exclusively to their parks and to the highways. The few footpaths in their vicinities "are gradually vanishing," says Wilkinson, "under the encroachments of the proprietors." He proposes that the people's right to them be asserted and defended and that they be kept in a passable state at the public expense. "This," says he, "would be easily done by means of asphalt laid upon a good foundation"!!! So much for walking, and the prospects of walking, in the neighborhood of English large towns.

I should die from mere nervousness at the thought of such confinement. I should hesitate before I were born, if those terms could be made known to me beforehand. Fenced in forever by those green barriers of fields, where gentlemen are seated! Can they be said to be inhabitants of this globe? Will they be content to inhabit heaven thus partially?

Sept. 4. We drink in the meadow at Second Division Brook, then sit awhile to watch its yellowish pebbles and the cress (?) in it and other weeds. The ripples cover its surface like a network and are faithfully reflected on the bottom. In some places, the sun reflected from ripples on a flat stone looks like a golden comb. The whole brook seems as busy as a loom: it is a woof and warp of ripples; fairy fingers are throwing the shuttle at every step, and the long, waving brook is the fine product. The water is wonderfully clear.

In the summer we lay up a stock of experiences for the winter, as the squirrel of nuts,—something for conversation in winter evenings. I love to think then of the more distant walks I took in summer.

At the powder-mills the carbonic acid gas in the road from the building where they were making charcoal made us cough for twenty or thirty rods.

Saw some gray squirrels whirling their cylinder by the roadside. How fitted that cylinder to this animal! "A squirrel is easily taught to turn his cylinder" might be a saying frequently applicable. And as they turned, one leaped over or dodged under another most gracefully and unexpectedly, with interweaving motions. It was the circus and menagerie combined. So human they were, exhibiting themselves.

It is wise to write on many subjects, to try many themes, that so you may find the right and inspiring one. Be greedy of occasions to express your thought. Improve the opportunity to draw analogies. There are innumerable avenues to a perception of the truth. Improve the suggestion of each object however humble, however slight and transient the provocation. What else is there to be improved? Who knows what opportunities he may neglect? It is not in vain that the mind turns aside this way or that: follow its leading; apply it whither it inclines to go. Probe the universe in a myriad points. Be avaricious of these impulses. You must try a thousand themes before you find the right one, as nature makes a thousand acorns to get one oak. He is a wise man and experienced who has taken many views; to whom stones and plants and animals and a myriad objects have each suggested something, contributed something.

And now, methinks, this wider wood-path is not bad, for it admits of society more conveniently. Two can walk side by side in it in the ruts, aye, and one more in the horse-track.

As I looked back up the stream from near the bridge (I suppose on the road from Potter's house to Stow), I on the railroad, I saw the ripples sparkling in the sun, reminding me of the sparkling icy fleets which I saw last winter; and I saw how one corresponded to the other, ice waves to water ones; the erect ice-flakes were the waves stereotyped. It was the same sight, the reflection of the sun sparkling from a myriad slanting surfaces at a distance, a rippled water surface or a crystallized frozen one.

Here crossed the river and climbed the high hills on the west side. The walnut trees conformed in their branches to the slope of the hill, being just as high from the ground on the upper side as on the lower.

Saw quite a flock, for the first time, of goldfinches.

On hillside north of river above powder-mills the *Pycnanthemum incanum* (mountain mint, calamint) and the *Lespedeza violacea*.

Sept. 5. Wilkinson's book[*] to some extent realizes what I have dreamed of,—a return to the primitive analogical and derivative senses of words. His ability to trace analogies often leads him to a truer word than more remarkable writers have found; as when, in

---

*[James John Garth Wilkinson, *The Human Body and Its Connection with Man, Illustrated by the Principal Organs,* 1851.]

his chapter on the human skin, he describes the papillary cutis as "an encampment of small conical tents coextensive with the surface of the body." The faith he puts in old and current expressions as having sprung from an instinct wiser than science, and safely to be trusted if they can be interpreted. The man of science discovers no world for the mind of man with all its faculties to inhabit. Wilkinson finds a *home* for the imagination, and it is no longer outcast and homeless. All perception of truth is the detection of an analogy; we reason from our hands to our head.

Sept. 7. We sometimes experience a mere fullness of life, which does not find any channels to flow into. We are stimulated, but to no obvious purpose. I feel myself uncommonly prepared for *some* literary work, but I can select no work. I am prepared not so much for contemplation, as for forceful expression. I am braced both physically and intellectually. It is not so much the music as the marching to the music that I feel. I feel that the juices of the fruits which I have eaten, the melons and apples, have ascended to my brain and are stimulating it. They give me a heady force. Now I can write nervously. Carlyle's writing is for the most part of this character.

Our ecstatic states, which appear to yield so little fruit, have this value at least: though in the seasons when our genius reigns we may be powerless for expression, yet, in calmer seasons, when our talent is active, the memory of those rarer moods comes to color our picture and is the permanent paint-pot, as it were, into which we dip our brush. Thus no life or experience goes unreported at last; but if it be not solid gold it is gold-leaf, which gilds the furniture of the mind. It is an experience of infinite beauty on which we unfailingly draw, which enables us to exaggerate ever truly. Our moments of inspiration are not lost though we have no particular poem to show for them; for those experiences have left an indelible impression, and we are ever and anon reminded of them. When I despair to sing them, I will remember that they will furnish me with paint with which to adorn and preserve the works of talent one day. They are like a pot of pure ether. It is the difference between our river, now parched and dried up, exposing its unsightly and weedy bottom, and the same when, in the spring, it covers all the meads with a chain of placid lakes, reflecting the forests and the skies.

We are receiving our portion of the infinite. The art of life! I do not remember any page which will tell me how to spend this afternoon. I do not so much wish to know how to economize time as how to spend it.

The scenery, when it is truly seen, reacts on the life of the seer. How to live. How to get the most life. How to extract its honey from the flower of the world. That is my every-day business. I am as busy as a bee about it. I ramble over all fields on that errand, and am never so happy as when I feel myself heavy with honey and wax. I am like a bee searching the livelong day for the sweets of nature. Do I not impregnate and intermix the flowers, produce rare and finer varieties by transferring my eyes from one to another? I do as naturally and as joyfully, with my own humming music, seek honey all the day. With what honeyed thought any experience yields me I take a bee line to my cell. It is with flowers I would deal.

I am convinced that men are not well employed, that this is not the way to spend a day. If by patience, if by watching, I can secure one new ray of light, can feel myself elevated for an instant upon Pisgah, the world which was dead prose to me become living and divine, shall I not watch ever? shall I not be a watchman henceforth? If by watching a whole year on the city's walls I may obtain a communication from heaven, shall I not do well to shut up my shop and turn a watchman? We are surrounded by a rich and fertile mystery. May we not probe it, pry into it, employ ourselves about it, a little? To devote your life to the discovery of the divinity in nature or to the eating of oysters, would they not be attended with very different results?

I cannot *easily* buy a blank-book to write thoughts in; they are all ruled for dollars and cents.

If the wine, the water, which will nourish me grows on the surface of the moon, I will do the best I can to go to the moon for it.

We all have our states of fullness and of emptiness, but we overflow at different points. One overflows through the sensual outlets, another through his heart, another through his head, and another perchance only through the higher part of his head, or his poetic faculty. It depends on where each is tight and open. We can, perchance, then direct our nutriment to those organs we specially use.

To Conantum *via* fields, Hubbard's Grove, and grain-field, to Tupelo Cliff and Conantum and returning over peak same way. 6 P.M.

Sept. 12. I can hardly believe that there is so great a difference between one year and another as my journal shows. The 11th of this month last year, the river was as high as it commonly is in the spring, over the causeway on the Corner road. It is now quite low. Last year, October 9th, the huckleberries were fresh and abundant on Conantum. They are now already dried up.

On Monday, the 15th, I am going to perambulate the bounds of the town. As I am partial to across-lot routes, this appears to be a very proper duty for me to perform, for certainly no route can well be chosen which shall be more across-lot, since the roads in no case run round the town but ray out from its centre, and my course will lie across each one. It is almost as if I had undertaken to walk round the town at the greatest distance from its centre and at the same time from the surrounding villages. There is no public house near the line. It is a sort of reconnoissance of its frontiers authorized by the central government of the town, which will bring the surveyor in contact with whatever wild inhabitant or wilderness its territory embraces.

This appears to be a very ancient custom, and I find that this word "perambulation" has exactly the same meaning that it has at present in Johnson and Walker's dictionary. A hundred years ago they went round the towns of this State every three years. And the old selectmen tell me that, before the present split stones were set up in 1829, the bounds were marked by a heap of stones, and it was customary for each selectman to add a stone to the heap.

Sept. 14. A great change in the weather from sultry to cold, from one thin coat to a thick coat or two thin ones.

2 P.M.—To Cliffs.

SEPT. 15. MONDAY. Ice in the pail under the pump, and quite a frost.

Commenced perambulating the town bounds. At 7.30 A.M. rode in company with A. A. Kelsey and Mr. Tolman to the bound between Acton and Concord near Paul Dudley's. Mr. Tolman told a story of his wife walking in the fields somewhere, and, to keep the rain off, throwing her gown over her head and holding it in her mouth, and so being poisoned about her mouth from the skirts of her dress having come in contact with poisonous plants. At Dudley's, which house is handsomely situated, with five large elms in front, we met the selectmen of Acton, Ivory Keyes and Luther Conant. Here were five of us. It appeared that we weighed,— Tolman I think about 160, Conant 155, Keyes about 140, Kelsey 130, myself 127. —— described the wall about or at Forest Hills Cemetery in Roxbury as being made of stones upon which they were careful to preserve the moss, so that it cannot be distinguished from a very old wall.

Found one intermediate bound-stone near the powder-mill drying-house on the bank of the river. The workmen there wore shoes without iron tacks. He said that the kernel-house was the most dangerous, the drying-house next, the press-house next. One of the powder-mill buildings in Concord? The potato vines and the beans which were still green are now blackened and flattened by the frost.

SEPT. 16. Met the selectmen of Sudbury, Moore and Haines. I trust that towns will remember that they are supposed to be fairly represented by their *select* men. From the specimen which Acton sent, I should judge that the inhabitants of that town were made up of a mixture of quiet, respectable, and even gentlemanly farmer people, well to do in the world, with a rather boisterous, coarse, and a little self-willed class; that the inhabitants of Sudbury are farmers almost exclusively, exceedingly rough and countrified and more illiterate than usual, very tenacious of their rights and dignities and difficult to deal with; that the inhabitants of Lincoln yield sooner than usual to the influence of the rising generation, and are a mixture of rather simple but clever with a well-informed and trustworthy people; that the inhabitants of Bedford are mechanics, who aspire to keep up with the age, with some of the polish of society, mingled with substantial and rather intelligent farmers.

Moore of Sudbury thinks the river would be still lower now if it were not for the water in the reservoir pond in Hopkinton running into it.

SEPT. 17. Perambulated the Lincoln line.

Was it the small rough sunflower which I saw this morning at the brook near Lee's Bridge?*

Saw at James Baker's a buttonwood tree with a swarm of bees now three years in it, but honey and all inaccessible. John W. Farrar tells of sugar maples behind Miles's in the Corner.

Did I see privet in the swamp at the Bedford stone near Giles's house? Swamp all dry now; could not wash my hands.

SEPT. 18. Perambulated Bedford line.

Sept. 20. 3 P.M.—To Cliffs *via* Bear Hill.

As I go through the fields, endeavoring to recover my tone and sanity and to perceive things truly and simply again, after having been perambulating the bounds of the town all the week, and dealing with the most commonplace and worldly-minded men, and emphatically *trivial* things, I feel as if I had committed suicide in a sense. I am again forcibly struck with the truth of the fable of Apollo serving King Admetus, its universal applicability. A fatal coarseness is the result of mixing in the trivial affairs of men. Though I have been associating even with the *select* men of this and the surrounding towns, I feel inexpressibly begrimed. My Pegasus has lost his wings; he has turned a reptile and gone on his belly. Such things are compatible only with a cheap and superficial life.

The poet must keep himself unstained and aloof. Let him perambulate the bounds of Imagination's provinces, the realms of

---

*Probably great bidens.

faery, and not the insignificant boundaries of towns. The excursions of the imagination are so boundless, the limits of towns are so petty.

Sept. 22. To the Three Friends' Hill over Bear Hill.

Yesterday and to-day the stronger winds of autumn have begun to blow, and the telegraph harp has sounded loudly. I heard it especially in the Deep Cut this afternoon, the tone varying with the tension of different parts of the wire. The sound proceeds from near the posts, where the vibration is apparently more rapid. I put my ear to one of the posts, and it seemed to me as if every pore of the wood was filled with music, labored with the strain,—as if every fibre was affected and being seasoned or timed, rearranged according to a new and more harmonious law. Every swell and change or inflection of tone pervaded and seemed to proceed from the wood, the divine tree or wood, as if its very substance was transmuted. What a recipe for preserving wood, perchance,—to keep it from rotting,—to fill its pores with music!

Shall we not add a tenth Muse to the immortal Nine? And that the invention thus divinely honored and distinguished—on which the Muse has condescended to smile—is this magic medium of communication for mankind!

To read that the ancients stretched a wire round the earth, attaching it to the trees of the forest, by which they sent messages by one named Electricity, father of Lightning and Magnetism, swifter far than Mercury, the stern commands of war and news of peace, and that the winds caused this wire to vibrate so that it emitted a harp-like and æolian music in all the lands through which it passed, as if to express the satisfaction of the gods in this invention. Yet this is fact, and we have yet attributed the invention to no god.

Sept. 23. Notwithstanding the fog, the fences this morning are covered with so thick a frost that you can write your name anywhere with your nail.

Sept. 24. 8 A.M.—To Lee's Bridge *via* Conantum.

It is a cool and windy morning, and I have donned a thick coat for a walk. The wind is from the north, so that the telegraph harp does not sound where I cross. This windy autumnal weather is very exciting and bracing, clear and cold, after the rain of yesterday, it having cleared off in the night.

What can be handsomer for a picture than our river scenery now? Take this view from the first Conantum Cliff. First this smoothly shorn meadow on the west side of the stream, with all the swaths distinct, sprinkled with apple trees casting heavy shadows black as ink, such as can be seen only in this clear air, this strong light, one cow wandering restlessly about in it and lowing; then the blue river, scarcely darker than and not to be distinguished from the sky, its waves driven southward, or up-stream, by the wind, making it appear to flow that way, bordered by willows and button-bushes; then the narrow meadow beyond, with varied lights and shades from its waving grass, which for some reason has not been cut this year, though so dry, now at length each grass-blade bending south before the wintry blast, as if bending for aid in that direction; then the hill rising sixty feet to a terrace-like plain covered with shrub oaks, maples, etc., now variously tinted, clad all in a livery of gay colors, every bush a feather in its cap; and further in the rear the woodcrowned Cliff some two hundred feet high, where gray rocks here and there project from amidst the bushes, with its orchard on the slope; and to the right of the Cliff the distant Lincoln hills in the horizon. The landscape so handsomely colored, the air so clear and wholesome; and the surface of the earth is so pleasingly varied, that it seems rarely fitted for the abode of man.

In Cohush Swamp the sumach leaves have turned a very deep red, but have not lost their fragrance. I notice wild apples growing luxuriantly in the midst of the swamp, rising red over the colored, painted leaves of the sumach, and reminding me that they were ripened and colored by the same influences,—some green, some yellow, some red, like the leaves.

Fell in with a man whose breath smelled of spirit which he had drunk. How could I but feel that it was his own spirit that I smelt? Behind Miles's, Darius Miles's, that was, I asked an Irishman how many potatoes he could dig in a day, wishing to know how well they yielded. "Well, I don't keep any account," he answered; "I scratch away, and let the day's work praise itself." Aye, there's the difference between the Irishman and the Yankee; the Yankee keeps an account. The simple honesty of the Irish pleases me. A sparrow hawk, hardly so big as a nighthawk, flew over high above my head,—a pretty little graceful fellow, too small and delicate to be rapacious.

Such near hills as Nobscot and Nashoba have lost all their azure in this clear air and plainly belong to earth. Give me clearness nevertheless, though my heavens be moved further off to pay for it.

Get home at noon.

At sundown the wind has all gone down.

Sept. 25. The season of flowers may be considered as past now that the frosts have come. Fires have become comfortable. The evenings are pretty long.

2 P.M.—To bathe in Hubbard's meadow, thence to Cliffs. I find the water suddenly cold, and that the bathing days are over.

I see numerous butterflies still, yellow and small red, though not in fleets. Examined the hornets' nest near Hubbard's Grove, suspended from contiguous huckleberry bushes. The tops of the bushes appearing to grow out of it, little leafy sprigs, had a pleasing effect.

SEPT. 26. Since I perambulated the bounds of the town, I find that I have in some degree confined myself,—my vision and my walks. On whatever side I look off I am reminded of the mean and narrow-minded men whom I have lately met there. What can be uglier than a country occupied by grovelling, coarse, and low-lived men? No scenery will redeem it. What can be more beautiful than any scenery inhabited by heroes? Any landscape would be glorious to me, if I were assured that its sky was arched over a single hero. Hornets, hyenas, and baboons are not so great a curse to a country as men of a similar character. It is a charmed circle which I have drawn around my abode, having walked not with God but with the devil. I am too well aware when I have crossed this line.

Most New England biographies and journals—John Adams's not excepted—affect me like opening of the tombs.

The prudent and seasonable farmers are already plowing against another year.

Sept. 28. 2 P.M.—To Conantum.

A warm, damp, mistling day, without much wind. The white pines in Hubbard's Grove have now a pretty distinct parti-colored look,—green and yellow mottled,—reminding me of some plants like the milkweed, expanding with maturity and pushing off their downy seeds. They have a singularly soft look. For a week or ten days I have ceased to look for new flowers or carry my botany in my pocket.

I see where the squirrels have carried off the ears of corn more than twenty rods from the corn-field into the woods. A little further on, beyond Hubbard's Brook, I saw a gray squirrel with an ear of yellow corn a foot long sitting on the fence, fifteen rods from the field. He dropped the corn, but continued to sit on the rail, where I could hardly see him, it being of the same color with himself, which I have no doubt he was well aware of. He next took to a red maple, where his policy was to conceal himself behind the stem, hanging perfectly still there till I passed, his fur being exactly the color of the bark. When I struck the tree and tried to frighten him, he knew better than to run to the next tree, there being no continuous row by which he might escape; but he merely fled higher up and put so many leaves between us that it was difficult to discover him. When I threw up a stick to frighten him, he disappeared entirely, though I kept the best watch I could, and stood close to the foot of the tree. They are wonderfully cunning.

Sept. 30. The white ash has got its autumnal mulberry hue. What is the autumnal tint of the black ash? The former contrasts strongly with the other shade-trees on the village street—the elms and buttonwoods—at this season, looking almost black at the first glance. The different characters of the trees appear more clearly at this season, when their leaves, so to speak, are ripe, than at any other. It is with leaves as with fruits and woods, and animals and men; when they are mature their different characters appear.

Oct. 1. 5 P.M.—Just put a fugitive slave, who has taken the name of Henry Williams, into the cars for Canada. He escaped from Stafford County, Virginia, to Boston last October; has been in Shadrach's place at the Cornhill Coffee-House; had been corresponding through an agent with his master, who is his father, about buying himself, his master asking $600, but he having been able to raise only $500. Heard that there were writs out for two Williamses, fugitives, and was informed by his follow-servants and employer that Augerhole Burns and others of the police had called for him when he was out. Accordingly fled to Concord last night on foot, bringing a letter to our family from Mr. Lovejoy of Cambridge and another which Garrison had formerly given him on another occasion. He lodged with us, and waited in the house till funds were collected with which to forward him. Intended to dispatch him at noon through to Burlington, but when I went to buy his ticket, saw one at the depot who looked and behaved so much like a Boston policeman that I did not venture that time. An intelligent and very well-behaved man, a mulatto.

The slave said he could guide himself by many other stars than the north star, whose rising and setting he knew. They steered for the north star even when it had got round and appeared to them to be in the south. They frequently followed the telegraph when there was no railroad. The slaves bring many superstitions from Africa. The fugitives sometimes superstitiously carry a turf in their hats, thinking that their success depends on it.

These days when the trees have put on their autumnal tints are the gala days of the year, when the very foliage of trees is colored like a blossom. It is a proper time for a yearly festival, an agricultural show.

Oct. 4. Minott used the word "gavel" to describe a parcel of stalks cast on the ground to dry. His are good old English words, and I am always sure to find them in the dictionary, though I never heard them before in my life.

I was admiring his corn-stalks disposed about the barn to dry, over or astride the braces and the timbers, of such a fresh, clean, and handsome green, retaining their strength and nutritive properties so, unlike the gross and careless husbandry of speculating, money-making farmers, who suffer their stalks to remain out till they are dry and dingy and black as chips.

Minott is, perhaps, the most poetical farmer—who most realizes to me the poetry of the farmer's life—that I know. He does nothing with haste and drudgery, but as if he loved it. He makes the most of his labor, and takes infinite satisfaction in every part of it. He is not looking forward to the sale of his crops or any pecuniary profit, but he is paid by the constant satisfaction which his labor yields him. He has not too much land to trouble him,—too much work to do,—no hired man nor boy,—but simply to amuse himself and live. He cares not so much to raise a large crop as to do his work well. He knows every pin and nail in his barn. If another linter is to be floored, he lets no hired man rob him of that amusement, but he goes slowly to the woods and, at his leisure, selects a pitch pine tree, cuts it, and hauls it or gets it hauled to the mill; and so he knows the history of his barn floor.

He always prophesies a failure of the crops, and yet is satisfied with what he gets. His barn floor is fastened down with oak pins, and he prefers them to iron spikes, which he says will rust and give way. He handles and amuses himself with every ear of his corn crop as much as a child with its playthings, and so his small crop goes a great way. He might well cry if it were carried to market. The seed of weeds is no longer in his soil.

He loves to walk in a swamp in windy weather and hear the wind groan through the pines. He keeps a cat in his barn to catch the mice. He indulges in no luxury of food or dress or furniture, yet he is not penurious but merely simple. If his sister dies before him, he may have to go to the almshouse in his old age; yet he is not poor, for he does not want riches. He gets out of each manipulation in the farmers' operations a fund of entertainment which the speculating drudge hardly knows. With never-failing rheumatism and trembling hands, he seems yet to enjoy perennial health. Though he never reads a book,—since he has finished the "Naval Monument,"—he speaks the best of English.

Oct. 5. Sunday. I noticed on Friday, October 3d, that the willows generally were green and unchanged. The red maples varied from green through yellow to bright red. The black cherry was green inclining to yellow. (I speak of such trees as I chanced to see.) The apple trees, green but shedding their leaves like most of the trees. Elm, a dingy yellow. White ash, from green to dark purple or mulberry. White oak, green inclining to yellow. Tupelo, reddish yellow and red; tree bushed about the head, limbs small and slanting downward. Some maples when ripe are yellow or whitish yellow, others reddish yellow, others bright red, by the accident of the season or position,—the more or less light and sun, being on the edge or in the midst of the wood; just as the fruits are more or less deeply colored. Birches, green and yellow. Swamp white oak, a yellowish green. Black ash, greenish yellow and now sered by frost. Bass, sered yellowish.

Color in the maturity of foliage is as variable and little characteristic as naturalists have found it to be for distinguishing fishes and quadrupeds, etc.

Oct. 6. Monday. 12 M.—To Bedford line to set a stone by river on Bedford line.

7.30 P.M.—To Fair Haven Pond by boat, the moon four-fifths full, not a cloud in the sky; paddling all the way.

In the middle of the pond we tried the echo. As we paddled down the stream with our backs to the moon, we saw the reflection of every wood and hill on both sides distinctly. These answering reflections—shadow to substance—impress the voyager with a sense of harmony and symmetry, as when you fold a blotted paper and produce a regular figure,—a dualism which nature loves. What you commonly see is but half. Home at ten.

VIII.

Oct. 8. By the side of J.P. Brown's grain-field I picked up some white oak acorns in the path by the wood-side, which I found to be unexpectedly sweet and palatable, the bitterness being scarcely perceptible. To my taste they are quite as good as chestnuts. No wonder the first men lived on acorns. Such as these are no mean food, such as they are represented to be. Their sweetness is like the sweetness of bread, and to have discovered this palatableness in this neglected nut, the whole world is to me the sweeter for it. To find that acorns are edible,—it is a greater addition to one's stock of life than would be imagined. I should be at least equally pleased if I were to find that the grass tasted sweet and nutritious. It increases the number of my friends; it diminishes the number of my foes. How easily at this season I could feed myself in the woods!

The farmers are ditching,—redeeming more meadow,—getting corn, collecting their apples, threshing, etc.

This warm day is a godsend to the wasps. The puffballs are split open and rayed out on the sand like five or *ten* (!) fingers. The milkweed seeds must be carried far, for it is only when a strong wind is blowing that they are loosened from their pods. An arrowhead. Filled my pockets with acorns. Found another gouge on Dennis's Hill. To have found the Indian gouges and tasted sweet acorns,—is it not enough for one afternoon?

Oct. 9. Heard two screech owls in the night. Boiled a quart of acorns for breakfast, but found them not so palatable as raw, having acquired a bitterish taste, perchance from being boiled with the shells and skins; yet one would soon get accustomed to this.

2 P.M.—To Conantum.

The witch-hazel here is in full blossom on this magical hillside, while its broad yellow leaves are falling. It is an extremely interesting plant,—October and November's child, and yet reminds me of the very earliest spring. Its blossoms smell like the spring, like the willow catkins; by their color as well as fragrance they belong to the saffron dawn of the year, suggesting amid all these signs of autumn, falling leaves and frost, that the life of Nature, by which she eternally flourishes, is untouched. While its leaves fall, its blossoms spring. The autumn, then, is indeed a spring. All the year is a spring.

Oct. 10. The air this morning is full of bluebirds, and again it is spring. There are many things to indicate the renewing of spring at this season. The blossoming of spring flowers,—not to mention the witch-hazel,—the notes of spring birds, the springing of grain and grass and other plants.

Plants have two states, certainly,—the green and the dry. The lespedeza and primrose heads, etc., etc.,—I look on these with interest, as if they were newly blossoming plants.

Going through Britton's clearing, I find a black snake out enjoying the sun. I perceive his lustrous greenish blackness. He holds up his head and threatens; then dashes off into the woods, making a great rustling among the leaves. This might be called snake summer or snakes' week.

Another warm night.

OCT. 17. Surveying for Loring. A severe frost this morning, which puts us one remove further from summer.

OCT. 23. It is never too late to learn. I observed to-day the Irishman who helped me survey *twisting* the branch of a birch for a withe, and *before* he cut it off; and also, wishing to stick a tall, smooth pole in the ground, cut a notch in the side of it by which to drive it with a hatchet.

OCT. 26. I awoke this morning to infinite regret. In my dream I had been riding, but the horses bit each other and occasioned endless trouble and anxiety, and it was my employment to hold their heads apart. Next I sailed over the sea in a small vessel such as the Northmen used, as it were to the Bay of Fundy, and thence overland I sailed, still over the shallows about the sources of rivers toward the deeper *channel* of a stream which emptied into the Gulf beyond,—the Miramichi, was it? Again I was in my own small pleasure-boat, learning to sail on the sea, and I raised my sail before my anchor, which I dragged far into the sea. I saw the buttons which had come off the coats of drowned men, and suddenly I saw my dog—when I knew not that I had one—standing in the sea up to his chin, to warm his legs, which had been wet, which the cool wind numbed. And then I was walking in a meadow, where the dry season permitted me to walk further than usual, and there I met Mr. Alcott, and we fell to quoting and referring to grand and pleasing couplets and single lines which we had read in times past; and I quoted one which in my waking hours I have no knowledge of, but in my dream it was familiar enough. I only know that those which I quoted expressed regret, and were like the following, though they were not these, *viz.:*—

"The short parenthesis of life was sweet,"
"The remembrance of youth is a sigh," etc.

It had the word "memory" in it!! And then again the instant that I awoke, methought I was a musical instrument from which I heard a strain die out,—a bugle, or a clarionet, or a flute. My body was the organ and channel of melody, as a flute is of the music that is breathed through it. My flesh sounded and vibrated still to the strain, and my nerves were the chords of the lyre. I awoke, therefore, to an infinite regret,—to find myself, not the thoroughfare of glorious and world-stirring inspirations, but a scuttle full of dirt, such a thoroughfare only as the street and the kennel, where, perchance, the wind may sometimes draw forth a strain of music from a straw.

I can partly account for this. Last evening I was reading Laing's account of the Northmen, and though I did not write in my Journal, I remember feeling a fertile regret, and deriving even an inexpressible satisfaction, as it were, from my ability to feel regret, which made that evening richer than those which had preceded it. I heard the last strain or flourish, as I woke, played on my body as the instrument. Such I knew I had been and might be again, and my regret arose from the consciousness how little like a musical instrument my body was now.

Oct. 27. This morning I wake and find it snowing and the ground covered with snow; quite unexpectedly, for last night it was rainy but not cold.

The obstacles which the heart meets with are like granite blocks which one alone cannot move. She who was as the morning light to me is now neither the morning star nor the evening star. We meet but to find each other further asunder, and the oftener we meet the more rapid our divergence.

The night is oracular. What have been the intimations of the night? I ask. How have you passed the night? Good-night!

The cold numbs my fingers this morning. The strong northwest wind blows the damp snow along almost horizontally. The birds fly about as if seeking shelter.

Winter, with its *inwardness*, is upon us. A man is constrained to sit down, and to think.

Nov. 1. Saturday. Man recognizes laws little enforced, and he condescends to obey them. In the moment that he feels his superiority to them as compulsatory, he, as it were, courteously reënacts them but to obey them.

This on my way to Conantum, 2.30 P.M. It is a bright, clear, warm November day. I feel blessed. I love my life. I warm toward all nature. The woods are now much more open than when I last observed them; the leaves have fallen, and they let in light, and I see the sky through them as through a crow's wing in every direction. For the most part only the pines and oaks (white?) retain their leaves. At a distance, accordingly, the forest is green and reddish. The crickets now sound faintly and from very deep in the sod.

Nov. 9. In our walks C. takes out his note-book sometimes and tries to write as I do, but all in vain. He soon puts it up again, or contents himself with scrawling some sketch of the landscape. Observing me still scribbling, he will say that he confines himself to the ideal, purely ideal remarks; he leaves the facts to me. Sometimes, too, he will say a little petulantly, "*I* am universal; I have nothing to do with the particular and definite." He is the moodiest person, perhaps, that I ever saw. As naturally whimsical as a cow is brindled, both in his tenderness and his roughness he belies himself. He can be incredibly selfish and unexpectedly generous. He is conceited, and yet there is in him far more than usual to ground conceit upon.

I, too, would fain set down something beside facts. Facts should only be as the frame to my pictures; they should be material to the mythology which I am writing; not facts to assist men to make money, farmers to farm profitably, in any common sense; facts to tell who I am, and where I have been or what I have thought: as now the bell rings for evening meeting, and its volumes of sound, like smoke which rises from where a cannon is fired, make the tent in which I dwell. My facts shall be falsehoods to the common sense. I would so state facts that they shall be significant, shall be myths or mythologic. Facts which the mind perceived, thoughts which the body thought.

Nov. 11. 2 P.M.—A bright, but cold day, finger-cold. One must next wear gloves, put his hands in winter quarters.

White Pond is prepared for winter. The view of the southern horizon from the lane this side still attracts me, but not so much as before I had explored those Wayland hills, which look so much fairer, perhaps, than they are. To-day you may write a chapter on the advantages of travelling, and to-morrow you may write another chapter on the advantages of not travelling. The horizon has one kind of beauty and attraction to him who has never explored the hills and mountains in it, and another, I fear a less ethereal and glorious one, to him who has. That blue mountain in the horizon is certainly the most heavenly, the most elysian, which we have not climbed, on which we have not camped for a night. But only our horizon is moved thus further off, and if our whole life should prove thus a failure, the future which is to atone for all, where still there must be some success, will be more glorious still.

"Says I to myself" should be the motto of my journal.

It is fatal to the writer to be too much possessed by his thought. Things must lie a little remote to be described.

Nov. 12. Write often, write upon a thousand themes, rather than long at a time, not trying to turn too many feeble somersets in the air,—and so come down upon your head at last. Antæus-like, be not long absent from the ground. Those sentences are good and well discharged which are like so many little resiliencies from the spring floor of our life,—a distinct fruit and kernel itself, springing from terra firma. Let there be as many distinct plants as the soil and the light can sustain. Take as many bounds in a day as possible. Sentences uttered with your back to the wall. Those are the admirable bounds when the performer has lately touched the spring-board.

C. is one who will not stoop to rise (to change the subject). He wants something for which he will not pay the going price. He will only learn slowly by failure,—not a noble, but disgraceful, failure. This is not a noble method of learning, to be educated by inevitable suffering, like De Quincey, for instance. Better dive like a muskrat into the mud, and pile up a few weeds to sit on during the floods, a foundation of your own laying, a house of your own building, however cold and cheerless.

Methinks the hawk that soars so loftily and circles so steadily and apparently without effort has earned this power by faithfully creeping on the ground as a reptile in a former state of existence. You must creep before you can run; you must run before you can fly.

Nov. 13. To Fair Haven Hill.

A cold and dark afternoon, the sun being behind clouds in the west. The landscape is barren of objects, the trees being leafless, and so little light in the sky for variety. Such a day as will almost oblige a man to eat his own heart. A day in which you must hold on to life by your teeth. You can hardly ruck up any skin on Nature's bones. The sap is down; she won't peel. Now is the time to cut timber for yokes and ox-bows, leaving the tough bark on,— yokes for your own neck. Finding yourself yoked to Matter and to Time. Truly a hard day, hard times these! Not a mosquito left. Not an insect to hum. Crickets gone into winter quarters. Friends long since gone there, and you left to walk on frozen ground, with your hands in your pockets. Ah, but is not this a glorious time for your deep inward fires? And will not your green hickory and white oak burn clear in this frosty air? No Indian summer have we had this November. I see but few traces of the perennial spring. Now is there nothing, not even the cold beauty of ice crystals and snowy architecture, nothing but the echo of your steps over the frozen ground, no voice of birds nor frogs. You are dry as a farrow cow. The earth will not admit a spade. All fields lie fallow.

I see snow on the Peterboro hills, reflecting the sun. It is pleasant thus to look from afar into winter. We look at a condition which we have not reached. Notwithstanding the poverty of the immediate landscape, in the horizon it is simplicity and grandeur. I look into valleys white with snow and now lit up by the sun, while all this country is in shade. This accounts for the cold northwest wind.

Just spent a couple of hours (eight to ten) with Miss Mary Emerson at Holbrook's. The wittiest and most vivacious woman that I know, certainly that woman among my acquaintance whom it is most profitable to meet, the least frivolous, who will most surely provoke to good conversation and the expression of what is in you. She is singular, among women at least, in being really and perseveringly interested to know what thinkers think. She relates herself surely to the intellectual where she goes. It is perhaps her greatest praise and peculiarity that she, more surely than any other woman, gives her companion occasion to utter his best thought. In spite of her own biases, she can entertain a large thought with hospitality, and is not prevented by any intellectuality in it, as women commonly are. In short, she is a genius, as woman seldom is, reminding you less often of her sex than any woman whom I know.

The cattle-train came down last night from Vermont with snow nearly a foot thick upon it. It is as if, in the fall of the year, a swift traveller should come out of the north with snow upon his coat. So it snows. Such, some years, may be our first snow.

NOV. 14. *Friday.* Surveying the Ministerial Lot in the southwestern part of the town. Unexpectedly find Hayward's Pond frozen over thinly, it being shallow and coldly placed.

In the evening went to a party. It is a bad place to go to,—thirty or forty persons, mostly young women, in a small room, warm and noisy. Was introduced to two young women. The first one was as lively and loquacious as a chickadee; had been accustomed to the society of watering-places, and therefore could get no refreshment out of such a dry fellow as I. The other was said to be pretty-looking, but I rarely look people in their faces, and, moreover, I could not hear what she said, there was such a clacking,—could only see the motion of her lips when I looked that way. I could imagine better places for conversation, where there should be a certain degree of silence surrounding you, and less than forty talking at once. Why, this afternoon, even, I did better. There was old Mr. Joseph Hosmer and I ate our luncheon of cracker and cheese together in the woods. I heard all he said, though it was not much, to be sure, and he could hear me. And then he talked out of such a glorious repose, taking a leisurely bite at the cracker and cheese between his words; and so some of him was communicated to me, and some of me to him, I trust.

These parties, I think, are a part of the machinery of modern society, that young people may be brought together to form marriage connections.

What is the use of going to see people whom yet you never see, and who never see you? I begin to suspect that it is not necessary that we should see one another.

Some of my friends make singular blunders. They go out of their way to talk with certain young women of whom they think, or have heard, that they are pretty, and take pains to introduce me to them. That may be a reason why they should look at them, but it is not a reason why they should talk with them. I confess that I am lacking a sense, perchance, in this respect, and I derive no pleasure from talking with a young woman half an hour simply because she has regular features. The society of young women is the most un-profitable I have ever tried. They are so light and flighty that you can never be sure whether they are there or not there. I prefer to talk with the more staid and settled, *settled for life*, in every sense.

I met a man yesterday afternoon in the road who behaved as if he was deaf, and I talked with him in the cold in a loud tone for fifteen minutes, but that uncertainty about his ears, and the neces-sity I felt to talk loudly, took off the fine edge of what I had to say and prevented my saying anything satisfactory. It is bad enough when your neighbor does not understand you, but if there is any uncertainty as to whether he hears you, so that you are obliged to become your own auditor, you are so much the poorer speaker, and so there is a double failure.

Nov. 15. Here is a rainy day, which keeps me in the house.

I am pleased to read in Stoever's Life of Linnæus (Trapp's trans-lation) that his father, being the first learned man of his family, changed his family name and borrowed that of Linnæus (Linden-tree-man) from a lofty linden tree which stood near his native place,—"a custom," he says, "not unfrequent in Sweden, to take fresh appellations from natural objects." What more fit than that the advent of a new man into a family should acquire for it, and trans-mit to his posterity, a new patronymic? It is refreshing to get to a man whom you will not be satisfied to call John's son or Johnson's son, but a new name applicable to himself alone, he being the first of his kind. Get yourself therefore a name, and better a nickname than none at all. There was one enterprising boy came to school to me whose name was "Buster," and an honorable name it was. He was the only boy in the school, to my knowledge, who was named.

I think it would be a good discipline for Channing, who writes poetry in a sublimo-slipshod style, to write Latin, for then he would be compelled to say something always, and frequently have recourse to his grammar and dictionary. Methinks that what a man might write in a dead language could be more surely translated into good sense in his own language, than his own language could be translated into good Latin, or the dead language.

Nov. 16. Sunday. If it were not for death and funerals, I think the institution of the Church would not stand longer. The necessity that men be decently buried—our fathers and mothers, brothers and sisters and children (notwithstanding the danger that they be buried alive)—will long, if not forever, prevent our laying violent hands on it. If salaries were stopped off, and men walked out of this world bodily at last, the minister and his vocation would be gone. What is the churchyard but a graveyard?

Plenty of ripe checkerberries now. Do they blossom again in the spring?*

Nov. 25. That kind of sunset which I witnessed on Saturday and Sunday is perhaps peculiar to the late autumn. The sun is unseen behind a hill. Only this bright white light like a fire falls on the trembling needles of the pine.

Dec. 12. Ah, dear nature, the mere remembrance, after a short forgetfulness, of the pine woods! I come to it as a hungry man to a crust of bread.

I have been surveying for twenty or thirty days, living coarsely, even as respects my diet,—for I find that that will always alter to suit my employment,—indeed, leading a quite trivial life; and tonight, for the first time, had made a fire in my chamber and endeavored to return to myself. I wished for leisure and quiet to let my life flow in its proper channels, with its proper currents; when I might not waste the days, might establish daily prayer and thanksgiving in my family; might do my own work and not the work of Concord and Carlisle, which would yield me better than money.

---

*Only once.

(How much forbearance, aye, sacrifice and loss, goes to every accomplishment! I am thinking by what long discipline and at what cost a man learns to speak simply at last.)

Dec. 13. Saturday. While surveying to-day, we had one hour of almost Indian summer weather in the middle of the day. I felt the influence of the sun. It melted my stoniness a little. The pines looked like old friends again. Cutting a path through a swamp where was much brittle dogwood, etc., etc., I wanted to know the name of every shrub. This varied employment, to which my necessities compel me, serves instead of foreign travel and the lapse of time. If it makes me forget some things which I ought to remember, it no doubt enables me to forget many things which it is well to forget. By stepping aside from my chosen path so often, I see myself better and am enabled to criticise myself. Of this nature is the only true lapse of time. It seems an age since I took walks and wrote in my journal, and when shall I revisit the glimpses of the moon? To be able to see ourselves, not merely as others see us, but as we are, that service a *variety* of absorbing employments does us.

Dec. 14. The boys have been skating for a week, but I have had no time to skate for surveying. I have hardly realized that there was ice, though I have walked over it about this business. As for the weather, all seasons are pretty much alike to one who is actively at work in the woods.

There is a beautifully pure greenish-blue sky under the clouds now in the southwest just before sunset. I hear the ice along the edge of the river cracking as the water settles. It has settled about two feet, leaving ice for the most part without water on the meadows, all uneven and cracked over the hummocks, so that you cannot run straight for sliding. The ice takes the least hint of a core to eke out a perfect plant; the wrecks of bulrushes and meadow grass are expanded into palm leaves and other luxuriant foliage. I see delicate-looking green pads frozen into the ice, and, here and there, where some tender and still green weeds from the warm bottom of the river have lately been cast up on to the ice.

There are certain places where the river will always be open, where perchance warmer springs come in. There are such places in every character, genial and open in the coldest seasons.

Dec. 21. Sunday. My difficulties with my friends are such as no frankness will settle. There is no precept in the New Testament that will assist me. My nature, it may be, is secret. Others can confess and explain; I cannot. It is not that I am too proud, but that is not what is wanted.

I feel sometimes as if I could say to my friends, "My friends, I am aware how I have outraged you, how I have seemingly preferred hate to love, seemingly treated others kindly and you unkindly." I can imagine how I might utter something like this in some moment never to be realized. But let me say frankly that at the same time I feel, it may be with too little regret, that I am under an awful necessity to be what I am. If the truth were known, which I do not know, I have no concern with those friends whom I misunderstand or who misunderstand me.

I am of the nature of stone. It takes the summer's sun to warm it.

My acquaintances sometimes imply that I am too cold; but each thing is warm enough of its kind. Is the stone too cold which absorbs the heat of the summer sun and does not part with it during the night? Crystals, though they be of ice, are not too cold to melt, but it was in melting that they were formed. Cold! I am most sensible of warmth in winter days. It is not the warmth of fire that you would have, but everything is warm and cold according to its nature. It is not that I am too cold, but that our warmth and coldness are not of the same nature; hence when I am absolutely warmest, I may be coldest to you. Crystal does not complain of crystal any more than the dove of its mate. You who complain that I am cold find Nature cold. To me she is warm. My heat is latent to you. Fire itself is cold to whatever is not of a nature to be warmed by it. A cool wind is warmer to a feverish man than the air of a furnace. That I am cold means that I am of another nature.

The dogwood and its berries in the *swamp* by the railroad, just above the red house, pendent on long stems which hang short down as if broken, betwixt yellowish (?) and greenish (?), white, ovoid, pearly (?) or waxen (?) berries. What is the color of them? Ah, give me to walk in the dogwood swamp, with its few coarse branches! Beautiful as Satan.

DEC. 25. *Thursday. Via* spruce swamp on Conantum to hilltop, returning across river over shrub oak plain to Cliffs.

A wind is now blowing the light snow which fell a day or two ago into drifts, especially on the lee, now the south, side of the walls, the outlines of the drifts corresponding to the chinks in the walls and the eddies of the wind. The snow glides, unperceived for the most part, over the open fields without rising into the air (unless the ground is elevated), until it reaches an opposite wall, which it sifts through and is blown over, blowing off from it like steam when seen in the sun. As it passes through the chinks, it does not drive straight onward, but curves gracefully upwards into fantastic shapes, somewhat like the waves which curve as they break upon the shore; that is, as if the snow that passes through a chink were one connected body, detained by the friction of its lower side. It takes the form of saddles and shells and porringers. It builds up a fantastic alabaster wall behind the first,—a snowy sierra. It is wonderful what sharp turrets it builds up,—builds up, *i.e.* by accumulation though seemingly by attrition, though the curves upward to a point like the prows of ancient vessels look like sharp carving, or as if the material had been held before the blowpipe. So what was blown up into the air gradually sifts down into the road or field, and forms the slope of the sierra. Astonishingly sharp and thin overhanging eaves it builds, even this dry snow, where it has the least suggestion from a wall or bank,—less than a mason ever springs his brick from. This is the architecture of the snow. On high hills exposed to wind and sun, it curls off like the steam from a damp roof in the morning. Such sharply defined forms it takes as if the core had been the flames of gaslights.

I go forth to see the sun set. Who knows how it will set, even half an hour beforehand? whether it will go down in clouds or a clear sky? I feel that it is late when the mountains in the north and northwest have ceased to reflect the sun. The shadow is not partial but universal.

In a winter day the sun is almost all in all.

I witness a beauty in the form or coloring of the clouds which addresses itself to my imagination, for which you account scientifically to my understanding, but do not so account to my imagination. It is what it suggests and is the symbol of that I care for, and if, by any trick of science, you rob it of its symbolicalness, you do me no service and explain nothing. I, standing twenty miles off, see a crimson cloud in the horizon. You tell me it is a mass of vapor which absorbs all other rays and reflects the red, but that is nothing to the purpose, for this red vision excites me, stirs my blood, makes my thoughts flow, and I have new and indescribable fancies, and you have not touched the secret of that influence. If there is not something mystical in your explanation, something unexplainable to the understanding, some elements of mystery, it is quite insufficient. If there is nothing in it which speaks to my imagination, what boots it? What sort of science is that which enriches the understanding, but robs the imagination? not merely robs Peter to pay Paul, but takes from Peter more than it ever gives to Paul? That is simply the way in which it speaks to the understanding, and that is the account which the understanding gives of it; but that is not the way it speaks to the imagination, and that is not the account which the imagination gives of it. Just as inadequate to a pure mechanic would be a poet's account of a steam-engine.

If we knew all things thus mechanically merely, should we know anything really?

It would be a truer discipline for the writer to take the least film of thought that floats in the twilight sky of his mind for his theme, about which he has scarcely one idea (that would be teaching his ideas how to shoot), faintest intimations, shadowiest subjects, make a lecture on this, by assiduity and attention get perchance two views of the same, increase a little the stock of knowledge, clear a new field instead of manuring the old; instead of making a lecture out of such obvious truths, hackneyed to the minds of all thinkers. We seek too soon to ally the perceptions of the mind to the experience of the hand, to prove our gossamer truths practical, to show their connection with our every-day life (better show their distance from our every-day life), to relate them to the cider-mill and the banking institution. Ah, give me pure mind, pure thought! Let me not be in haste to detect the *universal law*; let me see more clearly a particular instance of it! Much finer themes I aspire to, which will yield no satisfaction to the vulgar mind, not one sentence for them. Perchance it may convince such that there are more things in heaven and earth than are dreamed of in their philosophy. Dissolve one nebula, and so destroy the nebular system and hypothesis. Do not seek expressions, seek thoughts to be expressed. By perseverance you get two views of the same rare truth.

That way of viewing things you know of, least insisted on by you, however, least remembered,—take that view, adhere to that, insist on that, see all things from that point of view. Will you let these intimations go unattended to and watch the door-bell or knocker? That is your text. Do not speak for other men; speak for yourself. They show you as in a vision the kingdoms of the world, and of all the worlds, but you prefer to look in upon a puppet-show. Though you should only speak to one kindred mind in all time, though you should not speak to one, but only utter aloud, that you may the more completely realize and live in the idea which contains the reason of your life, that you may build yourself up to the height of your conceptions, that you may remember your Creator in the days of your youth and justify His ways to man, that the end of life may not be its amusement, speak—though your thought presupposes the non-existence of your hearers—thoughts that transcend life and death. What though mortal ears are not fitted to hear absolute truth! Thoughts that blot out the earth are best conceived in the night, when darkness has already blotted it out from sight.

We look upward for inspiration.

Dec. 29. Snow all gone from Minott's hillside. The willow at the red house shines in the sun. The boys have come out under the hill to pitch coppers. Watts sits on his door-step. It is like the first of April. The wind is west. It feels as warm as in summer; you sit on any fence-rail and vegetate in the sun, and realize that the earth may produce peas again. Yet they say that this open and mild weather is unhealthy; that is always the way with them. How admirable it is that we can never foresee the weather,—that that is always novel! Yesterday nobody dreamed of to-day; nobody dreams of tomorrow. Hence the weather is ever the news. What a fine and measureless joy the gods grant us thus, letting us know nothing about the day that is to dawn! This day, yesterday, was as incredible as any other miracle.

Dec. 31. There is a low mist in the woods. It is a good day to study lichens. The view so confined it compels your attention to near objects, and the white background reveals the disks of the lichens distinctly. They appear more loose, flowing, expanded, flattened out, the colors brighter for the damp. The round greenish-yellow lichens on the white pines loom through the mist (or are seen dimly) like shields whose devices you would fain read. The trees appear all at once covered with their crop of lichens and mosses of all kinds,—flat and tearful are some, distended by moisture. This is their solstice, and your eyes run swiftly through the mist to these things only. Nature has a day for each of her creatures, her creations. To-day it is an exhibition of lichens at Forest Hall, the livid green of some, the fruit of others. They eclipse the trees they cover. Ah, beautiful is decay! True, as Thales said, the world was made out of water. That is the principle of all things.

Jan. 1. I have observed that one mood is the natural critic of another. When possessed with a strong feeling on any subject foreign to the one I may be writing on, I know very well what of good and what of bad I have written on the latter. It looks to me now as it will ten years hence. My life is then earnest and will tolerate no makeshifts nor nonsense. What is tinsel or euphuism or irrelevant is revealed to such a touchstone. I wish to survey my composition for a moment from the least favorable point of view. I wish to be translated to the future, and look at my work as it were at a structure on the plain, to observe what portions have crumbled under the influence of the elements.

McKean has sawed another of the pines under Fair Haven. He says it made eighty-two feet in length of mill-logs, and was so straight that it would have made a first-rate mast eighty feet long.

JAN. 4. To Fair Haven on the ice partially covered with snow.

The cracks in the ice showing a white cleavage. What is their law? Somewhat like foliage, but too rectangular, like the characters of some Oriental language. I feel as if I could get grammar and dictionary and go into it. They are of the form which a thin flake of ice takes in melting, somewhat rectangular with an irregular edge.

The pond is covered,—dappled or sprinkled,—more than half covered, with flat drifts or patches of snow which has lodged, of graceful curving outlines. One would like to skim over it like a hawk, and detect their law.

Jan. 9. The sky shut out by snow-clouds. It spits a little snow and then holds up. Where a path has been shovelled through drifts in the road, and the cakes of snow piled up, I see little azures, little heavens, in the crannies and crevices. The deeper they are, and the larger masses they are surrounded by, the darker-blue they are. Some are a very light blue with a tinge of green. Methinks I oftenest see this when it is snowing. At any rate the atmosphere must be in a peculiar state. Apparently the snow absorbs the other rays and reflects the blue. It has strained the air, and only the blue rays have passed through the sieve. Is, then, the blue water of Walden snow-water? I see the heaven hiding in nooks and crevices in the snow. Into every track which the teamster makes, this elysian, empyrean atmosphere rushes. The blue of my eye sympathizes with this blue in the snow.

I never saw the pitch pines better snowed up. They look like Chinese pagodas.

IX.

Jan. 12. Monday. C. says that he studied lichens a little while, but he found that if you pursued that study you must give up man. It was so thin, and there was so little of man in it! Why, the whole of it was n't more than an inch thick.

Jan. 13. Would not snow-drifts be a good study,—their philosophy and poetry? Are they not worthy of a chapter? Are they always built up, or not rather carved out of the heaps of snow by the wind passing through the chinks in the walls? I do not see yet but they are builded. They are a sort of ripple-marks which the atmospheric sea makes on the snow-covered bottom.

Jan. 14. The shrub oaks here have lost their leaves, *i.e.* the small scrubby kind on this hill. I can see at a distance above the level of the snow a few bushes and grasses which mark the edge of the river. They seem to write the word *rivus* there. That is all or most to indicate that there is a river there. It is betrayed by that thin sedgy and willowy line or border marking the snow yonder.

As usual, there was no blueness in the ruts and crevices in the snow to-day. What kind of atmosphere does this require? When I observed it the other day, it was a rather moist air, some snow falling, the sky completely overcast, and the weather not very cold. It is one of the most interesting phenomena of the winter.

Jan. 15. It is a good school the farmers' sons go to these afternoons, loading and hauling great mill-logs bigger than any cannon,—a sort of battle in the forest. I think there must be an excitement derived from their labor such as they cannot tell. After reading of the life and battles of the Northmen in Snorro Sturleson's Chronicle, these labors most remind me of that. How they renew and wear out the paths through the woods! They think I'm loafing. I think they are drudging for gain. But no doubt our employment is more alike than we suspect, and we are each serving the great Master's ends more than our own. I have my work in the woods where I meet them, though my logs do not go to the same mill.

Jan. 18. To-day, again, I saw some of the *blue* in the crevices of the snow. It is snowing, but not a moist snow. Perhaps the snow in the air, as well as on the ground, takes up the white rays and reflects the blue. There is no blue to be seen overhead, and it has as it were taken refuge in the chinks and crevices in the snow.

Jan. 20. I do not know but it is too much to read one newspaper in a week, for I now take the weekly *Tribune*, and for a few days past, it seems to me, I have not dwelt in Concord; the sun, the clouds, the snow, the trees say not so much to me. You cannot serve two masters. To read of things distant and sounding betrays us into slighting these which are then apparently near and small.

Greeley says of London, "The morning to sleep, the afternoon to business, and the evening to enjoyment, seems the usual routine with the favored classes." They have no morning life then. They are afternoon men. To begin the day at noon!

The days are now sensibly longer, and half past five is as light as five was.

Jan. 21. This winter they are cutting down our woods more seriously than ever,—Fair Haven Hill, Walden, Linnæa Borealis Wood, etc., etc. Thank God, they cannot cut down the clouds!

Jan. 22. To set down such choice experiences that my own writings may inspire me and at last I may make wholes of parts. Certainly it is a distinct profession to rescue from oblivion and to fix the sentiments and thoughts which visit all men more or less generally, that the contemplation of the unfinished picture may suggest its harmonious completion. Associate reverently and as much as you can with your loftiest thoughts. Each thought that is welcomed and recorded is a nest egg, by the side of which more will be laid. Thoughts accidentally thrown together become a frame in which more may be developed and exhibited. Perhaps this is the main value of a habit of writing, of keeping a journal,—that so we remember our best hours and stimulate ourselves. My thoughts are my company. They have a certain individuality and separate existence, aye, personality. Having by chance recorded a few disconnected thoughts and then brought them into juxtaposition, they suggest a whole new field in which it was possible to labor and to think. Thought begat thought.

I love to look at Ebby Hubbard's oaks and pines on the hillside from Brister's Hill. Am thankful that there is one old miser who will not sell nor cut his woods, though it is said that they are wasting. It is an ill wind that blows nobody any good.

It is a sharp, cutting cold day, stiffening the face. Thermometers have lately sunk to 20°.

The surface of the snow in the fields is that of pretty large waves on a sea over which a summer breeze is sweeping.

Jan. 24. P.M.—Down the Flint's Pond road and return across.

Even the dry leaves are gregarious, and they collect in little heaps in the hollows in the snow, or even on the plane surfaces, driven in flocks by the wind. How like shrinking maidens wrapping their scarfs about them they flutter along! The oaks are made thus to retain their leaves, that they may play over the snow-crust and add variety to the winter landscape. If you wished to collect leaves, you would only have to make holes in the snow for traps. I see that my tracks are often filled two feet deep with them. They are blown quite across Walden on the wavy snow. Two flitting along together by fits and starts, now one running ahead, then another, remind me of squirrels. Mostly white oak leaves, but the other oaks, *i.e.* especially red oaks, also. There is a certain refinement or cultivation, even feminineness, suggested by the rounded lobes, the scalloped edge, of the white oak leaf, compared with the wild, brusque points of the red and black and scarlet and shrub oaks.

These woods! Why do I not feel their being cut more sorely? Does it not affect me nearly? The axe can deprive me of much. Concord is sheared of its pride. I am certainly the less attached to my native town in consequence. One, and a main, link is broken. I shall go to Walden less frequently.

Jan. 26. Men have ever associated the verdure of evergreen trees—hemlocks, firs, spruces, etc.—with the moisture and coolness of mountains. Our word pine is from the Celtic "*pin* or *pen*, a rock or mountain," from which is derived the name of this genus in many languages. Hence the name "Apennines" (*Alpes pennines*). "*Pinaster* is Pliny's name for the wild pine." (All this from Lindley in Loudon.) But *Pinus* does not include hemlock or larch or fir.

When the thermometer is down to 20°, the streams of thought tinkle underneath like the rivers under the ice. Thought like the ocean is nearly of one temperature. Ideas,—are they the fishes of thought?

Poetry *implies* the whole truth. Philosophy *expresses* a particle of it.

Would you see your mind, look at the sky. Would you know your own moods, be weather-wise. He whom the weather disappoints, disappoints himself.

The word is well naturalized or rooted that can be traced back to a Celtic original. It is like getting out stumps and fat pine roots.

In few countries do they enjoy so fine a contrast of summer and winter. We really have four seasons, each incredible to the other. Winter cannot be mistaken for summer here. Though I see the boat turned up on the shore and half buried under snow, as I walk over the invisible river, summer is far away, with its rustling reeds. It only suggests the want of thrift, the carelessness, of its owner.

Nature never indulges in exclamations, never says Ah! or Alas!

She is not of French descent. She is a plain writer, uses few gestures, does not add to her verbs, uses few adverbs, uses no expletives. I find that I use many words for the sake of emphasis which really add nothing to the force of my sentences, and they look relieved the moment I have cancelled these. Words by which I express my mood, my conviction, rather than the simple truth.

Yesterday, though warm, it was clear enough for water and windows to sparkle.

Thaw with his gentle persuasion is more powerful than Thor with his hammer. The one melts, the other but breaks in pieces.

Jan. 27. The snow has been slowly melting, without rain or mist, the last two or three days. It has settled very much, though the eaves have not been heard to run by me. In going across lots, I walk in the woods, where the snow is not so deep, part having been caught in the trees and dissipated in the air, and a part melted by the warmth of the wood and the reflection.

The poison sumach, with its stems hanging down on every side, is a very agreeable object now, seen against the snow.

I do not know but thoughts written down thus in a journal might be printed in the same form with greater advantage than if the related ones were brought together into separate essays. They are now allied to life, and are seen by the reader not to be far-fetched. It is more simple, less artful. I feel that in the other case I should have no proper frame for my sketches. Mere facts and names and dates communicate more than we suspect. Whether the flower looks better in the nosegay than in the meadow where it grew and we had to wet our feet to get it! Is the scholastic air any advantage?

Jan. 28. Perhaps I can never find so good a setting for my thoughts as I shall thus have taken them out of. The crystal never sparkles more brightly than in the cavern. The world have always loved best the fable with the moral. The children could read the fable alone, the grown-up read both. The truth so told has the best advantages of the most abstract statement, for it is not the less universally applicable. Where else will you ever find the true cement for your thoughts? How will you ever rivet them together without leaving the marks of the file? Yet Plutarch did not so; Montaigne did not so. Men have written travels in this form, but perhaps no man's daily life has been rich enough to be journalized.

It is remarkable that no pains is taken to teach children to distinguish colors. I am myself uncertain about the names of many.

Jan. 30. Friday. One must not complain that his friend is cold, for heat is generated between them.

I doubt if Emerson could trundle a wheelbarrow through the streets, because it would be out of character. One needs to have a comprehensive character.

Do nothing merely out of good resolutions. Discipline yourself only to yield to love; suffer yourself to be attracted. It is in vain to write on chosen themes. We must wait till they have kindled a flame in our minds. There must be the copulating and generating force of love behind every effort destined to be successful. The cold resolve gives birth to, begets, nothing. The theme that seeks me, not I it. The poet's relation to his theme is the relation of lovers. It is no more to be courted. Obey, report.

Jan. 31. Emerson is too grand for me. He belongs to the nobility and wears their cloak and manners; is attracted to Plato, not to Socrates, I fear partly because the latter's life and associates were too humble. I am a commoner. To me there is something devilish in manners. The best manners is nakedness of manners. I should value E.'s praise more, which is always so discriminating, if there were not some alloy of patronage and hence of flattery about it. In that respect he is like [*erased*]; they flatter you, but themselves more.

Feb. 3. I have been to the libraries (yesterday) at Cambridge and Boston. How happens it that I find not in the country, in the fields and woods, the *works* even of like-minded naturalists and poets. Those who have expressed the purest and deepest love of nature have not recorded it on the bark of the trees with the lichens; they have left no memento of it there; but if I would read their books I must go to the city,—so strange and repulsive both to them and to me,—and deal with men and institutions with whom I have no sympathy. When I have just been there on this errand, it seems too great a price to pay for access even to the works of Homer, or Chaucer, or Linnæus. I have sometimes imagined a library, *i.e.* a collection of the works of true poets, philosophers, naturalists, etc., deposited not in a brick or marble edifice in a crowded and dusty city, guarded by cold-blooded and methodical officials and preyed on by bookworms, in which you own no share, and are not likely to, but rather far away in the depths of a primitive forest, like the ruins of Central America, where you can trace a series of crumbling alcoves, the older books protecting the most modern from the elements, partially buried by the luxuriance of nature, which the heroic student could reach only after adventures in the wilderness amid wild beasts and wild men. That, to my imagination, seems a fitter place for these interesting relics, which owe no small part of their interest to their antiquity, and whose occasion is nature, than the well-preserved edifice, with its well-preserved officials on the side of a city's square. More terrible than lions and tigers these Cerberuses.

About 6 P.M. walked to Cliffs *via* railroad.

Snow quite deep. The sun had set without a cloud in the sky,—a rare occurrence, but I missed the clouds, which make the glory of evening. The sky must have a few clouds, as the mind a few moods; nor is the evening the less serene for them. There is only a tinge of red along the horizon. The moon is nearly full tonight, and the moment is passed when the light in the east (*i.e.* of the moon) balances the light in the west.

Selenite "is a stone (as is said) in Arabia, wherein is a white, which decreases and increases with the moon" (Dictionary). My summer journal was selenitic in this sense. It had this white spot in it.

Is not the sky unusually blue to-night? dark blue? Is it not always bluer when the ground is covered with snow in the winter than in summer?

The forcible writer stands bodily behind his words with his experience. He does not make books out of books, but he has been *there* in person.

Feb. 4. Heard Professor Blasius lecture on the tornado this evening. He said that nine vessels were wrecked daily in the world on an average; that Professor Dove of Berlin was the best meteorologist in his opinion, but had not studied the effects of wind in the fields so much as some here.

The audience are never tired of hearing how far the wind carried some man, woman, or child, or family Bible, but they are immediately tired if you undertake to give them a scientific account of it.

Feb. 6. Dioscorides, "the second father of Botany,"—what a flowery name!

The artificial system has been very properly called the dictionary, and the natural method, the grammar, of the science of botany, by botanists themselves. But are we to have nothing but grammars and dictionaries in this literature? Are there no works written in the language of the flowers?

I asked a learned and accurate naturalist, who is at the same time the courteous guardian of a public library, to direct me to those works which contained the more particular *popular* account, or *biography*, of particular flowers, from which the botanies I had met with appeared to draw sparingly,—for I trusted that each flower had had many lovers and faithful describers in past times,—but he informed me that I had read all; that no one was acquainted with the flowers, they were only catalogued like his books.

It is still thawy. A mistiness makes the woods look denser, darker, and more imposing. Seen through this veil, they are more grand and primitive.

Feb. 8. Night before last, our first rain for a long time; this afternoon, the first crust to walk on. It is pleasant to walk over the fields raised a foot or more above their summer level, and the prospect is altogether new.

Thoughts of different dates will not cohere.

Feb. 11. Wednesday. When the thermometer is down to 20° in the morning, as last month, I think of the poor dogs who have no masters. If a poor dog has no master, everybody will throw a billet of wood at him. It never rains but it pours.

It now rains,—a drizzling rain mixed with mist, which ever and anon fills the air to the height of fifteen or twenty feet.

Perhaps the best evidence of an amelioration of the climate—at least that the snows are less deep than formerly—is the snow-shoes which still lie about in so many garrets, now useless, though the population of this town has not essentially increased for seventy-five years past, and the travelling within the limits of the town accordingly not much facilitated. No man ever uses them now, yet the old men used them in their youth.

FEB. 15. Perhaps I am descended from that Northman named "Thorer the Dog-footed." Thorer Hund—"he was the most powerful man in the North"—to judge from his name belonged to the same family. Thorer is one of the most, if not the most, common name in the chronicles of the Northmen.

Feb. 16. Laing says that "the Heimskringla has been hardly used by the learned men of the period in which it was first published. It appeared first in the literary world in 1697, frozen into the Latin of the Swedish antiquary, Peringskiold."

Snorro Sturleson says, "From Thor's name comes Thorer, also Thorarinn." Again: "Earl Rognvald was King Harald's dearest friend, and the king had the greatest regard for him. He was married to Hilda, a daughter of Rolf Naefia, and their sons were Rolf and Thorer...Rolf became a great viking, and was of so stout a growth that no horse could carry him, and wheresoever he went he must go on foot; and therefore he was called Gange-Rolf." (Laing says in a note, what Sturleson also tells in the text, Gange-Rolf, Rolf Ganger, Rolf the Walker, was the conqueror of Normandy.) "Gange-Rolf's son was William, father to Richard, and grandfather to another Richard, who was the father of Richard Longspear, and grandfather of William the Bastard, from whom all the following English kings are descended."

King Harald "set Earl Rognvald's son Thorer over Möre, and

gave him his daughter Alof in marriage. Thorer, called the Silent, got the same territory his father Rognvald had possessed." His brother Einar, going into battle to take vengeance on his father's murderers, sang a kind of reproach against his brothers Rollang and Rolf for their slowness and concludes,—

> "And silent Thorer sits and dreams
> At home, beside the mead-bowl's streams."

So it seems that from one branch of the family were descended the kings of England, and from the other myself.

Feb. 18. Hakon had a daughter *Thora*.

Thorer Klakke was one "who had been long on Viking expeditions."

Thorer Hiort "was quicker on foot than any man."

I have a commonplace-book for facts and another for poetry, but I find it difficult always to preserve the vague distinction which I had in my mind, for the most interesting and beautiful facts are so much the more poetry and that is their success. They are *translated* from earth to heaven. I see that if my facts were sufficiently vital and significant,—perhaps transmuted more into the substance of the human mind,—I should need but one book of poetry to contain them all.

FEB. 21. "As fat as a hen in the forehead,"—a saying which I heard my father use this morning.

Feb. 29. For the past month there has been more sea-room in the day, without so great danger of running aground on one of those two promontories that make it arduous to navigate the winter day, the morning or the evening. It is a narrow pass, and you must go through with the tide. Might not some of my pages be called "The Short Days of Winter"?

MARCH 1. Linnæus, speaking of the necessity of precise and adequate terms in any science, after naming some which he invented for botany, says, "Termini praeservarunt Anatomiam, Mathesin, Chemiam, ab idiotis; Medicinam autem eorum defectus conculcavit." (Terms (well defined) have preserved anatomy, mathematics, and chemistry from idiots; but the want of them has ruined medicine.) But I should say that men generally were not enough interested in the first-mentioned sciences to meddle with and degrade them. There is no interested motive to induce them to listen to the quack in mathematics, as they have to attend to the quack in medicine; yet chemistry has been converted into alchemy, and astronomy into astrology.

However, I can see that there is a certain advantage in these hard and precise terms, such as the lichenist uses, for instance. No one masters them so as to use them in writing on the subject without being far better informed than the rabble about it. New books are not written on chemistry or cryptogamia of as little worth comparatively as are written on the *spiritual* phenomena of the day. No man writes on lichens, using the terms of the science intelligibly, without having something to say, but every one thinks himself competent to write on the relation of the soul to the body, as if that were a *phænogamous* subject.

After having read various books on various subjects for some months, I take up a report on Farms by a committee of Middlesex Husbandmen, and read of the number of acres of bog that some farmer has redeemed, and the number of rods of stone wall that he has built, and the number of tons of hay he now cuts, or of bushels of corn or potatoes he raises there, and I feel as if I had got my foot down on to the solid and sunny earth, the basis of all philosophy, and poetry, and religion even. I have faith that the man who redeemed some acres of land the past summer redeemed also some parts of his character. I shall not expect to find him ever in the almshouse or the prison. He is, in fact, so far on his way to heaven. When he took the farm there was not a grafted tree on it, and now he realizes something handsome from the sale of fruit. These, in the absence of other facts, are evidence of a certain moral worth.

March 4. It is discouraging to talk with men who will recognize no principles. How little use is made of reason in this world! You argue with a man for an hour, he agrees with you step by step, you are approaching a triumphant conclusion, you think that you have converted him; but ah, no, he has a habit, he takes a pinch of snuff, he remembers that he entertained a different opinion at the commencement of the controversy, and his reverence for the past compels him to reiterate it now. You began at the butt of the pole to curve it, you gradually bent it round according to rule, and planted the other end in the ground, and already in imagination saw the vine curling round this segment of an arbor, under which a new generation was to re-create itself; but when you had done, just when the twig was bent, it sprang back to its former stubborn and unhandsome position like a bit of whalebone.

If I were to paint the short days of winter, I should represent two towering icebergs, approaching each other like promontories, for morning and evening, with cavernous recesses, and a solitary traveller, wrapping his cloak about him and bent forward against a driving storm, just entering the narrow pass. I would paint the light of a taper at midday, seen through a cottage window half buried in snow and frost, and some pale stars in the sky, and the sound of the woodcutter's axe. The icebergs with cavernous recesses. In the foreground should appear the harvest, and far in the background, through the pass, should be seen the sowers in the fields and other evidences of spring. The icebergs should gradually approach, and on the right and left the heavens should be shaded off from the light of midday to midnight with its stars. The sun low in the sky.

March 9. A warm spring rain in the night.

3 P.M.—Down the railroad.

Cloudy but springlike. When the frost comes out of the ground, there is a corresponding thawing of the man.

Again it rains, and I turn about.

The sound of water falling on rocks and of air falling on trees are very much alike.

Though cloudy, the air excites me. Yesterday all was tight as a stricture on my breast; to-day all is loosened. It is a different element from what it was.

March 10. I see flocks of a dozen bluebirds together. The warble of this bird is innocent and celestial, like its color. A woodchopper tells me he heard a robin this morning. What is the little chick-weed-like plant already springing up on the top of the Cliffs? There are some other plants with bright-green leaves which have either started somewhat or have never suffered from the cold under the snow.

March 14. Sunday. Rain, rain, rain; but even this is fair weather after so much snow.

March 15. This afternoon I throw off my outside coat. A mild spring day. I must hie to the Great Meadows. The air is full of bluebirds. The ground almost entirely bare. The villagers are out in the sun, and every man is happy whose work takes him outdoors. My life partakes of infinity. The air is as deep as our natures. I go forth to make new demands on life. I wish to begin this summer well; to do something in it worthy of it and of me; to transcend my daily routine and that of my townsmen; to have my immortality now, that it be in the *quality* of my daily life; to pay the greatest price, the greatest tax, of any man in Concord, and enjoy the most!! I will give all I am for *my* nobility. I will pay all my days for *my* success. I pray that the life of this spring and summer may ever lie fair in my memory. May I dare as I have never done! May I persevere as I have never done! I am eager to report the glory of the universe; may I be worthy to do it; to have got through with regarding human values, so as not to be distracted from regarding divine values. It is reasonable that a man should be something worthier at the end of the year than he was at the beginning.

March 16. Before sunrise.
    Spent the day in Cambridge Library.
    The Library a wilderness of books. The volumes of the Fifteenth,

Sixteenth, and Seventeenth Centuries, which lie so near on the shelf, are rarely opened, are effectually forgotten and not implied by our literature and newspapers. When I looked into Purchas's Pilgrims, it affected me like looking into an impassable swamp, ten feet deep with sphagnum, where the monarchs of the forest, covered with mosses and stretched along the ground, were making haste to become peat. Those old books suggested a certain fertility, an Ohio soil, as if they were making a humus for new literatures to spring in. I heard the bellowing of bullfrogs and the hum of mosquitoes reverberating through the thick embossed covers when I had closed the book. Decayed literature makes the richest of all soils.

March 18. This afternoon the woods and walls and the whole face of the country wear once more a wintry aspect, though there is more moisture in the snow and the trunks of the trees are whitened now on a more southerly or southeast side. These slight falls of snow which come and go again so soon when the ground is partly open in the spring, perhaps helping to open and crumble and prepare it for the seed, are called "the poor man's manure." They are, no doubt, more serviceable still to those who are rich enough to have some manure spread on their grass ground, which the melting snow helps dissolve and soak in and carry to the roots of the grass. At any rate, it is all the poor man has got, whether it is good or bad. There is more rain than snow now falling.

X.

March 30. Having occasion to-day to put up a long ladder against the house, I found, from the trembling of my nerves with the exertion, that I had not exercised that part of my system this winter. How much I may have lost! It would do me good to go forth and work hard and sweat. Though the frost is nearly out of the ground, the winter has not broken up in me. It is a backward season with me. Perhaps we grow older and older till we no longer sympathize with the revolution of the seasons, and our winters never break up.

March 31. Intended to get up early this morning and commence a series of spring walks, but clouds and drowsiness prevented.

Perhaps after the thawing of the trees their buds universally swell before they can be said to spring.

Perchance as we grow old we cease to spring with the spring, and we are indifferent to the succession of years, and they go by without epoch as months. Woe be to us when we cease to form new resolutions on the opening of a new year!

A cold, raw day with alternating hail-like snow and rain.

It would be worth the while to tell why a swamp pleases us, what kinds please us, also what weather, etc., etc.,—analyze our impressions. Why the moaning of the storm gives me pleasure. I sometimes feel that I need to sit in a far-away cave through a three weeks' storm, cold and wet, to give a tone to my system. The spring has its windy March to usher it in, with many soaking rains reaching into April. Methinks I would share every creature's suffering for the sake of its experience and joy. The song sparrow and the transient fox-colored sparrow,—have they brought me no message this year? Have I heard what this tiny passenger has to say, while it flits thus from tree to tree? I love the birds and beasts because they are mythologically in earnest. I reproach myself because I have regarded with indifference the passage of the birds; I have thought them no better than I.

April 1. Saw the first bee of the season on the railroad causeway, also a small red butterfly and, later, a làrge dark one with buff-edged wings.

Walden is all white ice, but little melted about the shores. The very sight of it carries my thoughts back at once some weeks toward winter, and a chill comes over them.

We have had a good solid winter, which has put the previous summer far behind us; intense cold, deep and lasting snows, and clear, tense winter sky. It is a good experience to have gone through with.

April 2. 6 A.M.—The sun is up. The air is full of the notes of birds,— song sparrows, red-wings, robins (singing a strain), bluebirds,— and I hear also a lark,—as if all the earth had burst forth into song. A few weeks ago, before the birds had come, there came to my mind in the night the twittering sound of birds in the early dawn of a spring morning, a semiprophecy of it, and last night I attended mentally as if I heard the spray-like dreaming sound of the midsummer frog and realized how glorious and full of revelations it was. Expectation may amount to prophecy. The clouds are *white* watery, not such as we had in the winter.

It appears to me that man is altogether too much insisted on. The poet says the proper study of mankind is man. I say, study to forget all that; take wider views of the universe. That is the egotism of the race. What is this our childish, gossiping, social literature, mainly in the hands of the publishers? Look at our literature. What a poor, puny, social thing, seeking sympathy! The author troubles himself about his readers,—would fain have one before he dies. He stands too near his printer; he corrects the proofs. Not satisfied with defiling one another in this world, we would all go to heaven together.

I do not value any view of the universe into which man and the institutions of man enter very largely and absorb much of the attention. Man is but the place where I stand, and the prospect hence is infinite. It is not a chamber of mirrors which reflect me. When I reflect, I find that there is other than me. The universe is larger than enough for man's abode.

Landed on Tall's Island. On the rocky point, where the wind is felt, the waves are breaking merrily, and now for half an hour our dog has been standing in the water under the small swamp white oaks, and ceaselessly snapping at each wave as it broke, as if it were a living creature. He, regardless of cold and wet, thrusts his head into each wave to gripe it. A dog snapping at the waves as they break on a rocky shore. He then rolls himself in the leaves for a napkin. We hardly set out to return, when the water looked sober and rainy. There was more appearance of rain in the water than in the sky,—April weather look. And soon we saw the dimples of drops on the surface. I forgot to mention before the cranberries seen on the bottom, as we pushed over the meadows, and the red beds of pitcher-plants.

April 3. It is a clear day with a cold westerly wind, the snow of yesterday being melted. When the sun shines unobstructedly the landscape is full of light, for it is reflected from the withered fawn-colored grass, as it cannot be from the green grass of summer. (On the back of the hill behind Gourgas's.)

The bluebird carries the sky on his back.

April 4. Sunday. I have got to that pass with my friend that our words do not pass with each other for what they are worth. We speak in vain; there is none to hear. He finds fault with me that I walk alone, when I pine for want of a companion; that I commit my thoughts to a diary even on my walks, instead of seeking to share them generously with a friend; curses my practice even. Awful as it is to contemplate, I pray that, if I am the cold intellectual skeptic whom he rebukes, his curse may take effect, and wither and dry up those sources of my life, and my journal no longer yield me pleasure nor life.

April 11. The sight of Nut Meadow Brook in Brown's land reminds me that the attractiveness of a brook depends much on the character of its bottom. I love just now to see one flowing through soft sand like this, where it wears a deep but irregular channel, now wider and shallower with distinct ripple-marks, now shelving off suddenly to indistinct depths, meandering as much up and down as from side to side, deepest where narrowest, and ever gullying under this bank or that, its bottom lifted up to one side or the other, the current inclining to one side. I stop to look at the circular shadows of the dimples over the yellow sand, and the dark-brown clams on their edges in the sand at the bottom. (I hear the sound of the piano below as I write this, and feel as if the winter in me were at length beginning to thaw, for my spring has been even more backward than nature's. For a month past life has been a thing incredible to me. None but the kind gods can make me sane. If only they will let their south winds blow on me! I ask to be melted. You can only ask of the metals that they be tender to the fire that *melts* them. To naught else can they be tender.) The sweet flags are now starting up under water two inches high, and minnows dart. A pure brook is a very beautiful object to study minutely. It will bear the closest inspection, even to the fine air-bubbles, like minute globules of quicksilver, that lie on its bottom. The minute particles or spangles of golden mica in these sands, when the sun shines on them, remind one of the golden sands we read of. Everything is washed clean and bright, and the water is the best glass through which to see it.

April 12. Saw the first blossoms (bright-yellow stamens or pistils) on the willow catkins to-day. The speckled alders and the maples are earlier then. The yellow blossom appears first on one side of the ament and is the most of bright and sunny color the spring has shown, the most decidedly flower-like that I have seen. It is fit that this almost earliest spring flower should be yellow, the color of the sun.

I am made somewhat sad this afternoon by the coarseness and vulgarity of my companion, because he is one with whom I have made myself intimate. He inclines latterly to speak with coarse jesting of facts which should always be treated with delicacy and reverence. I lose my respect for the man who can make the mystery of sex the subject of a coarse jest, yet, when you speak earnestly and seriously on the subject, is silent. I feel that this is to be truly irreligious. Whatever may befall me, I trust that I may never lose my respect for purity in others. Can I walk with one who by his jests and by his habitual tone reduces the life of men and women to a level with that of cats and dogs? I can have no really serious conversation with my companion. He seems not capable of it.

In the New Forest in Hampshire they had a chief officer called the Lord Warden and under him two distinct officers, one to preserve the *venison* of the forest, another to preserve its *vert, i.e.* woods, lawns, etc. Does not our Walden need such? The Lord Warden was a person of distinction, as the Duke of Gloucester.

Walden Wood was my forest walk.

The English forests are divided into "walks," with a keeper presiding over each. My "walk" is ten miles from my house every way.

There is, this afternoon and evening, a rather cool April rain. Pleasant to hear its steady dripping.

April 13. A driving snow-storm in the night and still raging; five or six inches deep on a level at 7 A.M. All birds are turned into snow-birds. Trees and houses have put on the aspect of winter. The traveller's carriage wheels, the farmer's wagon, are converted into white disks of snow through which the spokes hardly appear. But it is good now to stay in the house and read and write. We do not now go wandering all abroad and dissipated, but the imprisoning storm condenses our thoughts. I can hear the clock tick as not in pleasant weather. My life is enriched. I love to hear the wind howl. I have a fancy for sitting with my book or paper in some mean and apparently unfavorable place, in the kitchen, for instance, where the work is going on, rather a little cold than comfortable.

April 15. Would it not be a fine office to preserve the *vert* of this forest in which I ramble?

Channing calls our walks along the banks of the river, taking a boat for convenience at some distant point, *riparial* excursions. It is a pleasing epithet, but I mistrust such, even as good as this, in which the mere name is so agreeable, as if it would ring hollow ere long; and rather the thing should make the true name poetic at last. Alcott wished me to name my book *Sylvania!*

April 16. As I turned round the corner of Hubbard's Grove, saw a woodchuck, the first of the season, in the middle of the field, six or seven rods from the fence which bounds the wood, and twenty rods distant. I ran along the fence and cut him off, or rather overtook him, though he started at the same time. When I was only a rod and a half off, he stopped, and I did the same; then he ran again, and I ran up within three feet of him, when he stopped again, the fence being between us. I squatted down and surveyed him at my leisure. His eyes were dull black and rather inobvious, with a faint chestnut (?) iris, with but little expression and that more of resignation than of anger. The general aspect was a coarse grayish brown, a sort of grisel (?). A lighter brown next the skin, then black or very dark brown and tipped with whitish rather loosely. The head between a squirrel and a bear, flat on the top and dark brown, and darker still or black on the tip of the nose. The whiskers black, two inches long. The ears very small and roundish, set far back and nearly buried in the fur. Black feet, with long and slender claws for digging. It appeared to tremble, or perchance shivered with cold. When I moved, it gritted its teeth quite loud, sometimes striking the under jaw against the other chatteringly, sometimes grinding one jaw on the other, yet as if more from instinct than anger. Whichever way I turned, that way it headed. I took a twig a foot long and touched its snout, at which it started forward and bit the stick, lessening the distance between us to two feet, and still it held all the ground it gained. I played with it tenderly awhile with the stick, trying to open its gritting jaws. Ever its long incisors, two above and two below, were presented. But I thought it would go to sleep if I stayed long enough. It did not sit upright as sometimes, but *standing* on its fore feet with its head down, *i.e.* half sitting, half standing. We sat looking at one another about half an hour, till we began to feel mesmeric influences. When I was tired, I moved away, wishing to see him run, but I could not start him. He would not stir as long as I was looking at him or could see him. I walked round him; he turned as fast and fronted me still. I sat down by his side within a foot. I talked to him *quasi* forest lingo, baby-talk, at any rate in a conciliatory tone, and thought that I had some influence on him. He gritted his teeth less. I chewed checkerberry leaves and presented them to his nose at last without a grit; though I saw that by so much gritting of the teeth he had worn them rapidly and they were covered with a fine white powder, which, if you measured it thus, would have made his anger terrible. He did not mind any noise I might make. With a little stick I lifted one of his paws to examine it, and held it up at pleasure. I turned him over to see what color he was beneath (darker or more purely brown), though he turned himself back again sooner than I could have wished. His tail was also all brown, though not very dark, rat-tail like, with loose hairs standing out on all sides like a caterpillar brush. He had a rather mild look. I spoke kindly to him. I reached checkerberry leaves to his mouth. I stretched my hands over him, though he turned up his head and still gritted a little. I laid my hand on him, but immediately took it off again, instinct not being wholly overcome. If I had had a few fresh bean leaves, thus in advance of the season, I am sure I should have tamed him completely. Could easily have wrapped him in my handkerchief. He was not fat nor particularly lean. I finally had to leave him without seeing him move from the place. A large, clumsy, burrowing squirrel. *Arctomys*, bearmouse. I respect him as one of the natives. He lies there, by his color and habits so naturalized amid the dry leaves, the withered grass, and the bushes. A sound nap, too, he has enjoyed in his native fields, the past winter. I think I might learn some wisdom of him.

The two states of the meadow are to be remembered: first in a March or April wind, as I have described it; second in a perfectly calm and beautiful mild morning or evening or midday, as lately, at the same season, such as I have also partially described, when there are no gulls circling over it. What different thoughts it suggests! Would it not be worth the while to describe the different states of our meadows which cover so large a portion of the town? It is not as if we had a few acres only of water surface. They answer to moods of the Concord mind. There might be a chapter: The Sudbury Meadows, the Humors of the Town.

April 17. Observed in the second of the chain of ponds between Fair Haven and Walden a large (for the pond) island patch of the dwarf andromeda, I sitting on the east bank; its fine brownish-red color very agreeable and memorable to behold. In the last long pond, looking at it from the south, I saw it filled with a slightly grayish shrub which I took for the sweet-gale, but when I had got round to the east side, chancing to turn round, I was surprised to see that all this pond-hole also was filled with the same warm brownish-red-colored andromeda. The fact was I was opposite to the sun, but from every other position I saw only the sun reflected from the surface of the andromeda leaves, which gave the whole a grayish-brown hue tinged with red; but from this position alone I saw, as it were, through the leaves which the opposite sun lit up, giving to the whole this charming warm, what I call *Indian*, red color,—the mellowest, the ripest, red imbrowned color; but when I looked to the right or left, *i.e.* north or south, the more the swamp had the mottled light or grayish aspect where the light was reflected from the surfaces of the leaves. And afterward, when I had risen higher up the hill, though still opposite the sun, the light came reflected upward from the surfaces, and I lost that warm, rich red tinge, surpassing cathedral windows. Let me look again at a different hour of the day, and see if it is really so. It is a very interesting piece of magic. It is the autumnal tints in spring, only more subdued and mellow. These leaves are so slow to decay. *Vide* when they fall. Already these ponds are greened with frog-spittle. I see the tracks of muskrats through it. Hear the faint croak of frogs and the still rather faint peeping of hylas. It is about 4.30 P.M.

April 18.* The most interesting fact, perhaps, at present is these few tender yellow blossoms, these half-expanded sterile aments of the willow, seen through the rain and cold,—signs of the advancing year, pledges of the sun's return. Anything so delicate, both in structure, in color and in fragrance, contrasts strangely with surrounding nature and feeds the faith of man. The fields are acquiring a greenish tinge.

The birds which I see and hear in the midst of the storm are robins, song sparrows, blackbirds, and crows occasionally.

This is the spring of the year. Birds are migrating northward to their breeding-places; the melted snows are escaping to the sea. We have now the unspeakable rain of the Greek winter. The element of water prevails. The river has far overflowed its channel.

For the first time I perceive this spring that the year is a circle. I see distinctly the spring arc thus far. It is drawn with a firm line. Every incident is a parable of the Great Teacher. The cranberries washed up in the meadows and into the road on the causeways now yield a pleasant acid.

Why should just these sights and sounds accompany our life? Why should I hear the chattering of blackbirds, why smell the skunk each year? I would fain explore the mysterious relation between myself and these things. I would at least know what these things unavoidably are, make a chart of our life, know how its shores trend, that butterflies reappear and when, know why just this circle of creatures completes the world. Can I not by expectation affect the revolutions of nature, make a day to bring forth something new?

Observe all kinds of coincidences, as what kinds of birds come with what flowers.

An east wind. I hear the clock strike plainly ten or eleven P.M.

---

*Storm begins this morning and continues five days incessantly.

April 19. 6 A.M.—Rain still, a fine rain. The birds must live on expectation now. There is nothing in nature to cheer them yet.

That oak by Derby's is a grand object, seen from any side. It stands like an athlete and defies the tempests in every direction. It has not a weak point. It is an agony of strength. Its branches look like stereotyped gray lightning on the sky. But I fear a price is set upon its sturdy trunk and roots for ship-timber, for knees to make stiff the sides of ships against the Atlantic billows. Like an athlete, it shows its well-developed muscles.

How sweet is the perception of a new natural fact! suggesting what worlds remain to be unveiled. That phenomenon of the andromeda seen against the sun cheers me exceedingly. When the phenomenon was not observed, it was not at all. I think that no man ever takes an original or detects a principle, without experiencing an inexpressible, as quite infinite and sane, pleasure, which advertises him of the dignity of that truth he has perceived. The thing that pleases me most within these three days is the discovery of the andromeda phenomenon. It makes all those parts of the country where it grows more attractive and elysian to me. It is a natural magic. These little leaves are the stained windows in the cathedral of my world. At sight of any redness I am excited like a cow.

Scared up three blue herons in the little pond close by, quite near us. It was a grand sight to see them rise, so slow and stately, so long and limber, with an undulating motion from head to foot, undulating also their large wings, undulating in two directions, and looking warily about them. With this graceful, limber, undulating  motion they arose, as if so they got under way, their two legs trailing parallel far behind like an earthy residuum to be left behind. They are large, like birds of Syrian lands, and seemed to oppress the earth, and hush the hillside to silence, as they winged their way over it, looking back toward us. It would affect our thoughts, deepen and perchance darken our reflections, if such huge birds flew in numbers in our sky. The legs hang down like a weight which they raise, to pump up as it were with its wings and convey out of danger.

April 23. The water has risen one and a half inches at six this morning since last night. There is absolutely no passing, in carriages or otherwise, over Hubbard's and the Red Bridge roads, and over *none* of the bridges for foot-travellers. Throughout this part of the country most people do not remember so great a flood, but, judging from some accounts, it was probably as high here thirty-five years ago. I hear this morning, in the pine woods above the railroad bridge, for the first time, that delicious cool-sounding *wetter-wetter-wetter-wetter-wet'* from that small bird (pine warbler?) in the tops of the pines. I associate it with the *cool, moist, evergreen spring* woods.

April 26. P.M.—Rambled amid the shrub oak hills beyond Hayden's.

Lay on the dead grass in a cup-like hollow sprinkled with half-dead low shrub oaks. As I lie flat, looking close in among the roots of the grass, I perceive that its endless ribbon has pushed up about one inch and is green to that extent,—such is the length to which the spring has gone here,—though when you stand up the green is not perceptible. It is a dull, rain dropping and threatening afternoon, inclining to drowsiness. I feel as if I could go to sleep under a hedge. The landscape wears a subdued tone, quite soothing to the feelings; no glaring colors.

XI.

April 28. I scarcely know why I am excited when, in M. Huc's book, I read of the country of the Mongol Tartars as the "Land of Grass," but I am, as much as if I were a cow.[*]

2.30 P.M.—To Cliffs and Heywood's Brook.

Are not the flowers which appear earliest in the spring the most primitive and simplest? They have been in this town thus far, as I have observed them this spring, putting them down in the order in which I think they should be named, using Gray's names:—

[1] *Symplocarpus fœtidus*	(well advanced Feb. 13th, '51)[†]
[2] *Alnus incana*	April 11
[3] *Alnus serrulata*	8
[4] *Acer ~~rubrum~~ dasycarpum*	April 9 one by Red Bridge
[5] *Salix,* willow, earliest	12
[6] *Ulmus Americana* (?)	15 one, Cheney's (others ten days or fourteen later)
[7] *Populus tremuloides*	15
[8] *Corylus tremuloides*	16 perhaps before the last[‡]
[9] *Carex Pennsylvanica* (?)	22
[10] *Caltha palustris*	25 many
[11] *Stellaria media* (?)	26 Cheney's garden
[12] *Capsella Bursa-pastoris*	26 Cheney's garden

---

*Drive about the 10th of May to Ashburnham.
†N.B. Spring of '51 ten days or more earlier.
‡*Corylus rostrata* when?

[13] *Taraxacum Dens-leonis*	25 one in water (seen by another the 20th)
[14] *Equisetum arvense*	25 in water
[15] *Gnaphalium purpureum*	27 (about April 16th, '51)
[16] *Saxifraga Virginiensis*	27 (April 22d, '51)
[17] *Antennaria plantaginifolia*	27
[18] *Ranunculus fascicularis*	28 only two (abundant April 22d, '51)

All but the 3d, 8th, 11th, 12th observed in the very best season, and these within a day (?) of their flowering.*

I observe that the first six are decidedly water or water-loving plants, and the 10th, 13th, and 14th were found in the water and are equally if not more confined to that element. The 7th and 8th belong to the cooler zones of the earth, the 7th, according to [*George B.*] Emerson, as far north as 64° and comes up (is it this?) on burnt lands first and will grow in dry, cool, dreary places. The 9th on a dry, warm rocky hillside,—the earliest (?) grass to blossom,—also the 18th; the 11th and 12th in cold, damp gardens, like the earth first made dry land; the 15th and 17th on dry (scantily clad with grass) fields and hills, hardy; the 16th, sunny bare rocks, in seams on moss, where also in a day or two the columbine will bloom. The 18th is also indebted to the warmth of the rocks.

This may, perhaps, be nearly the order of the world's creation. Thus we have in the spring of the year the spring of the world represented. —Such were the first localities afforded for plants,—water-bottoms, bare rocks, and scantily clad lands, and land recently bared of water.

May 1. The little peeping frogs which I got last night resemble the description of the *Hylodes Pickeringii* and in some respects the peeping hyla, but they are probably the former, though every way considerably smaller (*vide* pencil mark in report). Mine are about

---

*N.B. Is the *Hepatica triloba* found here?

three quarters of an inch long as they sit, seven eighths if stretched; thigh five sixteenths, leg same; tarsus and toes one half; four-fingered and five-toed with *small* tubercles on the ends of them. Some difference in their color; one is like a pale oak leaf at this season, streaked with brown; two others more ashy. Two have crosses like this on back, of dark brown. On the head thus, with transverse bands on the legs. I keep them in a tumbler. Peep at twilight and evening, occasionally at other times. One that got out in the evening on to the carpet was found soon after by his peeping *on the piano*. They easily ascend the glass of the window; jump eighteen inches and more. When they peep, the loose wrinkled skin of the throat is swelled up into a globular bubble, very large and transparent and quite round, except on the throat side, behind which their little heads are lost, mere protuberances on the side of this sphere; and the peeping wholly absorbs them; their mouths shut, or apparently so. Will sit half a day on the side of a smooth tumbler. Made that trilling note in the house. Remain many hours at the bottom of the water in the tumbler, or sit as long on the leaves above. A pulse in the throat always, except in one for an hour or two apparently asleep. They change their color to a darker or lighter shade, chameleon-like.

May 2. 6 A.M.—Is not the chipping sparrow the commonest heard in the village streets in the mornings now, sitting on an elm or apple tree? Was it the black and white warbler that I saw this morning? It did not stop to creep round the trunks; was very shy. Or was it the myrtle-bird? Might it have been the log-cock woodpecker that I saw yesterday morning? Reptiles must not be omitted, especially frogs; their croaking is the most earthy sound now, a rustling of the scurf of the earth, not to be overlooked in the awakening of the year. It is such an earth-sound.

May 3. 5 A.M.—To Cliffs.

Hear the first brown thrasher,—two of them. Minott says he heard one yesterday, but does he know it from a catbird? They drown all the rest. He says *cherruwit, cherruwit; go ahead, go ahead; give it to him, give it to him;* etc., etc., etc. Plenty of birds in the woods this morning.

P.M.—Cinquefoil or five-finger (*Potentilla Canadensis*). Also the golden saxifrage (what a name!) (*Chrysosplenium Americanum*), in the meadow at Brister's Hill, in the water, in moss-like beds. It may have been in bloom some time; an obscure flower.

Going through the Depot Field, I hear the dream frog at a distance. The little peeping frogs make a background of sound in the horizon, which you do not hear unless you attend. The former is a trembling note, some higher, some lower, along the edge of the earth, an all-pervading sound. Nearer, it is a blubbering or rather bubbling sound, such as children, who stand nearer to nature, can and do often make,—this and many others, ~~remembering the frog state~~. There is no dew (I have observed none yet). The dream of the frog sounds best at a distance,—most dreamy. The little peeper prefers a pool on the edge of a wood, which mostly dries up at midsummer, whose shore is covered with leaves and where twigs lie in the water, as where choppers have worked.

Summer is coming apace. Within three or four days the birds have come so fast I can hardly keep the run of them,—much faster than the flowers. I did not watch for the *very earliest*, however.

May 4. R. W. E. tells me he does not like Haynes as well as I do. I tell him that he makes better manure than most men.

May 5. Heard the first cricket singing, on a lower level than any bird, observing a lower tone—the sane, wise one—than all the singers. He came not from the south, but from the depths. He has felt the heats at last,—that migrates downward. The smallest of birds. The myrtle-bird again, rather tame. In the small ponds I hear a slight bullfroggy note. The andromeda is now a brownish-green; very little of the redness left. Seen from the sun side, now the sun is getting low, it looks like a large bed of greenish-gray moss, reflecting the light. What has become of its red leaves? Does it shed them, and the present fresher ones not till next spring?

A fine scarlet sunset. As I sit by my window and see the clouds reflected in the meadow, I think it is important to have water, because it multiplies the heavens.

MAY 6. 3 P.M.—To Conantum.

Heard the first warbling vireo this morning on the elms. This almost makes a summer. Heard also, as I sat at my desk, the unusual low of cows being driven to their country pastures. Sat all day with the window open, for the outer air is the warmest. The balm-of-Gilead was well blossomed out yesterday, and has been for three or four days probably. The woods seen a mile off in the horizon are more indistinct yesterday and today, these two summerlike days (it is a summer heat), the green of the pines being blended with the gray or ash of the deciduous trees; partly, perhaps, because the fine haze in the air is the color of the twigs, and partly because the buds are expanded into leaves on many; but this last cause is hardly admissible. Now the wasps have come.

My dream frog turns out to be a toad. I watched half a dozen a long time at 3.30 this afternoon in Hubbard's Pool, where they were frogging (?) lustily. They sat in the shade, either partly in the water, or on a stick; looked darker and narrower in proportion to their length than toads usually do, and moreover are aquatic. I see them jump into the ditches as I walk. After an interval of silence, one appeared to be gulping the wind into his belly, inflating himself so that he was considerably expanded; then he discharged it all into his throat while his body or belly collapsed suddenly, expanding his throat to a remarkable size. Was nearly a minute inflating itself; then swelled out its sac, which is rounded and reminded me of the bag to a work-table, holding its head up the while. It is whitish specked (the bag) on a dull bluish or slate ground, much bigger than all the rest of the head, and nearly an inch in diameter. It was a ludicrous sight, with their so serious prominent eyes peering over it; and a deafening sound, when several were frogging at once, as I was leaning over them. The mouth [seemed] to be shut always, and perhaps the air was expelled through the nostrils. The strain appeared prolonged as long as the air lasted, and was sometimes quavered or made intermittent, apparently by closing the orifice, whatever it was, or the blast. One, which I brought home, answers well enough to the description of the common toad (*Bufo Americanus*), though it is hardly so gray. Their piping (?) was evidently connected with their loves. Close by, it is an unmusical monotonous deafening sound, a steady blast,—not a peep nor a croak, but a *kind* of piping,—but, far away, it is a dreamy, lulling sound, and fills well the crevices of nature. Out of its place, as very near, it would be as intolerable as the thrumming of children. The plower yesterday disturbed a toad in the garden, the first I have heard of. I must catch him and compare them. Their heads are well above the water when they pipe.

Saw a striped snake lying by the roadside as if watching for toads, though they must be scarce now, his head just on the edge of the road. The most flexible of creatures, it is so motionless it appears the most rigid, in its waving line.

The yellow willows on the causeways are now fairly leaving out. They are more forward in this respect than that early willow, or any other that I see. The trees are already a mass of green, partly concealing the yellow stems,—a tender, fresh light green. No *trees* look so forward in this respect, and, being in rows, they make the more show, their branches are so thick and numerous, close together. If some have leaves as large, they are much more scattered and make no such show. I did not observe what time the willow bark would strip and make whistles. The female maple is more crimson, the male more scarlet. The horse-chestnut buds are so advanced that they are larger than the leaves of any tree. The elder, the wild cherry, thimble-berries, sweet-briars, cultivated cherry, and early apples, etc., white birches, hazels, aspens, hornbeams, maples, etc., etc.,—not quite the hickory and alder,—are opening their buds; the alders are beginning to.

It is pleasant when the road winds along the side of a hill with a thin fringe of wood through which to look into the low land. It furnishes both shade and frame for your pictures,—as this Corner road. The first *Anemone nemorosa*, wind-flower or wood anemone, its petals more slightly tinged with purple than the rue-leaved. See the ferns here at the spring curling up like the proboscis of the sphinx moth. The first *Viola blanda* (sweet-scented white), in the moist ground, also, by this spring. It is pretty numerous and may have been out a day or two. I think I could not find so many blue ones. It has a rather strong scent like heliotrope (?). The *Convallaria bifolia* budded. Sometimes the toad reminds me of the cricket, its note also proceeding from the ground. See now the woodchuck rollicking across a field toward his hole and tumbling into it. See where he has just dug a new hole. Their claws long and rather weak-looking for digging. The wood-peckers tapping. The first columbine (*Aquilegia Canadensis*) to-day, on Conantum. Shade is grateful, and the walker feels a desire to bathe in some pond or stream for cool-ness and invigoration.

Cowslips show at a distance in the meadows (Miles's). The new butter is white still, but with these *cows' lips* in the grass it will soon be yellow, I trust. This yellowness in the spring, derived from the sun, affects even the cream in the cow's bag, and flowers in yellow butter at last. Who has not turned pale at the sight of hay butter? These are the cows' lips.

The music of all creatures has to do with their loves, even of toads and frogs. Is it not the same with man?

There are odors enough in nature to remind you of everything, if you had lost every sense but smell. The fever-bush is an apothe-cary's shop.

The farmers are very busily harrowing and rolling in their grain. The dust flies from their harrows across the field. The tearing, toothed harrow and the ponderous cylinder, which goes creaking and rumbling over the surface, heard afar, and vying with the sphere. The cylinder is a simple machine, and must go into the new symbols. It is an interesting object, seen drawn across a grain-field. The willows are now suddenly of a light, fresh, tender yellowish-green. A green bittern, a gawky bird. As I return over the bridge, shadflies very numerous. Many insects now in the evening sun-shine, especially over the water.

Houstonia (*Hedyotis cœrulea*), bluets, now just begun. Dewey calls it Venus' Pride. Gray says truly, "a very delicate little herb, . . .

producing in spring a profusion of handsome bright blue blossoms fading to white, with a yellow eye." I should say bluish-white. The dwarf andromeda (*A. calyculata*) just begun; leaves called evergreen; flowers on "one-sided leafy racemes." Methinks its leaves remain two years, and fall in the spring, the small ones continuing to grow. (?) The ground is now strewn with the old red-brown lower leaves, and only the smaller and fresher green ones remain.

The common toad, with which I compared the dream toad I brought home, has two horn-like dark marks reaching over the eyes. It is not depressed, but rather has a tubercle, on the top of the head between the eyes. It is also much wider in proportion to length, and is triangular, as I have drawn in report. Yet they are probably the same. The garden toad made the same faint chicken-like, musical croak, when I held him in my hand, with the other, and in the same manner swelling his bag. The garden toad was yellowish beneath, the other white with some small spots. The latter turned much lighter-colored,—from brown to a yellowish and light-brown green, or rather greenish-brown,—while I had him. They have a bright eye, with coppery or golden-coppery iris. It is their redeeming feature. But why do I not hear them in the garden? They appear to frequent the water first, and breed there, then hop to the gardens, and turn lighter and grow thicker.

May 7. I would fain see the sun as a moon, more weird. Methinks the birds sing more some mornings than others, when I cannot see the reason.

I think that birds vary their notes considerably with the seasons. When I hear a bird singing, I cannot think of any words that will imitate it. What word can stand in place of a bird's note? You would have to surround it with a *chevaux de frise* of accents, and exhaust the art of the musical composer besides with your different bars, to represent it, and finally get a bird to sing it, to perform it. It has so little relation to words. The wood thrush says *ah-tully-tully* for one strain.

I fear that the dream of the toads will not sound so musical now that I know whence it proceeds. But I will not fear to *know*. They will awaken new and more glorious music for me as I advance, still farther in the horizon, not to be traced to toads and frogs in slimy pools.

P.M.—To Nawshawtuct.

May 9. It is impossible to remember a week ago. A river of Lethe flows with many windings the year through, separating one season from another. The heavens for a few days have been lost. It has been a sort of *paradise* instead.

Saw a green snake, twenty or more inches long, on a bush, hanging over a twig with its head held forward six inches into the air, without support and motionless. What there for? Leaves generally are most beautiful when young and tender, before insects or weather has defaced them.

These are the warm-west-wind, dream-frog, leafing-out, willowy, haze days. Is not this summer, whenever it occurs, the vireo and yellowbird and golden robin being here? The young birch leaves reflect the light in the sun.

Mankind seen in a dream. The gardener asks what kind of beans he shall plant. Nobody is looking up into the sky.

May 10. This Monday the streets are full of cattle being driven up-country,—cows and calves and colts. The rain is making the grass grow apace. It appears to stand upright,—its blades,—and you can almost see it grow. For some reason I now remember the autumn,—the succory and the goldenrod. We remember autumn to best advantage in the spring; the finest aroma of it reaches us then. How closely the flower follows upon, if it does not precede, the leaf! The leaves are but calyx and escort to the flower. Some beds of clover wave.

Some look out only for the main chance, and do not regard appearances nor manners; others—others regard these mainly. It is an immense difference. I feel it frequently. It is a theme I must dwell upon.

May 13. P.M.—To Walden in rain.

A May storm, yesterday and to-day; rather cold. The fields are green now, and the cows find good feed. All these expanding leaves and flower-buds are much more beautiful in the rain,—covered with clear drops. They have lost some of their beauty when I have shaken the drops off. They who do not walk in the woods in the rain never behold them in their freshest, most radiant and blooming beauty.

May 14. Hastily reviewing this Journal, I find the flowers to have appeared in this order since the 28th of April (perhaps *some note* in my Journal has escaped me):*—

Acer rubrum	April 28 male; a female 30th; first date is perhaps early enough for both.
Populus grandidentata	29
Epigæa repens	30 (April 25, '51).
Sweet-gale	30 probably a *day* or *two* before.
Viola ovata	May 1 (April 25, '51).
[*Etc.—32 more.*]	

BIRDS SINCE 28TH APRIL

Saw the last *Fringilla hyemalis*	May 4.
First	
Savannah (?)† sparrow	May 1 or a day or two before.
Ground robin	May 1
Catbird	1
Black and white creeper	1
Purple finch	1
Myrtle-bird	2
[*Etc.—22 more.*]	

---

*The Latin Gray's. By last of June, '51 is apparently three or four days earlier than '52.

†["Seringo" in pencil written over "Savannah" and "Baywinged" under.]

Snow in hollows?	April 28
Saw frog spawn	28
Rushes at Second Division	
one foot high, highest of	
grasslike herbs	29
A *large* water-bug	29
Heard toad (dreaming)	30
Bull(?)frog (saw him)	30
Flies buzz outdoors	
Gooseberry leaves	
(earliest of leaves?)	April 30
Sit without fire to-night.	
Spearing.	
Chickadee's *tull-a-lull*	May 4
First cricket on Cliff	5
Shad-fly	5
Toad in garden	5
Wasps	6
Willows suddenly green	6
Cows going up-country	
Many trees *just beginning*	
to expand leaves	6
First fog, very slight	
Ant-hills	7
Humblebee	7
Partridge drums	7
Stinkpot tortoise	8 How much earlier?
Birch leaves, sweet-scented	8
Ground still frozen in some places	8
Barn swallows twitter	8
Apple and cherry trees	
begin to show green	9
Elms darkened with samaræ	
A green snake	9
Reduce neck-cloth	
Clover waves	10

Frogs snore in the river	10
One oak in the gray	13
Pines start	13
A May storm	13

These pages do not contain the earliest phenomena of the spring, for which see the previous journal, as far as observed.

May 26. Wednesday. Surveying the Brooks farm.

The early thalictrum has been in bloom some time. Perceive the rank smell of brakes. Observe the yellow bark of the barberry.

The air is full of the odor of apple blossoms, yet the air is fresh as from the salt water. The meadow smells sweet as you go along low places in the road at sundown. To-night I hear many crickets. They have commenced their song. They bring in the summer.

May 27. My early willow is either the swamp willow or the bog willow of Bigelow. The *Salix nigra*, or black willow, of Gray, in bloom. *Myosotis laxa*, water mouse-ear, by Depot Field Brook. The fruit of the sweet flag is now just fit to eat, and reminds me of childhood,—the critchicrotches. They would help sustain a famished traveller. The inmost tender leaf, also, near the base, is quite palatable, as children know. I love it as well as muskrats(?) The smooth speedwell, the minute pale-blue striated flower by the roadsides and in the short sod of fields common now. I hear but few toads and peepers now. The tall crowfoot out. The fringed polygala near the Corner Spring is a delicate flower, with very fresh tender green leaves and red-purple blossoms; beautiful from the contrast of its clear red-purple flowers with its clear green leaves. The cuckoo. Caught a wood frog (*Rana sylvatica*), the color of a dead leaf. He croaked as I held him, perfectly frog-like. A humblebee is on my bunch of flowers laid down.

May 30. Sunday. Now is the summer come. A breezy, washing day. A day for shadows, even of moving clouds, over fields in which the grass is beginning to wave. Senecio in bloom. A bird's nest in grass, with coffee-colored eggs. Cinquefoil and houstonia cover the ground, mixed with the grass and contrasting with each other. Strong lights and shades now.

June 5. The lupine is now in its glory. It is the more important because it occurs in such extensive patches, even an acre or more together, and of such a pleasing variety of colors,—purple, pink, or lilac, and white,—especially with the sun on it, when the transparency of the flower makes its color changeable. It paints a whole hillside with its blue, making such a field (if not meadow) as Proserpine might have wandered in. Its leaf was made to be covered with dewdrops. I am quite excited by this prospect of blue flowers in clumps with narrow intervals. Such a profusion of the heavenly, the elysian, color, as if these were the Elysian Fields. They say the seeds look like babies' faces, and hence the flower is so named. No other flowers exhibit so much blue. That is the value of the lupine. The earth is blued with them. Yet a third of a mile distant I do not detect their color on the hillside. Perchance because it is the color of the air.

JUNE 6. *Sunday.* First devil's-needles in the air, and some smaller, bright-green ones on flowers. The earliest blueberries are now forming as greenberries. The wind already injures the just-expanded leaves, tearing them and making them turn black. I see the effects of recent frosts on the young oaks in hollows in the woods. The leaves are turned dry, black, and crisp. The side-flowering sandwort, an inconspicuous white flower like a chickweed.

JUNE 7. Surveying for Sam. Pierce. Found piece of an Indian soapstone pot.

June 9. The season of waving boughs; and the lighter under sides of the new leaves are exposed. This is the first half of June. Already the grass is not so fresh and liquid-velvety a green, having much of it blossomed and some even gone to seed, and it is mixed with reddish ferns and other plants, but the general leafiness, shadiness, and waving of grass and boughs in the breeze characterize the season. The weather is very clear, and the sky bright. The river shines like silver. Methinks this is a traveller's month. The locust in bloom. The waving, undulating rye. The deciduous trees have filled up the intervals between the evergreens, and the woods are bosky now.

Evelyn* has collected the fine exaggerations of antiquity respecting the virtues and habits of trees and added some himself. If the oft-repeated glorification of the forest from age to age smacks of religion, is even druidical, Evelyn is as good as several old druids, and his "Silva" is a new kind of prayerbook, a glorifying of the trees and enjoying them forever, which was the chief end of his life.

Evelyn speaks of "mel-dews" attracting bees. Can mildews be corrupted from this? Says that the alder, laid under water, "will harden like a very stone," and speaks of their being used "for the draining of grounds by placing them... in the trenches," which I have just seen done here under Clamshell Hill.

Evelyn's love of his subject teaches him to use many expressive words, some imported from the Latin, which I wonder how we can do without. He says of the "oziers or aquatic salix," "It likewise yields more limber and flexible twigs for baskets, flaskets, hampers, cages, lattices, cradles,... the bodies of coaches and waggons,... for chairs, hurdles, stays, bands," etc.; "likewise for fish-weirs, and to support the banks of impetuous rivers: In fine, for all wicker and *twiggy* works;

'Viminibus Salices'—VIRG."

Many of his words show a poetic genius.

Evelyn well says "a *sobbing* rain."

He speaks of pines "pearling out into gums." Things raised in a garden he calls "*hortular furniture.*" He talks of modifying the air as well as the soil, about plants, "and make the remedy as well regional as topical." This suggests the propriety of Shakespeare's expression the "*region* cloud," region meaning then oftener upper regions relatively to the earth.

---

*[John Evelyn, *Silva: or a Discourse of Forest Trees.*]

He speaks of a "dewie *sperge* or brush," to be used instead of a watering-pot, which "gluts" the earth. He calls the kitchen-garden the "olitory garden." In a dedication of his "Kalendarium Hortense" to Cowley, he inserts two or three good sentences or quotations, *viz.:* "As the philosopher in Seneca desired only bread and herbs to dispute felicity with Jupiter," so of Cowley's simple retired life. "Who would not, like you, *cacher sa vie?*" "Delivered from the gilded impertinences of life."

June 12. How difficult, if not impossible, to do the things we have done! as fishing and camping out. They seem to me a little fabulous now.

Boys are bathing at Hubbard's Bend, playing with a boat (I at the willows). The color of their bodies in the sun at a distance is pleasing, the not often seen flesh-color. I hear the sound of their sport borne over the water. As yet we have not man in nature. What a singular fact for an angel visitant to this earth to carry back in his notebook, that men were forbidden to expose their bodies under the severest penalties! A pale pink, which the sun would soon tan. White men! There are no white men to contrast with the red and the black; they are of such colors as the weaver gives them.

Hedge-mustard. Some fields are almost wholly covered with sheep's-sorrel, now turned red,—its valves (?). It helps thus agreeably to paint the earth, contrasting even at a distance with the greener fields, blue sky, and dark or downy clouds. It is red, marbled, watered, mottled, or waved with greenish, like waving grain,—three or four acres of it. To the farmer or grazier it is a troublesome weed, but to the landscape-viewer an agreeable red tinge laid on by the painter. I feel well into summer when I see this redness. It appears to be avoided by the cows.

The color of the earth at a distance where a wood has been cut off is a reddish brown. Nature has put no large object on the face of New England so glaringly white as a white house.

June 15. Very warm. Now for a thin coat. This melting weather makes a stage in the year. The drouth begins. The dry z-ing of the locust is heard. Bathing cannot be omitted. The conversation of all boys in the streets is whether they will or not or who will go in a-swimming, and how they will not tell their parents. You lie with open windows and hear the sounds in the streets.

I will note such birds as I observe in this walk, beginning on the railroad causeway in middle of this hot day. The chuckling warble of martins heard over the meadow, from a village box. The lark. The fields are blued with blue-eyed grass,—a slaty blue. The epilobium shows some color in its spikes.

How rapidly new flowers unfold! as if Nature would get through her work too soon. One has as much as he can do to observe how flowers successively unfold. It is a flowery revolution, to which but few attend. Hardly too much attention can be bestowed on flowers. We follow, we march after, the highest color; that is our flag, our standard, our "color." Flowers were made to be seen, not overlooked. Their bright colors imply eyes, spectators.

The oven-bird, chewink, pine warbler (?), thrasher, swallows on the wire, cuckoo, phœbe, red-eye, robin, veery. The maple-leaved viburnum is opening with a purplish tinge. Wood thrush.

Young robins, dark-speckled, and the pigeon wood-pecker flies up from the ground and darts away. I forget that there are lichens at this season.

On Mt. Misery, panting with heat, looking down the river. Methinks there is a male and female shore to the river, one abrupt, the other flat and meadowy. Have not all streams this contrast more or less, on the one hand eating into the bank, on the other depositing their sediment? The year is in its manhood now. The very river looks warm, and there is none of that light celestial blue seen in far reaches in the spring.

8 P.M.—On river.

No moon. A deafening sound from the toads, and intermittingly from bullfrogs. What I have thought to be frogs prove to be toads, sitting by thousands along the shore and trilling short and loud,—not so long a quaver as in the spring. (I do not know what to think of my midsummer frog now.)

June 19. Saturday. These are the clover days. The light of June is not golden but silvery, not a torrid but somewhat temperate heat. See it reflected from the bent grass and the under sides of leaves.

Grape in bloom; agreeable perfume to many, to me not so.

What subtile differences between one season and another! The warmest weather has, perchance, arrived and the longest days, but not the driest. When I remember gathering ripe blackberries on sandy fields or stones by the roadside, the very berries warmed by the sun, I am convinced of this. The seasons admit of infinite degrees in their revolutions.

June 23. These are very agreeable pastures to me; no house in sight, no cultivation. I sit under a large white oak, upon its swelling instep, which makes an admirable seat, and look forth over these pleasant rocky and bushy pastures, where for the most part there are not even cattle to graze them, but patches of huckleberry bushes, and birches, and pitch pines, and barberry bushes, and creeping juniper in great circles, its edges curving upward, and wild roses spotting the green with red, and numerous tufts of indigo-weed, and, above all, great gray boulders lying about far and near, with some barberry bush, perchance, growing half-way up them; and, between all, the short sod of the pasture here and there appears.

The beauty and fragrance of the wild rose are wholly agreeable and wholesome and wear well, and I do not wonder much that men have given the preference to this family of flowers, notwithstanding their thorns. It is hardy and more complete in its parts than most flowers,—its color, buds, fragrance, leaves, the whole bush, frequently its stem in particular, and finally its red or scarlet hips. I take the wild rose buds to my chamber and put them in a pitcher of water, and they will open there the next day, and a single flower will perfume a room; and then, after a day, the petals drop off, and new buds open.

I am inclined to think that my hat, whose lining is gathered in midway so as to make a shelf, is about as good a botany-box as I could have and far more convenient, and there is something in the darkness and the vapors that arise from the head—at least if you take a bath—which preserves flowers through a long walk. Flowers will frequently come fresh out of this botany-box at the end of the day, though they have had no sprinkling.

This grassy road now dives into the wood, as if it were entering a cellar or bulkhead, the shadow is so deep. June is the first month for shadows. How is it in July?

The sweet-briar bud which I brought home opened in the night. Is that the habit of roses?

June 25. 8.30 P.M.—To Conantum.

The great story of the night is the moon's adventures with the clouds. What innumerable encounters she has had with them!

June 26. I have not put darkness, duskiness, enough into my night and moonlight walks. Every sentence should contain some twilight or night. At least the light in it should be the yellow or creamy light of the moon or the fine beams of stars, and not the white light of day. The peculiar dusky serenity of the sentences must not allow the reader to forget that it is evening or night, without my saying that it is dark. Otherwise he will, of course, presume a daylight atmosphere.

P.M.—Boated up the Assabet.

The *Nymphæa odorata*, water nymph, sweet water-lily, pond-lily, in bloom. A superb flower, our lotus, queen of the waters. Now is the solstice in still waters. How sweet, innocent, wholesome its fragrance! How pure its white petals, though its root is in the mud! It must answer in my mind for what the Orientals say of the lotus flower. Probably the first a day or two since. To-morrow, then, will be the first Sabbath when the young men, having bathed, will walk slowly and soberly to church in their best clothes, each with a lily in his hand or bosom,—with as long a stem as he could get. At least I used to see them go by and come into church smelling a pond-lily, when I used to go myself. So that the flower is to some extent associated with bathing in Sabbath mornings and going to church, its odor contrasting and atoning for that of the sermon. We now have roses on the land and lilies on the water,—both land and water have done their best,—now *just* after the longest day. Nature says, "You behold the utmost I can do." And the young women carry their finest roses on the other hand. Roses and lilies. The floral days. The highest, intensest color belongs to the land, the purest, perchance, to the water.

June 27. Saw a very large white ash tree, three and a half feet in diameter, in front of the house which White formerly owned, under this hill, which was struck by lightning the 22d, about 4 P.M. The lightning apparently struck the top of the tree and scorched the bark and leaves for ten or fifteen feet downward, then began to strip off the bark and enter the wood, making a ragged narrow furrow or crack, till, reaching one of the upper limbs, it apparently divided, descending on both sides and entering deeper and deeper into the wood. At the first general branching, it had got full possession of the tree in its centre and tossed off the main limbs butt foremost, making holes in the ground where they struck; and so it went down in the midst of the trunk to the earth, where it apparently exploded, rending the trunk into six segments, whose tops, ten or twenty feet long, were rayed out on every side at an angle of about 30° from a perpendicular, leaving the ground bare directly under where the tree had stood, though they were still fastened to the earth by their roots. The lightning appeared to have gone off through the roots, furrowing them as the branches, and through the earth, making a furrow like a plow, four or five rods in one direction, and in another passing through the cellar of the neighboring house, about thirty feet distant, scorching the tin milk-pans and throwing dirt into the milk, and coming out the back side of the house in a furrow, splitting some planks there. The main body of the tree was completely stripped of bark, which was cast in every direction two hundred feet; and large pieces of the inside of the tree, fifteen feet long, were hurled with tremendous force in various directions, one into the side of a shed, smashing it, another burying itself in a wood-pile. The heart of the tree lay by itself. Probably a piece as large as a man's leg could not have been sawn out of the trunk which would not have had a crack in it, and much of it was very finely splintered. The windows in the house were broken and the inhabitants knocked down by the concussion. All this was accomplished in an instant by a kind of fire out of the heavens called lightning, or a thunderbolt, accompanied by a crashing sound. For what purpose? The ancients called it Jove's bolt, with which he punished the guilty, and we moderns understand it no better.

This is one of those instances in which a man hesitates to refer his safety to his prudence, as the putting up of a lightning-rod. There is no lightning-rod by which the sinner can finally avert the avenging Nemesis. Though I should put up a rod if its utility were satisfactorily demonstrated to me, yet, so mixed are we, I should feel myself safe or in danger quite independently of the senseless rod. Yet there is a degree of faith and righteousness in putting up a rod, as well as trusting without one, though the latter, which is the rarest, I feel to be the most effectual rod of the two. The savage's and the civilized man's instincts are right. Science affirms too much. Science assumes to show *why* the lightning strikes a tree, but it does not show us the moral *why* any better than our instincts did. Why should trees be struck? It is not enough to say because they are in the way. All the phenomena of nature need to be seen from the point of view of wonder and awe, like lightning; and, on the other hand, the lightning itself needs to be regarded with serenity, as the most familiar and innocent phenomena are. Men are probably nearer to the essential truth in their superstitions than in their science.

June 29. In my experience nothing is so opposed to poetry—not crime—as business. It is a negation of life.

Children bring you the early blueberry to sell now. It is considerably earlier on the tops of hills which have been recently cut off than on the plains or in vales. The girl that has Indian blood in her veins and picks berries for a living will find them out as soon as they turn.

July 1. Thursday. 9.30 A.M.—To Sherman's Bridge by land and water.

A cloudy and slightly showery morning, following a thunder-shower the previous afternoon. One object to see the white lilies in blossom.

Borrowed Brigham the wheelwright's boat at the Corner Bridge. He was quite ready to lend it, and took pains to shave down the handle of a paddle for me, conversing the while on the subject of spiritual knocking, which he asked if I had looked into,—which made him the slower. An obliging man, who understands that I am abroad viewing the works of Nature and not loafing, though he makes the pursuit a semi-religious one, as are all more serious ones to most men. All that is not sporting in the field, as hunting and fishing, is of a religious or else love-cracked character. Another hard-featured but talkative character at the bridge inquired, as I was unlocking the boat, if I knew anything that was good for the rheumatism; but I answered that I had heard of so many and had so little faith in any that I had forgotten them all. (On Conantum I had found *Krigia Virginica*, one of the smallest compound flowers.) The white lilies were in all their splendor, fully open, sometimes their lower petals lying flat on the surface. The largest appeared to grow in the shallower water, where some stood five or six inches out of water, and were five inches in diameter. Two which I examined had twenty-nine petals each.

The freshly opened lilies were a pearly white, and though the water amid the pads was quite unrippled, the passing air gave a slight oscillating, boat-like motion to and fro to the flowers, like boats held fast by their cables. Some of the lilies had a beautiful rosaceous tinge, most conspicuous in the half-opened flower, extending through the calyx to the second row of petals, on those parts of the petals between the calyx-leaves which were most exposed to the influence of the light. They were tinged with red, as they are very commonly tinged with green, as if there were a gradual transition from the stamens to the petals. Yet these rosaceous ones are chiefly interesting to me for variety, and I am contented that lilies should be white and leave those higher colors to the land. I wished to breathe the atmosphere of lilies, and get the full impression which lilies are fitted to make.

After eating our luncheon at Rice's landing, we observed that every white lily in the river was shut. It would be interesting to observe how instantaneously these lilies close at noon.

July 2. Bigelow tells me that saddlers sometimes use the excrescence, the whitish fungus, on the birch to stick their awls in. Men find a use for everything at last. I saw one nailed up in his shop with an awl in it.

Last night, as I lay awake, I dreamed of the muddy and weedy river on which I had been paddling, and I seemed to derive some vigor from my day's experience, like the lilies which have their roots at the bottom.

I have plucked a white lily bud just ready to expand, and, after keeping it in water for two days,* have cut its stem short and placed it in a broad dish of water, where it sailed about under the breath of the beholder with a slight undulatory motion. The breeze of his half-suppressed admiration it was that filled its sail. It was a rare-tinted one.

Nature is reported not by him who goes forth consciously as an observer, but in the fullness of life. To such a one she rushes to make her report. To the full heart she is all but a figure of speech. This is my year of observation, and I fancy that my friends are also more devoted to outward observation than ever before, as if it were an epidemic. At this season, methinks, we do not regard the larger features of the landscape, as in the spring, but are absorbed in details. Then, when the meadows were flooded, I looked far over them to the distant woods and the outlines of hills, which were more distinct. I should not have so much to say of extensive water or landscapes at this season. You are a little bewildered by the variety of objects. There must be a certain meagreness of details and nakedness for wide views.

July 4. Sunday. 3 A.M.—To Conantum, to see the lilies open.

I hear an occasional crowing of cocks in distant barns, as has

---

*Till July 3d.

been their habit for how many thousand years. It was so when I was young; and it will be so when I am old. I hear the croak of a tree-toad as I am crossing the yard. I am surprised to find the dawn so far advanced. Now, on the Corner road, the hedges are alive with twittering sparrows, a bluebird or two, etc. The daylight now balances the moonlight. How short the nights! The last traces of day have not disappeared much before 10 o'clock, or perchance 9.30, and before 3 A.M. you see them again in the east,—probably 2.30,—leaving about five hours of solid night, the sun so soon coming round again.

July 5. There is a meadow on the Assabet just above Derby's Bridge,—it may contain an acre,—bounded on one side by the river, on the other by alders and a hill, completely covered with small hummocks which have lodged on it in the winter, covering it like the mounds in a graveyard at pretty regular intervals. Their edges are rounded like the latter, and they and the paths between are covered with a firm, short greensward, with here and there hardhacks springing out of them, so that they make excellent seats, especially in the shade of an elm that grows there. They are completely united with the meadow, forming little oblong hillocks from one to ten feet long, flat as a mole to the sward. I am inclined to call it the elfin burial-ground, or perchance it might be called the Indian burial-ground. It is a remarkably firm-swarded meadow, and convenient to walk on. I love to ponder the natural history thus written on the banks of the stream, for every higher freshet and intenser frost is recorded by it. The stream keeps a faithful and a true journal of every event in its experience, whatever race may settle on its banks; and it purls past this natural graveyard with a storied murmur, and no doubt it could find endless employment for an old mortality in renewing its epitaphs.

The progress of the season is indescribable. It is growing warm again, but the warmth is different from that we have had. We lie in the shade of locust trees. Haymakers go by in a hay-rigging. I am reminded of berrying. I scent the sweet-fern and the dead or dry pine leaves. Cherry-birds alight on a neighboring tree. The warmth is something more normal and steady, ripening fruits. Nature offers fruits now as well as flowers. We have become accustomed to the summer. It has acquired a certain eternity. The earth is dry. Perhaps the sound of the locust expresses the season as well as anything. The farmers say the abundance of the grass depends on wet in June. I might make a separate season of those days when the locust is heard.

I see many devil's-needles zigzagging along the Second Division Brook, some green, some blue, both with black and perhaps velvety wings. They are confined to the brook. How lavishly they are painted! How cheap was the paint! How free the fancy of their creator! I caught a handful of small water-bugs, fifteen or twenty, about as large as apple seeds. Some country people call them apple seeds, it is said, from their scent. I perceived a strong scent, but I am not sure it was like apples. I should rather think they were so called from their shape.

The robin, the red-eye, the veery, the wood thrush, etc., etc.

How fitting to have every day in a vase of water on your table the wild-flowers of the season which are just blossoming! Can any house be said to be furnished without them? Shall we be so forward to pluck the fruits of Nature and neglect her flowers? These are surely her finest influences. So may the season suggest the fine thoughts it is fitted to suggest. Shall we say, "A penny for your thoughts," before we have looked into the face of Nature? Let me know what picture she is painting, what poetry she is writing, what ode composing, now.

The sun has set. We are in Dennis's field. The dew is falling fast. Some fine clouds, which have just escaped being condensed in dew, hang on the skirts of day and make the attraction in our western sky,—that part of day's gross atmosphere which has escaped the clutches of the night and is not enough condensed to fall to earth. They are remarkably finely divided clouds, a very fine mackerel sky, or, rather, as if one had sprinkled that part of the sky with a brush, the outline of the whole being that of several large sprigs of fan coral. C., as usual, calls it a Mediterranean sky.

July 6. Hosmer is haying, but inclined to talk as usual. I blowed on his horn at supper-time. I asked if I should do any harm if I sounded it. He said no, but I called Mrs. Hosmer back, who was on her way to the village, though I blowed it but poorly. I was surprised to find how much skill and breath it took, depending on the size of the throat. Let blow a horn, says Robin, that good fellowship may us know. Where could a man go to practice on the horn, unless he went round to the farmer's at meal-time?

I am disappointed that Hosmer, the most intelligent farmer in Concord, and perchance in Middlesex, who admits that he has property enough for his use without accumulating more, and talks of leaving off hard work, letting his farm, and spending the rest of his days easier and better, cannot yet think of any method of employing himself but in work with his hands; only he would have a little less of it. Much as he is inclined to speculation in conversation—giving up any work to it for the time—and long-headed as he is, he talks of working for a neighbor for a day now and then and taking his dollar. He "would not like to spend his time sitting on the mill-dam." He has not even planned an essentially better life.

July 8. P.M.—Down river in boat to the Holt.

It is perhaps the warmest day yet.

We held on to the abutments under the red bridge to cool ourselves in the shade. No better place in hot weather, the river rippling away beneath you and the air rippling through beneath the abutments, if only in sympathy with the river, while the planks afford a shade, and you hear all the travel and the travellers' talk without being seen or suspected. The bullfrog it is, methinks, that makes the dumping sound. There is generally a current of air circulating over water, always, methinks, if the water runs swiftly, as if it put the air in motion. There is quite a breeze here this sultry day. Commend me to the sub-pontean, the under-bridge, life.

I found a remarkable moth lying flat on the still water as if asleep (they appear to sleep during the day), as large as the smaller birds. Five and a half inches in alar extent and about three inches long, something like the smaller figure in one position of the wings (with a re-

markably narrow lunar-cut tail), of a sea-green color, with four conspicuous spots whitish within, then a red line, then yellowish border below or toward the tail, but brown, brown orange, and black above, toward head; a very robust body, covered with a kind of downy plumage, an inch and a quarter long by five eighths thick. The sight affected me as tropical, and I suppose it is the northern verge of some species. It suggests into what productions Nature would run if all the year were a July. By night it is active, for, though I thought it dying at first, it made a great noise in its prison, a cigar-box, at night. When the day returns, it apparently drops wherever it may be, even into the water, and dozes till evening again. Is it called the emperor moth?

XII.

July 9. Friday. 4 A.M.—To Cliffs.

No dew; no dewy cobwebs. The sky looks mist-like, not clear blue. An aurora fading into a general saffron color. At length the redness travels over, partly from east to west, before sunrise, and there is little color in the east. There is no name for the evening red corresponding to aurora. It is the blushing foam about the prow of the sun's boat, and at eve the same in its wake.

Morton, in his "Crania Americana," says, referring to Wilkinson as his authority, that "vessels of porcelain of Chinese manufacture have of late been repeatedly found in the catacombs of Thebes, in Egypt," some as old as the Pharaonic period, and the inscriptions on them "have been read with ease by Chinese scholars, and in three instances record the following legend: The flower opens, and lo! another year." There is something sublime in the fact that some of the oldest written sentences should thus celebrate the coming in of spring. How many times have the flowers opened and a new year begun! Hardly a more cheering sentence could have come down to us. How old is spring, a phenomenon still so fresh! Do we perceive any decay in Nature? How much evidence is contained in this short and simple sentence respecting the former inhabitants of this globe! It is a sentence to be inscribed on vessels of porcelain. Suggesting that so many years had gone before. An observation as fit then as now.

Bathing is an undescribed luxury. To feel the wind blow on your body, the water flow on you and lave you, is a rare physical enjoyment this hot day. The water is remarkably warm here, especially in the shallows,—warm to the hand, like that which has stood long in a kettle over a fire. The pond water being so warm made the water of the brook feel very cold; and this kept close on the bottom of the pond for a good many rods about the mouth of the brook, as I could feel with my feet; and when I thrust my arm down where it was only two feet deep, my arm was in the warm water of the pond, but my hand in the cold water of the brook.

July 13. A journal, a book that shall contain a record of all your joy, your ecstasy.

July 14. A writer who does not speak out of a full experience uses torpid words, wooden or lifeless words, such words as "humanitary," which have a paralysis in their tails.

Saw to-day for the first time this season fleets of yellow butterflies dispersing before us, we rode along berrying on the Walden road. Their yellow fleets are in the offing. Do I ever see them in numbers off the road? They are a yellow flower that blossoms generally about this time. Like a mackerel fleet, with their small hulls and great sails. Collected now in compact but gorgeous assembly in the road, like schooners in a harbor, a haven; now suddenly dispersing on our approach and filling the air with yellow snowflakes in their zigzag flight, or as when a fair wind calls those schooners out and disperses them over the broad ocean.

How deep or perhaps slaty sky-blue are those blueberries that grow in the shade! It is an unexpected and thrilling discovery to find such ethereal fruits in dense drooping clusters under the fresh green of oak and hickory sprouts. Those that grow in the sun appear to be the same species, only to have lost their bloom and freshness, and hence are darker.

The youth gets together his materials to build a bridge to the moon, or perchance a palace or temple on the earth, and at length the middle-aged man concludes to build a wood-shed with them.

July 16. The bass on Conantum is a very rich sight now. Its twigs are drooping, weighed down with pendulous flowers, so that, when you stand directly under it and look up, you see one mass of flowers, a flowery canopy. Its conspicuous leaf-like bracts, too, have the effect of flowers. The tree resounds with the hum of bees,—bumblebees and honey-bees; rose-bugs and butterflies, also, are here,— a perfect susurrus, a sound, as C. says, unlike any other in nature, —not like the wind, as that is like the sea. The bees abound on the flowers of the smooth sumach now. The branches of this tree touch the ground, and it has somewhat the appearance of being weighed down with flowers. The air is full of sweetness. The tree is full of poetry.

I observe the yellow butterflies everywhere in the fields and on the pontederias, which now give a faint blue tinge to the sides of the rivers. I hear the *link link*, fall-like note of the bobolink (?) in the meadows; he has lost the *bobo* off. This is a still, thoughtful day, the air full of vapors which shade the earth, preparing rain for the morrow.

July 17. P.M.—A summer rain. A gentle steady rain, long a-gathering, without thunder or lightning,—such as we have not, and, methinks, could not have had, earlier than this.

I pick raspberries dripping with rain beyond Sleepy Hollow. This weather is rather favorable to thought. On all sides is heard a gentle dripping of the rain on the leaves, yet it is perfectly warm. It is a day of comparative leisure to many farmers. Some go to the mill-dam and the shops; some go a-fishing.

July 18. Sunday. 8.30 A.M.—To the Sudbury meadows in boat.

I observe that even in these meadows, where no willows nor button-bushes line the shore, there is still a pretty constant difference between the shores. The border of pontederia is rarely of equal depth on both sides at once, but it keeps that side in the meander where the sediment is deposited, the shortest course which will follow the shore, as I have dotted it, crossing from this side to that as the river meanders; for on the longest side the river is active, not

passive, wearing into the bank, and runs there more swiftly.

This is the longest line of blue that nature paints with flowers in our fields, though the lupines may have been more densely blue within a small compass. Thus by a natural law a river, instead of flowing straight through its meadows, meanders from side to side and fertilizes this side or that, and adorns its banks with flowers. The river has its active and its passive side, its right and left breast.

Every poet has trembled on the verge of science.

Got green grapes to stew.

July 22. We have more of the furnace-like heat to-day, after all. The *Rhus glabra* flowers are covered with bees, *large* yellowish wasps, and butterflies; they are all alive with them. How much account insects make of some flowers! There are other botanists than I. The *Asclepias syriaca* is going to seed. Here is a kingfisher frequenting the Corner Brook Pond. They find out such places. Huckleberrying and blackberrying have commenced.

July 24. The cardinal-flower probably open to-day. The quails are heard whistling this morning near the village.

I sympathize with weeds perhaps more than with the crop they choke, they express so much vigor. They are the truer crop which the earth more willingly bears.

Just after sunrise this morning I noticed Hayden walking beside his team, which was slowly drawing a heavy hewn stone swung under the axle, surrounded by an atmosphere of industry, his day's work begun. Honest, peaceful industry, conserving the world, which all men respect, which society has consecrated. A reproach to all sluggards and idlers. Honest, manly toil. His brow has commenced to sweat. Honest as the day is long. One of the sacred band doing the needful but irksome drudgery. The day went by, and at evening I passed a rich man's yard, who keeps many servants and foolishly spends much money while he adds nothing to the common stock, and there I saw Hayden's stone lying beside a whimsical structure intended to adorn this Lord Timothy Dexter's mansion, and the dignity forthwith departed from Hayden's labor, in my eyes. How much of the industry of the boor, traced to the end, is found thus to be subserving some rich man's foolish enterprise! There is a coarse, boisterous, money-making fellow in the north part of the town who is going to build a bank wall under the hill along the edge of his meadow. The powers have put this into his head to keep him out of mischief, and he wishes me to spend three weeks digging there with him. The result will be that he will perchance get a little more money to hoard, or leave for his heirs to spend foolishly when he is dead. Now, if I do this, the community will commend me as an industrious and hardworking man; but, as I choose to devote myself to labors which yield more real profit, though but little money, they regard me as a loafer. But, as I do not need this police of meaningless labor to regulate me, and do not see anything absolutely praiseworthy in his undertaking, however amusing it may be to him, I prefer to finish my education at a different school.

July 25. 4 A.M.—To Cliffs.

This early twitter or breathing of chip-birds in the dawn sounds like something organic in the earth. This is a morning celebrated by birds. This morning is all the more glorious for a white fog, which, though not universal, is still very extensive over all lowlands, some fifty feet high or more, though there was none at ten last night. There are white cobwebs on the grass. The battalions of the fog are continually on the move.

When I return this way I find two farmers loading their cart with dirt, and they are so unmanly as to excuse themselves to me for working this Sunday morning by saying with a serious face that they are burying a cow which died last night after some months of sickness,—which, however, they unthinkingly admit that they killed last night, being the most convenient time for them, and I see that they are now putting more loads of soil over her body to save the manure. How often men will betray their sense of guilt, and hence their actual guilt, by their excuses, where no guilt necessarily was.

July 26. By my intimacy with nature I find myself withdrawn from man. My interest in the sun and the moon, in the morning and the evening, compels me to solitude.

My desire for society is infinitely increased; my fitness for any actual society is diminished.

Went to Cambridge and Boston to-day. Dr. Harris says that my great moth is the *Attacus luna*; may be regarded as one of several emperor moths. They are rarely seen, being very liable to be snapped up by birds. Once, as he was crossing the College Yard, he saw the wings of one coming down, which reached the ground just at his feet. What a tragedy! The wings came down as the only evidence that such a creature had soared,—wings large and splendid, which were designed to bear a precious burthen through the upper air. So most poems, even epics, are like the wings come down to earth, while the poet whose adventurous flight they evidence has been snapped up by the ravenous vulture of this world. If this moth ventures abroad by day, some bird will pick out the precious cargo and let the sails and rigging drift, as when the sailor meets with a floating spar and sail and reports a wreck seen in a certain latitude and longitude. For what were such tender and defenseless organizations made? The wreck of an argosy in the air.

July 30. The fore part of this month was the warmest weather we have had; the last part, sloping toward autumn, has reflected some of its coolness, for we are very forward to anticipate the fall. Perhaps I may say the spring culminated with the commencement of haying, and the summer side of the year in mid-July.

Do not all flowers that blossom after mid-July remind us of the fall? After midsummer we have a belated feeling as if we had all been idlers, and are forward to see in each sight and hear in each sound some presage of the fall, just as in middle age man anticipates the end of life.

Caught in a thunder-shower, when south of Flint's Pond. Stood under thick trees. I care not how hard it rains, if it does not rain more than fifteen minutes. I can shelter myself effectually in the woods. It is a grand sound, that of the rain on the leaves of the forest a quarter of a mile distant, approaching. But I got wet through, after all, being caught where there were no trees.

Aug. 2. Wachusett from Fair Haven Hill looks like this:—

the dotted line being the top of the surrounding forest. Even on the low principle that misery loves company and is relieved by the consciousness that it is shared by many, and therefore is not so insignificant and trivial, after all, this blue mountain outline is valuable. In many moods it is cheering to look across hence to that blue rim of the earth, and be reminded of the invisible towns and communities, for the most part also unremembered, which lie in the further and deeper hollows between me and those hills. Towns of sturdy uplandish fame, where some of the morning and primal vigor still lingers, I trust. Ashburnham, Rindge, Jaffrey, etc.,—it is cheering to think that it is with such communities that we survive or perish. Yes, the mountains do thus impart, in the mere prospect of them, some of the New Hampshire vigor. The melancholy man who had come forth to commit suicide on this hill might be saved by being thus reminded how many brave and contented lives are lived between him and the horizon. Those hills extend our plot of earth; they make our native valley or indentation in the earth so much the larger.

Aug. 5. Hearing that one with whom I was acquainted had committed suicide, I said I did not know when I had planted the seed of that fact that I should hear of it.

P.M.—To C. Miles's blueberry swamp.

That is a glorious swamp of Miles's,—an extensive rich moss-like bed, in which you sink three feet to a dry bottom of moss or dead twigs; surrounded all by wild-looking woods, with the wild white spruce advancing into it and the pitch pine here and there, and high blueberry and tall pyrus and holly and other bushes under their countenance and protection. These are the wildest and richest gardens that we have. Such a depth of verdure into which you sink.

Aug. 6. Gathered some of those large, sometimes pear-shaped, sweet blue huckleberries which grow amid the rubbish where woods have just been cut.

Milkweeds and trumpet-flowers are important now, to contrast with the cool, dark, shaded sides and recesses of moist copses. I see their red under the willows and alders everywhere against a dark ground. Methinks that blue, next to red, attracts us in a flower. Blue vervain is now very attractive to me, and then there is that interesting progressive history in its rising ring of blossoms. It has a story. Next to our blood is our prospect of heaven. Does not the blood in fact show blue in the covered veins and arteries, when distance lends enchantment to the view? The sight of it is more affecting than I can describe or account for.

Methinks there are few new flowers of late. An abundance of small fruits takes their place. Summer gets to be an old story. Birds leave off singing, as flowers blossoming, *i.e.* perhaps in the same proportion.

Aug. 8. I only know myself as a human entity, the scene, so to speak, of thoughts and affections, and am sensible of a certain doubleness by which I can stand as remote from myself as from another. However intense my experience, I am conscious of the presence and criticism of a part of me which, as it were, is not a part of me, but spectator, sharing no experience, but taking note of it, and that is no more I than it is you. When the play—it may be the tragedy of life—is over, the spectator goes his way. It was a kind of fiction, a work of the imagination only, so far as he was concerned.

Ambrosia artemisiæfolia. July was a month of dry, torrid heat and drouth, especially the fore part. August, thus far, of gentle rain-storms and fogs, dog-days. Things mildew now. I notice now, along the North River, horse-mint, arrowhead, cardinal-flower, trumpet-weed (just coming out), water parsnip, skull-cap (*lateriflora*), monkey-flower, etc., etc. Rivers meander most not amid rugged mountains, but through soft level meadows. In some places the ground is covered now with the black umbelled berries of the sarsaparilla. No man ever makes a discovery, ever an observation of the least importance, but he is advertised of the fact by a joy that surprises him. The powers thus celebrate all discovery. The squirrels are now devouring the hazelnuts fast.

Aug. 21. Weeds in potato-fields are now very rank. What should we come to if the season were longer, and the reins were given to vegetation? Young turkeys are straying in the grass, which is alive with grasshoppers.

The bees, wasps, etc., are on the goldenrods, impatient to be interrupted, improving their time before the sun of the year sets. A man killed by lightning would have a good answer ready in the next world to the question "How came *you* here?" which he need not hesitate to give.

The sound of the crickets gradually prevails more and more. I hear the year falling asleep.

Aug. 23. About 8 P.M.—Now I sit on the Cliffs and look abroad over the river and Conantum hills. I live so much in my habitual thoughts, a routine of thought, that I forget there is any outside to the globe, and am surprised when I behold it as now,—yonder hills and river in the moonlight, the monsters. Yet it is salutary to deal with the surface of things. What are these rivers and hills, these hieroglyphics which my eyes behold? There is something invigorating in this air, which I am peculiarly sensible is a real wind, blowing from over the surface of a planet. I look out at my eyes, I come to my window, and I feel and breathe the fresh air. It is a fact equally glorious with the most inward experience. Why have we ever slandered the outward? The perception of surfaces will always have the effect of miracle to a sane sense.

Aug. 24. The year is but a succession of days, and I see that I could assign some office to each day which, summed up, would be the history of the year. Everything is done in season, and there is no time to spare. The bird gets its brood hatched in season and is off. I looked into the nest where I saw a vireo feeding its young a few days ago, but it is empty; it is fledged and flown.

XIII.

Sept. 18. The poor student begins now to seek the sun. In the forenoons I move into a chamber on the east side of the house, and so follow the sun round. It is agreeable to stand in a new relation to the sun. They begin to have a fire occasionally below-stairs.

3.30 P.M.—A-barberrying to Flint's Pond.

How much handsomer in fruit for being bent down in wreaths by the weight! The increasing weight of the fruits adds gracefulness to the form of the bush. I get my hands full of thorns, but my basket full of berries.

Sept. 26. Dreamed of purity last night. The thoughts seemed not to originate with me, but I was invested, my thought was tinged, by another's thought. It was not I that originated, but I that *entertained* the thought.

The river is getting to be too cold for bathing.

Sept. 27. Monday. P.M.—The flashing clearness of the atmosphere. More light appears to be reflected from the earth, less absorbed.

The touch-me-not seed-vessels go off like pistols,—shoot their seeds off like bullets. They explode in my hat.

Sept. 30. Thursday. 10 A.M.—To Fair Haven Pond, bee-hunting,—Pratt, Rice, Hastings, and myself, in a wagon.

A fine, clear day after the coolest night and severest frost we have had. The apparatus was, first a simple round tin box about four and a half inches in diameter and one and a half inches deep, containing a piece of empty honeycomb of its own size and form, filling it within a third of an inch of the top; also another, *wooden* box about two and a half inches square every way, with a glass window occupying two thirds the upper side under a slide, with a couple of narrow slits in the wood, each side of the glass, to admit air, but too narrow for the bees to pass; the whole resting on a circular bottom a little larger than the lid of the tin box, with a sliding door in it. We were earnest to go this week, before the flowers were gone, and we feared the frosty night might make the bees slow to come forth.

After we got to the Baker Farm, to one of the open fields nearest to the tree I had marked, the first thing was to find some flowers and catch some honey-bees. We followed up the bank of the brook for some distance, but the goldenrods were all dried up there, and the asters on which we expected to find them were very scarce. We had no better luck at Clematis Brook. Not a honey-bee could we find, and we concluded that we were too late,—that the weather was too cold.

After eating our lunch, we set out on our return. By the roadside at Walden, on the sunny hillside sloping to the pond, we saw a large mass of goldenrod and aster several rods square and comparatively fresh. Getting out of our wagon, we found it to be resounding with the hum of bees. (It was about 1 o'clock.) There were far more flowers than we had seen elsewhere. Here were bees in great numbers, both bumblebees and honey-bees, as well as butterflies and wasps and flies. So, pouring a mixture of honey and water into the empty comb in the tin box, and holding the lid of the tin box in one hand and the wooden box with the slides shut in the other, we proceeded to catch the honey-bees by shutting them in suddenly between the lid of the tin box and the large circular bottom of the wooden one, cutting off the flower-stem with the edge of the lid at the same time. Then, holding the lid still against the wooden box, we drew the slide in the bottom and also the slide covering the window at the top, that the light might attract the bee to pass up into the wooden box. As soon as he had done so and was buzzing against the glass, the lower slide was closed and the lid with the flower removed, and more bees were caught in the same way. Then, placing the other, tin, box containing the comb filled with honeyed water close under the wooden one, the slide was drawn again, and the upper slide closed, making it dark; and in about a minute they went to feeding, as was ascertained by raising slightly the wooden box. Then the latter was wholly removed, and they were left feeding or sucking up the honey in broad daylight. In from two to three minutes one had loaded himself and commenced leaving the box. He would buzz round it back and forth a foot or more, and then, sometimes, finding that he was too heavily loaded, alight to empty himself or clean his feet. Then, starting once more, he would begin to circle round irregularly, at first in a small circle only a foot or two in diameter, as if to examine the premises that he might know them again, till, at length, rising higher and higher and circling wider and wider and swifter and swifter, till his orbit was ten or twelve feet in diameter and as much from the ground,—though its centre might be moved to one side,—so that it was very difficult to follow him, especially if you looked against a wood or the hill, and you had to lie low to fetch him against the sky (you must operate in an open space, not in a wood); all this as if to ascertain the course to his nest; then, in a minute or less from his first starting, he darts off in a bee-line, that is, as far as I could see him, which might be eight or ten rods, looking against the sky (and you had to follow his whole career very attentively indeed to see when and where he went off at a tangent), in a waving or sinuous (right and left) line, toward his nest.

We sent forth as many as a dozen bees, which flew in about three directions, but all toward the village, or where we knew there were hives. They did not fly so almost absolutely straight as I had heard, but within three or four feet of the same course for half a dozen rods, or as far as we could see. Those belonging to one hive all had to digress to get round an apple tree. As none flew in the right direction for us, we did not attempt to line them. In less than half

an hour the first returned to the box still lying on the wood-pile,—
for not one of the bees on the surrounding flowers discovered it,—
and so they came back, one after another, loaded themselves and
departed; but now they went off with very little preliminary circling, as if assured of their course. We were furnished with little
boxes of red, blue, green, yellow, and white paint, in dry powder,
and with a stick we sprinkled a little of the red powder on the back
of one while he was feeding,—gave him a little dab,—and it settled
down amid the fuzz of his back and gave him a distinct red jacket.
He went off like most of them toward some hives about three quarters of a mile distant, and we observed by the watch the time of his
departure. In just twenty-two minutes red jacket came back, with
enough of the powder still on his back to mark him plainly. He
may have gone more than three quarters of a mile. At any rate, he
had a head wind to contend with while laden. They fly swiftly and
surely to their nests, never resting by the way, and I was surprised—
though I had been informed of it—at the distance to which the
village bees go for flowers.

The rambler in the most remote woods and pastures little thinks
that the bees which are humming so industriously on the rare wild
flowers he is plucking for his herbarium, in some out-of-the-way
nook, are, like himself, ramblers from the village, perhaps from his
own yard, come to get their honey for his hives. All the honey-bees
we saw were on the blue-stemmed goldenrod (*Solidago cæsia*),
which is late, lasts long, which emitted a sweet agreeable fragrance,
not on the asters. I feel the richer for this experience. It taught me
that even the insects in my path are not loafers, but have their spe-
cial errands. Not merely and vaguely in this world, but in this hour,
each is about its business. If, then, there are any sweet flowers still
lingering on the hillside, it is known to the bees both of the forest
and the village. The botanist should make interest with the bees if
he would know when the flowers open and when they close. Those
I have named were the only common and prevailing flowers at this
time to look for them on.

Our red jacket had performed the voyage in safety; no bird had
picked him up. Are the kingbirds gone? Now is the time to hunt

bees and take them up, when the combs are full of honey and before the flowers are so scarce that they begin to consume the honey they have stored.

Rees's Cyclopædia says that "Philliscus retired into a desert wood, that he might have the opportunity of observing them [bees] to better advantage." Paul Dudley wrote the Royal Society about 1723 that the Indians had no word for bee; called it "Englishman's fly."

OCT. 9. Touch-me-not, self-heal, *Bidens cernua*, ladies'-tresses, cerastium, dwarf tree-primrose, butter-and-eggs (abundant), prenanthes, sium, silvery cinquefoil, mayweed. My rainbow rush must be the *Juncus militaris*, not yet colored.

OCT. 10. Burdock, *Ranunculus acris*, rough hawkweed. A drizzling rain to-day. The air is full of falling leaves. The streets are strewn with elm leaves. The trees begin to look thin. The butternut is perhaps the first on the street to lose its leaves. Rain, more than wind, makes the leaves fall. Glow-worms in the evening.

Oct. 15. 9 A.M.—The first snow is falling (after not very cool weather), in large flakes, filling the air and obscuring the distant woods and houses, as if the inhabitants above were emptying their pillow-cases. Like a mist it divides the uneven landscape at a little distance into ridges and vales. The ground begins to whiten, and our thoughts begin to prepare for winter. Whiteweed. The snow lasted but half an hour. Ice a week or two ago.

P.M.—Walden.

The rain of the night and morning, together with the wind, had strewn the ground with chestnuts. The burs, generally empty, come down with a loud sound, while I am picking the nuts in the woods. It is a pleasure to detect them in the woods amid the firm, crispy, crackling chestnut leaves. There is somewhat singularly refreshing in the color of this nut, the chestnut color. No wonder it gives a name to a color. One man tells me he has bought a wood-lot in Hollis to cut, and has let out the picking of the chestnuts to women at the halves. As the trees will probably be cut for them, they will make rapid work of it.

Oct. 20. Canada snapdragon, tansy, white goldenrod, blue-stemmed ditto. *Aster undulatus*, autumnal dandelion, tall buttercup, yarrow, mayweed. Picking chestnuts on Pine Hill.

Oct. 25. Monday. P.M.—Down river to Ball's Hill in boat.

Mint is still green and wonderfully recreating to smell. I had put such things behind me. It is hard to remember lilies now.

Oct. 28. Four months of the green leaf make all our summer, if I reckon from June 1st to October 1st, the growing season, and methinks there are about four months when the ground is white with snow. That would leave two months for spring and two for autumn. October the month of ripe or painted leaves; November the month of withered leaves and bare twigs and limbs.

I heard one boy say to another in the street to-day "You don't know much more than a piece of putty."

Nov. 1. Day before yesterday to the Cliffs in the rain, misty rain. In November, a man will eat his heart, if in any month. The birches have almost all lost their leaves. On the river this afternoon, the leaves, now crisp and curled, when the wind blows them on to the water become rude boats which float and sail about awhile conspicuously before they go to the bottom,—oaks, walnuts, etc.

Nov. 4. Autumnal dandelion and yarrow.

Must be out-of-doors enough to get experience of wholesome reality, as a ballast to thought and sentiment. Health requires this relaxation, this aimless life. This life in the present. Let a man have thought what he will of Nature in the house, she will still be novel outdoors. I keep out of doors for the sake of the mineral, vegetable, and animal in me.

My thought is a part of the meaning of the world, and hence I use a part of the world as a symbol to express my thought.

NOV. 18. Measured a stick of round timber, probably white pine, on the cars this afternoon,—ninety-five feet long, nine and ten twelfths in circumference at butt, and six and two twelfths in circumference at small end, quite straight. From Vermont. Yarrow and tansy still. These are cold, gray days.

Nov. 23. There is something genial even in the first snow, and Nature seems to relent a little of her November harshness.

This, then, may be considered the end of the flower season for this year, though this snow will probably soon melt again.

I had a thought in a dream last night which surprised me by its strangeness, as if it were based on an experience in a previous state of existence, and could not be entertained by my waking self. Both the thought and the language were equally novel to me, but I at once perceived it to be true and to coincide with my experience in this state.

Nov. 27. Like many of my contemporaries I had rarely for many years used animal food, or tea or coffee, etc., etc., not so much because of any ill effects which I had traced to them in my own case, though I could theorize extensively in that direction, as because it was not agreeable to my imagination. It appeared more beautiful to live low and fare hard in many respects; and though I never did so, I went just far enough to please my imagination. But now I find myself somewhat less particular in these respects. I carry less religion to the table, ask no blessing, not because I am wiser than I was, but, I am obliged to confess, because, however much it is to be regretted with years I have grown more coarse and indifferent.

Nov. 29, 30, and Dec. 1. The snow which fell the 23d whitened the ground but a day or two. These have been the mildest and pleasantest days since November came in.

Dec. 2. The pleasantest day of all.

Started in boat before 9 A.M. down river to Billerica with W. E. C.

Not wind enough for a sail. I do not remember when I have taken a sail or a row on the river in December before. Still no snow.

Dec. 5. P.M.—Rowed over Walden!
A dark, but warm, misty day, completely overcast.

Dec. 7. P.M.—Perhaps the warmest day yet. True Indian summer. The walker perspires. The shepherd's-purse is in full bloom; the andromeda not turned red.

Jan. 3. The evergreens appear to relieve themselves soonest of the ice, perhaps because of the reflection from their leaves. Those trees, like the maples and hickories, which have most spray and branches make the finest show of ice. This afternoon it snows, the snow lodging on the ice, which still adheres to the trees. The more completely the trees are changed to ice trees, to spirits of trees, the finer. Instead of the minute frostwork on a window, you have whole forests of silver boughs. The "brattling" of the ice. Is not that the word?

I love Nature partly *because* she is not man, but a retreat from him. None of his institutions control or pervade her. There a different kind of right prevails. In her midst I can be glad with an entire gladness. If this world were all man, I could not stretch myself, I should lose all hope. He is constraint, she is freedom to me. He makes me wish for another world. She makes me content with this.

Methinks that these prosers, with their saws and their laws, do not know how glad a man can be. What wisdom, what warning, can prevail against gladness? There is no law so strong which a little gladness may not transgress. I have a room all to myself; it is nature. It is a place beyond the jurisdiction of human governments. There is a prairie beyond your laws. Nature is a prairie for outlaws. There are two worlds, the post-office and nature. I know them both. I continually forget mankind and their institutions, as I do a bank.

Well, now this afternoon the snow is lodging on all this ice. Walden not yet frozen.

The air is thick and darkened with falling snow, and the woods are being draped with it in white wreaths. This is winter. They are putting on their white greatcoats.

Jan. 4. I must call that swamp of E. Hubbard's west of the Hunt Pasture, Yellow Birch Swamp. How pleasing to stand beside a new or rare tree! And few are so handsome as this. The sight of these trees affects me more than California gold. We have the silver and the golden birch. This is like a fair, flaxen-haired sister of the dark-complexioned black birch, with golden ringlets. How lustily it takes hold of the swampy soil, and braces itself! In an undress, this tree. Ah, time will come when these will be all gone. Among the primitive trees. What sort of dryads haunt these? Blond nymphs.

XIV.

Jan. 9. As I walked the railroad this springlike day, I heard from time to time the sound of stones and earth falling and rolling down the bank in the cuts. The earth is almost entirely bare. We have not yet had snow more than one inch deep!!!

As I climbed the Cliff, I paused in the sun and sat on a dry rock, dreaming. I thought of those summery hours when time is tinged with eternity,—runs into it and becomes of one stuff with it. How much—how, perhaps, all—that is best in our experience in middle life may be resolved into the memory of our youth! I remember how I expanded. If the genius visits me now I am not quite taken off my feet, but I remember how this experience is like, but less than, that I had long since.

Jan. 14. Snows all day. P.M.—To Walden and Andromeda Ponds.

It is a very light snow, lying like down or feathery scales. Examined closely, the flakes are beautifully regular six-rayed stars or wheels with a centre disk, perfect geometrical figures in thin scales like this: far more perfect than I can draw. These thin crystals are piled about a foot deep all over the country, but as light as bran. The surface of fields, as I look toward the western light, appears waved or watered on a large scale, as if different kinds of flakes drifted together, some glistening scales, others darker; or perhaps the same reflected the light differently from different sides of slight drifts or undulations on the surface. Thus beautiful the snow.

I suppose that the meadow mouse can still pick up chestnuts under the snow. The nuts commonly lie as they fell from the bur, two or three together.

The bones of children soon turn to dust again.

JAN. 16. *Sunday.* Cold, with blustering winds drifting the snow. Yesterday the hounds were heard. It was a hunter's day. All tracks were fresh, the snow deep and light. I met Melvin with his bag full.

Trench[*] says that "'rivals,' in the primary sense of the word, are those who dwell on the banks of the same stream" or "on opposite banks," but as he says, in many words, since the use of water-rights is a fruitful source of contention between such neighbors, the word has acquired this secondary sense. My friends are my *rivals* on the Concord, in the primitive sense of the word. There is no strife between us respecting the use of the stream. The Concord offers many privileges, but none to quarrel about. It is a peaceful, not a brawling, stream. It has not made *rivals* out of neighbors *that lived on its banks*, but friends. My friends are my *rivals*; we dwell on opposite banks of the stream, but that stream is the Concord, which flows without a ripple or a murmur, without a rapid or a brawl, and offers no petty privileges to quarrel about.[†]

Jan. 21. A fine, still, warm moonlight evening.

I easily read the moral of my dreams. Yesterday I was influenced with the rottenness of human relations. They appeared full of death and decay, and offended the nostrils. In the night I dreamed of delving amid the graves of the dead, and soiled my fingers with their rank mould. It was *sanitarily*, *morally*, and *physically* true.

JAN. 27. Trench says a wild man is a *willed* man. Well, then, a man of will who does what he wills or wishes, a man of hope and of the future tense, for not only the obstinate is willed, but far more the constant and persevering. The obstinate man, properly speaking, is one who will not. The perseverance of the saints is positive willed-

---

*[Richard Trench's Emersonian *On the Study of Words*, 1851.]
†Bailey, I find, has it: "Rival (*Rivalis* L.q.d. qui juxta eundem rivum pascit)." My friends my rivals are.

ness, not a mere passive willingness. The fates are wild, for they *will*; and the Almighty is wild above all, as fate is.

What are our fields but *felds* or *felled* woods. They bear a more recent name than the woods, suggesting that previously the earth was covered with woods. Always in the new country a field is a clearing.

Feb. 11. While surveying on the Hunt farm the other day, behind Simon Brown's house I heard a remarkable echo. In the course of surveying, being obliged to call aloud to my assistant from every side and almost every part of a farm in succession, and at various hours of a day, I am pretty sure to discover an echo if any exists, and the other day it was encouraging and soothing to hear it. After so many days of comparatively insignificant drudgery with stupid companions, this leisure, this sportiveness, this generosity in nature, sympathizing with the better part of me; somebody I could talk with,—one degree, at least, better than talking with one's self. Some voice of somebody I pined to hear, with whom I could form a community. I did wish, rather, to linger there and call all day to the air and hear my words repeated, but a vulgar necessity dragged me along round the bounds of the farm, to hear only the stale answers of my chain-man shouted back to me.

I am surprised that we make no more ado about echoes. They are almost the only kindred voices that I hear.

It was the memorable event of the day, not anything my companions said, or the travellers whom I met, or my thoughts, for they were all mere repetitions or echoes in the worst sense of what I had heard and thought before many times; but this echo was accompanied with novelty, and by its repetition of my voice it did more than double that. It was a profounder Socratic method of suggesting thoughts unutterable to me the speaker. There was one I heartily loved to talk with. Under such favorable auspices I could converse with myself, could reflect.

Feb. 23. I think myself in a wilder country, and a little nearer to primitive times, when I read in old books which spell the word savages with an *l* (salvages), like John Smith's "General Historie of Virginia, etc.," reminding me of the derivation of the word from *sylva*. There is some of the wild wood and its bristling branches still left in their language. The savages they described are really *salvages*, men of the *woods*.

Feb. 27. A week or two ago I brought home a handsome pitch pine cone which had freshly fallen and was closed perfectly tight. It was put into a table drawer. To-day I am agreeably surprised to find that it has there dried and opened with perfect regularity, filling the drawer, and from a solid, narrow, and sharp cone, has become a broad, rounded, open one,—has, in fact, expanded with the regularity of a flower's petals into a conical flower of rigid scales, and has shed a remarkable quantity of delicate-winged seeds. Each scale, which is very elaborately and perfectly constructed, is armed with a short spine, pointing downward, as if to protect its seed from squirrels and birds. That hard closed cone, which defied all violent attempts to open it, has thus yielded to the gentle persuasion of warmth and dryness. The expanding of the pine cones, that, too, is a season.

March 5. The secretary of the Association for the Advancement of Science requests me, as he probably has thousands of others, by a printed circular letter from Washington the other day, to fill the blank against certain questions, among which the most important one was what branch of science I was specially interested in, using the term science in the most comprehensive sense possible. Now, though I could state to a select few that department of human inquiry which engages me, and should be rejoiced at an opportunity to do so, I felt that it would be to make myself the laughing-stock of the scientific community to describe or attempt to describe to them that branch of science which specially interests me, inasmuch as they do not believe in a science which deals with the higher law. So I was obliged to speak to their condition and describe to them that poor part of me which alone they can understand. The fact is

I am a mystic, a transcendentalist, and a natural philosopher to boot. Now I think of it, I should have told them at once that I was a transcendentalist. That would have been the shortest way of telling them that they would not understand my explanations.

How absurd that, though I probably stand as near to nature as any of them, and am by constitution as good an observer as most, yet a true account of my relation to nature should excite their ridicule only! If it had been the secretary of an association of which Plato or Aristotle was the president, I should not have hesitated to describe my studies at once and particularly.

March 6. Sunday. Last Sunday I plucked some alder (apparently speckled) twigs, some (apparently *tremuloides*) aspen, and some swamp (?) willow, and put them in water in a warm room. Immediately the alder catkins were relaxed and began to lengthen and open, and by the second day to drop their pollen; like handsome pendants they hung round the pitcher, and at the same time the smaller female flower expanded and brightened. In about four days the aspens began to show their red anthers and feathery scales, being an inch in length and still extending. March 2d, I added the andromeda; March 3d, the rhodora.

March 7. What is the earliest sign of spring? The motion of worms and insects? The flow of sap in trees and the swelling of buds? Do not the insects awake with the flow of the sap? Bluebirds, etc., probably do not come till insects come out. Or are there earlier signs in the water?—the tortoises, frogs, etc.

March 8. Saw two or three hawks sailing. Saw the remains of four cows and a horse that were burned in a barn a month ago. Where the paunch was, a large bag of coarse hay and stalks was seen in the midst of an indistinct circumference of ribs. Saw some very large willow buds expanded (their silk) to thrice the length of their scales, indistinctly carved or waved with darker lines around them. They look more like, are more of, spring than anything I have seen.

Heard the *phebe*, or spring note of the chickadee, now, before any spring bird has arrived.

Heard the first flies buzz in the sun on the south side of the house.

XV.

March 10. This is the first really spring day. The sun is brightly reflected from all surfaces, and the north side of the street begins to be a little more passable to foot-travellers. You do not think it necessary to button up your coat.

I see many middling-sized black spiders on the edge of the snow, very active. The radical leaves of innumerable plants (as here a dock in and near the water) are evidently affected by the spring influences. Many plants are to some extent evergreen, like the buttercup now beginning to start. Methinks the first obvious evidence of spring is the pushing out of the swamp willow catkins, then the relaxing of the earlier alder catkins, then the pushing up of skunk-cabbage spathes (and pads at the bottom of water). This is the order I am inclined to,* though perhaps any of these may take precedence of all the rest in any particular case.

At Nut Meadow Brook crossing we rest awhile on the rail, gazing into the eddying stream. The ripple-marks on the sandy bottom, where silver spangles shine in the river with black wrecks of caddis-cases lodged under each shelving sand, the shadows of the invisible dimples reflecting prismatic colors on the bottom, the minnows already stemming the current with restless, wiggling tails, ever and anon darting aside, probably to secure some invisible mote in the water, whose shadows we do not at first detect on the sandy bottom,—when detected so much more obvious as well as larger and more interesting than the substance,—in which each fin is distinctly seen, though scarcely to be detected in the substance;

*Vide next page.

these are all very beautiful and exhilarating sights, a sort of diet drink to heal our winter discontent. Have the minnows played thus all winter? The equisetum at the bottom has freshly grown several inches. Then should I not have given the precedence on the last page to this and some other water-plants? I suspect that I should, and the flags appear to be starting.

What was that sound that came on the softened air? It was the warble of the first bluebird from that scraggy apple orchard yonder. When this is heard, then has spring arrived.

It must be that the willow twigs, both the yellow and green, are brighter-colored than before. I cannot be deceived.

March 12. Last night it snowed, a sleety snow again, and now the ground is whitened with it, and where are gone the bluebirds whose warble was wafted to me so lately like a blue wavelet through the air?

The greater part of the alder catkins (as well as the willow) are still in their winter condition, but some have their scales conspicuously loosened and elevated, showing their lighter-colored edges and interstices. They are actually beginning to blossom, certainly in advance of the willows. The sweet-gale is the prettiest flower which I have found expanded yet.

It is essential that a man confine himself to pursuits—a scholar, for instance, to studies—which lie next to and conduce to his life, which do not go against the grain, either of his will or his imagination. The scholar finds in his experience some studies to be most fertile and radiant with light, others dry, barren, and dark. If he is wise, he will not persevere in the last, as a plant in a cellar will strive toward the light. He will confine the observations of his mind as closely as possible to the experience or life of his senses. His thought must live with and be inspired with the life of the body. Some men endeavor to live a constrained life, to subject their whole lives to their wills, as he who said he would give a sign if he were conscious after his head was cut off,—but he gave no sign. Dwell as near as possible to the channel in which your life flows. A man may associate with such companions, he may pursue such employments, as will darken the day for him. Men choose darkness rather than light.

March 14. P.M.—Repairing my boat.

High winds, growing colder and colder, ground stiffening again. My ears have not been colder the past winter. March is rightly famous for its winds.

March 15. There were few colder nights last winter than the last. The water in the flower-stand containing my pet tortoise froze solid,—completely enveloping him, though I had a fire in my chamber all the evening,—also that in my pail pretty thick. But the tortoise, having been thawed out on the stove, leaving the impression of his back shell in the ice, was even more lively than ever. His efforts at first had been to get under his chip, as if to go into the mud. To-day the weather is severely and remarkably cold. It is not easy to keep warm in my chamber. I have not taken a more blustering walk the past winter than this afternoon.

March 18. P.M.—To Conantum.

I find it unexpectedly mild. It appears to be clearing up but will be wet underfoot.

Now, then, spring is beginning again in earnest after this short check. Is it not always thus? Is there not always an early promise of spring, something answering to the Indian summer, which succeeds the summer, so an Indian or false spring preceding the true spring,—first false promise which merely excites our expectations to disappoint them, followed by a short return of winter? Yet all things appear to have made progress, even during these wintry days, for I cannot believe that they have thus instantaneously taken a start. I no sooner step out of the house than I hear the bluebirds in the air, and far and near, everywhere except in the woods, throughout the town you may hear them,—the blue curls of their warblings,—harbingers of serene and warm weather, little azure rills of melody trickling here and there from out the air, their short warble trilled in the air reminding of so many corkscrews assaulting and thawing the torpid mass of winter, assisting the ice and snow to melt and the streams to flow. Everywhere also, all over the town, within an hour or two have come out little black two-winged gnats with plumed or fuzzy shoulders. When I catch one in my hands, it looks like a bit of black silk ravelling. They have suddenly come forth everywhere.

I came forth expecting to hear new birds, and I am not disappointed. We know well what to count upon. Their coming is more sure than the arrival of the sailing and steaming packets.

It grows more and more fair. Yesterday at this hour it was more raw and blustering than the past winter; to-day it seems more mild and balmy than summer. I have rarely known a greater contrast.

To-day first I smelled the earth.

March 20. (Yesterday I forgot to say I painted my boat. Spanish brown and raw oil were the ingredients. I found the painter had sold me the brown in hard lumps as big as peas, which I could not reduce with a stick; so I passed the whole when mixed through an old coffee-mill, which made a very good paint-mill, catching it in an old coffeepot, whose holes I puttied up, there being a lack of vessels; and then I broke up the coffee-mill and nailed a part over the bows to protect them, the boat is made so flat. I had first filled the seams with some grafting-wax I had, melted.)

It is evident that the English do not enjoy that contrast between winter and summer that we do,—that there is too much greenness and spring in the winter. There is no such wonderful resurrection of the year. Birds kindred with our first spring ones remain with them all winter, and flowers answering to our earliest spring ones put forth there in January. In one sense they have no winter but such as our spring. Our April is their March; our March, their February; our February, January, and December are not theirs at all under any name or sign.

The peculiarity of to-day is that now first you perceive that dry, warm, summer-presaging scent from dry oak and other leaves, on the sides of hills and ledges. You smell the summer from afar. The warm makes a man young again. There is also some dryness, almost dustiness, in the roads. The mountains are white with snow, and sure as the wind is northwest it is wintry; but now it is more westerly.

March 21. Morning along the river.

Might not my Journal be called "Field Notes?"

I see a honey-bee about my boat, apparently attracted by the beeswax (if there is any) in the grafting-wax with which I have luted it. There are many; one is caught and killed in it.

P.M.—To Kibbe Place.

It is a genial and reassuring day; the mere warmth of the west wind amounts almost to balminess. The softness of the air mollifies our own dry and congealed substance. I sit down by a wall to see if I can muse again. We are affected like the earth, and yield to the elemental tenderness; winter breaks up within us; the frost is coming out of me, and I am heaved like the road; accumulated masses of ice and snow dissolve, and thoughts like a freshet pour down unwonted channels. Roads lead elsewhither than to Carlisle and Sudbury. Our experience does not wear upon us. It is seen to be fabulous or symbolical, and the future is worth expecting. In all my walking I have not reached the top of the earth yet.

March 22. No sap flows from the maples I cut into, except that one in Lincoln. What means it? *Hylodes Pickeringii*, a name that is longer than the frog itself! A description of animals, too, from a dead specimen only, as if, in a work on man, you were to describe a dead man only, omitting his manners and customs, his institutions and divine faculties, from want of opportunity to observe them, because you do not live in the country. Only dindons and dandies. Nothing is known of his habits. Food: seeds of wheat, beef, pork, and potatoes.

P.M.—To Martial Miles Meadow, by boat to Nut Meadow Brook.

Launched my new boat. It is very steady, too steady for me; does not toss enough and communicate the motion of the waves. Beside, the seats are not well arranged; when there are two in it, it requires a heavy stone in the stern to trim. But it holds its course very well with a side wind from being so flat from stem to stern.

The cranberries now make a show under water, and I always make it a point to taste a few.

March 23. 5 A.M.—I hear the robin sing before I rise.

6 A.M.—Up the North River.

A fresh, cool spring morning.

The cat-tail down puffs and swells in your hand like a mist, or the conjurer's trick of filling a hat with feathers, for when you have rubbed off but a thimbleful, and can close and conceal the wound completely, the expanded down fills your hand to overflowing. Apparently there is a spring to the fine elastic threads which compose the down, which, after having been so long closely packed, on being the least relieved at the base, spring open apace into the form of parachutes to convey the seed afar. Where birds or the winds or ice have assaulted them, this has spread like an eruption.* Again, when I rub off the down of its spike with my thumb, I am surprised at the sensation of warmth it imparts to my hand, as it flushes over it magically, at the same time revealing a faint purplish-crimson tinge at the base of the down, as it rolls off and expands. It is a very pleasing experiment to try.

Man cannot afford to be a naturalist, to look at Nature directly, but only with the side of his eye. He must look through and beyond her. To look at her is fatal as to look at the head of Medusa. It turns the man of science to stone. I feel that I am dissipated by so many observations. I should be the magnet in the midst of all this dust and filings. I knock the back of my hand against a rock, and as I smooth back the skin, I find myself prepared to study lichens there. I look upon man but as a fungus. I have almost a slight, dry headache as the result of all this observing. How to observe is how to behave. O for a little Lethe! To crown all, lichens, which are so thin, are described in the *dry* state, as they are most commonly, not most truly, seen. Truly, they are *dryly* described.

Vide amount of seed in *Tribune,* Mar. 16, 1860.

I am surprised as well as delighted when any one wishes to know what I think. It is such a rare use they would make of me, as if they were acquainted with the tool. Commonly, if men want anything of me, it is only to know how many acres I make of their land, or, at most, what trivial news I have burdened myself with. They never will go to law for my meat. They prefer the shell.

March 24. Since the cold snap of the 14th, 15th, etc., have walked for the most part with unbuttoned coat, and for the most part without mittens.

There are very slight but white mists on the river these mornings.

It spits a little snow this afternoon.

The white pine wood, freshly cut, piled by the side of the Charles Miles road, is agreeable to walk beside. I like the smell of it, all ready for the borers, and the rich light-yellow color of the freshly split wood and the purple color of the sap at the ends of the quarters, from which distill perfectly clear and crystalline tears, colorless and brilliant as diamonds, tears shed for the loss of a forest in which is a world of light and purity, its life oozing out. These beautiful accidents that attend on man's works! I am surprised to find that these terebinthine (?) tears have a hard (seemingly soft as water) not film but transparent skin over them. How many curiosities are brought to us with our wood! The trees and the lichens that clothe them, the forest warrior and his shield adhering to him.

March 25. When I saw the fungi in my lamp, I was startled and awed, as if I were stooping too low, and should next be found classifying carbuncles and ulcers. Is there not sense in the mass of men who ignore and confound these things, and never see the cryptogamia on the one side any more than the stars on the other? Underfoot they catch a transient glimpse of what they call toad-stools, mosses, and frog-spittle, and overhead of the heavens, but they can all read the pillars on a Mexican quarter. They ignore the worlds above and below, keep straight along, and do not run their boots down at the heel as I do. How to keep the heels up I have been obliged to study carefully, turning the nigh foot painfully on side-hills. I find that the shoemakers, to save a few iron heel-pegs, do not complete the rows on the inside by three or four,—the very place in the whole boot where they are most needed,—which has fatal consequences to the buyer. I often see the tracks of them in the paths. It is as if you were to put no under-pinning under one corner of your house. I have managed to cross very wet and miry places dry-shod by moving rapidly on my heels. I always use leather strings tied in a hard knot; they untie but too easily even then.

The various lights in which you may regard the earth, *e.g.* the dry land as sea bottom, or the sea bottom as a dry down.

March 26. Saw about 10 A.M. a gaggle of geese, forty-three in number, in a very perfect harrow flying northeasterly. One side the harrow was a little longer than the other. They appeared to be four or five feet apart. It is remarkable that we commonly see geese go over in the spring about 10 o'clock in the morning, as if they were accustomed to stop for the night at some place southward whence they reached us at that time. Goodwin saw six geese in Walden about the same time.

March 27. The hazel is fully out. The 23d was perhaps full early to date them. It is in some respects the most interesting flower yet, though so minute that only an observer of nature, or one who looked for them, would notice it. It is the highest and richest colored yet,—ten or a dozen little rays at the end of the buds which are the ends and along the sides of the bare stems. Some of the flowers are a light, some a dark crimson. The high color of this minute, unobserved flower, at this cold, leafless, and almost flowerless season! Moreover, they are so tender that I never get one home in good condition. They wilt and turn black.

Tried to see the faint-croaking frogs at J. P. Brown's Pond in the woods. They are remarkably timid and shy; had their noses and eyes out, croaking, but all ceased, dove, and concealed themselves, before I got within a rod of the shore. Stood perfectly still amid the bushes on the shore, before one showed himself; finally five or six, and all eyed me, gradually approached me within three feet to re-connoitre, and, though I waited about half an hour, would not ut-ter a sound nor take their eyes off me,—were plainly affected by curiosity. Dark brown and some, perhaps, dark green, about two inches long; had their noses and eyes out when they croaked.

March 28. My Aunt Maria asked me to read the life of Dr. Chal-mers, which however I did not promise to do. Yesterday, Sunday, she was heard through the partition shouting to my Aunt Jane, who is deaf, "Think of it! He stood half an hour to-day to hear the frogs croak, and he would n't read the life of Chalmers."

6 A.M.—To Cliffs.

I do not now think of a bird that *hops* so distinctly, rapidly, and commonly as the robin, with its head up.

Why is the pollen of flowers commonly yellow?

March 29. 6 A.M.—To Leaning Hemlocks, by boat.

The sun has just risen, but there is only a now clear saffron belt next the east horizon; all the rest of the sky is covered with clouds, broken into lighter and darker shades. An agreeable yellow sun-light falls on the western fields and the banks of the river. Whence this yellow tinge? Probably a different light would be reflected if there were no dark clouds above.

This is one of those days divided against itself, when there is a cool wind but a warm sun, when there is little or no coolness proper to this locality, but it is wafted to us probably from the snow-clad northwest, and hence in sheltered places it is very warm. However, the sun is rapidly prevailing over the wind, and it is already warmer than when I came out.

Four ducks, two by two, are sailing conspicuously on the river. There appear to be two pairs. In each case one two-thirds white and another grayish-brown and, I think, smaller. They are very shy and fly at fifty rods' distance. Are they whistlers? The white are much more white than those I saw the other day and at first thought summer ducks.* Would it not be well to carry a spy-glass in order to watch these shy birds such as ducks and hawks? In some respects, methinks, it would be better than a gun. The latter brings them nearer dead, but the former alive. You can identify the species better by killing the bird, because it was a dead specimen that was so minutely described, but you can study the habits and appearance best in the living specimen.

Walking along near the edge of the meadow under Lupine Hill, I slumped through the sod into a muskrat's nest, for the sod was only two inches thick over it, which was enough when it was frozen. I laid it open with my hands. There were three or four channels or hollowed paths, a rod or more in length, not merely worn but made in the meadow, and centring at the mouth of this burrow. They were three or four inches deep, and finally became indistinct and were lost amid the cranberry vines and grass toward the river. The entrance to the burrow was just at the edge of the upland, here a gently sloping bank, and was probably just beneath the surface of the water six weeks ago. It was about twenty-five rods distant from the true bank of the river. From this a straight gallery, about six inches in diameter every way, sloped upward about eight feet into the bank just beneath the turf, so that the end was about a foot higher than the entrance. There was a somewhat circular enlargement about one foot in horizontal diameter and the same depth with the gallery; and it was nearly a peck of coarse meadow stubble, showing the marks of the scythe, with which was mixed accidentally a very little of the moss which grew with it. Three short galleries, only two feet long, were continued from this centre somewhat like rays toward the high land, as if they had been prepared in order to be ready for a sudden rise of the water, or had been actually made so far under such an emergency. The nest was of course thoroughly wet and, humanly speaking, uncomfortable, though the creature could breathe in it. But it is plain that the muskrat cannot be subject to the toothache. I have no doubt this

---

*These were either mergansers or the golden-eye; I think the former, *i.e. Mergus serrator*, or red-breasted merganser (?), or sheldrake.

was made and used last winter, for the grass was as fresh as that in the meadow (except that it was pulled up), and the sand which had been taken out lay partly in a flattened heap in the meadow, and no grass had sprung up through it.

In the course of the above examination I made a very interesting discovery. When I turned up the thin sod from over the damp cavity of the nest, I was surprised to see at this hour of a pleasant day what I took to be beautiful frost crystals of a rare form,—frost bodkins I was in haste to name them, for around the fine white roots of the grass, apparently the herd's-grass, which were from one to two or more inches long, reaching downward into the dark, damp cavern (though the green blades had scarcely made so much growth above; indeed, the growth was scarcely visible there), appeared to be lingering still into the middle of this warm afternoon rare and beautiful frost crystals exactly in the form of a bodkin, about one sixth of an inch wide at base and tapering evenly to the lower end, sometimes the upper part of the core being naked for half an inch, which last gave them a slight resemblance to feathers, though they were not flat but round, and at the abrupt end of the rootlet (as if cut off) a larger, clear drop. On examining them more closely, feeling and tasting them, I found that it was not frost but a clear, crystalline dew in almost invisible drops, concentrated from the dampness of the cavern, and perhaps melted frost still reserving by its fineness its original color, thus regularly arranged around the delicate white fibre; and, looking again, incredulous, I discerned extremely minute white threads or gossamer standing out on all sides from the main rootlet in this form and affording the core for these drops. Yet on those fibres which had lost their dew, none of these minute threads appeared. There they pointed downward somewhat like stalactites, or very narrow caterpillar brushes. It impressed me as a wonderful piece of chemistry, that the very grass we trample on and esteem so cheap should be thus wonderfully nourished, that this spring greenness was not produced by coarse and cheap means, but in sod, out of sight, the most delicate and magical processes are going on. The half is not shown. The very sod is replete with mechanism far finer than that of a watch, and yet it is cast under our feet to be trampled on. The process that goes on in the sod and the dark, about the minute fibres of the grass,—the chemistry and the mechanics,—before a single green blade can appear above the withered herbage, if it could be adequately described, would supplant all other revelations. We are acquainted with but one side of the sod. I brought home some tufts of the grass in my pocket, but when I took it out I could not at first find those pearly white fibres and thought that they were lost, for they were shrunk to dry brown threads; and, as for the still finer gossamer which supported the roscid droplets, with few exceptions they were absolutely undiscoverable,—they no longer stood out around the core,—so fine and delicate was their organization. It made me doubt almost if there were not actual, substantial, though invisible cores to the leaflets and veins of the hoar frost. And can these almost invisible and tender fibres penetrate the earth where there is no cavern? Or is what we call the solid earth porous and cavernous enough for them?

The trout glances like a film from side to side and under the bank.

Tried several times to catch a skater. Got my hand close to him; grasped at him as quick as possible; was sure I had got him this time; let the water run out between my fingers; hoped I had not crushed him; opened my hand; and lo! he was not there. I never succeeded in catching one. What are those common snails in the mud in ditches, with their feet out, for some time past?

The early willow will bloom to-morrow. Its catkins have lost many of their scales. The crowded yellow anthers are already bursting out through the silvery down, like the sun of spring through the clouds of winter.

March 30. Now commences the season for fires in the woods. The winter, and now the sun and winds, have dried the old leaves more thoroughly than ever, and there are no green leaves to shade the ground or to check the flames, and these high March winds are the very ones to spread them. The woods look peculiarly dry and russet. There is as yet no new greenness in the landscape. With these thoughts and impressions I had not gone far before I saw the smoke of a fire on Fair Haven Hill. Some boys were going *sassafrasing*, for boys will have some pursuit peculiar to every season. A match came in contact with a marble, nobody knew how, and suddenly the fire flashed up the broad open hillside, consuming the low grass and sweet-fern and leaving a smoking, blackened waste. A few glowing stumps, with spadefuls of fresh earth thrown on them, the white ashes here and there on the black ground, and the not disagreeable scent of smoke and cinders was all that was left when I arrived.

Dry leaves, which I at first mistake for birds, go sailing through the air in front of the Cliff.

The motions of a hawk correcting the flaws in the wind by raising his shoulder from time to time, are much like those of a leaf yielding to them.

Ah, those youthful days! are they never to return? when the walker does not too curiously observe particulars, but sees, hears, scents, tastes, and feels only himself,—the phenomena that show themselves in him,—his expanding body, his intellect and heart. No worm or insect, quadruped or bird, confined his view, but the unbounded universe was his. A bird is now become a mote in his eye.

March 31. Brown has these birds set up which I may wish to examine:—

Turtle-dove, green heron, *Ardea Herodias*, pileated woodpecker, fox-colored sparrow, young of purple finch, white-eyed vireo, goldfinch, brown creeper, scarlet tanager (male and female), white-breasted nuthatch, solitary vireo, red-eyed vireo, yellow redpoll warbler, hermit thrush (killed here), cardinal grosbeak, pine grosbeak, black-billed cuckoo, mockingbird, woodcock, *Totanus flavipes* (or small yellow-leg), (great ditto ?), Bartram's tatler (or upland plover), golden ditto, *Falco sparverius*, sharp-shinned or slate-colored hawk, or *F. Pennsylvanicus* of Wilson, green-winged teal, blue-winged teal, wood duck (young drakes).

April 3. The last two *Tribunes* I have not looked at. I have no time to read newspapers.

April 6. 6 A.M.—To Cliffs.

How many walks along the brooks I take in the spring! What shall I call them? Lesser riparial excursions? Prairial? rivular?

When I came out there was not a speck of mist in the sky, but the morning without a cloud is not the fairest. Now, 8.30 A.M., it rains. Such is April.

April 7. 10 A.M.—Down river in boat to Bedford, with C.

If you make the least correct observation of nature this year, you will have occasion to repeat it with illustrations the next, and the season and life itself is prolonged.

May 1. Sunday. The oak leaves on the plain are fallen. The colors are now: light blue above (where is my cyanometer? Saussure invented one, and Humboldt used it in his travels); landscape russet and greenish, spotted with fawn-colored plowed lands, with green pine and gray or reddish oak woods intermixed, and dark-blue or slate-colored water here and there. It is greenest in the meadows and where water has lately stood, and a strong, invigorating scent comes up from the fresh meadows. It is like the greenness of an apple faintly or dimly appearing through the russet.

The columbines have been out some days. How ornamental to these dark-colored perpendicular cliffs, nodding from the clefts and shelves!

May 6. The whole landscape is many shades greener for the rain, almost a blue green.

May 10. 5 A.M. I proceed down the Turnpike. The masses of the golden willow are seen in the distance on either side the way, twice as high as the road is wide, conspicuous against the distant, still half-russet hills and forests, for the green grass hardly yet prevails over the dead stubble, and the woods are but just beginning to gray. The female willow is a shade greener. At this season the travel-ler passes through a golden gate on causeways where these willows are planted, as if he were approaching the entrance to Fairyland;

and there will surely be found the yellowbird, and already from a distance is heard his note, a *tche tche tche tcha tchar tcha*,—ah, willow, willow. And as he passes between the portals, a sweet fragrance is wafted to him; he not only breathes but scents and tastes the air, and he hears the low humming or susurrus of a myriad insects which are feeding on its sweets. It is, apparently, these that attract the yellowbird. The golden gates of the year, the *May*-gate. The traveller cannot pass out of Concord by the highways in any direction without passing between such portals,—graceful, curving, drooping, wand-like twigs, on which leaves and blossoms appear together.

He is the richest who has most use for nature as raw material of tropes and symbols with which to describe his life. If these gates of golden willows affect me, they correspond to the beauty and promise of some experience on which I am entering. If I am overflowing with life, am rich in experience for which I lack expression, then nature will be my language full of poetry,—all nature will *fable*, and every natural phenomenon be a myth.

The hornbeam (*Carpinus*) is just ready to bloom.* I was in search of this, and, not observing it at first, and having forgotten it, I sat down on a rock, with the thought that if I sat there quietly a little while I might see some flower or other object about me; unexpectedly, as I cast my eyes upward, over my head stretched a spreading branch of the carpinus full of small catkins with anthers now reddish, spread like a canopy just over my head. As it is best to sit in a grove and let the birds come to you, so, as it were, even the flowers will come to you.

I sit here surrounded by hellebores eighteen inches high or more, with handsome, regular, plaited leaves, regularly arranged around the erect stems, and a multitude of ferns are unrolling themselves, altogether making the impression of a tropical vegetation.

I leave the woods and begin to ascend Smith's Hill along the course of the rill. From the hill, I look westward over the landscape. As you ascend, the near and low hills sink and flatten into

---

*Does next morning in pitcher.

the earth; no sky is seen behind them; the distant mountains rise. The truly great are distinguished. You see, not the domes only, but the body, the façade, of these terrene temples. You see that the foundation answers to the superstructure. Moral structures. (The sweet-fern leaves among odors now.) The value of the mountains in the horizon,—would not that be a good theme for a lecture? The text for a discourse on real values, and permanent; a sermon on the mount. They are stepping-stones to heaven,—as the rider has a horse-block at his gate,—by which to mount when we would commence our pilgrimage to heaven—from this bare actual earth, which has so little of the hue of heaven. They make it easier to die and easier to live. They let us off.

They are valuable to mankind as is the iris of the eye to a man. They are the path of the translated. They are the pastures to which we drive our thoughts on these 20ths of May. (George Baker told me the other day that he had driven cows to Winchendon, forty miles, in one day.)

May 11. The late pipes (*limosum?*), now nearly a foot high, are very handsome, like Oriental work, their encircled columns of some precious wood or gem, or like small bamboos, from Oriental jungles. Very much like art. The gold-thread, apparently for a day or two, though few flowers compared with buds. A high blueberry by Potter's heater piece. A yellow lily.

As I stand by the river in the truly warm sun, I hear the low trump of a bullfrog, but half sounded,—doubting if it be really July,—some bassoon sounds, as it were the tuning that precedes the summer's orchestra; and all is silent again. How the air is saturated with sweetness on causeways these willowy days!

Some grass is seen to wave in the distance on the side of N. Barrett's warm hill, showing the lighter under sides. That is a soft, soothing, June-like impression when the most forward grass is seen to wave and the sorrel looks reddish. The year has the down of youth on its cheek. Now it is too late to retreat from the summer adventure. You have passed the Rubicon, and will spend your summer here.

May 14. Saturday. 9 A.M.—To Wayland by boat. Close under the lee of the button-bushes which skirt the pond, as I look south, there is a narrow smooth strip of water, silvery and contrasting with the darker rippled body of the pond. Its edge, or the separation between this, which I will call the polished silvery border of the pond, and the dark and ruffled body, is not a straight line or film, but an ever-varying, irregularly and finely serrated or fringed border, ever changing as the breeze falls over the bushes at an angle more or less steep, so that this moment it is a road wide, the next not half so much. Every feature is thus fluent in the landscape.

May 15. The golden willow catkins begin to fall; their prime is past. And buttercups and silvery cinquefoil, and the first apple blossoms, and waving grass beginning to be tinged with sorrel, introduce us to a different season. The huckleberry, *resinosa*, its red flowers are open, in more favorable places several days earlier, probably; and the earliest shrub and red and black oaks in warm exposures may be set down to to-day. A red butterfly goes by. Methinks I have seen them before. The painted-cup is now abundantly and fully out. Six or eight inches high above its spidery leaves, almost like a red flame, it stands on edge of the hill just rising from the meadow,—on the instep of the hill. It tells of July with its fiery color. It promises a heat we have not experienced yet. This is a field which lies nearer to summer. Yellow is the color of spring; red, of midsummer. Through pale golden and green we arrive at the yellow of the buttercup; through scarlet, to the fiery July red, the red lily.

May 16. It has been oppressively warm to-day, the first really warm, sultry-like weather, so that we were prepared for a thunder-storm at evening. At 5 P.M., dark, heavy, wet-looking clouds are seen in the northern horizon, perhaps over the Merrimack Valley. People stand at their doors in the warm evening, listening to the muttering of distant thunder and watching the forked lightning, now descending to the earth, now ascending to the clouds. This the first really warm day and thunder-shower. Nature appears to have passed a crisis. All slimy reptile life is wide awake. We smell the fresher and cooler air from where the storm has passed. And now that it has grown dark, the skirts of the cloud seem to promise us a shower. We look out into the dark, and ever and anon comes a sudden illumination blinding our eyes, like a vast glow-worm, succeeded ere long by the roll of thunder. The first pattering of drops is heard; all west windows are hastily shut. The weak-eyed sit with their backs to windows and close the blinds.

May 21. P.M.—Up Assabet to cress, with Sophia.

May 22. Sunday. It is clear June, the first day of summer. The rye, which, when I last looked, was one foot high, is now three feet high and waving and tossing its heads in the wind. We ride by these bluish-green waving rye-fields in the woods, as if an Indian juggler had made them spring up in a night. Though I walk every day I am never prepared for this magical growth of the rye. I am advanced by whole months, as it were, into summer. Sorrel reddens the fields. Cows are preparing the milk for June butter.

When yesterday Sophia and I were rowing past Mr. Prichard's land, where the river is bordered by a row of elms and low willows, at 6 P.M., we heard a singular note of distress as it were from a catbird—a loud, vibrating, catbird sort of note, as if the catbird's mew were imitated by a smart vibrating spring. Blackbirds and others were flitting about, apparently attracted by it. At first, thinking it was merely some peevish catbird or red-wing, I was disregarding it, but on second thought turned the bows to the shore, looking into the trees as well as over the shore, thinking some bird might be in distress, caught by a snake or in a forked twig. The hovering birds dispersed at my approach; the note of distress sounded louder and nearer as I approached the shore covered with low osiers. The sound came from the ground, not from the trees. I saw a little black animal making haste to meet the boat under the osiers. A young muskrat? a mink? No, it was a little dot of a kitten. It was scarcely six inches long from the face to the base—or I might as well say the tip—of the tail, for the latter was a short, sharp pyramid, perfectly perpendicular but not swelled in the least. It was a very handsome and very precocious kitten, in perfectly good condition, its breadth being considerably more than one third of its length. Leaving its mewing, it came scrambling over the stones as fast as its weak legs would permit, straight to me. I took it up and dropped it into the boat, but while I was pushing off it ran the length of the boat to Sophia, who held it while we rowed homeward. Evidently it had not been weaned—was smaller than we remembered that kittens ever were—almost infinitely small; yet it had hailed a boat, its life being in danger, and saved itself. Its performance, considering its age and amount of experience, was more wonderful than that of any young mathematician or musician that I have read of. Various were the conjectures as to how the kitten came there, a quarter of a mile from a house. The possible solutions were finally reduced to three: first, it must either have been born there, or, secondly, carried there by its mother, or, thirdly, by human hands. In the first case, it had possibly brothers and sisters, one or both, and its mother had left them to go a-hunting on her own account and might be expected back. In the second, she might equally be expected to return. At any rate, not having thought of all this till we got home, we found that we had got ourselves into a scrape; for this kitten, though exceedingly interesting, required one nurse to attend it constantly for the present, and, of course, another to spell the first; and, beside, we had already a cat wellnigh grown, who manifested such a disposition toward the young stranger that we had no doubt it would have torn it in pieces in a moment if left alone with it. As nobody made up his or her mind to have it drowned, and still less to drown it,—having once looked into its innocent extremely pale blue eyes (as of milk thrice skimmed) and had his finger or his chin sucked by it, while, its eyes being shut, its little paws played a soothing tune,—it was resolved to keep it till it could be suitably disposed of. It rested nowhere, in no lap, under no covert, but still faintly cried for its mother and its accustomed supper. It ran toward every sound or movement of a human being, and whoever crossed the room it was sure to follow at a rapid pace. It had all the ways of a cat of the maturest years; could purr divinely and raised its back to rub all boots and shoes. When it raised its foot to scratch its ear, which by the way it never hit, it was sure to fall over and roll on the floor. It climbed straight up the sitter, faintly mewing all the way, and sucked his chin. In vain, at first, its head was bent down into saucers of milk which its eyes did not see, and its chin was wetted. But soon it learned to suck a finger that had been dipped in it, and better still a rag; and then at last it slept and rested. The street was explored in vain to find its owner, and at length an Irish family took it into their cradle. Soon after we learned that a neighbor who had heard the mewing of kittens in the partition had sent for a carpenter, taken off a board, and found two the very day at noon that we sailed. That same hour it was first brought to the light a coarse Irish cook had volunteered to drown it, had carried it to the river, and without bag or sinker had cast it in! It saved itself and hailed a boat! What an eventful life! What a precocious kitten! We feared it owed its first plump condition to the water. How strong and effective the instinct of self-preservation!

Our quince blossomed yesterday. Saw many low blackberries in bloom to-day.

May 23. To-day I am surprised by the dark orange-yellow of the senecio. At first we had the lighter, paler spring yellows of willows (cowslips even, for do they not grow a little darker afterward?), dandelion, cinquefoil, then the darker (methinks it is a little darker than the cowslip) and deeper yellow of the buttercup; and then this broad distinction between the buttercup and the krigia and senecio, as the seasons revolve toward July. Every new flower that opens, no doubt, expresses a new mood of the human mind. Have I any dark or ripe orange-yellow thoughts to correspond? The *flavor* of my thoughts begins to correspond. Lupines now for some days, probably about the 19th.

White clover. I see the light purple of the rhodora enlivening the edges of swamps—another color the sun wears. Is it not the most showy *high-colored* flower or shrub? Flowers are the different colors of the sunlight.

An abundance of pure white fringed polygalas, very delicate, by the path at Harrington's mud-hole. Thus many flowers have their nun sisters, dressed in white. At Loring's Wood heard and saw a tanager. That contrast of a *red* bird with the green pines and the blue sky! Even when I have heard his note and look for him and find the bloody fellow, sitting on a dead twig of a pine, I am always startled. (They seem to love the darkest and thickest pines.) That incredible red, with the green and blue, as if these were the trinity we wanted. Yet with his hoarse note he pays for his color. I am transported; these are not the woods I ordinarily walk in. How he enhances the wildness and wealth of the woods! This and the emperor moth make the tropical phenomena of our zone.

May 25. I quarrel with most botanists' description of different species, say of willows. It is a difference without a distinction. No stress is laid upon the peculiarity of the species in question, and it requires a very careful examination and comparison to detect any difference in the description. Having described you one species, he begins again at the beginning when he comes to the next and describes it *absolutely*, wasting time; in fact does not describe the species, but rather the genus or family; as if, in describing the particular races of men, you should say of each in its turn that it is but dust and to dust it shall return. The object should be to describe not those particulars in which a species resembles its genus, for they are many and that would be but a negative description, but those in which it is peculiar, for they are few and positive.

Steady fisherman's rain, without wind, straight down, flooding the ground and spattering on it, beating off the blossoms of apples and thorns, etc. Within the last week or so the grass and leaves have grown many shades darker, and if we had leaped from last Wednesday to this, we should have been startled by the change—the dark bluish green of rank grass especially. How rapidly the young twigs shoot—the herbs, trees, shrubs no sooner leaf out than they shoot forward surprisingly, as if they had acquired a head by being re-pressed so long. They do not grow nearly so rapidly at any other season. Many do most of their growing for the year in a week or two at this season. They *shoot*—they *spring*—and the rest of the year they harden and mature, and perhaps have a second spring in the latter part of summer or in the fall.

May 27. 5.30 A.M.—To Island.

A turtle walking is as if a man were to try to walk by sticking his legs and arms merely out the windows.

May 29. Cattle stand in the river by the bridge for coolness. Place my hat lightly on my head that the air may circulate beneath. Fields are whitened with mouse-ear gone to seed—a mass of white fuzz blowing off one side—and also with dandelion globes of seeds. Some plants have already reached their fall. How still the hot noon; people have retired behind blinds. I see men and women through open windows in white undress taking their Sunday-afternoon nap, overcome with heat.

May 31. Some incidents in my life have seemed far more allegorical than actual; they were so significant that they plainly served no other use. That is, I have been more impressed by their allegorical significance and fitness; they have been like myths or passages in a myth, rather than mere incidents or history which have to wait to become significant. Quite in harmony with my subjective philoso-phy. This, for instance: that, when I thought I knew the flowers so well, the beautiful purple azalea or pinxter-flower should be shown me by the hunter who found it. Such facts are lifted quite above the level of the actual. They are all just such events as my imagination prepares me for, no matter how incredible. Ever and anon some-thing will occur which my philosophy has not dreamed of. The limits of the actual are set some thoughts further off. That which had seemed a rigid wall of vast thickness unexpectedly proves a thin and undulating drapery. The boundaries of the actual are no more fixed and rigid than the elasticity of our imaginations. The fact that a rare and beautiful flower which we never saw, perhaps never heard, for which therefore there was no place in our thoughts, may at length be found in our immediate neighborhood, is very suggestive.

P.M.—A change in the weather. It is comparatively cool since last night, and the air is very clear accordingly; none of that haze in it occasioned by the late heat. The leaves are now fairly expanded—that has been the work of May—and are of a dark summer greenness. It is surprising to see how many leaves are already attacked by insects,—leafrollers, pincushion galls, one kind of oak-balls, etc., etc.; and many a shrub and tree, black cherry and shrub oak, is no sooner leaved out than it is completely stripped by its caterpillar foes.

I am going in search of the *Azalea nudiflora*. Sophia brought home a single flower without twig or leaf from Mrs. Brooks's last evening. Mrs. Brooks, I find, has a large twig in a vase of water, still pretty fresh, which she says George Melvin gave to her son George. I called at his office. He says that Melvin came in to Mr. Gourgas's office, where he and others were sitting Saturday evening, with his arms full and gave each a sprig, but he does n't know where he got it. Somebody, I heard, had seen it at Captain Jarvis's; so I went there. I found that they had some still pretty fresh in the house. Melvin gave it to them Saturday night, but they did not know where he got it. A young man working at Stedman Buttrick's said it was a secret; there was only one bush in the town; Melvin knew of it and Stedman knew; when asked, Melvin said he got it in the swamp, or from a bush, etc. The young man thought it grew on the Island across the river on the Wheeler farm. I went on to Melvin's house, though I did not expect to find him at home at this hour, so early in the afternoon. (Saw the wood-sorrel out, a day or two perhaps, by the way.) At length I saw his dog by the door, and knew he was at home.

He was sitting in the shade, bareheaded, at his back door. He had a large pailful of the azalea recently plucked and in the shade behind his house, which he said he was going to carry to town at evening. He had also a sprig set out. He had been out all the forenoon and said he had got seven pickerel—perhaps—apparently he had been drinking and was just getting over it. At first he was a little shy about telling me where the azalea grew, but I saw that I should get it out of him. He dilly-dallied a little; called to his neighbor Farmer, whom he called "Razor," to know if he could tell me where that flower grew. He called it, by the way, the "red honeysuckle." This was to prolong the time and make the most of his secret. I felt pretty sure the plant was to be found on Wheeler's land beyond the river, as the young man had said, for I had remembered how, some weeks before this, when I went up the Assabet after the yellow rocket, I saw Melvin, who had just crossed with his dog, and when I landed to pluck the rocket he appeared out of the woods, said he was after a fish-pole, and asked me the name of my flower. Did n't think it was very handsome,—"not so handsome as the honey-suckle, is it?" And now I knew it was his "red honeysuckle," and not the columbine, he meant. Well, I told him he had better tell me where it was; I was a botanist and ought to know. But he thought I could n't possibly find it by his directions. I told him he'd better tell me and have the glory of it, for I should surely find it if he did n't; I'd got a clue to it, and should n't give it up. I should go over the river for it. I could smell it a good way, you know. He thought I could smell it half a mile, and he wondered that I had n't stumbled on it, or Channing. Channing, he said, came close by it once, when it was in flower. He thought he'd surely find it then; but he did n't, and he said nothing to him.

He told me he found it about ten years ago, and he went to it every year. It blossomed at the old election time, and he thought it "the handsomest flower that grows." Yarrow just out.

In the meanwhile, Farmer, who was hoeing, came up to the wall, and we fell into a talk about Dodge's Brook, which runs through his farm. A man in Cambridge, he said, had recently writ-ten to Mr. Monroe about it, but he did n't know why. All he knew about the brook was that he had seen it dry and then again, after a week of dry weather in which no rain fell, it would be full again, and either the writer or Monroe said there were only two such brooks in all North America. One of its sources—he thought the principal one—was in his land. We all went to it. It was in a meadow,—rather a dry one, once a swamp. He said it never ceased to flow at the head now, since he dug it out, and never froze there. He ran a pole down eight or nine feet into the mud to show me the depth. He had minnows there in a large deep pool, and cast an insect into the water, which they presently rose to and swallowed. Fifteen years ago he dug it out nine feet deep and found spruce logs as big as his leg, which the beavers had gnawed, with the marks of their teeth very distinct upon them; but they soon crumbled away on coming to the air. Melvin, meanwhile, was telling me of a pair of geese he had seen which were breeding in the Bedford Swamp. He had seen them within a day. Last year he got a large brood (11?) of black ducks there.

We went on down the brook,—Melvin and I and his dog,—and crossed the river in his boat, and he conducted me to where the *Azalea nudiflora* grew,—it was a little past its prime, perhaps,—and showed me how near Channing came. ("You won't tell him what I said; will you?" said he.) I offered to pay him for his trouble, but he would n't take anything. He had just as lief I'd know as not. He thought it first came out last Wednesday, on the 25th.

Azalea nudiflora,—purple azalea, pinxter-flower,—but Gray and Bigelow say nothing about its *clamminess*. It is a conspicuously beautiful flowering shrub, with the sweet fragrance of the common swamp-pink, but the flowers are larger and, in this case, a fine lively rosy pink, not so clammy as the other. With a broader, somewhat downy pale-green leaf. Growing in the shade of large wood, like the laurel. Eaton says the *nudiflora* is "not viscous;" names half a dozen varieties and among them *A. partita* (flesh-colored flowers, 5-parted to the base), but then this is viscous. And it cannot be his species *A. nitida*, with glabrous and shining and small leaves. It must be an undescribed variety—a viscous one—of *A. nudiflora*.

There is a little danger of a frost to-night.

June 1. The pincushion galls on young white oaks are now among the most beautiful objects in the woods, coarse woolly white to appearance, spotted with bright red or crimson on the exposed side. It is remarkable that a mere gall, which at first we are inclined to regard as something abnormal, should be made so beautiful, as if it were the *flower* of the tree; that a disease, an excrescence, should prove, perchance, the greatest beauty,—as the tear of the pearl. Beautiful scarlet sins they may be. Through our temptations,—aye, and our falls,—our virtues appear. As in many a character,—many a poet,—we see that beauty exhibited in a gall, which was meant to have bloomed in a flower, unchecked. Such, however, is the accomplishment of the world. The poet cherishes his chagrins and sets his sighs to music. This gall is the tree's "Ode to Dejection."

June 2. 3.30 A.M.—When I awake I hear the low universal chirping or twittering of the chip-birds, like the bursting bead on the surface of the uncorked day. First come, first served! You must taste the first glass of the day's nectar, if you would get all the spirit of it.

4 A.M.—I go to the river in a fog through which I cannot see more than a dozen rods,—three or four times as deep as the houses.

Now I have reached the hilltop above the fog at a quarter to five, about sunrise, and all around me is a sea of fog, level and white, reaching nearly to the top of this hill, only the tops of a few high hills appearing as distant islands in the main. It resembles nothing so much as the ocean. You can get here the impression which the ocean makes, without ever going to the shore. Men—poor simpletons as they are—will go to a panorama by families, to see a Pilgrim's Progress, perchance, who never yet made progress so far as to the top of such a hill as this at the dawn of a foggy morning. All the fog they know is in their brains. The seashore exhibits nothing more grand or on a larger scale. It is as boundless as the view from the highlands of Cape Cod.

Meanwhile my hands are numb with cold and my wet feet ache with it. Now, at 5.15, before this southwest wind, it is already grown thin as gossamer in that direction, and woods and houses are seen through it, while it is heaped up toward the sun, and finally becomes so thick there that for a short time it appears in one place a dark, low cloud, such as else can only be seen from mountains; and now long, dark ridges of wood appear through it, and now the sun reflected from the river makes a bright glow in the fog, and now, at 5.30, I see the green surface of the meadows and the water through the trees, sparkling with bright reflections.

June 4. Saturday. Looked over the oldest town records at the clerk's office this evening, the old book containing grants of land. Am surprised to find such names as "Walden Pond" and "Fair Haven" as early as 1653, and apparently 1652; also, under the first date at least, "Second Division," the rivers as North and South Rivers (no Assabet at that date), "Swamp bridge," apparently on back road, "Goose Pond," "Mr. Flints Pond," "Nutt Meadow," "Willow Swamp," "Spruce Swamp," etc., etc. "Dongy," "Dung Hole," or what-not, appears to be between Walden and Fair Haven. Is Rocky Hill Mr. Emerson's or the Cliffs? Where are South Brook, Frog Ponds, etc., etc., etc.? It is pleasing to read these evergreen wilderness names, *i.e.* of particular swamps and woods, then applied to now perchance cleared fields and meadows said to be redeemed. The Second Division appears to have been a very large tract between the two rivers.

June 7. P.M.—To Walden.

Visited my nighthawk on her nest. Could hardly believe my eyes when I stood within seven feet and beheld her sitting on her eggs, her head to me. She looked so Saturnian, so one with the earth, so sphinx-like, a relic of the reign of Saturn which Jupiter did not destroy, a riddle that might well cause a man to go dash his head against a stone. It was not an actual living creature, far less a winged creature of the air, but a figure in stone or bronze, a fanciful production of art, like the gryphon or phœnix. It was enough to fill one with awe. All the while, this seemingly sleeping bronze sphinx, as motionless as the earth, was watching me with intense anxiety through those narrow slits in its eyelids. Another step, and it fluttered down the hill close to the ground, with a wabbling motion, as if touching the ground now with the tip of one wing, now with the other, so ten rods to the water, which it skimmed close over a few rods, then rose and soared in the air above me. Wonderful creature, which sits motionless on its eggs on the barest, most exposed hills, through pelting storms of rain or hail, as if it were a rock or a part of the earth itself, the outside of the globe, with its eyes shut and its wings folded, and, after the two days' storm, when you think it has become a fit symbol of the rheumatism, it suddenly rises into the air a bird, one of the most aerial, supple, and graceful of creatures, without stiffness in its wings or joints! It was a fit prelude to meeting Prometheus bound to his rock on Caucasus.

June 9. I was amused by the account which Mary, the Irish girl who left us the other day, gave of her experience at Joseph Brown, the milkman's, in the north part of the town. She said that twenty-two lodged in the house the first night, including two pig men, that Mr. Brown kept ten men, had six children and a deaf wife, and one of the men had his wife with him, who helped sew, beside taking care of her own child. Also all the cooking and washing for his father and mother, who live in another house and whom he is bound to carry through, is done in his house, and she, Mary, was the only girl they hired; and the workmen were called up at four by an alarm clock which was set a quarter of an hour ahead of the clock downstairs,—and that more than as much ahead of the town clock,—and she was on her feet from that hour till nine at night. Each man had two pairs of overalls in the wash, and the cans to be scalded were countless. Having got through washing the breakfast dishes by a quarter before twelve, Sunday noon, by Brown's time, she left, no more to return. He had told her that the work was easy, that girls had lived with him to recover their health, and then went away to be married. He is regarded as one of the most enterprising and thrifty farmers in the county, and takes the premiums of the Agricultural Society. He probably exacts too much of his hands.

The steam of the engine streaming far behind is regularly divided, as if it were the vertebræ of a serpent, probably by the strokes of the piston. The reddish seeds or glumes of grasses cover my boots now in the dewy or foggy morning. The first white lily bud.

8 A.M.—To Orchis Swamp; Well Meadow.

I have come with a spy-glass to look at the hawks. They have detected me and are already screaming over my head more than half a mile from the nest. I find no difficulty in looking at the young hawk (there appears to be one only, standing on the edge of the nest), resting the glass in the crotch of a young oak. I can see every wink and the color of its iris. It watches me more steadily than I it, now looking straight down at me with both eyes and outstretched neck, now turning its head and looking with one eye. How its eye and its whole head express anger! Its anger is more in its eye than in its beak. It is quite hoary over the eye and on the chin. The mother meanwhile is incessantly circling about and above its charge and me, farther or nearer, sometimes withdrawing a quarter of a mile, but occasionally coming to alight for a moment almost within gunshot, on the top of a tall white pine; but I hardly bring my glass fairly to bear on her, and get sight of her angry eye through the pine-needles, before she circles away again. Thus for an hour that I lay there, screaming every minute or oftener with open bill. Now and then pursued by a kingbird or a blackbird, who appear merely to annoy it by dashing down at its back. Meanwhile the male is soaring, apparently quite undisturbed, at a great height above, evidently not hunting, but amusing or recreating himself in the thinner and cooler air, as if pleased with his own circles, like a geometer, and enjoying the sublime scene. I doubt if he has his eye fixed on any prey, or the earth. He probably descends to hunt.

Prunella out. The meadows are now yellow with the golden senecio, a more orange yellow, mingled with the light glossy yellow of the buttercup. The green fruit of the sweet-fern now. The *Juniperus repens* appears, though now dry and effete, to have blossomed recently.

The tall white *Erigeron annuus* (?), for this is the only one described as white tinged with purple, just out.*

June 13. 9 A.M.—To Orchis Swamp.

Find that there are two young hawks; one has left the nest and

---

*I think it is *strigosus*, but tinged with purple sometimes.

is perched on a small maple seven or eight rods distant. This one appears much smaller than the former one. I am struck by its large, naked head, so vulture-like, and large eyes, as if the vulture's were an inferior stage through which the hawk passed. Its feet, too, are large, remarkably developed, by which it holds to its perch securely like an old bird, before its wings can perform their office. It has a buff breast, striped with dark brown. Pratt, when I told him of this nest, said he would like to carry one of his rifles down there. But I told him that I should be sorry to have them killed. I would rather save one of these hawks than have a hundred hens and chickens. It was worth more to see them soar especially now that they are so rare in the landscape. It is easy to buy eggs, but not to buy hen-hawks. My neighbors would not hesitate to shoot the last pair of hen-hawks in the town to save a few of their chickens! But such economy is narrow and grovelling. It is unnecessarily to sacrifice the greater value to the less. I would rather never taste chickens' meat nor hens' eggs than never to see a hawk sailing through the upper air again. This sight is worth incomparably more than a chicken soup or a boiled egg. So we exterminate the deer and substitute the hog. It was amusing to observe the swaying to and fro of the young hawk's head to counterbalance the gentle motion of the bough in the wind.

June 14. C. says he saw a "lurker" yesterday in the woods on the Marlborough road. He heard a distressing noise like a man sneezing but long continued, but at length found it was a man wheezing. He was oldish and grizzled, the stumps of his grizzled beard about an inch long, and his clothes in the worst possible condition,—a wretched-looking creature, an escaped convict hiding in the woods, perhaps. He appeared holding on to his paunch, and wheezing as if it would kill him. He appeared to have come straight through the swamp, and—what was most interesting about him, and proved him to be a lurker of the first class,—one of our party, as C. said,— he kept straight through a field of rye which was fully grown, not regarding it in the least; and, though C. tried to conceal himself on the edge of the rye, fearing to hurt his feelings if the man should mistake him for the proprietor, yet they met, and the lurker, giving him a short bow, disappeared in the woods on the opposite side of the road. He went through everything.

June 15. A great fog this morning.

Clover now in its prime. What more luxuriant than a clover-field? The poorest soil that is covered with it looks incomparably fertile. This is perhaps the most characteristic feature of June, resounding with the hum of insects. It is so massive, such a blush on the fields. The rude health of the sorrel cheek has given place to the blush of clover. Painters are wont, in their pictures of Paradise, to strew the ground too thickly with flowers. There should be moderation in all things. Though we love flowers, we do not want them so thick under our feet that we cannot walk without treading on them. But a clover-field in bloom is some excuse for them.

June 17. Here have been three ultra-reformers, lecturers on Slavery, Temperance, the Church, etc., in and about our house and Mrs. Brooks's the last three or four days,—A.D. Foss, once a Baptist minister in Hopkinton, N.H.; Loring Moody, a sort of travelling pattern-working chaplain; and H.C. Wright, who shocks all the old women with his infidel writings. Though Foss was a stranger to the others, you would have thought them old and familiar cronies. (They happened here together by accident.) They addressed each other constantly by their Christian names, and rubbed you continually with the greasy cheeks of their kindness. They would not keep their distance, but cuddle up and lie spoon-fashion with you, no matter how hot the weather nor how narrow the bed,—chiefly Wright. I was awfully pestered with his benignity; feared I should get greased all over with it past restoration; tried to keep some starch in my clothes. He wrote a book called "A Kiss for a Blow," and he behaved as if there were no alternative between these, or as if I had given him a blow. I would have preferred the blow, but he was bent on giving me the kiss, when there was neither quarrel nor agreement between us. I wanted that he should straighten his back, smooth out those ogling wrinkles of benignity about his eyes, and,

with a healthy reserve, pronounce something in a downright manner. It was difficult to keep clear of his slimy benignity, with which
he sought to cover you before he swallowed you and took you fairly
into his bowels. It would have been far worse than the fate of Jo-
nah. I do not wish to get any nearer to a man's bowels than usual.
They lick you as a cow her calf. They would fain wrap you about
with their bowels. W. addressed me as "Henry" within one minute
from the time I first laid eyes on him, and when I spoke, he said
with drawling, sultry sympathy, "Henry, I know all you would say;
I understand you perfectly; you need not explain anything to me;"
and to another, "I am going to dive into Henry's inmost depths." I
said, "I trust you will not strike your head against the bottom." He
could tell in a dark room, with his eyes blinded and in perfect stillness, if there was one there whom he loved. One of the most attractive things about the flowers is their beautiful reserve. The truly
beautiful and noble puts its lover, as it were, at an infinite distance,
while it attracts him more strongly than ever. I do not like the men
who come so near me with their bowels. It is the most disagreeable
kind of snare to be caught in. Men's bowels are far more slimy than
their brains. They must be ascetics indeed who approach you by
this side.

June 18. Saturday. 4 A.M.—By boat to Nawshawtuct; to Azalea
Spring, or Pinxter Spring.

As I was going up the hill, I was surprised to see rising above the
June-grass, near a walnut, a whitish object, like a stone with a white
top, or a skunk erect, for it was black below. It was an enormous
toadstool, or fungus, a sharply conical parasol in the form of a
sugar loaf, slightly turned up at the edges, which were rent half an
inch in every inch or two. The whole height was sixteen inches. The
pileus or cap was six inches long by seven in width at the rim,
though it appeared longer than wide. There was no veil, and the
stem was about one inch in diameter and naked.

It looked much like an old felt hat that is pushed up into a cone
and its rim all ragged and with some meal shaken on to it; in fact,
it was almost big enough for a child's head. It was so delicate and

fragile that its whole cap trembled on the least touch, and, as I could not lay it down without injuring it, I was obliged to carry it home all the way in my hand and erect, while I paddled my boat with one hand. It was a wonder how its soft cone ever broke through the earth. Such growths ally our age to former periods, such as geology reveals. I wondered if it had not some relation to the skunk, though not in odor, yet in its colors and the general impression it made. It suggests a vegetative force which may almost make man tremble for his dominion. It carries me back to the era of the formation of the coal-measures—the age of the saurus and pleiosaurus and when bullfrogs were as big as bulls. Its stem had something massy about it like an oak, large in proportion to the weight it had to support (though not perhaps to the size of the cap), like the vast hollow columns under some piazzas, whose caps have hardly weight enough to hold their tops together. It made you think of parasols of Chinese mandarins; or it might have been used by the great fossil bullfrog in his walks. What part does it play in the economy of the world?

I have just been out (7.30 A.M.) to show my fungus. The milk-man and the butcher followed me to inquire what it was, and children and young ladies addressed me in the street who never spoke to me before. It is so fragile I was obliged to walk at a funereal pace for fear of jarring it. It is so delicately balanced on its stem that it falls to one side across it on the least inclination; falls about like an umbrella that has lost its stays. It is rapidly curling up on the edge, and the rents increasing, until it is completely fringed, and is an inch wider there. It is melting in the sun and light, and black drops and streams falling on my hand and fragments of the black fringed rim falling on the sidewalk. Evidently such a plant can only be seen in perfection in the early morning. It is a creature of the night, like the great moths. They wish me to send it to the first of a series of exhibitions of flowers and fruits to be held at the court-house this afternoon, which I promise to do if it is presentable then. Perhaps it might be placed in the court-house cellar and the company be invited at last to walk down and examine it. Think of placing this giant parasol fungus in the midst of all their roses; yet they admit that it would overshadow and eclipse them all. It is to be remarked that this grew, not in low and damp soil, but high up on the open side of a dry hill, about two rods from a walnut and one from a wall, in the midst of and rising above the thin June-grass. The last night was warm; the earth was very dry, and there was a slight sprinkling of rain.

I believe the 14th was the first day I began to wear my single thin sack in my walk and at night sleep with both windows open; say, when the swamp-pink opens.

I think the blossom of the sweet-briar, now in prime,—eglantine,—is more delicate and interesting than that of the common roses, though smaller and paler and without their spicy fragrance; but its fragrance is in its leaves all summer, and the form of the bush is handsomer, curving over from a considerable height in wreaths sprinkled with numerous flowers. They open out flat soon after sunrise. Flowers whitish in middle, then pinkish-rose inclining to purple toward the edges.

I put the parasol fungus in the cellar to preserve it, but it went on rapidly melting and wasting away from the edges upward, spreading as it dissolved, till it was shaped like a dish cover. By night, though kept in the cellar all the day, there was not more than two of the six inches of the height of the cap left, and the barrel-head beneath it and its own stem looked as if a large bottle of ink had been broken there. It defiled all it touched. Probably one night produced it, and in one day, with all our pains, it wasted away. Is it not a giant mildew or mould? The Pyramids and other monuments of Egypt are a vast mildew or toadstools which have met with no light of day sufficient to waste them away. Slavery is such a mould, and superstition,—which are most rank in the warm and humid portions of the globe. Luxor sprang up one night out of the slime of the Nile. The humblest, puniest weed that can endure the sun is thus superior to the largest fungus, as is the peasant's cabin to those foul temples. It is a temple consecrated to Apis. All things flower, both vices and virtues, but the one is essentially foul, the other fair. In hell, toadstools should be represented as overshadowing men.

At the Flower Exhibition, saw the rhododendron plucked yesterday in Fitzwilliam, N.H. It was the earliest to be found there, and only one bud yet fully open. They say it is in perfection there the 4th of July, nearer Monadnock than the town.

This unexpected display of flowers culled from the gardens of the village suggests how many virtues also are cultivated by the villagers, more than meet the eye.

It would be an interesting subject,—the materials with which different birds line their nests, or, more generally, *construct* them. The hickory catkins, etc., of the cuckoo, the hypnum and large nest of the phœbe.

8.30 P.M.—To Cliffs.

Moon not quite full. There is no motion nor sound in the woods (Hubbard's Grove) along which I am walking. The trees stand like great screens against the sky. The distant village sounds are the barking of dogs, that animal with which man has allied himself, and the rattling of wagons, for the farmers have gone into town a-shopping this Saturday night. The dog is the tamed wolf, as the villager is the tamed savage. But near, the crickets are heard in the grass, chirping from everlasting to everlasting, a mosquito sings near my ear, and the humming of a dor-bug drowns all the noise of the village, so roomy is the universe. The moon comes out of the mackerel cloud, and the traveller rejoices. How can a man write the same thoughts by the light of the moon, resting his book on a rail by the side of a remote potato-field, that he does by the light of the sun, on his study table? The light is but a luminousness. My pencil seems to move through a creamy, mystic medium. The moonlight is rich and somewhat opaque, like cream, but the daylight is thin and blue, like skimmed milk. I am less conscious than in the presence of the sun; my instincts have more influence.

June 21.

The warmest day yet. For the last two days I have worn nothing about my neck. This change or putting off of clothing is, methinks, as good an evidence of the increasing warmth of the weather as meteorological instruments. I thought it was hot weather perchance, when, a month ago, I slept with a window wide open and laid aside a comfortable, but by and by I found that I had got two windows open, and to-night two windows and the door are far from enough.

At sunset to Island.

Between the heavy masses of clouds, mouse-colored, with dark-blue bases, the patches of clear sky are a glorious cobalt blue, as Sophia calls it. How happens it that the sky never appears so intensely, brightly, memorably blue as when seen between clouds and, it may be, as now in the south at sunset? This, too, is like the blue in snow. For the last two or three days it has taken me all the forenoon to wake up.

June 24. There were piles of dried heart-leaf on shore at the bathing-place, a foot high and more. Were they torn up and driven ashore by the wind? I suspect it is the wind in both cases. As storms at sea tear up and cast ashore the seaweeds from the rocks. These are our seaweeds cast ashore in storms, but I see only the eel-grass and the heart-leaf thus served. Our most common in the river appears to be between the *Potamogeton natans* and *pulcher*; it answers to neither, but can be no other described. All these have a strong fresh-water marsh smell, rather agreeable sometimes as a bottle of salts, like the salt marsh and seaweeds, invigorating to my imagination. In our great stream of distilled water going slowly down to ocean to be salted. There are the heart-leaf ponds, but I cannot say the potamo-geton rivers on account of the tautology, and, beside, I do not like this last name,* which signifies that it grows in the neighborhood of rivers, when it is not a neighbor but an indweller. You might as well describe the seaweeds as growing in the neighborhood of the sea.

June 25. Great orange lily beyond stone bridge. Found in the Glade (?) Meadows an unusual quantity of amelanchier berries now in their prime. These are the first berries after strawberries, or the first, and I think the sweetest, *bush* berries. Somewhat like high blueberries, but not so hard. Much eaten by insects, worms, etc. As

---

*[From Greek: *potamo* = river; *geiton* = neighbor.]

big as the largest blueberries or peas. These are the "service-berries" which the Indians of the north and the Canadians use. *La poire* of the latter (*vide* Indian books, No. 6, p. 13). I felt all the while I was picking them, in the low, light, wavy shrubby wood they make, as if I were in a foreign country. Several old farmers say, "Well, though I have lived seventy years, I never saw nor heard of them." I think them a delicious berry, and no doubt they require only to be more abundant every year to be appreciated.

JUNE 28. Nettle out a few days. Pepper-grass, a week or more. Catnep, also, a few days. We have warmer weather now again.

July 1. I am surveying the Bedford road these days, and have no time for my Journal. Saw one of those great pea-green emperor moths, like a bird, fluttering over the top of the woods this forenoon, 10 A.M., near Beck Stow's. Gathered the early red blackberry in the swamp or meadow this side of Pedrick's, where I ran a pole down nine feet.

July 12. White vervain. Checkerberry, maybe some days. Spikenard, not quite yet. The green-flowered lanceolate-leafed orchis at Azalea Brook will soon flower. Wood horse-tail very large and handsome there.

July 21. 2 P.M.—Went, in pursuit of boys who had stolen my boat-seat, to Fair Haven.

July 24. With or without reason, I find myself associating with the idea of summer a certain cellar-like coolness, resulting from the depth of shadows and the luxuriance of foliage. I think that after this date the crops never suffer so severely from drought as in June, because of their foliage shading the ground and producing dews. We had fog this morning, and no doubt often the last three weeks, which my surveying has prevented my getting up to see.

How far behind the spring seems now,—farther off, perhaps, then ever, for this heat and dryness is most opposed to spring.

Where most I sought for flowers in April and May I do not think to go now; it is either drought and barrenness or fall there now. The reign of moisture is long since over. For a long time the year feels the influence of the snows of winter and the long rains of spring, but now how changed! It is like another and a fabulous age to look back on, when earth's veins were full of moisture, and violets burst out on every hillside. Spring is the reign of water; summer, of heat and dryness; winter, of cold. Summer is one long drought. Rain is the exception. All the signs of it fail, for it is dry weather. Though it may seem so, the current year is not peculiar in this respect.

The shaggy hazelnuts now greet the eye, always an agreeable sight to me, with which when a boy I used to take the stains of berries out of my hands and mouth. These and green grapes are found at berry time.

July 25. I have for years had a great deal of trouble with my shoe-strings, because they get untied continually. They are leather, rolled and tied in a hard knot. But some days I could hardly go twenty rods before I was obliged to stop and stoop to tie my shoes. My companion and I speculated on the distance to which one tying would carry you,—the length of a shoe-tie,—and we thought it nearly as appreciable and certainly a more simple and natural measure of distance than a stadium, or league, or mile. Ever and anon we raised our feet on whatever fence or wall or rock or stump we chanced to be passing, and drew the strings once more, pulling as hard as we could. It was very vexatious, when passing through low scrubby bushes, to become conscious that the strings were already getting loose again before we had fairly started. What should we have done if pursued by a tribe of Indians? My companion sometimes went without strings altogether, but that loose way of proceeding was not to be thought of by me. One shoemaker sold us shoe-strings made of the hide of a South American jackass, which he recommended; or rather he gave them to us and added their price to that of the shoes we bought of him. But I could not see that these were any better than the old. I wondered if anybody had exhibited a better article at the World's Fair, and whether England did not bear the palm from America in this respect. I thought of strings with recurved prickles and various other remedies myself. At last the other day it occurred to me that I would try an experiment, and, instead of tying two simple knots one over the other the same way, putting the end which fell to the right over each time, that I would reverse the process, and put it under the other. Greatly to my satisfaction, the experiment was perfectly successful, and from that time my shoe-strings have given me no trouble, except sometimes in untying them at night.

On telling this to others I learned that I had been all the while tying what is called a granny's knot, for I had never been taught to tie any other, as sailors' children are; but now I had blundered into a square knot, I think they called it, or two running slip-nooses. Should not all children be taught this accomplishment, and an hour, perchance, of their childhood be devoted to instruction in tying knots?

Aug. 6. More dog-days.

I see the sunflower's broad disk now in gardens, probably a few days,—a true sun among flowers, monarch of August. Do not the flowers of August and September generally resemble suns and stars?—sunflowers and asters and the single flowers of the golden-rod. I once saw one as big as a milk-pan, in which a mouse had its nest.

I have seen some red leaves on the low choke-berry. Now begins the vintage of their juices. Nature is now a Bacchanal, drunk with the wines of a thousand plants and berries.

Aug. 7. I think that within a week I have heard the alder cricket,— a clearer and shriller sound from the leaves in low grounds, a clear shrilling out of a cool moist shade, an autumnal sound. The year is in the grasp of the crickets, and they are hurling it round swiftly on its axle. Some wasps (I am not sure there's more than one) are building a nest in my room, of mud, these days, buzzing loudly while at work, but at no other time.

Now for the herbs,—the various mints. The pennyroyal is out

abundantly on the hills. I do not scent these things enough. Would it not be worth the while to devote a day to collecting the mountain mint, and another to the peppermint?

How trivial and uninteresting and wearisome and unsatisfactory are all employments for which men will pay you money! The ways by which you may get money all lead downward. To have done anything by which you earned money merely is to have been truly idle. If the laborer gets no more than the wages his employer pays him, he is cheated, he cheats himself. Those services which the world will most readily pay for, it is most disagreeable to render. You are paid for being something less than a man. The state will pay a genius only for some service which it is offensive to him to render. Even the poet-laureate would rather not have to celebrate the accidents of royalty.

Dangle-berries have begun.

It is worth the while to walk in wet weather; the earth and leaves are strewn with pearls.

As I was walking along a hillside the other day, I smelled pennyroyal, but it was only after a considerable search that I discovered a single minute plant, which I had trodden on, the only one near. When, yesterday, a boy spilled his huckleberries in the pasture, I saw that Nature was making use of him to disperse her berries, and I might have advised him to pick another dishful.* The three kinds of epilobium grow rankly where Hubbard burned his swamp this year, also erechthites. I think that I have observed that this last is a true fireweed.

---

*["Then there were huckleberrying parties. These were under the guidance of Thoreau, because he alone knew the precise locality of every variety of the berry. I recall an occasion when little Edward Emerson, carrying a basket of fine huckleberries, had a fall and spilt them all. Great was his distress, and our offers of berries could not console him for the loss of those gathered by himself. But Thoreau came, put his arm around the troubled child, and explained to him that if the crop of huckleberries was to continue it was necessary that some should be scattered. Nature had provided that little boys should now and then stumble and sow the berries. We shall have a grand lot of bushes and berries in this spot, and we shall owe them to you. Edward began to smile."—Moncure Daniel Conway, *Autobiography*, Boston, 1904, vol. I, p. 148.]

Is it not as language that all natural objects affect the poet? He sees a flower or other object, and it is beautiful or affecting to him because it is a symbol of his thought, and what he indistinctly feels or perceives is matured in some other organization. The objects I behold correspond to my mood.

The past has been a remarkably wet week, and now the earth is strewn with fungi. The earth itself is mouldy. I see a white mould in the path.

I was struck by the perfect neatness, as well as elaborateness and delicacy, of a lady's dress the other day. She wore some worked lace or gauze over her bosom, and I thought it was beautiful, if it indicated an equal inward purity and delicacy,—if it was the soul she dressed and treated thus delicately.

Aug. 10. Alcott spent the day with me yesterday. He spent the day before with Emerson. He observed that he had got his wine and now he had come after his venison. Such was the compliment he paid me. The question of a livelihood was troubling him. He knew of nothing which he could do for which men would pay him. He could not compete with the Irish in cradling grain. His early education had not fitted him for a clerkship. He had offered his services to the Abolition Society, to go about the country and speak for freedom as their agent, but they declined him. This is very much to their discredit; they should have been forward to secure him. Such a connection with him would confer unexpected dignity on their enterprise. But they cannot tolerate a man who stands by a head above them. They are as bad—Garrison and Phillips, etc.—as the overseers and faculty of Harvard College. They require a man who will train well *under* them.

Aug. 11. Evening draws on while I am gathering bundles of pennyroyal on the further Conantum height. I find it amid the stubble mixed with blue-curls and, as fast as I get my hand full, tie it into a fragrant bundle. Evening draws on, smoothing the waters and lengthening the shadows, now half an hour or more before sundown. What constitutes the charm of this hour of the day? Is it the condensing of dews in the air just beginning, or the grateful increase of shadows in the landscape?

What shall we name this season?—this very late afternoon, or very early evening, this severe and placid season of the day.

Aug. 12. 9 A.M.—To Conantum by boat, berrying, with three ladies.

Carried watermelons for drink. What more refreshing and convenient! This richest wine in a convenient cask, and so easily kept cool! No foreign wines could be so grateful. The first muskmelon to-day. If you would cool a watermelon, do not put it in water, which keeps the heat in, but cut it open and set it in a cellar or in the shade.* If you have carriage, carry these green bottles of wine.

Aug. 14. In the low woodland paths full of rank weeds, there are countless great fungi of various forms and colors, the produce of the warm rains and muggy weather of a week ago, now rapidly dissolving. One great one, more than a foot in diameter, with a stem 2½+ inches through and 5 inches high, and which has sprung up since I passed here on the 10th, is already sinking like lead into that portion already melted. The ground is covered with foul spots where they have dissolved, and for *most* of my *walk* the air is tainted with a musty, carrion-like odor, in some places very offensive, so that I at first suspected a dead horse or cow. They impress me like humors or pimples on the face of the earth, toddy-blossoms, by which it gets rid of its corrupt blood. A sort of excrement they are. It never occurred to me before to-day that those different forms belong to one species.

Aug. 17. Rain, rain, rain again! Good for grass and apples; said to be bad for potatoes, making them rot; makes the fruit now ripening decay,—apples, etc.

Aug. 18. Rain again.

---

*Or in a draught.

Now again I am caught in a heavy shower in Moore's pitch pines on edge of Great Fields, and am obliged to stand crouching under my umbrella till the drops turn to streams, which find their way through my umbrella, and the path up the hillside is all afloat, a succession of puddles at different levels, each bounded by a ridge of dead pine-needles.

What means this sense of lateness that so comes over one now,—as if the rest of the year were down-hill, and if we had not performed anything before, we should not now? The season of flowers or of promise may be said to be over, and now is the season of fruits; but where is our fruit? The night of the year is approaching. What have we done with our talent? All nature prompts and reproves us. How early in the year it begins to be late! It matters not by how little we have fallen behind; it seems irretrievably late. The year is full of warnings of its shortness, as is life.

XVI.

Aug. 19. Friday. 9 A.M.—To Sudbury by boat with W.E.C.

Cooler weather. Last Sunday we were sweltering here and one hundred died of the heat in New York; to-day they have fires in this village. After more rain, with wind in the night, it is now clearing up cool. A considerable wind wafts us along with our one sail and two umbrellas, sitting in thick coats. I was going to sit and write or mope all day in the house, but it seems wise to cultivate animal spirits, to embark in enterprises which employ and recreate the whole body.

We landed at the first cedar hills above the causeway and ate our dinner and watermelon on them. A great reddish-brown marsh hawk circling over the meadow there. How freshly, beautifully green the landscape after all these rains! The poke-berry ripe.

Aug. 23. Observing the blackness of the foliage, especially between me and the light, I am reminded that it begins in the spring, the dewy dawn of the year, with a silvery hoary downiness, changing to a yellowish or light green,—the saffron-robed morn,—then to a pure, spotless, glossy green with light under sides reflecting the light,—the forenoon,—and now the dark green, or early after-noon, when shadows begin to increase, and next it will turn yellow or red,—the sunset sky,—and finally sere brown and black, when the night of the year sets in.

I am again struck by the perfect correspondence of a day—say an August day—and the year. I think that a perfect parallel may be drawn between the seasons of the day and of the year. Perhaps after middle age man ceases to be interested in the morning and in the spring.

Live in each season as it passes; breathe the air, drink the drink, taste the fruit, and resign yourself to the influences of each. In August live on berries, not dried meats and pemmican, as if you were on shipboard making your way through a waste ocean, or in a northern desert. Be blown on by all the winds. Open all your pores and bathe in all the tides of Nature, in all her streams and oceans, at all seasons. Why, "nature" is but another name for health, and the seasons are but different states of health.

Aug. 26. Saw the comet in the west to-night. It made me think of those imperfect white seeds in a watermelon,—an immature, ineffectual meteor.

Aug. 27. September is at hand; the first month (after the summer heat) with a *burr* to it, month of early frosts; but December will be tenfold rougher. January relents for a season at the time of its thaw, and hence that liquid *r* in its name.

Aug. 29. The 25th and 26th I was surveying Tuttle's farm. The northeast side bounds on the Mill Brook and its tributary and is very irregular. I find, after surveying accurately the windings of several brooks and of the river, that their meanders are not such regular serpentine curves as is commonly supposed, or at least represented. They flow as much in a zigzag as serpentine manner. The eye is very much deceived when standing on the brink, and one who had only surveyed a brook so would be inclined to draw a succession of pretty regular serpentine curves. But, accurately plotted, the regularity disappears, and there are found to be many straight lines and sharp turns. I want no better proof of the inaccuracy of some maps than the regular curving meanders of the streams, made evidently by a sweep of the pen. No, the Meander no doubt flowed in a very crooked channel, but depend upon it, it was as much zigzag as serpentine. This last brook I observed was doubly zigzag, or compoundly zigzag; *i.e.*, there was a zigzag on a large scale including the lesser. To the eye this meadow is perfectly level. Probably all streams are (generally speaking) far more meandering in low and level and soft ground near their mouths, where they flow slowly, than in high and rugged ground which offers more obstacles. The meadow being so level for long distances, no doubt as high in one direction as another, how, I asked myself, did the feeble brook, with all its meandering, ever find its way to the distant lower end? What kind of instinct conducted it forward in the right direction? How unless it is the relict of a lake which once stood high over all these banks, and knew the different levels of its distant shores? How unless a flow which commenced above its level first wore its channel for it? Thus, in regard to most rivers, did not lakes first find their mouths for them, just as the tide now keeps open the mouths of sluggish rivers? And who knows to what extent the sea originally channelled the submerged globe?

Sept. 1. The character of the past month, as I remember, has been, at first, very thick and sultry, dogdayish, the height of summer, and throughout very rainy, followed by crops of toadstools, and latterly, after the dogdays and most copious of the rains, autumnal, somewhat cooler, with signs of decaying or ripening foliage. The month of green corn and melons and plums and the earliest apples,—and now peaches,—of rank weeds. As July, perchance, has its spring side, so August has its autumnal side.

Sept. 2. P.M.—Collected and brought home in a pail of water this afternoon the following asters and diplopappi, going by Turnpike and Hubbard's Close to Saw Mill Brook, and returning by Goose Pond: (1) *A. Tradescanti*, now well under way, most densely flowered, by low roadsides; (2) *dumosus*, perhaps the most prevalent of the small whitish ones, especially in wood-paths; [*etc.—ten more*].

These twelve placed side by side, Sophia and I decided that, regarding only individual flowers, the handsomest was—

1st, *A. patens*, deep bluish-purple ("deep blue-purple" are Gray's very words), large!

2d, *lævis* bright lilac-purple, large.

3d, perhaps *Radula*, pale bluish-purple, turning white, large!
[*Etc. for all 12.*]

The first (*patens*) has broader rays than the second, paler within toward the large handsome yellow disk. Its rough leaves are not so handsome.

The *lævis* is more open and slender-rayed than the last, with a rather smaller disk, but, including its stem and leaves, it is altogether the most delicate and graceful, and I should incline to put it before the last. [*Etc. for all 12.*]

Sept. 7. Yesterday and to-day and day before yesterday, some hours of very warm weather, as oppressive as any in the year, one's thermometer at 93°.

Sept. 11. Sunday. Cool weather. Sit with windows shut, and many by fires. A great change since the 6th, when the heat was so oppressive. The air has got an autumnal coolness which it will not get rid of again.

Signs of frost last night in M. Miles's cleared swamp. Potato vines black. How much farther it is back to frost from the greatest heat of summer, *i.e.* from the 6th back to the 1st of June, three months, than forward to it, four days!

OCT. 12. To-day I have had the experience of borrowing money for a poor Irishman who wishes to get his family to this country. One will never know his neighbors till he has carried a subscription paper among them. Ah! it reveals many and sad facts to stand in this relation to them. To hear the selfish and cowardly excuses some make,—that *if* they help any they must help the Irishman who lives with them,—and him they are sure never to help! Others, with whom public opinion weighs, will think of it, trusting you never will raise the sum and so they will not be called on again; who give stingily after all. What a satire in the fact that you are much more inclined to call on a certain slighted and so-called crazy woman in moderate circumstances rather than on the president of the bank! But some are generous and save the town from the distinction which threatened it, and *some* even who do not lend, plainly would if they could.

Oct. 20. How pleasant to walk over beds of these fresh, crisp, and rustling fallen leaves,—young hyson, green tea, clean, crisp, and wholesome! How beautiful they go to their graves! how gently lay themselves down and turn to mould!—painted of a thousand hues and fit to make the beds of us living. So they troop to their graves, light and frisky. They put on no weeds.

Oct. 22. A week or more of fairest Indian summer ended last night, for to-day it rains. It was so warm day before yesterday, I worked in my shirt-sleeves in the woods.

I cannot easily dismiss the subject of the fallen leaves. How densely they cover and conceal the water for several feet in width, under and amid the alders and button-bushes and maples along the shore of the river,—still light, tight, and dry boats, dense cities of boats, their fibres not relaxed by the waters, undulating and rustling with every wave, of such various pure and delicate, though fading, tints,—of hues that might make the fame of teas,—dried on great Nature's coppers. And then see this great fleet of scattered leaf boats, still tight and dry, each one curled up on every side by the sun's skill, like boats of hide, scarcely moving in the sluggish current,—like the great fleets with which you mingle on entering some great mart, some New York which we are all approaching together.

Consider what a vast crop is thus annually shed upon the earth. This, more than any mere grain or seed, is the great harvest of the year. This annual decay and death, this dying by inches, before the whole tree at last lies down and turns to soil. As trees shed their leaves, so deer their horns, and men their hair or nails. The year's great crop. They teach us how to die. How many flutterings before they rest quietly in their graves! By what subtle chemistry they will mount up again, climbing by the sap in the trees.

For beautiful variety can any crop be compared with them?

Yesterday, toward night, gave Sophia and mother a sail as far as the Battle-Ground. One-eyed John Goodwin, the fisherman, was loading into a hand-cart and conveying home the piles of drift-wood which of late he had collected with his boat. It was a beauti-ful evening, and a clear amber sunset lit up all the eastern shores; and that man's employment, so simple and direct,—though he is regarded by most as a vicious character,—whose whole motive was so easy to fathom,—thus to obtain his winter's wood,—charmed me unspeakably. So much do we love actions that are simple. They are all poetic. We, too, would fain be so employed. So unlike the pursuits of most men, so artificial or complicated. Consider how the broker collects his winter's wood, what sport he makes of it, what is his boat and hand-cart! Postponing instant life, he makes haste to Boston in the cars, and there deals in stocks, not quite relishing his employment,—and so earns the money with which he buys his fuel. And when, by chance, I meet him about this indirect and complicated business, I am not struck with the beauty of his employment. It does not harmonize with the sunset. How much more the former consults his genius, some genius at any rate!

No *trade* is simple, but artificial and complex. It postpones life and substitutes death. It goes against the grain. The oldest, wisest politician grows not more human so, but is merely a gray wharf rat at last. He makes a habit of disregarding the moral right and wrong for the legal or political, commits a slow suicide, and thinks to re-cover by retiring on to a farm at last. This simplicity it is, and the vigor it imparts, that enables the simple vagabond, though he does get drunk and is sent to the house of correction so often, to hold up his head among men.

Oct. 23. Sunday. I find my clothes all bristling as with a *chevaux-de-frise* of beggar-ticks, which hold on for many days. A storm of ar-rows these weeds have showered on me, as I went through their moats. How irksome the task to rid one's self of them! We are fain to let some adhere. Through thick and thin I wear some; hold on many days. In an instant a thousand seeds of the bidens fastened themselves firmly to my clothes, and I carried them for miles, planting one here and another there. They are as thick on my clothes as the teeth of a comb.

It is the season of fuzzy seeds,—goldenrods, everlasting, senecio, asters, epilobium, etc., etc. *Viburnum Lentago*, with ripe berries and dull-glossy red leaves; young black cherry, fresh green or yellow; mayweed. The chestnuts have mostly fallen. One *Diplopappus linariifolius* in bloom, its leaves all yellow or red. This and *A. undulatus* the asters seen to-day.

The red oak now red, perhaps inclining to scarlet; the white, with that peculiar ingrained redness; the shrub oak, a clear thick leather-color; some dry black oak, darker brown; chestnut, light brown; hickory, yellow, turning brown. These the colors of some leaves I brought home.

Oct. 24. It has rained all day, filling the streams. Just after dark, high southerly winds arise, but very warm, blowing the rain against the windows and roof and shaking the house. It is very dark withal, so that I can hardly find my way to a neighbor's. We think of vessels on the coast, and shipwrecks, and how this will bring down the remaining leaves and to-morrow morning the street will be strewn with rotten limbs of the elms amid the leaves and puddles, and some loose chimney or crazy building will have fallen. Some fear to go to bed, lest the roof be blown off.

Oct. 26. I well remember the time this year when I first heard the dream of the toads. I was laying out house-lots on Little River in Haverhill. We had had some raw, cold and wet weather. But this day was remarkably warm and pleasant, and I had thrown off my outside coat. I was going home to dinner, past a shallow pool, which was green with springing grass, and where a new house was about being erected, when it occurred to me that I heard the dream of the toad. It rang through and filled all the air, though I had not heard it once. And I turned my companion's attention to it, but he did not appear to perceive it as a new sound in the air. Loud and prevailing as it is, most men do not notice it at all. It is to them, perchance, a sort of simmering or seething of all nature. That afternoon the dream of the toads rang through the elms by Little River and affected the thoughts of men, though they were not conscious that they heard it.

How watchful we must be to keep the crystal well that we were made, clear!—that it be not made turbid by our contact with the world, so that it will not reflect objects. What other liberty is there worth having, if we have not freedom and peace in our minds,—if our inmost and most private man is but a sour and turbid pool? Often we are so jarred by chagrins in dealing with the world, that we cannot reflect.

Ah! the world is too much with us, and our whole soul is stained by what it works in, like the dyer's hand. A man had better starve at once than lose his innocence in the process of getting his bread.

It is surprising how any reminiscence of a different season of the year affects us. When I meet with any such in my Journal, it affects me as poetry, and I appreciate that other season and that particular phenomenon more than at the time. The world so seen is all one spring, and full of beauty. You only need to make a faithful record of an average summer day's experience and summer mood, and read it in the winter, and it will carry you back to more than that summer day alone could show. Only the rarest flower, the purest melody, of the season thus comes down to us.

When, after feeling dissatisfied with my life, I aspire to something better, am more scrupulous, more reserved and continent, as if expecting somewhat, suddenly I find myself full of life as a nut of meat,—am overflowing with a quiet, genial mirthfulness. I think to myself, I must attend to my diet; I must get up earlier and take a morning walk; I must have done with luxuries and devote myself to my muse. So I dam up my stream, and my waters gather to a head. I am freighted with thought.

Oct. 27. Some less obvious and commonly unobserved signs of the progress of the seasons interest me most, like the loose, dangling catkins of the hop-hornbeam or of the black or yellow birch. I can recall distinctly to my mind the image of these things, and that time in which they flourished is glorious as if it were before the fall of man. I see all nature for the time under this aspect. These features are particularly prominent; as if the first object I saw on approaching this planet in the spring was the catkins of the hop-hornbeam on the hillsides. As I sailed by, I saw the yellowish waving sprays.

Oct. 28. Rain in the night and this morning, preparing for winter.

For a year or two past, my *publisher*, falsely so called, has been writing from time to time to ask what disposition should be made of the copies of "A Week on the Concord and Merrimack Rivers" still on hand, and at last suggesting that he had use for the room they occupied in his cellar. So I had them all sent to me here, and they have arrived to-day by express, filling the man's wagon,—706 copies out of an edition of 1000 which I bought of Munroe four years ago and have been ever since paying for, and have not quite paid for yet. The wares are sent to me at last, and I have an opportunity to examine my purchase. They are something more substantial than fame, as my back knows, which has borne them up two flights of stairs to a place similar to that to which they trace their origin. Of the remaining two hundred and ninety and odd, seventy-five were given away, the rest sold. I have now a library of nearly nine hundred volumes, over seven hundred of which I wrote myself. Is it not well that the author should behold the fruits of his labor? My works are piled up on one side of my chamber half as high as my head, my *opera omnia*. This is authorship; these are the work of my brain. There was just one piece of good luck in the venture. The unbound were tied up by the printer four years ago in stout paper wrappers, and inscribed,—

H. D. Thoreau's

Concord River

50 cops.

So Munroe had only to cross out "River" and write "Mass." and deliver them to the expressman at once. I can see now what I write for, the result of my labors.

Nevertheless, in spite of this result, sitting beside the inert mass of my works, I take up my pen to-night to record what thought or experience I may have had, with as much satisfaction as ever. Indeed, I believe that this result is more inspiring and better for me than if a thousand had bought my wares. It affects my privacy less and leaves me freer.

Oct. 31. 7 A.M.—By river to Nawshawtuct.

The flood and wind have washed up great quantities of cranberries loosened by the rake, which now line the shore, mixed with the wrecked grass and weeds. We gathered five quarts, partly frostbitten.

I slowly discover that this is a gossamer day. I first see the fine lines stretching from one weed or grass stem or rush to another, sometimes seven or eight feet distant, horizontally and only four or five inches above the water. When I look further, I find that they are everywhere and on everything, sometimes forming conspicuous fine white gossamer webs on the heads of grasses, or suggesting an Indian bat. They are so abundant that they seem to have been suddenly produced in the atmosphere by some chemistry,—spun out of air,—I know not for what purpose. These gossamer lines are not visible unless between you and the sun. We pass some black willows, now of course quite leafless, and when they are between us and the sun they are so completely covered with these fine cobwebs or lines, mainly parallel to one another, that they make one solid woof, a misty woof, against the sun. They are not drawn taut, but curved downward in the middle, like the rigging of vessels,—the ropes which stretch from mast to mast,—as if the fleets of a thousand Lilliputian nations were collected one behind another under bare poles. But when we have floated a few feet further, and thrown the willow out of the sun's range, not a thread can be seen on it.

I am at a loss to say what purpose they serve, and am inclined to think that they are to some extent attached to objects as they float through the atmosphere; for I noticed, before I had gone far, that my grape-vines in a basket in the boat had got similar lines stretching from one twig to another, a foot or two, having undoubtedly caught them as we paddled along. It might well be an electric phenomenon. The air appeared crowded with them. It was a wonder they did not get into the mouth and nostrils, or that we did not feel them on our faces, or continually going and coming amid them did not whiten our clothes more. And yet one with his back to the sun, walking the other way, would observe nothing of all this. Only stand so as to bring the south side of any tree, bush, fence, or other object between you and the sun. Methinks it is only on these very finest days late in autumn that this phenomenon is seen, as if that fine vapor of the morning were spun into these webs.

According to Kirby and Spence, "in Germany these flights of gossamer appear so constantly in autumn that they are there metaphorically called 'Der fliegender Sommer' (the flying or departing summer)." What can possess these spiders thus to run all at once to every the least elevation, and let off this wonderful stream? Sophia thought that thus at last they emptied themselves and wound up, or, I suggested, unwound, themselves,—cast off their mortal coil. It looks like a mere frolic spending and wasting of themselves, of their vigor, now that there is no further use for it, their prey, perchance, being killed or banished by the frost.

Nov. 1. 6.30 A.M.—To Hubbard's Bridge to see the gossamer.

About three weeks ago my indignation was roused by hearing that one of my townsmen, notorious for meanness, was endeavoring to get and keep a premium of four dollars which a poor Irish laborer whom he hired had gained by fifteen minutes' spading at our Agricultural Fair. To-night a free colored woman is lodging at our house, whose errand to the North is to get money to buy her husband, who is a slave to one Moore in Norfolk, Virginia. She persuaded Moore, though not a kind master, to buy him that he might not be sold further South. Moore paid six hundred dollars for him, but asks her eight hundred. My most natural reflection was that he was even meaner than my townsman. As mean as a slaveholder!

Nov. 3. Heard a bluebird about a week ago.

There are very few phenomena which can be described indifferently as occurring at different seasons of the year, for they will occur with some essential difference.

A warm westerly wind, the sky concealed and a storm gathering. A sober, cloudy afternoon. To-day I see yarrow, very bright; red clover; autumnal dandelion; the silvery potentilla, and one *Canadensis*; and the *Norvegica*; and a dandelion; *Veronica arvensis*; and gnawel; one *Aster lœvis* (!) by the Hosmer Ditch; and, to my surprise, that solidago of September 11th, still showing some fresh yellow petals and a very fresh stem and leaves.

I make it my business to extract from Nature whatever nutriment she can furnish me, though at the risk of endless iteration. I milk the sky and the earth.

Nov. 6. Still the Canada snapdragon, yarrow, autumnal dandelion, tansy, shepherd's-purse, silvery cinquefoil, witch-hazel.

The witch-hazel spray is peculiar and interesting, with little knubs at short intervals, zigzag, crinkle-crankle. How happens it? Did the leaves grow so close? The bud is long against the stem, with a neck to it.

Nov. 8. 10 A.M.—Our first snow, the wind southerly, the air chilly and moist; a very fine snow, looking like a mist toward the woods or horizon, which at 2 o'clock has not whitened the ground. The children greet it with a shout when they come out at recess.

Nov. 12. I cannot but regard it as a kindness in those who have the steering of me that, by the want of pecuniary wealth, I have been nailed down to this my native region so long and steadily, and made to study and love this spot of earth more and more. What would signify in comparison a thin and diffused love and knowledge of the whole earth instead, got by wandering? The traveller's is but a barren and comfortless condition. It is insignificant, and a merely negative good fortune, to be provided with thick garments against cold and wet, an unprofitable, weak, and defensive condition, compared with being able to extract some exhilaration, some warmth even, out of cold and wet themselves, and to clothe them with our sympathy. The rich man buys woollens and furs, and sits naked and shivering still in spirit, besieged by cold and wet. But the poor Lord of Creation, cold and wet he makes to warm him, and be his garments.

Tasted to-day a black walnut, a spherical and corrugated nut with a large meat, but of a strong oily taste.

NOV. 13. Rain all day.

Nov. 15. After having some business dealings with men, I am occasionally chagrined, and feel as if I had done some wrong, and it is hard to forget the ugly circumstance. I see that such intercourse long continued would make one thoroughly prosaic, hard, and coarse. But the longest intercourse with Nature, though in her rudest moods, does not thus harden and make coarse. A hard, insensible man whom we liken to a rock is indeed much harder than a rock. From hard, coarse, insensible men with whom I have no sympathy, I go to commune with the rocks, whose hearts are comparatively soft.

Together with the barberry, I dug up a brake root by chance. This, too, should have gone into the witches' caldron. It is large and black, almost like a cinder without, and within curiously black and white in parallel fibres, with a sort of mildewiness as if it were rotting; yet fresh shoots are ready for the spring with a cottony point.

This afternoon has wanted no condition to make it a gossamer day, it seems to me, but a calm atmosphere. Plainly the spiders cannot be abroad on the water unless it is smooth. The one I witnessed this fall was at time of flood. May it be that they are driven out of their retreats like muskrats and snow-fleas, and spin these lines for their support?

I see many cranberries on the vines at the bottom, making a great show. It might be worth the while, where possible, to flood a cranberry meadow as soon as they are ripe and before the frosts, and so preserve them plump and sound till spring.

NOV. 18. Conchologists call those shells "which are fished up from the depths of the ocean" and are never seen on the shore, which are the rarest and most beautiful, *Pelagii*, but those which are cast on shore and are never so delicate and beautiful as the former, on account of exposure and abrasion, *Littorales*. So it is with the thoughts of poets: some are fresh from the deep sea, radiant with unimagined beauty,—*Pelagii*; but others are comparatively worn, having been tossed by many a tide,—*Littorales*,—scaled off, abraded, and eaten by worms.

Nov. 19. What is the peculiarity of the Indian summer? From the 14th to the 21st October inclusive, this year, was perfect Indian summer; and this day the next? Methinks that any particularly pleasant and warmer weather after the middle of October is thus called. Has it not fine, calm spring days answering to it? Autumnal dandelion quite fresh. Tansy very fresh yesterday.

Nov. 20. What enhances my interest in dew—I am thinking of the summer—is the fact that it is so distinct from rain, formed most abundantly after bright, starlit nights, a product especially of the clear, serene air. That nightly rain called dew, which gathers and falls in so low a stratum that our heads tower above it like mountains in an ordinary shower. A writer in *Harper's Magazine* (vol. vii, page 505) says that the mist at evening does not rise, "but gradually forms higher up in the air." He calls it the moisture of the air become visible. Says there is most dew in clear nights, because clouds prevent the cooling down of the air; they radiate the heat of the earth back to it; and that a strong wind, by keeping the air in motion, prevents its heat from passing off. Therefore, I proceed, for a plentiful dew it must not only be clear but calm. The above writer says bad conductors of heat have always most dew on them, and that wool or swan's-down is "good for experimenting on the quantity of dew falling,"—weight before and after. Thinks it not safe to walk in clear nights, especially after midnight, when the dew is most abundantly forming; better in cloudy nights, which are drier. Also thinks it not prudent to venture out until the sun begins to rise and warms the air. But methinks this prudence begets a tenderness that will catch more cold at noonday than the opposite hardiness at midnight.

Nov. 22. I see still, here and there, a few deep-sunk yellow and de-cayed pads, the bleared, dulled, drowned eyes of summer.

I was just thinking it would be fine to get a specimen leaf from each changing tree and shrub and plant in autumn, in September and October, when it had got its brightest characteristic color, the intermediate ripeness in its transition from the green to the russet or brown state, outline and copy its color exactly with paint in a book,—a book which should be a memorial of October, be entitled October Hues or Autumnal Tints. I remember especially the beau-tiful yellow of the *Populus grandidentata* and the tint of the scarlet maple. What a memento such a book would be, beginning with the earliest reddening of the leaves, woodbine and ivy, etc., etc., and the lake of radical leaves, down to the latest oaks! I might get the impression of their veins and outlines in the summer with lampblack, and after color them.

Nov. 24. At noon, after a drizzling forenoon, the weather suddenly changed to clear and wintry, freezing cold with strong wind from a northerly quarter. It seems like the beginning of winter. Ice forms in my boat at 5 P.M., and what was mud in the street is fast becom-ing a rigid roughness.

Nov. 27. Now a man will eat his heart, if ever, now while the earth is bare, barren and cheerless, and we have the coldness of winter without the variety of ice and snow; but methinks the variety and compensation are in the stars now. How bright they are now by contrast with the dark earth! The days are short enough now. The sun is already setting before I have reached the ordinary limit of my walk, but the 21st of next month the day will be shorter still by about twenty-five minutes.

It is too cold to-day to use a paddle; the water freezes on the handle and numbs my fingers.

Dec. 5. P.M.—Got my boat in. The river frozen over thinly in most places and whitened with snow, which was sprinkled on it this noon.

It is a startling thought that the Assyrian king who with so much pains recorded his exploits in stone at Nineveh, that the story might come down to a distant generation, has indeed succeeded by those means which he used. All was not vanity, quite.

DEC. 10. Another still more glorious day, if possible; Indian-summery even. These are among the finest days in the year, on account of the wholesome bracing coolness and clearness.

Paddled Cheney's boat up Assabet.

Passed in some places between shooting ice-crystals, extending from both sides of the stream. Upon the thinnest black ice-crystals, just cemented, was the appearance of broad fern leaves, or ostrich-plumes, or flat fir trees with branches bent down. The surface was far from even, rather in sharp-edged plaits or folds. The form of the crystals was oftenest that of low, flattish, three-sided pyramids; when the base was very broad the apex was imperfect, with many irregular rosettes of small and perfect pyramids, the largest with bases equal to two or three inches. All this appeared to advantage only while the ice (one twelfth of an inch thick, perhaps) rested on the black water.

What I write about at home I understand so well, comparatively! and I write with such repose and freedom from exaggeration.

Dec. 22. Surveying the last three days. They have not yielded much that I am aware of. All I find is old bound-marks, and the slowness and dullness of farmers reconfirmed. They even complain that I walk too fast for them. This coarse and hurried outdoor work compels me to live grossly or be inattentive to my diet; that is the worst of it. Like work, like diet; that, I find, is the rule. Left to my chosen pursuits, I should never drink tea nor coffee, nor eat meat. The diet of any class or generation is the natural result of its employment and locality. It is remarkable how unprofitable it is for the most part to talk with farmers. They commonly stand on their good behavior and attempt to moralize or philosophize in a serious conversation. Sportsmen and loafers are better company. For society a man must not be too *good* or well-disposed, to spoil his natural disposition. The bad are frequently good enough to let you see how bad they are, but the good as frequently endeavor to get between you and themselves.

I have dined out five times and tea'd once within a week. Four times there was tea on the dinner-table, always meat, but once baked beans, always pie, but no puddings. I suspect tea has taken the place of cider with farmers. I am reminded of Haydon the painter's experience when he went about painting the nobility. I go about to the houses of the farmers and squires in like manner. This is my portrait-painting,—when I would fain be employed on higher subjects. I have offered myself much more earnestly as a lecturer than a surveyor. Yet I do not get any employment as a lecturer; was not invited to lecture once last winter, and only once (without pay) this winter. But I can get surveying enough, which a hundred others in this county can do as well as I, though it is not boasting much to say that a hundred others in New England cannot lecture as well as I on my themes. But they who do not make the highest demand on you shall rue it. It is because they make a low demand on themselves. All the while that they use only your humbler faculties, your higher unemployed faculties, like an invisible cimetar, are cutting them in twain. Woe be to the generation that lets any higher faculty in its midst go unemployed! That is to deny God and know him not, and he, accordingly, will know not of them.

DEC. 27. High wind with more snow in the night. The snow is damp and covers the panes, darkening the room. At first I did not know that more snow had fallen, it was so drifted. Snowy ridges cross the village street and make it look as wild and bleak as a pass of the Rocky Mountains or the Sierra Nevada.

P.M.—To Fair Haven Pond up meadows and river.

The snow blows like spray, fifteen feet high, across the fields, while the wind roars in the trees as in the rigging of a vessel. It is altogether like the ocean in a storm. The wind, eddying through and over the wall, is scooping it out in fantastic forms,—shells and troughs and glyphs of all kinds. Sometimes the drift is pierced with many holes as big as one's fist, where the fine snow-drift is passing through like steam. As it flows over, it builds out eaves to the bank of razor sharpness.

It is surprising what things the snow betrays. I had not seen a meadow mouse all summer, but no sooner does the snow come and spread its mantle over the earth than it is printed with the tracks of countless mice and larger animals. I see where the mouse has dived into a little hole in the snow, not larger than my thumb, by the side of a weed, and a yard further reappeared again, and so on alternately above and beneath. A snug life it lives. The crows come nearer to the houses, alight on trees by the roadside, apparently being put to it for food. I saw them yesterday also.

The wind has now shaken the snow from the trees, and it lies in irregular little heaps on the snow beneath, except that there is a white ridge up and down their trunks on the northwest side, showing which side the storm came from, which, better than the moss, would enable one to find his way in the night. It is a true winter sunset, almost cloudless, clear, cold indigo-y along the horizon. The evening (?) star is seen shining brightly, before the twilight has begun. A rosy tint suffuses the eastern horizon. The outline of the mountains is wonderfully distinct and hard, and they are a dark blue and very near. Wachusett looks like a right whale over our bow, plowing the continent, with his flukes well down. He has a vicious look, as if he had a harpoon in him.

I wish that I could buy at the shops some kind of india-rubber that would rub out at once all that in my writing which it now costs me so many perusals, so many months if not years, and so much reluctance, to erase.

Dec. 29. All day a driving snow-storm, imprisoning most, stopping the cars, blocking up the roads. No school to-day. I cannot see a house fifty rods off from my window through;* yet in midst of all I see a bird, probably a tree sparrow, partly blown, partly flying, over

---

*In an ordinary snow-storm, when snowing fast, Jan. 1st, '54, I can see E. Wood's house, or about a mile.

the house to alight in a field. The snow penetrates through the smallest crevices under doors and side of windows.

P.M.—Tried my snow-shoes. They sink deeper than I expected, and I throw the snow upon my back. When I returned, twenty minutes after, my great tracks were not to be seen. It is the worst snow-storm to bear that I remember. The strong wind from the north blows the snow almost horizontally, and, beside freezing you, almost takes your breath away. The driving snow blinds you, and where you are protected, you can see but little way, it is so thick. Yet in spite, or on account, of all, I see the first flock of arctic snowbirds (*Emberiza nivalis*) near the depot, white and black, with a sharp, whistle-like note. An hour after I discovered half a pint of snow in each pocket of my greatcoat.

What a contrast between the village street now and last summer! The leafy elms then resounding with the warbling vireo, robins, bluebirds, and the fiery hangbird, etc., to which the villagers, kept indoors by the heat, listen through open lattices. Now it is like a street in Nova Zembla,—if they were to have any there. I wade to the post-office as solitary a traveller as ordinarily in a wood-path in winter. The snow is mid-leg deep, while drifts as high as one's head are heaped against the houses and fences, and here and there range across the street like snowy mountains. There is not a track leading from any door to indicate that the inhabitants have been forth today, any more than there is track of any quadruped by the wood-paths. It is all pure untrodden snow, banked up against the houses now at 4 P.M., and no evidence that a villager has been abroad today. In one place the drift covers the front-yard fence and stretches thence upward to the top of the front door, shutting all in, and frequently the snow lies banked up three or four feet high against the front doors, and the windows are all snowed up, and there is a drift over each window, and the clapboards are all hoary with it. It is as if the inhabitants were all frozen to death, and now you threaded the desolate streets weeks after that calamity. Yet they are warmer, merrier than ever there within. At the post-office they ask each traveller news of the cars,—"Is there any train up or down?"— or how deep the snow is on a level.

The thoughts and associations of summer and autumn are now as completely departed from our minds as the leaves are blown from the trees. Some withered deciduous ones are left to rustle, and our cold immortal evergreens. Some lichenous thoughts still adhere to us.

Dec. 31. Walden froze completely over last night. It is, however, all snow ice, as it froze while it was snowing hard, and it looks like frozen yeast somewhat. I waded about in the woods through the snow, which certainly averaged considerably more than two feet deep where I went. It stuck to my clothes and melted, and so was more inconvenient than yesterday. Saw probably an otter's track, very broad and deep, as if a log had been drawn along. It was nearly as obvious as a man's track. It was made before last night's snow fell. The creature from time to time went beneath the snow for a few feet, to the leaves. This animal probably I should never see the least trace of, were it not for the snow, the great revealer.

Jan. 1. The drifts mark the standstill or equilibrium between the currents of air or particular winds. In our greatest snow-storms, the wind being northerly, the greatest drifts are on the south sides of the houses and fences and accordingly on the left-hand side of the street going down it. I notice that in the angle made by our house and shed, a southwest exposure, the snow-drift does not lie close about the pump, but is a foot off, forming a circular bowl, showing that there was an eddy about it. It shows where the wind has been, the form of the wind. The snow is like a mould, showing the form of the eddying currents of air which have been impressed on it, while the drift and all the rest is that which fell between the currents or where they counterbalanced each other. These boundary lines are mountain barriers.

The snow is the great betrayer. It not only shows the tracks of mice, otters, etc., etc., which else we should rarely if ever see, but the tree sparrows are more plainly seen against its white ground, and they in turn are attracted by the dark weeds which it reveals. It also drives the crows and other birds out of the woods to the villages for food. If one could detect the meaning of the snow, would he not be on the trail of some higher life that has been abroad in the night? Are there not hunters who seek for something higher than foxes? Is the great snow of use to the hunter only, and not to the saint, or him who is earnestly building up a life? Do the Indian and hunter only need snow-shoes, while the saint sits indoors in embroidered slippers?

The Indians might have imagined a large snow bunting to be the genius of the storm.

This morning it is snowing again fast, and about six inches has already fallen by 10 A.M., of a moist and heavy snow.

I would fain be a fisherman, hunter, farmer, preacher, etc., but fish, hunt, farm, preach other things than usual.

Jan. 2. I noticed yesterday that the damp snow, falling gently without wind on the top of front-yard posts, had quite changed the style of their architecture,—to the dome style of the East, a four-sided base becoming a dome at top. I observe other revelations made by the snow. The team and driver have long since gone by, but I see the marks of his whip-lash on the snow,—its recoil,—but alas! these are not a complete tally of the strokes which fell upon the oxen's back. The unmerciful driver thought perchance that no one saw him, but unwittingly he recorded each blow on the un-spotted snow behind his back as in the book of life. To more searching eyes the marks of his lash are in the air.

Jan. 9. P.M.—To Heywood's Pond with Tappan.

T. has a singularly elastic step. He will run through the snow, lifting his knees like a child who enjoys the motion. When he slumped once through to water and called my attention to it, with an indescribable flash of his eye, he reminded me forcibly of Hawthorne's little son Julian. He used the greatest economy in speech of any man I know. Speaks low, beside, and without emphasis; in monosyllables. I cannot guess what the word was for a long time.

Jan. 10. When we were walking last evening, Tappan admired the soft rippling of the Assabet under Tarbell's bank. One could have lain all night under the oaks there listening to it. Westward forty rods, the surface of the stream reflected a silvery whiteness, but gradually darkened thence eastward, till beneath us it was almost quite black.

What you can recall of a walk on the second day will differ from what you remember on the first day, as the mountain chain differs in appearance, looking back the next day, from the aspect it wore when you were at its base, or generally, as any view changes to one who is journeying amid mountains when he has increased the distance.

With Tappan, his speech is frequently so frugal and reserved, in monosyllables not fairly uttered clear of his thought, that I doubt if he did not cough merely, or let it pass for such, instead of asking what he said or meant, for fear it might turn out that he coughed merely.

I mistook the creaking of a tree in the woods the other day for the scream of a hawk. How numerous the resemblances of the animate to the inanimate!

Jan. 11. The north side of all stubble, weeds, and trees, and the whole forest is covered with a hoar frost a quarter to a half inch deep. It is easily shaken off. The air is still full of mist. No snow has fallen, but, as it were, the vapor has been caught by the trees like a cobweb. The trees are bright hoary forms, the ghosts of trees. In fact, the warm breath of the earth is frozen on its beard. Closely examined or at a distance, it is just like the sheaf-like forms of vegetation and the diverging crystals on the window-panes. Even birds' nests have a white beard.

Birches, especially, are the trees for these hoar frosts and also for glazes. They are so thickly twigged and of such graceful forms and attitudes. I can distinguish a birch now further off than ever. As I stand by its north side (Hubbard's Grove), almost the whole forest is concealed by the hoar frost. It is as if the mist had been caught on an invisible net spread in the air. Yet the white is tinged with the ground color of reddish oak leaves and even green pine-needles. Nature is now gone into her winter palace.

The humblest weed is indescribably beautiful, of purest white and richest form. The hogweed becomes a fairy's wand. The blue-curls, rising from bare gray sand, is perhaps particularly beautiful. Every part of the plant is concealed. Its expression is changed or greatly enriched by this exaggeration or thickening of the mere linear original. It is an exquisitely delicate frost plant, trembling like swan's-down. As if Nature had sprinkled her breast with down this cold season. The character of each tree and weed is rendered with spirit,—the pine plumes and the cedar spires. All this you see going from north to south; but, going the other way (*perchance?*), you might not be struck with the aspect of the woods.

Jan. 13. I saw yesterday my snow-shoe tracks quite distinct, though made January 2d. Though they pressed the snow down four or five inches, they consolidated it, and it now endures and is two or three inches above the general level there, and more white.

Jan. 14. Cato makes the vineyard of first importance to a farm; second, a well-watered garden; third, a willow plantation (*salictum*); fourth, an olive-yard (*oletum*); fifth, a meadow or grass ground (?) (*pratum*); sixth, a grain-field ortillage (?) (*campus frumentarius*); seventh, a copsewood (?) for fuel (?) (*silva caedua*) (Varro speaks of planting and cultivating this); eighth, an arbustum (Columella says it is a plantation of elms, etc., for vines to rest on) (*arbustum*); ninth, a wood that yields mast (*glandaria silva*). He says elsewhere the *arbustum* yields *ligna et virgae*.

He says: "In earliest manhood the master of a family must study to plant his ground; as for building he must think a long time about it (*diu cogitare*); he must not think about planting, but do it. When he gets to be thirty-six years old, then let him build, if he has his ground planted. So build, that the villa may not have to seek the farm, nor the farm the villa." This contains sound advice, as pertinent now as ever.

"If you have done one thing late, you will do all your work late," says Cato to the farmer.

Jan. 22. Once or twice of late I have seen the mother-o'-pearl tints and rainbow flocks in the western sky. The usual time is when the air is clear and pretty cool, about an hour before sundown. Yesterday I saw a very permanent specimen, like a long knife-handle of mother-of-pearl, very pale with an interior blue and rosaceous tinges. Methinks the summer sky never exhibits this so finely.

When I was at C.'s the other evening, he punched his cat with the poker because she purred too loud for him.

No second snow-storm in the winter can be so fair and interesting as the first. Last night was very windy, and to-day I see the dry oak leaves collected in thick beds in the little hollows of the snow-crust. These later falls of the leaf.

Jan. 27. I have an old account-book, found in Deacon R. Brown's garret since his death. The first leaf or two is gone. Its cover is brown paper, on which, amid many marks and scribblings, I find written:—

> "Mr. Ephraim Jones
> His Wast Book
> Anno Domini
> 1742"

It extends from November 8th, 1742, to June 20th, 1743 (inclusive). It appears without doubt from the contents of this book that he is the one of whom Shattuck writes in his history that he "married Mary Hayward, 1728, and died November 29th, 1756, aged 51; having been captain, town-clerk, and otherwise distinguished." His father's name was Ephraim, and he had a son Ephraim. The entries are made apparently by himself, or a boy, or his wife, or some other when he was out. The book is filled with familiar Concord names, the grandfathers and great-grandfathers of the present generation. Dr. Hartshorn—he lived to be ninety-two—and Dr. Temple send to the store once or twice. It is more important now what was bought than who bought it.

The articles most commonly bought were mohair (commonly with buttons) (a kind of twist to sew on buttons with), rum (often only a gill to drink at the store),—more of these than anything;

salt, molasses, shalloon, fish, calico, some sugar, a castor hat, almanac, psalter (and sometimes primer and testament), paper, knee-buckles and shoe-buckles, garters and spurs by the pair, deer skins, a fan, a cart whip, various kinds of cloth and trimmings,—as half-thick, osnaburg, a very little silk, ferret, quality, serge for breeches, etc., etc.,—gloves, a spring knife, an ink-horn, a gun, cap, spice, a pocket case, timber, iron, etc., earthenware; no tea (?) (I am in doubt about one or perhaps two entries), nor coffee, nor meal, nor flour. Of the last two they probably raised all they wanted. Credit is frequently given for timber and once for cloth brought to the store.

On the whole, it is remarkable how little provision was sold at the store. The inhabitants raised almost everything for themselves. Chocolate is sold once. Rum, salt, molasses, fish, a biscuit with their drink, a little spice, and the like are all that commonly come under this head that I remember.

On a loose piece of paper is a bill for "todey," "a bowl of punch," etc., and on another piece is Jonathan Dwight's (innholder's?) bill against the Estate of Capt. Ephraim Jones for entertainment, etc., etc. (apparently he treated his company) at divers times for half a dozen years, amounting to over £146. One entry is "Dea Brown to flip & rum."

The people apparently made their own cloth and even thread, and hence for the most part bought only buttons and mohair and a few trimmings.

> Feb. 1, 1742. "Town of Concord Dr to sundry
>   for the funerel of Widow Williams daughter
>   to 5 pr gloves @ 1/9 1 DP. @ 2/1½   0–10–10½ "
> Jan. 10, 1742 (3). "Jonᵃ Edes to 3 Raccoon skins⎫
>   @ 2/9 2 minks @ 1/6 4 musquash @ / 3½   ⎬ 0–12– 5 "
>   ⎭
> Jan. 18, 1742 (3). "John Melven Cr by 1 Grey fox   0– 2– 3   "
> Feb. 14, 1742 (3). "Aaron Parker Cr by 100
>   squirell skins   0– 6– 3   "

Deer skins were sold at from ten to seventeen shillings. Sometimes it is written "old" or "new tenor."

Many of the customers came from as far as Harvard, or much farther.

A fan, a jack-knife, or a pair of garters are much more important relatively to the other goods sold than now.

No butter, nor rice, nor oil, nor candles are sold. They must have made their own butter and done without rice. There is no more authentic history of those days than this "Wast Book" contains, and, being money matters, it is more explicit than almost any other statement; something *must* be said. Each line contains and states explicitly a fact. It is the best of evidence of several facts. It tells distinctly and authoritatively who sold, who bought, the article, amount, and value, and the date. You could not easily crowd more facts into one line. You are warned when the doctor or deacon had a new suit of clothes, by the charge for mohair, buttons, and trimmings, or a castor hat; and here also is entered the rum which ran down their very throats.

Jan. 29. A very cold morning. Thermometer, or mercury, 18° below zero.

The village is the place to which the roads tend, a sort of expansion of the highway, as a lake of a river, the thoroughfare and ordinary of travellers, a trivial or quadrivial place. It is the body of which roads are the arms and legs. It is from the Latin *villa*, which, together with *via* (a way), or more anciently *vea* and *vella*, Varro derives from *veho* (to carry), because the villa is the place to and from which things are carried. And whence the Latin *vilis* and our word *villain* (?). The inhabitants are way-worn by the travel that goes by and over them without travelling themselves.

Jan. 30. This morning, though not so cold by a degree or two as yesterday morning, the cold has got more into the house, and the frost visits nooks never known to be visited before. The sheets are frozen about the sleeper's face; the teamster's beard is white with ice. Last night I felt it stinging cold as I came up the street at 9 o'clock; it bit my ears and face, but the stars shone all the brighter. The windows are all closed up with frost, as if they were ground glass.

The winter, cold and bound out as it is, is thrown to us like a bone to a famishing dog, and we are expected to get the marrow out of it. While the milkmen in the outskirts are milking so many scores of cows before sunrise these winter mornings, it is our task to milk the winter itself. It is true it is like a cow that is dry, and our fingers are numb, and there is none to wake us up. But the winter was not given to us for no purpose. We must thaw its cold with our genialness. If it is a cold and hard season, its fruit, no doubt, is the more concentrated and nutty.

Shall we take refuge in cities in November? Shall the nut fall green from the tree? Let not the year be disappointed of its crop. I knew a crazy man who walked into an empty pulpit one Sunday and, taking up a hymn-book, remarked: "We have had a good fall for getting in corn and potatoes. Let us sing Winter." So I say, "Let us sing winter." What else can we sing, and our voices be in harmony with the season?

Jan. 31. The wind is more southerly, and now the warmth of the sun prevails, and is felt on the back. The snow softens and melts. It is a beautiful clear and mild winter day. Our washwoman says she is proud of it. But I do not melt; there is no thaw in me; I am bound out still.

Feb. 2. Up river on ice to Clematis Brook.

Another warm, melting day, like yesterday. You can see some softening and relenting in the sky.

Already we begin to anticipate spring, and this is an important difference between this time and a month ago. We begin to say that the day is springlike.

Is not January the hardest month to get through? When you have weathered that, you get into the gulf-stream of winter, nearer the shores of spring.

Feb. 9. My ink was frozen last month, and is now pale.

Is not January alone pure winter? December belongs to the fall; is a wintry November: February, to the spring; it is a snowy March.

Feb. 12. Another cold morning. The snow-fleas look like little patches of rust on the ice.

At first, in clear cold weather, we may be walking on dry snow, which we cronch with squeaking sound under our feet. Then comes a thaw, and we slump about in slosh half a foot deep. Then, in a single night, the surface of the earth is all dried and stiffened, and we stagger over the rough, frozen ground and ice on which it is torture to walk. It becomes quite a study how a man will shoe himself for a winter. For outdoor life in winter, I use three kinds of shoes or boots: first and chiefly, for the ordinary dry snows or bare ground, cowhide boots; secondly, for shallow thaws, half-shoe depth, and spring weather, light boots and india-rubbers; third, for the worst sloshy weather, about a week in the year, india-rubber boots.

P.M.—Skate to Pantry Brook.

I was not aware till I came out how pleasant a day it was. It was very cold this morning, and I have been putting on wood in vain to warm my chamber, and lo! I come forth, and am surprised to find it warm and pleasant. There is very little wind, here under Fair Haven especially. I begin to dream of summer even. I take off my mittens.

To make a perfect winter day like this, you must have a clear, sparkling air, with a sheen from the snow, sufficient cold, little or no wind; and the warmth must come directly from the sun. It must not be a thawing warmth. The tension of nature must not be relaxed.

The sun being low, I see as I skate, reflected from the surface of the ice, flakes of rainbow somewhat like cobwebs, where the great slopes of the crystallization fall at the right angle, six inches or a foot across, but at so small an angle with the horizon that they had seemed absolutely flat and level before. Think of this kind of mosaic and tessellation for your floor! A floor made up of surfaces not absolutely level,—though level to the touch of the feet and to the noonday eye,—composed of crystals variously set, but just enough inclined to reflect the colors of the rainbow when the sun gets low.

XVII.

Feb. 16. Saw two large hawks circling over the woods by Walden, hunting,—the first I have seen since December 15th. That Indian trail on the hillside about Walden was revealed with remarkable distinctness to me standing on the middle of the pond, by the slight snow which had lodged on it forming a clear white line unobscured by weeds and twigs. (For snow is a great revealer not only of tracks made in itself, but even in the earth before it fell.) It was quite distinct in many places where you would not have noticed it before. A light snow will often reveal a faint foot or cart track in a field which was hardly discernible before, for it reprints it, as it were, in clear white type, alto-relievo.

Feb. 18. The last part of January and all February thus far have been alternate thaw and freeze and snow. It has more thaws, even as the running "r" (root of ῥέω) occurs twice in it and but once in January. It does not take so much fuel to keep us warm of late. I begin to think that my wood will last. We begin to have days precursors of spring.

I read some of the speeches in Congress about the Nebraska Bill,—a thing the like of which I have not done for a year. What trifling upon a serious subject!

De Quincey says that "the ancients had no experimental knowledge of severe climates." Neither have the English at home as compared with us of New England, nor we, compared with the Esquimaux.

This is a common form of the birch scale,—black, I think, —not white, at any rate.

Feb. 19. For several weeks the fall has seemed far behind, spring comparatively near. Yet I cannot say that there is any positive sign of spring yet; only we feel that we are sloping toward it. The sky has sometimes a warmth in its colors more like summer. A few birds have possibly strayed northward further than they have wintered.

The large moths apparently love the neighborhood of water, and are wont to suspend their cocoons over the edge of the meadow and river, places more or less inaccessible, to men at least. I saw the light ash-colored cocoons of the *A. Promethea*, four or five, with the completely withered and faded leaves wrapped around them, and so artfully and admirably secured to the twigs by fine silk wound round the leaf-stalk and the twig,—which last add nothing to its strength, being deciduous, but aid its deception,—they are taken at a little distance for a few curled and withered leaves left on. Each and all such disguises and other resources remind us that not some poor worm's instinct merely, as we call it, but the mind of the universe rather, which we share, has been intended upon each particular object. All the wit in the world was brought to bear on each case to secure its end. It was long ago, in a full senate of all intellects, determined how cocoons had best be suspended,—kindred mind with mine that admires and approves decided it so.

Feb. 20. We have had but one* (and that I think was the first) of those gentle moist snows which lodge perfectly on the trees and make perhaps the most beautiful sight of any. Much more common is what we have now, *i.e.*—

Feb. 21. A.M.—A fine, driving snow-storm. Have seen no good samples of the blue in snow this winter. At noon clears up.

Feb. 27. Morning.—Rain over; water in great part run off; wind rising; river risen and meadows flooded.

---

*No more this winter.

It looks as if Nature had a good deal of work on her hands between now and April, to break up and melt twenty-one inches of ice on the ponds,—beside melting all the snow,—and before planting-time to thaw from one to two and a half or three feet of frozen ground.

March 5. Sunday. Channing, talking with Minott the other day about his health, said, "I suppose you'd like to die now." "No," said Minott, "I've toughed it through the winter, and I want to stay and hear the bluebirds once more."

March 8. I wrote a letter for an Irishman night before last, sending for his wife in Ireland to come to this country. One sentence which he dictated was, "Don't mind the rocking of the vessel, but take care of the children that they be not lost overboard."

Lightning this evening, after a day of successive rains.

March 10. Misty rain, rain,—the third day of more or less rain.

It occurs to me that heavy rains and sudden meltings of the snow, such as we had a fortnight ago (February 26th), before the ground is thawed, so that all the water, instead of being soaked up by the ground, flows rapidly into the streams and ponds, is necessary to swell and break them up. If we waited for the direct influence of the sun on the ice and the influence of such water as would reach the river under other circumstances, the spring would be very much delayed. In the violent freshet there is a mechanic force added to the chemic. Saw a skunk in the Corner road, which I followed sixty rods or more. Out now about 4 P.M.,—partly because it is a dark, foul day. It is a slender black (and white) animal, with its back remarkably arched, standing high behind and carrying its head low; runs, even when undisturbed, with a singular teeter or undulation, like the walking of a Chinese lady. Very slow; I hardly have to run to keep up with it. It has a long tail, which it regularly

erects when I come too near and prepares to discharge its liquid. It has a remarkably long, narrow, pointed head and snout, which enable it to make those deep narrow holes in the earth by which it probes for insects. Its eyes have an innocent, childlike, bluish-black expression. It made a singular loud patting sound repeatedly, on the frozen ground under the wall, undoubtedly with its fore feet (I saw only the upper part of the animal), which reminded me of what I have heard about your stopping and stamping in order to stop the skunk. Probably it has to do with its getting its food,— patting the earth to get the insects or worms. Though why it did so then I know not.

March 13. To Boston.

Bought a telescope to-day for eight dollars.

P.M.—To Great Meadows.

Counted over forty robins with my glass in the meadow north of Sleepy Hollow, in the grass and on the snow. A large company of fox-colored sparrows in Heywood's maple swamp close by.

March 30. 6 A.M.—To Island.

First still hour since the afternoon of the 17th. March truly came in like a lamb and went out like a lion this year. Remarkably and continuously pleasant weather from the very first day till the 18th. Apparently an early spring,—buds and birds well advanced,— then suddenly very severe cold and high winds cold enough to skim the river over in broad places at night, and commencing with the greatest and most destructive gale for many a year, felt far and wide; and it has never ceased to blow since till this morning. Vegetation is accordingly put back.

April 1. April has begun like itself. It is warm and showery, while I sail away with a light southwest wind toward the Rock. Sometimes the sun seems just ready to burst out, yet I know it will not. The meadow resounds with the sprayey notes of blackbirds. The birds sing this warm, showery day after a fortnight's cold (yesterday was wet too), with a universal burst and flood of melody. The lines of sawdust from Barrett's mill at different heights on the steep, wet bank under the hemlocks rather enhance the impression of freshness and wildness, as if it were a new country.

April 5. These days, when a soft west or southwest wind blows and it is truly warm, and an outside coat is oppressive,—these bring out the butterflies and the frogs, and the marsh hawks which prey on the last. Just so simple is every year. Whatever year it may be, I am surveying, perhaps, in the woods; I have taken off my outside coat, perhaps for the first time, and hung it on a tree; the zephyr is positively agreeable on my cheek; I am thinking what an elysian day it is, and how I seem always to be keeping the flocks of Admetus such days—that is my luck; when I hear a single, short, well-known stertorous croak from some pool half filled with dry leaves.

April 8. At Nut Meadow Brook saw, or rather heard, a muskrat plunge into the brook before me, and saw him endeavoring in vain to bury himself in the sandy bottom, looking like an amphibious animal. I stooped and, taking him by his tail, which projected, tossed him ashore. He did not lose the points of compass, but turned directly to the brook again, though it was toward me, and, plunging in, buried himself in the mud, and that was the last I saw of him.

Hazel, the very first male, open.

I find that I can criticise my composition best when I stand at a little distance from it,—when I do not see it, for instance. I make a little chapter of contents which enables me to recall it page by page to my mind, and judge it more impartially when my manuscript is out of the way. The distraction of surveying enables me rapidly to take new points of view. A day or two surveying is equal to a journey.

April 10. April rain. How sure a rain is to bring the tree sparrows into the yard, to sing sweetly, canary-like!

I bought me a spy-glass some weeks since. I buy but few things, and those not till long after I begin to want them, so that when I do get them I am prepared to make a perfect use of them and extract their whole sweet.

April 13. The golden-brown tassels of the alder are very rich now. The poplar (*tremuloides*) by Miles's Swamp has been out—*the earliest catkins*—maybe two or three days. On the evening of the 5th the body of a man was found in the river between Fair Haven Pond and Lee's, much wasted. How these events disturb our associations and tarnish the landscape! It is a serious injury done to a stream. One or two crowfoots on Lee's Cliff, fully out, surprise me like a flame bursting from the russet ground. The saxifrage is pretty common, ahead of the crowfoot now.

April 15. Morning.—Snow and snowing; four inches deep. Yesterday was very cold. Now, I trust, it will come down and out of the air. Many birds must be hard put to it.

April 17. Snows again.

It is remarkable how the American mind runs to statistics. Consider the number of meteorological observers and other annual phenomena. The Smithsonian Institution is a truly national institution. Every shopkeeper makes a record of the arrival of the first martin or bluebird to his box. Dodd, the broker, told me last spring that he knew when the first bluebird came to his boxes, he made a memorandum of it: John Brown, merchant, tells me this morning that the martins first came to his box on the 13th, he "made a minute of it." Beside so many entries in their day-books and ledgers, they record these things.

April 19. Do I ever see the marsh hawk?* Is it not the sharp-shinned which I have mistaken for it? A man came to me yesterday to offer me as a naturalist a two-headed calf which his cow had brought

---

*I think the early large hawk was it.

forth, but I felt nothing but disgust at the idea and began to ask myself what enormity I had committed to have such an offer made to me. I am not interested in mere phenomena, though it were the explosion of a planet, only as it may have lain in the experience of a human being.

April 20. I find some advantage in describing the experience of a day on the day following. At this distance it is more ideal, like the landscape seen with the head inverted, or reflections in water.

April 23. Saw my white-headed eagle again, first at the same place, the outlet of Fair Haven Pond. It was a fine sight, he is mainly—*i.e.* his wings and body—so black against the sky, and they contrast so strongly with his white head and tail. Lying on the ground with my glass, I could watch him very easily, and by turns he gave me all possible views of himself. When I observed him edgewise I noticed that the tips of his wings curved upward slightly the more, like a stereotyped undulation. He rose very high at last, till I almost lost him in the clouds, circling or rather *looping* along westward, high over river and wood and farm, effectually concealed in the sky. We who live this plodding life here below never know how many eagles fly over us. They are concealed in the empyrean. I think I have got the worth of my glass now that it has revealed to me the white-headed eagle. Now I see him edgewise like a black ripple in the air, his white head still as ever turned to earth, and now he turns his under side to me, and I behold the full breadth of his broad black wings, somewhat ragged at the edges.

May 6. P.M.—To epigæa *via* Clamshell Hill.

There is no such thing as pure *objective* observation. Your observation, to be interesting, *i.e.* to be significant, must be *subjective.* The sum of what the writer of whatever class has to report is simply some human experience, whether he be poet or philosopher or man of science. The man of most science is the man most alive, whose life is the greatest event. Senses that take cognizance of outward things merely are of no avail. It matters not where or how far you travel,—the farther commonly the worse,—but how much alive you are. If it is possible to conceive of an event outside to humanity, it is not of the slightest significance, though it were the explosion of a planet. No mere willful activity whatever, whether in writing verses or collecting statistics, will produce true poetry or science. If you are really a sick man, it is indeed to be regretted, for you cannot accomplish so much as if you were well. All that a man has to say or do that can possibly concern mankind, is in some shape or other to tell the story of his love,—to sing; and, if he is fortunate and keeps alive, he will be forever in love. This alone is to be alive to the extremities. It is a pity that this divine creature should ever suffer from cold feet; a still greater pity that the coldness so often reaches to his heart. I look over the report of the doings of a scientific association and am surprised that there is so little life to be reported; I am put off with a parcel of dry technical terms. Anything living is easily and naturally expressed in popular language. I cannot help suspecting that the life of these learned professors has been almost as inhuman and wooden as a rain-gauge or self-registering magnetic machine. They communicate no fact which rises to the temperature of blood-heat. It does n't all amount to one rhyme.

Dandelions, perhaps the first, yesterday. This flower makes a great show,—a sun itself in the grass. How emphatic it is! You cannot but observe it set in the liquid green grass even at a distance. I am surprised that the sight of it does not affect me more, but I look at it as unmoved as if but a day had elapsed since I saw it in the fall.

May 7. Flowers, *e.g.* willow and hazel catkins, are self-registering indicators of *fair* weather. I remember how I waited for the hazel catkins to become relaxed and shed their pollen, but they delayed, till at last there came a pleasanter and warmer day and I took off my greatcoat while surveying in the woods, and then, when I went to dinner at noon, hazel catkins in full flower were dangling from the banks by the roadside and yellowed my clothes with their pollen. If man is thankful for the serene and warm day, much more are the flowers.

May 8. P.M.—By boat to Fair Haven.

It is long since I have sailed on so broad a tide. How dead would the globe seem, especially at this season, if it were not for these water surfaces! We are slow to realize water,—the beauty and magic of it. It is interestingly strange to us forever. Immortal water, alive even in the superficies, restlessly heaving now and tossing me and my boat, and sparkling with life! I look round with a thrill on this bright fluctuating surface on which no man can walk, whereon is no trace of footstep, unstained as glass. When I got off this end of the Hollowell place I found myself in quite a sea with a smacking wind directly aft. I felt no little exhilaration, mingled with a slight awe, as I drove before this strong wind over the great black-backed waves I judged to be at least twenty inches or two feet high, cutting through them, and heard their surging and felt them toss me. I was even obliged to head across them and not get into their troughs, for then I could hardly keep my legs. They were crested with a dirty-white foam and were ten or twelve feet from crest to crest. They were so black,—as no sea I have seen,—large and powerful, and made such a roaring around me, that I could not but regard them as gambolling monsters of the deep. They were *melainai*—what is the Greek for waves? This is our black sea. You see a *perfectly black* mass about two feet high and perhaps four or five feet thick and of indefinite length, round-backed, or perhaps forming a sharp ridge with a dirty-white crest, tumbling like a whale unceasingly before you. Only one of the epithets which the poets have applied to the color of the sea will apply to this water,—*melaina*, μέλαινα θάλασσα. I was delighted to find that our usually peaceful river could toss me so. How much more exciting than to be planting potatoes with those men in the field! What a different world!

May 13. The portion of the peach trees in bloom in our garden shows the height of the snow-drifts in the winter.

May 15. Have just been looking at Nuttall's "North American Sylva." Much research, fine plates and print and paper, and unobjectionable periods, but no turpentine, or balsam, or quercitron, or salicin, or birch wine, or the aroma of the balm-of-Gilead, no gallic, or ulmic, or even malic acid. The plates are greener and higher-colored than the words, etc., etc. It is sapless, if not leafless.

May 16. On Hubbard's meadow, saw a motion in the water as if a pickerel had darted away; approached and saw a middle-sized snapping turtle on the bottom; managed at last, after stripping off my coat and rolling up my shirt-sleeve, by thrusting in my arm to the shoulder, to get him by the tail and lift him aboard. He tried to get under the boat. He snapped at my shoe and got the toe in his mouth. His back was covered with green moss (?), or the like, mostly concealing the scales. In this were small leeches. Great, rough, but not hard, scales on his legs. He made a pretty loud hissing like a cross dog, by his breathing. It was wonderful how suddenly this sluggish creature would snap at anything. As he lay under the seat, I scratched his back, and, filling himself with air and rage, his head would suddenly fly upward, his shell striking the seat, just as a steel trap goes off, and though I was prepared for it, it never failed to startle me, it was so swift and sudden. He slowly inflated himself, and then suddenly went off like a percussion lock snapping the air. Thus undoubtedly he catches fishes, as a toad catches flies. His laminated tail and great triangular points in the rear edge of his shell. Nature does not forget beauty of outline even in a mud turtle's shell.

May 17. 5.30 A.M.—To Island.

I found a large snapping turtle on the bottom. He appeared of a dirty brown there, very nearly the color of the bottom at present. With his great head, as big as an infant's, and his vigilant eyes as he paddled about on the bottom in his attempts to escape, he looked not merely repulsive, but to some extent terrible even as a crocodile. At length, after thrusting my arm in up to the shoulder two or three times, I succeeded in getting him into the boat, where I secured him with a lever under a seat. I could get him from the landing to the house only by turning him over and drawing him by the tail, the hard crests of which afforded a good hold; for he was so heavy that I could not hold him off so far as to prevent his snapping at my legs. He weighed thirty and a half pounds.

Extreme length of shell	15½ inches
Length of shell in middle	15 inches
Greatest width of shell	12½ inches
(This was toward the rear.)	
Tail (beyond shell)	11½ inches

His head and neck it was not easy to measure, but, judging from the proportions of one described by Storer, they must have been 10 inches long at least, which makes the whole length 37 inches. Width of head 4½ inches; with the skin of the neck, more than 5. He had a very ugly and spiteful face (with a vigilant gray eye, which was never shut in any position of the head), surrounded by the thick and ample folds of the skin about his neck. His shell was comparatively smooth and free from moss,—a dirty black. He was a *dirty* or speckled white beneath. He made the most remarkable and awkward appearance when walking. The edge of his shell was lifted about eight inches from the ground, tilting now to this side, then to that, his great scaly legs or flippers hanging with flesh and loose skin,—slowly and gravely (?) hissing the while. His walking was perfectly elephantine. Thus he stalked along,—a low conical mountain,—dragging his tail, with his head turned upward with the ugliest and most venomous look, on his flippers, half leg half fin. But he did not proceed far before he sank down to rest. If he could support a world on his back when lying down, he certainly could not stand up under it. All said that he walked like an elephant. When lying on his back, showing his *dirty* white and warty under side, with his tail curved round, he reminded you forcibly of pictures of the dragon. He could not easily turn himself back; tried many times in vain, resting betweenwhiles. Would inflate himself and convulsively spring with head and all upward, so as to lift his shell from the ground, and he would strike his head on the ground lift up his shell, and catch at the earth with his claws.

The turtle was very sluggish, though capable of putting forth great strength. He would just squeeze into a flour barrel and would not quite lie flat in it when his head and tail were drawn in. I hear of a man who injured his back seriously for many years by carry- ing one some distance at arm's length to prevent his biting him. They are frequently seen fighting and their shells heard striking together.

The turtle's snapping impressed me as something mechanical, like a spring, as if there were no volition about it. Its very sudden- ness seemed too great for a conscious movement. Perhaps in these cold-blooded and sluggish animals there is a near approach to the purely material and mechanical. Their very tenacity of life seems to be owing to their insensibility or small amount of life,—indeed, to be an irritation of the muscles. One man tells me of a turtle's head which, the day after it was cut off, snapped at a dog's tail and made him run off yelping, and I have witnessed something similar my- self. I can think of nothing but a merely animated jaw, as it were a piece of mechanism.

Observed a rill emptying in above the stone-heaps, and after- ward saw where it ran out of June-berry Meadow, and I considered how surely it would have conducted me to the meadow, if I had traced it up. I was impressed as it were by the intelligence of the brook, which for ages in the wildest regions, before science is born, knows so well the level of the ground and through whatever woods or other obstacles finds its way. Who shall distinguish between the *law* by which a brook finds its river, the *instinct* by which a bird performs its migrations, and the *knowledge* by which a man steers his ship round the globe? The globe is the richer for the variety of its inhabitants.

Saw a large gray squirrel near the split rock in the Assabet. He went skipping up the limb of one tree and down the limb of an- other, his great gray rudder undulating through the air, and occa- sionally hid himself behind the main stem. The *Salix nigra* will open to-morrow.

May 23. We soon get through with Nature. She excites an expecta- tion which she cannot satisfy. The merest child which has rambled into a copsewood dreams of a wilderness so wild and strange and inexhaustible as Nature can never show him. I expected a fauna more infinite and various, birds of more dazzling colors and more celestial song. How many springs shall I continue to see the common sucker (*Catostomus Bostoniensis*) floating dead on our river! Will not Nature select her types from a new fount? This earth which is spread out like a map around me is but the lining of my inmost soul exposed. In me is the sucker that I see. No wholly extraneous object can compel me to recognize it. I am guilty of suckers. I go about to look at flowers and listen to the birds. There was a time when the beauty and the music were all within, and I sat and listened to my thoughts, and there was a song in them. I sat for hours on rocks and wrestled with the melody which possessed me. When you walked with a joy which knew not its own origin. Man *should be* the harp articulate. When your cords were tense.

May 29. These days it is left to one Mr. Loring to say whether a citizen of Massachusetts is a slave or not.[*] Does any one think that Justice or God awaits Mr. Loring's decision? Such a man's existence in this capacity under these circumstances is as impertinent as the gnat that settles on my paper. We do not ask him to make up his mind, but to make up his pack. Why, the United States Government never performed an act of justice in its life!

It is really the trial of Massachusetts. Every moment that she hesitates to set this man free, she is convicted. The Commissioner on her case is God. Perhaps the most saddening aspect of the matter is the tone of almost all the Boston papers, connected with the fact that they are and have been of course sustained by a majority of their readers. They are feeble indeed, but only as sin compared with righteousness and truth. They are eminently time-serving. I never look at them except at such a time as this. Their life is abject even as that of the marines. Will mankind never learn that policy is not

---

[*][On May 24, the fugitive slave Anthony Burns was arrested in Boston; under the Fugitive Slave Law of 1850 he had to be returned to his master in Virginia. This law made the north more obviously complicit in the slave system, and the Burns case radicalized many northerners into abolitionists. Edward G. Loring was the judge in the case. Cf. July 4, p. 268 below.]

morality, that it never secures any moral right, but always considers merely what is "expedient,"—chooses the available candidate, who, when moral right is concerned, is always the devil? Witness the President of the United States. I do not vote at the polls. I wish to record my vote here. The majority of the men of the North, and of the South and East and West, are not men of principle. If they vote, they do not send men to Congress on errands of humanity; but, while their brothers and sisters are being scourged and hung for loving liberty, while (insert here all the inhumanities that pandemonium can conceive of), it is the mismanagement of wood and iron and stone and gold which concerns them. Do what you will, O Government, with my mother and brother, my father and sister, I will obey your command to the letter. It will, indeed, grieve me if you hurt them, if you deliver them to overseers to be hunted by hounds, and to be whipped to death; but, nevertheless, I will peaceably pursue my chosen calling on this fair earth, until, perhaps, one day I shall have persuaded you to relent. Such is the attitude, such are the words of Massachusetts. Rather than thus consent to establish hell upon earth,—to be a party to this establishment,—I would touch a match to blow up earth and hell together. As I love my life, I would side with the Light and let the Dark Earth roll from under me, calling my mother and my brother to follow me.

June 5. 6 P.M.—To Cliffs.

Large yellow butterflies with black spots since the 3d. Carrion-flower, maybe a day. Dangle-berry, probably June 3d at Trillium Woods. Now, just before sundown, a nighthawk is circling, imp-like, with undulating, irregular flight over the sprout-land on the Cliff Hill, with an occasional squeak and showing the spots on his wings. He does not circle away from this place, and I associate him with two gray eggs somewhere on the ground beneath and a mate there sitting. I have come to this hill to see the sun go down, to recover sanity and put myself again in relation with Nature. I would fain drink a draft of Nature's serenity. I love to sit here and look off into the broad deep vale in which the shades of night are beginning to prevail. When the sun has set, the river becomes more white and distinct in the landscape. The caterpillars are and have been very numerous this year. I see large trees (wild cherry and apple) completely stripped of leaves. Some of the latter, twenty or thirty feet high, are full of blossoms without a single leaf. I return by moonlight.

June 9. The mosquitoes encircle my head and torment me, and I see a great moth go fluttering over the tree-tops and the water, black against the sky, like a bat. A full moon.

While the whole military force of the State, if need be, is at the service of a slaveholder, to enable him to carry back a slave, not a soldier is offered to save a citizen of Massachusetts from being kidnapped. Is this what all these arms, all this "training," has been for these seventy-eight years past? What is wanted is men of principle, who recognize a higher law than the decision of the majority. The marines and the militia whose bodies were used lately were not men of sense nor of principle; in a high moral sense they were not *men* at all.

June 15. 5.30 A.M.—To Island and Hill.

A young painted tortoise on the surface of the water, as big as a quarter of a dollar, with a reddish or orange sternum. Found a nest of tortoise eggs, apparently buried last night, which I brought home, ten in all,—one lying wholly on the surface,—and buried in the garden.

7 P.M.—To Cliff by railroad.

Cranberry. Methinks the birds sing a little feebler nowadays. The sun has set, or is at least concealed in a low mist.

June 16. Heart-leaf. *Nymphæa odorata.* Again I scent the white water-lily, and a season I had waited for is arrived. How indispensable all these experiences to make up the summer! It is the emblem of purity, and its scent suggests it. Growing in stagnant and muddy water, it bursts up so pure and fair to the eye and so sweet to the scent, as if to show us what purity and sweetness reside in, and can be extracted from, the slime and muck of earth. I think I have plucked the first one that has opened for a mile at least. What confirmation of our hopes is in the fragrance of the water-lily! I shall not so soon despair of the world for it, notwithstanding slavery, and the cowardice and want of principle of the North. It suggests that the time may come when man's deeds will smell as sweet. Such, then, is the odor our planet emits. It reminds me that Nature has been partner to no Missouri compromise. So behave that the odor of your actions may enhance the general sweetness of the atmosphere, that, when I behold or scent a flower, I may not be reminded how inconsistent are your actions with it; for all odor is but one form of advertisement of a moral quality.

The effect of a good government is to make life more valuable,—of a bad government, to make it less valuable. Every man in New England capable of the sentiment of patriotism must have lived the last three weeks with the sense of having suffered a vast, indefinite loss. I had never respected this government, but I had foolishly thought that I might manage to live here, attending to my private affairs, and forget it. For my part, my old and worthiest pursuits have lost I cannot say how much of their attraction, and I feel that my investment in life here is worth many per cent. less since Massachusetts last deliberately and forcibly restored an innocent man, Anthony Burns, to slavery. I dwelt before in the illusion that my life passed somewhere only *between* heaven and hell, but now I cannot persuade myself that I do not dwell wholly within hell. The sight of that political organization called Massachusetts is to me morally covered with scoriæ and volcanic cinders, such as Milton imagined. If there is any hell more unprincipled than our rulers and our people, I feel curious to visit it. Life itself being worthless, all things with it, that feed it, are worthless. Suppose you have a small library, with pictures to adorn the walls,—a garden laid out around,—and contemplate scientific and literary pursuits, etc., etc., and discover suddenly that your villa, with all its contents, is located in hell, and that the justice of the peace is one of the devil's angels, has a cloven foot and a forked tail,—do not these things suddenly lose their value in your eyes? Are you not disposed to sell at a great sacrifice?

Autumnal dandelion, some time, in Emerson's meadow pasture. *Potentilla Norvegica*, a day or two, in low ground; very abundant at Baker Ditch with other weeds, on a cleared and ditched swamp. Veiny-leaved hawkweed at Heywood Peak appears shut up at midday,—also the autumnal dandelion.

There is a cool east wind,—and has been afternoons for several days,—which has produced a very thick haze or a fog. I find a tortoise egg on this peak at least sixty feet above the pond. There is a fine ripple and sparkle on the pond, seen through the mist. But what signifies the beauty of nature when men are base? We walk to lakes to see our serenity reflected in them. When we are not serene, we go not to them. Who can be serene in a country where both rulers and ruled are without principle? The remembrance of the baseness of politicians spoils my walks. My thoughts are murder to the State; I endeavor in vain to observe nature; my thoughts involuntarily go plotting against the State. I trust that all just men will conspire.

It is eight days since I plucked the great orchis; one is perfectly fresh still in my pitcher. It may be plucked when the spike is only half opened, and will open completely and keep perfectly fresh in a pitcher more than a week. Do I not live in a garden,—in paradise? I can go out each morning before breakfast—I do—and gather these flowers with which to perfume my chamber where I read and write, all day. The note of the cherry-bird is fine and ringing, but peculiar and very noticeable. With its crest it is a resolute and combative-looking bird.

June 19. Men may talk about measures till all is blue and smells of brimstone, and then go home and sit down and expect their measures to do their duty for them. The only measure is integrity and manhood.

JULY 4. A sultry night the last; bear no covering; all windows open.
8 A.M.—To Framingham.*

---

*[There, at an antislavery rally where William Lloyd Garrison burned a copy of the Constitution, Thoreau gave his passionate lecture "Slavery in Massachusetts."]

Great orange-yellow lily, some days, wild yellow lily, drooping, well out. *Asclepias obtusifolia*, also day or two. Some chestnut trees show at distance as if blossoming. Buckwheat, how long? I probably saw *Asclepias purpurascens* (??) over the walls. A very hot day.

July 10. Monday. Took up one of the small tortoise eggs which I had buried June 15th. The eye was remarkable, developed in the colorless and almost formless head, one or two large dark circles of the full diameter; a very distinct pulsation where the heart should be and along the neck was perceptible; but there seemed to be no body but a mass of yellow yolk.

The following are the birds I chanced to hear in this walk (did not attend much): The seringos on fences, *link* of bobolink, crow, oven-bird, tanager, chewink, huckleberry-bird (pretty often and loud), flicker cackle, wood thrush, robin (?), before 3 P.M.; then red-eye, veery trill, catbird rigmarole, etc., etc.

The singing birds at present are:—

Villageous: Robin, chip-bird, warbling vireo, swallows.

Rural: Song sparrow, seringos, flicker, kingbird, goldfinch, *link* of bobolink, cherry-bird.

Sylvan: Red-eye, tanager, wood thrush, chewink, veery, oven-bird,—all even at midday. Catbird full strain, whip-poor-will, crows.

July 14. Friday. Awake to day of gentle rain,—very much needed; none to speak of for nearly a month, methinks. The cooler and stiller day has a valuable effect on my spirits.

It holds up from time to time, and then a fine, misty rain falls. It lies on the fine reddish tops of some grasses, thick and whitish like morning cobwebs. The stillness is very soothing. This is a summer rain. The earth is being bedewed. There is no storm or violence to it. Health is a sound relation to nature.

July 17. 11 A.M.—By river to Fair Haven.

I go to observe the lilies. I see a rail lodged in the weeds with seven tortoises on it, another with ten, another with eleven, all in a row sunning now at midday, hot as it is. They are mostly the painted tortoise. Apparently no weather is too hot for them thus to bask in the sun. The pontederia is in its prime, alive with butterflies, yellow and others. I see its tall blue spikes reflected beneath the edge of the pads on each side, pointing down to a heaven beneath as well as above. Earth appears but a thin crust or pellicle.

I am surprised to see crossing my course in middle of Fair Haven Pond great yellowish devil's-needles, flying from shore to shore, from Island to Baker's Farm and back, about a foot above the water, some against a head wind; also yellow butterflies; suggesting that these insects see the distant shore and resolve to visit it. In fact, they move much faster than I can toward it, yet as if they were conscious that they were on a journey, flying for the most part straight forward. It shows more enterprise and a wider range than I had suspected. It looks very bold. If devil's-needles cross Fair Haven, then man may cross the Atlantic.

July 18. We have very few bass trees in Concord, but walk near them at this season and they will be betrayed, though several rods off, by the wonderful susurrus of the bees, etc., which their flowers attract. It is worth going a long way to hear. I was warned that I was passing one in two instances on the river,—the only two I passed,—by this remarkable sound. At a little distance it is like the sound of a waterfall or of the cars; close at hand like a factory full of looms. They were chiefly humblebees, and the great globose tree was all alive with them. I heard the murmur distinctly fifteen rods off. You will know if you pass within a few rods of a bass tree at this season in any part of the town, by this loud murmur, like a waterfall, which proceeds from it.

July 22. The hottest night,—the last.

It was almost impossible to pursue any work out-of-doors yesterday. There were but few men to be seen out. You were prompted often, if working in the sun, to step into the shade to avoid a sunstroke. At length a shower passing in the west slightly cooled the air. The domestic animals suffer much. Saw a dog which had crawled into a corner and was apparently dying of heat.

July 26. To-day I see in various parts of the town the yellow butterflies in fleets in the road, on bare damp sand (not dung), twenty or more collected within a diameter of five or six inches in many places. They are a greenish golden, sitting still near together, and apparently headed one way if the wind blows. At first, perhaps, you do not notice them, but, as you pass along, you disturb them, and the air is suddenly all alive with them fluttering over the road, and, when you are past, they soon settle down in a new place. How pretty these little greenish-golden spangles! Some are a very pale greenish yellow. I do not know what attracts them thus to sit near together, like a fleet in a haven; why they collect in groups. I see many small red ones elsewhere on the sericocarpus, etc., etc.

JULY 28. *Friday.* Clethra. Methinks the season culminated about the middle of this month,—that the year was of indefinite promise before, but that, after the first intense heats, we postponed the fulfillment of many of our hopes for this year, and, having as it were attained the ridge of the summer, commenced to descend the long slope toward winter, the afternoon and down-hill of the year. Last evening it was much cooler, and I heard a decided fall sound of crickets.

Partridges begin to go off in packs.

Lark still sings, and robin.

Small sparrows still heard.

Kingbird lively.

Veery and wood thrush (?) not very lately, nor oven-bird.

Red-eye and chewink common.

Night-warbler and evergreen-forest note not lately.

Cherry-bird common.

Turtle dove seen.

July 30. Opened one of the snapping turtle's eggs at Dugan Desert, laid June 7th. There is a little mud turtle squirming in it, apparently perfect in outline, shell and all, but all *soft* and of one consistency,—a bluish white, with a mass of yellowish yolk (?) attached. Perhaps it will be a month more before it is hatched.

Aug. 2. Wednesday.

Surveyed east part of Lincoln.

5 P.M.—To Conantum on foot.

My attic chamber has compelled me to sit below with the family at evening for a month. I feel the necessity of deepening the stream of my life; I must cultivate privacy. It is very dissipating to be with people too much. As C. says, it takes the edge off a man's thoughts to have been much in society. I cannot spare my moonlight and my mountains for the best of man I am likely to get in exchange.

I am inclined now for a pensive evening walk. Methinks we think of spring mornings and autumn evenings. July has been to me a trivial month. It began hot and continued drying, then rained some toward the middle, bringing anticipations of the fall, and then was hot again about the 20th. It has been a month of haying, heat, low water, and weeds.

As I go up the hill, surrounded by its shadow, while the sun is setting, I am soothed by the delicious stillness of the evening, save that on the hills the wind blows. I was surprised by the sound of my own voice. For the first time for a month, at least, I am reminded that thought is possible. The din of trivialness is silenced. I float over or through the deeps of silence. It is the first silence I have heard for a month. My life had been a River Platte, tinkling over its sands but useless for all great navigation, but now it suddenly became a fathomless ocean. It shelved off to unimagined depths.

The surface of the forest on the east of the river presents a singularly cool and wild appearance,—cool as a pot of green paint,—stretches of green light and shade, reminding me of some lonely mountainside. A few fireflies in the meadows. I am uncertain whether that so large and bright and high was a firefly or a shooting star. Shooting stars are but fireflies of the firmament. The crickets on the causeway make a *steady* creak, on the dry pasture-tops an *interrupted* one. I was compelled to stand to write where a soft, faint light from the western sky came in between two willows.

Fields to-day sends me a specimen copy of my "Walden." It is to be published on the 12th.

Aug. 5. I find that we are now in the midst of the meadow-haying season, and almost every meadow or section of a meadow has its band of half a dozen mowers and rakers, either bending to their manly work with regular and graceful motion or resting in the shade, while the boys are turning the grass to the sun. I passed as many as sixty or a hundred men thus at work to-day. They stick up a twig with the leaves on, on the river's brink, as a guide for the mowers, that they may not exceed the owner's bounds. I hear their scythes cronching the coarse weeds by the river's brink as I row near. In one place I see one sturdy mower stretched on the ground amid his oxen in the shade of an oak, trying to sleep; or I see one wending far inland with a jug to some well-known spring.

There is very little air stirring to-day.

Aug. 7. It is inspiriting at last to hear the wind whistle and moan about my attic, after so much trivial summer weather, and to feel cool in my thin pants.

Do you not feel the fruit of your spring and summer beginning to ripen, to harden its seed within you? Do not your thoughts begin to acquire consistency as well as flavor and ripeness? How can we expect a harvest of thought who have not had a seed-time of character?

P.M.—To Peter's, Beck Stow's, and Walden.

Still autumnal, breezy with a cool vein in the wind; so that, passing from the cool and breezy into the sunny and warm places, you begin to love the heat of summer. It is the contrast of the cool wind with the warm sun. I walk over the pinweed-field. It is just cool enough in my thin clothes. There is a light on the earth and leaves, as if they were burnished. It is the glistening autumnal side of summer. I feel a cool vein in the breeze, which braces my thought, and I pass with pleasure over sheltered and sunny portions of the sand where the summer's heat is undiminished, and I realize what a friend I am losing. This off side of summer glistens like a burnished shield. Tansy is apparently now in its prime, and the early goldenrods have acquired a brighter yellow. From this off side of the year, this imbricated slope, with alternating burnished surfaces and shady ledges, much more light and heat are reflected (less absorbed), methinks, than from the springward side. In mid-summer we are of the earth,—confounded with it,—and covered with its dust. Now we begin to erect ourselves somewhat and walk upon its surface. I am not so much reminded of former years, as of existence prior to years.

A wasp stung me at one high blueberry bush on the forefinger of my left hand, just above the second joint. It was very venomous; a white spot with the red mark of the sting in the centre, while all the rest of the finger was red, soon showed where I was stung, and the finger soon swelled much below the joint, so that I could not com-pletely close the finger, and the next finger sympathized so much with it that at first there was a *little* doubt which was stung. These insects are effectively weaponed. But there was not enough venom to prevail further than the finger.

AUG. 9. *Wednesday.*—To Boston.
"Walden" published. Elder-berries. Waxwork yellowing.

Aug. 12. The wind is autumnal and at length compels me to put on my coat. I bathe at Hubbard's. The water is rather cool, compara-tively. As I look down-stream from southwest to northeast, I see the red under sides of the white lily pads about half exposed, turned up by the wind to an angle of 45° or more. These hemispherical red shields are so numerous as to produce a striking effect on the eye, as of an endless array of forces with shields advanced; sometimes four or five rods in width.

On Conantum saw a cow looking steadily up into the sky for a minute. It gave to her face an unusual almost human or wood-god, faun-like expression, and reminded me of some frontispieces to Vir-gil's Bucolics. She was gazing upward steadily at an angle of about 45°. There were only some downy clouds in that direction. It was so unusual a sight that any one would notice it. It suggested adoration.

Aug. 18. A great drought now for several weeks. The haymakers have been remarkably uninterrupted this year by rain. Corn and potatoes are nearly spoiled. Our melons suffer the more because there was no drought in June and they ran to vine, which now they cannot support. Hence there is little fruit formed, and that small and dying ripe. Almost everywhere, if you dig into the earth, you find it all dusty. Even wild black cherries and choke-cherries are drying before fairly ripe, all shrivelled. Many are digging potatoes half grown. Trees and shrubs recently set out, and many old ones, are dying. A good time to visit swamps and meadows.

Aug. 19. The near meadow is very beautiful now, seen from the railroad through this dog-day haze, which softens to velvet its fresh green of so many various shades, blending them harmoniously,— darker and lighter patches of grass and the very light yellowish-green of the sensitive fern which the mowers have left. It has an indescribable beauty to my eye now, which it could not have in a clear day. The haze has the effect both of a wash or varnish and of a harmonizing tint. It destroys the idea of definite distance which distinctness suggests. It is as if you had painted a meadow of fresh grass springing up after the mower,—here a dark green, there lighter, and there again the yellowish onoclea,—then washed it over with some gum like a map and tinted the paper of a fine misty blue. This is an effect of the dog-days.

Aug. 22. P.M.—To Great Meadows on foot along bank into Bedford meadows; thence to Beck Stow's and Gowing's Swamp.

Walking may be a science, so far as the direction of a walk is concerned. I go again to the Great Meadows, to improve this remarkably dry season and walk where in ordinary times I cannot go. There is, no doubt, a particular season of the year when each place may be visited with most profit and pleasure, and it may be worth the while to consider what that season is in each case.

This was a prairial walk. I went along the river and meadows from the first.

At the lower end of these meadows, between the river and the firm land, are a number of shallow muddy pools or pond-holes, where the yellow lily and pontederia, etc., grow, where apparently the surface of the meadow was floated off some spring and so a permanent pond-hole was formed in which, even in this dry season, there is considerable water left.

In these shallow muddy pools, but a few inches deep and few feet in diameter, I was surprised to observe the undulations produced by pretty large fishes endeavoring to conceal themselves. In one little muddy basin where there was hardly a quart of water, caught half a dozen little breams and pickerel, only an inch long, as perfectly distinct as full grown, and in another place, where there was little else than mud left, breams two or three inches long still alive. In many dry hollows were dozens of small breams, pickerel, and pouts, quite dead and dry. Hundreds, if not thousands, of fishes had here perished on account of the drought.

Saw a blue heron—apparently a young bird, of a brownish blue—fly up from one of these pools, and a stake-driver from another, and also saw their great tracks on the mud, and the feathers they had shed,—some of the long, narrow white neck-feathers of the heron. The tracks of the heron were about six inches long. Here was a rare chance for the herons to transfix the imprisoned fish. It is a wonder that any have escaped. I was surprised that any dead were left on the mud, but I judge from what the book says that they do not touch dead fish. To these remote shallow and muddy pools, usually surrounded by reeds and sedge, far amid the wet meadows,—to these, then, the blue heron resorts for its food. Here, too, is an abundance of the yellow lily, on whose seeds they are said to feed. There, too, are the paths of muskrats.

I find at length a pitcher-plant with a spoonful of water in it. It must be last night's dew. It is wonderful that in all this drought it has not evaporated.

Aug. 25. I think I never saw the haze so thick as now, at 11 A.M., looking from my attic window. I cannot quite distinguish J. Hosmer's house, only the dark outline of the woods behind it.

Aug. 26. Opened one of my snapping turtle's eggs. The egg was not warm to the touch. The young is now larger and darker-colored, shell and all, more than a hemisphere, and the yolk which maintains it is much reduced. Its shell, very deep, hemispherical, fitting close to the shell of the egg, and, if you had not just opened the egg, you would say it could not contain so much. Its shell is considerably hardened, its feet and claws developed, and also its great head, though held in for want of room. Its eyes are open. It puts out its head, stretches forth its claws, and liberates its tail, though all were enveloped in a gelatinous fluid. With its great head it has already the ugliness of the full-grown, and is already a hieroglyphic of snappishness. It may take a fortnight longer to hatch it.

How much lies quietly buried in the ground that we wot not of! We unconsciously step over the eggs of snapping turtles slowly hatching the summer through. Not only was the surface perfectly dry and trackless there, but blackberry vines had run over the spot where these eggs were buried and weeds had sprung up above. If Iliads are not composed in our day, snapping turtles are hatched and arrive at maturity. It already thrusts forth its tremendous head,—for the first time in this sphere,—and slowly moves from side to side,—opening its small glistening eyes for the first time to the light,—expressive of dull rage, as if it had endured the trials of this world for a century. When I behold this monster thus steadily advancing toward maturity, all nature abetting, I am convinced that there must be an irresistible necessity for mud turtles. With what tenacity Nature sticks to her idea!

Grapes ripe, owing to the hot dry weather.

Passing by M. Miles's, he told me he had a mud turtle in a box in his brook, where it had lain since the last of April, and he had given it nothing to eat. He wished he had known that I caught some in the spring and let them go. He would have bought them of me. He is very fond of them. He bought one of the two which Ed. Garfield caught on Fair Haven in the spring; paid him seventy-five cents for it. Garfield was out in his boat and saw two fighting on the pond. Approached carefully and succeeded in catching both and getting them into the boat. He got them both home by first carrying one along a piece, then putting him down and, while he was crawling off, going back for the other. One weighed forty-three or forty-four pounds and the other forty-seven. Miles gave me the shell of the one he bought, which weighed forty-three or forty-four. It is fifteen and six eighths inches long by fourteen and a half broad, of a roundish form, broadest backward. The upper shell is more than four and a half inches deep and would make a good dish to bail out a boat with. He said he had no trouble in killing them. It was of no great use to cut off their heads. He thrust his knife through the soft thin place in their sternum and killed them at once. Told of one Artemas (?) Wheeler of Sudbury who used to keep fifteen or twenty in a box in a pond-hole, and fat them and eat them from time to time, having a great appetite for them. Some years ago, in a January thaw, many came out on the Sudbury meadows, and, a cold snap suddenly succeeding, a great many were killed. One man counted eighty or more dead, some of which would weigh eighty to a hundred pounds. Miles himself found two shells on his river meadow of very large ones. Since then they have been scarce. It increases my respect for our river to see these great products of it. No wonder the Indians made much of them. Such great shells must have made convenient household utensils for them.

Even the hinder part of a mud turtle's shell is scalloped, one would say rather for beauty than use.

Hear by telegraph that it rains in Portland and New York.

In the evening, some lightning in the horizon, and soon after a *little* gentle rain, which—

(*Aug. 27*) I find next day has moistened the ground about an inch down only. But now it is about as dry as ever.

Many red oak acorns have fallen.[*] The great green acorns in broad, shallow cups. How attractive these forms! No wonder they are imitated on pumps, fence and bed posts. Is not this a reason that the pigeons are about? The yellow birch is yellowed a good deal, the leaves spotted with green. The dogsbane a clear yellow. On the Walden road some maples are yellow and some chestnuts brownish-yellow and also sere. From Heywood's Peak I am sur-

---

[*]Were they not cast down?

prised to see the top of Pine Hill wearing its October aspect,—yellow with changed maples and here and there faintly blushing with changed red maples. This is the effect of the drought. Among other effects of the drought I forgot to mention the fine dust, which enters the house and settles everywhere and also adds to the thickness of the atmosphere. Fences and roadside plants are thickly coated with it.

When I awake in the morning, I remember what I have seen and heard of snapping turtles, and am in doubt whether it was dream or reality. I slowly raise my head and peeping over the bedside see my great mud turtle shell lying bottom up under the table, showing its prominent ribs, and realize into what world I have awaked. Before I was in doubt how much prominence my good Genius would give to that fact. That the first object you see on awakening should be an empty mud turtle's shell!! Will it not make me of the earth earthy? Or does it not indicate that I am of the earth earthy? What life, what character, this has shielded, which is now at liberty to be turned bottom upward! I can put specimens of all our other turtles into this cavity. This too was once an infant in its egg. When I see this, then I am sure that I am not dreaming, but am awake to this world. I do not know any more terrene fact. It still carries the earth on its back. Its life is between the animal and vegetable; like a seed it is planted deep in the ground and is all summer germinating. Does it not possess as much the life of the vegetable as the animal?

Would it not be well to describe some of those rough all-day walks across lots?—as that of the 15th, picking our way over quaking meadows and swamps and occasionally slipping into the muddy batter midleg deep; jumping or fording ditches and brooks; forcing our way through dense blueberry swamps, where there is water beneath and bushes above; then brushing through extensive birch forests all covered with green lice, which cover our clothes and face; then, relieved, under larger wood, more open beneath, steering for some more conspicuous trunk; now along a rocky hillside where the sweet-fern grows for a mile, then over a recent cutting, finding our uncertain footing on the cracking tops and trimmings of trees left by the choppers; now taking a step or two of smooth walking across a highway; now through a dense pine wood, descending into a rank, dry swamp, where the cinnamon fern rises above your head, with isles of poison-dogwood; now up a scraggy hill covered with shrub oak, stooping and winding one's way for half a mile, tearing one's clothes in many places and putting out one's eyes, and find at last that it has no bare brow, but another slope of the same character; now through a corn-field diagonally with the rows; now coming upon the hidden melon-patch; seeing the back side of familiar hills and not knowing them,—the nearest house to home, which you do not know, seeming further off than the farthest which you do know;—in the spring defiled with the froth on various bushes, etc., etc., etc.; now reaching on higher land some open pigeon-place, a breathing-place for us.

Aug. 28. The meadow is drier than ever, and new pools are dried up. The breams, from one to two and a half inches long, lying on the sides and quirking from time to time, a dozen together where there is but a pint of water on the mud, are a handsome but sad sight,— pretty green jewels, dying in the sun. I saved a dozen or more by putting them in deeper pools. Saw a whole school of little pouts, hundreds of them one and a half inches long, many dead, all apparently fated to die, and some full-grown fishes. The muddy bottom of these pools dried up is cracked into a sort of regular crystals. In the soft mud, the tracks of the great bittern and the blue heron. Scared up one of the former and saw a small dipper on the river.

In my experience, at least *of late years*, all that depresses a man's spirits is the sense of remissness,—duties neglected, unfaithfulness,—or shamming, impurity, falsehood, selfishness, inhumanity, and the like.

Aug. 29. Early for several mornings I have heard the sound of a flail. It leads me to ask if I have spent as industrious a spring and summer as the farmer, and gathered as rich a crop of experience. If so, the sound of my flail will be heard by those who have ears to hear, separating the kernel from the chaff all the fall and winter, and a sound no less cheering it will be. If the drought has destroyed the corn, let not all harvests fail. Have you commenced to thresh your grain? The lecturer must commence his threshing as early as August, that his fine flour may be ready for his winter customers.

Aug. 30. The clearness of the air which began with the cool morning of the 28th makes it delicious to gaze in any direction. *Though there has been no rain*, the valleys are emptied of haze, and I see with new pleasure to distant hillsides and farmhouses and a river-reach shining in the sun, and to the mountains in the horizon. Coolness and clarity go together. Was not that a meadow-hen  which I scared up in two places by the river-side,—of a dark brown like a small woodcock, though it flew *straight* and low? I go along the flat Hosmer shore to Clamshell Hill. The sparganium seed balls begin to brown and come off in the hand. Are they not young hen-hawks which I have seen sailing for a week past, without red tails?

Sept. 2. The second still, misty, mizzling and rainy day. We all lie abed late. Now many more sparrows in the yard, larger than chip-birds and showing ashy under sides as they fly.

P.M.—By boat to Purple Utricularia Shore.

To my great surprise I find this morning (September 3d) that the little unhatched turtle, which I thought was sickly and dying, and left out on the grass in the rain yesterday morn, thinking it would be quite dead in a few minutes—I find the shell alone and the turtle a foot or two off vigorously crawling, with neck outstretched (holding up its head and looking round like an old one) and feet surmounting every obstacle. It climbs up the nearly perpendicular side of a basket with the yolk attached. They thus not only continue to live after they are dead, but begin to live before they are alive!

[*Noted on the inside back cover:*] My faults are:—

Paradoxes,—saying just the opposite,—a style which may be imitated.

Ingenious.

Playing with words,—getting the laugh,—not always simple, strong, and broad.

Using current phrases and maxims, when I should speak for myself.

Not always earnest.

"In short," "in fact," "alas!" etc.

Want of conciseness.

Walden published, Wednesday, Aug. 9th, '54.

Sent Fields 12 copies of the *Week*, Oct. 18th, '54.

XVIII.

Sept. 3. Woodbine berries purple. Even at this season I see some fleets of yellow butterflies in the damp road after the rain, as earlier. Close to the left-hand side of bridle-road, about a hundred rods south of the oak, a bayberry bush without fruit, probably a male one. It made me realize that this was only a more distant and elevated sea-beach and that we were within reach of marine influences. My thoughts suffered a sea-turn.

Sept. 4. Monday. I have provided my little snapping turtle with a tub of water and mud, and it is surprising how fast he learns to use his limbs and this world. He actually runs, with the yolk still trailing from him, as if he had got new vigor from contact with the mud. The insensibility and toughness of his infancy make our life, with its disease and low spirits, ridiculous. He impresses me as the rudiment of a man worthy to inhabit the earth. He is born with a shell. That is symbolical of his toughness. His shell being so rounded and sharp on the back at this age, he can turn over without trouble.

Sept. 6. My little turtle, taken out of the shell September 2d, has a shell one and seven fortieths inches long, or four fortieths longer than the diameter of the egg-shell, to say nothing of head and tail. Warm weather again, and sultry nights the last two. The last a splendid moonlight and quite warm.

Sept. 8. I have brought home a half-bushel of grapes to scent my chamber with. It is impossible to get them home in a basket with all their rich bloom on them, which, no less than the form of the clusters, makes their beauty. As I paddled home with my basket of grapes in the bow, every now and then their perfume was wafted to me in the stern, and I thought that I was passing a richly laden vine on shore. Some goldfinches twitter over, while I am pulling down the vines from the birchtops.

Sept. 9. This morning I find a little hole, three quarters of an inch or an inch over, above my small tortoise eggs, and find a young tortoise coming out (apparently in the rainy night) just beneath. It is the *Sternothærus odoratus*—already has the strong scent—and now has drawn in its head and legs. I see no traces of the yolk, or what-not, attached. It may have been out of the egg some days. *Only one* as yet. I buried them in the garden June 15th.

I am affected by the thought that the earth nurses these eggs. They are planted in the earth, and the earth takes care of them; she is genial to them and does not kill them. It suggests a certain vitality and intelligence in the earth, which I had not realized. This mother is not merely inanimate and inorganic. Though the immediate mother turtle abandons her offspring, the earth and sun are kind to them. The old turtle on which the earth rests takes care of them while the other waddles off. Earth was not made poisonous and deadly to them. The earth has some virtue in it; when seeds are put into it, they germinate; when turtles' eggs, they hatch in due time. Though the mother turtle remained and brooded them, it would still nevertheless be the universal world turtle which, through her, cared for them as now. Thus the earth is the mother of all creatures.

Sept. 10. Yesterday and to-day the first regular rain-storm, bringing down more leaves,—elms, button woods, and apple tree,—and decidedly raising the river and brooks. Already the grass both in meadows and on hills looks greener, and the whole landscape, this overcast rainy day, darker and more verdurous. Hills which have been russet and tawny begin to show some greenness.

On account of the drought one crop has almost entirely failed this year thus far, which the papers have not spoken of. Last year, for the last three weeks of August, the woods were filled with the strong musty scent of decaying fungi, but this year I have seen very few fungi and have not noticed that odor at all,—a failure more perceptible to frogs and toads, but no doubt serious to those whom it concerns.

As for birds:—

> About *ten* days ago *especially* I saw many large hawks, probably hen-hawks and young, about.
>
> Within a week several of the small slate-colored and black-tipped hawks.
>
> August 20th, saw a sucker which I suppose must have been caught by a fish hawk.
>
> Hear screech owls and hooting owls these evenings.
>
> Have not noticed blue jays of late.
>
> Bats common.
>
> [*Etc.—40 more.*]

Sept. 11. Measured to-day the little *Sternothærus odoratus* which came out the ground in the garden September 9th. Its shell is thirty-two fortieths of an inch long, by twenty-five fortieths wide. It has a distinct dorsal ridge, and its head and flippers are remarkably developed. Its raised back and dorsal ridge, as in the case of the mud turtle, enable it to turn over very easily. It may have been hatched some time before it came out, for not only there was no trace of the *yolk* (?), but its shell was much wider than the egg, when it first came out of the ground. I put it into the tub on the edge of the mud. It seems that it does not have to learn to walk, but walks at once. It seems to have no infancy such as birds have. It is surprising how much cunning it already exhibits. It is defended both by its form and color and its instincts. As it lay on the mud, its color made it very inobvious, but, besides, it kept its head and legs drawn in and perfectly still, as if feigning death; but this was not sluggishness. At a little distance I watched it for ten minutes or more. At length it put its head out far enough to see if the coast was clear, then, with its flippers, it turned itself toward the water (which element it had never seen before), and suddenly and with rapidity launched itself into it and dove to the bottom. Its whole behavior was calculated to enable it to reach its proper element safely and without attracting attention. Not only was it made of a color and form (like a bit of coal) which alone almost effectually concealed it, but it was made, infant as it was, to be perfectly still as if inanimate and then to move with rapidity when unobserved. The oldest turtle does not show more, if so much, cunning. I think I may truly say that it uses cunning and meditates how it may reach the water in safety. When I first took it out of its hole on the morning of the 9th, it shrunk into its shell and was motionless, feigning death. That this was not sluggishness, I have proved. When to-day it lay within half an inch of the water's edge, it knew it for a friendly element and, without deliberation or experiment, but at last, when it thought me and all foes unobservant of its motions, with remarkable precipitation it committed itself to it as if realizing a long-cherished idea. Plainly all its motions were as much the result of what is called instinct as is the act of sucking in infants. Our own subtlest is likewise but another kind of instinct. The wise man is a wise infant obeying his finest and never-failing instincts. It does not so much impress me as an infantile beginning of life as an epitome of all the past of turtledom and of the earth. I think of it as the result of all the turtles that have been.

The little snapping turtle lies almost constantly on the mud with its snout out of water. It does not keep under water long. Yesterday in the cold rain, however, it lay buried in the mud all day!

This is a *cold* evening with a white twilight, and threatens frost, the first in *these respects* decidedly autumnal evening. It makes us think of wood for the winter. For a week or so the evenings have been sensibly longer, and I am beginning to throw off my summer idleness. This twilight is succeeded by a brighter starlight than heretofore.

Sept. 14. 8 A.M.—To opposite Pelham's Pond by boat.

Quite cool, with some wind from east and southeast. Took a watermelon for drink. Now, instead of haying, they are raking cranberries all along the river. The raker moves slowly along with a basket before him, into which he rakes (hauling) the berries, and his wagon stands one side. It is now the middle of the cranberry season.

We see half a dozen herons in this voyage. Their wings are so long in proportion to their bodies that there seems to be more than one undulation to a wing as they are disappearing in the distance, and so you can distinguish them. You see another begin before the first has ended. It is remarkable how common these birds are about our sluggish and marshy river. We must attract them from a wide section of country. It abounds in those fenny districts and meadow pond-holes in which they delight. A flock of thirteen telltales, great yellow-legs, start up with their shrill whistle from the midst of the great Sudbury meadow, and away they *sail in a flock,—a sailing* (or skimming) *flock*, that is something rare methinks,—showing their white tails, to alight in a more distant place. The great bittern, too, rises from time to time, slowly flapping his way along at no great height above the meadow.

Sept. 16. Sophia and mother returned from Wachusett. S. saw much bayberry in Princeton.

Another little sternothærus has come out of the ground since eight this morning (it is now 11 A.M.).* The first sternothærus has remained buried in the mud in the tub from the first, and the snapping turtle also for the last few days.

Sept. 19. Thinking this afternoon of the prospect of my writing lectures and going abroad to read them the next winter, I realized

---

*Another, Sept. 17th, found in morning. Another the 18th, between 8 and 11 A.M. Another the 18th, between 11 A.M. and 1 P.M. Another between 1 and 3 P.M. the 18th. Another found out on the morning of the 19th. Another was dug out the 25th. (All hatched, then, but one egg which I have.)

A snapping turtle had come out on the morning of the 20th, one at least. Another on the morning of the 23d Sept. Another on the morning of the 26th.

how incomparably great the advantages of obscurity and poverty which I have enjoyed so long (and may still perhaps enjoy). I thought with what more than princely, with what poetical, leisure I had spent my years hitherto, without care or engagement, fancy-free. I have given myself up to nature; I have lived so many springs and summers and autumns and winters as if I had nothing else to do but *live* them, and imbibe whatever nutriment they had for me; I have spent a couple of years, for instance, with the flowers chiefly, having none other so binding engagement as to observe when they opened; I could have afforded to spend a whole fall observing the changing tints of the foliage. Ah, how I have thriven on solitude and poverty! I cannot overstate this advantage. I do not see how I could have enjoyed it, if the public had been expecting as much of me as there is danger now that they will. If I go abroad lecturing, how shall I ever recover the lost winter?

It has been my vacation, my season of growth and expansion, a prolonged youth.

An upland plover goes off from Conantum top (though with a white belly), uttering a sharp *white, tu white.*

That drought was so severe that a *few* trees here and there—birch, maple, chestnut, apple, oak—have lost nearly all their leaves.

Sept. 21. Thursday. P.M.—To Flint's Pond.

The first frost in our yard last night, the grass white and stiff in the morning. The muskmelon vines are now blackened in the sun. There have been some frosts in low grounds about a week. The forenoon is cold, and I have a fire, but it is a fine clear day, as I find when I come forth to walk in the afternoon, a fine grained air with a seething or shimmering in it, as I look over the fields,—days which remind me of the Indian summer that is to come. Do not these days always succeed the first frosty mornings?

I sometimes seem to myself to owe all my little success, all for which men commend me, to my vices. I am perhaps more willful than others and make enormous sacrifices, even of others' happiness, it may be, to gain my ends. It would seem even as if nothing good could be accomplished without some vice to aid in it.

Sept. 24. Sunday. 6 A.M.—To Hill.

Low fog-like veil on meadows.

Man identifies himself with earth or the material, just as he who has the least tinge of African blood in his veins regards himself as a negro and is identified with that race. Spirit is strange to him; he is afraid of ghosts.

What name of a natural object is most poetic? That which he has given for convenience whose life is most nearly related to it, who has known it longest and best.

Sept. 26. Took my last bath the 24th. Probably shall not bathe again this year. It was chilling cold. It is a warm and very pleasant afternoon, and I walk along the riverside in Merrick's pasture.

Sept. 30. The clear bright-scarlet leaves of the smooth sumach in many places are curled and drooping, hanging straight down, so as to make a funereal impression, reminding me of a red sash and a soldier's funeral. They impress me quite as black crape similarly arranged, the bloody plants.

The conventional acorn of art is of course of no particular species, but the artist might find it worth his while to study Nature's varieties again.

Oct. 7. Went to Plymouth to lecture and survey Watson's grounds. Returned the 15th.

NOV. II. Minott heard geese go over night before last, about 8 P.M. Therien, too, heard them "yelling like anything" over Walden, where he is cutting, the same evening. He cut down a tree with a flying squirrel on it; often sees them. Receive this evening a letter in French and three "ouvrages" from the Abbé Rougette in Louisiana.*

---

*[Abbé Adrien Rougette of New Orleans—Louisiana Creole, authority on monastic solitude, friend of the Choctaw Indians, and nature writer—praised *Walden* and sent Thoreau three of his own books: *La Thébaïde en Amérique*, *Wild Flowers*, and *Les Savanes*.]

Nov. 20. To Philadelphia. 7 A.M., to Boston; 9 A.M., Boston to New York, by express train, land route.

See the reddish soil (red sandstone?) all through Connecticut. Pleasantest part of the whole route between Springfield and Hartford, along the river; perhaps include the hilly region this side of Springfield. Reached Canal Street at 5 P.M., or candle-light.

Started for Philadelphia from foot of Liberty Street at 6 P.M. Saw only the glossy panelling of the cars reflected out into the dark, like the magnificent lit façade of a row of edifices reaching all the way to Philadelphia, except when we stopped and a lanthorn or two showed us a ragged boy and the dark buildings of some New Jersey town. Arrive at 10 P.M.; time, four hours from New York, thirteen from Boston, fifteen from Concord. Put up at Jones's Exchange Hotel, 77 Dock Street; lodgings thirty-seven and a half cents per night, meals separate.

Nov. 21. Looked from the cupola of the State-House, where the Declaration of Independence was declared. The best view of the city I got. Was interested in the squirrels, gray and black, in Independence and Washington Squares. Heard that they have, or have had, deer in Logan Square. The squirrels are fed, and live in boxes in the trees in the winter.

In the narrow market-houses in the middle of the streets, was struck by the neat-looking women marketers with full cheeks. There was a mosquito about my head at night.

Nov. 22. Left at 7.30 A.M. for New York. Went to Crystal Palace; admired the houses on Fifth Avenue, the specimens of coal at the Palace, one fifty feet thick as it was cut from the mine, in the form of a square column, iron and copper ore, etc. Saw sculptures and paintings innumerable, and armor from the Tower of London, some of the Eighth Century. Saw Greeley; Snow, the commercial editor of the *Tribune*; Solon Robinson; Fry, the musical critic, etc.; and others. Greeley carried me to the new opera-house, where I heard Grisi and her troupe. First, at Barnum's Museum, I saw the camelopards, said to be one eighteen the other sixteen feet high. I should say the highest stood about fifteen feet high at most (twelve or thirteen ordinarily). The body was only about five feet long. Why has it horns, but for ornament? Looked through his diorama, and found the houses all over the world much alike. Greeley appeared to know and be known by everybody; was admitted free to the opera, and we were led by a page to various parts of the house at different times.

Dec. 6. To Providence to lecture.

I see thick ice and boys skating all the way to Providence, but know not when it froze, I have been so busy writing my lecture; probably the night of the 4th.

Was struck with the Providence depot, its towers and great length of brick. Lectured in it.

After lecturing twice this winter I feel that I am in danger of cheapening myself by trying to become a successful lecturer, *i.e.*, to interest my audiences. I am disappointed to find that most that I am and value myself for is lost, or worse than lost, on my audience. I fail to get even the attention of the mass. I should suit them better if I suited myself less. I feel that the public demand an average man,—average thoughts and manners,—not originality, nor even absolute excellence. You cannot interest them except as you are like them and sympathize with them. I would rather that my audience come to me than that I should go to them, and so they be sifted; *i.e.*, I would rather write books than lectures. That is fine, this coarse. To read to a promiscuous audience who are at your mercy the fine thoughts you solaced yourself with far away is as violent as to fatten geese by cramming, and in this case they do not get fatter.

Dec. 8. Winter has come unnoticed by me, I have been so busy writing. This is the life most lead in respect to Nature. How different from my habitual one! It is hasty, coarse, and trivial, as if you were a spindle in a factory. The other is leisurely, fine, and glorious, like a flower. In the first case you are merely getting your living; in the second you live as you go along. You travel only on roads of the proper grade without jar or running off the track, and sweep round the hills by beautiful curves.

Dec. 20. 7 A.M.—To Hill.

Said to be the coldest morning as yet. The river appears to be frozen everywhere. Where was water last night is a firm bridge of ice this morning. The snow which has blown on to the ice has taken the form of regular star-shaped crystals, an inch in diameter. Sometimes these are arranged in a spear three feet long quite straight. The woodchoppers are making haste to their work far off, walking fast to keep warm, before the sun has risen, their ears and hands well covered, the dry, cold snow squeaking under their feet. They will be warmer after they have been at work an hour.

P.M.—Skated to Fair Haven with C.

C.'s skates are not the best, and beside he is far from an easy skater, so that, as he said, it was killing work for him. Time and again the perspiration actually dropped from his forehead on to the ice, and it froze in long icicles on his beard. Yet he kept up his spirits and his fun, said he had seen much more suffering than I, etc., etc.

It has been a glorious winter day, its elements so simple,—the sharp clear air, the white snow everywhere covering the earth, and the polished ice. Cold as it is, the sun seems warmer on my back even than in summer, as if its rays met with less obstruction. And then the air is so beautifully still; there is not an insect in the air, and hardly a leaf to rustle. I am surprised to find how fast the dog can run in a straight line on the ice. I am not sure that I can beat him on skates, but I can turn much shorter. It is very fine skating for the most part.

Dec. 21. What a grovelling appetite for profitless jest and amusement our countrymen have! Next to a good dinner, at least, they love a good joke,—to have their sides tickled, to laugh sociably, as in the East they bathe and are shampooed. Curators of lyceums write to me:—

DEAR SIR,—I hear that you have a lecture of some humor. Will you do us the favor to read it before the Bungtown Institute?

Dec. 26. At Ricketson's [*in New Bedford on the coast*].

I do not remember to have ever seen such a day as this in

Concord. There is no snow here (though there has been excellent sleighing at Concord since the 5th), but it is very muddy, the frost coming out of the ground as in spring with us. I went to walk in the woods with R. It was wonderfully warm and pleasant, and the cockerels crowed just as in a spring day at home. I felt the winter breaking up in me, and if I had been at home I should have tried to write poetry. They told me that this was not a rare day there, that they had little or no winter such as we have, and it was owing to the influence of the Gulf Stream, which was only sixty miles from Nantucket at the nearest, or one hundred and twenty miles from them. In midwinter, when the wind was southeast or even southwest, they frequently had days as warm and debilitating as in summer. There is a difference of about a degree in latitude between Concord and New Bedford, but far more in climate.

The American holly is quite common there, with its red berries still holding on, and is now their Christmas evergreen. I heard the larks sing strong and sweet, and saw robins. There is a Quaker meeting-house there. Such an ugly shed, without a tree or bush about it, which they call their meeting-house (without steeple, of course) is altogether repulsive to me, like a powder-house or grave. And even the quietness and perhaps unworldliness of an aged Quaker has something ghostly and saddening about it, as it were a mere preparation for the grave.

Dec. 28. Visited the museum at the Athenæum. Various South Sea implements, etc., etc., brought home by whalers.

The last Indian, not of pure blood, died this very month, and I saw his picture with a basket of huckleberries in his hand.

Jan. 4. To Worcester to lecture.

Visited the Antiquarian Library of twenty-two or twenty-three thousand volumes. It is richer in pamphlets and newspapers than Harvard. One alcove contains Cotton Mather's library, chiefly theological works, reading which exclusively you might live in his days and believe in witchcraft. Old leather-bound tomes, many of them as black externally as if they had been charred with fire. Time

and fire have the same effect. Haven said that the Rev. Mr. Somebody had spent almost every day the past year in that alcove.

Saw after my lecture a young negro who introduced himself as
a native of Africa, Leo L. Lloyd, who lectures on "Young Africa"!!
I never heard of anything but old Africa before.

Jan. 5. At Quinsigamond Village, a Mr. Washburn showed me the
wire rolling and drawing mill in which he is concerned. All sorts of
scrap iron is first heated to a welding heat in masses of about two
hundredweight, then rolled between vast iron rollers in successive
grooves till it is reduced to long rods little more than an inch in
diameter. These are cut up by powerful shears into lengths of about
three feet, heated again, and rolled between other rollers in grooves
successively of various forms,—square, oval, round, diamond, etc.,
which part of the work only one man in the concern fully understood and kept secret. It was here rolled and reduced to a large-
sized wire maybe three eighths of an inch in diameter, of which
screws are made. At this stage, first, it begins to be *drawn*, though
it must be heated again in the course of the drawing to restore its
ductility. Make a great deal of telegraph-wire, and for pail-bails,
etc. About twenty miles of telegraph-wire in a day, of the best
Swedish iron for strength. Cannot make so good iron in this country, because we cannot afford to work it over so much, labor being
higher. I saw a part of the glowing mass which had been heated to
a welding heat, ready to be rolled, but had dropped on its way. I
could still trace the outlines of the various scraps which composed
it,—screws, bolts, bar iron, an old axe curiously twisted, etc.,
etc.,—all which by mere pressure would have been rolled into a
homogeneous mass. It was now in the condition of many a piece of
composition, which, however, mere compression would weld together into a homogeneous mass or a continuous rod. Washburn
said the workmen were like sailors; their work was exciting and
they drank more spirit than other laborers. In hot weather would
sometimes drink two quarts of water an hour and sweat as much.
If they could not sweat, left off work. Showed me a peculiar coarse
yellow sand which they imported from the shore of Long Island,

whose quartz, examined by a microscope, was seen to be perfect crystals. This they used on the floor of their furnace to repair and level it when their iron bars had furrowed it. In the cavernous furnace I saw the roof *dripping* with dark stalactites from the mortar and bricks.

Higginson showed me a new translation of the Vishnu Sarma. Spoke of the autobiography of a felon older than Stephen Burroughs, one Fitch of Revolutionary days.

R.W.E. told of Mr. Hill, his classmate, of Bangor, who was much interested in my "Walden," but relished it merely as a capital satire and joke, and even thought that the survey and map of the pond were not real, but a caricature of the Coast Surveys. Also of Mr. Frost, the botanist, of Brattleboro, who has found five or six new species of lichens thereabouts.

Jan. 7. Sunday. Cloudy and misty. On opening the door I feel a very warm southwesterly wind, contrasting with the cooler air of the house, and find it unexpectedly wet in the street, and the manure is being washed off the ice into the gutter. It is, in fact, a January thaw. The channel of the river is quite open in many places, and in others I remark that the ice and water alternate like waves and the hollow between them. I hear the pleasant sound of running water.

The delicious soft, spring-suggesting air,—how it fills my veins with life! Life becomes again credible to me. A certain dormant life awakes in me, and I begin to love nature again. Here is my Italy, my heaven, my New England. I understand why the Indians hereabouts placed heaven in the southwest,—the soft south.

The bank is tinged with a most delicate pink or bright flesh-color—where the *Bæomyces roseus* grows. It is a lichen day. How full of life and of eyes is the damp bark! It would not be worth the while to die and leave all this life behind one.

Jan. 9. P.M.—To Conantum.

A cloudy day, threatening snow; wet under foot. How pretty the evergreen radical shoots of the St. John's-wort now exposed, partly red or lake, various species of it. Have they not grown since fall? I put a stone at the end of one to try it. A little wreath of green and red lying along on the muddy ground amid the melting snows. I am attracted at this season by the fine bright-red buds of the privet andromeda, sleeping couchant along the slender light-brown twigs. They look brightest against a dark ground.

This winter I hear the axe in almost every wood of any consequence left standing in the township.

What a strong and hearty but reckless, hit-or-miss style had some of the early writers of New England, like Josselyn and William Wood and others elsewhere in those days; as if they spoke with a relish, smacking their lips like a coach-whip, caring more to speak heartily than scientifically true. They are not to be caught napping by the wonders of Nature in a new country, and perhaps are often more ready to appreciate them than she is to exhibit them. They give you one piece of nature, at any rate, and that is themselves. (Cotton Mather, too, has a rich phrase.) They use a strong, coarse, homely speech which cannot always be found in the dictionary, nor sometimes be heard in polite society, but which brings you very near to the thing itself described. The strong new soil speaks through them. I have just been reading some in Wood's "New England's Prospect." He speaks a good word for New England, indeed will come very near lying for her, and when he doubts the justness of his praise, he brings it out not the less roundly; as who cares if it is not so? we love her not the less for all that. Certainly that generation stood nearer to nature, nearer to the facts, than this, and hence their books have more life in them.

They speak like men who have backs and stomachs and bowels, with all the advantages and disadvantages that attach to them. Ready to find lions here, some having "heard such terrible roarings," "which must be either Devils or Lions; there being no other creatures which use to roar." What a gormandizing faith (or belief) he has, ready to swallow all kinds of portents and prodigies!

Jan. 11. P.M.—Skated to Lee's Bridge and Farrar's Swamp—call it Otter Swamp.

A fine snow had just begun to fall, so we made haste to improve the skating before it was too late. Our skates made tracks often nearly an inch broad in the slight snow which soon covered the ice. All along the shores and about the islets the water had broadly overflowed the ice of the meadows, and frequently we had to skate through it, making it fly. The snow soon showed where the water was. It was a pleasant time to skate, so still, and the air so thick with snowflakes that the outline of near hills was seen against it and not against the more distant and higher hills. Single pines stood out distinctly against it in the near horizon.

Jan. 12. Where are the shiners now, and the trout? I see none in the brook. Have the former descended to the deep water of the river? Ah, may I be there to see when they go down! Why can they not tell me? Or gone into the mud? There are few or no insects for them now.

The strong scent of this red oak, just split and corded, is a slight compensation for the loss of the tree.

How cheering the sight of the evergreens now, on the forest floor, fresh as in summer!

What is that mint whose seed-vessels rubbed are so spicy to smell—minty—at the further end of the pond by the Gourgas wood-lot?*

Well may the tender buds attract us at this season, no less than partridges, for they are the hope of the year, the spring rolled up. The summer is all packed in them.

Observed this afternoon the following oak leaves:—

1st, the white oak, the most withered and faded and curled; many spotted with black dot lichens.

2d, the bear scrub, the most firm and fresh-colored and flat. [*Etc.—5 more.*]

For color, perhaps all may be called brown, and vary into each other more or less.

The 1st, as both sides are seen, pale-brown with a salmon tinge beneath.

———————————

*Lycopus.

2d, clear reddish-brown, leather-like, above, often paler, whitish or very light beneath, silveryish. [*Etc.*]

The oak leaves now resemble the different kinds of calf, sheep, Russia leather, and Morocco (a few scarlet oaks), of different ages.

Jan. 14. Skated to Baker Farm with a rapidity which astonished myself, before the wind, feeling the rise and fall,—the water having settled in the suddenly cold night,—which I had not time to see. A man feels like a new creature, a deer, perhaps, moving at this rate. He takes new possession of nature in the name of his own majesty. There was I, and there, and there, as Mercury went down the Idæan Mountains.

JAN. 15. P.M.—Skated to Bedford.

It had just been snowing, and this lay in shallow drifts or waves on the Great Meadows, alternate snow and ice. Skated into a crack, and slid on my side twenty-five feet.

The river-channel dark and rough with fragments of old ice,—polygons of various forms,—cemented together, not strong.

Jan. 19. 7 A.M.—Yesterday it rained hard all day, washing off the little snow that was left down to the ice, the gutters being good-sized mill-brooks and the water over shoes in the middle of the road.

In the night it turned to snow, which still falls, and now covers the wet ground three or four inches deep. It is a very damp snow or sleet, perhaps mixed with rain, which the strong northwest wind plasters to that side of the trees and houses. I never saw the blue in snow so bright as this damp, dark, stormy morning at 7 A.M., as I was coming down the railroad. I did not have to make a hole in it, but I saw it some rods off in the deep, narrow ravines of the drifts and under their edges or eaves, like the serenest blue of heaven, though the sky was, of course, wholly concealed by the driving snow-storm; suggesting that in darkest storms we may still have the hue of heaven in us.

P.M.—The damp snow still drives from the northwest nearly

horizontally over the fields, while I go with C. toward the Cliffs and Walden. Though considerable snow has fallen, it lies chiefly in drifts under the walls. It was worth the while to see what a burden of damp snow lay on the trees notwithstanding the wind. Pitch pines were bowed to the ground with it, and birches also, and white oaks. I saw one of the last, at least twenty-five feet high, splintered near the ground past recovery. The snow, a little damp, had lodged not only on the oak leaves and the evergreens, but on every twig and branch, and stood in upright walls or ruffs five or six inches high, like miniature Chinese walls, zigzag over hill and dale, making more conspicuous than ever the arrangement and the multitude of the twigs and branches; and the trunks also being plastered with snow, a peculiar soft light was diffused around, very unlike the ordinary darkness of the forest, as if you were inside a drift or snow house. This even when you stood on the windward side. In most directions you could not see more than four or five rods into this labyrinth or maze of white arms. This is to be insisted on. They were so thick that they left no crevice through which the eye could penetrate further. The path was for the most part blocked up with the trees bent to the ground, which we were obliged to go round by zigzag paths in the woods, or carefully creep under at the risk of getting our necks filled with an avalanche of snow. Often we touched a tree with our foot or shook it with our hand, and so relieved it of a part of its burden, and, rising a little, it made room for us to pass beneath. Often singular portals and winding passages were left between the pitch pines, through which, stooping and grazing the touchy walls, we made our way. Where the path was open in the midst of the woods, the snow was about seven or eight inches deep. The trunks of the trees so uniformly covered on the northerly side, as happens frequently every winter, and sometimes continuing so for weeks, suggested that this might be a principal reason why the lichens watered by the melting snow flourished there most. The snow lay in great continuous masses on the pitch pines and the white, not only like napkins, but great white tablespreads and counter panes, when you looked off at the wood from a little distance. Some white pine boughs hung down like fans or the webbed feet of birds. On some pitch pines it lay in fruit-like balls as big as one's head, like cocoanuts. Where the various oaks were bent down, the contrast of colors of the snow and oak leaves and the softened tints through the transparent snow—often a delicate fawn-color—were very agreeable.

As we returned over the Walden road the damp, driving snow-flakes, when we turned partly round and faced them, hurt our eye-balls as if they had been dry scales.

It may be that the linarias come into the gardens now not only because all nature is a wilderness to-day, but because the woods where the wind has not free play are so snowed up, the twigs are so deeply covered, that they cannot readily come at their food. We saw only one indistinct, snow-covered trail of an animal. Where are the crows now? I never see them at such a time. The channel ice is lifted up by the freshet, and there is dry white snow, but on each side are broad dirty or yellowish green strips of slosh. Whence comes this green color?

The houses have that peculiarly wintry aspect now on the west side, being all plastered over with snow adhering to the clapboards and half concealing the doors and windows.

You would not have believed there were so many twigs and branches in a wood as were revealed by the snow resting on them; perfect walls of snow; no place for a bird to perch.*

Jan. 20. You can tell by the ridges of the drifts on the south side of the walls which way the wind was. They all run from north to south; *i.e.*, the common drift is divided into ridges or plaits in this direction, frequently down to the ground between; which separate drifts are of graceful outlines somewhat like fishes, with a sharp ridge or fin gracefully curved, both as you look from one side and down on them, their sides curving like waves about to break. The thin edge of some of these drifts at the wall end, where the air has come through the wall

---

*Vide 20th and 26th.

and made an eddy, are remarkably curved, like some shells, even thus, more than once round: I would not have believed it.

T. admired much the addition to the red house, with its steep bevelled roof. Thought he should send Mr. Upjohn to see it. The whole house, methought, was well planted, rested solidly on the earth, with its great bank (green in summer) and few stately elms before, it so much simpler and more attractive than a front yard with its knickknacks. To contrast with this pleasing structure, which is painted a wholesome red, was a modern addition in the rear, perhaps no uglier than usual, only by contrast,—such an outline alone as our carpenters have learned to produce. I see that I cannot draw anything so bad as the reality. So you will often see an ugly new barn beside a pleasing old house.

I doubt if I can convey an idea of the appearance of the woods yesterday, as you stood in their midst and looked round on their boughs and twigs laden with snow. It seemed as if there could have been none left to reach the ground. These countless zigzag white arms crossing each other at every possible angle completely closed up the view, like a light drift within three or four rods on every side. The wintriest prospect imaginable. That snow which sifted down into the wood-path was much drier and lighter than elsewhere.

Jan. 24. I am reading William Wood's "New England's Prospect." He left New England August 15th, 1633, and the last English edition referred to in this American one of 1764 is that of London, 1639.

The wild meadow-grasses appear to have grown more rankly in those days. He describes them as "thick and long, as high as a man's middle; some as high as the shoulders." (*Vide* Indian book.)[*] Strawberries too were more abundant and large before they were so cornered up by cultivation, "some being two inches about; one may gather half a bushel in a forenoon;" and no doubt many other berries were far more abundant, as gooseberries, raspberries, and especially currants, which last so many old writers speak of, but so few moderns find wild. We can perhaps imagine how the primitive

---

[*][Thoreau's notebook on Indians.]

wood looked from the sample still left in Maine. "Here no doubt might be good done with saw mills; for I have seene of these stately high grown trees [he is speaking of pines particularly] ten miles together close by the river [probably Charles River] side." He says at first "fir and pine," as if the fir once grew in this part of the State abundantly, as now in Maine and further west. Of the oaks he says, "These trees afford much mast for hogs, especially every third year." Does not this imply many more of them than now? "The hornbound tree is a tough kind of wood, that requires so much pains in riving as is almost incredible, being the best to make bowls and dishes, not being subject to crack or leak," and he speaks, both in prose and verse, of the vines being particularly inclined to run over this tree. If this is the true hornbeam it was probably larger then, but I am inclined to think it the tupelo, and that it was both larger and more abundant than commonly now, for he says it was good for bowls, and it has been so used since. Of the plums of the country he says, "They be black and yellow, about the bigness of damsons, of a reasonable good taste." Yet Emerson has not found the yellow plum, *i.e.* Canada, growing wild in Massachusetts.

Of quadrupeds no longer found in Concord, he names the lion,—that Cape Ann Lion "which some affirm that they have seen," which may have been a cougar, for he adds, "Plimouth men have traded for Lions skins in former times,"—bear, moose, deer, porcupines, "the grim-fac'd Ounce, and rav'nous howling Wolf," and beaver. Martens.

For moose and deer see Indian book.

Complains of the wolf as the great devourer of bear, moose, and deer, which kept them from multiplying more.

For porcupine and raccoon *vide* Indian book.

Gray squirrels were evidently more numerous than now.

I do not know whether his ounce or wild cat is the Canada lynx[*] or wolverine. He calls it wild cat and does not describe the little wildcat. (*Vide* Indian book.) Says they are accounted "very good meat. Their skins be a very deep kind of fur, spotted white and

---

[*]Probably this.

black on the belly." Audubon and Bachman make the *Lynx rufus* black and white beneath.

Says the beaver are so cunning the English "seldom or never kill any of them, being not patient to lay a long siege" and not having experience.

Eagles are probably less common; pigeons of course (*vide* Indian book); heath cocks all gone (price "four pence"); and turkeys (good cock, "four shillings"). Probably more owls then, and cormorants, etc., etc., sea-fowl generally (of humilities he "killed twelve score at two shots"), and swans. Of the crane, "almost as tall as a man," probably blue heron,—possibly the whooping crane or else the sandhill,—he says, "I have seen many of these fowls, yet did I never see one that was fat, though very sleaky;" neither did I. "There be likewise many Swans, which frequent the fresh ponds and rivers, seldom consorting themselves with ducks and geese; these be very good meat, the price of one is six shillings." Think of that!

Sturgeon were taken at Cape Cod and in the Merrimack especially, "pickled and brought to England, some of these be 12, 14, and 18 feet long." An abundance of salmon, shad, and bass,—

> "The stately Bass old Neptune's fleeting post,
>
> That tides it out and in from sea to coast;"

"one of the best fish in the country," taken "sometimes two or three thousand at a set," "some four foot long," left on the sand behind the seine; sometimes used for manure. "Alewives...in the latter end of April come up to the fresh rivers to spawn, in such multitudes as is almost incredible, pressing up in such shallow waters as will scarce permit them to swim, having likewise such longing desire after the fresh water ponds, that no beatings with poles, or forcive agitations by other devices, will cause them to return to the sea, till they have cast their spawn."

"The Oysters be great ones in form of a shoe-horn, some be a foot long; these breed on certain banks that are bare every spring tide. This fish without the shell is so big, that it must admit of a division before you can well get it into your mouth." For lobsters, "their plenty makes them little esteemed and seldom eaten." Speaks of "a great oyster bank" in the middle of Back Bay, just off the true mouth of the Charles, and of another in the Mistick. These obstructed the navigation of both rivers. *Vide* book of facts.

P.M.—To Walden and Andromeda Ponds.

I was surprised to find the ice in the middle of the last pond a beautiful delicate rose-color for two or three rods, deeper in spots. It reminded me of red snow, and may be the same. I tried to think it the blood of wounded muskrats, but it could not be. It extended several inches into the ice, at least, and had been spread by the flowing water recently. As for vegetable pigments, there were buttonbushes in and about it. It was quite conspicuous fifteen rods off, and the color of spring-cranberry juice. This beautiful blushing ice! What are we coming to?

Was surprised to see oak-balls on a bear scrub oak. Have them, then, on black, scarlet, red, and bear scrub.

Saw a young (apparently) red oak (it did not taste bitter) ten feet high, the ends of whose twigs looked at first sight as if they had been twisted off by some hungry browsing bird, leaving the fibres streaming. These I found were the strong woody fibres of last year's leaf-stalk, standing out white, in some cases two inches in all directions, from the ends of the twigs, in others rolled together like strong twine; sometimes four or five leaf-stalks' fibres, with wonderful regularity, as if braided,—like braided horse-tails. It was wonderful how they could have become so wonderfully knotted or braided together, but Nature had made up in assiduity for want of skill. I think it must be that these leaves died (perhaps in the great drought of last year) while their fibres were still strongly united with their twigs and so preserving their flexibility without losing their connection, and so the wind flapping the leaves, which hang short down, has twisted them together and commonly worn out the leaves entirely, without loosening or breaking the tough leaf-stalk. Here is self-registered the flutterings of a leaf in this twisted, knotted, and braided twine. So fickle and unpredictable, not to say insignificant, a motion does yet get permanently recorded in some sort. Not a leaf flutters, summer or winter, but its variation and dip and intensity are registered in THE BOOK.

Jan. 25. I have come with basket and hatchet to get a specimen of the rose-colored ice. It is covered with snow. I push it away with my hands and feet. At first I detect no rose tint, and suspect it may have disappeared,—faded or bleached out,—or it was a dream. But the surrounding snow and the little body of the ice I had laid bare was what hindered. At length I detect a faint tinge; I cut down a young white oak and sweep bare a larger space; I then cut out a cake. The redness is all about an inch below the surface, the little bubbles in the ice there for half an inch vertically being coated interruptedly within or without with what looks like a minute red dust when seen through a microscope, as if it had dried on. Little balloons, with some old paint almost scaled off their spheres. It has no beauty nor brightness thus seen, more than brick-dust. And this it is which gave the ice so delicate a tinge, seen through that inch of clear white ice. What is it? Can it be blood?

Jan. 26. I am afraid I have not described vividly enough the aspect of that Lodging Snow of the 19th and to-day partly. Imagine the innumerable twigs and boughs of the forest (as you stand in its still midst), crossing each other at every conceivable angle on every side from the ground to thirty feet in height, with each its zigzag wall of snow four or five inches high, so innumerable at different distances one behind another that they completely close up the view like a loose-woven downy screen, into which, however, stooping and winding, you ceaselessly advance. The wintriest scene,—which perhaps can only be seen in perfection while the snow is yet falling, before wind and thaw begin. Else you miss, you lose, the delicate touch of the master. A coarse woof and warp of snowy batting, leaving no space for a bird to perch.

In many places where you knew there was a thrifty young wood, there appears to be none, for all is bent down and almost completely buried in the snow, and you are stepping over them. The pitch pines are most round-headed, and the young white oaks are most leaved at top, and hence suffer most.

What changes in the aspect of the earth! one day russet hills, and muddy ice, and yellow and greenish pools in the fields; the next all painted white, the fields and woods and roofs laid on thick. The great sloshy pools in the fields, freezing as they dried away, look like bread that has spewed in the baking, the fungi of a night, an acre in extent; but trust not your feet on it, for the under side is not done; there the principle of water still prevails.

Jan. 27. P.M.—Up meadow to Cliffs and Walden road.

I came upon a fox's track under the north end of the Cliffs and followed it. It was made last night, after the sleet and probably the rain was over, before it froze; it must have been at midnight or after. The tracks were commonly ten or twelve inches apart and each one and three quarters or two inches wide. Sometimes there was a longer interval and two feet fell nearer together, as if in a canter. It did not wind round the prominent rocks, but leaped upon them as if to reconnoitre. At length, after going perhaps half a mile, it turned as if to descend a dozen rods beyond the juniper, and suddenly came to end. Looking closely I found the entrance (apparently) to its hole, under a prominent rock which seemed to lie loose on the top of the ledge and about two feet from the nearest track. By stooping it had probably squeezed under this and passed into its den beneath. I could find no track leading from it.

Their tracks are larger than you would expect, as large as those of a much heavier dog, I should think. What a life is theirs, venturing forth only at night for their prey, ranging a great distance, trusting to pick up a sleeping partridge or a hare, and at home again before morning! With what relish they must relate their midnight adventures to one another there in their dens by day, if they have society! I had never associated that rock with a fox's den, though perhaps I had sat on it many a time. There are more things in heaven and earth, Horatio, etc., etc. They are the only outlaws, the only Robin Hoods, here nowadays. Do they not stand for gypsies and all outlaws? Wild dogs, as Indians are wild men.

Jan. 31. Wednesday. A clear, cold, beautiful day. Fine skating. An unprecedented expanse of ice.

As I skated near the shore under Lee's cliff, I saw what I took to be some scrags or knotty stubs of a dead limb lying on the bank beneath a white oak, close by me. Yet while I looked directly at them I could not but admire their close resemblance to partridges. I had come along with a rapid whir and suddenly halted right against them, only two rods distant, and, as my eyes watered a little from skating against the wind, I was not convinced that they were birds till I had pulled out my glass and deliberately examined them. They sat and stood, three of them, perfectly still with their heads erect, some darker feathers like ears, me-thinks, increasing their resemblance to scrabs, as where a small limb is broken off. I was much surprised at the remarkable stillness they preserved, instinctively rely-ing on the resemblance to the ground for their protec-tion, *i.e.* withered grass, dry oak leaves, dead scrags, and broken twigs. I thought at first that it was a dead oak limb with a few stub ends or scrabbs sticking up, and it was not till I brought my glass to bear on them and saw their eyes distinctly, steadily glaring on me, their necks and every muscle tense with anxiety, that I was convinced. At length, on some signal which I did not perceive, they went with a whir, as if shot, off over the bushes.

It was quite an adventure getting over the bridgeways or cause-ways, for on every shore there was either water or thin ice which would not bear. Returning, I saw a large hawk flapping and sailing low over the meadow. There was some dark color to its wings.

You were often liable to be thrown when skating fast, by the shallow puddles on the ice formed in the middle of the day and not easy to be distinguished. These detained your feet while your un-impeded body fell forward.

Feb. 2. Snowed again half an inch more in the evening, after which, at ten o'clock, the moon still obscured, I skated on the river and meadows. Our skates make but little sound in this coating of snow about an inch thick, as if we had on woollen skates, and we can eas-ily see our tracks in the night. We seem thus to go faster than be-fore by day, not only because we do not see (but feel and imagine) our rapidity, but because of the impression which the mysterious muffled sound of our feet makes. Now and then we skated into some chippy, crackling white ice, where a superficial puddle had run dry before freezing hard, and got a tumble.

Feb. 3. This morning it is snowing again. This will deserve to be called the winter of skating.

Skated up the river with Tappan in spite of the snow and wind. It was a novel experience, this skating through snow, sometimes a mile without a bare spot, this blustering day. In many places a crack ran across our course where the water had oozed out, and the driving snow catching in it had formed a thick batter with a stiffish crust in which we were tripped up and measured our lengths on the ice. The few thin places were concealed, and we avoided them by our knowledge of the localities. Sometimes a thicker drift, too, threw us, or a sudden unevenness in the concealed ice; but on the whole the snow was but a slight obstruction. We skated with much more facility than I had anticipated, and I would not have missed the experience for a good deal.

We went up the Pantry Meadow above the old William Wheeler house, and came down this meadow again with the wind and snow dust, spreading our coat-tails, like birds, though somewhat at the risk of our necks if we had struck a foul place. I found that I could sail on a tack pretty well, trimming with my skirts. Sometimes we had to jump suddenly over some obstacle which the snow had concealed before, to save our necks. It was worth the while for one to look back against the sun and wind and see the other sixty rods off coming, floating down like a graceful demon in the midst of the broad meadow all covered and lit with the curling snow-steam, between which you saw the ice in dark, waving streaks, like a mighty river Orellana braided of a myriad steaming currents,— like the demon of the storm driving his flocks and herds before him. In the midst of this tide of curling snow-steam, he sweeps and surges this way and that and comes on like the spirit of the whirl-wind.

At Lee's Cliff we made a fire, kindling with white pine cones, after oak leaves and twigs,—else we had lost it; these saved us, for there is a resinous drop at the point of each scale,—and then we forgot that we were outdoors in a blustering winter day.

Some little boys ten years old are as handsome skaters as I know. They sweep along with a graceful floating motion, leaning now to this side, then to that, like a marsh hawk beating the bush.

I still recur in my mind to that skate of the 31st. I was thus enabled to get a bird's-eye view of the river,—to survey its length and breadth within a few hours, connect one part (one shore) with another in my mind, and realize what was going on upon it from end to end,—to know the whole as I ordinarily knew a few miles of it only. I connected the chestnut-tree house, near the shore in Wayland, with the chimney house in Billerica, Pelham's Pond with Nutting's Pond in Billerica. There is good skating from the mouth to Saxonville, measuring in a straight line some twenty-two miles, by the river say thirty now, Concord midway. It is all the way of one character,—a meadow river, or dead stream,—Musketicook,—the abode of muskrats, pickerel, etc., crossed by some twenty low wooden bridges, *sublicii pontes*, connected with the mainland by willowy causeways. Thus the long, shallow lakes divided into reaches. These long causeways all under water and ice now, only the bridges peeping out from time to time like a dry eyelid.

Feb. 5. It was quite cold last evening, and I saw the scuttle window reflecting the lamp from a myriad brilliant points when I went up to bed. It sparkled as if we lived inside of a cave, but this morning it has moderated considerably and is snowing. Already one inch of snow has fallen.

According to Webster, in Welsh a hare is "furze or gorse-cat." Also, "Chuk, a word used in calling swine. It is the original name of that animal, which our ancestors brought with them from Persia, where it is still in use. Pers. *chuk*," etc. "Sans. *sugara*. Our ancestors while in England adopted the Welsh *hwc*, hog; but *chuck* is retained in our popular name of woodchuck, that is, wood hog."

In a journal it is important in a few words to describe the weather, or character of the day, as it affects our feelings. That which was so important at the time cannot be unimportant to remember.

Feb. 6. The coldest morning this winter. Our thermometer stands at −14° at 9 A.M.; others, we hear, at 6 A.M. stood at −18°, at Gorham, N.H., −30°. There are no loiterers in the street, and the wheels of wood wagons squeak as they have not for a long time,—actually shriek. Frostwork keeps its place on the window within three feet of the stove *all day* in my chamber. At 4 P.M. the thermometer is at −10°; at six it is at −14°.

I was walking at five, and found it stinging cold. It stung the face. The setting sun no sooner leaves our west windows than a solid but beautiful crystallization coats them, except perhaps a triangularish bare spot at one corner, which perhaps the sun has warmed and dried. (I believe the saying is that by the 1st of February the meal and grain for a horse are half out.)

Feb. 7. The coldest night for a long, long time was last. Sheets froze stiff about the faces. Cat mewed to have the door opened, but was at first disinclined to go out. When she came in at nine she smelt of meadow hay. We all took her up and smelled of her, it was so fragrant. Had cuddled in some barn. People dreaded to go to bed. The ground cracked in the night as if a powder-mill had blown up, and the timbers of the house also. My pail of water was frozen in the morning so that I could not break it. Must leave many buttons unbuttoned, owing to numb fingers. Iron was like fire in the hands. Thermometer at about 7.30 A.M. gone into the bulb, −19° at least. The cold has stopped the clock. Every bearded man in the street is a graybeard. Bread, meat, milk, cheese, etc., etc., all frozen. Pity the poor who have not a large wood-pile. The latches are white with frost, and every nail-head in entries, etc., has a white cap. The chopper hesitates to go to the woods. Yet I see S. Wetherbee stumping past, three quarters of a mile, for his morning's dram. Neighbor Smith's thermometer stood at −26° early this morning. But this day is at length more moderate than yesterday.

This, *i.e.* yesterday, the 6th, will be remembered as the cold Tuesday. The old folks still refer to the Cold Friday, when they sat before great fires of wood four feet long, with a fence of blankets behind them, and water froze on the mantelpiece. But they say this is as cold as that was.

Feb. 15. All day a steady, warm, imprisoning rain carrying off the snow, not unmusical on my roof. It is a rare time for the student and reader who cannot go abroad in the afternoon, provided he can keep awake, for we are wont to be drowsy as cats in such weather. Without, it is not walking but wading. The fire needs no replenishing, and we save our fuel. It seems like a distant forerunner of spring.

Feb. 18. After a thaw old tracks in the snow, from *basso*, become *alto relievo*. The snow which was originally compressed and hardened beneath the feet,—also, perhaps, by the influence of the sun and maybe rain,—being the last to melt, becomes protuberant, the highest part and most lasting. The track becomes a raised almost icy type. How enduring these trails! How nature clings to these types. The track even of small animals like a skunk will outlast a considerable thaw.

Feb. 21. A clear air, with a northwesterly, March-like wind, as yesterday. What is the peculiarity in the air that both the invalid in the chamber and the traveller on the highway say these are perfect March days?

A warmth begins to be reflected from the partially dried ground here and there in the sun in sheltered places, very cheering to invalids who have weak lungs, who think they may weather it till summer now.

Mar. 1. The last day for skating. It is a very pleasant and warm day, the finest yet, with considerable coolness in the air, however,— winter still. The dusty banks of snow by the railroad reflect a wonderfully dazzling white from their pure crannies, being melted into an uneven, sharp, wavy surface. This more dazzling white must be due to the higher sun.

Examined again the ice and meadow-crust deposited just south of Derby's Bridge.

I think the meadow is lifted in this wise: First, you have a considerable freshet in midwinter, succeeded by severe cold before the water has run off much. Then, as the water goes down, the ice for a certain width on each side the river meadows rests on the ground, which freezes to it.* Then comes another freshet, which rises a little higher than the former. This gently lifts up the river ice, and that meadow ice on each side of it which still has water under it, without breaking them, but overflows the ice which is frozen to the bottom. Then, after some days of thaw and wind, the latter ice is broken up and rises in cakes, larger or smaller with or without the meadow-crust beneath it, and is floated off before the wind and current till it grounds somewhere, or melts and so sinks, frequently three cakes one upon another, on some swell in the meadow or the edge of the upland. The ice is thus with us a wonderful agent in changing the aspect of the surface of the river-valley. I think that there has been more meadow than usual moved this year, because we had so great a freshet in midwinter succeeded by severe cold, and that by another still greater freshet before the cold weather was past.

I did well to walk in the forenoon, the fresh and inspiring half of this bright day, for now, at midafternoon, its brightness is dulled, and a fine stratus is spread over the sky.

March 4. Sunday. We go over the Cliffs. At the Bee Hill-side, a striped squirrel, which quickly dives into his hole at our approach.† May not this season of springlike weather between the first decidedly springlike day and the first blue-bird, already fourteen days long, be called the *striped squirrel spring*? In which we go listening for the blue-bird, but hear him not.

March 6. Our woods are now so reduced that the chopping of this winter has been a cutting to the quick. At least we walkers feel it as

---

*Or rather all the water freezes where it is shallow and the grass is frozen into it. *Vide* Mar. 11th.
† *Vide* Mar. 7th.

such. There is hardly a wood lot of any consequence left but the chopper's axe has been heard in it this season. They have even infringed fatally on White Pond, on the south of Fair Haven Pond, shaved off the topknot of the Cliffs, the Colburn farm, Beck Stow's, etc., etc.

March 7. We were walking along the sunny hillside on the south of Fair Haven Pond (on the 4th), which the choppers had just laid bare, when, in a sheltered and warmer place, we heard a rustling amid the dry leaves on the hillside and saw a striped squirrel eying us from its resting-place on the bare ground. It sat still till we were within a rod, then suddenly dived into its hole, which was at its feet, and disappeared. The first pleasant days of spring come out like a squirrel and go in again.

March 10. I am not aware of growth in any plant yet, unless it be the further peeping out of willow catkins. They have crept out further from under their scales, and, looking closely into them, I detect a little redness along the twigs even now. You are always surprised by the sight of the first spring bird or insect; they seem premature, and there is no such evidence of spring as themselves, so that they literally *fetch* the year about. It is thus when I hear the first robin or bluebird or, looking along the brooks, see the first water-bugs out circling. But you think, They have come, and Nature cannot recede.

March 11. On Abel Hosmer's pasture, just southeast of the stone bridge, I see where the sod was lifted up over a great space in the flood of the 17th of February. The sod carried off is from four to six inches thick commonly. Pieces of this crust are resting within ten or twenty rods. One has sunk against the causeway bridge, being too wide to go through. I see one piece of crust, twelve feet by six, turned completely topsyturvy with its ice beneath it. This has prevented the ice from melting, and on examining it I find that the ice did not settle down on to the grass after the water went down and then freeze to it, for the blades of grass penetrate one inch into the ice, showing that, the water being shallow, the whole froze, and the grass was frozen in, and thus, when the water rose again, was lifted up.

Saw a cake of recent ice very handsomely marked as it decayed, with darker marks for the original crystals centred with the original white. It would be a rare pattern for a carpet, because it contains a variety of figures agreeable to the eye without regularity.

March 13. Northern lights last night. Rainbow in east this morning.

March 20. A flurry of snow at 7 A.M. I go to turn my boat up. Four or five song sparrows are flitting along amid the willows by the waterside. Probably they came yesterday with the bluebirds.

It is remarkable by what a gradation of days which we *call* pleasant and warm, beginning in the last of February, we come at last to real summer warmth. At first a sunny, calm, serene winter day is pronounced spring, or reminds us of it; and even the first pleasant spring day perhaps we walk with our greatcoat buttoned up and gloves on.

Trying the other day to imitate the honking of geese, I found myself flapping my sides with my elbows, as with wings, and uttering something like the syllables *mow-ack* with a nasal twang and twist in my head; and I produced their note so perfectly in the opinion of the hearers that I thought I might possibly draw a flock down.

March 22. I hear a song sparrow on an alder-top sing *ozit ozit oze-e-e* | (quick) *tchip tchip tchip tchip tchay* | *te tchip ter che ter tchay*; also the same shortened and *very much* varied. Heard one sing uninterruptedly, *i.e.* without a pause, almost a minute. I crossed Fair Haven Pond, including the river, on the ice, and probably can for three or four days yet.

Going along the steep side-hill on the south of the pond about 4 P.M., on the edge of the little patch of wood which the choppers have not yet levelled,—though they have felled many an acre around it this winter,—I observed a rotten and hollow hemlock stump about two feet high and six inches in diameter, and instinctively approached with my right hand ready to cover it. I found a flying squirrel in it, which, as my left hand had covered a small hole at the bottom, ran directly into my right hand. It struggled and bit not a little, but my cotton glove protected me, and I felt its teeth only once or twice. It also uttered three or four dry shrieks at first, something like *cr-r-rack cr-r-r-ack cr-r-r-ack.* I rolled it up in my handkerchief and, holding the ends tight, carried it home in my hand, some three miles. It struggled more or less all the way, especially when my feet made any unusual or louder noise going through leaves or bushes. I could count its claws as they appeared through the handkerchief, and once it got its head out a hole. It even bit through the handkerchief.

Color, as I remember, above a chestnut ash, inclining to fawn or cream color (?), slightly browned; beneath white, the under edge of its wings (?) tinged yellow, the upper dark, perhaps black, making a dark stripe. Audubon and Bachman do not speak of any such stripe! It was a very cunning little animal, reminding me of a mouse in the room. Its very large and prominent black eyes gave it an interesting innocent look. Its very neat flat, fawn-colored, distichous tail was a great ornament. Its "sails" were not very obvious when it was at rest, merely giving it a flat appearance beneath. It would leap off and upward into the air two or three feet from a table, spreading its "sails," and fall to the floor in vain; perhaps strike the side of the room in its upward spring and endeavor to cling to it. It would run up the window by the sash, but evidently found the furniture and walls and floor too hard and smooth for it and after some falls became quiet. In a few moments it allowed me to stroke it, though far from confident.

I put it in a barrel and covered it for the night. It was quite busy all the evening gnawing out, clinging for this purpose and gnawing at the upper edge of a sound oak barrel, and then dropping to rest from time to time. It had defaced the barrel considerably by morning, and would probably have escaped if I had not placed a piece of iron against the gnawed part. I had left in the barrel some bread, apple, shagbarks, and cheese. It ate some of the apple and one shagbark, cutting it quite in two transversely.

In the morning it was quiet, and *squatted* somewhat curled up amid the straw, with its tail passing under it and the end curled over its head very prettily, as if to shield it from the light and keep it warm. I always found it in this position by day when I raised the lid.

MARCH 23. P.M.—To Fair Haven Pond.

Carried my flying squirrel back to the woods in my handkerchief. I placed it, about 3.30 P.M., on the very stump I had taken it from. It immediately ran about a rod over the leaves and up a slender maple sapling about ten feet, then after a moment's pause sprang off and skimmed downward toward a large maple nine feet distant, whose trunk it struck three or four feet from the ground. This it rapidly ascended, on the opposite side from me, nearly thirty feet, and there clung to the main stem with its head downward, eying me. After two or three minutes' pause I saw that it was preparing for another spring by raising its head and looking off, and away it went in admirable style, more like a bird than any quadruped I had dreamed of and far surpassing the impression I had received from naturalists' accounts.* I marked the spot it started from and the place where it struck, and measured the height and distance carefully. It sprang off from the maple at the height of twenty-eight and a half feet, and struck the ground at the foot of a tree fifty and a half feet distant, measured horizontally. Its flight was not a *regular* descent; it varied from a direct line both horizontally and vertically. Indeed it skimmed much like a hawk and part of its flight was nearly horizontal, and it diverged from a right line eight or ten feet to the right, making a curve in that direction. There were six trees from six inches to a foot in diameter, one a hemlock, in a direct line between the two termini, and these it skimmed partly round, and passed through their thinner limbs; did not as I could perceive touch a twig. It skimmed its way like a hawk between and around the trees. Though it was a windy day, this was on a steep hillside away from the wind and covered with wood, so it was not aided by that. As the ground rose about, two feet, the distance was to the absolute height as fifty and a half to twenty-six and a half, or it advanced about two feet for every one

—————————

Vide next page.

foot of descent. After its vain attempts in the house, I was not pre-pared for this exhibition. It did not fall heavily as in the house, but struck the ground gently enough, and I cannot believe that the mere extension of the skin enabled it to skim so far. It must be still further aided by its organization. Perhaps it fills itself with air first. Perhaps I had a fairer view than common of its flight, now at 3.30 P.M. Audubon and Bachman say *he* saw it skim "about fifty yards," curving upwards at the end and alighting on the trunk of a tree. This in a meadow in which were scattered oaks and beeches. This near Philadelphia. Wesson says he has seen them fly five or six rods.

Kicking over the hemlock stump, which was a mere shell with holes below, and a poor refuge, I was surprised to find a little nest at the bottom, open above just like a bird's nest, a mere bed. It was composed of leaves, shreds of bark, and dead pine-needles. As I remember, it was not more than an inch and a half broad when at rest, but when skimming through the air I should say it was four inches broad. This is the impression I now have. Captain John Smith says it is said to fly thirty or forty yards. Audubon and Bach-man quote one Gideon B. Smith, M.D., of Baltimore, who has had much to do with these squirrels and speaks of their curving upward at the end of their flight to alight on a tree-trunk and of their "fly-ing" into his windows. In order to perform all these flights,—to strike a tree at such a distance, etc., etc.,—it is evident it must be able to steer. I should say that mine steered as a hawk that moves without flapping its wings, never being able, however, to get a new impetus after the first spring.

C. saw geese to-night.

March 24. Passing up the Assabet, by the Hemlocks, where there has been a slide and some rocks have slid down into the river, I think I see how rocks come to be found in the midst of rivers. Riv-ers are continually changing their channels,—eating into one bank and adding their sediment to the other,—so that frequently where there is a great bend you see a high and steep bank or hill on one side, which the river washes, and a broad meadow on the other. As the river eats into the hill, especially in freshets, it undermines the rocks, large and small, and they slide down, alone or with the sand and soil, to the water's edge. The river continues to eat into the hill, carrying away all the lighter parts of the sand and soil, to add to its meadows or islands somewhere, but leaves the rocks where they rested, and thus in course of time they occupy the middle of the stream and, later still, the middle of the meadow, perchance, though it may be buried under the mud. But this does not explain how so many rocks lying in streams have been split in the direction of the current. Again, rivers appear to have travelled back and worn into the meadows of their creating, and then they become more meandering than ever. Thus in the course of ages the rivers wriggle in their beds, till it feels comfortable under them. Time is cheap and rather insignificant. It matters not whether it is a river which changes from side to side in a geological period or an eel that wriggles past in an instant.

The last four days, including this, have been very cold and blustering. We have had several flurries of snow, when we hoped it would snow in earnest and the weather be warmer for it. It is too cold to think of those signs of spring which I find recorded under this date last year.

March 26. P.M.—Sail down to the Great Meadows. A strong wind with snow driving from the west and thickening the air. The farmers pause to see me scud before it.

March 28. I run about these cold and blustering days, on the whole perhaps the worst to bear in the year,—partly because they disappoint expectation,—looking almost in vain for some animal or vegetable life stirring. The warmest springs hardly allow me the glimpse of a frog's heel as he settles himself in the mud, and I think I am lucky if I see one winter-defying hawk or a hardy duck or two at a distance on the water. As for the singing of birds,—the few that have come to us,—it is too cold for them to sing and for me to hear. The bluebird's warble comes feeble and frozen to my ear. We still walk on frozen ground, though in the garden I can thrust a spade in about six inches.

March 30. He must have a great deal of life in him to draw upon, who can pick up a subsistence in November and March. Man comes out of his winter quarters this month as lean as a wood-chuck. Except for science, do not travel in such a climate as this in November and March. I tried if a fish would take the bait to-day; but in vain; I did not get a nibble. Where are they?

March 31. I see through the window that it is a very fine day, the first really warm one. I did not know the whole till I came out at 3 P.M. and walked to the Cliffs.

The fuzzy gnats are in the air, and bluebirds, whose warble is thawed out. I am uncomfortably warm, gradually unbutton both my coats, and wish that I had left the outside one at home.

It is suddenly warm, and this amelioration of the weather is in-comparably the most important fact in this vicinity. It is incredible what a revolution in our feelings and in the aspect of nature this warmer air alone has produced. Yesterday the earth was simple to barrenness, and dead,—*bound out.* Out-of-doors there was nothing but the wind and the withered grass and the cold though sparkling blue water, and you were driven in upon yourself. Now you would think that there was a sudden awakening in the very crust of the earth, as if flowers were expanding and leaves putting forth; but not so; I listen in vain to hear a frog or a new bird as yet; only the frozen ground is melting a little deeper, and the water is trickling down the hills in some places. No, the change is mainly in us. We feel as if we had obtained a new lease of life. Some juniper (*repens*) berries are blue now. Looking from the Cliffs I see that Walden is open to-day first, and Fair Haven Pond will open by day after to-morrow.*

April 1. The month comes in true to its reputation. We wake, though late, to hear the sound of a strong, steady, and rather warm rain on the roof, and see the puddles shining in the road.

When I look out the window I see that the grass on the bank on the south side of the house is already much greener than it was

------

*No.

yesterday. As it cannot have grown so suddenly, how shall I account for it? I suspect that the reason is that the few green blades are not merely washed bright by the rain, but erect themselves to imbibe its influence, and so are more prominent, while the withered blades are beaten down and flattened by it.

April 2. Not only the grass but the pines also were greener yesterday for being wet. To-day, the grass being dry, the green blades are less conspicuous than yesterday. It would seem, then, that this color is more vivid when wet, and perhaps all green plants, like lichens, are to some extent greener in moist weather. Green is essentially *vivid*, or the color of life, and it is therefore most brilliant when a plant is moist or most alive. A plant is said to be green in opposition to being withered and dead. The word, according to Webster, is from the Saxon *grene*, to grow, and hence is the color of herbage when growing.

High winds all night, rocking the house, opening doors, etc. To-day also. It is wintry cold also, and ice has formed nearly an inch thick in my boat.

P.M.—Down the river-bank.

April 15. 9 A.M.—To Atkins's boat-house.

Returning, we had a fine view of a blue heron, standing erect and open to view on a meadow island, by the great swamp south of the bridge, looking as broad as a boy on the side. When the heron takes to flight, what a change in size and appearance! It is *presto change*! There go two great undulating wings pinned together, but the body and neck must have been left behind somewhere.

April 19. 5 A.M.—Up Assabet.

Warm and still and somewhat cloudy. Am without greatcoat. Many tortoises have their heads out. The river has fallen a little. Going up the Assabet, two or three tortoises roll down the steep bank with a rustle. One tumbles on its edge and rolls swiftly like a disk cast by a boy, with its back to me, from eight or ten feet into the water.

P.M.—To Walden.

APRIL 20. Rains all day, taking out the frost and imprisoning me. You cannot set a post yet on account of frost.

April 22. Fair, but windy. The yellow willow catkins pushing out begin to give the trees a misty, downy appearance, dimming them. The bluish band on the breast of the kingfisher leaves the pure white beneath in the form of a heart. The blossoms of the sweet-gale are now on fire over the brooks, contorted like caterpillars.

April 29. That lake grass—or perhaps I should call it *purple* grass— is now apparently in perfection on the water. Long and slender blades (about an eighth of an inch wide and six to twelve inches long, the part exposed) lie close side by side straight and parallel on the surface, with a dimple at the point where they emerge. Some are a very rich purple, with apparently a bloom, and very suggestive of placidity. It is a true *bloom*, at any rate,—the first blush of the spring caught on these little standards elevated to the light. By the water they are left perfectly smooth and flat and straight, as well as parallel, and thus, by their mass, make the greater impression on the eye. It has a strong marshy, somewhat fishy, almost seaweed-like scent when plucked. Seen through a glass the surface is finely grooved.

April 30. I hear from far the scream of a hawk circling over the Holden woods and swamp. This accounts for those two men with guns just entering it. What a dry, shrill, angry scream! I see the bird with my glass resting upon the topmost plume of a tall white pine. Its back, reflecting the light, looks white in patches; and now it circles again. It is a red-tailed hawk. The tips of its wings are curved upward as it sails. How it scolds at the men beneath! I see its open bill. It must have a nest there. Hark! there goes a gun, and down it tumbles from a rod or two above the wood. So I thought, but was mistaken. In the meanwhile, I learn that there is a nest there, and the gunners killed one this morning, which I examined. They are now getting the young. Above it was brown, but not at all reddish brown except about head.

Powerful neck and legs. The claws pricked me as I handled it. It measured one yard and three eighths plus from tip to tip, *i.e.* four feet and two inches.* Some ferruginous on the neck; ends of wings nearly black.

May 1. Rained some in the night; cloudy in the forenoon; clears up in the afternoon.

P.M.—By boat with Sophia to Conantum, a maying.

There is an unaccountable sweetness as of flowers in the air,—a true May day. Raw and drizzling in the morning. The grackle still. What various brilliant and evanescent colors on the surface of this agitated water! It reminds me of the sea.

Went to Garfield's for the hawk of yesterday. It was nailed to the barn *in terrorem* and as a trophy. He gave it to me with an egg. He called it the female, and probably was right, it was so large. He tried in vain to shoot the male, which I saw circling about just out of gunshot and screaming, while he robbed the nest.

The hawk measures exactly 22½ inches in length and 4 feet 4½ inches in alar extent, and weighs 3¼ pounds. The ends of closed wings almost two inches short of end of tail. The wing-coverts and scapulars glossed with purple reflections. The twelve tail-feathers (which MacGillivray says is the number in all birds of prey, *i.e.* the *Falconinæ* and *Striginæ*) showing five and three quarters inches a clear brown red, or rather fox-color, above, with a narrow dark band within half an inch of the end, which is tipped with dirty white.

Bill very *blue* black, with a *short, stout* curved tip,—curving from the cere more than a quarter of a circle, extends not quite a quarter of an inch beyond the lower mandible. [*Etc.: 5 more pages of data—observation, dissection, reading*].

May 5. Looking over my book, I found I had done my errands, and said to myself I would find a crow's nest. (I had heard a crow scold at a passing hawk a quarter of an hour before.) I had hardly taken this resolution when, looking up, I saw a crow wending his way

---

*Vide forward. More.

across an interval in the woods towards the highest pines in the swamp, on which he alighted. I directed my steps to them and was soon greeted with an angry *caw*, and, within five minutes from my resolve, I detected a new nest close to the top of the tallest white pine in the swamp. A crow circled cawing about it within gunshot, then over me surveying, and, perching on an oak directly over my head within thirty-five feet, cawed angrily. But suddenly, as if having taken a new resolution, it flitted away, and was joined by its mate and two more, and they went off silently a quarter of a mile or more and lit in a pasture, as if they had nothing to concern them in the wood.

May 7. 5 A.M.—To Island. Finger-cold and windy.

A crow's nest near the top of a pitch pine about twenty feet high, just completed, betrayed by the birds' cawing and alarm.* As on the 5th, *one* came and sat on a bare oak within forty feet, cawed, reconnoitred; and then both flew off to a distance, while I discovered and climbed to the nest within a dozen rods. One comes near to spy you first.

P.M.—Climbed to two crows' nests,—or maybe one of them a squirrel's,—in Hubbard's Grove. Do they not sometimes use a squirrel's nest for a foundation? A ruby-crested wren is apparently attracted and eyes me. It is wrenching and fatiguing, as well as dirty, work to climb a tall pine with nothing, or maybe only dead twigs and stubs, to hold by. You must proceed with great deliberation and see well where you put your hands and your feet. Scared up two gray squirrels in the Holden wood, which ran glibly up the tallest trees on the opposite side to me, and leaped across from the extremity of the branches to the next trees, and so on very fast ahead of me. Remembering—aye, aching with—my experience in climbing trees this afternoon and morning, I could not but admire their exploits. To see them travelling with so much swiftness and ease that road over which I climbed a few feet with such painful exertion!

---

*A mistake.

A short distance beyond the hawk's-nest pine, I observed a middling-sized red oak standing a little aslant on the side-hill over the swamp, with a pretty large hole in one side about fifteen feet from the ground, where apparently a limb on which a felled tree lodged had been cut some years before and so broke out a cavity. I thought that such a hole was too good a one not to be improved by some inhabitant of the wood. Perhaps the gray squirrels I had just seen had their nest there. Or was not the entrance big enough to admit a screech owl? So I thought I would tap on it and put my ear to the trunk and see if I could hear anything stirring within it, but I heard nothing. Then I concluded to look into it. So I shinned up, and when I reached up one hand to the hole to pull myself up by it, the thought passed through my mind perhaps something may take hold my fingers, but nothing did. The first limb was nearly opposite to the hole, and, resting on this, I looked in, and, to my great surprise, there squatted, filling the hole, which was about six inches deep and five to six wide, a salmon-brown bird not so big as a partridge, seemingly asleep within three inches of the top and close to my face. It was a minute or two before I made it out to be an owl. It was a salmon-brown or fawn (?) above, the feathers shafted with small blackish-brown somewhat hastate (?) marks, *grayish* toward the ends of the wings and tail, as far as I could see. A large white circular space about or behind eye, banded in rear by a pretty broad (one third of an inch) and quite conspicuous perpendicular *dark*-brown stripe. It lay crowded in that small space, with its tail somewhat bent up and one side of its head turned up with one egret, and its large dark eye open only by a long slit about a sixteenth of an inch wide; visible breathing. After a little while I put in one hand and stroked it repeatedly, whereupon it reclined its head a little lower and closed its eye entirely. Though curious to know what was under it, I disturbed it no farther at that time.

In the meanwhile, the crows were making a great cawing amid and over the pine-tops beyond the swamp, and at intervals I heard the scream of a hawk, probably the surviving male hen-hawk, whom they were pestering (unless they had discovered the male screech owl), and a part of them came cawing about me. This was a very fit place for hawks and owls to dwell in,—the thick woods just over a white spruce swamp; the gray squirrels, partridges, hawks, and owls, all together. It was probably these screech owls which I heard in moonlight nights hereabouts last fall.

Returning by owl's nest, about one hour before sunset, I climbed up and looked in again. The owl was gone, but there were four nearly round *dirty brownish white**[*]* eggs, quite warm, on nothing but the bits of rotten wood which made the bottom of the hole. The eggs were very nearly as large at one end as the other, slightly oblong, 1⅜ inches by 1⅞, as nearly as I could measure. I took out one. It would probably have hatched within a week, the young being considerably feathered and the bill remarkably developed. Perhaps she heard me coming, and so left the nest.

Nuttall says, Little Screech-Owl: Greenland to Florida; chiefly prey on mice; also small birds, beetles, crickets, etc.; nest in May and June, and lined with etc., etc., eggs four to six; several bluebirds, blackbirds, and song sparrows in one. In cloudy weather come out earlier. Wilson's thrush attacked one. Note in autumn, "hō, hŏ, hŏ, hŏ, hŏ, hŏ, hŏ, proceeding from high and clear to a low guttural shake or trill."

May 11. You can hardly walk in a thick pine wood now, especially a swamp, but presently you will have a crow or two over your head, either silently flitting over, to spy what you would be at and if its nest is in danger, or angrily cawing. It is most impressive when, looking for their nests, you first detect the presence of the bird by its shadow.

May 12. As I approached the owl's nest, I saw her run past the hole up into that part of the hollow above it, and probably she was there when I thought she had flown on the 7th. I looked in, and at first did not know what I saw. One of the three remaining eggs was hatched, and a little downy *white* young one, two or three times as

---

[*]MacGillivray describes no eggs of this color,—only white,—and the same with Nuttall, except the great gray owl.

long as an egg, lay helpless between the two remaining eggs. Also a dead white-bellied mouse (*Mus leucopus*) lay with them, its tail curled round one of the eggs. Wilson says of his red owl (*Strix asio*),—with which this apparently corresponds, and not with the mottled, though my egg is not "pure white,"—that "the young are at first covered with a whitish down."

Just before sundown, took our seats before the owl's nest and sat perfectly still and awaited her appearance. We sat about half an hour, and it was surprising what various distinct sounds we heard there deep in the wood, as if the aisles of the wood were so many ear trumpets,—the cawing of crows, the peeping of hylas in the swamp and perhaps the croaking of a tree-toad, the oven-bird, the *yorrick* of Wilson's thrush, a distant stake-driver, the night-warbler and black and white creeper, the lowing of cows, the late supper horn, the voices of boys, the singing of girls,—not all together but separately, distinctly, and musically, from where the partridge and the red-tailed hawk and the screech owl sit on their nests.

XIX.

MAY 17. Waked up at 2.30 by the peep of robins, which were aroused by a fire at the pail-factory about two miles west. I hear that the air was full of birds singing thereabouts. It rained gently at the same time, though not steadily.

MAY 19. Put my little turtles into the river. They had not noticeably increased in size,—or hardly. Three had died within a week for want of attention,—two mud turtles and one musk turtle. Two were missing,—one mud and one musk. Five musk were put into the river.

May 25. Critchicrotches in prime.

Heard the first regular bullfrog's trump on the 18th; none since.[*]

Juniper, plucked yesterday, sheds pollen in house to-day, and probably in field.

The golden robin keeps whistling something like *Eat it, Potter, eat it!*

May 28. I see a tanager, the most brilliant and tropical-looking bird we have, bright-scarlet with black wings, the scarlet appearing on the rump again between wing-tips. He brings heat, or heat him. A remarkable contrast with the green pines.

June 11. What if we feel a yearning to which no breast answers? I walk alone. My heart is full. Feelings impede the current of my

---

[*]One in the evening.

thoughts. I knock on the earth for my friend. I expect to meet him at every turn; but no friend appears, and perhaps none is dreaming of me. I am tired of frivolous society, in which silence is forever the most natural and the best manners. I would fain walk on the deep waters, but my companions will only walk on shallows and puddles. I am naturally silent in the midst of twenty from day to day, from year to year. I am rarely reminded of their presence. Two yards of politeness do not make society for me. One complains that I do not take his jokes. I took them before he had done uttering them, and went my way. One talks to me of his apples and pears, and I depart with my secret untold. His are not the apples that tempt me.

Now (September 16, '55), after four or five months of invalidity and worthlessness, I begin to feel some stirrings of life in me.

What a difference between one red-wing blackbird's egg and another's! C. finds one long as a robin's, but narrow, with large black spots on larger end and on side, on or between the bushes by riverside; another much shorter, with a large black spot on the side. Both pale-blue ground.

I have noticed the green oak-balls some days. Now observe the dark *evergreen* of June.

AUG. 7. To Tarbell Hill again with the Emersons, a-berrying.

Very few berries this year.

Sept. 14. It costs so much to publish, would it not be better for the author to put his manuscripts in a safe?

Sept. 24. P.M.—Up river to Conantum with C.

A very bright and pleasant fall day. The button-bushes pretty well browned with frost (though the maples are but just beginning to blush), their pale-yellowish season past. Nowadays remark the more the upright and fresh green phalanxes of bulrushes when the pontederias are mostly prostrate.

Brought home quite a boat-load of fuel,—one oak rail, on which fishers had stood in wet ground at Bittern Cliff, a white pine rider (?) with a square hole in it made by a woodpecker anciently, so wasted the sap as to leave the knots projecting, several chestnut rails; and I obtained behind Cardinal Shore a large oak stump which I know to have been bleaching there for more than thirty years, with three great gray prongs sprinkled with lichens. It bore above the marks of the original burning. Also, at Clamshell Hill Shore, a chestnut boat-post with a staple in it, which the ice took up last winter, though it had an arm put through it two feet underground. Some much decayed perhaps old red maple stumps at Hubbard's Bath Place. It would be a triumph to get all my winter's wood thus. How much better than to buy a cord coarsely from a farmer, seeing that I get my money's worth! Then it only affords me a momentary satisfaction to see the pile tipped up in the yard. Now I derive a separate and peculiar pleasure from every stick that I find. Each has its history, of which I am reminded when I come to burn it, and under what circumstances I found it. Got home late. C. and I supped together after our work at wooding, and talked it over with great appetites.

Dr. Aikin, in his "Arts of Life," says that "the acorns of warm climates are fit for human food."

Sept. 25. A very fine and warm afternoon after a cloudy morning. Carry Aunt and Sophia a-barberrying to Conantum. Saw two marsh hawks skimming low over the meadows and another, or a hen-hawk, sailing on high.

We got about three pecks of barberries from four or five bushes, but I filled my fingers with prickles to pay for them. With the hands well defended, it would be pleasant picking, they are so handsome, and beside are so abundant and fill up so fast. I take hold the end of the drooping twigs with my left hand, raise them, and then strip downward at once as many clusters as my hand will embrace, commonly bringing away with the raceme two small green leaves or bracts, which I do not stop to pick out. When I come to a particularly thick and handsome wreath of fruit, I pluck the twig entire and bend it around the inside of the basket. Meanwhile the catbird mews in the alders by my side, and the scream of the jay is heard from the wood-side.

In the evening went to Welch's (?) circus with C. Approaching, I perceived the peculiar scent which belongs to such places, a certain sourness in the air, suggesting trodden grass and cigar smoke. The curves of the great tent, at least eight or ten rods in diameter,—the main central curve and wherever it rested on a post,—suggested that the tent was the origin of much of the Oriental architecture, the Arabic perhaps. There was the pagoda in perfection. It is remarkable what graceful attitudes feats of strength and agility seem to require.

Sept. 26. Went up Assabet for fuel. One old piece of oak timber looks as if it had been a brace in a bridge. I get up oak rails here and there, almost as heavy as lead, and leave them to dry somewhat on the bank. Stumps, partially burned, which were brought by the freshet from some newly cleared field last spring; bleached oak trees which were once lopped for a fence; alders and birches which the river ice bent and broke by its weight last spring. It is pretty hard and dirty work.

Oct. 2. Rode [*from New Bedford*] to Middleborough, thirteen miles. Many quails in road. Passed over a narrow neck between the two Quitticus ponds, after first visiting Great Quitticus on right of road and gathering clamshells there, as I had done at Long Pond and intend to do at Assawampsett. These shells labelled will be good mementos of the ponds.

Returning along the shore, we saw a man and woman putting off in a small boat, the first we had seen. The man was black. He rowed, and the woman steered. R. called to them. They approached within a couple of rods in the shallow water. "Come nearer," said R. "Don't be afraid; I ain't a-going to hurt you." The woman answered, "I never saw the man yet that I was afraid of." The man's name was Thomas Smith, and, in answer to R.'s very direct questions as to how much he was of the native stock, said that he was one-fourth Indian. He then asked the woman, who sat unmoved in the stern with a brown dirt-colored dress on, a regular country-woman with half an acre of face (squaw-like), having first inquired of Tom if she was his woman, how much Indian blood she had in her. She did not answer directly so home a question, yet at length as good as acknowledged to one-half Indian, and said that she came from Carver, where she had a sister; the only half-breeds about here. Said her name was Sepit, but could not spell it. R. said, "Your nose looks rather Indiany." Where will you find a Yankee and his wife going a-fishing thus? They lived on the shore. Tom said he had seen turtles in the pond that weighed between fifty and sixty; had caught a pickerel that morning that weighed four or five pounds; had also seen them washed up with another in their mouths.

Their boat was of peculiar construc- 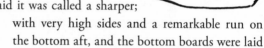 tion, and T. said it was called a sharper;

 with very high sides and a remarkable run on the bottom aft, and the bottom boards were laid across, coming out flush, and the sides set on them. An ugly model.

This boat had a singular "wooden grapple," as Tom called it, made in form of a cross, thus: with a stone within.

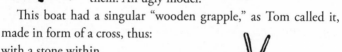

The arrowheads hereabouts are commonly white quartz.

R. says "gamble-roof." This should be "gambrel," apparently from the hind leg of a horse,—crooked like it.

Oct. 12. Carried home a couple of rails which I fished out of the bottom of the river and left on the bank to dry about three weeks ago. One was a chestnut which I have noticed for some years on the bottom of the Assabet, just above the spring on the east side, in a deep hole. It looked as if it had been there a hundred years. It was so heavy that C. and I had as much as we could do to lift it, covered with mud, on to the high bank. It was scarcely lighter to-day, and I amused myself with asking several to lift one half of it after I had sawed it in two. They failed at first, not being prepared to find it so heavy, though they could easily lift it afterward.

Oct. 16. P.M.—To the white pine grove beyond Beck Stow's.

How evenly the freshly fallen pine-needles are spread on the ground! quite like a carpet. Throughout this grove no square foot is left bare. I dug down with a stick and found that the layers of three or four years could be distinguished with considerable ease, and much deeper the old needles were raised in flakes or layers still. The topmost, or this year's, were fawn-colored; last year's, dark dull reddish; and so they went on, growing darker and more decayed, till, at the depth of three inches, where, perhaps, the needles were fifteen or twenty years old, they began to have the aspect of a dark loose-lying virgin mould, mixed with roots (pine cones and sticks a little higher). The freshly fallen needles lay as evenly strewn as if sifted over the whole surface, giving it a uniform neat fawn-color, tempting one to stretch himself on it. They rested alike on the few green leaves of weeds and the fallen cones and the cobwebs between them, in every direction across one another like joggle-sticks. In course of years they are beaten by rain and snow into a coarse, thick matting or felt to cover the roots of the trees with.

Oct. 18. Last night I was reading Howitt's account of the Australian gold-diggings, and had in my mind's eye the numerous valleys with their streams all cut up with foul pits, ten to a hundred feet deep and half a dozen feet across, as close as they can be dug, and half full of water, where men furiously rushed to probe for their fortunes, uncertain where they shall break ground, not knowing but the gold is under their camp itself; sometimes digging a hundred and sixty feet before they strike the vein, or then missing it by a foot; turned into demons and regardless of each other's rights in their thirst after riches; whole valleys for thirty miles suddenly honeycombed by the pits of the miners, so that hundreds are drowned in them. Standing in water and covered with mud and clay, they work night and day, dying of exposure and disease. Having read this and partly forgotten it, I was thinking of my own unsatisfactory life, doing as others do without any fixed star habitually in my eye, my foot not planted on any blessed isle. Then, with that vision of the diggings before me, I asked myself why I might not be washing some gold daily, though it were only the finest particles, or might not sink a shaft down to the gold within me and work that mine. There is a Ballarat or Bendigo for you. What though it were a "Sulky Gully"? Pursue some path, however narrow and crooked, in which you can walk with love and reverence. Wherever a man separates from the multitude and goes his own way, there is a fork in the road, though the travellers along the highway see only a gap in the paling.

P.M.—To Great Meadows to observe the hummocks left by the ice. I find the white fragments of a tortoise-shell in the meadow,—thirty or forty pieces, straight-sided polygons,—which apparently a hay-cart passed over. They look like broken crockery. I brought it home and amused myself with putting it together. It is a painted tortoise. The variously formed sections or component parts of the shell are not broken, but only separated. To restore them to their places is like the game which children play with pieces of wood completing a picture. It is surprising to observe how these different parts are knitted together by countless minute teeth on their edges. Then the scales, which are not nearly so numerous, and therefore larger commonly, are so placed over the former as to break joints always, as appears by the indented lines at their edges and the serrations of the shell. These scales, too, *slightly* overlap each other, *i.e.* the foremost over the next behind, so that they may not be rubbed off. Thus the whole case is bound together like a very stout band-box. The bared shell is really a very interesting study. The sternum in its natural position looks like a well-contrived drag, turned up at the sides in one solid piece.

When I was surveying for Legross, as we went to our work in the morning, we passed by the Dudley family tomb, and Legross remarked to me, all in good faith, "Would n't you like to see old Daddy Dudley? He lies in there. I'll get the keys if you'd like. I sometimes go in and look at him."

Those bright-red marks on the marginal scales of the painted tortoise remind me of some Chinese or other Oriental lacquer-work on waiters (?). This color fades to a pale yellow. The color is wholly in the scale above the bone. Of the bright colors, the yellow marks on tortoise-shells are the fastest.

How much beauty in decay! I pick up a white oak leaf, dry and stiff, but yet mingled red and green, October-like, whose pulpy part some insect has eaten beneath, exposing the delicate network of its veins. It is very beautiful held up to the light,—such work as only an insect eye could perform. Yet, perchance, to the vegetable kingdom such a revelation of ribs is as repulsive as the skeleton in the animal kingdom. In each case it is some little gourmand, working for another end, that reveals the wonders of nature. There are countless oak leaves in this condition now, and also with a submarginal line of network exposed.

Men rush to California and Australia as if the true gold were to be found in that direction; but that is to go to the very opposite extreme to where it lies. They go prospecting further and further away from the true lead, and are most unfortunate when most successful. Is not our native soil auriferous? Does not a stream from the golden mountains flow through our native valley? and has it not for more than geologic ages been bringing down the shining particles and the nuggets? Yet, strange to tell, if a digger steal away prospecting for this true gold into the unexplored solitudes, there is no danger, alas, that any will dog his steps and endeavor to supplant him. He may claim and undermine the whole valley, even the cultivated and uninhabited portions, his whole life long in peace, and no one will ever dispute his claim.

To rebuild the tortoise-shell is a far finer game than any geographical or other puzzle, for the pieces do not merely make part of a plane surface, but you have got to build a roof and a floor and the connecting walls. These are not only thus dovetailed and braced and knitted and bound together, but also held together by the skin and muscles within. It is a *band*-box.

Oct. 19. P.M.—To Pine Hill for chestnuts.

I see Mrs. Riordan and her little boy coming out of the woods with their bundles of fagots on their backs. It is surprising what great bundles of wood an Irish-woman will contrive to carry. I confess that though I could carry one I should hardly think of making such a bundle of them. They are first regularly tied up, and then carried on the back by a rope,—somewhat like the Indian women and their straps. There is a strange similarity; and the little boy carries his bundle proportionally large. The sticks about four feet long. They make haste to deposit their loads before I see them, for they do not know how pleasant a sight it is to me. The Irish-woman does the squaw's part in many respects.

When, returning at 5 o'clock, I pass the pond in the road, I see the sun, which is about entering the grosser hazy atmosphere above the western horizon, brilliantly reflected in the pond,—a dazzling sheen, a bright golden shimmer. His broad sphere extended stretches the whole length of the pond toward me. First, in the extreme distance, I see a few sparkles of the gold on the dark surface; then begins a regular and solid column of shimmering gold, straight as a rule, but at one place, where a breeze strikes the surface from one side, it is remarkably spread or widened, then recovers its straightness again, thus: Again it is remarkably curved, say thus: then broken into several pieces, then straight and entire again, then spread or blown aside at the point like smoke from a chimney, thus: Of course, if there were eyes enough to occupy all the east shore, the whole pond would be seen as one dazzling shimmering lake of melted gold. Such beauty and splendor adorns our walks!

Talking with Bellew this evening about Fourierism and communities, I said that I suspected any enterprise in which two were engaged together. "But," said he, "it is difficult to make a stick stand unless you slant two or more against it." "Oh, no," answered I, "you may split its lower end into three, or drive it single into the ground, which is the best way; but most men, when they start on a new enterprise, not only figuratively, but really, *pull up stakes*. When the sticks prop one another, none, or only one, stands erect."

He showed me a sketch of Wachusett. Spoke of his life in Paris, etc. I asked him if he had ever visited the Alps and sketched there.

He said he had not. Had he been to the White Mountains? "No," he answered, "the highest mountains I have ever seen were the Himalayas, though I was only two years old then." It seems that he was born in that neighborhood.

He complains that the Americans have attained to bad luxuries, but have no comforts.

Oct. 20. I have collected and split up now quite a pile of driftwood,—rails and riders and stems and stumps of trees,—perhaps half or three quarters of a tree. It is more amusing, not only to collect this with my boat and bring it up from the river on my back, but to split it also, than it would be to speak to a farmer for a load of wood and to saw and split that. Each stick I deal with has a history, and I read it as I am handling it, and, last of all, I remember my adventures in getting it, while it is burning in the winter evening. That is the most interesting part of its history. It has made part of a fence or a bridge, perchance, or has been rooted out of a clearing and bears the marks of fire on it. When I am splitting it, I study the effects of water on it, and, if it is a stump, the curiously winding grain by which it separates into so many prongs,—how to take advantage of its grain and split it most easily. I find that a dry oak stump will split pretty easily in the direction of its diameter, but not at right angles with it or along its circles of growth. I got out some good knees for a boat. Thus one half the value of my wood is enjoyed before it is housed, and the other half is equal to the whole value of an equal quantity of the wood which I buy.

Some of my acquaintances have been wondering why I took all this pains, bringing some nearly three miles by water, and have suggested various reasons for it. I tell them in my despair of making them understand me that it is a profound secret,—which it has proved,—yet I did hint to them that one reason was that I wanted to get it. I take some satisfaction in eating my food, as well as in being nourished by it. I feel well at dinner-time as well as after it. The world will never find out why you don't love to have your bed tucked up for you,—why you will be so perverse. I enjoy more drinking water at a clear spring than out of a goblet at a gentleman's table. I like best the bread which I have baked, the garment which I have made, the shelter which I have constructed, the fuel which I have gathered.

Oct. 21. It began to rain about 10 o'clock last evening after a cloudy day, and it still rains, gently but steadily, this morning. The wind must be east, for I hear the church bell very plainly; yet I sit with an open window, it is so warm.

I enjoyed getting that large oak stump from Fair Haven some time ago, and bringing it home in my boat. I tipped it in with the prongs up, and they spread far over the sides of the boat. There was no passing amidships. I much enjoyed this easy carriage of it, floating down the Musketaquid from far. It was a great stump and sunk my boat considerably, and its prongs were so in the way that I could take but a short stroke with my paddle. I enjoyed every stroke of my paddle, every rod of my progress, which advanced me so easily nearer to my port. It was as good as to sit by the best oak wood fire. I still enjoy such a conveyance, such a victory, as much as boys do riding on a rail. All the upper part of this, when I came to split it, I found to be very finely honeycombed, reduced to a coarse cellular mass, apparently by shrinkage and wasting; but it made excellent fuel, nevertheless, as if all the combustible part remained. Only the earthy had returned to earth.

I have been thinking over with Father the old houses in this street. There was the Hubbard (?) house at the fork of the roads; the Thayer house (now Garrison's); Sam Jones's (now Channing's); Willoughby Prescott's (a bevel-roof, which I do not remember), where Loring's is (Hoar's was built by a Prescott); Ma'm Bond's; the Jones Tavern (Bigelow's); the old Hurd (or Cumming's?) house; the Dr. Hurd house; the old mill; and the Richardson Tavern (which I do not remember). On this side, the Monroe house, in which we lived; the Parkman house, which William Heywood told me twenty years ago that he helped raise the rear of sixty years before (it then sloping to one story behind), and that then it was called an old house (Dr. Ripley said that a Bond built it); the Merrick house;

a rough-cast house where Bates's is (Betty?); and all the south side of the Mill-Dam. Still further from the centre the old houses and sites are about as numerous as above. Most of these houses slanted to one story behind.

Oct. 22. The Plymouth fishermen have just come home from the Banks, except one.

Oct. 23. The streets are strewn with buttonwood leaves, which rustle under your feet, and the children are busy raking them into heaps, some for bonfires. The sugar maples on the Common stand dense masses of rich yellow leaves with a deep scarlet blush,—far more than blush. They are remarkably brilliant this year on the exposed surfaces. The last are as handsome as any trees in the street. I am struck with the handsome form and clear, though very pale, say lemon, yellow of the black birch leaves on sprouts in the woods, finely serrate and distinctly *plaited* from the midrib. I plucked three leaves from the end of a red maple shoot, an underwood, each successively smaller than the last, the brightest and clearest scarlet that I ever saw. These and the birch attracted universal admiration when laid on a sheet of white paper and passed round the supper table, and several inquired particularly where I found them. I never saw such colors painted. They were without spot;[*] ripe leaves.

Now is the time for chestnuts. A stone cast against the trees shakes them down in showers upon one's head and shoulders. But I cannot excuse myself for using the stone. It is not innocent, it is not just, so to maltreat the tree that feeds us. I sympathize with the tree, yet I heaved a big stone against the trunks like a robber,—not too good to commit murder. I trust that I shall never do it again. It is worse than boorish, it is criminal, to inflict an unnecessary injury on the tree that feeds or shadows us. Old trees are our parents, and our parents' parents, perchance. If you would learn the secrets of Nature, you must practice more humanity than others. I was

---

[*]Yet some spots appeared and they were partly wilted the next morning, so delicate are they.

affected as if I had cast a rock at a sentient being,—with a duller sense than my own, it is true, but yet a distant relation.

Faded white ferns now at Saw Mill Brook. They press yellow or straw-color.

Oct. 26. I see a red squirrel dash out from the wall, snatch an apple from amid many on the ground, and, running swiftly up the tree with it, proceed to eat it, sitting on a smooth dead limb, with its back to the wind and its tail curled close over its back. It allows me to approach within eight feet. It holds the apple between its two fore paws and scoops out the pulp, mainly with its lower incisors, making a saucer-like cavity, high and thin at the edge, where it bites off the skin and lets it drop. It keeps its jaws a-going very fast, from time to time turning the apple round and round with its paws (as it eats), like a wheel in a plane at right angles to its body. It holds it up and twirls it with ease. Suddenly it pauses, having taken alarm at something, then drops the remainder of the apple in the hollow of the bough and glides off by short snatches, uttering a faint, sharp bird-like note.

I sometimes think that I must go off to some wilderness where I can have a better opportunity to play life,—can find more suitable materials to build my house with, and enjoy the pleasure of collecting my fuel in the forest. I have more taste for the wild sports of hunting, fishing, wigwam-building, making garments of skins, and collecting wood wherever you find it, than for butchering, farming, carpentry, working in a factory, or going to a wood market.

Oct. 28. As I paddle under the Hemlock bank this cloudy afternoon, about 3 o'clock, I see a screech owl sitting on the edge of a hollow hemlock stump about three feet high, at the base of a large hemlock. It sits with its head drawn in, eying me, with its eyes partly open, about twenty feet off. When it hears me move, it turns its head toward me, perhaps one eye only open, with its great glaring golden iris. You see two whitish triangular lines above the eyes meeting at the bill, with a sharp reddish-brown triangle between and a narrow curved line of black under each eye. At this distance and in this light, you see only a black spot where the eye is, and the question is whether the eyes are open or not. It sits on the lee side of the tree this raw and windy day. You would say that this was a bird without a neck. Its short bill, which rests upon its breast, scarcely projects at all, but in a state of rest the whole upper part of the bird from the wings is rounded off smoothly, excepting the horns, which stand up conspicuously or are slanted back. After watching it ten minutes from the boat, I landed two rods above, and, stealing quietly up behind the hemlock, though from the windward, I looked carefully around it, and, to my surprise, saw the owl still sitting there. So I sprang round quickly, with my arm outstretched, and caught it in my hand. It was so surprised that it offered no resistance at first, only glared at me in mute astonishment with eyes as big as saucers. But ere long it began to snap its bill, making quite a noise, and, as I rolled it up in my handkerchief and put it in my pocket, it bit my finger slightly. I soon took it out of my pocket and, tying the handkerchief, left it on the bottom of the boat. So I carried it home and made a small cage in which to keep it, for a night. When I took it up, it clung so tightly to my hand as to sink its claws into my fingers and bring blood.

When alarmed or provoked most, it snaps its bill and hisses. It puffs up its feathers to nearly twice its usual size, stretches out its neck, and, with wide-open eyes, stares this way and that, moving its head slowly and undulatingly from side to side with a curious motion. While I write this evening, I see that there is ground for much superstition in it. It looks out on me from a dusky corner of its box with its great solemn eyes, so perfectly still itself. I was surprised to find that I could imitate its note as I remember it, by a *guttural* whinnering.

A remarkably squat figure, being very broad in proportion to its length, with a short tail, and very catlike in the face with its horns and great eyes. Remarkably large feet and talons, legs thickly clothed with whitish down, down to the talons. It brought blood from my fingers by clinging to them. It would lower its head, stretch out its neck, and, bending it from side to side, peer at you with laughable circumspection; from side to side, as if to catch or absorb into its eyes every ray of light, strain at you with complacent yet earnest scrutiny. Raising and lowering its head and moving it from side to side in a slow and regular manner, at the same time snapping its bill smartly perhaps, and faintly hissing, and puffing itself up more and more,—cat-like, turtle-like, both in hissing and swelling. The slowness and gravity, not to say solemnity, of this motion are striking. There plainly is no jesting in this case.

General color of the owl a rather pale and perhaps slightly reddish brown, the feathers centred with black. Perches with two claws above and two below the perch. It is a slight body, covered with a mass of soft and light-lying feathers. Its head muffled in a great hood. It must be quite comfortable in winter. Dropped a pellet of fur and bones (?) in his cage. He sat, not really moping but trying to sleep, in a corner of his box all day, yet with one or both eyes slightly open all the while. I never once caught him with his eyes shut. Ordinarily stood rather than sat on his perch.

Oct. 29. P.M.—Up Assabet.

Carried my owl to the hill again. Had to shake him out of the box, for he did not go of his own accord. (He had learned to alight on his perch, and it was surprising how lightly and noiselessly he would hop upon it.) There he stood on the grass, at first bewildered, with his horns pricked up and looking toward me. In this strong light the pupils of his eyes suddenly contracted and the iris expanded till they were two great brazen orbs with a centre spot merely. His attitude expressed astonishment more than anything. I was obliged to toss him up a little that he might feel his wings, and then he flapped away low and heavily to a hickory on the hillside twenty rods off. (I had let him out in the plain just east of the hill.) Thither I followed and tried to start him again. As I moved around him, he turned his head always toward me, till he looked *directly* behind himself as he sat crosswise on a bough. He behaved as if bewildered and dazzled, gathering all the light he could and ever straining his great eyes toward you to make out who you are, but not inclining to fly. He never appeared so much alarmed as surprised and astonished.

When I moved him in his cage he would cling to the perch, though it was in a perpendicular position, one foot above another, suggesting his habit of clinging to and climbing the inside of hollow trees.

I have got a load of great hardwood stumps. For sympathy with my neighbors I might about as well live in China. They are to me barbarians, with their committee-works and gregariousness.

Nov. 1. Thursday. P.M.—Up Assabet, a-wooding.

After a rain-threatening morning it is a beautiful Indian-summer day, the most remarkable hitherto and equal to any of the kind. Yet we kept fires in the forenoon, the warmth not having got into the house. It is akin to sin to spend such a day in the house. The air is still and warm. This, too, is the *recovery* of the year,—as if the year, having nearly or quite accomplished its work, and abandoned all design, were in a more favorable and poetic mood, and thought rushed in to fill the vacuum. The river is perfectly smooth. The wool-grass, with its drooping head and the slender withered leaves dangling about its stem, stands in little sheaves upon its tussocks, clean dry straw, and is thus reflected in the water. This is the November shore.

I made out to get one great and heavy stump to the water twenty rods distant by ant-like turning it over and over laboriously. It sunk my craft low in the water.

Nov. 4. P.M.—To Hill by Assabet.

It is a dark, almost rainy day.

The winter is approaching. The birds are almost all gone. The autumnal dandelion sheltered by this apple-tree trunk is drooping and half closed and shows but half its yellow, this dark, late, wet day in the fall.

Nov. 5. I hate the present modes of living and getting a living. Farming and shopkeeping and working at a trade or profession are all odious to me. I should relish getting my living in a simple, primitive fashion. The life which society proposes to me to live is so artificial and complex—bolstered up on many weak supports, and sure to topple down at last—that no man surely can ever be inspired to live it, and only "old fogies" ever praise it. At best some think it their duty to live it. I believe in the infinite joy and satisfaction of helping myself and others to the extent of my ability. But what is the use in trying to live simply, raising what you eat, making what you wear, building what you inhabit, burning what you cut or dig, when those to whom you are allied insanely want and will have a thousand other things which neither you nor they can raise and nobody else, perchance, will pay for? The fellow-man to whom you are yoked is a steer that is ever bolting right the other way.

I was suggesting once to a man who was wincing under some of the consequences of our loose and expensive way of living, "But you might raise all your own potatoes, etc., etc." We had often done it at our house and had some to sell. At which he demurring, I said, setting it high, "You could raise twenty bushels even." "But," said he, "I use thirty-five." "How large is your family?" "A wife and three infant children." This was the real family; I need not enumerate those who were hired to *help* eat the potatoes and waste them. So he had to hire a man to raise his potatoes.

Thus men invite the devil in at every angle and then prate about the garden of Eden and the fall of man.

I know many children to whom I would fain make a present on some one of their birthdays, but they are so far gone in the luxury of presents—have such perfect museums of costly ones—that it would absorb my entire earnings for a year to buy them something which would not be beneath their notice.

P.M.—To foot of Fair Haven Hill *via* Hubbard's Grove. I see the shepherd's-purse, hedge-mustard, and red clover,—November flowers.

Nov. 6. A mizzling rain from the east drives me home from my walk.

A great many rainy or mizzling days the last fortnight, yet not much rain.

Pennyroyal has a long time stood withered and dark, blackish brown, in the fields, yet scented.

I can hardly resist the inclination to collect driftwood, to collect a great load of various kinds, which will sink my boat low in the water, and paddle or sail slowly home with it. I love this labor so much that I would gladly collect it for some person of simple habits who might want it.

Nov. 9. 7 A.M.—Grass white and stiff with frost.

9 A.M.—With Blake up Assabet.

A clear and beautiful day after frost.

Saw in the pool at the Hemlocks what I at first thought was a brighter leaf moved by the zephyr on the surface of the smooth dark water. We soon overhauled it again, and got a fair and long view of it. It was a splendid bird, a perfect floating gem, and Blake, who had never seen the like, was greatly surprised, not knowing that so splendid a bird was found in this part of the world. Above all, its breast, when it turns into the right light, all aglow with splendid purple (?) or ruby (?) reflections, *like the throat of the hummingbird*. It might not appear so close at hand. This was the most surprising to me. What an ornament to a river to see that glowing gem floating in contact with its waters! As if the hummingbird should recline its ruby throat and its breast on the water. Like dipping a glowing coal in water! It so affected me.

Found a good stone jug, small size, floating stopple up. I drew the stopple and smelled, as I expected, molasses and water, or something stronger (black-strap?), which it *had* contained. Probably some meadow-haymakers' jug left in the grass, which the recent rise of the river has floated off. It will do to put with the white pitcher I found and keep flowers in. Thus I get my furniture.

I deal so much with my fuel,—what with finding it, loading it, conveying it home, sawing and splitting it,—get so many values out of it, am warmed in so many ways by it, that the heat it will yield when in the stove is of a lower temperature and a lesser value in my eyes,—though when I feel it I am reminded of all my adventures. I just turned to put on a stick. I had my choice in the box of gray chestnut rail, black and brown snag of an oak stump, dead white pine top, gray and round, with stubs of limbs, or else old bridge plank, and chose the last.

I feel disposed, to this extent, to do the getting a living and the living for any three or four of my neighbors who really want the fuel and will appreciate the act, now that I have supplied myself. There was a fat pine plank, heavy as lead, I gave to Aunt L. for kindling.

That duck was all jewels combined, showing different lustres as it turned on the unrippled element in various lights, now brilliant glossy green, now dusky violet, now a rich bronze, now the reflections that sleep in the ruby's grain.

I see floating, just above the Hemlocks, the large sliding door of a railroad car, burnt to a cinder on one side and lettered in large bright-yellow letters on the other, "Cheshire 1510." It may have been cast over at the railroad bridge.

I affect what would commonly be called a mean and miserable way of living. I thoroughly sympathize with all savages and gypsies in so far as they merely assert the original right of man to the productions of Nature and a place in her. The highest law gives a thing to him who can use it.

Nov. 16. Mr. Rice asked me to-night if I knew how hard a head a goat had. When he lived in Roxbury a man asked him to kill a goat for him. He accordingly struck the goat with a hatchet, hard enough, as he supposed, to dash his brains out, but the goat instantly, with a bleat, leaped on to a wall and ran twenty rods on the wall faster than they could on the ground after him, and he saw him as much as a month afterward none the worse for the blow.

I think that by the "swamp robin" he means the veery.

Nov. 17. Just after dark the first snow is falling, after a chilly afternoon with cold gray clouds, when my hands were uncomfortably cold.

It is interesting to me to talk with Rice, he lives so thoroughly and satisfactorily to himself. He has learned that rare art of living, the very elements of which most professors do not know. His life has been not a failure but a success. Seeing me going to sharpen some plane-irons, and hearing me complain of the want of tools, he said that I ought to have a chest of tools. But I said it was not worth the while. I should not use them enough to pay for them. "You would use them more, if you had them," said he. "When I came to do a piece of work I used to find commonly that I wanted a certain tool, and I made it a rule first always to make that tool. I have spent as much as $3000 thus on my tools." Comparatively speaking, his life is a success; not such a failure as most men's. He gets more out of any enterprise than his neighbors, for he helps himself more and hires less. Whatever pleasure there is in it he enjoys. By good sense and calculation he has become rich and has invested his property well, yet practices a fair and neat economy, dwells not in untidy luxury. It costs him less to live, and he gets more out of life, than others. To get his living, or keep it, is not a hasty or disagreeable toil. He works slowly but surely, enjoying the sweet of it. He buys a piece of meadow at a profitable rate, works at it in pleasant weather, he and his son, when they are inclined, goes a-fishing or a-bee-hunting or a-rifle-shooting quite as often, and thus the meadow gets redeemed, and potatoes get planted, perchance, and he is very sure to have a good crop stored in his cellar in the fall, and some to sell. He always has the best of potatoes there. Their life is a long sport and they know not what hard times are.

Rice says there are no bees worth hunting about here now. He has sometimes been to a large wood in the west part of Sudbury, and also to Nagog, yet there was little honey there.

Labaume says that he wrote his journal of the Campaign in Russia each night, in the midst of incredible danger and suffering, with "a raven's quill, and a little gunpowder, mixed with some melted snow, in the hollow of my hand," the quill cut and mended with "the knife with which I had carved my scanty morsel of horse-flesh." Such a statement promises well for the writer's qualifications to treat such a theme.

Nov. 18. One man thinks that he has a right to burn his thirty cords in a year because he can give a certain sum of money in exchange for them, but that another has no right to pick up the fagots which else nobody would burn. They who will remember only this kind of right do as if they stood under a shed and affirmed that they were under the unobscured heavens. The shed has its use, but what is it to the heavens above?

The pleasure, the warmth, is not so much in *having* as in a true and simple manner *getting* these necessaries.

Men prefer foolishly the gold to that of which it is the symbol,—simple, honest, independent labor. Can gold be said to buy food, if it does not buy an appetite for food? It is fouler and uglier to have too much than not to have enough.

Nov. 19. Rice told his turtle story the other night: "One day I was going through Boston market and I saw a huddle of men around something or other. I edged my way between them and saw that they had got a great mud turtle on a plank, and a butcher stood over him with a cleaver in his hand. 'Eh,' said I, 'what are you trying to do?' 'We are waiting for him to put out his head so that we may cut it off. Look out,' they said; 'don't come so near, or he 'll bite you.' 'Look here,' said I, 'let me try. I guess I can make him put his head out.' 'Let him try. Let him try,' they said, with a laugh. So I stepped into the ring and stood astride of the turtle, while they looked on to see the sport. After looking at him a moment, I put down my hands and turned him over on to his back, where-upon he immediately ran out his head and pushed against the plank to turn himself back, but, as they were not ready to cut at once, or his neck was not in a good position, I seized his head in both hands and, putting my feet against his breast-bone, drew his head out the full length of his neck and said, 'Now cut away. Only take care you don't cut my fingers.' They cut, and I threw the head down on the floor. As I walked away, some one said, 'I guess that fellow has seen mud turtles before to-day.'"

Nov. 30. On the 27th, when I made my last voyage for the season, I found a large sound pine log about four feet long floating, and brought it home. Off the larger end I sawed two wheels, about a foot in diameter and seven or eight inches thick, and I fitted to them an axle-tree made of a joist, which also I found in the river, and thus I had a convenient pair of wheels on which to get my boat up and roll it about. The assessors called me into their office this year and said they wished to get an inventory of my property; asked if I had any real estate. No. Any notes at interest or railroad shares? No. Any taxable property? None that I knew of. "I own a boat," I said; and one of them thought that that might come under the head of a pleasure carriage, which is taxable. Now that I have wheels to it, it comes nearer to it. I was pleased to get my boat in by this means rather than on a borrowed wheelbarrow. It was fit that the river should furnish the material, and that in my last voyage on it, when the ice reminded me that it was time to put it in winter quarters.

I asked Aunt L. to-night why *Scheeter* Potter was so called. She said, because his neighbors regarded him as so small a man that they said in jest that it was his business to make mosquitoes' bills. He was accused of catching his neighbor's hens in a trap and eating them. But he was crazy.

Dec. 3. Every larger tree which I knew and admired is being gradually culled out and carried to mill. I see one or two more large oaks in E. Hubbard's wood lying high on stumps, waiting for snow to be removed. I miss them as surely and with the same feeling that I do the old inhabitants out of the village street. To me they were something more than timber; to their owner not so.

Dec. 11. P.M.—To Holden Swamp, Conantum. No snow; scarcely any ice to be detected. It is only an aggravated November.

When some rare northern bird like the pine grosbeak is seen thus far south in the winter, he does not suggest poverty, but dazzles us with his beauty. The woods and fields, now somewhat solitary, being deserted by their more tender summer residents, are now frequented by these rich but delicately tinted and hardy northern immigrants of the air. Here is no imperfection to be suggested. The winter, with its snow and ice, is not an evil to be corrected. It is as it was designed and made to be, for the artist has had leisure to add beauty to use. My acquaintances, angels from the north. I had a vision thus prospectively of these birds as I stood in the swamps. I saw this familiar—too *familiar*—fact at a different angle, and I was charmed and haunted by it. It is only necessary to behold thus the least fact or phenomenon, however familiar, from a point a hair's breadth aside from our habitual path or routine, to be overcome, enchanted by its beauty and significance. Only what we have touched and worn is trivial,—our scurf, repetition, tradition, conformity. To perceive freshly, with fresh senses, is to be inspired. Great winter itself looked like a precious gem, reflecting rainbow colors from one angle.

My body is all sentient. As I go here or there, I am tickled by this or that I come in contact with, as if I touched the wires of a battery. I can generally recall—have fresh in my mind—several scratches last received. These I continually recall to mind, reimpress, and harp upon. The age of miracles is each moment thus returned. Now it is wild apples, now river reflections, now a flock of lesser redpolls. In winter, too, resides immortal youth and perennial summer. Its head is not silvered; its cheek is not blanched but has a ruby tinge to it.

We get only transient and partial glimpses of the beauty of the world. Standing at the right angle, we are dazzled by the colors of the rainbow in colorless ice. From the right point of view, every storm and every drop in it is a rainbow. Beauty and music are not mere traits and exceptions. They are the rule and character. It is the exception that we see and hear. Then I try to discover what it was in the vision that charmed and translated me. What if we could daguerreotype our thoughts and feelings! for I am surprised and enchanted often by some quality which I cannot detect. I have seen an attribute of another world and condition of things. It is a wonderful fact that I should be affected, and thus deeply and powerfully, more than by aught else in all my experience,—that this fruit should be borne in me, sprung from a seed finer than the spores of fungi, floated from other atmospheres! finer than the dust caught in the sails of vessels a thousand miles from land! Here the invisible seeds settle, and spring, and bear flowers and fruits of immortal beauty.

Dec. 13. This morning it is snowing, and the ground is whitened. The countless flakes, seen against the dark evergreens like a web that is woven in the air, impart a cheerful and busy aspect to nature. It is like a grain that is sown, or like leaves that have come to clothe the bare trees.

How pleasant a sense of preparedness for the winter,—plenty of wood in the shed and potatoes and apples, etc., in the cellar, and the house banked up! Now it will be a cheerful sight to see the snows descend and hear the blast howl.

Dec. 26. I go to Walden *via* the almshouse and up the railroad. Trees seen in the west against the dark cloud, the sun shining on them, are perfectly white as frostwork, and their outlines very perfectly and distinctly revealed, great wisps that they are and ghosts of trees, with recurved twigs. The walls and fences are encased, and the fields bristle with a myriad of crystal spears.

But the low and spreading weeds in the fields and the wood-paths are the most interesting. Here are asters, savory-leaved, whose flat imbricated calyxes, three quarters of an inch over, are surmounted and inclosed in a perfectly transparent ice button, like a glass knob, through which you see the reflections of the brown calyx. These are very common. Each little blue-curls calyx has a spherical button like those brass ones on little boys' jackets,—little sprigs on them,—and the pennyroyal has still smaller spheres, more regularly arranged about its stem, chandelier-wise, and still smells through the ice. The finest grasses support the most wonderful burdens of ice and most branched on their minute threads. These weeds are spread and arched over into the snow again,—countless little arches a few inches high, each cased in ice, which you break with a tinkling crash at each step.

Thorny bushes look more thorny than ever; each thorn is prolonged and exaggerated.

Some boys have come out to a wood-side hill to coast. It must be sport to them, lying on their stomachs, to hear their sled cronching the crystalled weeds when they have reached the more weedy pasture below.

4 P.M.—Up railroad.

In a true history or biography, of how little consequence those events of which so much is commonly made! For example, how difficult for a man to remember in what towns or houses he has lived, or when! Yet one of the first steps of his biographer will be to establish these facts, and he will thus give an undue importance to many of them. I find in my Journal that the most important events in my life, if recorded at all, are not dated.

DEC. 27. Recalled this evening, with the aid of Mother, the various houses (and towns) in which I have lived and some events of my life.

Born, July 12, 1817, in the

Minott House,	on the Virginia Road, where Father occupied Grandmother's thirds, carrying on the farm. The Catherines the other half of the house. Bob Catherines and John threw up the turkeys. Lived there about eight months. Si Merriam next neighbor. Uncle David died when I was six weeks old. I was baptized in old M.H. by Dr. Ripley, when I was three months, and did not cry.
The Red House,	where Grandmother lived, we the west side till October, 1818, hiring of Josiah Davis, agent for Woodwards. (There were Cousin Charles and Uncle C. more or less.) According to day-book, Father hired of Proctor, October 16, 1818, and shop of *Spaulding, November 10, 1818.* Day-book first used by Grandfather, dated 1797. His part cut out and used by Father in Concord in 1808–9, and in Chelmsford, 1818–19–20–21.
Chelmsford,	till March, 1821. (Last charge in Chelmsford about middle of March, 1821.) Aunt Sarah taught me to walk there when fourteen months old. Lived next the meeting-house, where they kept the powder in the garret. Father kept shop and painted signs, etc.

Pope's House,	at South End in Boston, five or six (?) months, a ten-footer. Moved from Chelmsford through Concord, and may have tarried in Concord a little while. Day-book says, "Moved to Pinkney Street Sep 10th 1821 on Monday."
Whitwell's House,	Pinckney Street, Boston, to March, 1823 (?).
Brick House,	Concord, to spring of 1826.
Davis's House	(next to S. Hoar's) to May 7th, 1827.
Shattuck House (Hollis Hall, Cambridge)	(now William Monroe's) to spring of 1835. (Hollis, Cambridge, 1833.)
Aunt's House, (Hollis Hall and Canton)	to spring of 1837. At Brownson's while teaching in winter of 1835. Went to New York with Father, peddling, in 1836.
Parkman House, (Hollis, Cambridge)	to fall of 1844. Was graduated in 1837. Kept town school a fortnight in 1837 (?). Began the big Red Journal, October, 1837. Found first arrowheads, fall of 1837. Wrote a lecture (my first) on Society, March 14th, 1838, and read it before the Lyceum in the Masons' Hall, April 11th, 1838. Went to Maine for a school in May, 1838. Commenced school in the house in summer of 1838. Wrote an essay on Sound and Silence, December, 1838. Fall of 1839 up Merrimack to White Mountains. "Aulus Persius Flaccus," first printed paper of consequence, February 10th, 1840. The Red Journal of 546 pages ended, June, 1840. Journal of 396 pages ended January 31st, 1841.
(R.W.E.'s) (William Emerson's, Staten Island)	Went to R.W.E.'s in spring of 1841 and stayed there to summer of 1843. Went to Staten Island, June, 1843, and returned in December, 1843, or to Thanksgiving. Made pencils in 1844.
Texas House, (Walden) (R.W.E.'s)	to August 29th, 1850. At Walden, July, 1845 to fall of 1847, then at R.W.E.'s to fall of 1848, or while he was in Europe.
Yellow House,	reformed, till present.

Dec. 29. When two men, Billings and Prichard, were dividing the stock of my father and Hurd, the former acting for Father, P. was rather tight for Hurd. They came to a cracked bowl, at which P. hesitated and asked, "Well, what shall we do with this?" B. took it in haste and broke it, and, presenting him one piece, said, "There, that is your half and this is ours."

Dec. 31. It is one of the mornings of *creation*, and the trees, shrubs, etc., etc., are covered with a fine leaf frost, as if they had their morning robes on, seen against the sun.

Jan. 1. On the north shore, near the railroad, I see the track of a large rabbit, probably a white one, which was evidently on the full spring. Its tracks are four feet apart, and, unlike the others, which are on the surface even of this light snow, these break through deep, making a hole six inches over. Why was this one in such haste? I conclude to trace him back and find out. His bounds grow greater and greater as I go back, now six feet quite, and a few rods further are the tracks of a fox (*possibly* a dog, but I think not) exactly on the trail! A little further, where the rabbit was ascending a considerable slope, through this snow nearly a foot deep, the bounds measure full seven feet, leaving the snow untouched for that space between. It appeared that the fox had started the rabbit from a bank on which it was resting, near a young hemlock, and pursued it only a dozen rods up the hill, and then gave up the chase,—and well he might, methought.

This chase occurred probably in the night, either the last or night before, when there was not a man within a mile; but, treading on these very deep and distinct tracks, it was as if I had witnessed it, and in imagination I could see the sharp eyes of the crafty fox and the palpitating breast of the timorous rabbit, listening behind. We unwittingly traverse the scenery of what tragedies! Every square rod, perchance, was the scene of a life or death struggle last night. As you track the rabbit further off, its bounds becoming shorter and shorter, you follow also surely its changing moods from desperate terror till it walks calmly and reassured over the snow without breaking its very slight crust,—perchance till it gnaws some twig composedly,—and in the other direction you trace the retreating steps of the disappointed fox until he has forgotten this and scented some new game, maybe dreams of partridges or wild mice. Your own feelings are fluttered proportionably.

Jan. 2. As for the fox and rabbit race described yesterday, I find that the rabbit was going *the other way*, and possibly the fox was a rabbit, for, tracing back the rabbit, I found that it had first been walking with alternate steps, fox-like.

XX.

THE LONG, SNOWY WINTER

Jan. 4. A clear, cold day. To Walden to examine the ice.

Some fishermen had, apparently by accident, left two of their lines there, which were frozen in. They had, apparently, taken no fish, for they had cut no well to put them in. I cut out the lines, the ice being about an inch thick around them, and pulled up a fine yellow pickerel which would weigh two pounds or more. At first I thought there was none, for he was tired of struggling, but soon I felt him. The hook had caught in the outside of his jaws, and the minnow hung entire by his side. It was very cold, and he struggled but a short time, not being able to bend and quirk his tail; in a few minutes became quite stiff as he lay on the snowy ice. The water in his eyes was frozen, so that he looked as if he had been dead a week. About fifteen minutes after, thinking of what I had heard about fishes coming to life again after being frozen, on being put into water, I thought I would try it. This one was to appearance as completely dead as if he had been frozen a week. I stood him up on his tail without bending it. I put him into the water again without removing the hook. The ice melted off, and its eyes looked bright again; and after a minute or two I was surprised by a sudden, convulsive quirk of the fish, and a minute or two later by another, and I saw that it would indeed revive, and drew it out again. Yet I do not believe that if it had been frozen solid through and through it would have revived, but only when it is superficially frozen.

Jan. 5. The thin snow now driving from the north and lodging on my coat consists of those beautiful star crystals, not cottony and chubby spokes, as on the 13th December, but thin and partly transparent crystals. They are about a tenth of an inch in diameter, perfect little wheels with six spokes without a tire, or rather with six perfect little leafets, fern-like, with a distinct straight and slender midrib, raying from the centre. On each side of each midrib there is a transparent thin blade with a crenate edge, thus: How full of the creative genius is the air in which these are generated! I should hardly admire more if real stars fell and lodged on my coat. Nature is full of genius, full of the divinity; so that not a snowflake escapes its fashioning hand. Nothing is cheap and coarse, neither dewdrops nor snowflakes. Soon the storm increases, —it was already very severe to face,—and the snow comes finer, more white and powdery. Who knows but this is the original form of all snowflakes, but that when I observe these crystal stars falling around me they are but just generated in the low mist next the earth? I am nearer to the source of the snow, its primal, auroral, and golden hour or infancy, but commonly the flakes reach us travel-worn and agglomerated, comparatively without order or beauty, far down in their fall, like men in their advanced age.

As for the circumstances under which this phenomenon occurs, it is quite cold, and the driving storm is bitter to face,[*] though very little snow is falling. It comes almost horizontally from the north. Methinks this kind of snow never falls in any quantity.[†]

A divinity must have stirred within them before the crystals did thus shoot and set. Wheels of the storm-chariots. The same law that shapes the earth-star shapes the snow-star. As surely as the petals of a flower are fixed, each of these countless snow-stars comes whirling to earth, pronouncing thus, with emphasis, the number six. Order, κόσμος.[‡]

What a world we live in! where myriads of these little disks, so beautiful to the most prying eye, are whirled down on every traveller's coat, the observant and the unobservant, and on the restless

---

[*]*Vide* Mar. 19th.

[†] Yes, it does.

[‡]This was the beginning of a storm which reached far and wide and elsewhere was more severe than here.

squirrel's fur, and on the far-stretching fields and forests, the wooded dells, and the mountain-tops. There they lie, like the wreck of chariot-wheels after a battle in the skies. Meanwhile the meadow mouse shoves them aside in his gallery, the schoolboy casts them in his snowball, or the woodman's sled glides smoothly over them, these glorious spangles, the sweeping of heaven's floor. And they all sing, melting as they sing of the mysteries of the number six,—six, six, six.

Jan. 7. At breakfast time the thermometer stood at –12°. Earlier it was probably much lower. Smith's was at –24° early this morning. The latches are white with frost at noon. They say there was yet more snow at Boston, two feet even.

They tell how I swung on a gown on the stairway when I was at Chelmsford. The gown gave way; I fell and fainted, and it took two pails of water to bring me to, for I was remarkable for holding my breath in those cases.

Mother tells how, at the brick house, we each had a little garden a few feet square, and I came in one day, having found a potato just sprouted, which by her advice I planted in my garden. Ere long John came in with a potato which he had found and had it planted in his garden,—"Oh, mother, I have found a potato all sprouted. I mean to put it in my garden," etc. Even Helen is said to have found one. But next I came crying that somebody had got my potato, etc., etc., but it was restored to me as the youngest and original discoverer, if not inventor, of the potato, and it grew in *my* garden, and finally its crop was dug by myself and yielded a dinner for the family.

I was kicked down by a passing ox. Had a chicken given me by Lidy—Hannah—and peeped through the keyhole at it. Caught an eel with John. Went to bed with new boots on, and after with cap. "Rasselas" given me, etc., etc. Asked P. Wheeler, "Who owns all the land?" Asked Mother, having got the medal for geography, "Is Boston in Concord?" etc., etc.

Jan. 10. The weather has considerably moderated; −2° at breakfast time; but this has been the coldest night probably. You lie with your feet or legs curled up, waiting for morning, the sheets shining with frost about your mouth. Water left by the stove is frozen thickly, and what you sprinkle in bathing falls on the floor ice. The house plants are all frozen and soon droop and turn black. I look out on the roof of a cottage covered a foot deep with snow, wondering how the poor children in its garret, with their few rags, contrive to keep their toes warm. I mark the white smoke from its chimney, whose contracted wreaths are soon dissipated in this stinging air, and think of the size of their wood-pile, and again I try to realize how they panted for a breath of cool air those sultry nights last summer. Realize it now if you can. Recall the hum of the mosquito.

It seems that the snow-storm of Saturday night was a remarkable one, reaching many hundred miles along the coast. It is said that some thousands passed the night in cars.

The kitchen windows were magnificent last night, with their frost sheaves, surpassing any cut or ground glass.

I love to wade and flounder through the swamp now, these bitter cold days when the snow lies deep on the ground, and I need travel but little way from the town to get to a Nova Zembla solitude. There is but little life and but few objects, it is true. We are reduced to admire buds, even like the partridges, and bark, like the rabbits and mice. Even a little shining bud which lies sleeping behind its twig and dreaming of spring, perhaps half concealed by ice, is object enough.

Such is the piercing wind, no man loiters between his house and barn. You know only by an occasional white wreath of smoke from his chimney, which is at once snapped up by the hungry air, that he sits warming his wits there within, studying the almanac to learn how long it is before spring.

The windows give no sign of inhabitants, for they are frosted over as if they were ground glass, and the curtains are down beside. The path is snowed up, and all tracks to and fro. No sound issues from within. It remains only to examine the chimney's nostrils. I look long and sharp at it, and fancy that I see some smoke against sky there, but this is deceptive, for, as we are accustomed to walk up to an empty fireplace and imagine that we feel some heat from it, so I have convinced myself that I saw smoke issuing from the chimney of a house which had not been inhabited for twenty years. I had so vivid an idea of smoke curling up from a chimney's top that no painter could have matched my imagination. It was as if the spirits of the former inhabitants, revisiting their old haunts, were once more boiling a spiritual kettle below,—a small whitish-bluish cloud, almost instantly dissipated, as if the fire burned with a very clear flame.

P.M.—Worked on flower-press.

Jan. 11. The *January Sunsets.*

To-day I burn the first stick of the wood which I bought and did not get from the river. What I have still left of the river wood, added to what of it I reserve for other uses, would last me a week longer.

Jan. 12. Moderating, though at zero at 9 A.M.

P.M.—To Andromeda Swamps, measuring snow. I carry a four-foot stick marked in inches, striking it down as far as it will go at every tenth step. First, beginning in the first field west of the railroad causeway, four to six rods from the railroad, and walking parallel with the railroad,—open fields north to south:—[*A table of 177 measurements, averaged and analyzed and corrected later.*]

Jan. 15. A fine, clear winter day.

In the street not only fences but trees are obviously shortened, as by a flood. You are sensible that you are walking at a level a foot or more above the usual one. Seeing the tracks where a leaf had blown along and then tacked and finally doubled and returned on its trail, I thought it must be the tracks of some creature new to me.

Jan. 18. P.M.—To Walden to learn the temperature of the water. This is a very mild, melting winter day, but clear and bright, yet I see the blue shadows on the snow at Walden. The snow lies very level there, about ten inches deep, and for the most part bears me as I go across with my hatchet. I think I never saw a more elysian blue than my shadow. I am turned into a tall blue Persian from my cap to my boots, such as no mortal dye can produce, with an amethystine hatchet in my hand. I am in raptures at my own shadow. What if the substance were of as ethereal a nature? Our very shadows are no longer black, but a celestial blue. This has nothing to do with cold, methinks, but the sun must not be too low.

Jan. 20. In my experience I have found nothing so truly impoverishing as what is called wealth, *i.e.* the command of greater means than you had before possessed, though comparatively few and slight still, for you thus inevitably acquire a more expensive habit of living, and even the very same necessaries and comforts cost you more than they once did. Instead of gaining, you have lost some independence, and if your income should be suddenly lessened, you would find yourself poor, though possessed of the same means which once made you rich. Within the last five years I have had the command of a little more money than in the previous five years, for I have sold some books and some lectures; yet I have not been a whit better fed or clothed or warmed or sheltered, not a whit richer, except that I have been less concerned about my living, but perhaps my life has been the less serious for it, and, to balance it, I feel now that there is a possibility of failure. Who knows but I *may* come upon the town, if, as is likely, the public want no more of my books, or lectures (which last is already the case)? Before, I was much likelier to take the town upon my shoulders. That is, I have lost some of my independence on them, when they would say that I had gained an independence. If you wish to give a man a sense of poverty, give him a thousand dollars. The next hundred dollars he gets will not be worth more than ten that he used to get. Have pity on him; withhold your gifts.

Jan. 22. Most were not aware of the size of the great elm till it was cut down. I surprised some a few days ago by saying that when its trunk should lie prostrate it would be higher than the head of the tallest man in the town, and that two such trunks could not stand in the chamber we were then in, which was fifteen feet across; that there would be ample room for a double bedstead on the trunk, nay, that the very dinner-table we were sitting at, with our whole party of seven, chairs and all, around it, might be set there. On the decayed part of the butt end there were curious fine black lines, giving it a geographical look, here and there, half a dozen inches long, sometimes following the line of the rings; the boundary of a part which had reached a certain stage of decay.

I have attended the felling and, so to speak, the funeral of this old citizen of the town,—I who commonly do not attend funerals,—as it became me to do. I was the chief if not the only mourner there. I have taken the measure of his grandeur; have spoken a few words of eulogy at his grave, remembering the maxim *de mortuis nil nisi bonum* (in this case *magnum*). But there were only the choppers and the passers-by to hear me. Further the town was not represented; the fathers of the town, the selectmen, the clergy were not there. But I have not known a fitter occasion for a sermon of late. How have the mighty fallen! Its history extends back over more than half the whole history of the town. Since its kindred could not conveniently attend, I attended. Methinks its fall marks an epoch in the history of the town. It has passed away together with the clergy of the old school and the stage-coach which used to rattle beneath it. Its virtue was that it steadily grew and expanded from year to year to the very last. How much of old Concord falls with it! The town clerk will not chronicle its fall. I will, for it is of greater moment to the town than that of many a human inhabitant would be. Instead of erecting a monument to it, we take all possible pains to obliterate its stump, the only monument of a tree which is commonly allowed to stand. Another link that bound us to the past is broken. How much of old Concord was cut away with it! A few such elms would alone constitute a township. They might claim to send a representative to the General Court to look after their interests, if a fit one could be found, a native American one in a true and worthy sense, with catholic principles. Our town has lost some of its venerableness. No longer will our eyes rest on its massive gray trunk, like a vast Corinthian column by the wayside; no longer shall we walk in the shade of its lofty, spreading dome. You have laid the axe, you have made fast your tackle, to one of the king-posts of the town. I feel the whole building wracked by it. Is it not sacrilege to cut down the tree which has so long looked over Concord beneficently?

Supposing the first fifteen feet to average six feet in diameter, they would contain more than three cords and a foot of wood; but probably not more than three cords.

I brought home and examined some of the droppings of the crow mentioned four pages back. They were brown and dry, though partly frozen. After long study with a microscope, I discovered that they consisted of the seeds and skins and other indigestible parts of red cedar berries and some barberries and I knew whence it had probably come, *i.e.* from the cedar woods and barberry bushes by Flint's Pond. These, then, make part of the food of crows in severe weather when the snow is deep, as at present.

Jan. 24. A journal is a record of experiences and growth, not a preserve of things well done or said. I am occasionally reminded of a statement which I have made in conversation and immediately forgotten, which would read much better than what I put in my journal. It is a ripe, dry fruit of long-past experience which falls from me easily, without giving pain or pleasure. The charm of the journal must consist in a certain greenness, though freshness, and not in maturity. Here I cannot afford to be remembering what I said or did, my scurf cast off, but what I am and aspire to become.

Reading the hymns of the Rig Veda, translated by Wilson, which consist in a great measure of simple epithets addressed to the firmament, or the dawn, or the winds, which mean more or less as the reader is more or less alert and imaginative, and seeing how widely the various translators have differed, they regarding not the poetry, but the history and philology, dealing with very concise, Sanscrit, which must almost always be amplified to be understood,

I am sometimes inclined to doubt if the translator has not made something out of nothing,—whether a real idea or sentiment has been thus transmitted to us from so primitive a period. I doubt if learned Germans might not thus edit pebbles from the seashore into hymns of the Rig Veda, and translators translate them accordingly, extracting the meaning which the sea has imparted to them in very primitive times. While the commentators and translators are disputing about the meaning of this word or that, I hear only the resounding of the ancient sea and put into it all the meaning I am possessed of, the deepest murmurs I can recall, for I do not the least care where I get my ideas, or what suggests them.

P.M.—Up Assabet.

The snow is so deep along the sides of the river that I can now look into nests which I could hardly reach in the summer. I can hardly believe them the same. They have only an ice egg in them now. Thus we go about, raised, generally speaking, more than a foot above the summer level. So much higher do we carry our heads in the winter. What a great odds such a little difference makes! When the snow raises us one foot higher than we have been accustomed to walk, we are surprised at our elevation! So we soar.

Jan. 25. P.M.—Up river.

The hardest day to bear that we have had, for, beside being 5° at noon and at 4 P.M., there is a strong northwest wind. It is worse than when the thermometer was at zero all day. The travellers I meet have red faces. Their ears covered. Pity those who have not thick mittens. No man could stand it to travel far toward this wind. It stiffens the whole face, and you feel a tingling sensation in your forehead. Much worse to bear than a still cold. I see no life abroad, no bird nor beast. What a stern, bleak, inhospitable aspect nature now wears!

A closed pitch pine cone gathered January 22d opened last night in my chamber. If you would be convinced how differently armed the squirrel is naturally for dealing with pitch pine cones, just try to get one off with your teeth. He who extracts the seeds from a single closed cone with the aid of a knife will be constrained to confess that the squirrel earns his dinner. It is a rugged customer, and will make your fingers bleed. But the squirrel has the key to this conical and spiny chest of many apartments. He sits on a post, vibrating his tail, and twirls it as a plaything.

But so is a man commonly a locked-up chest to us, to open whom, unless we have the key of sympathy, will make our hearts bleed.

Jan. 26. They have cut and sawed off the butt of the great elm at nine and a half feet from the ground, and I counted the annual rings there with the greatest ease and accuracy. Indeed I never saw them so distinct on a large butt. The tree was quite sound there, not the least hollow even at the pith. There were one hundred and twenty-seven rings. Supposing the tree to have been five years old when nine and a half feet high, then it was one hundred and thirty-two years old, or came up in the year 1724, just before Lovewell's Fight.

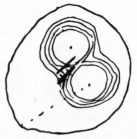

There were two centres, fourteen inches apart. The accompanying coarse sketch will give a *general* idea of it. [*More than a page of details.*]

P.M.—Walked as far as Flint's Bridge with Abel Hunt, where I took to the river. I told him I had come to walk on the river as the best place, for the snow had drifted somewhat in the road, while it was converted into ice almost entirely on the river. "But," asked he, "are you not afraid that you will get in?" "Oh, no, it will bear a load of wood from one end to the other." "But then there may be some weak places." Yet he is some seventy years old and was born and bred immediately on its banks. Truly one half the world does not know how the other half lives.

Men have been talking now for a week at the post-office about the age of the great elm, as a matter interesting but impossible to be determined. The very choppers and travellers have stood upon its prostrate trunk and speculated upon its age, as if it were a profound mystery. I stooped and read its years to them (127 at nine and a half feet), but they heard me as the wind that once sighed through its branches. They still surmised that it might be two hundred years old, but they never stooped to read the inscription. Truly they love darkness rather than light. One said it was probably one hundred and fifty, for he had heard somebody say that for fifty years the elm grew, for fifty it stood still, and for fifty it was dying. (Wonder what portion of his career he stood still!) Truly all men are not men of science. They dwell within an integument of prejudice thicker than the bark of the cork-tree, but it is valuable chiefly to stop bottles with. Tied to their buoyant prejudices, they keep themselves afloat when honest swimmers sink.

Talking with Miss Mary Emerson this evening, she said, "It was not the fashion to be so original when I was young." She is readier to take my view—look through my eyes for the time—than any young person that I know in the town.

Feb. 1. Our kitten Min, two-thirds grown, was playing with Sophia's broom this morning, as she was sweeping the parlor, when she suddenly went into a fit, dashed round the room, and, the door being opened, rushed up two flights of stairs and leaped from the attic window to the ice and snow by the side of the door-step,—a descent of a little more than twenty feet,—passed round the house and was lost. But she made her appearance again about noon, at the window, quite well and sound in every joint, even playful and frisky.

This has been a memorable January for snow and cold. It has been excellent sleighing ever since the 26th of December,—not less than a foot at any time since January 6th on a level in open fields, in swamps much more. We have completely forgotten the summer. There has been no January thaw, though one prophesied it a fortnight ago because he saw snow-fleas. The ponds are yielding a good crop of ice. The eaves have scarcely run at all. It has been what is called "an old-fashioned winter."

Feb. 3. It is a cold and windy Sunday. The wind whistles round the northwest corner of the house and penetrates every crevice and consumes the wood in the stoves,—soon blows it all away. An armful goes but little way. Such a day makes a great hole in the wood-pile. Whisks round the corner of the house, in at a crevice, and flirts off with all the heat before we have begun to feel it.

Mr. Emerson, who returned last week from lecturing on the Mississippi, having been gone but a month, tells me that he saw boys skating on the Mississippi and on Lake Erie and on the Hudson, and has no doubt they are skating on Lake Superior; and probably at Boston he saw them skating on the Atlantic.

In Barber's "Historical Collections," page 476, there is a letter by Cotton Mather, dated "Boston, 10th Dec. 1717," describing the great snow of the previous February, from which I quote:—

"On the twentieth of the last February there came on a snow, which being added unto what had covered the ground a few days before, made a thicker mantle for our mother than what was usual: And the storm with it was, for the following day, so violent as to make all communication between the neighbors everywhere to cease. People, for some hours, could not pass from one side of a street unto another.... On the 24th day of the month, comes Pelion upon Ossa: Another snow came on which almost buried the memory of the former, with a storm so famous that Heaven laid an interdict on the religious assemblies throughout the country, on this Lord's day, the like whereunto had never been seen before. The Indians near an hundred years old affirm that their fathers never told them of anything that equalled it. Vast numbers of cattle were destroyed in this calamity. Whereof some there were, of the stranger [stronger? mine] sort, were found standing dead on their legs, as if they had been alive many weeks after, when the snow melted away. And others had their eyes glazed over with ice at such a rate, that being not far from the sea, their mistake of their way drowned them there."

"A man had a couple of young hogs, which he gave over for dead, but on the 27th day after their burial, they made their way out of a snow-bank, at the bottom of which they had found a little tansy to feed upon."

"Hens were found alive after seven days; Turkeys were found

alive after five and twenty days, buried in the snow, and at a distance from the ground, and altogether destitute of anything to feed them."

"The wild creatures of the woods, the out-goings of the evening, made their descent as well as they could in this time of scarcity for them towards the sea-side. A vast multitude of deer, for the same cause, taking the same course, and the deep snow spoiling them of their only defence, which is to run, they became such a prey to these devourers that it is thought not one in twenty escaped."

"It is incredible how much damage is done to the orchards, for the snow freezing to a crust, as high as the bows of the trees, anon split them to pieces. The cattle, also, walking on the crusted snow a dozen foot from the ground, so fed upon the trees as very much to damnify them." "Cottages were totally covered with the snow, and not the very tops of their chimneys to be seen." These "odd accidents," he says, "would afford a story. But there not being any relation to Philosophy in them, I forbear them." He little thought that his simple testimony to such facts as the above would be worth all the philosophy he might dream of.

Feb. 4. I see that the partridges feed quite extensively on the sumach berries, *e.g.* at my old house. They come to them after every snow, making fresh tracks, and have now stripped many bushes quite bare.

I have often wondered how red cedars could have sprung up in some pastures which I knew to be miles distant from the nearest fruit-bearing cedar, but it now occurs to me that these and barberries, etc., may be planted by the crows, and probably other birds.

Feb. 25. Gathered some facts from Henry Bond's "Genealogies of the Families of Watertown, etc."

My mother's mother was *Mary Jones*, only daughter of "Col. Elisha Jones, Esq., of Weston. A Boston newspaper, of Feb. 15, 1775, says 'On Monday last, died, in this town, in the sixty-sixth year of his age, Elisha Jones Esq., late of Weston, for many years a magistrate, Col. of a Regiment of Militia, and member of the General

Assembly. In the many departments in which he acted, he eminently showed the man of principle, virtue,' &c. He married, Jan. 24, 1733–4, Mary Allen, and occupied his father's homestead." (Mary Allen was the daughter of Abel Allen, who was the son of Lewis Allen of Watertown Farms, who died 1707–8.)

The children of E. Jones and Mary Allen were (1) Nathan (2d son died in infancy), (3) Elisha, (4) Israel, (5) Daniel, (6) Elias, (7) Josiah, (8) Silas, (9) Mary (b. 1748), (10) Ephraim, (11) Simon (or Simeon), (12) Stephen, (13) Jonas, (14) Phillemore, (15) Charles.

Colonel Elisha Jones was born 1710, the son of *Captain Josiah Jones* (born, 1670, in Weston) and *Abigail Barnes*. Captain Josiah Jones was the son of *Josiah Jones* of Watertown Farms (born 1643) and *Lydia Treadway* (daughter of Nathaniel Treadway, who died in Watertown, 1689). Josiah Jones was son of *Lewis Jones* (who appears to have moved from Roxbury to Watertown about 1650, and died 1684) and Anna (perhaps Stone? born in England).

Feb. 27. The papers are talking about the prospect of a war between England and America. Neither side sees how its country can avoid a long and fratricidal war without sacrificing its honor. Both nations are ready to take a desperate step, to forget the interests of civilization and Christianity and their commercial prosperity and fly at each other's throats. When I see an individual thus beside himself, thus desperate, ready to shoot or be shot, like a blackleg who has little to lose, no serene aims to accomplish, I think he is a candidate for bedlam. What asylum is there for nations to go to? Nations are thus ready to talk of wars and challenge one another,* because they are made up to such an extent of poor, low-spirited, despairing men, in whose eyes the chance of shooting somebody else without being shot themselves exceeds their actual good fortune. Who, in fact, will be the first to enlist but the most desperate class, they who have lost all hope? And they may at last infect the rest.

---

*Will it not be thought disreputable at length, as duelling between individuals now is?

Feb. 28. Mother says that the cat lay on her bread one night and caused it to rise finely all around her.

Our young maltese cat Min, which has been absent five cold nights, the ground covered deep with crusted snow,—her first absence,—and given up for dead, has at length returned at daylight, awakening the whole house with her mewing and afraid of the strange girl we have got in the meanwhile. She is a mere wrack of skin and bones, with a sharp nose and wiry tail. She is as one returned from the dead. There is as much rejoicing as at the return of the prodigal son, and if we had a fatted calf we should kill it. Various are the conjectures as to her adventures,—whether she has had a fit, been shut up somewhere, or lost, torn in pieces by a certain terrier or frozen to death. In the meanwhile she is fed with the best that the house affords, minced meats and saucers of warmed milk, and, with the aid of unstinted sleep in all laps in succession, is fast picking up her crumbs. She has already found her old place under the stove, and is preparing to make a stew of her brains there.

Feb. 29. Minott said he saw Emerson come home from lecturing the other day with his knitting-bag (lecture-bag) in his hand. He asked him if the lecturing business was as good as it used to be. Emerson said he did n't see but it was as good as ever; guessed the people would want lectures "as long as he or I lived."

March 10. Thermometer at 7 A.M. 6° below zero. Dr. Bartlett's, between 6.30 and 7 A.M., was at –13°; Smith's at –13° or –14°, at 6 A.M.

The snow hard and dry, squeaking under the feet; excellent sleighing. A biting northwest wind *compels* to cover the ears. It is one of the hardest days of the year to bear. Truly a memorable 10th of March. A bluebird would look as much out of place now as the 10th of January.

I suspect that in speaking of the springing of plants in previous years I have been inclined to make them start too early generally.

The blue shadows on snow are as fine as ever. It is hard to believe the records of previous years.

The past has been a winter of such unmitigated severity that I have not chanced to notice a snow-flea, which are so common in thawing days.

I may say that I have not had to climb a fence this winter, but have stepped over them on the snow.

Still there is little or no chopping, for it will not pay to shovel the snow away from the trees; unless they are quite large, and then you must work standing in it two feet deep. There is an eddy about the large trees beside, which produces a hollow in the snow about them, but it lies close up to the small ones on every side.

10 P.M.—Thermometer at zero.

March 14. Tapped several white maples with my knife, but find no sap flowing; but, just above Pinxter Swamp, one red maple limb was moistened by sap trickling along the bark. Tapping this, I was surprised to find it flow freely. Where the sap had dried on the bark, shining and sticky, it tasted quite sweet. This is the only one of eight or ten white and red maples that flows. I do not see why it should be.

March 15. Put a spout in the red maple of yesterday, and hung a pail beneath to catch the sap.

March 16. 7 A.M.—The sap of that red maple has not begun to flow yet. The few spoonfuls in the pail and in the hole are frozen.

2 P.M.—The red maple is now about an inch deep in a quart pail,—nearly all caught since morning. It now flows at the rate of about six drops in a minute. Has probably flowed faster this forenoon. It is perfectly clear, like water. Going home, slipped on the ice, throwing the pail over my head to save myself, and spilt all but a pint. So it was lost on the ice of the river. When the river breaks up, it will go down the Concord into the Merrimack, and down the Merrimack into the sea, and there get salted as well as diluted, part being boiled into sugar. It suggests, at any rate, what various liquors, beside those containing salt, find their way to the sea,—the sap of how many kinds of trees!

There is, at any rate, such a phenomenon as the willows shining in the spring sun, however it is to be accounted for.

WHAT BEFELL AT MRS. BROOKS'S.

March 19. On the morning of the 17th, Mrs. Brooks's Irish girl Joan fell down the cellar stairs, and was found by her mistress lying at the bottom, apparently lifeless. Mrs. Brooks ran to the street-door for aid to get her up, and asked a Miss Farmer, who was passing, to call the blacksmith near by. The latter lady turned instantly, and, making haste across the road on this errand, fell flat in a puddle of melted snow, and came back to Mrs. Brooks's, bruised and dripping and asking for opodeldoc. Mrs. Brooks again ran to the door and called to George Bigelow to complete the unfinished errand. He ran nimbly about it and fell flat in another puddle near the former, but, his joints being limber, got along without opodeldoc and raised the blacksmith. He also notified James Burke, who was passing, and he, rushing in to render aid, fell off one side of the cellar stairs in the dark. They no sooner got the girl up-stairs than she came to and went raving, then had a fit.

Haste makes waste. It never rains but it pours. I have this from those who have heard Mrs. Brooks's story, seen the girl, the stairs, and the puddles.

March 21. 10 A.M.—To my red maple sugar camp. Between 10.30 and 11.30 A.M. this forenoon, I caught two and three quarters pints more, from six tubes, at the same tree, though it is completely overcast and threatening rain. Four and one half pints in all. This sap is an agreeable drink, like iced water (by chance), with a pleasant but slight sweetish taste. I boiled it down in the afternoon, and it made an ounce and a half of sugar, without any molasses, which appears to be the average amount yielded by the sugar maple in similar situations, *viz.* south edge of a wood, a tree partly decayed, two feet diameter.

It is worth the while to know that there is all this sugar in our woods, much of which might be obtained by using the refuse wood lying about, without damage to the proprietors, who use neither the sugar nor the wood.

I noticed that my fingers were purpled, evidently from the sap on my auger.

Had a dispute with Father about the *use* of my making this sugar when I knew it could be done and might have bought sugar cheaper at Holden's. He said it took me from my studies. I said I made it my study: I felt as if I had been to a university.

It dropped from each tube about as fast as my pulse beat, and, as there were three tubes directed to each vessel, it flowed at the rate of about one hundred and eighty drops in a minute into it. One maple, standing immediately north of a thick white pine, scarcely flowed at all, while a smaller, farther in the wood, ran pretty well. The south side of a tree bleeds first in spring. I hung my pails on the tubes or a nail. Had two tin pails and a pitcher. Had a three-quarters-inch auger. Made a dozen spouts, five or six inches long, hole as large as a pencil, smoothed with a pencil.

March 23. I spend a considerable portion of my time observing the habits of the wild animals, my brute neighbors. By their various movements and migrations they fetch the year about to me. Very significant are the flight of geese and the migration of suckers, etc., etc. But when I consider that the nobler animals have been exterminated here,—the cougar, panther, lynx, wolverene, wolf, bear, moose, deer, the beaver, the turkey, etc., etc.,—I cannot but feel as if I lived in a tamed, and, as it were, emasculated country. Would not the motions of those larger and wilder animals have been more significant still? Is it not a maimed and imperfect nature that I am conversant with? As if I were to study a tribe of Indians that had lost all its warriors. Do not the forest and the meadow now lack expression, now that I never see nor think of the moose with a lesser forest on his head in the one, nor of the beaver in the other? When I think what were the various sounds and notes, the migrations and works, and changes of fur and plumage which ushered in the spring and marked the other seasons of the year, I am reminded that this my life in nature, this particular round of natural phenomena which I call a year, is lamentably incomplete. I listen to a concert in which so many parts are wanting. The whole civilized country is to some extent turned into a city, and I am that citizen whom I pity. Primitive Nature is the most interesting to me. I take

infinite pains to know all the phenomena of the spring, for instance, thinking that I have here the entire poem, and then, to my
chagrin, I hear that it is but an imperfect copy that I possess and
have read, that my ancestors have torn out many of the first leaves
and grandest passages, and mutilated it in many places. I should
not like to think that some demigod had come before me and
picked out some of the best of the stars. I wish to know an entire
heaven and an entire earth. All the great trees and beasts, fishes and
fowl are gone. The streams, perchance, are somewhat shrunk.

I see that a shopkeeper advertises among his perfumes for hand-
kerchiefs "meadow flowers" and "new-mown hay."

P.M.—To Walden.

March 27. Uncle Charles died this morning, about midnight, aged
seventy-six.

March 28. Uncle Charles buried. He was born in February, 1780,
the winter of the Great Snow, and he dies in the winter of another
great snow,—a life bounded by great snows.

Cold, and the earth stiff again, after fifteen days of steady warm
and, for the most part, sunny days (without rain), in which the
snow and ice have rapidly melted.

Barrett has suffered all winter for want of water.

I think to say to my friend, There is but one interval between us.
You are on one side of it, I on the other. You know as much about
it as I,—how wide, how impassable it is. I will endeavor not to
blame you. Do not blame me. There is nothing to be said about it.
Recognize the truth, and pass over the intervals that are bridged.

Farewell, my friends, my path inclines to this side the mountain, yours to that.

We are no longer the representatives of our former selves.

March 30. P.M.—To Walden and Fair Haven *via* the Andromeda
Swamps. The snow is a foot and more in depth there still. I see already one blade, three or four inches long, of that purple or lake
grass, lying flat on some water, between snow-clad banks,—the

first leaf with a rich bloom on it. How silent are the footsteps of Spring! The spring advances in spite of snow and ice, and cold even. The ground under the snow has long since felt the influence of the spring sun, whose rays fall at a more favorable angle. In warm recesses and clefts in meadows and rocks in the midst of ice and snow, nay, even under the snow, vegetation commences and steadily advances.

April 1. It is a question whether it is better sleighing or wheeling now, taking all our roads together. At any rate we may say the sleighing lasted till April. In some places the snow still fills the roads level with the walls, and bears me up still in the middle of the day. It grows more and more solid, apparently freezing at night quite through. William Wheeler (of the Corner road) tells me that it was more solid this morning than any time in the winter, and he was surprised to find that it would bear his oxen where three or four feet deep behind his house. On some roads you walk in a path recently shovelled out, with upright walls of snow three or four feet high on each side and a foot of snow beneath you, for twenty or thirty rods; and this is old snow.

April 2. In the warm recess at the head of Well Meadow, which makes up on the northeast side of Fair Haven, I find many evidences of spring. This year, at least, the cabbage is the first flower; and perhaps it is always earlier than I have thought, if you seek it in a favorable place. It will take you half a lifetime to find out where to look for the earliest flower.

It is evident that it depends on the character of the season whether this flower or that is the most forward; whether there is more or less snow or cold or rain, etc. I am tempted to stretch myself on the bare ground above the Cliff, to feel its warmth in my back, and smell the earth and the dry leaves. I see and hear flies and bees about. A large buff-edged butterfly flutters by along the edge of the Cliff,—*Vanessa antiopa*. Though so little of the earth is bared, this frail creature has been warmed to life again. Here is the broken shell of one of those large white snails (*Helix albolabris*) on the top of the Cliff. It is like a horn with ample mouth wound on itself. I am rejoiced to find anything so pretty. I cannot but think it nobler, as it is rarer, to appreciate some beauty than to feel much sympathy with misfortune. The Powers are kinder to me when they permit me to enjoy this beauty than if they were to express any amount of compassion for me. I could never excuse them that.

April 3. When I awoke this morning I heard the almost forgotten sound of rain on the roof. I think there has not been any of any consequence since Christmas Day. The pattering of the rain is a soothing, slumberous sound, which tempts me to lie late, yet there is more fog than rain. Here, then, at last, is the end of the sleighing, which began the 25th of December. Not including that date and to-day it has lasted ninety-nine days.

Hosmer is overhauling a vast heap of manure in the rear of his barn, turning the ice within it up to the light; yet he asks despairingly what life is for, and says he does not expect to stay here long. But I have just come from reading Columella, who describes the same kind of spring work, in that to him new spring of the world, with hope, and I suggest to be brave and hopeful with nature. Human life may be transitory and full of trouble, but the perennial mind, whose survey extends from that spring to this, from Columella to Hosmer, is superior to change. I will identify myself with that which did not die with Columella and will not die with Hosmer.

People are talking about my Uncle Charles. Minott tells how he heard Tilly Brown once asking him to show him a peculiar (inside?) lock in wrestling. "Now, don't hurt me, don't throw me hard." He struck his antagonist inside his knees with his feet, and so deprived him of his legs. Hosmer remembers his tricks in the barroom, shuffling cards, etc. He could do anything with cards, yet he did not gamble. He would toss up his hat, twirling it over and over, and catch it on his head invariably. Once wanted to live at Hosmer's, but the latter was afraid of him. "Can't we study up something?" he asked.

He had a strong head and never got drunk; would drink gin sometimes, but not to excess. Did not use tobacco, except snuff out of another's box sometimes. Was very neat in his person. Was not profane, though vulgar.

Very few men take a wide survey; their knowledge is very limited and particular. I talked with an old man the other day about the snow, hoping he would give me some information about past winters. I said, "I guess you don't remember so much old snow on the ground at this season." He answered, "I never saw the snow so deep between my house and John's." It was n't a stone's throw.[*]

Uncle Charles used to say that he had n't a single tooth in his head. The fact was they were all double, and I have heard that he lost about all of them by the time he was twenty-one. Ever since I knew him he could swallow his nose.

The river is now generally and rapidly breaking up. It is surprising what progress has been made since yesterday.

April 6. As I am going along the Corner road by the meadow mouse brook, hear and see, a quarter of a mile northwest, on those conspicuous white oaks near the river in Hubbard's second grove, the crows buffeting some intruder. The crows had betrayed to me some large bird of the hawk kind which they were buffeting. I suspected it before I looked carefully. I saw several crows on the oaks, and also what looked to my naked eye like a cluster of the palest and most withered oak leaves with a black base about as big as a crow. Looking with my glass, I saw that it was a great bird. The crows sat about a rod off, higher up, while another crow was occasionally diving at him, and all were cawing. I am not sure whether it was a white-headed eagle or a fish hawk. It rose and wheeled, flapping several times, till it got under way; then, with its rear to me, presenting the least surface, it moved off steadily in its orbit over the woods northwest, with the slightest possible undulation of its wings,—a noble planetary motion, like Saturn with its ring seen edgewise. It is so rare that we see a large body self-sustained in the air. While crows sat still and silent and confessed their lord. Was it

---

[*]The same man in summer of '59 said he never saw the river so low!! Of what use to be old?

not the white-headed eagle in the state when it is called the sea eagle?

April 7. Monday. Launched my boat, through three rods of ice on the riverside, half of which froze last night. The meadow is skimmed over, but by mid-forenoon it is melted.

April 8. Noticed, returning, this afternoon, a muskrat sitting on the ice near a small hole in Willow Bay, so motionless and withal round and featureless, of so uniform a color, that half a dozen rods off I should not have detected him if not accustomed to observing them. Saw the same thing yesterday. It reminds me of the truth of the Indian's name for it,—"that sits in a round form on the ice." You would think it was a particularly round clod of meadow rising above the ice. But while you look, it concludes its meditations or perchance its meal, and deliberately takes itself off through a hole at its feet, and you see no more of it. I noticed five muskrats this afternoon without looking for them very carefully. You would think that so large an animal, sitting right out upon the ice, would be sure to be seen or detected, but not so.

April 9. Wednesday. Another fine day.
    7 A.M.—To Trillium Woods.
    Air full of birds.
    These birds give evidence that they prefer the fields of New England to all other climes, deserting for them the warm and fertile south. Here is their paradise. It is here they express the most happiness by song and action. Though these spring mornings may often be frosty and rude, they are exactly tempered to their constitutions, and call forth the sweetest strains.
    8 A.M.—See that broad, smooth vernal lake, like a painted lake. Not a breath disturbs it. I am surprised when I perceive men going about their ordinary occupations. I presume that before ten o'clock at least all the villagers will have come down to the bank and looked over this bright and placid flood,—the child and the man, the housekeeper and the invalid,—even as the village beholds itself

reflected in it. How much would be subtracted from the day if the water was taken away! It is certainly important that there be some priests, some worshippers of Nature. I do not imagine anything going on to-day away from and out of sight of the waterside.

P.M.—Up railroad. A very warm day. I go off a little to the right of the railroad, and sit there on the warm bank, above the broad, shallow, crystalline pool, on the sand. I hear one hyla peep faintly several times. This is, then, a degree of warmth sufficient for the hyla. He is the first of his race to awaken to the new year and pierce the solitudes with his voice. He shall wear the medal for this year. You hear him, but you will never find him. He is somewhere down amid the withered sedge and alder bushes there by the water's edge, but where? From that quarter his shrill blast sounded, but he is silent, and a kingdom will not buy it again.

The communications from the gods to us are still deep and sweet, indeed, but scanty and transient,—enough only to keep alive the memory of the past. I remarked how many old people died off on the approach of the present spring. It is said that when the sap begins to flow in the trees our diseases become more violent. It is now advancing toward summer apace, and we seem to be reserved to taste its sweetness, but to perform what great deeds? Do we detect the reason why we also did not die on the approach of spring?

The thermometer at 5 P.M. is 66°+, and it has probably been 70° or more; and the last two days have been nearly as warm.

April 10. Thursday. Fast-Day.—Some fields are dried sufficiently for the games of ball with which this season is commonly ushered in. I associate this day, when I can remember it, with games of baseball played over behind the hills in the russet fields toward Sleepy Hollow, where the snow was just melted and dried up, and also with the uncertainty I always experienced whether the shops would be shut, whether we should have an ordinary dinner, an extraordinary one, or none at all, and whether there would be more than one service at the meeting-house. This last uncertainty old folks share with me. This is a windy day, drying up the fields; the first we have had for a long time.

P.M.—I set out to sail, the wind northwest, but it is so strong, and I so feeble, that I gave it up. The waves dashed over into the boat and with their sprinkling wet me half through in a few moments. Our meadow looks as angry now as it ever can.

April 16. A moist, misty, rain-threatening April day. About noon it *does* mizzle a little. The robin sings throughout it. It is rather raw, tooth-achy weather.

I see a maple twig eaten off by a rabbit four and a quarter feet from the ground, showing how high the snow was there. Golden saxifrage at Hubbard's Close. Frogs sit round Callitriche Pool, where the tin is cast. We have waste places—pools and brooks, etc.,—where to cast tin, iron, slag, crockery, etc. No doubt the Romans and Ninevites had such places. To what a perfect system this world is reduced! A place for everything and everything in its place!

April 17. Was awakened in the night by a thunder and lightning shower and hail-storm—the old familiar burst and rumble, as if it had been rumbling somewhere else ever since I heard it last, and had not lost the knack. I heard a thousand hailstones strike and bounce on the roof at once. What a clattering! Yet it did not last long, and the hail took a breathing-space once or twice. I did not know at first but we should lose our windows, the blinds being away at the painters'. These sounds lull me into a deeper slumber than before. Hail-storms are milked out of the first summer-like warmth. The thunder, too, sounds like the final rending and breaking up of winter; thus precipitous is its edge.

P.M.—Start for Conantum in boat, wind southwest. A moist muggy afternoon, rain-threatening, true April weather, after a particularly warm and pleasant forenoon. It grows more and more rain-threatening,—all the air moist and muggy, a great ill-defined cloud darkening all the west,—but I push on till I feel the first drops, knowing that the wind will take me back again.

Now comes the rain with a rush. In haste I put my boat about, raise my sail, and, cowering under my umbrella in the stern, with the steering oar in my hand, begin to move homeward. The rain soon fulls up my sail, and it catches all the little wind. From under the umbrella I look out on the scene. The big drops pepper the watery plain, the *aequor*, on every side. It is not a hard, dry pattering, as on a roof, but a softer, liquid pattering, which makes the impression of a double wateriness. I make haste to take down my sail at the bridges, but at the stone arches forgot my umbrella, which was unavoidably crushed in part. Even in the midst of this rain I am struck by the variegated surface of the water, different portions reflecting the light differently, giving what is called a watered appearance. Broad streams of light water stretch away between streams of dark, as if they were different kinds of water unwilling to mingle, though all are equally dimpled by the rain, and you detect no difference in their condition. As if Nature loved variety for its own sake. It is a true April shower, or rain,—I think the first. It rains so easy,—has a genius for it and infinite capacity for it. Many showers will not exhaust the moisture of April.

When I get home and look out the window, I am surprised to see how it has greened the grass. It springs up erect like a green flame in the ditches on each side the road, where we had not noticed it before. Grass is born.

April 18. Walden is open entirely to-day for the first time, owing to the rain of yesterday and evening. I have observed its breaking up of different years commencing in '45, and the average date has been April 4th.

April 20. Rain, rain, rain,—a northeast storm. I see that it is raising the river somewhat again.

April 22. Soon after I turned about in Fair Haven Pond, it began to rain hard. I raised my sail and, cowering under my umbrella in the stern, wearing the umbrella like a cap and holding the handle between my knees, I steered and paddled, almost perfectly sheltered from the heavy rain. Yet my legs and arms were a little exposed sometimes, in my endeavors to keep well to windward so as to double certain capes ahead. For the wind occasionally drove me on to the western shore. From time to time, from under my umbrella, I could see the ducks spinning away before me, like great bees. For when they are flying low directly from you, you see hardly anything but their vanishing dark bodies, while the rapidly moving wings or paddles, seen edgewise, are almost invisible. Though my progress was slow and laborious, and at length I began to get a little wet, I enjoyed the adventure because it combined to some extent the advantages of being at home in my chamber and abroad in the storm at the same time.

It is highly important to invent a dress which will enable us to be abroad with impunity in the severest storms. We cannot be said to have fully invented clothing yet. In the meanwhile the rainwater collects in the boat, and you must sit with your feet curled up on a paddle, and you expose yourself in taking down your mast and raising it again at the bridges. These rain-storms—this is the third day of one—characterize the season, and belong rather to winter than to summer. Flowers delay their blossoming, birds tarry in their migrations, etc., etc. It is surprising how so many tender organizations of flowers and insects survive them uninjured.

XXI.

April 23. A very handsome little beetle, deep, about a quarter of an inch long, with *pale*-golden wing-cases, artificially and handsomely marked with burnished dark-green marks and spots, one side answering to the other; front and beneath burnished dark-green; legs brown or cinnamon-color. It was on the side of my boat. Brought it home in a clam's shells tied up,—a good insect-box.

April 24. I see some roadside lakes, where the grass and clover had already sprung, owing to previous rain or melted snow, now filled with perfectly transparent April rain-water, through which I see to their emerald bottoms,—paved with emerald. In the pasture beyond Nut Meadow Brook Crossing, the unsightly holes where rocks have been dug and blasted out are now converted into perfect jewels. Even these furnish goblets and vases of perfect purity to hold the dews and rains, and what more agreeable bottom can we look to than this which the earliest moisture and sun had tinged green? What wells can be more charming? If I see an early grasshopper drowning in one, it looks like a fate to be envied. Here is no dark unexplored bottom, with its imagined monsters and mud, but perfect sincerity, setting off all that it reveals.

April wells, call them, vases clean as if enamelled.

There is a slight sea-turn. I saw it like a smoke beyond Concord from Brown's high land, and felt the cool fresh east wind.

April 25. Anne Karney, our neighbor, looking over her garden yesterday with my father, saw what she said was shamrock, which the

Irish wear on their caps on St. Patrick's Day, the first she had ever seen in this country. My father pointed it out in his own garden to the Irishman who was working for him, and he was glad to see it, for he had had a dispute with another Irishman as to whether it grew in this country and now he could convince him, and he put it in his pocket. I saw it afterward and pronounced it common white clover, and, looking into Webster's Dictionary, I read, under Shamrock: "The Irish name for a three-leafed plant, the *Oxalis Acetosella*, or common wood-sorrel. It has been often supposed to be the *Trifolium repens*, white trefoil or white clover." This was very satisfactory, though perhaps Webster's last sentence should have been, The *Trifolium repens* has often been mistaken for it.

April 28. Surveying the Tommy Wheeler farm.[*]

Again, as so many times, I am reminded of the advantage to the poet, and philosopher, and naturalist, and whomsoever, of pursuing from time to time some other business than his chosen one,— seeing with the side of the eye. The poet will so get visions which no deliberate abandonment can secure. The philosopher is so forced to recognize principles which long study might not detect. And the naturalist even will stumble upon some new and unexpected flower or animal.

As I was measuring along the Marlborough road, a fine little blue-slate butterfly fluttered over the chain. Even its feeble strength was required to fetch the year about. How daring, even rash, Nature appears, who sends out butterflies so early!

Observing the young pitch pines by the road south of Loring's lot that was so heavily wooded, George Hubbard remarked that if they were cut down oaks would spring up, and sure enough, looking across the road to where Loring's white pines recently stood so densely, the ground was all covered with young oaks. *Mem.*—Let me look at the site of some thick pine woods which I remember, and see what has sprung up; *e.g.* the pitch pines on Thrush Alley

---

[*]I believe it was this morning there was quite a fog.

and the white pines on Cliffs, also at Baker's chestnuts, and the chestnut lot on the Tim. Brooks farm.

This was a very pleasant or rather warm day, looking a little rainy, but on our return the wind changed to easterly, and I felt the cool, fresh sea-breeze.

This has been a remarkably pleasant, and I think warm, spring. We have not had the usual sprinklings of snow, having had so much in the winter,—none since that I can remember. There is none to come down out of the air.

April 30. Surveying the Tommy Wheeler farm.

A fine morning. I hear the first brown thrasher singing within three or four rods of me on the shrubby hillside in front of the Hadley place. This, I think, is the very place to hear them early, a dry hillside sloping to the south, covered with young wood and shrub oaks. I am the more attracted to that house as a dwelling-place. To live where you would hear the first brown thrasher! Surveying seemed a noble employment which brought me within hearing of this bird. I was trying to get the exact course of a wall thickly beset with shrub oaks and birches, making an opening through them with axe and knife, while the hillside seemed to quiver or pulsate with the sudden melody. Again, it is with the side of the ear that you hear. The music or the beauty belong not to your work itself but some of its accompaniments. You would fain devote yourself to the melody, but you will hear more of it if you devote yourself to your work.

The Italian with his hand-organ stops to stare at my compass, just as the boys are curious about *his* machine. We have exchanged places.

May 4. About a foot above the water, about my boat, are many of those little fuzzy gnats. (On the 6th, our house being just painted, the paint is peppered with the *myriads* of the same insects which have stuck to it. They are particularly thick on the coping under the eaves, where they look as if they had been dusted on, and dense swarms of them are hovering within a foot. Paint a house now, and these are the insects you catch.)

Having fastened my boat at the maple, met, on the bank just above, Luke Dodge, whom I met in a boat fishing up that way once or twice last summer and previous years. Was surprised to hear him say, "I am in my eighty-third year." He still looks pretty strong and has a voice like a nutmeg-grater. Within two or three years at most, I have seen him walking, with that remarkable gait. It is encouraging to know that a man may fish and paddle in this river in his eighty-third year. He says he is older than Winn, though not the oldest man in the town. Mr. Tolman is in his eighty-sixth year.

May 11. The Roman writers Columella and Palladius warn not to build in a low valley or by a marsh, and the same rule is observed here to-day. In the West the prudent settler avoids the banks of rivers, choosing high and open land. It suggests that man is not completely at one with Nature, or that she is not yet fitted to be his abode. Adam soon found that he must give a marsh a wide berth,— that he must not put his bower in or near a swamp in the new country,—else he would get the fever and ague or an intermittent fever. Either nature may be changed or man. Some animals, as frogs and musquash, are fitted to live in the marsh. Only a portion of the earth is habitable by man. Is the earth improving or deteriorating in this respect? Does it require to be improved by the hands of man, or is man to live more naturally and so more safely?

May 13. Potter has a remarkable field of mulleins, sown as thickly as if done with a machine (under Bear Garden Hill). I remarked them last year. William Wheeler thinks the seed lies in the ground an indefinite period ready to come up. I thought that it might have been introduced with his grain when it was sown lately. Wheeler says that many a pasture, if you plow it up after it has been lying still ten years, will produce an abundant crop of wormwood, and its seeds must have lain in the ground. Why do not the chemists in their analyses of soils oftener mention the seeds of plants? Would not a careful analysis of old pasture sod settle the question?

I suspect that I can throw a little light on the fact that when a dense pine wood is cut down oaks, etc., may take its place. There were only pines, no other tree. They are cut off, and, after two years have elapsed, you see oaks, or perhaps a few other hard woods, springing up with scarcely a pine amid them, and you wonder how the acorns could have lain in the ground so long without decaying. There is a good example at Loring's lot. But if you look through a thick pine wood, even the exclusively pitch pine ones, you will detect many little oaks, birches, etc., sprung probably from seeds carried into the thicket by squirrels, etc., and blown thither, but which are overshadowed and choked by the pines. This planting under the shelter of the pines may be carried on annually, and the plants annually die, but when the pines are cleared off, the oaks, etc., having got just the start they want, and now secured favorable conditions, immediately spring up to trees. Scarcely enough allowance has been made for the agency of squirrels and birds in dispersing seeds.

May 15. Cleared out the Beech Spring, which is a copious one. So I have done some service, though it was a wet and muddy job. Cleared out a spring while you have been to the wars. Now that warmer days make the traveller thirsty, this becomes an important work.

May 18. *Sailed* back on Hubbard's redstart path, and there saw a mud turtle draw in his head, of which I saw the half, about eight rods off. Pushed to the spot, where the water was about a foot deep, and at length detected him spread out on the bottom, his monstrous head and tail and legs outspread, probably directly under where he had appeared. At first, I suspect, I mistook him for a rock, for he was thickly covered with a short green moss-like conferva (?),—a venerable object, a true son of the meadow, suggesting what vigor! what naturalness! Perchance to make the moss grow on your back without injuring your health! How many things can he sustain on his shell where the mosses grow? He looked like an antediluvian under that green, shaggy shell, tougher than the rock you mistake it for. No wonder the Indian reverenced him as a god. Think of the time when he was an infant. There is your native American, who was before Columbus, perchance. Grown, not gray, but green with the lapse of ages. Living with the life of the meadow. I took off my coat, stripped up my shirt-sleeve, and caught him by his great rough tail. He snapped at me and my paddle, striking his snout against the side of the boat till he made it bleed. Though I held him down with an oar for a lever and my foot on it, he would suddenly lift all together, or run out his head and knock the oar and my leg aside. He held up his head to me and, with his mouth wide open, hissed in his breathing like a locomotive for a quarter of an hour, and I could look straight down his monstrous gullet ten inches. The only way to hold him and paddle too was to turn him on his back, then, putting the end of a paddle under a seat, slant it over his sternum and press my foot on the other end. He was fourteen and one half inches long by twelve at the broadest places, and weighed twenty-five pounds and three ounces. The claws were an inch and a quarter long beyond the skin, and very stout. You had to exert yourself to turn him over on a plane surface, he held down so firmly with his claws, as if grown to it. He took my hand into his shell with his tail and took the skin off it.

I know of a young lady who, when riding, came across one in the road, which not wishing to run over, she got out and tried to drive it out of the way with her whip, but it "screamed" at and terrified her. A caravan could not make him budge under those circumstances.

May 20. Was awaked and put into sounder sleep than ever early this morning by the distant crashing of thunder, and now,—

P.M. (to Beck Stow's),—

I hear it in mid-afternoon, muttering, crashing in the muggy air in mid-heaven, a little south of the village as I go through it, like the tumbling down of piles of boards, and get a few sprinkles in the sun. Nature has found her hoarse summer voice again, like the lowing of a cow let out to pasture. It is Nature's rutting season. Even as the birds sing tumultuously and glance by with fresh and brilliant plumage, so now is Nature's grandest voice heard, and her sharpest flashes seen. The air has resumed its voice, and the light-ning, like a yellow spring flower, illumines the dark banks of the clouds. All the pregnant earth is bursting into life like a mildew, accompanied with noise and fire and tumult.

May 22. P.M.—To *Viola Muhlenbergii*, which is abundantly out; how long? A small pale-blue flower growing in dense bunches, but in spots a little drier than the *V. cucullata* and *blanda*. *Veronica peregrina*, apparently several days. A yellow butterfly over the middle of the flooded meadow. *Polygonatum pubescens* at rock. *Aralia nudicaulis*, apparently a day or two where heat is reflected from the rock on Island. Chokecherry and cratægus there in a day or two. The *Cornus florida* does not bloom this year. Hemlock and creeping juniper, not quite yet. The red and cream-colored cone-shaped staminate buds of the black spruce will apparently shed pollen in one to three days?

May 24. Humphrey Buttrick says he has caught as many as a dozen partridges in his hands. He lies right down on them, or where he knows them to be, then passes his hands back and forth under his body till he feels them. You must not lift your body at all or they will surely squeeze out, and when you feel one must be sure you get hold of their legs or head, and not feathers merely.

To-day is suddenly overpoweringly warm. Thermometer at 1 P.M., 94° in the shade! but in the afternoon it suddenly fell to 56, and it continued cold the next two days.

May 31. It has been *very* cold for two or three days, and to-night a frost is feared. The telegraph says it snowed in Bangor to-day. The hickory leaves are blackened by blowing in the cold wind.

June 21. Very hot day, as was yesterday,—98° at 2 P.M., 99° at 3, and 128° in sun. Nighthawks numerously squeak at 5 P.M. and boom. Saw them fly low and touch the water like swallows over Walden. All my birch wines are now more acid and very good indeed with sugar. Am surprised to see it effervesce, all white with white sugar only, like a soda-water.

June 22. Sunday. P.M.—To Walden.

Ricketson says that they say at New Bedford that the song sparrow says, *Maids, maids, maids,—hang on your tea-kettle-ettle-ettle-ettle-ettle.*

R.W.E. imitates the wood thrush by *he willy willy—ha willy willy—O willy O.*

June 26. [At New Bedford, visiting Ricketson.] Heard of, and sought out, the hut of Martha Simons, the only pure-blooded Indian left about New Bedford. She lives alone on the narrowest point of the Neck, near the shore, in sight of New Bedford. The squaw was not at home when we first called. It was a little hut not so big as mine. *Vide* sketch by R., with the bay not far behind it. No garden; only some lettuce amid the thin grass in front, and a great white pile of clam and quahog shells one side. She ere long came in from the seaside, and we called again. We knocked and walked in, and she asked us to sit down. She had half an acre of the real tawny Indian face, broad with high cheek-bones, black eyes, and straight hair, originally black but now a little gray, parted in the middle. Her hands were several shades darker than her face. She had a peculiarly vacant expression, perhaps characteristic of the Indian, and answered our questions listlessly, without being interested or implicated, mostly in monosyllables, as if hardly present there. To judge from her physiognomy, she might have been King Philip's own daughter. Yet she could not speak a word of Indian, and knew nothing of her race. Said she had lived with the whites, gone out to service to them when seven years old. Had lived part of her life at Squaw Betty's Neck, Assawampsett Pond. Did she know Sampson's? She'd ought to; she'd done work enough there. She said she was sixty years old, but was probably nearer seventy. She sat with her elbows on her knees and her face in her hands and that peculiar vacant stare, perhaps looking out the window between us, not repelling us in the least, but perfectly indifferent to our presence.

She was born on that spot. Her grandfather also lived on the same spot, though not in the same house. He was the last of her race who could speak Indian. She had heard him pray in Indian, but could only understand "Jesus Christ." Her only companion was a miserable tortoise-shell kitten which took no notice of us. She had stone chimney, a small cooking-stove without fore legs, set up on bricks within it, and a bed covered with dirty bed-clothes.

Said she hired out her field as pasture; better for her than to cultivate it. There were two young heifers in it. The question she answered with most interest was, "What do you call that plant?" and I reached her the aletris from my hat. She took it, looked at it a moment, and said, "That's husk-root. It's good to put into bitters for a weak stomach." The last year's light-colored and withered leaves surround the present green star like a husk. This must be the origin of the name. Its root is described as intensely bitter. I ought to have had my hat full of plants.

A conceited old Quaker minister, her neighbor, told me with a sanctified air, "I think that the Indians were human beings; dost thee not think so?" He only convinced me of his doubt and narrowness.

June 30. Monday. A.M.—To Middleborough ponds in the new town of Lakeville (some three years old). What a miserable name! It should have been Assawampsett or, perchance, Sanacus, if that was the name of the Christian Indian killed on the pond.

Saw a haymaker with his suspenders crossed before as well as behind. A valuable hint, which I think I shall improve upon, since I am much troubled by mine slipping off my shoulders.

July 12. Hear the plaintive note of young bluebirds, a reviving and gleaming of their blue ray. White vervain. Smooth sumach. Rue is beginning now to whiten the meadows on all hands.

Red lilies in prime, single upright fiery flowers, their throats how splendidly and *variously* spotted, hardly two of quite the same hue and not two spotted alike,—leopard-spotted,—averaging a foot or more in height, amid the huckleberry and lambkill, etc., in the moist, meadowy pasture.

July 14. While drinking at Assabet Spring in woods, noticed a cherry-stone on the bottom. A bird that came to drink must have brought it half a mile. So the tree gets planted!

July 17. Bathed at Clamshell. See great schools of minnows, apparently shiners, hovering in the clear shallow next the shore. They seem to choose such places for security. They take pretty good care of themselves and are harder to catch with the hands than you expect, darting out of the way at last quite swiftly. Caught three, however, between my hands. They have brighter golden irides, all the abdomen conspicuously pale-golden, the back and half down the sides pale-brown, a broad, distinct black band along sides (which methinks marks the shiner), and comparatively transparent beneath behind vent. When the water is gone I am surprised to see how they can skip or spring from side to side in my cup-shaped two hands for a long time. This to enable them to get off floating planks or pads on the shore when in fright they may have leaped on to them. But they are very tender, and the sun and air soon kill them. If there is any water in your hand they will pass out through the smallest crack between your fingers. They are about three quarters of an inch long generally, though of various sizes.

Half a dozen big bream come quite up to me, as I stand in the water. They are not easily scared in such a case.

A very warm afternoon. Thermometer at 97°.

July 23. Saw at Hydropeltis Meadow a small bullfrog in the act of swallowing a young but pretty sizable apparently *Rana palustris*, such as now hop about, an inch and a half long. He took it down head foremost, and as the legs were slowly taken in,—stuffing himself,—for the legs were often straightened out,—I wondered what satisfaction it could be to the larger to have that cold slimy fellow, entire, lying head to tail within him! I sprang to make him disgorge, but it was too late to save him. Though I tossed the bullfrog out of the water, the *palustris* was entombed. So little while had he been in the light when he fell into that recess!

Bathing in Walden, I find the water considerably colder at the bottom while I stand up to my chin, but the sandy bottom much warmer to my feet than the water. The heat passes *through* the water without being absorbed by it much.

July 29. Pratt says he one day walked out with Wesson, with their rifles, as far as Hunt's Bridge. Looking downstream, he saw a swallow sitting on a bush very far off, at which he took aim and fired with ball. He was surprised to see that he had touched the swallow, for it flew directly across the river toward Simon Brown's barn, always descending toward the earth or water, not being able to maintain itself; but what surprised him most was to see a second swallow come flying behind and repeatedly strike the other with all his force beneath, so as to toss him up as often as he approached the ground and enable him to continue his flight, and thus he continued to do till they were out of sight. Pratt said he resolved that he would never fire at a swallow again.

Looked at a Sharp's rifle, a Colt's revolver, a Maynard's, and a Thurber's revolver. The last fires fastest (by a steady pull), but not so smartly, and is not much esteemed.

Aug. 1. Since July 30th, inclusive, we have had perfect dog-days without interruption. The earth has suddenly invested with a thick musty mist. The sky has become a mere fungus. A thick blue musty veil of mist is drawn before the sun. The sun has not been visible, except for a moment or two once or twice a day, all this time, nor the stars by night. Moisture reigns. You cannot dry a napkin at the window, nor press flowers without their mildewing. You imbibe so much moisture from the atmosphere that you are not so thirsty, nor is bathing so grateful as a week ago. The burning heat is tempered, but as you lose sight of the sky and imbibe the musty, misty air, you exist as a vegetable, a fungus. Unfortunate those who have not got their hay. I see them wading in overflowed meadows and pitching the black and mouldy swaths about in vain that they may dry. In the meanwhile, vegetation is becoming rank, vines of all kinds are rampant. Squashes and melons *are said* to grow a foot in a night. But weeds grow as fast. The corn unrolls. Berries abound and attain their full size. Once or twice in the day there is an imperfect gleam of yellow sunlight for a moment through some thinner part of the veil, reminding us that we have not seen the sun so long, but no blue sky is revealed. The drooping spirits of mosquitoes revive, and they whet their stings anew. Legions of buzzing flies blacken the furniture. We have a dense fog every night, which lifts itself but a short distance during the day. At sundown I see it curling up from the river and meadows. However, I love this moisture in its season. I believe it is good to breathe, wholesome as a vapor bath. Toadstools shoot up in the yards and paths.

The Great Meadows being a little wet,—hardly so much as usual,—I took off my shoes and went barefoot some two miles through the cut-grass. The cut-grass is bad for tender feet, and you must be careful not to let it draw through your hands, for it will cut like a fine saw. I was surprised to see dense beds of rhexia in full bloom there. They make a splendid show, these brilliant rose-colored patches. It is about the richest color to be seen now. Yet few ever see them in this perfection, unless the haymaker who levels them, or the birds that fly over the meadow. These gay standards otherwise unfurled in vain.

Aug. 2. The lower leaves of some catnep are now of that delicate lake or claret color. Some waxwork leaves have felt the heat and slight drought. Their green is spotted with yellow, distinct yellow and green; others a very delicate clear yellow; others faded quite white.

Aug. 4. P.M.—Carried party a-berrying to Conantum in boat.

Conantum hillside is now literally black with berries. They are literally five or six species deep. This favorable moist weather has expanded some of the huckle-berries to the size of bullets. Each patch, each bush, seems fuller and blacker than the last. Such a profusion, yet you see neither birds nor beasts eating them, unless ants and the huckleberry-bug! I carried my hands full of bushes to the boat, and, returning, the two ladies picked fully three pints from these alone, casting the bare bushes into the stream.

Aug. 5. Choke-cherries near House-leek Rock begin to be ripe, though still red. They are scarcely edible, but their beauty atones for it. See those handsome racemes of ten or twelve cherries each, dark glossy red, semi-transparent. You love them not the less because they are not quite palatable. Along fences or hedgerows.

Aug. 6. Copious and continuous rain in the night, deluging, soaking rain, with thunder and lightning, beating down the crops; and this morning it is cooler and clearer and windier.

P.M.—To Walden.

Artificial, denaturalized persons cannot handle nature without being poisoned. If city-bred girls visit their country cousins,—go a-berrying with them,—they are sure to return covered with blueberry bumps at least. They exhaust all the lotions of the country apothecary for a week after. Unnamable poisons infect the air, as if they were pursued by imps. I have known those who forbade their children going into the woods at all.

AUG. 8. Rain, lightning, and thunder all day long in torrents. The ground was already saturated on the night of the 5th, and now it fills all gutters and low grounds. No sooner has one thunder-shower swept over and the sky begun to light up a little, than another darkens the west. We were told that lightning cleared the air and so cleared itself, but now we lose our faith in that theory, for we have thunder after thunder-shower and lightning is become a drug. Nature finds it just as easy to lighten the last time as at first, and we cannot believe that the air was so very impure.

3.30 P.M.—When I came forth, thinking to empty my boat and go a-meditating along the river,—for the full ditches and drenched grass forbade other routes, except the highway,—and this is one advantage of a boat,—I learned to my chagrin that Father's pig was gone. He had leaped out of the pen some time since his breakfast, but his dinner was untouched. Here was an ugly duty not to be shirked,—a wild shoat that weighed but ninety to be tracked, caught, and penned,—an afternoon's work, at least (if I were lucky enough to accomplish it so soon), prepared for me, quite different from what I had anticipated. I felt chagrined, it is true, but I could not ignore the fact nor shirk the duty that lay so near to me. Do the duty that lies nearest to thee. I proposed to Father to sell the pig as he was running (somewhere) to a neighbor who had talked of buying him, making a considerable reduction. But my suggestion was not acted on, and the responsibilities of the case all devolved on me, for I could run faster than Father. Father looked to me, and I ceased to look to the river. Well, let us see if we can track him. Yes, this is the corner where he got out, making a step of his trough. Thanks to the rain, his tracks are quite distinct. Here he went along the edge of the garden over the water and muskmelons, then through the beans and potatoes, and even along the front-yard walk I detect the print of his divided hoof, his two sharp toes (*ungulæ*). It 's a wonder we did not see him. And here he passed out under the gate, across the road,—how naked he must have felt!—into a grassy ditch, and whither next? Is it of any use to go hunting him up unless you have devised some mode of catching him when you have found? Of what avail to know where he has been, even where he is? He was so shy the little while we had him, of course he will never come back; he cannot be tempted by a swill-pail. Who knows how many miles off he is! Perhaps he has taken the back track and gone to Brighton, or Ohio! At most, probably we shall only have the satisfaction of glimpsing the nimble beast at a distance, from time to time, as he trots swiftly through the green meadows and corn-fields. But, now I speak, what is that I see pacing deliberately up the middle of the street forty rods off? It is *he*. As if to tantalize, to tempt us to waste our afternoon without further hesitation, he thus offers himself. He roots a foot or two and then lies down on his belly in the middle of the street. But think not to catch him a-napping. He has his eyes about, and his ears too. He has already been chased. He gives that wagon a wide berth, and now, seeing me, he turns and trots back down the street. He turns into a front yard. Now if I can only close that gate upon him ninety-nine hundredths of the work is done, but ah! he hears me coming afar off, he foresees the danger, and, with swinish cunning and speed, he scampers out. My neighbor in the street tries to head him; he jumps to this side the road, then to that, before him; but the third time the pig was there first and went by. "Whose is it?" he shouts. "It's ours." He bolts into that neighbor's yard and so across his premises. He has been twice there before, it seems; he knows the road; see what work he has made in his flower-garden! He must be fond of bulbs. Our neighbor picks up one tall flower with its bulb attached, holds it out at arm's length. He is excited about the pig; it is a subject he is interested in. But where is he gone now? The last glimpse I had of him was as he went through the cow-yard; here are his tracks again in this corn-field, but they are lost in the grass. We lose him; we beat the bushes in vain; he may be far away. But hark! I heard a grunt. Nevertheless for half an hour I do not see him that grunted. At last I find fresh tracks along the river, and again lose them. Each neighbor whose garden I traverse tells me some anecdote of losing pigs, or the attempt to drive them, by which I am not encouraged. Once more he crosses our first neighbor's garden and is said to be in the road. But I am not there yet; it is a good way off. At length my eyes rest on him again, after three quarters of an hour's separation. There he trots with the whole road to himself, and now again drops on his belly in a puddle. Now he starts again, seeing me twenty rods off, deliberates, considers which way I want him to go, and goes the other. There was some chance of driving him along the sidewalk, or letting him go rather, till he slipped under our gate again, but of what avail would that be? How corner and catch him who keeps twenty rods off? He never lets the open side of the triangle be less than half a dozen rods wide. There was one place where a narrower street turned off at right angles with the main one, just this side our yard, but I could not drive him past that. Twice he ran up the narrow street, for he knew I did not wish it, but though the main street was broad and open and no traveller in sight, when I tried to drive him past this opening he invariably turned his piggish head toward me, dodged from side to side, and finally ran up the narrow street or down the main one, as if there were a high barrier erected before him. But really he is no more obstinate than I. I cannot but respect his tactics and his independence. He will be he, and I may be I. He is not unreasonable because he thwarts me, but only the more reasonable. He has a strong will. He stands upon his idea. There is a wall across the path not where a man bars the way, but where he is resolved not to travel. Is he not superior to man therein? Once more he glides down the narrow street, deliberates at a corner, chooses wisely for him, and disappears through an openwork fence eastward. He has gone to fresh gardens and pastures new. Other neighbors stand in the doorways but half sympathizing, only observing, "Ugly thing to catch." "You have a job on your hands." I lose sight of him, but hear that he is far ahead in a large field. And there we try to let him alone a while, giving him a wide berth.

At this stage an Irishman was engaged to assist. "I can catch him," says he, with Buonapartean confidence. He thinks him a family Irish pig. His wife is with him, bareheaded, and his little flibbertigibbet of a boy, seven years old. "Here, Johnny, do you run right off there" (at the broadest possible angle with his own course). "Oh, but he can't do anything." "Oh, but I only want him to tell me where he is,—to keep sight of him." Michael soon discovers that he is not an Irish pig, and his wife and Johnny's occupation are soon gone. Ten minutes afterward I am patiently tracking him step by step through a corn-field, a near-sighted man helping me, and then into garden after garden far eastward, and finally into the highway, at the graveyard; but hear and see nothing. One suggests a dog to track him. Father is meanwhile selling him to the black-smith, who also is trying to get sight of him. After fifteen minutes since he disappeared eastward. I hear that he has been to the river twice far on [?] the north, through the first neighbor's premises. I wend that way. He crosses the street far ahead, Michael behind; he dodges up an avenue. I stand in the gap there, Michael at the other end, and now he tries to corner him. But it is a vain hope to corner him in a yard. I see a carriage-manufactory door open. "Let him go in there, Flannery." For once the pig and I are of one mind; he bolts in, and the door is closed. Now for a rope. It is a large barn, crowded with carriages. The rope is at length obtained; the windows are barred with carriages lest he bolt through. He is resting quietly on his belly in the further corner, thinking unutterable things.

Now the course recommences within narrower limits. Bump, bump, bump he goes, against wheels and shafts. We get no hold yet. He is all ear and eye. Small boys are sent under the carriages to drive him out. He froths at the mouth and deters them. At length he is stuck for an instant between the spokes of a wheel, and I am securely attached to his hind leg. He squeals deafeningly, and is silent. The rope is attached to a hind leg. The door is opened, and the *driving* commences. Roll an egg as well. You may drag him, but you cannot drive him. But he is in the road, and now another thundershower greets us. I leave Michael with the rope in one hand and a switch in the other and go home. He seems to be gaining a little westward. But, after long delay, I look out and find that he makes but doubtful progress. A boy is made to face him with a stick, and it is only when the pig springs at him savagely that progress is made homeward. He will be killed before he is driven home. I get a wheelbarrow and go to the rescue. Michael is alarmed. The pig is rabid, snaps at him. We drag him across the barrow, hold him down, and so, at last, get him home.

If a wild shoat like this gets loose, first track him if you can, or otherwise discover where he is. Do not scare him more than you can help. Think of some yard or building or other inclosure that will hold him and, by showing your forces—yet as if uninterested parties—fifteen or twenty rods off, let him of his own accord enter it. Then slightly shut the gate. Now corner and tie him and put him into a cart or barrow.

All progress in driving at last was made by facing and endeavoring to switch him from home. He rushed upon you and made a few feet in the desired direction. When I approached with the barrow he advanced to meet it with determination.

So I get home at dark, wet through and supperless, covered with mud and wheel-grease, without any rare flowers.

To the eyes of men there is something tragic in death. We hear of the death of any member of the human family with something more than regret,—not without a slight shudder and feeling of commiseration. The churchyard is a *grave* place.

Aug. 9. Saturday. Notwithstanding the very copious rain, with lightning, on the night of August 5th and the deluge which fell yesterday, raising the river still higher, it rained again and again with very vivid lightning, more copiously than ever, last night, and without long intervals all this day. Few, if any, can remember such a succession of thunder-storms merged into one long thunder-storm, lasting almost continuously (the storm does) two nights and two days. We are surprised to see that it can lighten just as vividly, thunder just as loud, rain just as copiously at last as at first.

The river is raised about two feet! My boat is nearly even full, though under the willows. There is more current. The pads are drowned; the utmost length of their tethers does not permit them to come within a foot or ten inches of the surface. They lay smoothly on the top before, with considerable spare coil beneath; now they strain in vain toward the surface.

Aug. 12. What a wilderness of weeds is Moore's Swamp now! Tall rough goldenrods, erechthites, poke, *Aster Radula*, dogwood, etc., etc. It looks as if the potatoes which grew there would be poisonous.

The late rains have tried the roofs severely. Tenants have complained to their landlords, and now I see carpenters setting up their staging and preparing to shingle on various sides.

Aug. 16. What a variety of old garden herbs—mints, etc.—are naturalized along an old settled road, like this to Boston which the British travelled! And then there is the site, apparently, of an old garden by the tan-yard, where the spearmint grows so rankly. I am intoxicated with the fragrance. Though I find only one new plant (the cassia), yet old acquaintances grow so rankly, and the spearmint intoxicates me so, that I am bewildered, as it were by a variety of new things. An infinite novelty. All the roadside is the site of an old garden where fragrant herbs have become naturalized,— hounds-tongue, bergamot, spearmint, elecampane, etc. I see even the tiger lily, with its bulbs, growing by the roadside far from houses (near Leighton's graveyard). I think I have found many new plants, and am surprised when I can reckon but one. A little distance from my ordinary walk and a little variety in the growth or luxuriance will produce this illusion. By the discovery of one new plant all bounds seem to be infinitely removed.

Am frequently surprised to find how imperfectly water-plants are known. Even good shore botanists are out of their element on the water. I would suggest to young botanists to get not only a botany-box but a boat, and know the water-plants not so much from the shore as from the water side.

My plants in press are in a sad condition; mildew has invaded them during the late damp weather, even those that were nearly dry. I find more and other plants than I counted on. Very bad weather of late for pressing plants. Give me the dry heat of July. Even growing leaves out of doors are spotted with fungi now, much more than mine in press.

Aug. 25. The farmers commonly say that the spring floods, being of cold water, do not injure the grass like later ones when the water is warm, but I suspect it is not so much owing to the warmth of the water as to the age and condition of the grass and whatever else is exposed to them. They say that if you let the water rise and stand some time over the roots of trees in warm weather it will kill them. This, then, may be the value of these occasional freshets in August: they steam and kill the shrubs and trees which had crept into the river meadows, and so keep them open perpetually, which, perchance, the spring floods alone might not do. It is commonly supposed that our river meadows were much drier than now originally, or when the town was settled. They were probably drier before the dam was built at Billerica, but if they were much or at all drier than now originally, I ask what prevented their being converted into maple swamps? Maples, alders, birches, etc., are creeping into them quite fast on many sides at present. If they had been so dry as is supposed they would not have been open meadows. It seems to be true that high water in mid-summer, when perchance the trees and shrubs are in a more tender state, kills them. It "steams" them, as it does the grass; and maybe the river thus asserts its rights, and possibly it would still to great extent, though the meadows should be considerably raised. Yet, I ask, why do maples, alders, etc., at present border the stream, though they do not spring up to any extent in the open meadow? Is it because the immediate bank is commonly more firm as well as higher (their seeds also are more liable to be caught there), and where it is low they are protected by willows and button-bushes, which can bear the flood? Not even willows and button-bushes prevail in the Great Meadows,—though many of the former, at least, spring up there,—except on the most elevated parts or hummocks. The reason for this cannot be solely in the fact that the water stands over them there a part of the year, because they are still more exposed to the water in many places on the shore of the river where yet they thrive. Is it then owing to the soft character of the ground in the meadow and the ice tearing up the meadow so extensively? On the immediate bank of the river that kind of sod and soil is not commonly formed which the ice lifts up. Why is the black willow so strictly confined to the bank of the river? What is the use, in Nature's economy, of these occasional floods in August? Is it not partly to preserve the meadows open?

I was suggesting yesterday, as I have often before, that the town should provide a stone monument to be placed in the river, so as to be surrounded by water at its lowest stage, and a dozen feet high, so as to rise above it at its highest stage; on this feet and inches to be permanently marked; and it be made some one's duty to record each high or low stage of the water. Now, when we have a remarkable freshet, we cannot tell surely whether it is higher than the one thirty or sixty years ago or not. It would be not merely interesting, but often practically valuable, to know this. Reuben Rice was telling me to-night that the great freshet of two or three years ago came, according to his brother Israel, within two inches of one that occurred about forty years ago. I asked how he knew. He said that the former one took place early (February?), and the surface froze so that boys skated on it, and the ice marked a particular apple tree, girdled it, so that it is seen to this day. But we wish to speak more confidently than this allows. It is important when building a causeway, or a bridge, or a house even, in some situations, to know exactly how high the river has ever risen. It would need to be a very large stone or pile of stones, which the ice could not move or break. Perhaps one corner of a bridge abutment would do.

Aug. 26. Tuesday. More wind and quite cold this morning, but very bright and sparkling, autumn-like air, reminding of frosts to be

apprehended,* also tempting abroad to adventure. The fall cricket—
or is it alder locust?—sings the praises of the day.

So about 9 A.M. up river to Fair Haven Pond.

I rest and take my lunch on Lee's Cliff, looking toward Baker
Farm. What is a New England landscape this sunny August day? A
weather-painted house and barn, with an orchard by its side, in
midst of a sandy field surrounded by green woods, with a small
blue lake on one side. A sympathy between the color of the weather-
painted house and that of the lake and sky. I speak not of a country
road between its fences, for this house lies off one, nor do I commonly approach them from this side. The weather-painted house.
This is the New England color, homely but fit as that of a toadstool.

Aug. 28. I open the painted tortoise nest of June 10th, and find a
young turtle partly out of his shell. He is already wonderfully
strong and precocious. Though those eyes never saw the light before, he watches me very warily, even at a distance. With what vigor
he crawls out of the hole I have made, over opposing weeds! He
struggles in my fingers with great strength; has none of the tenderness of infancy. His whole snout is convex, and curved like a beak.
Having attained the surface, he pauses and warily watches me.

Meanwhile a striped squirrel sits on the wall across the road
under a pine, eying me, with his cheek-pouches stuffed with nuts
and puffed out ludicrously, as if he had the mumps, while the wall
is strewn with the dry brown husks of hazelnuts he has stripped. A
bird, perhaps a thrasher, in the pine close above him is hopping
restlessly and scolding at him.

June, July, and August, the tortoise eggs are hatching a few
inches beneath the surface in sandy fields. You tell of active labors,
of works of art, and wars the past summer; meanwhile the tortoise
eggs underlie this turmoil. What events have transpired on the lit
and airy surface three inches above them! Sumner knocked down;
Kansas living an age of suspense. Think what is a summer to them!

---

*We see no effects of frost yet in garden, but hear a rumor of a little somewhere.
First muskmelon gathered.

June, July, and August,—the livelong summer,—what are they with their heats and fevers but sufficient to hatch a tortoise in. Be not in haste; mind your private affairs. Consider the turtle. Perchance you have worried yourself, despaired of the world, meditated the end of life, and all things seemed rushing to destruction; but nature has steadily and serenely advanced with a turtle's pace. Has not the tortoise also learned the true value of time?

Aug. 30. I have come out this afternoon a-cranberrying, chiefly to gather some of the small cranberry, *Vaccinium Oxycoccus*, which Emerson says is the common cranberry of the north of Europe. This was a small object, yet not to be postponed, on account of imminent frosts, *i.e.*, if I would know this year the flavor of the European cranberry as compared with our larger kind. I thought I should like to have a dish of this sauce on the table at Thanksgiving of my own gathering. I could hardly make up my mind to come this way, it seemed so poor an object to spend the afternoon on. I kept foreseeing a lame conclusion,—how I should cross the Great Fields, look into Beck Stow's, and then retrace my steps no richer than before. In fact, I expected little of this walk, yet it did pass through the side of my mind that somehow, on this very account (my small expectation), it would turn out well, as also the advantage of having some purpose, however small, to be accomplished,— of letting your deliberate wisdom and foresight in the house to some extent direct and control your steps. If you would really take a position outside the street and daily life of men, you must have deliberately planned your course, you must have business which is not your neighbors' business, which they cannot understand. For only absorbing employment prevails, succeeds, takes up space, occupies territory, determines the future of individuals and states, drives Kansas out of your head, and actually and permanently occupies the only desirable and free Kansas against all border ruffians. The attitude of resistance is one of weakness, inasmuch as it only faces an enemy; it has its back to all that is truly attractive. You shall have your affairs, I will have mine. You will spend this afternoon in setting up your neighbor's stove, and be paid for it; I will spend it in gathering the few berries of the *Vaccinium Oxycoc-cus* which Nature produces here, before it is too late, and *be paid for it also* after another fashion. I have always reaped unexpected and incalculable advantages from carrying out at last, however tardily, any little enterprise which my genius suggested to me long ago as a thing to be done,—some step to be taken, however slight, out of the usual course.

How many schools I have thought of which I might go to but did not go to! expecting foolishly that some greater advantage or schooling would come to me! It is these comparatively cheap and private expeditions that substantiate our existence and batten our lives, as, where a vine touches the earth in its undulating course, it puts forth roots and thickens its stock. Our employment generally is tinkering, mending the old worn-out teapot of society. Our stock in trade is solder. Better for me, says my genius, to go cranberrying this afternoon for the *Vaccinium Oxycoccus* in Gowing's Swamp, to get but a pocketful and learn its peculiar flavor, aye, and the flavor of Gowing's Swamp and of *life* in New England, than to go consul to Liverpool [*as Nathaniel Hawthorne had done*] and get I don't know how many thousand dollars for it, with no such flavor. Many of our days should be spent, not in vain expectations and lying on our oars, but in carrying out deliberately and faithfully the hundred little purposes which every man's genius must have suggested to him. Let not your life be wholly without an object, though it be only to ascertain the flavor of a cranberry, for it will not be only the quality of an insignificant berry that you will have tasted, but the flavor of your life to that extent, and it will be such a sauce as no wealth can buy.

Both a conscious and an unconscious life are good. Neither is good exclusively, for both have the same source. The wisely conscious life springs out of an unconscious suggestion. I have found my account in travelling in having prepared beforehand a list of questions which I would get answered, not trusting to my interest at the moment, and can then travel with the most profit. Indeed, it is by obeying the suggestions of a higher light within you that you escape from yourself and, in the transit, as it were see with the unworn sides of your eye, travel totally new paths. What is that pretended life that does not take up a claim, that does not occupy ground, that cannot build a causeway to its objects, that sits on a bank looking over a bog, singing its desires?

However, it was not with such blasting expectations as these that I entered the swamp. I saw bags of cranberries, just gathered and tied up, on the banks of Beck Stow's Swamp. They must have been raked out of the water, now so high, before they should rot. I left my shoes and stockings on the bank far off and waded bare-legged through rigid andromeda and other bushes a long way, to the soft open sphagnous centre of the swamp.

I found these cunning little cranberries lying high and dry on the firm uneven tops of the sphagnum,—their weak vine considerably on one side,—sparsely scattered about the drier edges of the swamp, or sometimes more thickly occupying some little valley a foot or two over, between two mountains of sphagnum. They were of two varieties, judging from the fruit. The one, apparently the ripest, colored most like the common cranberry but more scarlet, *i.e.* yellowish-green, blotched or checked with dark scarlet-red, commonly pear-shaped; the other, also pear-shaped, or more bulged out in the middle, thickly and finely dark-spotted or peppered on yellowish-green or straw-colored or pearly ground, and with a tinge of purple. A singular difference. The grayish speckled variety was particularly novel and pretty, though not easy to detect. It lay here and there snugly sunk in the sphagnum, whose drier parts it exactly resembled in color, just like some kind of swamp sparrows' eggs in their nest. I was obliged with my finger carefully to trace the slender pedicel through the moss to its vine, when I would pluck the whole together. Like jewels worn on, or set in, these sphagnous breasts of the swamp,—swamp pearls, call them.

I waded quite round the swamp for an hour, my bare feet in the cold water beneath, and it was a relief to place them on the warmer surface of the sphagnum. I filled one pocket with each variety, but sometimes, being confused, crossed hands and put them into the wrong pocket.

I enjoyed this cranberrying very much, notwithstanding the wet and cold, and the swamp seemed to be yielding its crop to me alone, for there are none else to pluck it or to value it. I told the proprietor once that they grew here, but he, learning that they were not abundant enough to be gathered for the market, has probably never thought of them since. I am the only person in the township who regards them or knows of them, and I do not regard them in the light of their pecuniary value. I have no doubt I felt richer wading there with my two pockets full, treading on wonders at every step, than any farmer going to market with a hundred bushels which he has raked, or hired to be raked. I got further and further away from the town every moment, and my good genius seemed to have smiled on me, leading me hither, and then the sun suddenly came out clear and bright, but it did not warm my feet. I would gladly share my gains, take one, or twenty, into partnership and get this swamp with them, but I do not know an individual whom this berry cheers and nourishes as it does me. When I exhibit it to them I perceive that they take but a momentary interest in it and commonly dismiss it from their thoughts with the consideration that it cannot be profitably cultivated. You could not get a pint at one haul of a rake, and Slocum would not give you much for them. But I love it the better partly for that reason even. I fill a basket with them and keep it several days by my side. If anybody else—any farmer, at least—should spend an hour thus wading about here in this secluded swamp, barelegged, intent on the sphagnum, filling his pocket only, with no rake in his hand and no bag or bushel on the bank, he would be pronounced insane and have a guardian put over him; but if he'll spend his time skimming and watering his milk and selling his small potatoes for large ones, or generally in skinning flints, he will probably be made guardian of somebody else.

I noticed also a few small peculiar-looking huckle-berries hanging on bushes amid the sphagnum, and, tasting, perceived that they were hispid, a new kind to me. *Gaylussacia dumosa* var. *hirtella* (perhaps just after *resinosa*), though Gray refers it to a "*sandy* low soil" and says nothing of the hispid fruit. Has a small black hairy or hispid berry, shining but insipid and inedible, with a tough, hairy skin left in the mouth; has very prominent calyx-lobes.

I seemed to have reached a new world, so wild a place that the very huckleberries grew hairy and were inedible. What's the need of visiting far-off mountains and bogs, if a half-hour's walk will carry me into such wildness and novelty? But why should not as wild plants grow here as in Berkshire, as in Labrador? Is Nature so easily tamed? Is she not as primitive and vigorous here as anywhere? How does this particular acre of secluded, unfrequented, useless (?) quaking bog differ from an acre in Labrador? Has any white man ever settled on it? Does any now frequent it? Not even the Indian comes here now. I see that there are some square rods within twenty miles of Boston just as wild and primitive and unfrequented as a square rod in Labrador, as unaltered by man. Here grows the hairy huckleberry as it did in Squaw Sachem's day and a thousand years before, and concerns me perchance more than it did her. I have no doubt that for a moment I experience exactly the same sensations as if I were alone in a bog in Rupert's Land, and it saves me the trouble of going there; for what in any case makes the difference between being here and being there but many such little differences of flavor and roughness put together? Rupert's Land is recognized as much by one sense as another. I felt a shock, a thrill, an agreeable surprise in one instant, for, no doubt, all the possible inferences were at once drawn, with a rush, in my mind,—I could be in Rupert's Land and supping at home within the hour! This beat the railroad. That wild hairy huckleberry, inedible as it was, was equal to a domain secured to me and reaching to the South Sea. That was an unexpected harvest. I hope you have gathered as much, neighbor, from your corn and potato fields. I have got in my huckleberries. I shall be ready for Thanksgiving. It is in vain to dream of a wildness distant from ourselves. There is none such. It is the bog in our brain and bowels, the primitive vigor of Nature in us, that inspires that dream. I shall never find in the wilds of Labrador any greater wildness than in some recess in Concord, *i.e.* than I import into it. A little more manhood or virtue will make the surface of the globe anywhere thrillingly novel and wild. That alone will provide

and pay the fiddler; it will convert the district road into an untrodden cranberry bog, for it restores all things to their original primitive flourishing and promising state.

A cold white horizon sky in the north, forerunner of the fall of
the year. I go to bed and dream of cranberry-pickers far in the cold
north. With windows partly closed, with continent concentrated
thoughts, I dream. I get my new experiences still.

Better it is to go a-cranberrying than to go a-huckleberrying.
For that is cold and bracing, leading your thoughts beyond the
earth, and you do not surfeit on crude or terrene berries. It feeds
your spirit, now in the season of white twilights, when frosts are
apprehended, when edible berries are mostly gone.

Those small gray sparrow-egg cranberries lay so prettily in the
recesses of the sphagnum, I could wade for hours in the cold water
gazing at them, with a swarm of mosquitoes hovering about my
bare legs,—but at each step the friendly sphagnum in which I sank
protected my legs like a buckler,—not a crevice by which my foes
could enter.

I see that all is not garden and cultivated field and crops, that
there are little oases of wildness in the desert of our civilization,
wild as a square rod on the moon, supposing it to be uninhabited.
I believe almost in the personality of such planetary matter, feel
something akin to reverence for it, can even worship it as terrene,
titanic matter extant in my day. We are so different we admire each
other, we healthily attract one another. I love it as a maiden. These
spots are meteoric, aerolitic, and such matter has in all ages been
worshipped. Aye, when we are lifted out of the slime and film of
our habitual life, we see the whole globe to be an aerolite, and reverence it as such, and make pilgrimages to it, far off as it is. How
happens it that we reverence the stones which fall from another
planet, and not the stones which belong to this,—another globe,
not this,—heaven, and not earth?

If I could, I would worship the parings of my nails. I would fain
improve every opportunity to wonder and worship, as a sunflower
welcomes the light. The more thrilling, wonderful, divine objects I
behold in a day, the more expanded and immortal I become.

Aug. 31. Sunday. P.M.—To Hubbard Bath Swamp by boat.

There sits one by the shore who wishes to go with me, but I cannot think of it. I must be fancy-free. I would rather attend to him earnestly for half an hour, on shore or elsewhere, and then dismiss him. He thinks I could merely take him into my boat and then not mind him. He does not realize that I should by the same act take him into my mind, where there is no room for him, and my bark would surely founder in such a voyage as I was contemplating. I know very well that I should never reach that expansion of the river I have in my mind, with him aboard with his broad terrene qualities. He would sink my bark (not to another sea) and never know it. I could better carry a heaped load of meadow mud and sit on the thole-pins. There would be more room for me, and I should reach that expansion of the river nevertheless.

I could better afford to take him into bed with me, for then I might, perhaps, abandon him in my dreams. Ah! you are a heavy fellow, but I am well disposed. If you could go without going, then you might go. It is because I trust that I shall ere long depart from your thoughts, and so you from mine, that I am encouraged to set sail at all. I make haste to put several meanders and some hills between us.

What is getting into a man's carriage when it is full, compared with putting your foot in his mouth and popping right into his mind without considering whether it is occupied or not?

The *Viburnum nudum* berries are now in prime, a handsome rose-purple. I brought home a bunch of fifty-three berries, all of this color, and the next morning thirty were turned dark purple. In this state they are soft and just edible, having somewhat of a cherry flavor, not a large stone.

A painted tortoise shedding its scales.

Sept. 1. P.M.—With R. W. E. to Saw Mill and *Solidago odora*.

He has just had four of his fir trees next his house cut, they shaded his windows so. They were set out by Coolidge, E. thinks twenty-eight years ago.

We go admiring the pure and delicate tints of fungi on the surface of the damp swamp there, following up along the north side of the brook past the right of the old camp. There are many very beautiful lemon-yellow ones of various forms, some shaped like buttons, some becoming finely scalloped on the edge, some club-shaped and hollow, of the most delicate and rare but decided tints, contrasting well with the decaying leaves about them. There are others also pure white, others a wholesome red, others brown, and some even a light indigo-blue above and beneath and through-out. When colors come to be taught in the schools, as they should be, both the prism (or the rainbow) and these fungi should be used by way of illustration, and if the pupil does not learn colors, he may learn fungi, which perhaps is better. You almost envy the wood frogs and toads that hop amid such gems.

I think it stands about thus with asters and golden-rods now:—

The early meadow aster is either quite withered or much the worse for the wear, partly on account of the freshet.

Diplopappus cornifolius, not seen of late.

D. umbellatus, perhaps in prime or approaching it, but not much seen.

A. patens, apparently now in prime and the most abundant of the larger asters.

[*Etc.—23 more, plus footnotes and cross-references, with long follow-up lists on Sept. 24 and Oct. 8.*]

Sept. 2. Clear bright days of late, with a peculiar sheen on the leaves,—light reflected from the surface of each one, for they are grown and worn and washed smooth at last, no infantile downiness on them. A sheeny light reflected from the burnished leaves as so many polished shields, and a steady creak from the locusts these days. Frank Harding has caught a dog-day locust which lit on the bottom of my boat, in which he was sitting, and *z*-ed there. When you hear him you have got to the end of the alphabet and may imagine the &. It has a mark somewhat like a small writing *w* on the top of its thorax.

I think we may detect that some sort of preparation and faint expectation preceded every discovery we have made. We blunder into no discovery but it will appear that we have prayed and disciplined ourselves for it. Some years ago I sought for Indian hemp (*Apocynum cannabinum*) hereabouts in vain, and concluded that it did not grow here. A month or two ago I read again, as many times before, that its blossoms were very small, scarcely a third as large as those of the common species, and for some unaccountable reason this distinction kept recurring to me, and I regarded the size of the flowers I saw, though I did not believe that it grew here; and in a day or two my eyes fell on it, aye, in three different places, and different varieties of it. Also, a short time ago, I was satisfied that there was but one kind of sunflower (*divaricatus*) indigenous here. Hearing that one had found another kind, it occurred to me that I had seen a taller one than usual lately, but not so distinctly did I remember this as to name it to him or even fully remember it myself. (I rather remembered it afterward.) But within that hour my genius conducted me to where I had seen the tall plants, and it was the other man's new kind. The next day I found a third kind, miles from there, and, a few days after, a fourth in another direction.

It commonly chances that I make my most interesting botanical discoveries when I am in a thrilled and expectant mood, perhaps wading in some remote swamp where I have just found something novel and feel more than usually remote from the town. Or some rare plant which for some reason has occupied a strangely prominent place in my thoughts for some time will present itself. My expectation ripens to discovery. I am prepared for strange things.

The botanist refers you, for wild and we presume wild plants, further inland or westward to so many miles from Boston, as if Nature or the Indians had any such preferences. Perchance the ocean seemed wilder to them than the woods. As if there were primarily and essentially any more wildness in a western acre than an eastern one!

Sept. 4. Butterflies in road a day or two. The crackling flight of grasshoppers. The grass also is all alive with them, and they trouble me by getting into my shoes, which are loose, and obliging me to empty them occasionally.

XXII.

THE COLD WINTER AND WARM FEBRUARY

Sept. 10. When the water is lowest, the river is contracted to sixteen feet here, and Peters's, an old history of Connecticut, says it was so condensed that you could not thrust a crowbar into it. It did me good to read his wholesale hearty statements,—strong, living, human speech, so much better than the emasculated modern histories, like Bancroft's and the rest, cursed with a style. I would rather read such histories, though every sentence were a falsehood, than our dull emasculated reports which bear the name of histories. The former, having a human breath and interest behind them, are nearer to nature and to truth, after all. The historian is required to feel a human interest in his subject and to so express it.

Sept. 15. Monday. Sophia says, bringing company into my sanctum, by way of apology, that I regard the dust on my furniture like the bloom on fruits, not to be swept off.

Sept. 21. Find, for first time in Concord, *Solanum nigrum*, berries apparently just ripe, by a rock northwest of corydalis. Thus I have within a week found in Concord two of the new plants I found up-country. Such is the advantage of going abroad,—to enable you to detect your own plants. I detected them first abroad, because there I was *looking for* the *strange*.

Sept. 22. A rainy day. Tried some pennyroyal tea, but found it too medicinal for my taste. Yet I collect these herbs, biding the time when their use shall be discovered.

SEPT. 23. Rainy day.

Sept. 29. I can hardly clamber along the grape cliff now without getting my clothes covered with desmodium ticks. Though you were running for your life, they would have time to catch and cling to your clothes. You pause at a convenient place and spend a long time picking them off, which it took so short a time to attach. They will even cling to your hand as you go by. They cling like babes to the mother's breast, by instinct. These almost invisible nets, as it were, are spread for us, and whole coveys of desmodium and bidens seeds and burs steal transportation out of us. I have found myself often covered, and had to spend a quarter of an hour or more picking them off at some convenient place; and so they got just what they wanted, deposited in another place.

Oct. 2. I am amused to see four little Irish boys only five or six years old getting a horse in a pasture, for their father apparently, who is at work in a neighboring field. They have all in a row got hold of a very long halter and are leading him. All wish to have a hand in it. It is surprising that he obeys such small specimens of humanity, but he seems to be very docile, a real family horse. At length, by dint of pulling and shouting, they get him into a run down a hill, and though he moves very deliberately, scarcely faster than a walk, all but the one at the end of the line soon cut and run to right and left, without having looked behind, expecting him to be upon them. They haul up at last at the bars, which are down, and then the family puppy, a brown pointer (?), about two-thirds grown, comes bounding to join them and assist. He is as youthful and about as knowing as any of them. The horse marches gravely behind, obeying the faint tug at the halter, or honestly stands still from time to time, as if not aware that they are pulling at all, though they are all together straining every nerve to start him. It is interesting to behold this faithful beast, the oldest and wisest of the company, thus implicitly obeying the lead of the youngest and weakest.

Oct. 5. It is well to find your employment and amusement in simple and homely things. These wear best and yield most. I think I would rather watch the motions of these cows in their pasture for a day, which I now see all headed one way and slowly advancing,—watch them and project their course carefully on a chart, and report all their behavior faithfully,—than wander to Europe or Asia and watch other motions there; for it is only ourselves that we report in either case, and perchance we shall report a more restless and worthless self in the latter case than in the first.

Oct. 14. A sudden change in the weather after remarkably warm and pleasant weather. Rained in the night, and finger-cold to-day. Your hands instinctively find their way to your pockets. Leaves are fast falling, and they are already past their brightness, perhaps earlier than usual* on account of wet. Any flowers seen now may be called late ones. I see perfectly fresh succory, not to speak of yarrow, a *Viola ovata*, some *Polygala sanguinea*, autumnal dandelion, tansy, etc., etc.

Oct. 16. Found amid the sphagnum on the dry bank on the south side of the Turnpike, just below Everett's meadow, a rare and remarkable fungus, such as I have heard of but never seen before. The

whole height six and three quarters inches, two thirds of it being buried in the sphagnum. It may be divided into three parts, pileus, stem, and base,—or scrotum, for it is a perfect phallus. One of those fungi named *impudicus*, I think.† In all respects a most disgusting object, yet very suggestive. It is hollow from top to bottom, the form of the hollow answering to that of the outside. The color of the outside white excepting the pileus, which is olive-colored and somewhat coarsely corrugated, with an oblong mouth at tip about one eighth of an inch long, or, measuring the white lips, half an inch. Longest diameter at base one and a half inches, at top (on edge of pileus) fif-

---

*No.

†This is very similar to if not the same with that represented in London's *Encyclopædia* and called "*Phallus impudicus*, Stinking Morel, very fetid."

teen sixteenths of an inch. Short diameters in both cases about two thirds as much. It is a delicate white cylinder of a finely honeycombed and crispy material about three sixteenths of an inch thick, or more, the whole very straight and regular. The base, or scrotum, is of an irregular bag form, about one inch by two in the extremes, consisting of a thick trembling gelatinous mass surrounding the bottom of the stem and covered with a tough white skin of a darker tint than the stem. The whole plant rather frail and trembling. There was at first a very thin delicate white collar (or *volva*?) about the base of the stem above the scrotum. It was as offensive to the eye as to the scent, the cap rapidly melting and defiling what it touched with a fetid, olivaceous, semiliquid matter. In an hour or two the plant scented the whole house wherever placed, so that it could not be endured. I was afraid to sleep in my chamber where it had lain until the room had been well ventilated. It smelled like a dead rat in the ceiling, in all the ceilings of the house. Pray, what was Nature thinking of when she made this? She almost puts herself on a level with those who draw in privies.

Oct. 17. Frost has now within three or four days turned almost all flowers to woolly heads,—their November aspect.

Some trees, as small hickories, appear to have dropped their leaves instantaneously, as at a signal, as a soldier grounds arms. The ground under such reflects a blaze of light from now crisped yellow leaves. Down they have come on all sides, as if touched by fairy fingers. Boys are raking leaves in the street, if only for the pleasure of dealing with such clean, crisp substances.

Oct. 19. I have often noticed the inquisitiveness of birds, as the other day of a sparrow, whose motions I should not have supposed to have any reference to me, if I had not watched it from first to last. I stood on the edge of a pine and birch wood. It flitted from seven or eight rods distant to a pine within a rod of me, where it hopped about stealthily and chirped awhile, then flew as many rods the other side and hopped about there a spell, then back to the pine again, as near me as it dared, and again to its first position, very restless all the while. Generally I should have supposed that there was more than one bird, or that it was altogether accidental,—that the chipping of this sparrow eight or ten rods away had no reference to me,—for I could see nothing peculiar about it. But when I brought my glass to bear on it, I found that it was almost steadily eying me and was all alive with excitement.

DEC. 1. P.M.—By path around Walden.

With this little snow of the 29th there is yet pretty good sledding, for it lies solid.

I see the old pale-faced farmer out again on his sled now for the five-thousandth time,—Cyrus Hubbard, a man of a certain New England probity and worth, immortal and natural, like a natural product, like the sweetness of a nut, like the toughness of hickory. He, too, is a redeemer for me. How superior actually to the faith he professes! He is not an office-seeker. What an institution, what a revelation is a man! We are wont foolishly to think that the creed which a man professes is more significant than the fact he is. It matters not how hard the conditions seemed, how mean the world, for a man is a prevalent force and a new law himself. He is a system whose law is to be observed. The old farmer condescends to countenance still this nature and order of things. It is a great encouragement that an honest man makes this world his abode. He rides on the sled drawn by oxen, world-wise, yet comparatively so young, as if they had seen scores of winters. The farmer spoke to me, I can swear, clean, cold, moderate as the snow. He does not melt the snow where he treads. Yet what a faint impression that encounter may make on me after all! Moderate, natural, true, as if he were made of earth, stone, wood, snow. I thus meet in this universe kindred of mine, composed of these elements. I see men like frogs; their peeping I partially understand.

I go by Hayden's and take A. Wheeler's wood-path to railroad.

Slate-colored snowbirds flit before me in the path, feeding on the seeds on the snow, the countless little brown seeds that begin to be scattered over the snow, so much the more obvious to bird and beast. A hundred kinds of indigenous grain are harvested now, broadcast upon the surface of the snow. Thus at a critical season these seeds are shaken down on to a clean white napkin, unmixed with dirt and rubbish, and off this the little pensioners pick them. Their clean table is thus spread a few inches or feet above the ground. Will wonder become extinct in me? Shall I become insensible as a fungus?

A ridge of earth, with the red cockscomb lichen on it, peeps out still at the rut's edge. The dear wholesome color of shrub oak leaves, so clean and firm, not decaying, but which have put on a kind of immortality, not wrinkled and thin like the white oak leaves, but full-veined and plump, as nearer earth. Well-tanned leather on the one side, sun-tanned, color of colors, color of the cow and the deer, silver-downy beneath, turned toward the late bleached and russet fields. What are acanthus leaves and the rest to this? Emblem of my winter condition. I love and could embrace the shrub oak with its scanty garment of leaves rising above the snow, lowly whispering to me, akin to winter thoughts, and sunsets, and to all virtue. Covert which the hare and the partridge seek, and I too seek. What cousin of mine is the shrub oak? How can any man suffer long? For a sense of want is a prayer, and all prayers are answered. Rigid as iron, clean as the atmosphere, hardy as virtue, innocent and sweet as a maiden is the shrub oak. In proportion as I know and love it, I am natural and sound as a partridge. I felt a positive yearning toward one bush this afternoon. There was a match found for me at last. I fell in love with a shrub oak. Tenacious of its leaves, which shrivel not but retain a certain wintry life in them, firm shields, painted in fast colors a rich brown. The deer mouse, too, knows the shrub oak and has its hole in the snow by the shrub oak's stem.

Now, too, I remark in many places ridges and fields of fine russet or straw-colored grass rising above the snow, and beds of empty straw-colored heads of ever-lasting and ragged-looking Roman wormwood.

The blue-curls' chalices stand empty, and waiting evidently to be filled with ice.

I see great thimble-berry bushes rising above the snow, with still a rich, rank bloom on them, as in July. Hypæthral mildew, elysian fungus! To see the bloom on a thimble-berry stem lasting into mid-winter! What a salve that would make, collected and boxed!

No, I am a stranger in your towns. I am not at home at French's, or Lovejoy's, or Savery's. I can winter more to my mind amid the shrub oaks. I have made arrangements to stay with them.

The shrub oak, lowly, loving the earth and spreading over it, tough, thick-leaved; leaves firm and sound in winter and rustling like leather shields; leaves fair and wholesome to the eye, clean and smooth to the touch. Tough to support the snow, not broken down by it. Well-nigh useless to man. A sturdy phalanx, hard to break through. Product of New England's surface. Bearing many striped acorns.

I have seen more chestnuts in the streets of New York than anywhere else this year, large and plump ones, roasting in the street, roasting and popping on the steps of banks and exchanges. Was surprised to see that the citizens made as much of the nuts of the wild-wood as the squirrels. Not only the country boys, all New York goes a-nutting. Chestnuts for cabmen and newsboys, for not only are squirrels to be fed.

Well named *shrub oak*. Low, robust, hardy, indigenous. Well known to the striped squirrel and the partridge and rabbit. The squirrel nibbles its nuts sitting upon an old stump of its larger cousins. What is Peruvian bark to your bark? How many rents I owe to you! how many eyes put out! how many bleeding fingers! How many shrub oak patches I have been through, stooping, winding my way, bending the twigs aside, guiding myself by the sun, over hills and valleys and plains, resting in clear grassy spaces! I love to go through a patch of shrub oak in a bee-line, where you tear your clothes and put your eyes out.

Dec. 2. P.M.—Got in my boat, which before I had got out and turned up on the bank. It made me sweat to wheel it home through the snow, I am so unused to the work of late.

Then walked up the railroad. The clear straw-colored grass and some weeds contrasting with the snow it rises above. Saw little in this walk. Saw Melvin's lank bluish-white black-spotted hound, and Melvin with his gun near, going home at eve. He follows hunting, praise be to him, as regularly in our tame fields as the farmers follow farming. Persistent Genius! How I respect him and thank him for him! I trust the Lord will provide us with another Melvin when he is gone. How good in him to follow his own bent, and not continue at the Sabbath-school all his days! What a wealth he thus becomes in the neighborhood! Few know how to take the census. I thank my stars for Melvin. I think of him with gratitude when I am going to sleep, grateful that he exists,—that Melvin who is such a trial to his mother. Yet he is agreeable to me as a tinge of russet on the hillside. I would fain give thanks morning and evening for my blessings. Awkward, gawky, loose-hung, dragging his legs after him. He is my contemporary and neighbor. He is one tribe, I am another, and we are not at war.

I saw but little in my walk. Saw no bird, only a crow's track in the snow.

As for the sensuality in Whitman's "Leaves of Grass," I do not so much wish that it was not written, as that men and women were so pure that they could read it without harm.

Dec. 3. Mizzles and rains all day, making sloshy walking which sends us all to the shoemaker's. Bought me a pair of cowhide boots, to be prepared for winter walks. The shoemaker praised them because they were made a year ago. I feel like an armed man now. The man who has bought his boots feels like him who has got in his winter's wood. There they stand beside me in the chamber, expectant, dreaming of far woods and woodpaths, of frost-bound or sloshy roads, or of being bound with skate-straps and clogged with ice-dust.

How I love the simple, reserved countrymen, my neighbors, who mind their own business and let me alone, who never waylaid nor shot at me, to my knowledge, when I crossed their fields, though each one has a gun in his house! For nearly twoscore years I have known, at a distance, these long-suffering men, whom I never spoke to, who never spoke to me, and now feel a certain tenderness for them, as if this long probation were but the prelude to an eternal friendship. What a long trial we have withstood, and how much more admirable we are to each other, perchance, than if we had been bedfellows! I am not only grateful because Veias, and Homer, and Christ, and Shakespeare have lived, but I am grateful for Minott, and Rice, and Melvin, and Goodwin, and Puffer even. I see Melvin all alone filling his sphere, in russet suit, which no other could fill or suggest. He takes up as much room in nature as the most famous.

Six weeks ago I noticed the advent of chickadees and their winter habits. As you walk along a wood-side, a restless little flock of them, whose notes you hear at a distance, will seem to say, "Oh, there he goes! Let's pay our respects to him." And they will flit after and close to you, and naïvely peck at the nearest twig to you, as if they were minding their own business all the while without any reference to you.

Dec. 4. Saw and heard cheep faintly one little tree sparrow, the neat chestnut crowned and winged and white-barred bird, perched on a large and solitary white birch. So clean and tough, made to withstand the winter. This color reminds me of the upper side of the shrub oak leaf. I love the few homely colors of Nature at this season,—her strong wholesome browns, her sober and primeval grays, her celestial blue, her vivacious green, her pure, cold, snowy white.

In the sprout-land by the road, in the woods this side of C. Miles's, much gray goldenrod is mixed with the shrub oak. It reminds me of the color of the rabbits which run there. Thus Nature feeds her children chiefly with color. I have no doubt that it is an important relief to the eyes which have long rested on snow, to rest on brown oak leaves and the bark of trees. We want the greatest variety within the smallest compass, and yet without glaring diversity, and we have it in the colors of the withered oak leaves. The white, so curled and shrivelled and *pale*; the black (?), more flat and glossy and darker brown; the red, much like the black, but *perhaps* less dark, and less deeply cut. The scarlet still occasionally retains some blood in its veins.

Sophia says that just before I came home Min caught a mouse and was playing with it in the yard. It had got away from her once or twice, and she had caught it again; and now it was stealing off again, as she lay complacently watching it with her paws tucked under her, when her friend Riordan's stout but solitary cock stepped up inquisitively, looked down at it with one eye, turning his head, then picked it up by the tail and gave it two or three whacks on the ground, and giving it a dexterous toss into the air, caught it in its open mouth, and it went head foremost and alive down his capacious throat in the twinkling of an eye, never again to be seen in this world, Min, all the while, with paws comfortably tucked under her, looking on unconcerned. What matters it one mouse more or less to her? The cock walked off amid the currant bushes, stretched his neck up, and gulped once or twice, and the deed was accomplished, and then he crowed lustily in celebration of the exploit. Min sits composedly sentinel, with paws tucked under her, a good part of her days at present, by some ridiculous little hole, the possible entryway of a mouse. She has a habit of stretching or sharpening her claws on all smooth hair-bottomed chairs and sofas, greatly to my mother's vexation.

When I bought my boots yesterday, Hastings ran over his usual rigmarole. Had he any stout old-fashioned cowhide boots? Yes, he thought he could suit me. "There's something that 'll turn water about as well as anything. Billings had a pair just like them the other day, and he said they kept his feet as dry as a bone. But what's more than that, they were made above a year ago upon honor. They are just the thing, you may depend on it. I had an eye to you when I was making them." "But they are too soft and thin for me. I want them to be thick and stand out from my foot." "Well, there is another pair, maybe a little thicker. I'll tell you what it is, these were made of dry hide."

Both were warranted single leather and not split. I took the last. But after wearing them round this cold day I found that the little snow which rested on them and melted wet the upper leather through like paper and wet my feet, and I told H. of it, that he might have an offset to Billings's experience. "Well, you can't expect a new pair of boots to turn water at first. I tell the farmers that the time to buy boots is at midsummer, or when they are hoeing their potatoes, and the pores have a chance to get filled with dirt."

My first botany, as I remember, was Bigelow's "Plants of Boston and Vicinity," which I began to use about twenty years ago, looking chiefly for the popular names and the short references to the localities of plants, even without any regard to the plant. I also learned the names of many, but without using any system, and forgot them soon. I was not inclined to pluck flowers; preferred to leave them where they were, liked them best there. I was never in the least interested in plants in the house. But from year to year we look at Nature with new eyes. About half a dozen years ago I found myself again attending to plants with more method, looking out the name of each one and remembering it. I began to bring them home in my hat, a straw one with a scaffold lining to it, which I called my botany-box. I never used any other, and when some whom I visited were evidently surprised at its dilapidated look, as I deposited it on their front entry table, I assured them it was not so much my hat as my botany-box. I remember gazing with interest at the swamps about those days and wondering if I could ever attain to such familiarity with plants that I should know the species of every twig and leaf in them, that I should be acquainted with every plant (excepting grasses and cryptogamous ones), summer and winter, that I saw. Though I knew most of the flowers, and there were not in any particular swamp more than half a dozen shrubs that I did not know, yet these made it seem like a maze to me, of a thousand strange species, and I even thought of commencing at one end and looking it faithfully and laboriously through till I knew it all. I little thought that in a year or two I should have attained to that knowledge without all that labor. Still I never studied botany, and do not to-day systematically, the most natural system is still so artificial. I wanted to know my neighbors, if possible,—to get a little nearer to them. I soon found myself observing when plants first blossomed and leafed, and I followed it up early and late, far and near, several years in succession, running to different sides of the town and into the neighboring towns, often between twenty and thirty miles in a day. I often visited a particular plant four or five miles distant, half a dozen times within a fortnight, that I might know exactly when it opened, beside attending to a great many others in different directions and some of them equally distant, at the same time. At the same time I had an eye for birds and whatever else might offer.

Dec. 5. It is a perfectly cloudless and simple winter sky. A white moon, half full, in the pale or dull blue heaven and a whiteness like the reflection of the snow, extending up from the horizon all around a quarter the way up to the zenith. This at 4 P.M. About the sun it is only whiter than elsewhere, or there is only the faintest possible tinge of yellow there.

There are a great many walnuts on the trees, seen black against the sky, and the wind has scattered many over the snow-crust. It would be easier gathering them now than ever.

My themes shall not be far-fetched. I will tell of homely every-day phenomena and adventures. Friends! Society! It seems to me that I have an abundance of it, there is so much that I rejoice and sympathize with, and men, too, that I never speak to but only know and think of. What you call bareness and poverty is to me simplicity. God could not be unkind to me if he should try. I love the winter, with its imprisonment and its cold, for it compels the prisoner to try new fields and resources. I love best to have each thing in its season only, and enjoy doing without it at all other times. It is the greatest of all advantages to enjoy no advantage at all. I find it invariably true, the poorer I am, the richer I am. I have never got over my surprise that I should have been born into the most estimable place in all the world, and in the very nick of time, too.

Dec. 6. On all sides, in swamps and about their edges and in the woods, the bare shrubs are sprinkled with buds, more or less noticeable and pretty, their little gemmæ or gems, their most vital and attractive parts now, almost all the greenness and color left, greens and salads for the birds and rabbits. Our eyes go searching along the stems for what is most vivacious and characteristic, the concentrated summer gone into winter quarters. For we are hunters pursuing the summer on snow-shoes and skates, all winter long. There is really but one season in our hearts.

Dec. 7. Sunday. P.M.—Take my first skate to Fair Haven Pond.

It takes my feet a few moments to get used to the skates. I see the track of one skater who has preceded me this morning. This is the first skating. I keep mostly to the smooth ice about a rod wide next the shore commonly, where there was an overflow a day or two ago. Now I go shaking over hobbly places, now shoot over a bridge of ice only a foot wide between the water and the shore at a bend,— Hubbard Bath,—always so at first there. I am confined to a very narrow edging of ice in the meadow, gliding with unexpected ease through withered sedge, but slipping sometimes on a twig; again taking to the snow to reach the next ice, but this rests my feet; straddling the bare black willows, winding between the button-bushes, and following narrow threadings of ice amid the sedge, which bring me out to clear fields unexpectedly. Occasionally I am obliged to take a few strokes over black and thin-looking ice, where the neighboring bank is springy, and am slow to acquire confidence in it, but, returning, how bold I am! Where the meadow seemed only sedge and snow, I find a complete ice connection.

At Cardinal Shore, as usual, there is a great crescent of hobbly ice, where, two or three days ago, the north-west wind drove the

waves back up-stream and broke up the edge of the ice. This crescent is eight or ten rods wide and twice as many long. It is like skating over so many rails, or the edges of saws.

That grand old poem called Winter is round again without any connivance of mine. I see with surprise the pond a dumb white surface of ice speckled with snow, just as so many winters before, where so lately were lapsing waves or smooth reflecting water. It seemed as if winter had come without any interval since midsummer, and I was prepared to see it flit away by the time I again looked over my shoulder. It was as if I had dreamed it. But I see that the farmers have had time to gather their harvests as usual, and the seasons have revolved as slowly as in the first autumn of my life. The winters come now as fast as snowflakes. It is wonderful that old men do not lose their reckoning. It was summer, and now again it is winter. Nature loves this rhyme so well that she never tires of repeating it. So sweet and wholesome is the winter, so simple and moderate, so satisfactory and perfect, that her children will never weary of it. What a poem! an epic in blank verse, enriched with a million tinkling rhymes. It is solid beauty. It has been subjected to the vicissitudes of millions of years of the gods, and not a single superfluous ornament remains. The severest and coldest of the immortal critics have shot their arrows at and pruned it till it cannot be amended.

DEC. 8. Thermometer at 8 A.M. 8° above zero. Probably the coldest day yet.

Bradford, in his "History of the Plymouth Plantation," remembering the condition of the Pilgrims on their arrival in Cape Cod Bay the 11th of November, 1620, Old Style (page 79): "Which way soever they turned their eyes (save upward to the heavens) they could have little solace or content in respect of any outward objects. For summer being done, all things stand upon them with a weather-beaten face; and the whole country, full of woods and thickets, represented a wild and savage hue." Such was a New England November in 1620 to Bradford's eyes, and such, no doubt, it would be to his eyes in the country still. However, it required no little courage to found a colony here at that season of the year.

The earliest mention of anything like a glaze in New England that I remember is in Bradford's "History of the Plymouth Plantation," page 83, where he describes the second expedition with the shallop from Cape Cod Harbor in search of a settlement, the 6th of December, O.S. "The weather was very cold, and it froze so hard as the spray of the sea lighting on their coats, they were as if they had been glazed." Bradford was one of the ten principal ones. That same night they reached the bottom of the Bay and saw the Indians cutting up a blackfish. Nature has not changed one iota.

Dec. 9. The northwest wind, meeting the current in an exposed place, produces that hobbly ice which I described at Cardinal Shore day before yesterday. This is the case in this place every year, and no doubt this same phenomenon occurred annually at this point on this river a thousand years before America was discovered. This regularity and permanence make these phenomena more interesting to me.

Dec. 10. It is remarkable how suggestive the slightest drawing as a memento of things seen. For a few years past I have been accustomed to make a rude sketch in my journal of plants, ice, and various natural phenomena, and though the fullest accompanying description may fail to recall my experience, these rude outline drawings do not fail to carry me back to that time and scene. It is as if I saw the same thing again, and I may again attempt to describe it in words if I choose.

It has been a warm, clear, glorious winter day, the air full of that peculiar vapor. How short the afternoons! I hardly get out a couple of miles before the sun is setting. The nights are light on account of the snow, and, there being a moon, there is no distinct interval between the day and night.

Bradford, in his "History of the Plymouth Plantation," written between 1630 and 1650, uses, on page 235, the word "kilter," speaking of guns being out of kilter, proving that this is an old word; yet it is not in my dictionaries.

Dec. 15. I still recall to mind that characteristic winter eve of December 9th; the cold, dry, and wholesome diet my mind and senses necessarily fed on,—oak leaves, bleached and withered weeds that rose above the snow, the now dark green of the pines, and perchance the faint metallic chip of a single tree sparrow; the hushed stillness of the wood at sundown, aye, all the winter day; the short boreal twilight; the smooth serenity and the reflections of the pond, still alone free from ice; the melodious hooting of the owl, heard at the same time with the yet more distant whistle of a locomotive, more aboriginal, and perchance more enduring here than that, heard above the voices of all the wise men of Concord, as if they were not (how little he is Anglicized!); the last strokes of the woodchopper, who presently bends his steps homeward; the gilded bar of cloud across the apparent outlet of the pond, conducting my thoughts into the eternal west; the deepening horizon glow; and the hasty walk homeward to enjoy the long winter evening. The hooting of the owl! That is a sound which my red predecessors heard here more than a thousand years ago. It rings far and wide, occupying the spaces rightfully,—grand, primeval, aboriginal sound. There is no whisper in it of the Buckleys, the Flints, the Hosmers who recently squatted here, nor of the first parish, nor of Concord Fight, nor of the last town meeting.

Mrs. Moody very properly calls eating nuts "a mouse-like employment." It is quite too absorbing; you can't read at the same time, as when you are eating an apple.

Dec. 17. When I returned from the South the other day, I was greeted by withered shrub oak leaves which I had not seen there. It was the most homely and agreeable object that met me. I found that I had no such friend as the shrub oak hereabouts. A farmer once asked me what shrub oaks were made for, not knowing any use they served. But I can tell him that they do me good. They never did any man harm that I know.

Dec. 18. 12 M. Start for Amherst, N.H.

A very cold day. Thermometer at 8 A.M. −8°.

At my lecture, the audience attended to me closely, and I was satisfied; that is all I ask or expect generally. Not one spoke to me afterward, nor needed they. I have no doubt that they liked it, in the main, though few of them would have dared say so, provided they were conscious of it. Generally, if I can only get the ears of an audience, I do not care whether they say they like my lecture or not. I think I know as well as they can tell. At any rate, it is none of my business, and it would be impertinent for me to inquire. The stupidity of most of these country towns, not to include the cities, is in its innocence infantile. Lectured in basement (vestry) of the orthodox church, and I trust helped to undermine it.

Dec. 19. Withered leaves! this is our frugal winter diet, instead of the juicy salads of spring and summer. I think I could write a lecture on "Dry Leaves," carrying a specimen of each kind that hangs on in the winter into the lecture-room as the heads of my discourse. They have long hung to some extent in vain, and have not found their poet yet. The pine has been sung, but not, to my knowledge, the shrub oak. Most think it is useless. The citizen who has just bought a sprout-land on which shrub oaks alone come up only curses it. But it serves a higher use than they know.

Dec. 24. More snow in the night and to-day, making nine or ten inches.

P.M.—To Walden and Baker Farm with Ricketson, it still snowing a little.

It was very pleasant walking thus before the storm was over, in the soft, subdued light.

Dec. 25. Take long walks in stormy weather or through deep snows in the fields and woods, if you would keep your spirits up. Deal with brute nature. Be cold and hungry and weary.

Dec. 28. I thrive best on solitude. If I have had a companion only one day in a week, unless it were one or two I could name, I find that the value of the week to me has been seriously affected. It dissipates my days, and often it takes me another week to get over it.

Dec. 29. We must go out and re-ally ourselves to Nature every day. We must make root, send out some little fibre at least, even every winter day. I am sensible that I am imbibing health when I open my mouth to the wind. Staying in the house breeds a sort of insanity always. Every house is in this sense a hospital. A night and a forenoon is as much confinement to those wards as I can stand. I am aware that I recover some sanity which I had lost almost the instant that I come abroad.

Jan. 4. After spending four or five days surveying and drawing a plan incessantly, I especially feel the necessity of putting myself in communication with nature again, to recover my tone, to withdraw out of the wearying and unprofitable world of affairs. The things I have been doing have but a fleeting and accidental importance, however much men are immersed in them, and yield very little valuable fruit. I would fain have been wading through the woods and fields and conversing with the sane snow. I thus from time to time break off my connection with eternal truths and go with the shallow stream of human affairs, grinding at the mill of the Philistines; but when my task is done, with never-failing confidence I devote myself to the infinite again. It would be sweet to deal with men more, I can imagine, but where dwell they? Not in the fields which I traverse.

Jan. 7. I should not be ashamed to have a shrub oak for my coat-of-arms.

It is bitter cold, with a cutting northwest wind. The pond is now a plain snow-field, but there are no tracks of fishers on it. It is too cold for them. The surface of the snow there is finely waved and grained, giving it a sort of slaty fracture, the appearance which hard, dry *blown* snow assumes. All animate things are reduced to their lowest terms. This is the fifth day of cold, blowing weather.

There is nothing so sanative, so poetic, as a walk in the woods and fields even now, when I meet none abroad for pleasure. In the street and in society I am almost invariably cheap and dissipated, my life is unspeakably mean. No amount of gold or respectability would in the least redeem it,—dining with the Governor or a member of Congress!! But alone in distant woods or fields, I come to myself, I once more feel myself grandly related, and that cold and solitude are friends of mine. I suppose that this value, in my case, is equivalent to what others get by churchgoing and prayer. I thus dispose of the superfluous and see things as they are, grand and beautiful. I have told many that I walk every day about half the daylight, but I think they do not believe it. I wish to get the Concord, the Massachusetts, the America, out of my head and be sane a part of every day. If there are missionaries for the heathen, why not send them to me? I wish to know something; I wish to be made better. I wish to forget, a considerable part of every day, all mean, narrow, trivial men (and this requires usually to forego and forget all personal relations so long), and therefore I come out to these solitudes, where the problem of existence is simplified. I enter some glade in the woods, perchance, where a few weeds and dry leaves alone lift themselves above the surface of the snow, and it is as if I had come to an open window. I see out and around myself. Our *skylights* are thus far away from the ordinary resorts of men. I am not satisfied with ordinary windows. I must have a true *skylight*. My true sky light is on the outside of the village. It is as if I always met in those places some grand, serene, immortal, infinitely encouraging, though invisible, companion, and walked with him. There at last my nerves are steadied, my senses and my mind do their office. I am aware that most of my neighbors would think it a hardship to be compelled to linger here one hour, especially this bleak day, and yet I receive this sweet and ineffable compensation for it. It is the most agreeable thing I do. Truly, my coins are uncurrent with them.

I love and celebrate nature, even in detail, merely because I love the scenery of these interviews and translations. I love to remember every creature that was at this *club*. I thus get off a certain social scurf and scaliness. I do not consider the other animals brutes in the common sense. I am attracted toward them undoubtedly because I never heard any nonsense from them. I have not convicted them of folly, or vanity, or pomposity, or stupidity, in dealing with me. Their vices, at any rate, do not interfere with me. My fairies invariably take to flight when a man appears upon the scene. In a caucus, a meeting-house, a lyceum, a club-room, there is nothing like it in my experience. But away out of the town, on Brown's scrub oak lot, which was sold the other day for six dollars an acre,

I have company such as England cannot buy, nor afford. This society is what I live, what I survey, for. I subscribe generously to *this*—all that I have and am.

There, in that Well Meadow Field, perhaps, I feel in my element again, as when a fish is put back into the water. I wash off all my chagrins. All things go smoothly as the axle of the universe. I can remember that when I was very young I used to have a dream night after night, over and over again, which might have been named Rough and Smooth. All existence, all satisfaction and dissatisfaction, all event was symbolized in this way. Now I seemed to be lying and tossing, perchance, on a horrible, a fatal rough surface, which must soon, indeed, put an end to my existence, though even in the dream I knew it to be the symbol merely of my misery; and then again, suddenly, I was lying on a delicious smooth surface, as of a summer sea, as of gossamer or down or softest plush, and life was such a luxury to live. My waking experience *always* has been and is such an alternate Rough and Smooth. In other words it is Insanity and Sanity.

This snow which fell last Saturday so moist and heavy is now surprisingly dry and light and powdery. In the wood-path between the Well Meadow Field and the Cliff, it is all scored with the tracks of leaves that have scurried over it. Some might not suspect the cause of these fine and delicate traces, for the cause is no longer obvious. Here and there is but a leaf or two to be seen in the snow-covered path. The myriads which scampered here are now at rest perhaps far on one side. I have listened to the whispering of the dry leaves so long that whatever meaning it has for my ears, I think that I must have heard it.

Going down path to the spring, I see where some fox (apparently) has passed down it, and though the rest of the broad path is else perfectly unspotted white, each track of the fox has proved a trap which has caught from three or four to eight or ten leaves each, snugly packed; and thus it is reprinted.

Jan. 8. Miss Minott tells me that she does not think her brother George has ever been to Boston more than once (though she tells me he says he has been twice),[*] and certainly not since 1812. He was born in the Casey house, *i.e.* the same in which C. lived. Casey was a Guinea negro. Casey used to weep in his latter days when he thought of his wife and two children in Africa from whom he was kidnapped. The house he now lives in is about sixty years old, was moved from beside Casey's to where it now stands before it was roofed. Minott says he has lived where he now does as much as sixty years. He has not been up in town for three years, on account of his rheumatism. Does nothing whatever in the house but read the newspapers and few old books they have, the Almanac especially, and hold the cats, and very little indeed out of the house. Is just able to saw and split the wood.

Jan. 11. Began snowing yesterday afternoon, and it is still snowing this forenoon.

The other day a man came "just to get me to run a line in the woods." This is the usual request. "Do you know where one end of it is?" I asked. (It was the Stratton lot.) "No," said he, "I don't know either end; that is what I want to find." "Do you know either of the next sides of the lot?" Thinking a moment, he answered, "No." "Well, do you know any one side of the whole lot, or any corner?" After a little hesitation he said that he did not. Here, then, was a wood-lot of half a dozen acres, well enough described in a deed dated 1777, courses and distances given, but he could not tell exactly in what part of the universe any particular part of it was, but he expected me to find out. This was what he understood by "running." On the strength of this deed he had forbidden a man to chop wood somewhere.

Frequently, when my employer does not know where his land lies, and has put into my hands an ancient and tattered piece of paper called his deed, which throws no light at all on the question, he turns away, saying, "I want you to make it all right. Give me all that belongs to me."

There was wit and even poetry in the negro's answer to the man

------

[*]*He* since tells me *once*.

who tried to persuade him that the slaves would not be obliged to work in heaven. "Oh, you g' way, Massa. I know better. If dere 's no work for cullud folks up dar, dey 'll *make* some fur 'em, and if dere 's nuffin better to do, dey 'll make 'em *shub de clouds along*. You can't fool this chile, Massa."

I was describing the other day my success in solitary and distant woodland walking outside the town. I do not go there to get my dinner, but to get that sustenance which dinners only preserve me to enjoy, without which dinners are a vain repetition. But how little men can help me in this! only by having a kindred experience. Of what use to tell them of my happiness?

Jan. 20. At R.W.E.'s this evening, at about 6 P.M., I was called out to see Eddy's cave in the snow. It was a hole about two and a half feet wide and six feet long, into a drift, a little winding, and he had got a lamp at the inner extremity. I observed, as I approached in a course at right angles with the length of the cave, that the mouth of the cave was lit as if the light were close to it, so that I did not suspect its depth. Indeed, the light of this lamp was remarkably reflected and distributed. The snowy walls were one universal reflector with countless facets. I think that one lamp would light sufficiently a hall built of this material. The snow about the mouth of the cave within had the yellow color of the flame to one approaching, as if the lamp were close to it. We afterward buried the lamp in a little crypt in this snow-drift and walled it in, and found that its light was visible, even in this *twilight*, through fifteen inches' thickness of snow. The snow was all aglow with it. If it had been darker, probably it would have been visible through a much greater thickness. But, what was most surprising to me, when Eddy crawled into the extremity of his cave and shouted at the top of his voice, it sounded ridiculously faint, as if he were a quarter of a mile off, and at first I could not believe that he spoke loud, but we all of us crawled in by turns, and though our heads were only six feet from those outside, our loudest shouting only amused and surprised them. Apparently the porous snow drank up all the sound. The voice was, in fact, muffled by the surrounding snow walls, and

I saw that we might lie in that hole screaming for assistance in vain, while travellers were passing along twenty feet distant. It had the effect of ventriloquism. So you only need make a snow house in your yard and pass an hour in it, to realize a good deal of Esquimau life.

Jan. 22. I never knew it to make such a business of snowing and bring so little to pass. The air is filled, so that you cannot see far against it, *i.e.* looking north-northwest, yet but an inch or two falls all day.

I asked Minott about the Cold Friday. He said, "It was plaguy cold; it stung like a wasp." He remembers seeing them toss up water in a shoemaker's shop, usually a very warm place, and when it struck the floor it was frozen and rattled like so many shot. Old John Nutting used to say, "When it is cold it is a sign it's going to be warm," and "When it's warm it's a sign it's going to be cold."

JAN. 23. The coldest day that I remember recording, clear and bright, but very high wind, blowing the snow. Ink froze. Had to break the ice in my pail with a hammer. Thermometer at 6.45 A.M., −18°; at 10.30, −14° (Smith's, −20°; Wilds', −7°, the last being in a more sheltered place); at 12.45, −9°; at 4 P.M., −5 ½°; at 7.30 P.M., −8°. I may safely say that −5° has been the highest temperature to-day by our thermometer.

Walking this afternoon, I notice that the face inclines to stiffen, and the hands and feet get cold soon. On first coming out in very cold weather, I find that I breathe fast, though without walking faster or exerting myself any more than usual.

Jan. 24. Thermometer about 6.30 A.M. in the bulb!! Would have stood at −26° if the thermometer had been long enough.

Feb. 3. To Fitchburg to lecture.

Though the snow was not deep, I noticed that an unbroken snow-crust stretched around Fitchburg, and its several thousand inhabitants had been confined so long to the narrow streets, some of them a track only six feet wide. Hardly one individual had any-where departed from this narrow walk and struck out into the sur-rounding fields and hills. If I had had my cowhide boots, I should not have confined myself to those narrow limits, but have climbed some of the hills. It is surprising to go into a New England town in midwinter and find its five thousand inhabitants all living thus on the limits, confined at most to their narrow moose-yard in the snow. Scarcely here and there has a citizen stepped aside one foot to let a sled pass. And almost as circumscribed is their summer life, going only from house to shop and back to house again. It is as if some vigilance committee had given notice that if any should transgress those narrow limits he should be outlawed and his blood should be upon his own head. You don't see where the inhabitants get sufficient exercise, unless they swing dumb-bells down cellar.

Feb. 4. Yet along that sled-track (*vide* the 3d) they will have their schools and lyceums and churches, like the snow-heaps crowded up by the furrow, and consider themselves liberally educated, not-withstanding their narrow views and range. And the bare track that leads to the next town and seaboard, only six inches' breadth of iron rails! and a one-eighth-inch wire in the air!

Sometimes when, in conversation or a lecture, I have been grasping at, or even standing and reclining upon, the serene and everlasting truths that underlie and support our vacillating life, I have seen my auditors standing on their *terra firma*, the quaking earth, crowded together on their Lisbon Quay, and compassion-ately or timidly watching my motions as if they were the antics of a rope-dancer or mountebank pretending to walk on air; or here and there one creeping out upon an overhanging but cracking bough, unwilling to drop to the adamantine floor beneath, or per-chance even venturing out a step or two, as if it were a dangerous kittly-bender, timorously sounding as he goes. So the other day, as I stood on Walden, drinking at a puddle on the ice, which was probably two feet thick, and thinking how lucky I was that I had not got to cut through all that thickness, I was amused to see an Irish laborer on the railroad, who had come down to drink, timidly tiptoeing toward me in his cowhide boots, lifting them nearly two feet at each step and fairly trembling with fear, as if the ice were already bending beneath his ponderous body and he were about to be engulfed. "Why, my man," I called out to him, "this ice will bear a loaded train, half a dozen locomotives side by side, a whole herd of oxen," suggesting whatever would be a weighty argument with him. And so at last he fairly straightened up and quenched his thirst. It was very ludicrous to me, who was thinking, by chance, what a labor it would be to get at the water with an axe there and that I was lucky to find some on the surface.

Though the farmer has been all winter teaming wood along the river, the timid citizen that buys it, but who has not stepped out of the road, thinks it all kittly-benders there and warns his boys not to go near it.

Feb. 6. One who has seen them tells me that a covey of thirteen quails daily visits Hayden's yard and barn, where he feeds them and can almost put his hands on them.

Thermometer at noon 52°.

Winckelmann says in his "History of Ancient Art," vol. i, page 95: "I am now past forty, and therefore at an age when one can no longer sport freely with life. I perceive, also, that a certain delicate spirit begins to evaporate, with which I raised myself, by powerful soarings, to the contemplation of the beautiful."

Feb. 8. I see one of those great ash-colored puffballs with a tinge of purple, open like a cup, four inches in diameter. Though it is but just brought to light from beneath the deep snow, and the last two days have been misty or rainy without sun, it is just as dry and dusty as ever, and the drops of water rest on it, at first undetected, being coated with its dust, looking like unground pearls. I brought it home and held it in a basin of water. To my surprise, when held under water it looked like a mass of silver or melted lead, it was so coated with air, and when I suffered it to rise,—for it had to be kept down by force,—instead of being heavy like a sponge which has soaked water, it was as light as a feather, and its surface perfectly dry, and when touched it gave out its dust the same as ever. It was impossible to wet. It seems to be encased in a silvery coat of air which is water-tight. The water did not penetrate into it at all, and running off as you lifted it up, it was just as dry as before, and on the least jar floating in dust above your head.

And now another friendship is ended. I do not know what has made my friend doubt me, but I know that in love there is no mistake, and that every estrangement is well founded. But my destiny is not narrowed, but if possible the broader for it. The heavens withdraw and arch themselves higher. I am sensible not only of a moral, but even a grand physical pain, such as gods may feel, about my head and breast, a certain ache and fullness. My life is like a stream that is suddenly dammed and has no outlet; but it rises the higher up the hills that shut it in, and will become a deep and silent lake. Perchance there is none beside who knows us for a god, and none whom we know for such. Each man and woman is a veritable god or goddess, but to the mass of their fellows disguised. There is only one in each case who sees through the disguise. That one who does not stand so near to any man as to see the divinity in him is truly alone.

Feb. 18. Another remarkably warm and pleasant day. The snow is nearly all gone, and it is so warm and springlike that I walk over to the hill, listening for the note of the bluebird or other comer. The very grain of the air seems to have undergone a change and is ready to split into the form of the bluebird's warble. Methinks if it were visible, or I could cast up some fine dust which would betray it, it would take a corresponding shape. The bluebird does not come till the air consents and his wedge will enter easily. The air over these fields is a foundry full of moulds for casting bluebirds' warbles. Any sound uttered now would take that form, not of the harsh, vibrating, rending scream of the jay, but a softer, flowing, curling warble, like a purling stream or the lobes of flowing sand and clay.

What a poem is this of spring, so often repeated! I am thrilled when I hear it spoken of,—as the *spring* of such a year, that fytte of the glorious epic.

Feb. 20. What is the relation between a bird and the ear that appreciates its melody, to whom, perchance, it is more charming and significant than to any else? Certainly they are intimately related, and the one was made for the other. It is a natural fact. If I were to discover that a certain kind of stone by the pond-shore was affected, say partially disintegrated, by a particular natural sound, as of a bird or insect, I see that one could not be completely described without describing the other. I am that rock by the pond-side.

What is hope, what is expectation, but a seed-time whose harvest cannot fail, an irresistible expedition of the mind, at length to be victorious?

March 18. I meet Goodwin paddling up the still, dark river on his first voyage to Fair Haven for the season, looking for muskrats and from time to time picking drift-wood—logs and boards, etc.—out of the water and laying it up to dry on the bank, to eke out his wood-pile with. Says that when you hear a woodpecker's *rat-tat-tat-tat-tat* on a dead tree it is a sign of rain. While Emerson sits writing in his study this still, overcast, moist day, Goodwin is paddling up the still, dark river. Emerson burns twenty-five cords of wood and fourteen (?) tons of coal; Goodwin perhaps a cord and a half, much of which he picks out of the river. He says he 'd rather have a boat leak some for fishing.

March 24. If you are describing any occurrence, or a man, make two or more distinct reports at different times. Though you may think you have said all, you will to-morrow remember a whole new class of facts which perhaps interested most of all at the time, but did not present themselves to be reported. If we have recently met and talked with a man, and would report our experience, we commonly make a very partial report at first, failing to seize the most significant, picturesque, and dramatic points; we describe only what we have had time to digest and dispose of in our minds, without being conscious that there were other things really more novel and interesting to us, which will not fail to recur to us and impress us suitably at last. How little that occurs to us in any way are we prepared at once to appreciate! We discriminate at first only a few features, and we need to reconsider our experience from many points of view and in various moods, to preserve the whole fruit of it.

March 26. Stopped at Farrar's little stithy. He is making two nuts to mend a mop with, and when at length he has forged and filed them and cut the thread, he remarks that it is a puttering job and worth a good deal more than he can charge. He has sickness in the house, a daughter in consumption, which he says is a flattering disease, up one day and down the next. Seeing a monstrous horseshoe nailed against his shop inside, with a little one within it, I asked what that was for. He said that he made the big one when he was an apprentice (of three months' standing) for a sign, and he picked up the little one the other day in the road and put it within it for the contrast. But he thought that the big one was hardly too big for one of the fore feet of the horse Columbus, which he had seen.

The first croaking frogs, the hyla, the white maple blossoms, the skunk-cabbage, and the alder's catkins are observed about the same time.

Farrar spoke of horses driven "tantrum."

Are not March and November *gray* months?

Men will hardly believe me when I tell them of the thickness of snow and ice at this time last year.

March 27. I would fain make two reports in my Journal, first the incidents and observations of to-day; and by to-morrow I review the same and record what was omitted before, which will often be the most significant and poetic part. I do not know at first what it is that charms me. The men and things of to-day are wont to lie fairer and truer in to-morrow's memory.

I saw quail-tracks some two months ago, much like smaller partridge-tracks.

Men talk to me about society as if I had none and they had some, as if it were only to be got by going to the sociable or to Boston.

March 28. Often I can give the truest and most interesting account of any adventure I have had after years have elapsed, for then I am not confused, only the most significant facts surviving in my memory. Indeed, all that continues to interest me after such a lapse of time is sure to be pertinent, and I may safely record all that I remember.

XXIII.

April 23. I saw at Ricketson's a young woman, Miss Kate Brady, twenty years old, her father an Irishman, a worthless fellow, her mother a smart Yankee. The daughter formerly did sewing, but now keeps school for a livelihood. She was born at the Brady house, I think in Freetown, where she lived till twelve years old and helped her father in the field. There she rode horse to plow and was knocked off the horse by apple tree boughs, kept sheep, caught fish, etc., etc. I never heard a girl or woman express so strong a love for nature. She purposes to return to that lonely ruin, and dwell there alone, since her mother and sister will not accompany her; says that she knows all about farming and keeping sheep and spinning and weaving, though it would puzzle her to shingle the old house. There she thinks she can "live free." I was pleased to hear of her plans, because they were quite cheerful and original, not professedly reformatory, but growing out of her love for "Squire's Brook and the Middleborough ponds." A strong love for outward nature is singularly rare among both men and women. The scenery immediately about her homestead is quite ordinary, yet she appreciates and can use that part of the universe as no other being can. Her own sex, so tamely bred, only jeer at her for entertaining such an idea, but she has a strong head and a love for good reading, which may carry her through. I would by no means discourage, nor yet particularly encourage her, for I would have her so strong as to succeed in spite of all ordinary discouragements.

It is very rare that I hear one express a strong and imperishable attachment to a particular scenery, or to the whole of nature,—I mean such as will control their whole lives and characters. They alone are naturalized, but most are tender and callow creatures that wear a house as their outmost shell and must get their lives insured when they step abroad from it. They are lathed and plastered in from all natural influences, and their delicate lives are a long battle with the dyspepsia. The others are fairly rooted in the soil, and are the noblest plant it bears, more hardy and natural than sorrel. Children of the Golden Age. Hospitals and almshouses are not their destiny. When I hear of such an attachment in a reasonable, a divine, creature to a particular portion of the earth, it seems as if then first the earth succeeded and rejoiced, as if it had been made and existed only for such a use. How rarely a man's love for nature becomes a ruling principle with him, like a youth's affection for a maiden, but more enduring! All nature is my bride. That nature which to one is a stark and ghastly solitude is a sweet, tender, and genial society to another.

April 24. Scudding over the Great Meadows, I see the now red crescents of the red maples in their prime round about, above the gray stems. The willow osiers require to be seen endwise the rows, to get an intense color. The clouds are handsome this afternoon: on the north, some dark, windy clouds, with rain falling thus beneath:—

but it is chiefly wind; southward, those summer clouds in numerous isles, light above and dark-barred be-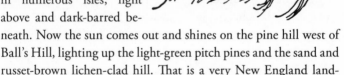

neath. Now the sun comes out and shines on the pine hill west of Ball's Hill, lighting up the light-green pitch pines and the sand and russet-brown lichen-clad hill. That is a very New England landscape. Buttrick's yellow farmhouse near by is in harmony with it.

April 25. It is cool and windy this afternoon. Some sleet falls, but as we sit on the east side of Smith's chestnut grove, the wood, though so open and leafless, makes a perfect lee for us, apparently by breaking the force of the wind. A dense but bare grove of slender chestnut trunks a dozen rods wide is a perfect protection against this violent wind, and makes a perfectly calm lee.

I find that I can very easily make a convenient box of the birch bark, at this season at least, when the sap is running, to carry a moss or other thing in safely. I have only to make three cuts and strip off a piece from a clear space some ten inches long, and then, rolling it up wrong side outward, as it naturally curls backward as soon as taken off (the dry side shrinking, the moist swelling) and so keeps its place, I bend or fold the ends back on it, as if it were paper, and so close them, and, if I please, tie it round with a string of the same bark. This is resilient or elastic, and stands out from a plant, and also is not injured by moisture like paper. This box dries yellow or straw-colored, with large clouds of green derived from the inner bark.

The dense, green, rounded beds of mosses in springs and old water-troughs are very handsome now,—intensely cold green cushions.

April 26. P.M.—Up Assabet to White Cedar Swamp.

See on the water over the meadow, north of the boat's place, twenty rods from the nearest shore and twice as much from the opposite shore, a very large striped snake swimming. It swims with great case, and lifts its head a foot above the water, darting its tongue at us. A snake thus met with on the water appears far more monstrous, not to say awful and venomous, than on the land. It is always something startling and memorable to meet with a serpent in the midst of a broad water, careering over it. But why had this one taken to the water? Is it possible that snakes ever hibernate in meadows which are subject to be overflown? This one when we approached swam toward the boat, apparently to rest on it, and when I put out my paddle, at once coiled itself partly around it and allowed itself to be taken on board. It did not hang down from the paddle like a dead snake, but stiffened and curved its body in a loose coil about it.

This snake was two feet and eleven inches long; the tail alone, seven and a quarter. There were one hundred and forty-five large abdominal plates, besides the three smaller under the head, and sixty-five pairs of caudal scales. The central stripe on the back was not bright-yellow, as Storer describes, but a pale brown or clay-color. Beneath the tail in centre, a dark, somewhat greenish line.

This snake was killed about 2 P.M.; *i.e.*, the head was perfectly killed then; yet the posterior half of the body was apparently quite alive and would curl strongly around the hand at 7 P.M. It had been hanging on a tree in the meanwhile.

I have the same objection to killing a snake that I have to the killing of any other animal, yet the most humane man that I know never omits to kill one.

I see a great many beetles, etc., floating and struggling on the flood.

We sit on the shore at Wheeler's fence, opposite Merriam's. At this season still we go seeking the sunniest, most sheltered, and warmest place. C. says this is the warmest place he has been in this year. We are in this like snakes that lie out on banks. By and by we shall seek the shadiest and coolest place. How well adapted we are to our climate! In the winter we sit by fires in the house; in spring and fall, in sunny and sheltered nooks; in the summer, in shady and cool groves, or over water where the breeze circulates. Thus the average temperature of the year just suits us.

A great part of our troubles are literally domestic or originate in the house and from living indoors. I could write an essay to be entitled "Out of Doors,"—undertake a crusade against houses. What a different thing Christianity preached to the house-bred and to a party who lived out of doors! Also a sermon is needed on economy of fuel. What right has my neighbor to burn ten cords of wood, when I burn only one? Thus robbing our half-naked town of this precious covering. Is he so much colder than I? It is expensive to maintain him in our midst. One man makes a little of the drift-wood of the river or of the dead and refuse (unmarketable!) of the forest suffice, and Nature rejoices in him. Another, Herod-like, requires ten cords of the best of young white oak or hickory, and he is commonly esteemed a virtuous man. He who burns the most wood on his hearth is the least warmed by the sight of it growing. Leave the trim wood-lots to widows and orphan girls. Let men tread gently through nature.

May 3. Sunday. A remarkably warm and pleasant morning.

Now, thinks many a one, is the time to paddle or push gently far up or down the river. It will be a grand forenoon for a cruise, to explore these meadow shores and inundated maple swamps which we have never explored. Now we shall be recompensed for the week's confinement to shop or garden.

Up and down the town, men and boys that are under subjection are polishing their shoes and brushing their go-to-meeting clothes. I, a descendant of Northmen who worshipped Thor, spend my time worshipping neither Thor nor Christ; a descendant of Northmen who sacrificed men and horses, sacrifice neither men nor horses. I care not for Thor nor for the Jews. I sympathize not to-day with those who go to church in newest clothes and sit quietly in straight-backed pews. I sympathize rather with the boy who has none to look after him, who borrows a boat and paddle and in common clothes sets out to explore these temporary vernal lakes. I meet such a boy paddling along under a sunny bank, with bare feet and his pants rolled up above his knees, ready to leap into the water at a moment's warning. Better for him to read "Robinson Crusoe" than Baxter's "Saints' Rest."

May 4. Perhaps the most generally interesting event at present is a perfectly warm and pleasant day. It affects the greatest number, the well out of doors and the sick in chambers. No wonder the weather is the universal theme of conversation.

A warm rain; and the ring of the toads is heard all through it.

May 8. Within a week I have had made a pair of corduroy pants, which cost when done $1.60. They are of that peculiar clay-color, reflecting the light from portions of their surface. They have this advantage, that, beside being very strong, they will look about as well three months hence as now,—or as ill, some would say. Most of my friends are disturbed by my wearing them. I can get four or five pairs for what one ordinary pair would cost in Boston, and each of the former will last two or three times as long under the same circumstances. The tailor said that the stuff was not made in this country; that it was worn by the Irish at home, and now they would not look at it, but others would not wear it, durable and cheap as it is, because it is worn by the Irish. Moreover, I like the color on other accounts. Anything but black clothes. The birds and beasts are not afraid of me now. A mink came within twenty feet of me the other day as soon as my companion had left me, and if I had had my gray sack on as well as my corduroys, it would perhaps have come quite up to me.

May 21. Rains still, more or less, all day.

I saw yesterday a parrot exceedingly frightened in its cage at a window. It rushed to the bars and struggled to get out. A piece of board had been thrown from the window above to the ground, which probably the parrot's instinct had mistaken for a hawk. Their eyes are very open to danger from above.

May 23. Tortoises out again abundantly. Each particularly warm and sunny day brings them out on to every floating rail and stump. I count a dozen within three or four feet on a rail. It is a tortoise day.

The first goldfinch twitters over, and at evening I hear the *spark* of a nighthawk.

May 26. My mother was telling to-night of the sounds which she used to hear summer nights when she was young and lived on the Virginia Road,—the lowing of cows, or cackling of geese, or the beating of a drum as far off as Hildreth's, but above all Joe Merriam whistling to his team, for he was an admirable whistler. Says she used to get up at midnight and go and sit on the door-step when all in the house were asleep, and she could hear nothing in the world but the ticking of the clock in the house behind her.

May 29. The sun came out an hour or more ago, rapidly drying the foliage, and for the first time this year I noticed the little shades produced by the foliage which had expanded in the rain, and long narrow dark lines of shade along the hedges or willow-rows. It was like the first bright flashings of an eye from under dark eyelashes after shedding warm tears.

Soon I hear the low all-pervading hum of an approaching hummingbird circling above the rock, which afterward I mistake several times for the gruff voices of men approaching, unlike as these sounds are in some respects, and I perceive the resemblance even when I know better. Now I am sure it is a hummingbird, and now that it is two farmers approaching. But presently the hum becomes more sharp and thrilling, and the little fellow suddenly perches on an ash twig within a rod of me, and plumes himself while the rain is fairly beginning. He is quite out of proportion to the size of his perch. It does not acknowledge his weight.

With all this opportunity, this comedy and tragedy, how near all men come to doing nothing! It is strange that they did not make us more intense and emphatic, that they do not goad us into some action. Generally, with all our desires and restlessness, we are no more likely to embark in any enterprise than a tree is to walk to a more favorable locality. The seaboard swarms with adventurous and rowdy fellows, but how unaccountably they train and are held in check! They are as likely to be policemen as anything. The Americans are very busy and adventurous sailors, but all in somebody's employ,—as hired men. I have not heard of one setting out in his own bark, if only to run down our own coast on a voyage of adventure or observation, on his own account.

May 31. That central meadow and pool in Gowing's Swamp is its very navel, *omphalos*, where the umbilical cord was cut that bound it to creation's womb. Methinks every swamp tends to have or suggests such as interior tender spot. The sphagnous crust that surrounds the pool is pliant and quaking, like the skin or muscles of the abdomen; you seem to be slumping into the very bowels of the swamp.

June 5. I am interested in each contemporary plant in my vicinity, and have attained to a certain acquaintance with the larger ones. They are cohabitants with me of this part of the planet, and they bear familiar names. Yet how essentially wild they are! as wild, really, as those strange fossil plants whose impressions I see on my coal. Yet I can imagine that some race gathered those too with as much admiration, and knew them as intimately as I do these, that even they served for a language of the sentiments. Stigmariæ stood for a human sentiment in that race's flower language. Chickweed, or a pine tree, is but little less wild. I assume to be acquainted with these, but what ages between me and the tree whose shade I enjoy! It is as if it stood substantially in a remote geological period.

June 6. This is June, the month of grass and leaves. The deciduous trees are investing the evergreens and revealing how dark they are. Already the aspens are trembling again, and a new summer is offered me. I feel a little fluttered in my thoughts, as if I might be too late. Each season is but an infinitesimal point. It no sooner comes than it is gone. It has no duration. It simply gives a tone and hue to my thought. Each annual phenomenon is a reminiscence and prompting. Our thoughts and sentiments answer to the revolutions of the seasons, as two cog-wheels fit into each other. We are conversant with only one point of contact at a time, from which we receive a prompting and impulse and instantly pass to a new season or point of contact. A year is made up of a certain series and number of sensations and thoughts which have their language in nature. Now I am ice, now I am sorrel. Each experience reduces itself to a mood of the mind. I see a man grafting, for instance. What this imports chiefly is not apples to the owner or bread to the grafter, but a certain mood or train of thought to my mind. That is what this grafting is to me. Whether it is anything at all, even apples or bread, to anybody else, I cannot swear, for it would be worse than swearing *through glass.* For I only see those other facts as through a glass darkly.

Cratægus Crus-Galli, maybe a day. Early iris. *Viburnum Lentago,* a day or more. Krigias, with their somewhat orange yellow, spot the dry hills all the forenoon and are very common, but as they are closed in the afternoon, they are but rarely noticed by walkers.

June 8. Mother was saying to-day that she bought no new clothes for John until he went away into a store, but made them of his father's old clothes, which made me say that country boys could get enough cloth for their clothes by robbing the scarecrows. So little it need cost to live.

June 10. In Julius Smith's yard, a striped snake (so called) was running about this forenoon, and in the afternoon it was found to have shed its slough, leaving it halfway out a hole, which probably it used to confine it in. It was about in its new skin. Many creatures—devil's-needles, etc., etc.—cast their sloughs now. Can't I?

June 12. Friday. 8.30 A.M.—Set out for CAPE COD.

June 18. Thursday. From Traveller's Home to Small's in Truro.

A mizzling and rainy day with thick driving fog; a drizzling rain, or "drisk," as one called it.

June 20. This was the third foggy day. It is a serious objection to visiting or living on the Cape that you lose so many days by fog. From time to time the sun almost or quite shines, and you can see half a mile, or to Provincetown even, and then, against all your rules, it thickens up again. An inlander would think it was going to clear up twenty times when it may last a week. I have now visited the Cape four times in as many different years, once in October, twice in June, and once in July, having spent in all about one month there, and about one third the days were foggy, with or without rain. According to Alden (in Massachusetts Historical Collections, vol. v, First Series, page 57), Nantucket was discovered by a famous old Indian giant named Maushop, who waded the sea to it, and there filling his pipe with "poke," his smoke made fog. Whence that island is so much in the fog, and the aborigines on the opposite portion of the Cape, seeing a fog over the water at a distance, would say, "There comes old Maushop's smoke."

The Cape people with whom I talked very generally denied that it was a phenomenon in any degree peculiar to the Cape. They said that it was just such weather at Boston. Indeed, some denied that it was fog at all. They said with some asperity that it was rain. Yet more rain would have fallen in a smart shower in the country in twenty minutes than in these five days on the Cape. When I got home I found that there had been an abundance of cloudy weather and rain within a week, but not one foggy day in Concord.

July 2. *Calla palustris* (with its convolute point like the cultivated) at the south end of Gowing's Swamp. Having found this in one place, I now find it in another. Many an object is not seen, though it falls within the range of our visual ray, because it does not come within the range of our intellectual ray, *i.e.*, we are not looking for it. So, in the largest sense, we find only the world we look for.

July 11. I see more berries than usual of the *Rubus triflorus* in the open meadow near the southeast corner of the Hubbard meadow blueberry swamp. Call it, perhaps, Cymbidium Meadow. They are dark shining red and, when ripe, of a very agreeable flavor and somewhat of the raspberry's *spirit*.

Thermometer at 93°+ this afternoon.

July 12. I drink at every cooler spring in my walk these afternoons and love to eye the bottom there, with perchance a luxurious frog cooling himself next my nose. Sometimes the farmer, foreseeing haying, has been prudent enough to sink a tub in one, which secures a clear deep space. It would be worth the while, methinks, to make a map of the town with all the good springs on it, indicating whether they were cool, perennial, copious, pleasantly located, etc. The farmer is wont to celebrate the virtues of some one on his own farm above all others. Some cool rills in the meadows should be remembered also, for some such in deep, cold, grassy meadows are as cold as springs. I have sometimes drank warm or foul water, not knowing such cold streams were at hand. By many a spring I know where to look for the dipper or glass which some mower has left. When a spring has been allowed to fill up, to be muddied by cattle, or, being exposed to the sun by cutting down the trees and bushes, to dry up, it affects me sadly, like an institution going to decay. Sometimes I see, on one side the tub,—the tub overhung with various wild plants and flowers, its edge almost completely concealed even from the searching eye,—the white sand freshly cast up where the spring is bubbling in. Often I sit patiently by the spring I have cleaned out and deepened with my hands, and see the foul water rapidly dissipated like a curling vapor and giving place to the cool and clear. Sometimes I can look a yard or more into a crevice under a rock, toward the sources of a spring in a hillside, and see it come cool and copious with incessant murmuring down to the light. There are few more refreshing sights in hot weather.

I find many strawberries deep in the grass of the meadow near this Hosmer Spring; then proceed on my way with reddened and fragrant fingers, till it gets washed off at new springs. It is exceedingly sultry this afternoon, and few men are abroad. The cows stand up to their bellies in the river, lashing their sides with their tails from time to time.

July 13. I sometimes awake in the night and think of friendship and its possibilities, a new life and relation to me, which perhaps I had not experienced for many months. Such transient thoughts have been my nearest approach to realization of it, thoughts which I know of no one to communicate to. I suddenly erect myself in my thoughts, or find myself erected, infinite degrees above the possibility of ordinary endeavors, and see for what grand stakes the game of life may be played. I catch an echo of the great strain of Friendship played somewhere, and feel compensated for months and years of commonplace. It is as if I were serenaded, and the highest and truest compliments were paid me. The universe gives me three cheers.

Friendship is the fruit which the year should bear; it lends its fragrance to the flowers, and it is in vain if we get only a large crop of apples without it.

July 15. When I entered the woods there, I was at once pursued by a swarm of those wood flies which gyrate around your head and strike your hat like rain-drops. As usual, they kept up with me as I walked, and gyrated about me still, as if I were stationary, advancing at the same time and receiving reinforcements from time to time. Though I switched them smartly for half a mile with some indigo-weed, they did not mind it in the least, but though I knocked down many of them, they soon picked themselves up and came on again. They had a large black spot on their wings and some yellowish rings about their abdomens. They keep up a smart buzzing all the while. They did not once sting, though they endeavored sometimes to alight on my face. What they got by their perseverance I do not know,—unless it were a switching.

XXIV.

Aug. 10. How meanly and miserably we live for the most part! We escape fate continually by the skin of our teeth, as the saying is. We are practically desperate. What kind of gift is life unless we have spirits to enjoy it and taste its true flavor? if, in respect to spirits, we are to be forever cramped and in debt? Have the gods sent us into this world,—to this *muster*,—to do chores, hold horses, and the like, and not given us any spending money?

I heard some ladies the other day laughing about some one of their *help* who had *helped* herself to a real hoop from off a hogshead for her gown. I laughed too, but which party do you think I laughed at? Is n't hogshead as good a word as crinoline?

Sept. 9. The cones are now all flowing with pitch, and my hands are soon so covered with it that I cannot easily cast down the cones where I would, they stick to my hands so. I cannot touch the basket, but carry it on my arm; nor can I pick up my coat, which I have taken off, unless with my teeth, or else I kick it up and catch it on my arm. Thus I go from tree to tree, from time to time rubbing my hands in brooks and mud-holes, in the hope of finding something that will remove pitch like grease, but in vain. It is the stickiest work I ever did. I do not see how the squirrels that gnaw them off and then open them scale by scale keep their paws and whiskers clean. They must know of, or possess, some remedy for pitch that we know nothing of. How fast I could collect cones, if I could only contract with a family of squirrels to cut them off for me! The cones collected in my chamber have a strong spirituous scent, almost rummy, or like a molasses hogshead, agreeable to some.

Sept. 12. Saturday. P.M.—To Owl Swamp.

In an open part of the swamp, started a very large wood frog, which gave one leap and squatted still. I put down my finger, and, though it shrank a little at first, it permitted me to stroke it as long as I pleased. Having passed, it occurred to me to return and cultivate its acquaintance. To my surprise, it allowed me to slide my hand under it and lift it up, while it squatted cold and moist on the middle of my palm, panting naturally. I brought it close to my eye and examined it. It was very beautiful seen thus nearly, not the dull dead-leaf color which I had imagined, but its back was like burnished bronze armor defined by a varied line on each side, where, as it seemed, the plates of armor united. It had four or five dusky bars which matched exactly when the legs were folded, showing that the painter applied his brush to the animal when in that position, and reddish-orange soles to its delicate feet. There was a conspicuous dark-brown patch along the side of the head, whose upper edge passed directly through the eye horizontally, just above its centre, so that the pupil and all below were dark and the upper portion of the iris golden. I have since taken up another in the same way.[*]

Sept. 18. Friday. P.M.—Round Walden with C. We started a pack of grouse, which went off with a whir like cannon-balls.

Sept. 24. Thursday. I saw a red squirrel run along the bank under the hemlocks with a nut in its mouth. He stopped near the foot of a hemlock, and, hastily pawing a hole with his fore feet, dropped the nut, covered it up, and retreated part way up the trunk of the tree, all in a few moments. I approached the shore to examine the deposit, and he, descending betrayed no little anxiety for his treasure and made two or three motions to recover the nut before he retreated. Digging there, I found two pignuts joined together, with their green shells on, buried about an inch and a half in the soil, under the red hemlock leaves. This, then, is the way forests are planted. This nut must have been brought twenty rods at least and

---

[*]Indeed they can generally be treated so. Some are reddish, as burnished copper.

was buried at just the right depth. If the squirrel is killed, or neglects its deposit, a hickory springs up.*

P.M.—I walked to that very dense and handsome white pine grove east of Beck Stow's Swamp. It is about fifteen rods square, the trees large, ten to twenty inches in diameter. It is separated by a wall from another pine wood with a few oaks in it on the southeast, and about thirty rods north and west are other pine and oak woods. Standing on the edge of the wood and looking through it,—for it is quite level and free from underwood, *mostly* bare, red-carpeted ground,—you would have said that there was not a hardwood tree in it, young or old, though I afterward found on one edge a middling-sized sassafras, a birch, a small tupelo, and two little scarlet oaks, but, what was more interesting, I found, on looking closely over its floor, that, alternating with thin ferns and small blueberry bushes, there was, as often as every five feet, a little oak, three to twelve inches high, and in one place I found a green acorn dropped by the base of a tree. I was surprised, I confess, to find my own theory so perfectly proved. These oaks, apparently, find such a locality unfavorable to their growth as long as the pines stand.

Sept. 25. The red maple has fairly begun to blush in some places by the river. I see one, by the canal behind Barrett's mill, all aglow against the sun. These first trees that change are most interesting, since they are seen against others still freshly green,—such brilliant red on green. I go half a mile out of my way to examine such a red banner.

As I came round the island, I took notice of that little ash tree on the opposite shore. It has been cut or broken off about two feet from the ground, and seven small branches have shot up from its circumference, all together forming a perfectly regular oval head about twenty-five feet high and very beautiful. With what harmony they work and carry out the idea of the tree, one twig not straying farther on this side than its fellow on that! That the tree thus has its idea to be lived up to, and, as it were, fills an invisible

---

*These nuts were there Oct. 8th. Gone Nov. 21st.

mould in the air, is the more evident, because if you should cut away one or all but one, the remaining branch or branches would still in time form a head in the main similar to this.

Brought home my first boat-load of wood.

Sept. 28. I planted six seeds sent from the Patent Office and labelled, I think, "*Poitrine jaune grosse*" (large yellow pumpkin (or squash?)). Two came up, and one bore a squash which weighs   123½lbs.

the other bore four,	1	weighing	72¾
	2d	weighing	54
	3d	weighing	37¾
	4th	weighing	21¾
			309¾

Who would have believed that there was 310 pounds of *poitrine jaune grosse* in that corner of our garden? Yet that little seed found it.

Sept. 30. According to the Upanishads, "As water, when rained down on elevated ground, runs scattered off in the valleys, so ever runs after difference a person who beholds attributes different (from the soul)."

"As pure water, which is thrown down on pure ground, remains alike, so also, O Gautama, is the soul of the thinker who knows."

Minott says he is seventy-five years old.

He says that that tall clock which still ticks in the corner belonged to old John Beatton, who died before he was born; thought it was two hundred years old!! Some of the rest of the furniture came from the same source. I read on John Beatton's tombstone near the powder-house that he died in 1776, aged seventy-four.

Oct. 3. How much more agreeable to sit in the midst of old furniture like Minott's clock and secretary and looking-glass, which have come down from other generations, than in that which was just brought from the cabinet-maker's and smells of varnish, like a coffin! To sit under the face of an old clock that has been ticking one hundred and fifty years,—there is something mortal, not to say immortal, about it! A clock that began to tick when Massachusetts was a province. Meanwhile John Beatton's heavy tombstone is cracked quite across and widely opened.

Oct. 5.* P.M.—To Yellow Birch Swamp.

I hear the alarum of a small red squirrel. I see him running by fits and starts along a chestnut bough toward me. His head looks disproportionately large for his body, like a bulldog's, perhaps because he has his chaps full of nuts. He chirrups and vibrates his tail, holds himself in, and scratches along a foot as if it were a mile. He finds noise and activity for both of us. It is evident that all this ado does not proceed from fear. There is at the bottom, no doubt, an excess of inquisitiveness and caution, but the greater part is make-believe and a love of the marvellous. He can hardly keep it up till I am gone, however, but takes out his nut and tastes it in the midst of his agitation. "*See there, see there,*" says he, "who's that? O dear, what shall I do?" and makes believe run off, but does n't get along an inch,—lets it all pass off by flashes through his tail, while he clings to the bark as if he were holding in a race-horse. He gets down the trunk at last on to a projecting knot, head downward, within a rod of you, and chirrups and chatters louder than ever. Tries to work himself into a fright. The hind part of his body is urging the forward part along, snapping the tail over it like a whip-lash, but the fore part, for the most part, clings fast to the bark with desperate energy. *Squirr*, "to throw with a jerk," seems to have quite as much to do with the name as the Greek *skia oura*, shadow and tail.

Oct. 6. Think what a change, unperceived by many, has within a month come over the landscape! Then the general, the universal, hue was green. Now see those brilliant scarlet and glowing yellow

---

*Begins now ten days of perfect Indian summer without rain; and the eleventh and twelfth days equally warm, though rainy.

trees in the lowlands a mile off! Or see that crowd in the swamp half a mile through, all vying with one another, a blaze of glory. We are not prepared to believe that the earth is now so particolored, and would present to a bird's eye such distinct masses of bright color. A great painter is at work. The very pumpkins yellowing in the fields become a feature in the landscape, and thus they have shone, maybe, for a thousand years here.

I have just read Ruskin's "Modern Painters." I am disappointed in not finding it a more out-of-door book, for I have heard that such was its character, but its title might have warned me. He does not describe Nature as Nature, but as Turner painted her, and though the work betrays that he has given a close attention to Nature, it appears to have been with an artist's and critic's design. How much is written about Nature as somebody has portrayed her, how little about Nature as she is, and chiefly concerns us, *i.e.* how much prose, how little poetry!

Oct. 7. I do not see what the Puritans did at that season when the maples blazed out in scarlet. They certainly could not have worshipped in groves then. Perhaps that is what they built meeting-houses and surrounded them with horse-sheds for.

It is the reign of crickets now. You see them gliding busily about over all sunny surfaces. They sometimes get into my shoes; but oftener I have to empty out the seeds of various shrubs and weeds which I have been compelled to transport.

When I turn round half-way up Fair Haven Hill, by the orchard wall, and look northwest, I am surprised for the thousandth time at the beauty of the landscape, and I sit down to behold it at my leisure. I think that Concord affords no better view. It is always incredibly fair, but ordinarily we are mere objects in it, and not witnesses of it.

I do not know how to entertain one who can't take long walks. The first thing that suggests itself is to get a horse to draw them, and that brings us at once into contact with stablers and dirty harness, and I do not get over my ride for a long time. I give up my forenoon to them and get along pretty well, the very elasticity of the air and promise of the day abetting me, but they are as heavy as dumplings by mid-afternoon. If they can't walk, why won't they take an honest nap and let me go in the afternoon? But, come two o'clock, they alarm me by an evident disposition to sit. In the midst of the most glorious Indian-summer afternoon, there they sit, breaking your chairs and wearing out the house, with their backs to the light, taking no note of the lapse of time.

As I sat on the high bank at the east end of Walden this afternoon, at five o'clock, I saw, by a peculiar intention or dividing of the eye, a very striking subaqueous rainbow-like phenomenon. A passer-by might, perhaps would, have noticed that the bright-tinted shrubs about the high shore on the sunny side were reflected from the water; but, unless on the alert for such effects, he would have failed to perceive the full beauty of the phenomenon. Unless you look for reflections, you commonly will not find them. Those brilliant shrubs, which were from three to a dozen feet in height, were all reflected, dimly so far as the details of leaves, etc., were concerned, but brightly as to color, and, of course, in the order in which they stood,—scarlet, yellow, green, etc.; but, there being a slight ripple on the surface, these reflections were not true to their height though true to their breadth, but were extended downward with mathematical perpendicularity, three or four times too far, forming sharp pyramids of the several colors, gradually reduced to mere dusky points. The effect of this prolongation of the reflection was a very pleasing softening and blending of the colors, especially when a small bush of one bright tint stood directly before another of a contrary and equally bright tint. It was just as if you were to brush firmly aside with your hand or a brush a fresh line of paint of various colors, or so many lumps of friable colored powders. There was, accordingly, a sort of belt, as wide as the whole height of the hill, extending downward along the whole north or sunny side of the pond, composed of exceedingly short and narrow inverted pyramids of the most brilliant colors intermixed. I have seen, indeed, similar inverted pyramids in the old drawings of tattooing about the waists of the aborigines of this country. Walden, too, like an Indian maiden, wears this broad rainbow-like belt of brilliant-colored points or cones round her waist in October. The color seems to be reflected and re-reflected from ripple to ripple, losing brightness each time by the softest possible gradation, and tapering toward the beholder, since he occupies a mere point of view. This is one of the prettiest effects of the autumnal change.

Oct. 9. It has come to this,—that the lover of art is one, and the lover of nature another, though true art is but the expression of our love of nature. It is monstrous when one cares but little about trees but much about Corinthian columns, and yet this is exceedingly common.

Oct. 10. You see now in sprout-lands young scarlet oaks of every degree of brightness from green to dark scarlet. It is a beautifully formed leaf, with its broad, free, open sinuses,—worthy to be copied in sculpture. A very agreeable form, a bold, deep scallop, as if the material were cheap. Like tracery.

Oct. 11. This is the seventh day of glorious weather. Perhaps these might be called Harvest Days. Within the week most of the apples have been gathered; potatoes are being dug; corn is still left in the fields, though the stalks are being carried in. Others are ditching and getting out mud and cutting up bushes along fences,—what is called "brushing up,"—burning brush, etc.

These are cricket days.

Oct. 12. I see a very distant mountain house in a direction a little to the west of Carlisle, and two elms in the horizon on the right of it. Measuring carefully on the map of the county, I think it must be the Baptist Church in North Tewksbury, within a small fraction of fourteen miles from me. I think that this is the greatest distance at which I have seen an elm without a glass. There is another elm in the horizon nearly north, but not so far. It looks very much larger than it is. Perhaps it looms a little. The elm, I think can be distinguished further than any other tree.

This was what those scamps did in California. The trees were so grand and venerable that they could not afford to let them grow a hair's breadth bigger, or live a moment longer to reproach themselves. They were so big that they resolved they should never be bigger. They were so venerable that they cut them right down. It was not for the sake of the wood; it was only because they were very grand and venerable.

Oct. 14. P.M.—To White Pond.

Another, the tenth of these memorable days. We have had some fog the last two or three nights, and this forenoon it was slow to disperse, dog-day-like, but this afternoon it is warmer even than yesterday. I should like it better if it were not so warm. I am glad to reach the shade of Hubbard's Grove; the coolness is refreshing. It is indeed a golden autumn. These ten days are enough to make the reputation of any climate. A tradition of these days might be handed down to posterity. They deserve a notice in history, in the history of Concord. All kinds of crudities have a chance to get ripe this year. Was there ever such an autumn? And yet there was never such a panic and hard times in the commercial world. The merchants and banks are suspending and failing all the country over, but not the sand-banks, solid and warm, and streaked with bloody blackberry vines. You may run upon them as much as you please,— even as the crickets do, and find their account in it. They are the stockholders in these banks, and I hear them creaking their content. In these banks, too, and such as these, are my funds deposited, a fund of health and enjoyment. Their (the crickets) prosperity and happiness and, I trust, mine do not depend on whether the New York banks suspend or no. Invest, I say, in these country banks. Let your capital be simplicity and contentment. Withered goldenrod (*Solidago nemoralis*) is no failure, like a broken bank, and yet in its most golden season nobody counterfeits it. Nature needs no counterfeit-detector. I have no compassion for, nor sympathy with, this miserable state of things. Banks built of granite, after some Grecian or Roman style, with their porticoes and their safes of iron, are not so permanent, and cannot give me so good security for capital invested in them, as the heads of withered hardhack in the meadow. I do not suspect the solvency of these. I know who is their president and cashier.

I take all these walks to every point of the compass, and it is always harvest-time with me. I am always gathering my crop from these woods and fields and waters, and no man is in my way or interferes with me. My crop is not their crop. I am not gathering beans and corn. Do they think there are no fruits but such as these? I am a reaper; I am not a gleaner.

On the causeway I pass by maples here and there which are bare and smoke-like, having lost their brilliant clothing; but there it lies, nearly as bright as ever, on one side on the ground, making nearly as regular a figure as lately on the tree. I should rather say that I first observed the trees thus flat on the ground like a permanent colored and substantial shadow, and they alone suggested to look for the trees that had borne them.

Looking now toward the north side of the pond, I perceive that the reflection of the hillside seen from an opposite hill is not so broad as the hillside itself appears, owing to the different angle at which it is seen. The reflection exhibits such an aspect of the hill, *apparently*, as you would get if your eye were placed at that part of the surface of the pond where the reflection seems to be. In this instance, too, then, Nature avoids repeating herself. Not even reflections in still water are like their substances as seen by us. Is the reflection of a hillside, however, such an aspect of it as can be obtained by the eye directed to the hill itself from any single point of view? If not, then the reflection is never a true copy or repetition of its substance, but a new composition, and this may be the source of its novelty and attractiveness, and of this nature, too, may be the charm of an echo. I doubt if you can ever get Nature to repeat herself exactly.

Oct. 15. Rain at last, and end of the remarkable days. The springs and rivers have been very low.

Our staghorn sumach has just become a very rich scarlet. So, apparently, has the large one at Mrs. Simmonds's. They are later than the others; a yellower scarlet, almost orange.

It is another example of the oddity of the Orientals that yellow "is in the east a regal color, more especially so in China, where it is exclusively royal." (Field on Colors, 139.) Further west it was purple, regal and imperial.

The river lower this morning than before this year. Concord Bank has suspended.

Oct. 16. I see a delicate pale brown-bronze wood frog. I think I can always take them up in my hand. They, too, vary in color, like the leaves of many species of plants at present, having now more yellow, now more red; and perhaps for the same reason.

What is acorn-color! Is it not as good as chestnut?

Oct. 18. I should say that the autumnal change and brightness of foliage began fairly with the red maples (not to speak of a very few premature trees in water) September 25th, and ends this year, say generally October 22d, or maybe two or three days earlier. The fall of the leaf, in like way, began fairly with the fall of the red maple leaves, October 13th, and ended at least as early as when the pitch pines had *generally* fallen, November 5th (the larches are about a week later). The red maples are now fairly bare, though you may occasionally see one full of leaves.

So gradually the leaves fall, after all,—though individuals will be completely stripped in one short windy rain-storm,—that you scarcely miss them out of the landscape; but the earth grows more bare, and the fields more hoary, and the heavy shadows that began in June take their departure, November being at hand.

Oct. 20. P.M.—To the Easterbrooks Country.

I had gone but little way on the old Carlisle road when I saw Brooks Clark, who is now about eighty and bent like a bow, hastening along the road, barefooted, as usual, with an axe in his hand; was in haste perhaps on account of the cold wind on his bare feet. When he got up to me, I saw that besides the axe in one hand, he had his shoes in the other, filled with knurly apples and a dead robin. He stopped and talked with me a few moments; said that we had had a noble autumn and might now expect some cold weather. I asked if he had found the robin dead. No, he said, he found it with its wing broken and killed it. He also added that he had found some apples in the woods, and as he had n't anything to carry them in, he put 'em in his shoes. They were queer-looking trays to carry fruit in. How many he got in along toward the toes, I don't know. I noticed, too, that his pockets were stuffed with them. His old tattered frock coat was hanging in strips about the skirts, as were his pantaloons about his naked feet. He appeared to have been out on a scout this gusty afternoon, to see what he could find, as the youngest boy might. It pleased me to see this cheery old man, with such a feeble hold on life, bent almost double, thus enjoying the evening of his days. Far be it from me to call it avarice or penury, this childlike delight in finding something in the woods or fields and carrying it home in the October evening, as a trophy to be added to his winter's store. Oh, no; he was happy to be Nature's pensioner still, and birdlike to pick up his living. Better his robin than your turkey, his shoes full of apples than your barrels full; they will be sweeter and suggest a better tale. Like an old squirrel shuffling to his hole with a nut.

This old man's cheeriness was worth a thousand of the church's sacraments and *memento mori*'s. It was better than a prayerful mood. It proves to me old age as tolerable, as happy, as infancy. I was glad of an occasion to suspect that this afternoon he had not been at "work" but living somewhat after my own fashion (though he did not explain the axe),—had been out to see what nature had for him, and now was hastening home to a burrow he knew, where he could warm his old feet. If he had been a young man, he would probably have thrown away his apples and put on his shoes when he saw me coming, for shame. But old age is manlier; it has learned to live, makes fewer apologies, like infancy. This seems a very manly man. I have known him within a few years building stone wall by himself, barefooted.

Warren Brown, who owns the Easterbrooks place, the west side the road, is picking barberries. Allows that the soil thereabouts is excellent for fruit, but it is so rocky that he has not patience to plow it. That is the reason this tract is not cultivated.

There was Melvin, too, a-barberrying and nutting. He had got two baskets, one in each hand, and his game-bag, which hung from his neck, all full of nuts and barberries, and his mouth full of tobacco. Trust him to find where the nuts and berries grow. He is hunting all the year and he marks the bushes and the trees which are fullest, and when the time comes, for once leaves his gun, though not his dog, at home, and takes his baskets to the spot.

What a wild and rich domain that Easterbrooks Country! Not a cultivated, hardly a cultivatable field in it, and yet it delights all natural persons, and feeds more still. Such great rocky and moist tracts, which daunt the farmer, are reckoned as unimproved land, and therefore worth but little; but think of the miles of huckleberries, and of barberries, and of wild apples, so fair, both in flower and fruit, resorted to by men and beasts; Clark, Brown, Melvin, and the robins, these, at least, were attracted thither this afternoon.

Wesson is so gouty that he rarely comes out-of-doors, and is a spectacle in the street; but he loves to tell his old stories still! How, when he was stealing along to get a shot at his ducks, and was just upon them, a red squirrel sounded the alarm, *chickaree chickaree chickaree*, and off they went; but he turned his gun upon the squirrel to avenge himself.

Oct. 21. I see a robin eating prinos berries. Is not the robin the principal berry-eating bird nowadays? There must be more about the barberry bushes in Melvin's Preserve than anywhere.

It is pitiful to see a man of sixty, a philosopher, perchance, inquiring for a bearing apple orchard for sale. If he must have one, why did he not set it out when he was thirty? How mean and lazy, to be plucking the fruit of another man's labor. The old man I saw yesterday lives on peaches and milk in their season, but then he planted them.

Is not the poet bound to write his own biography? Is there any other work for him but a good journal? We do not wish to know how his imaginary hero, but how he, the actual hero, lived from day to day.

That big swamp white oak limb or tree which I found prostrate in the swamp was longer than my boat and tipped it well. These old stumps stand like anchorites and yogees, putting off their earthy garments, more and more sublimed from year to year, ready to be translated, and then they are ripe for my fire. I administer the last sacrament and purification.

Oct. 22. Ground pretty white with frost. The stiffened and frosted weeds and grass have an aggrieved look. The lately free-flowing blades of grass look now like mourning tresses sculptured stiffly in marble; they lie stiff and dishevelled. A very narrow strip of ice has formed along the riverside, in which I see a pad or two, wearing the same aggrieved look, like the face of the child that cried for spilt milk, its summer irrevocably gone.

P.M.—As I go through the woods now, so many oak and other leaves have fallen the rustling noise somewhat disturbs my musing. However, Nature in this may have intended some kindness to the ducks, which are now loitering hereabouts on their migration southward, mostly young and inexperienced birds, for, as they are feeding in Goose Pond, for instance, the rustling of the leaves betrays the approach of the sportsman and his dog, or other foe; so perhaps the leaves on the ground protect them more than when on the trees.

What a perfect chest the chestnut is packed in! With such wonderful care Nature has secluded and defended these nuts, as if they were her most precious fruits, while diamonds are left to take care of themselves. First it bristles all over with sharp green prickles, some nearly half an inch long, like a hedgehog rolled into a ball; these rest on a thick, stiff, bark-like rind, one sixteenth to one eighth of an inch thick, which, again, is most daintily lined with a kind of silvery fur or velvet plush one sixteenth of an inch thick, even rising in a ridge between the nuts, like the lining of a casket in which the most precious commodities are kept. The chest is packed quite full; half-developed nuts are the waste paper used in the packing, to fill the vacancies. At last Frost comes to unlock this chest; it alone holds the true key.

Such is the cradle, thus daintily lined, in which they have been rocked in their infancy. See how tenderly it has been reared before its green and tender skin hardened into a shell. The October air comes in, and the light too, and proceed to paint the nuts that clear, handsome reddish (?) brown which we call chestnut. Nowadays the brush that paints chestnuts is very active. It is entering into every open bur over the stretching forests' tops for hundreds of miles, without horse or ladder, and putting on rapid coats of this wholesome color. Otherwise the boys would not think they had got perfect nuts. And that this may be further protected, perchance, both within the bur and afterward, the nuts themselves are partly covered toward the top, where they are first exposed, with that same soft velvety down. And then Nature drops it on the rustling leaves, a *done* nut, prepared to begin a chestnut's course again. Within itself, again, each individual nut is lined with a reddish velvet, as if to preserve the seed from jar and injury in falling and, perchance, from sudden damp and cold, and, within that, a thin white skin enwraps the germ. Thus it is lining within lining and unwearied care,—not to count closely, six coverings at least before you reach the contents!

But it is a barbarous way to jar the tree, and I trust I do repent of it. Gently shake it only, or let the wind shake it for you. You are gratified to find a nut that has in it no bitterness, altogether palatable.

Oct. 23. Sal Cummings, a thorough countrywoman, conversant with nuts and berries, calls the soapwort gentian "blue vengeance," mistaking the word. A masculine wild-eyed woman of the fields. Somebody has her daguerreotype. When Mr. —— was to lecture on Kansas, she was sure "she wa'n't going to hear him. None of her folks had ever had any."

Oct. 24. P.M.—To Smith's chestnut grove.

I get a couple of quarts of chestnuts by patiently brushing the thick beds of leaves aside with my hand in successive concentric circles till I reach the trunk; more than half under one tree. I believe I get more by resolving, where they are reasonably thick, to pick all under one tree first. Begin at the tree and brush the leaves with your right hand in toward the stump, while your left holds the basket, and so go round and round it in concentric circles, each time laying bare about two feet in width, till you get as far as the boughs extend. You may presume that you have got about all then. It is best to reduce it to a system. Of course you will shake the tree first, if there are any on it. The nuts lie commonly two or three together, as they fell.

I find one of those small, hard, dark-brown millipede worms partly crawled into a hole in a chestnut.

I find my account in this long-continued monotonous labor of picking chestnuts all the afternoon, brushing the leaves aside without looking up, absorbed in that, and forgetting better things awhile. My eye is educated to discover anything on the ground, as chestnuts, etc. It is probably wholesomer to look at the ground much than at the heavens. As I go stooping and brushing the leaves aside by the hour, I am not thinking of chestnuts merely, but I find myself humming a thought of more significance. This occupation affords a certain broad pause and opportunity to start again afterward,—turn over a new leaf.

I hear the dull thump of heavy stones against the trees from far through the rustling wood, where boys are ranging for nuts.

Oct. 26. Hard rain in the night and almost steady rain through the day, the second day.

A driving east or northeast storm. I can see through the drisk only a mile. The river is getting partly over the meadows at last, and my spirits rise with it. Methinks this rise of the waters must affect every thought and deed in the town. It qualifies my sentence and life. I trust there will appear in this Journal some flow, some gradual filling of the springs and raising of the streams, that the accumulating grists may be ground. I see two great fish hawks (*possibly* blue herons) slowly beating northeast against the storm, by what a curious tie circling ever near each other and in the same direction, as if you might expect to find the very motes in the air to be paired; two long undulating wings conveying a feathered body through the misty atmosphere, and this inseparably associated with another planet of the same species I can just glimpse their undulating lines. Damon and Pythias they must be. The waves beneath, which are of kindred form, are still more social, multitudinous, ἀνήριθμον. Where is my mate, beating against the storm with me?

These regular phenomena of the seasons get at last to be—they were *at first*, of course—simply and plainly phenomena or phases of my life. The seasons and all their changes are in me. I see not a dead eel or floating snake, or a gull, but it rounds my life and is like a line or accent in its poem. Almost I believe the Concord would not rise and overflow its banks again, were I not here. After a while I learn what my moods and seasons are. I would have nothing subtracted. I can imagine nothing added. My moods are thus periodical, not two days in my year alike. The perfect correspondence of Nature to man, so that he is at home in her!

At the hewing-place on the flat above, many sparrows are flitting past amid the birches and sallows. They are chiefly *Fringilla hyemalis*. How often they may be seen thus flitting along in a straggling manner from bush to bush, so that the hedgerow will be all alive with them, each uttering a faint *chip* from time to time, as if to keep together, bewildering you so that you know not if the greater part are gone by or still to come. One rests but a moment on the tree before you and is gone again. You wonder if they know whither they are bound, and how their leader is appointed.

Those sparrows, too, are thoughts I have. They come and go; they flit by quickly on their migrations, uttering only a faint *chip*, I know not whither or why exactly. One will not rest upon its twig for me to scrutinize it. The whole copse will be alive with my rambling thoughts, bewildering me by their very multitude, but they will be all gone directly without leaving me a feather.

Spring is brown; summer, green; autumn, yellow; winter, white; November, gray.

Oct. 27. The third day of steady rain; wind northeast.

I go up the river as far as Hubbard's Second Grove, in order to share the general commotion and excitement of the elements,—wind and waves and rain. I sailed swiftly, standing up and tipping my boat to make a keel of its side, though at first it was hard to keep off a lee shore. I looked for cranberries drifted up on the lee side of the meadows, but saw few. It was exciting to feel myself tossed by the dark waves and hear them surge about me. The reign of water now begins, and how it gambols and revels! Waves are its leaves, foam its blossoms. How they run and leap in great droves, deriving new excitement from each other! Schools of porpoises and blackfish are only more animated waves and have acquired the gait and game of the sea itself.

The fall (strictly speaking) is approaching an end in this probably annual northeast storm. Thus the summer winds up its accounts. The winter's wood is bargained for and being hauled. This storm reminds men to put things on a winter footing. There is not much more for the farmer to do in the fields.

The real facts of a poet's life would be of more value to us than any work of his art. Shakespeare has left us his fancies and imaginings, but the truth of his life, with its becoming circumstances, we know nothing about. The writer is reported, the liver not at all. But we want the basis of fact, of an actual life, to complete our Shakespeare, as much as a statue wants its pedestal.

Oct. 28. I look up and see a male marsh hawk with his clean-cut wings, that has just skimmed past above my head,—not at all disturbed, only tilting his body a little, now twenty rods off, with demi-semi-quaver of his wings. He is a very neat flyer. Steady as a planet in its orbit, with his head bent down, but on second thought that small sprout-land seems worthy of a longer scrutiny, and he gives one circle backward over it. His scream is somewhat like the whinnering of a horse, if it is not rather a *split squeal*. It is a hoarse, tremulous breathing forth of his winged energy. But why is it so regularly repeated at that height? Is it to scare his prey, that he may see by its motion where it is, or to inform its mate or companion of its whereabouts? Now he crosses the at present broad river steadily, deserving to have one or two rabbits at least to swing about him. What majesty there is in this small bird's flight! The hawks are large-souled.

Oct. 29. There is a large square-sided black rock, say five or six feet high, eight long, and five wide, on Mrs. Ripley's shore, wedged close between two small elms, and your first thought on seeing it is that it has according to some law occupied that space between the trees, not reflecting that it is more ancient than the trees by a geological period, and that the latter have but recently sprung up under its protection. I thought the rock had been accurately fitted into that space.

There are some things of which I cannot at once tell whether I have dreamed them or they are real; as if they were just, perchance, establishing, or else losing, a real basis in my world. This is especially the case in the early morning hours, when there is a gradual transition from dreams to waking thoughts, from illusions to actualities, as from darkness, or perchance moon and star light, to sunlight. Dreams are real, as is the light of the stars and moon, and theirs is said to be a *dreamy* light. Such early morning thoughts as I speak of occupy a debatable ground between dreams and waking thoughts. They are a sort of permanent dream in my mind. At least, until we have for some time changed our position from prostrate to erect, and commenced or faced some of the duties of the day, we cannot tell what we have dreamed from what we have actually experienced.

This morning, for instance, for the twentieth time at least, I thought of that mountain in the easterly part of our town (where no high hill actually is) which once or twice I had ascended, and often allowed my thoughts alone to climb. I now contemplate it in my mind as a familiar thought which I have surely had for many years from time to time, but whether anything could have reminded me of it in the middle of yesterday, whether I ever before remembered it in broad daylight, I doubt. I can now eke out the vision I had of it this morning with my old and yesterday forgotten dreams.

My way up used to lie through a dark and unfrequented wood at its base,—I cannot now tell exactly, it was so long ago, under what circumstances I first ascended, only that I shuddered as I went along (I have an indistinct remembrance of having been out overnight alone),—and then I steadily ascended along a rocky ridge half clad with stinted trees, where wild beasts haunted, till I lost myself quite in the upper air and clouds, seeming to pass an imaginary line which separates a hill, mere earth heaped up, from a mountain, into a superterranean grandeur and sublimity. What distinguishes that summit above the earthy line, is that it is unhandselled, awful, grand. It can never become familiar; you are lost the moment you set foot there. You know no path, but wander, thrilled, over the bare and pathless rock, as if it were solidified air and cloud. That rocky, misty summit, secreted in the clouds, was far more thrillingly awful and sublime than the crater of a volcano spouting fire.

This is a business we can partly understand. The perfect mountain height is already thoroughly purified. It is as if you trod with awe the face of a god turned up, unwittingly but helplessly, yielding to the laws of gravity. And are there not such mountains, east or west, from which you may look down on Concord in your thought, and on all the world? In dreams I am shown this height from time to time, and I seem to have asked my fellow once to climb there with me, and yet I am constrained to believe that I never actually ascended it. It chances, now I think of it,* that it rises in my mind where lies the Burying-Hill. You might go through its gate to enter that dark wood,† but that hill and its graves are so concealed and obliterated by the awful mountain that I never thought of them as underlying it. Might not the graveyards of the just always be hills, ways by which we ascend and overlook the plain?

But my old way down was different, and, indeed, this was another way up, though I never so ascended. I came out, as I descended, breathing the thicker air. I came out the belt of wood into

---

*Now *first think of it*, at this stage of my description, which makes it the more singularly symbolical. The interlineations on the last page were made before this.

†Perchance that was the grave.

a familiar pasture, and along down by a wall. Often, as I go along the low side of this pasture, I let my thoughts ascend toward the mount, gradually entering the stinted wood (Nature subdued) and the thinner air, and drape themselves with mists. There are ever two ways up: one is through the dark wood, the other through the sunny pasture. That is, I reach and discover the mountain only through the dark wood, but I see to my surprise, when I look off between the mists from its summit, how it is ever adjacent to my native fields, nay, imminent over them, and accessible through a sunny pasture. Why is it that in the lives of men we hear more of the dark wood than of the sunny pasture?

A hard-featured god reposing, whose breath hangs about his forehead.

Oct. 30. There's a very large and complete circle round the moon this evening, which part way round is a faint rainbow. It is a clear circular space, sharply and mathematically cut out of a thin mackerel sky. You see no mist within it, large as it is, nor even a star.

Oct. 31. In the Lee farm swamp, by the old Sam Barrett mill site, I see two kinds of ferns still green and much in fruit, apparently the *Aspidium spinulosum* (?) and *cristatum* (?). They are also common in other swamps now. You are inclined to approach and raise each frond in succession, moist, trembling, fragile greenness. What means this persistent vitality, invulnerable to frost and wet? They stay as if to keep up the spirits of the cold-blooded frogs which have not yet gone into the mud; that the summer may die with decent and graceful moderation, gradually. Even in them I feel an argument for immortality. Death is so far from being universal. The same destroyer does not destroy all. How valuable they are (with the lycopodiums) for cheerfulness. Greenness at the end of the year, after the fall of the leaf, as in a hale old age. What virtue is theirs that enables them to resist the frost?

If you are afflicted with melancholy at this season, go to the swamp and see the brave spears of skunk-cabbage buds already advanced toward a new year. Their gravestones are not bespoken yet.

Is it the winter of their discontent? Do they seem to have lain down to die, despairing of skunk-cabbagedom? "Up and at 'em," "Give it to 'em," "Excelsior," "Put it through,"—these are their mottoes. Mortal human creatures must take a little respite in this fall of the year; their spirits do flag a little. There is a little questioning of destiny, and thinking to go like cowards to where the "weary shall be at rest." But not so with the skunk-cabbage. Are these false prophets? Is it a lie or a vain boast underneath the skunk-cabbage bud, pushing it upward and lifting the dead leaves with it? They rest with spears advanced; they rest to shoot!

I say it is good for me to be here, slumping in the mud, a trap covered with withered leaves. See those green cabbage buds lifting the dry leaves in that watery and muddy place. There is no can't nor cant to them. They see over the brow of winter's hill. They see another summer ahead.

Nov. 2. P.M.—To Bateman's Pond.

Row up Assabet as far as the Pokelogan, thence on foot. It is very pleasant and cheerful nowadays, when the brown and withered leaves strew the ground and almost every plant is fallen or withered, to come upon a patch of polypody on some rocky hillside in the woods, where, in the midst of the dry and rustling leaves, defying frost, it stands so freshly green and full of life. The mere greenness, which was not remarkable in the summer, is positively interesting now. My thoughts are with the polypody a long time after my body has passed. Why is not this form copied by our sculptors instead of the foreign acanthus leaves and bays? The sight of this unwithering green leaf excites me like red at some seasons. Are not the wood frogs the philosophers who walk (?) in these groves? Methinks I imbibe a cool, composed, frog-like philosophy when I behold them. I don't care for acanthus leaves; they are far-fetched. I do love this form, however, and would like to see it painted or sculptured, whether on your marble or my butter. How fit for a tuft about the base of a column!

How contagious are boys' games! A short time ago they were spinning tops, as I saw and heard, all the country over. Now every

boy has a stick curved at the end, a *hawkie* (?), in his hand,
whether in yards or in distant lanes I meet them.

The form of the polypody is *strangely* interesting; it is
even outlandish. Some forms, though common in our midst, are
thus perennially foreign as the growths of other latitudes; there being a greater interval between us and their kind than usual. We all
feel the ferns to be further from us, essentially and sympathetically,
than the phænogamous plants, the roses and weeds, for instance. It
needs no geology nor botany to assure us of that. We feel it, and
told *them* of it first. It is a fabulous, mythological form, such as
prevailed when the earth and air and water were inhabited by those
extinct fossil creatures that we find. It is contemporary with them,
and affects as the sight of them.

Nov. 5. Sometimes I would rather get a transient glimpse or side
view of a thing than stand fronting to it,—as those polypodies. The
object I caught a glimpse of as I went by haunts my thoughts a long
time, is infinitely suggestive, and I do not care to front it and scrutinize it, for I know that the thing that really concerns me is not
there, but in my relation to that. That is a mere reflecting surface.
It is not the polypody in my pitcher or herbarium, or which I may
possibly persuade to grow on a bank in my yard, or which is described in botanies, that interests me, but the one that I pass by in
my walks a little distance off, when in the right mood. Its influence
is sporadic, wafted through the air to me. Do you imagine its fruit
to stick to the back of the leaf all winter? At this season polypody
is in the air. It is worth the while to walk in swamps now, to bathe
your eyes with greenness. The terminal shield fern is the handsomest and glossiest green.

I think that the man of science makes this mistake, and the mass
of mankind along with him: that you should coolly give your chief
attention to the phenomenon which excites you as something independent on you, and not as it is related to you. The important fact
is its effect on me. He thinks that I have no business to see anything
else but just what he defines the rainbow to be, but I care not whether
my vision of truth is a waking thought or dream remembered,

whether it is seen in the light or in the dark. It is the subject of the vision, the truth alone, that concerns me. The philosopher for whom rainbows, etc., can be explained away never saw them. With regard to such objects, I find that it is not they themselves (with which the men of science deal) that concern me; the point of interest is somewhere *between* me and them (*i.e.* the objects).

Nov. 6. Very warm but rather cloudy weather, after rain in the night. Wind southwest. Thermometer on north of the house 70° at 12 M. Indian summer. The cocks crow in the soft air. They are very sensitive to atmospheric changes.

Nov. 7. P.M.—To Bateman's Pond with R.W.E.

Stedman Buttrick, speaking of R.W.E.'s. cow that was killed by lightning and not found for some days, said that they heard a "bellering" of the cows some days before they found her, and they found the ground much trampled about the dead cow; that that was the way with cows in such cases; if such an accident happened to one of their number, they would have spells of gathering around her and "bellering."

Minott adorns whatever part of nature he touches; whichever way he walks he transfigures the earth for me. If a common man speaks of Walden Pond to me, I see only a shallow, dull-colored body of water without reflections or peculiar color, but if Minott speaks of it, I see the green water and reflected hills at once, for he *has been* there. I hear the rustle of the leaves from woods which he goes through.

Nov. 8. About 10 A.M. a long flock of geese are going over from northeast to southwest, or parallel with the general direction of the coast and great mountain-ranges. The sonorous, quavering sounds of the geese are the voice of this cloudy air,—a sound that comes from directly between us and the sky, an aerial sound, and yet so distinct, heavy, and sonorous, a clanking chain drawn through the heavy air. I saw through my window some children looking up and pointing their tiny bows into the heavens, and I knew at once that the geese were in the air. It is always an exciting event. The children, instinctively aware of its importance, rushed into the house to tell their parents. These travellers are revealed to you by the upward-turned gaze of men.

P.M.—I have no doubt that a good farmer, who, of course, loves his work, takes exactly the same kind of pleasure in draining a swamp, seeing the water flow out in his newly cut ditch, that a child does in its mud dikes and water-wheels. Both alike love to play with the natural forces.

Ah, my friends, I know you better than you think, and love you better, too. The day after never, we will have an explanation.

Nov. 9. Surveying for Stedman Buttrick and Mr. Gordon.

Jacob Farmer tells me that one Sunday he went to his barn, having nothing to do, and thought he would watch the swallows, republican swallows. The old bird was feeding her young, and he sat within fifteen feet, overlooking them. There were five young, and he was curious to know how each received its share; and as often as the bird came with a fly, the one at the door (or opening) took it, and then they all hitched round one notch, so that a new one was presented at the door, who received the next fly; and this was the invariable order, the same one never receiving two flies in succession. At last the old bird brought a very small fly, and the young one that swallowed it did not desert his ground but waited to receive the next, but when the bird came with another, of the usual size, she commenced a loud and long scolding at the little one, till it resigned its place, and the next in succession received the fly.

Nov. 14. This morning it was considerably colder than for a long time, and by noon very much colder than heretofore, with a pretty strong northerly wind. I find my hands stiffened and involuntarily finding their way to my pockets. No wonder that the weather is a standing subject of conversation, since we are so sensitive. If we had not gone through several winters, we might well be alarmed at the approach of cold weather. With this keener blast from the north, my hands suddenly fail to fulfill their office, as it were begin to die.

What a story to tell an inhabitant of the tropics,—perchance that you went to walk, after many months of warmth, when suddenly the air became so cold and hostile to your nature, that it benumbed you so that you lost the use of some of your limbs, could not untie your shoe-strings or unbutton your clothes!

Such is the first freezing day. Such are the first advances of winter. The thermometer is 27° at 6 P.M. The mud in the street is stiffened under my feet this evening.

Nov. 18. The sunlight is a peculiarly thin and clear yellow, falling on the pale-brown bleaching herbage of the fields at this season. There is no redness in it. This is November sunlight. Much cold, slate-colored cloud, bare twigs seen gleaming toward the light like gossamer, pure green of pines whose old leaves have fallen, reddish or yellowish brown oak leaves rustling on the hillsides, very pale brown, bleaching, almost hoary fine grass or hay in the fields, akin to the frost which has killed it, and flakes of clear yellow sunlight falling on it here and there,—such is November.

In one light, these are old and worn-out fields that I ramble over, and men have gone to law about them long before I was born, but I trust that I ramble over them in a new fashion and redeem them.

In sickness all is deranged. I had yesterday a kink in my back and a general cold, and as usual it amounted to a cessation of life. I lost for the time my *rapport* or relation to nature. Sympathy with nature is an evidence of perfect health. You cannot perceive beauty but with a serene mind. The cheaper your amusements, the safer and saner. They who think much of theatres, operas, and the like, are beside themselves. Each man's necessary path, though as obscure and apparently uneventful as that of a beetle in the grass, is the way to the deepest joys he is susceptible of; though he converses only with moles and fungi and disgraces his relatives, it is no matter if he knows what is steel to his flint.

Nov. 20. In books, that which is most generally interesting is what comes home to the most cherished private experience of the greatest number. It is not the book of him who has travelled the farthest over the surface of the globe, but of him who has lived the deepest and been the most at home. If an equal emotion is excited by a familiar homely phenomenon as by the Pyramids, there is no advantage in seeing the Pyramids. It is on the whole better, as it is simpler, to use the common language. The poet has made the best roots in his native soil of any man, and is the hardest to transplant. If a man is rich and strong anywhere, it must be on his native soil. Here I have been these forty years learning the language of these fields that I may the better express myself. If I should travel to the prairies, I should much less understand them, and my past life would serve me but ill to describe them. Many a weed here stands for more of life to me than the big trees of California would if I should go there. We only need travel enough to give our intellects an airing. In spite of Malthus and the rest, there will be plenty of room in this world, if every man will mind his own business. I have not heard of any planet running against another yet.

I observed this afternoon how some bullocks had a little sportiveness forced upon them. They were running down a steep declivity to water, when, feeling themselves unusually impelled by gravity downward, they took the hint even as boys do, flourished round gratuitously, tossing their hind quarters into the air and shaking their heads at each other, but what increases the ludicrousness of it to me is the fact that such capers are never accompanied by a smile. Who does not believe that their step is less elastic, their movement more awkward, for their long domesticity?

Nov. 24. P.M.—To Andromeda Ponds.
Cold Thanksgiving weather again, the pools freezing.

Nov. 25. A clear, cold, windy afternoon. The cat crackles with electricity when you stroke her, and the fur rises up to your touch.

This is November of the hardest kind,—bare frozen ground covered with pale-brown or straw-colored herbage, a strong, cold, cutting northwest wind which makes me seek to cover my ears, a perfectly clear and cloudless sky. The cattle in the fields have a cold, shrunken, shaggy look, their hair standing out every way, as if with electricity, like the cat's. Ditches and pools are fast skimming over, and a few slate-colored snowbirds, with thick, shuffling twitter, and fine-chipping tree sparrows flit from bush to bush in the otherwise deserted pastures. This month taxes a walker's resources more than any. For my part, I should sooner think of going into quarters in November than in the winter. If you do feel any fire at this season out of doors, you may depend upon it, it is your own. It is but a short time, these afternoons, before the night cometh, in which no man can walk. November Eat-heart,—is that the name of it? Not only the fingers cease to do their office, but there is often a benumbing of the faculties generally. You can hardly screw up your courage to take a walk when all is thus tightly locked or frozen up and so little is to be seen in field or wood. Nature has herself become like the few fruits which she still affords, a very thick-shelled nut with a shrunken meat within. I am obliged to go abroad willfully and against my inclinations at first. The prospect looks so barren, so many springs are frozen up, not a flower perchance and but few birds left, not a companion abroad in all these fields for me, I am slow to go forth. I seem to anticipate a fruitless walk. I think to myself hesitatingly, Shall I go there, or there, or there? and cannot make up my mind to any route, all seem so unpromising, mere surface walking and fronting the cold wind, so that I have to force myself to it often and at random. But then I am often unexpectedly compensated, and the thinnest yellow light of November is more warming and exhilarating than any wine they tell of; and then the mite which November contributes becomes equal in value to the bounty of July. I may meet with something which interests me, and immediately it is as warm as in July.

Pools under the north sides of hills are frozen pretty thick. That cold one of Stow's is nearly an inch and a half thick. The roar of the wind in the trees over my head sounds as cold as the wind feels.

I shiver about awhile on Pine Hill, waiting for the sun to set. Methinks the air is dusky soon after four these days. The landscape looks darker than at any season,—like arctic scenery.

XXV.

THE OPEN WINTER

Nov. 27. Standing before Stacy's large glass windows this morning, I saw that they were gloriously ground by the frost. I never saw such beautiful feather and firlike frosting. His windows are filled with fancy articles and toys for Christmas and New-Year's presents, but this delicate and graceful outside frosting surpassed them all infinitely. I saw countless feathers with very distinct midribs and fine pinnæ. Other crystals looked like pine plumes the size of life. If glass could be ground to look like this, how glorious it would be!

You can tell which shopman has the hottest fire within by the frost being melted off. I was never so struck by the gracefulness of the curves in vegetation, and wonder that Ruskin does not refer to frostwork.

Dec. 2. I find that, according to the deed of Duncan Ingraham to John Richardson in 1797, my old bean-field on Walden Pond then belonged to George Minott. (Minott thinks he bought it of an Allen.) This was Deacon George Minott, who lived in the house next below the East Quarter schoolhouse, and was a brother of my grandfather-in-law. He was directly descended from Thomas Minott, who, according to Shattuck, was secretary of the Abbot of Walden (!) in Essex and whose son George was born at Saffron Walden (!) and afterwards was one of the early settlers of Dorchester.

Dec. 7. Running the long northwest side of Richardson's Fair Haven lot. It is a fair, sunny, and warm day in the woods for the season. We eat our dinners on the middle of the line, amid the young oaks in a sheltered and very unfrequented place. I cut some leafy shrub oaks and cast them down for a dry and springy seat. As I sit there amid the sweet-fern, talking with my man Briney, I observe that the recent shoots of the sweet-fern—which, like many larger bushes and trees, have a few leaves in a tuft still at their extremities— toward the sun are densely covered with a bright, warm, silvery down, which looks like frost, so thick and white. Looking the other way, I see none of it, but the bare reddish twigs. Even this is a cheering and compensating discovery in my otherwise barren work. I get thus a few positive values, answering to the bread and cheese which make my dinner. I owe thus to my weeks at surveying a few such slight but positive discoveries.

Dec. 8. Staples says he came to Concord some twenty-four years ago a poor boy with a dollar and three cents in his pocket, and he spent the three cents for drink at Bigelow's tavern, and now he's worth "twenty hundred dollars clear." He remembers many who inherited wealth whom he can buy out to-day. I told him that he had done better than I in a pecuniary respect, for I had only earned my living. "Well," said he, "that's all I've done, and I don't know as I've got much better clothes than you." I was particularly poorly clad then, in the woods; my hat, pants, boots, rubbers, and gloves would not have brought four-pence, and I told the Irishman that it was n't everybody could afford to have a fringe round his legs, as I had, my corduroys not preserving a selvage.

Dec. 27. One while we do not wonder that so many commit suicide, life is so barren and worthless; we only live on by an effort of the will. Suddenly our condition is ameliorated, and even the barking of a dog is a pleasure to us. So closely is our happiness bound up with our physical condition, and one reacts on the other.

I am disappointed by most essays and lectures. I find that I had expected the authors would have some life, some very private experience, to report, which would make it comparatively unimportant in what style they expressed themselves, but commonly they have only a talent to exhibit. The new magazine which all have been expecting may contain only another love story as naturally told as the last, perchance, but without the slightest novelty in it. It may be a mere vehicle for Yankee phrases.

JAN. I. There are many words which are genuine and indigenous and have their root in our natures, not made by scholars, and as well understood by the illiterate as others. There are also a great many words which are spurious and artificial, and can only be used in a bad sense, since the thing they signify is not fair and substantial,—such as the *church*, the *judiciary*, to *impeach*, etc., etc. They who use them do not stand on solid ground. It is in vain to try to preserve them by attaching other words to them as the *true* church, etc. It is like towing a sinking ship with a canoe.

I have lately been surveying the Walden woods so extensively and minutely that I now see it mapped in my mind's eye—as, indeed, on paper—as so many men's wood-lots, and am aware when I walk there that I am at a given moment passing from such a one's wood-lot to such another's. I fear this particular dry knowledge may affect my imagination and fancy, that it will not be easy to see so much wildness and native vigor there as formerly. No thicket will seem so unexplored now that I know that a stake and stones may be found in it. In these respects those Maine woods differed essentially from ours. There you are never reminded that the wilderness which you are threading is, after all, some villager's familiar wood-lot from which his ancestors have sledded their fuel for generations, or some widow's thirds, minutely described in some old deed, which is recorded, of which the owner has got a plan, too, and old bound marks may be found every forty rods if you will search. What a history this Concord wilderness which I affect so much may have had! How many old deeds describe it,—some particular wild spot,—how it passed from Cole to Robinson, and Robinson to Jones, and Jones finally to Smith, in course of years! Some have cut it over three times during their lives, and some burned it and sowed it with rye, and built walls and made a pasture of it, perchance. All have renewed the bounds and reblazed the trees many times. Here you are not reminded of these things. 'T is true the map informs you that you stand on land granted by the State to such an academy, or on Bingham's Purchase, but these names do not impose on you, for you see nothing to remind you of the academy or of Bingham.

Jan. 3. About, in his lively "Greece and the Greeks," says, "These are the most exquisite delights to be found in Greece, next to, or perhaps before, the pleasure of admiring the masterpieces of art,— a little cool water under a genial sun." I have no doubt that this is true. Why, then, travel so far when the same pleasures may be found near home?

Going to the Andromeda Ponds, I was greeted by the warm brown-red glow of the *Andromeda calyculata* toward the sun. I see where I have been through, the more reddish under sides apparently being turned up. It is long since a human friend has met me with such a glow.

Jan. 6. I derive a certain excitement, not to be refused, even from going through Dennis's Swamp on the opposite side of the railroad, where the poison-dogwood abounds. It impresses me as the most fruitful shrub thereabouts. I cannot refrain from plucking it and bringing home some pretty sprigs.

I was feeling very cheap, nevertheless, reduced to make the most of dry dogwood berries. Very little evidence of God or man did I see just then, and life not as rich and inviting an enterprise as it should be, when my attention was caught by a snowflake on my coat-sleeve. It was one of those perfect, crystalline, star-shaped ones, six-rayed, like a flat wheel with six spokes, only the spokes were perfect little pine trees in shape, arranged around a central spangle. This little object, which, with many of its fellows, rested unmelting on my coat, so perfect and beautiful, reminded me that Nature had not lost her pristine vigor yet, and why should man lose heart? This was at mid-afternoon, and it has not quite ceased snowing yet (at 10 P.M.). We are rained and snowed on with gems. I confess that I was a little encouraged, for I was beginning to believe that Nature was poor and mean, and I was now convinced that she turned off as good work as ever. What a world we live in!

JAN. 11. *Monday. Rain, rain*—washes off almost every vestige of snow.

Jan. 23. Saturday. The wonderfully mild and pleasant weather continues. The ground has been bare since the 11th. There has been but little use for gloves this winter, though I have been surveying a great deal for three months. The sun, and cockcrowing, bare ground, etc., etc., remind me of March.

It is in vain to write on the seasons unless you have the seasons in you.

Jan. 24. Sunday. The river is broadly open, as usual this winter. But I do not quite like this warm weather and bare ground at this season. What is a winter without snow and ice in this latitude? The bare earth is unsightly. This winter is but unburied summer.

At Nut Meadow Brook the small-sized water-bugs are as abundant and active as in summer. I see forty or fifty circling together in the smooth and sunny bays all along the brook. This is something new to me. What must they think of this winter? It is like a child waked up and set to playing at midnight. At night, of course, they dive to the bottom and bury themselves, and if in the morning they perceive no curtain of ice drawn over their sky, and the pleasant weather continues, they gladly rise again and resume their gyrations in some sunny bay amid the alders and the stubble. But I fear for their nervous systems, lest this be too much activity, too much excitement. What a funny way they have of going to bed! They do not take a light and retire up-stairs; they go below. Suddenly it is heels up and heads down, and they go down to their muddy bed and let the unresting stream flow over them in their dreams. They go to bed in another element. What a deep slumber must be theirs, and what dreams, down in the mud there! So the insect life is not withdrawn far off, but a warm sun would soon entice it forth. Suppose you were to plot the course of one for a day; what kind of a figure would it make? Probably this feat too will one day be performed by science, that maid of all work. I see one chasing a mote, and the wave the creature makes always causes the mote to float away from it. I would like to know what it is they communicate to one another, they who appear to value each other's society so much. How many water-bugs make a quorum? How many hundreds does their Fourier think it takes to make a complete bug? Where did they get their backs polished so? They will have occasion to remember this year, that winter when we were waked out of our annual sleep! What is their precise hour for retiring?

Jan. 27. Time never passes so quickly and unaccountably as when I am engaged in composition, *i.e.* in writing down my thoughts. Clocks seem to have been put forward.

Jan. 29. Found some splendid fungi on old aspens used for a fence; quite firm; reddish-white above and bright-vermilion beneath, or perhaps more scarlet, reflecting various shades as it is turned. It is remarkable that the upper side of this fungus, which must, as here, commonly be low on decaying wood, so that we look down on it, is not bright-colored nor handsome, and it was only when I had broken it off and turned it over that I was surprised by its brilliant color. This intense vermilion (?) face, which would be known to every boy in the town if it were turned upward, faces the earth and is discovered only by the curious naturalist. Its ear is turned down, listening to the honest praises of the earth. It is like a light-red velvet or damask.

Feb. 4. P.M.—To C. Miles Swamp.

There are many small spruce thereabouts, with small twigs and leaves, an abnormal growth, reminding one of strange species of evergreen from California, China, etc. I brought some home and had a cup of tea made, which, in spite of a slight piny or turpentine flavor, I thought unexpectedly good.

Feb. 18. George Minott tells me that he, when young, used often to go to a store by the side of where Bigelow's tavern was and kept by Ephraim Jones,—the Goodnow store. That was probably the one kept by my old trader. Told me how Casey, who was a slave to a man—Whitney—who lived where Hawthorne owns,—the same house,—before the Revolution, ran off one Sunday, was pursued by the neighbors, and hid himself in the river up to his neck till nightfall, just across the Great Meadows. He ran through Gowing's Swamp and came back that night to a Mrs. Cogswell, who lived where Charles Davis does, and got something to eat; then cleared far away, enlisted, and was freed as a soldier after the war. Whitney's boy threw snowballs at him the day before, and finally C., who was chopping in the yard, threw his axe at him, and W. said he was an ugly nigger and he must put him in jail. He may have been twenty years old when stolen from Africa; left a wife and one child there. Used to say that he went home to Africa in the night and came back again in the morning; *i.e.*, he dreamed of home. Lived to be old. Called Thanksgiving "Tom Kiver."

FEB. 20. Snows all day. The most wintry day of the winter; yet not more than three inches on a level is fallen.

We hear the names of the worthies of Concord,—Squire Cuming and the rest,—but the poor slave Casey seems to have lived a more adventurous life than any of them. Squire Cuming probably never had to run for his life on the plains of Concord.

March 4. Thermometer 14° this morning, and this makes decent sleighing of the otherwise soft snow.

Father Rasle's dictionary of the Abenaki language amounts to a very concentrated and trustworthy natural history of that people, though it was not completed. What they have a word for, they have a thing for. A traveller may tell us that he *thinks* they used a pavement, or built their cabins in a certain form, or soaked their seed corn in water, or had no beard, etc., etc.; but when one gives us the word for these things, the question is settled,—that is a clincher. Let us know what words they had and how they used them, and we can infer almost all the rest. The lexicographer not only *says* that a certain people have or do a certain thing, but, being evidently a disinterested party, it may be allowed that he brings sufficient evidence to prove it. He does not so much assert as exhibit. He has no transient or private purpose to serve.

March 16. How conversant the Indian who lived out of doors, who lay on the ground, must have been with mouse-ear leaves, pine-needles, mosses, and lichens, which form the crust of the earth. No doubt he had names accordingly for many things for which we have no popular names.

I walk in muddy fields, hearing the tinkling of newborn rills. Where the melted snow has made a swift rill in the rut of a cart-path, flowing over an icy bottom and between icy banks, I see, just below a little fall of one inch, a circular mass of foam or white bubbles nearly two inches in diameter, slowly revolving but never moving off. The swift stream at the fall appears to strike one side, as it might the side of a water-wheel, and so cause it to revolve, but in the angle between this and the fall, and half an inch distant, is another circle of bubbles, individually larger and more evanescent, only half an inch in diameter, revolving very rapidly in the opposite direction. The laws, perchance, by which the world was made, and according to which the systems revolve, are seen in full operation in a rill of melted snow.

March 18. 7 A.M.—By river.

How much more habitable a few birds make the fields! The note of the first bluebird in the air answers to the purling rill of melted snow beneath. It is eminently soft and soothing, and, as surely as the thermometer, indicates a higher temperature. It is the accent of the south wind, its vernacular. The song sparrow is more sprightly, mingling its notes with the rustling of the brash along the watersides, but it is at the same time more *terrene* than the bluebird. The first woodpecker comes screaming into the empty house and throws open doors and windows wide, calling out each of them to let the neighbors know of its return. I was not aware that the capacity to hear the woodpecker had slumbered within me so long. When the blackbird gets to a *conqueree* he seems to be dreaming of the sprays that are to be and on which he is to perch. The robin does not come singing, but utters a somewhat anxious or inquisitive peep at first. The song sparrow is immediately most at home of any that I have named. I see this afternoon as many as a dozen bluebirds on the warm side of a wood.

Each new year is a surprise to us. We find that we had virtually forgotten the note of each bird, and when we hear it again it is remembered like a dream, reminding us of a previous state of existence. How happens it that the associations it awakens are always pleasing, never saddening; reminiscences of our sanest hours? The voice of nature is always encouraging.

I sit on the Cliff, and look toward Sudbury. How circumscribed are our walks, after all! With the utmost industry we cannot expect to know well an area more than six miles square, and yet we pretend to be travellers, to be acquainted with Siberia and Africa!

March 19. Another pleasant and warm day. Painted my boat this afternoon. These spring impressions are not repeated the same year, at least not with the same force, for the next day the same phenomenon does not surprise us. Our appetite has lost its edge. The other day the face of the meadow wore a peculiar appearance, as if it were beginning to wake up under the influence of the southwest wind and the warm sun, but it cannot again this year present precisely that appearance to me. I have taken a step forward to a new position and must see something else. You perceive, and are affected by, changes too subtle to be described.

March 20. In the sluiceway of Pole Brook, by the road just beyond, I found another kind of Indian pot. It was an eel-pot (?) or creel, a wattled basket or wickerwork, made of willow osiers with the bark on, very artfully. It was about four feet long and shaped thus:

 About a dozen (or more) willow sticks, as big as one's finger or larger, being set small end down in a circle, in a thin

round board which made the bottom, and then smaller osiers interwoven at right angles with them, close and firm. Another funnel-shaped basket was secured within this, extending about half-way down it, as represented by the dotted lines, with an opening hardly two inches wide at the bottom, where only a dozen sharped sticks approached each other. There was a square door in the board bottom, by which the fishes could be taken out. This was set in that sluiceway, with the mouth or broad end down-stream, all sunk beneath the surface, the fishes being now evidently running up the brooks from the river and ponds, the ice being mostly gone out of the meadows and brooks. We raised this and found eight or ten small pickerel in it, the biggest a foot long, and one good-sized perch. It was pleasant to find that any were practicing such cunning art in the outskirts.* I am not sure whether this invention is Indian or derived from our own ancestors. "Creel" appears to be an old English word. But I have no doubt that the Indians used something very like this. How much more we might have learned of the aborigines if they had not been so reserved! Suppose they had generally become the laboring class among the whites, that my father had been a farmer and had an Indian for his hired man, how many aboriginal ways we children should have learned from them! It was very pleasant to meet with this kind of textile or basket in our walk, to know that some had leisure for other things than farming and town meeting, and that they felt the spring influence in their way. That man was not fitting for the State prison when he was weaving that creel. He was meditating a small poem in his way. It was equal to a successful stanza whose subject was spring.

We, too, are out, obeying the same law with all nature. Not less important are the observers of the birds than the birds themselves.

March 21. Warm rain, April-like, the first of the season, holding up from time to time, though always completely overcast.

This first spring rain is very agreeable. I love to hear the patter-

---

*Minott has known them to be set for musquash, and sometimes the musquash gnaw out, if not drowned.

ing of the drops on my umbrella, and I love also the wet scent of the umbrella.

March 29. By a pool southeast of Nathan Barrett's, see five or six painted turtles in the sun,—probably some were out yesterday,—and afterward, along a ditch just east of the pine hill near the river, a great many more, as many as twenty within a rod. I must have disturbed this afternoon one hundred at least. They have crawled out on to the grass on the sunny side of the ditches where there is a sheltering bank. Some have very broad yellow lines on the back; others are almost uniformly dark above. They hurry and tumble into the water at your approach, but several soon rise to the surface and just put their heads out to reconnoitre. Each trifling weed or clod is a serious impediment in their path, catching their flippers and causing them to tumble back. They never lightly skip over it. But then they have patience and perseverance, and plenty of time. The narrow edges of the ditches are almost paved in some places with their black and muddy backs.

March 30. The frogs are now heard leaping into the ditches on your approach, and their dimple is seen. I find a smallish bullfrog (?) under my boat. I do not remember that I ever hear this frog in the river or ponds. They seem to be an early frog, peculiar to pools and small ponds in the woods and fields.

March 31. C. says he saw a great many wood turtles on the bank of the Assabet to-day. The painted and wood turtles have seemed to be out in surprising abundance at an unusually early date this year, but I think I can account for it. The river is remarkably low, almost at summer level. I am not sure that I remember it so low at this season. Now, probably, these tortoises would always lie out in the sun at this season, if there were any bank at hand to lie on. Ordinarily at this season, the meadows being flooded, together with the pools and ditches in which the painted turtles lie, there is no bank exposed near their winter quarters for them to come out on, and I first noticed them under water on the meadow. But this year it is but a step for them to the sunny bank, and the shores of the Assabet and of ditches are lined with them.

April 8. Surveying Kettell farm.

Polly Houghton comes along and says, half believing it, of my compass, "This is what regulates the moon and stars."

April 15. Having stood quite still on the edge of the ditch close to the north edge of the maple swamp some time, and heard a slight rustling near me from time to time, I looked round and saw a mink under the bushes within a few feet. It was pure reddish-brown above, with a blackish and somewhat bushy tail, a blunt nose, and somewhat innocent-looking head. It crept along toward me and around me, *within two feet*, in a semicircle, snuffing the air, and pausing to look at me several times. Part of its course when nearest me was in the water of the ditch. It then crawled slowly away, and I saw by the ripple where it had taken to the ditch again. Perhaps it was after a frog, like myself.

The naturalist accomplishes a great deal by patience, more perhaps than by activity. He must take his position, and then wait and watch. It is equally true of quadrupeds and reptiles. Sit still in the midst of their haunts.

April 18. Frogs are strange creatures. One would describe them as peculiarly wary and timid, another as equally bold and imperturbable. All that is required in studying them is patience. You will sometimes walk a long way along a ditch and hear twenty or more leap in one after another before you, and see where they rippled the water, without getting sight of one of them. You sit down on the brink and wait patiently for his reappearance. After a quarter of an hour or more he is sure to rise to the surface and put out his nose quietly without making a ripple, eying you steadily. At length he becomes as curious about you as you can be about him. He suddenly hops straight toward you, pausing within a foot, and takes a near and leisurely view of you. Perchance you may now scratch its nose with your finger and examine it to your heart's content, for it is become as imperturbable as it was shy before. You conquer them by superior patience and immovableness; not by quickness, but by slowness; not by heat, but by coldness.*

April 19. Spend the day hunting for my boat, which was stolen. As I go up the riverside, I see a male marsh hawk hunting. He skims along exactly over the edge of the water, on the meadowy side, not more than three or four feet from the ground and winding with the shore, looking for frogs, for in such a tortuous line do the frogs sit. They probably know about what time to expect his visits, being regularly decimated. Particular hawks farm particular meadows. It must be easy for him to get a breakfast. Far as I can see with a glass, he is still tilting this way and that over the water-line.

May 1. The old *Salix sericea* is now all alive with the hum of honey-bees. This would show that it is in bloom. I see and hear one humblebee among them, inaugurating summer with his deep bass. May it be such a summer to me as it suggests. It sounds a little like mockery, however, to cheat me again with the promise of such tropical opportunities. I have learned to suspect him, as I do all fortune-tellers. But no sound so brings round the summer again. It is like the drum of May training.

May 2. If I were to be a frog hawk for a month I should soon know some things about the frogs. How patiently they skim the meadows,

---

*[A Concord farmer's perspective: "Why, one morning I went out in my field across there to the river, and there, beside that little old mud pond, was standing *Da*-a-vid Henry, and he wasn't doin' nothin' but just standin' there—lookin' at that pond, and when I came back at noon, there he was standin' with his hands behind him just lookin' down into that pond, and after dinner when I come back again if there wasn't *Da*-a-vid standin' there just like as if he had been there all day, gazin' down into that *pond*, and I stopped and looked at him and I says, 'Da-a-vid Henry, what air you a-doin'?' And he didn't turn his head and he didn't look at me. He kept on lookin' down at that pond, and he said, as if he was thinkin' about the stars in the heavens, 'Mr. Murray, I'm a-studyin'—the habits—of the bullfrog!' And there that darned fool had been standin'—the livelong day—a-studyin'—the habits—of the bull-frog!" (Quoted in Mrs. Daniel Chester French, *Memories of a Sculptor's Wife*, 1928.)]

occasionally alighting, and fluttering as if it were difficult ever to stand still on the ground. I have seen more of them than usual since I too have been looking for frogs.

May 4. I find hopping in the meadow a *Rana halecina*, much brighter than any I have seen this year. There is not only a vivid green halo about each spot, but the back is vivid light-green between the spots. I think this was not the case with any of the hundreds I saw a month ago!! Why??

Coming back, I talk with Witherell at William Wheeler's landing. He comes pushing Wheeler's square-ended boat down-stream with a fish-spear. Says he caught a snapping turtle in the river May 1st. He sits on the side of my boat by the shore a little while, talking with me. There is a hole in the knee of his pants as big as your hand, and he keeps passing his hand over this slowly, to hide his bare skin, which is sunburnt and the color of his face, though the latter is reddened by rum, of which his breath smells. But how intimate he is with mud and its inhabitants.

May 6. About 9 P.M. I went to the edge of the river to hear the frogs. Each shore of the river now for its whole length is all alive with this stertorous purring. In the mornings now, I hear no *R. palustris* and no hylodes, but a few toads still, but now, at night, all ring together, the toads ringing through the day, the hylodes beginning in earnest toward night and the *palustris* at evening. I think that the different epochs in the revolution of the seasons may perhaps be best marked by the notes of reptiles. They express, as it were, the very feelings of the earth or nature. They are perfect thermometers, hygrometers, and barometers.

No exercise implies more real manhood and vigor than joining thought to thought. How few men can tell what they have thought! I hardly know half a dozen who are not too lazy for this. They cannot get over some difficulty, and therefore they are on the long way round. You conquer fate by thought. If you think the fatal thought of men and institutions, you need never pull the trigger. The consequences of thinking inevitably follow. There is no more Herculean task than to think a thought about this life and then get it expressed.

May 7. Plant melons.

I see a wood tortoise by the river there, half covered with the old withered leaves. Taking it up, I find that it must have lain perfectly still there for some weeks, for though the grass is all green about it, when I take it up, it leaves just such a bare cavity, in which are seen the compressed white roots of the grass only, as when you take up a stone. This shows how sluggish these creatures are. It lets the season slide.

May 9. A dandelion perfectly gone to seed, a complete globe, a system in itself.

May 12. Saw some unusually broad chestnut planks, just sawed, at the mill. Barrett said that they came from Lincoln; whereupon I said that I guessed I knew where they came from, judging by their size alone, and it turned out that I was right. I had often gathered the nuts of those very trees and had observed within a year that they were cut down. So it appears that we have come to this, that if I see any peculiarly large chestnuts at the sawmill, I can guess where they came from, even know them in the log.

May 14. 5.30 A.M.—Up railroad.

I discovered this morning that a large rock three feet in diameter was partially hollow, and broke into it at length with a stone in order to reach some large black crystals which I could partly see. I found that it had been the retreat of a squirrel, and it had left many nuts there. It had entered a small hole bristling with crystals, and there found a chamber or grotto a foot long at least, surrounded on all sides by crystals.

Celandine by cemetery.

May 16. A hummingbird yesterday came into the next house and was caught. Flew about our parlor to-day and tasted Sophia's flowers.

In some lights you saw none of the colors of its throat. In others, in the shade the throat was a clear bright scarlet, but in the sun it glowed with splendid metallic, *fiery* reflections about the neck and throat. It uttered from time to time, as it flew, a faint squeaking chirp or chirrup. The hum sounded more hollow when it approached a flower. Its wings fanned the air so forcibly that you felt the cool wind they raised a foot off, and nearer it was very remarkable. Does not this very motion of the wings keep a bird cool in hot weather?

P.M.—To Flint's Pond.

Sat down in the sun but soon, hearing a slight rustling, I looked round and saw a very large black snake about five feet long on the dry leaves, about a rod off. When I moved, it vibrated its tail very rapidly and smartly, which made quite a loud rustling or rattling sound, reminding me of the rattlesnake, as if many snakes obeyed the same instinct as the rattlesnake when they vibrate their tails. Once I thought I heard a low hiss. Suddenly, as it moved along, it erected itself half its length, and when I thought it was preparing to strike at me, to my surprise it glided up a slender oak sapling about an inch in diameter at the ground and ten feet high. It moved up in a somewhat zigzag manner, availing itself of the branches, yet also in part spirally about the main stem. It finds a rest (or hold if necessary) for its neck or forward part of its body, moving crosswise the small twigs, then draws up the rest of its body. From the top of this little oak it passed into the top of a white pine of the same height an inch and a half in diameter at the ground and two feet off; from this into another oak, fifteen feet high and three feet from the pine; from this to another oak, three feet from the last and about the same height; from this to a large oak about four feet off and three or four inches in diameter, in which it was about fourteen feet from the ground; thence through two more oaks, a little lower, at intervals of four feet, and so into a white pine; and at last into a smaller white pine and thence to the ground. It moved quite deliberately for the most part, choosing its course from tree to tree with great skill, and resting from time to time while it watched me, only my approach compelling it to move again. It surprised me very much to see it cross from tree to tree exactly like a squirrel, where there appeared little or no support for such a body. It would glide down the proper twig, its body resting at intervals of a foot or two, on the smaller side twigs, perchance, and then would easily cross an interval of two feet, sometimes in an ascending, sometimes a descending, direction. If the latter, its weight at last bent the first twig down nearer to the opposite one. It would extend its neck very much, as I could see by the increased width of the scales exposed, till its neck rested across the opposite twig, hold on all the while tightly to some part of the last twig by the very tip of its tail, which was curled round it just like a monkey's. I have hardly seen a squirrel *rest* on such slight twigs as it would rest on in mid-air, while its body stretched *clear* a foot at least between two trees. It was not at all like creeping over a coarse basketwork, but suggested long practice and skill, like the ropedancer's. There were no limbs for it to use comparable for size with its own body, and you hardly noticed the few slight twigs it rested on, as it glided through the air. When its neck rested on the opposite twig, it was, as it were, glued to it. It helped itself over or up them as surely as if it grasped with a hand. There were, no doubt, rigid kinks in its body when they were needed for support. It is a sort of endless hook, and, by its ability to bend its body in every direction, it finds some support on every side. Perhaps the edges of its scales give it a hold also. It is evident that it can take the young birds out of a sapling of any height, and no twigs are so small and pliant as to prevent it. I have no doubt that this snake could have reached many of the oriole-nests which I have seen. I noticed that in its anger its rigid neck was very much flattened or compressed vertically. At length it coiled itself upon itself as if to strike, and, I presenting a stick, it struck it smartly and then darted away, running swiftly down the hill toward the pond.

Yellow butterflies. Nabalus leaves are already up and coming up in the wood-paths.

May 17. When the hummingbird flew about the room yesterday, his body and tail hung in a singular manner between the wings, swinging back and forth with a sort of oscillating motion, not hanging directly down, but yet pulsating or teetering up and down.

I see a chewink flit low across the road with its peculiar flirting, undulating motion.

It is remarkable how little way most men get in their account of the mysteries of nature. Puffer, after describing the habits of a snake or turtle,—some peculiarity which struck him in its behavior,—would say with a remarkable air as if he were communicating or suggesting something, possibly explaining something, "Now I take it *that* is Nature; Nature did that."

May 24. Monday. To New York by railroad.

In the evening, looked at the aquarium at Barnum's. The glass boxes with nothing but water (labelled fresh or salt) and pebbles seemed sufficiently interesting. The sea-anemones were new and interesting to me. The ferns, etc., under glass a fine parlor ornament.

May 25. Visited the Egyptian Museum.

The chariot wheel might have been picked out of a ditch in Carlisle, and the infant's shoe have been found with it.

June 2. 8.30 A.M.—Start for Monadnock. Blake joins me at Fitchburg. Arrived at Troy Station at 11.5 and shouldered our knapsacks, steering northeast to the mountain, some four miles off,—its top.

Almost without interruption we had the mountain in sight before us,—its sublime gray mass—that antique, brownish-gray, Ararat color. Probably these crests of the earth are for the most part of one color in all lands, that gray color of antiquity, which nature loves; color of unpainted wood, weather-stain, time-stain; not glaring nor gaudy; the color of all roofs, the color of things that endure, and the color that wears well; color of Egyptian ruins, of mummies and all antiquity; baked in the sun, done brown; not scarlet, like the crest of the bragging cock, but that hard, enduring gray; a terrene sky-color; solidified air with a tinge of earth.

Notwithstanding the newspaper and egg-shell left by visitors, these parts of nature are still peculiarly unhandselled and untracked.

One, who was probably a blacksmith, had sculptured the emblems of his craft, an anvil and hammer, beneath his name. Apparently a part of the regular outfit of mountain-climbers is a hammer and cold-chisel. It reminds what kinds of steeps do climb the false pretenders to fame, whose chief exploit is the carriage of the tools with which to inscribe their names. For speaking epitaphs they are, and the mere name is a sufficient revelation of the character. They are all of one trade,—stone-cutters, defacers of mountain-tops. "Charles & Lizzie!" Charles carried the sledge-hammer, and Lizzie the cold-chisel. Some have carried up a paint-pot, and painted their names on the rocks.

[*16 pages of nature notes on this trip, covering birds, flowers, rocks, bogs, toad spawn, spruce trees, lichens, pools, views, sandy or gravelly scars, and clouds (their height, their shadows).*]

XXVI.

June 7. I sit in my boat in the twilight by the edge of the river. Toads are now in full blast along the river. Some sit quite out at the edge of the pads, and hold up their heads so high when they ring, and make such a large bubble, that they look as if they would tumble over backward. Bullfrogs now are in full blast. I do not hear other frogs; their notes are probably drowned. I perceive that this generally is the rhythm of the bullfrog: *er | er-r | er-r-r |* (growing fuller and fuller and more tremendous) and then doubling, *er, er | er, err | er, er, er | er, er, er |* and finally *er, er, er, er | er, er, er, er.* Or I might write it *oorar | oorar | oorar | oorar-hah | oorar-hah hah | oorar hah hah hah.* What lungs, what health, what terrenity (if not serenity) it suggests! Seeing a large head, with its prominent eyes, projecting above the middle of the river, I found it was a bullfrog coming across. It swam under water a rod or two, and then came up to see where it was, or its way. It is thus they cross when sounds or sights attract them to more desirable shores.

Fireflies pretty numerous over the river, though we have had no thunder-showers of late. Mosquitoes quite troublesome here.

JUNE 12. Rains all day. Much water falls.

June 18. Coming across the level pasture west of E. Hubbard's swamp, toward Emerson's, I find a young *Emys insculpta*, apparently going to lay, though she had not dug a hole. It was four and a quarter inches long by three and a half wide, and altogether the handsomest turtle of this species, if not of any, that I have ever seen. It was quite fresh and perfect, without wound or imperfection; its claws quite sharp and slender, and the annual striæ so distinct on all the scales above and below that I could count them with ease. It was nine years old, though it would be like an infant among turtles, the successive striæ being perfectly parallel at equal distances apart. The sternum, with a large black spot on the rear angle of each scale and elsewhere a rich brown color, even reminded me of the turtle-shell of commerce. While its upper shell was of a uniform wholesome brown, very prettily marked indeed, not only by the outlines of the scales, but more distinctly by the lines of prominences raying out from the starting-point of each scale, perfectly preserved in each year's growth, a most elaborate coat of mail, worthy the lifelong labor of some reptilian Vulcan. This must have been a belle among the *E. insculpta.* Nevertheless I did discover that all the claws but one of one hind foot were gone! Had not a bird pecked them off? So liable are they to injury in their long lives. Then they are so well-behaved; can be taken up and brought home in your pocket, and make no unseemly efforts to escape. The upper shell was remarkably spreading and curving upward on the rear edges.

June 20. I notice that when turtles are floating dead their necks and legs are stretched out. What kills them?

June 29. P.M.—To Walden.

Bathing in the cove by railroad. When I hold my head near the surface and look down, in two or three feet of water, the bottom appears concave, just as the sky does.

July 2. A.M.—Start for White Mountains in a private carriage with Edward Hoar.

Spent the noon close by the old Dunstable graveyard, by a small stream north of it.

Walked to and along the river and bathed in it.

What a relief and expansion of my thoughts when I come out to this broad river's shore! This vista was incredible there. Suddenly I see a broad reach of blue beneath, with its curves and headlands, liberating me from the more terrene earth. What a difference it makes whether I spend my four hours' nooning between the hills by yonder roadside, or on the brink of this fair river, within a quarter of a mile of that! This current allies me to all the world. Be careful to sit in an elevating and inspiring place. It is equal to a different season and country and creates a different mood. There is something in the scenery of a broad river equivalent to culture and civilization. Its channel conducts our thoughts as well as bodies to classic and famous ports, and allies us to all that is fair and great. I like to remember that at the end of half a day's walk I can stand on the bank of the Merrimack. It is just wide enough to interrupt the land and lead my eye and thoughts down its channel to the sea. A river is superior to a lake in its liberating influence. It has motion and indefinite length. A river touching the back of a town is like a wing, it may be unused as yet, but ready to waft it over the world. With its rapid current it is a slightly fluttering wing. River towns are winged towns.

[*This trip takes up 57 pages in the Journal, including Mt. Washington and Mt. Lafayette, treacherous fog, a badly sprained ankle, accidentally starting a scrub fire, "the grandest mountain view I ever got," and speculation about why peaks seem pyramidal from a distance, along with pages of botanical observation and reading notes.*]

XXVII.

July 18. Sunday. A marked difference when we enter Massachusetts, in roads, farms, houses, trees, fences, etc.,—a great improvement, showing an older-settled country. In New Hampshire there is a greater want of shade trees, but long bleak or sunny roads from which there is no escape. What barbarians we are!

July 19. Get home at noon.

For such an excursion as the above, carry and wear:—

Three strong check shirts.

Two pairs socks.

Neck ribbon and handkerchief.

Three pocket-handkerchiefs.

One thick waistcoat.

One thin (or half-thick) coat.

One thick coat (for mountain).

A large, broad india-rubber knapsack, with a *broad* flap.

A flannel shirt.

India-rubber coat.

Three bosoms (to go and come in).

A napkin.

Pins, needles, thread.

A blanket.

A cap to lie in at night.

Tent (or a large simple piece of india-rubber cloth for the mountain tops?).

Veil and *gloves* (or enough millinet to cover all at night).

Map and compass.

Plant book and paper.

Paper and stamps.

Botany, spy-glass, microscope.

Tape, insect-boxes.

Jack-knife and clasp-knife.

Fish-line and hooks.

Matches.

Soap and dish-cloths.

Waste-paper and twine.

Iron spoon.

Pint dipper with a pail-handle added (not to put out the fire), and perhaps a bag to carry water in.

Frying-pan, only if you ride.

Hatchet (sharp), if you ride, and perhaps in any case on mountain, with a sheath to it.

Hard-bread (sweet crackers good); a moist, sweet plum cake very good and lasting; pork, corned beef or tongue, sugar, tea or coffee, and a little salt.

It is surprising how much more bewildering is a mountain-top than a level area of the same extent. Its ridges and shelves and ravines add greatly to its apparent extent and diversity. You may be separated from your party by only stepping a rod or two out of the path.

July 29. In the Chinese novel "Ju-Kiao-Li, or The Two Fair Cousins," I find in a motto to a chapter (quoted): "He who aims at success should be continually on his guard against a thousand accidents. How many preparations are necessary before the sour plum begins to sweeten! ... But if supreme happiness was to be attained in the space of an hour, of what use would be in life the noblest sentiments?" (Page 227.) Also these verses on page 230:—

"Nourished by the study of ten thousand different works,

The pen in hand, one is equal to the gods.

Let not humility take its rank amongst virtues:

Genius never yields the palm that belongs to it."
Again, page 22, vol. ii:—

> "If the spring did not announce its reign by the return of the
> leaves,
> The moss, with its greenish tints, would find favor in men's
> eyes."

Aug. 6. I think that I speak impartially when I say that I have never met with a stream so suitable for boating and botanizing as the Concord, and fortunately nobody knows it. I know of reaches which a single country-seat would spoil beyond remedy, but there has not been any important change here since I can remember. The willows slumber along its shore, piled in light but low masses, even like the cumuli clouds above. We pass haymakers in every meadow, who may think that we are idlers. But Nature takes care that every nook and crevice is explored by some one. While they look after the open meadows, we farm the tract between the river's brinks and behold the shores from that side. We, too, are harvesting an annual crop with our eyes, and think you Nature is not glad to display her beauty to us?

This is pure summer; no signs of fall in this, though I have seen some maples, as above the Assabet Spring, already prematurely reddening, owing to the water.

Every board and chip cast into the river is soon occupied by one or more turtles of various sizes. The sternothærus oftenest climbs up the black willows, even three or more feet.

I hear of pickers ordered out of the huckleberry-fields, and I see stakes set up with written notices forbidding any to pick there. Some let their fields, or allow so much for the picking. *Sic transit gloria ruris.* We are not grateful enough that we have lived part of our lives before these evil days came. What becomes of the true value of country life? What if you must go to market for it? Shall things come to such a pass that the butcher commonly brings round huckleberries in his cart? It is as if the hangman were to perform the marriage ceremony, or were to preside at the communion table.

Such is the inevitable tendency of *our* civilization,—to reduce huckleberries to a level with beef-steak.

Aug. 7. Saturday. P.M.—Up Assabet.

The most luxuriant groves of black willow, *as I recall them*, are on the inside curves, or on sandy capes between the river and a bay, or sandy banks parallel with the firmer shore. They also grow on both sides sometimes, where the river runs straight through stagnant meadows or swamps,—*e.g.* above Hollowell Bridge,—or on one side, though straight, along the edge of a swamp,—as above Assabet Spring,—but rarely ever against a firm bank or hillside, the positive male shore. Measured the two largest of three below Dove Rock.

The *Sternothærus odoratus* knows them well, for it climbs highest up their stems, three or four feet or more nowadays, sometimes seven or eight along the slanting branches, and is frequently caught and hung by the neck in its forks. They do not so much jump as tumble off when disturbed by a passer. They will climb four feet up a stem not more than two inches in diameter, and yet undo all their work in an instant by tumbling off when your boat goes by. The trunk is covered with coarse, long, and thick upraised scales. It is this turtle's castle and path to heaven. He is on the upward road along the stem of the willow, and by its dark stem it is partially concealed.

How long will it be after we have passed before the mud tortoise has climbed to its perch again?

The author of the Chinese novel "Ju-Kiao-Li," some eight hundred years ago, appears to have appreciated the beauty of willows. Pe, his principal character, moved out of the city late in life, to a stream bordered with willows, about twenty miles distant, in order to spend the rest of his days drinking wine and writing verses there. He describes the eyebrow of his heroine as like a willow leaf floating on the surface of the water.

Aug. 8. Looking north from Hubbard's Bridge about 4 P.M., the wind being southeasterly, I am struck by the varied lights of the river. The wind, which is a considerable breeze, strikes the water by a very irregular serrated edge about mid-channel, and then abruptly leaves it on a distinct and regular meandering line, about eight feet from the outer edge of the pads on the west side. The rippled portion of the river is blue, the rest smooth, silvery. Thus to my eye the river is divided into five portions,—first the weedy and padded borders, then a smooth, silvery stripe, eight or ten feet wide, and next the blue rippled portion, succeeded by the broader silver, and the pads of the eastern side. How many aspects the river wears, depending on the height of the water, the season of the year and state of vegetation, the wind, the position of the sun and condition of the heavens, etc., etc.! Apparently such is the angle at which the wind strikes the river from over the bushes that it falls about mid-channel, and then it is either obliged to leave it at a nearly similar angle on account of the opposite shore and bushes, or, perchance,

the smoothing influence of the pads is felt to some distance beyond their edges. The line which separates the smooth from the rippled portion is as distinct and continuous as that which marks the edge of the pads. I think that 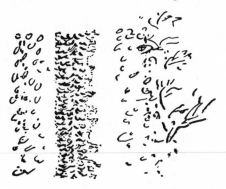 there is more oily matter floating on the stiller sides of the river, and this too may have something to do with the above phenomenon. Then there is the watered appearance of the surface in a shower.

Aug. 11. The great bullfrogs, of various colors from dark brown to greenish yellow, lie out on the surface of these slimy pools or in the shallow water by the shore, motionless and philosophic. Toss a chip to one, and he will instantly leap and seize and drop it as quick. Motionless and indifferent as they appear, they are ready to leap upon their prey at any instant.

Aug. 12. When I came down-stairs this morning, it raining hard and steadily, I found an Irishman sitting with his coat on his arm in the kitchen, waiting to see me. He wanted to inquire what I thought the weather would be to-day! I sometimes ask my aunt, and she consults the almanac. So we shirk the responsibility.

It clears up before noon and is now very warm and clear. When I look at the sparrows on the fences, yellow-browed and bay-wings, they all have their bills open and are panting with heat. Apparently the end of the very wet weather we have had about a fortnight.

Aug. 13. As I am paddling up the north side above the Hemlocks, I am attracted by the singular shadows of the white lily pads on the rich-brown muddy bottom. It is remarkable how light tends to pre-vail over shadow there. It steals in under the densest curtain of pads and illustrates the bottom. The shadows of these pads, seen (now at 3 P.M.) a little one side, where the water is eighteen inches or two feet deep, are rarely orbicular or entire-edged or resembling the leaf, but are more or less perfect rosettes, generally of an oval form, with five to fifteen or more regularly rounded petals, open half-way to the centre: or You cannot com-monly refer the shadow to its sub-stance but by touching the leaf with your paddle. Light knows a thousand tricks by which it pre-vails. Light is the rule, shadow the exception. The leaf fails to cast a shadow equal in area to itself. While it is a regular and almost solid disk, the shadow is a rosette or palmate, as if the sun, in its haste to illustrate every nook, shone round the shortest corner. Generally the two sharp angles of the pad are almost entirely eroded in the shadow. The shadows, too, have a slight halo about them. Such endless and varied play of light and shadow is on the river bottom! It is protean and somewhat weird even. The shadow of the leaf might be mistaken for that of the flower. The sun play-ing with a lily leaf draws the outline of a lily on the bottom with its shadow.

I landed in the Lee Wood. Perhaps those woods might be called Mantatukwet's, for he says he lived at the foot of Nawshawtuct about fifty years before 1684.

Aug. 14. Suggesting to C. an Indian name for one of our localities, he thought it had too many syllables for a place so near the middle of the town,—as if the more distant and less frequented place might have a longer name, less understood and less alive in its syllables.

To speak from recollection, the birds which I *have chanced to hear* of late are (running over the whole list):—

The squealing notes of young hawks.

Occasionally a red-wing's *tchuck*.

The *link* of bobolinks.

The *chickadee* and *phebe* note of the chickadees, five or six together occasionally.

The *fine* note of the cherry-bird, pretty often.

The twitter of the kingbird, pretty often.

The wood pewee, with its young, peculiarly common and prominent.

Only the *peep* of the robin.

The pine warbler, occasionally.

The bay-wing, pretty often.

The seringo, pretty often.

The song sparrow, often.

The field sparrow, often.

The goldfinch, a prevailing note, with variations into a fine song.

The ground-robin, *once* of late.

The flicker's cackle, *once* of late.

The nighthawk, as usual.

I have not been out early nor late, nor attended particularly to the birds. The more characteristic notes would appear to be the wood pewee's and the goldfinch's, with the squeal of young hawks. These might be called the pewee-days.

Aug. 15. Rain in the night and dog-day weather again, after two clear days. I do not like the name "dog-days." Can we not have a new name for this season? It is the season of mould and mildew, and foggy, muggy, often rainy weather.

The black willows are already being imbrowned. It must be the effect of the water, for we have had no drought.

Might not the potamogeton be called *waving weed*?

Aug. 16. In my boating of late I have several times scared up a couple of summer ducks of this year, bred in our meadows. They allowed me to come quite near, and helped to people the river. I have not seen them for some days. Would you know the end of our intercourse? Goodwin shot them, and Mrs. ——, who never sailed on the river, ate them. Of course, she knows not what she did. What if I should eat her canary? Thus we share each other's sins as well as burdens. The lady who watches admiringly the matador shares his deed. They belonged to me, as much as to any one, when they were alive, but it was considered of more importance that Mrs. —— should taste the flavor of them dead than that I should enjoy the beauty of them alive.

Talked with Minott, who sits in his wood-shed, having, as I notice, several seats there for visitors,—one a block on the saw-horse, another a patchwork mat on a wheelbarrow, etc., etc. His half-grown chickens which roost overhead, perch on his shoulder or knee. He tells me some of his hunting stories again. He always lays a good deal of stress on the kind of gun he used, as if he had bought a new one every year, when probably he never had more than two or three in his life. In this case it was a "half-stocked" one, a little "cocking-piece," and whenever he finished his game he used the word "gavel," I think in this way, "gave him gavel," *i.e.* made him bite the dust, or settled him. He used to love to hear the goldfinches sing on the hemp which grew near his gate.

Aug. 17. Minott has only lately been reading Shattuck's "History of Concord," and he says that his account is not right by a jugful, that he does not come within half a mile of the truth, not as he has heard tell.

Aug. 18. Having left my note-book at home, I strip off a piece of birch bark for paper. It begins at once to curl up, yellow side out, but I hold that side to the sun, and as soon as it is dry it gives me no more trouble.

Heard a nuthatch.*

Last evening one of our neighbors, who has just completed a costly house and front yard, the most showy in the village, illuminated in honor of the Atlantic telegraph. I read in great letters before the house the sentence "Glory to God in the highest." But it seemed to me that that was not a sentiment to be illuminated, but to keep dark about. A simple and genuine sentiment of reverence would not emblazon these words as on a signboard in the streets. They were exploding countless crackers beneath it, and gay company, passing in and out, made it a kind of housewarming. I felt a kind of shame for it, and was inclined to pass quickly by, the ideas of indecent exposure and cant being suggested. What is religion? That which is never spoken.

Aug. 22. P.M.—I have spliced my old sail to a new one, and now go out to try it in a sail to Baker Farm. It is a "square sail," some five feet by six. I like it much. It pulls like an ox, and makes me think there's more wind abroad than there is. The yard goes about with a pleasant force, almost enough, I would fain imagine, to knock me overboard. How sturdily it pulls, shooting us along, catching more wind than I knew to be wandering in this river valley! It suggests a new power in the sail, like a Grecian god. I can even worship it, after a heathen fashion. And then, how it becomes my boat and the river,—a simple homely square sail, all for use not show, so low and broad! The boat is like a plow drawn by a winged bull. If I had had this a dozen years ago, my voyages would have been performed more quickly and easily. But then probably I should have lived less in them. I land on a remote shore at an unexpectedly early hour, and have time for a long walk there.

As for the beauty of the river's brim: now that the mikania begins to prevail the button-bush has done, the pontederia is waning, and the willows are already somewhat crisped and imbrowned

---

*And a week later. Not heard since spring.

(though the last may be none the worse for it); lilies, too, are as good as gone. So perhaps I should say that the brim of the river was in its prime about the 1st of August this year, when the pontederia and button-bush and white lilies were in their glory. The cyperus now yellows edges of pools and half-bare low grounds.

See one or two blue herons every day now, driving them far up or down the river before me.

Aug. 23. Cooler than ever. Some must have fires, and I close my window.

Everywhere in woods and swamps I am already reminded of the fall. I see the spotted sarsaparilla leaves and brakes, and, in swamps, the withering and blackened skunk-cabbage and hellebore, and, by the river, the already blackening pontederias and pipes. There is no plateau on which Nature rests at midsummer, but she instantly commences the descent to winter.

High blackberries now in their prime, their great racemes of shining black fruit, mixed with red and green, bent over amid the sweet-fern and sumach on sunny hillsides, or growing more rankly with larger fruit by rich roadsides and in lower ground.

Smooth sumach berries all turned crimson.

Emerson says that he and Agassiz and Company broke some dozens of ale-bottles, one after another, with their bullets, in the Adirondack country, using them for marks! It sounds rather Cockneyish. He says that he shot a peetweet for Agassiz, and this, I think he said, was the first game he ever bagged. He carried a double-barrelled gun,—rifle and shotgun,—which he bought for the purpose, which he says received much commendation,—all parties thought it a very pretty piece. Think of Emerson shooting a peetweet (with shot) for Agassiz, and cracking an ale-bottle (after emptying it) with his rifle at six rods! They cut several pounds of lead out of the tree. It is just what Mike Saunders, the merchant's clerk, did when he was there.

Aug. 24. It is a strong but fitful northwest wind, stronger than before. Under my new sail, the boat dashes off like a horse with the bits in his teeth. Coming into the main stream below the island, a sudden flaw strikes me, and in my efforts to keep the channel I run one side under, and so am compelled to beach my boat there and bail it.

I am flattered because my stub sail frightens a haymakers' horse tied under a maple while his masters are loading. His nostrils dilate; he snorts and tries to break loose. He eyes with terror this white wind steed. No wonder he is alarmed at my introducing such a competitor into the river meadows.

Now and of late we remember hazel bushes,—we become aware of such a fruit-bearing bush. They have their turn, and every clump and hedge seems composed of them.

Aug. 28. Soaking rain last night, straight down. Especially the scarlet leaves of the cultivated cherry are seen to have fallen. When, as I go to the post-office this morning, I see these bright leaves strewing the moist ground on one side of the tree and blown several rods from it into a neighboring yard, I am reminded that I have crossed the summit ridge of the year and have begun to descend the other slope. The prospect is now toward winter. These are among the first-fruits of the leafy harvest.

Aug. 29. Has not the mind, too, its harvest? Do not some scarlet leaves of thought come scatteringly down, though it may be prematurely, some which, perchance, the summer's drought has ripened, and the rain loosened?

How hard one must work in order to acquire his language,— words by which to express himself! I have known a particular rush, for instance, for at least twenty years, but have ever been prevented from describing some of its peculiarities, because I did not know its name nor any one in the neighborhood who could tell me it. With the knowledge of the name comes a distincter recognition and knowledge of the thing. That shore is now more describable, and poetic even. My knowledge was cramped and confined before, and grew rusty because not used,—for it could not be used. My knowledge now becomes communicable and grows by communication. I can now learn what others know about the same thing.

Sept. 6. On the hillside above Clamshell Ditch, grows that handsome grass of Sept. 1st (*vide* September 4th), evidently *Sorghum nutans* (*Andropogon* of Bigelow), chestnut beard grass, Indian grass, wood grass. It is much larger than what I saw before; is still abundantly in flower; four and a half feet high. It is a very handsome, wild-looking grass, well enough called Indian grass, and I should have named it with the other andropogons, August 26th. It stands like an Indian chief taking a last look at his beloved hunting-grounds. The expression of this grass haunted me for a week after I first passed and noticed it, like the glance of an eye.

Sept. 7. I turn Anthony's corner. It is an early September afternoon, melting warm and sunny; the thousands of grasshoppers leaping before you reflect gleams of light; a little distance off the field is yellowed with a Xerxean army of *Solidago nemoralis* between me and the sun; the earth-song of the cricket comes up through all; and ever and anon the hot z-ing of the locust is heard. (Poultry is now fattening on grasshoppers.) The dry deserted fields are one mass of yellow, like a color shoved to one side on Nature's palette. You literally wade in yellow flowers knee-deep.

What a contrast to sink your head so as to cover your ears with water, and hear only the confused noise of the rushing river, and then to raise your ears above water and hear the steady creaking of crickets in the aerial universe!

Sept. 9. It requires a different intention of the eye in the same locality to see different plants, as, for example, *Juncaceæ* and *Gramineæ* even; *i.e.*, I find that when I am looking for the former, I do not see the latter in their midst. How much more, then, it requires different intentions of the eye and of the mind to attend to different departments of knowledge! How differently the poet and the naturalist look at objects! A man sees only what concerns him. A botanist absorbed in the pursuit of grasses does not distinguish the grandest pasture oaks. He as it were tramples down oaks unwittingly in his walk.

Sept. 29. Two blue herons, or "herns," as Goodwin calls them, fly sluggishly up the stream. Interesting even is a stake, with its reflection, left standing in the still river by some fisherman.

Again we have smooth waters, yellow foliage, and faint warbling birds, etc., as in spring. The year thus repeats itself.

Oct. 2. The garden is alive with migrating sparrows these mornings. The cat comes in from an early walk amid the weeds. She is full of sparrows and wants no more breakfast this morning, unless it be a saucer of milk, the dear creature. I saw her studying ornithology between the corn-rows.

Oct. 18. Let us have willows for spring, elms for summer, maples and walnuts and tupelos for autumn, evergreens for winter, and oaks for all seasons. What is a gallery in a house to a gallery in the streets! An avenue of elms as large as our largest, and three miles long, would seem to lead to some admirable place, though only Concord were at the end of it.

Oct. 19. A remarkably warm day. The thermometer says 74° at 1 P.M. This must be Indian summer.

P.M.—Ride to Sam Barrett's mill.

Am pleased again to see the cobweb drapery of the mill. Each fine line hanging in festoons from the timbers overhead and on the sides, and on the discarded machinery lying about, is covered and greatly enlarged by a coating of meal, by which its curve is revealed, like the twigs under their ridges of snow in winter. It is like the tassels and tapestry of counterpane and dimity in a lady's bedchamber, and I pray that the cobwebs may not have been brushed away from the mills which I visit. All things in the mill wear the same livery or drapery, down to the miller's hat and coat. I knew Barrett forty rods off in the cranberry meadow by the meal on his hat.

Barrett's apprentice, it seems, makes trays of black birch and of red maple, in a dark room under the mill. I was pleased to see this work done here, a wooden tray is so handsome. You could count the circles of growth on the end of the tray, and the dark heart of the tree was seen at each end above, producing a semicircular orna-ment. To see the tree reappear on the table, instead of going to the fire or some equally coarse use, is some compensation for having it cut down.

Standing on Hunt's Bridge at 5 o'clock, the sun just ready to set, I notice that its light on my note-book is quite rosy or purple, though the sun itself and its halo are merely yellow, and there is no purple in the western sky. Perhaps I might have detected a purple tinge already in the eastern sky, had I looked, and I was exactly at that distance this side the sunset where the foremost of the rosy waves of light roll in the wake of the sun, and the white page was the most suitable surface to reflect it.[*]

I was the more pleased with the sight of the trays because the tools used were so simple, and they were made by hand, not by machinery. They may make equally good pails, and cheaper as well as faster, at the pail-factory with the home-made ones, but that interests me less, because the man is turned partly into a machine there himself. In this case, the workman's relation to his work is more poetic, he also shows more dexterity and is more of a man. You come away from the great factory saddened, as if the chief end of man were to make pails; but, in the case of the countryman who makes a few by hand, rainy days, the relative importance of human life and of pails is preserved, and you come away thinking of the simple and helpful life of the man,—you do not turn pale at the thought,—and would fain go to making pails yourself.

Oct. 22. I can see the red of young oaks as far as the horizon on some sides.

I see, from the Cliffs, that color has run through the shrub oak plain like a fire or a wave, not omitting a single tree, though I had not expected it,—large oaks do not turn so completely,—and now

---

[*]*Vide* Sept. 24, 1851.

is for the most part burnt out for want of fuel, *i.e.* excepting the scarlet ones. The brown and chocolate colors prevail there.

These bright leaves are not the exception but the rule, for I believe that *all* leaves, even grasses, etc., etc.,—*Panicum clandestinum*,—and mosses, as sphagnum, under favorable circumstances acquire brighter colors just before their fall. When you come to observe faithfully the changes of each humblest plant, you find, it may be unexpectedly, that each has sooner or later its peculiar autumnal tint or tints, though it may be rare and unobserved, as many a plant is at all seasons.

Oct. 24. A northeast storm, though not much rain falls to-day, but a fine driving mizzle or "drisk." This, as usual, brings the geese, and at 2.30 P.M. I see two flocks go over.

P.M.—To Woodis Park over Hill.

The brilliant autumnal colors are red and yellow and the various tints, hues, and shades of these. Blue is reserved to be the color of the sky, but yellow and red are the colors of the earth flower. Every fruit, on ripening, and just before its fall, acquires a bright tint. So do the leaves; so the sky before the end of the day, and the year near its setting. October is the red sunset sky, November the later twilight. Color stands for all ripeness and success. We have dreamed that the hero should carry his color aloft, as a symbol of the ripeness of his virtue.

That large hornets' nest which I saw on the 4th is now deserted, and I bring it home. But in the evening, warmed by my fire, two or three come forth and crawl over it, and I make haste to throw it out the window.

Oct. 26. Minott remembers how he used to chop beech wood. He says that when frozen it is hard and brittle just like glass, and you must look out for the chips, for, if they strike you in the face, they will cut like a knife.

He says that some call the stake-driver "belcher-squelcher," and some, "wollerkertoot." I used to call them "pump-er-gor´." Some say "slug-toot."

I wear a thicker coat, my single thick fall coat, at last, and begin to feel my fingers cool early and late.

One shopkeeper has hung out woollen gloves and even thick buckskin mittens by his door, foreseeing what his customers will want as soon as it is finger-cold, and determined to get the start of his fellows.

Oct. 27. The bayonet rush has partly changed, and now, the river being perhaps lower than before this season, shows its rainbow colors, though dull. I distinguish four colors now, perfectly horizontal and parallel bars, as it were, six or eight inches wide as you look at the side of a dense patch along the shallow shore. The lowest is a dull red, the next clear green, then dull yellowish, and then dark brown. These colors, though never brilliant, are yet noticeable, and, when you look at a long and dense patch, have a rainbow-like effect. The red (or pinkish) is that part which has been recently submerged; the green, that which has not withered; the yellowish, what has changed; and the brown, the withered extremity, since it dies downward gradually from the tip to the bottom. The amount of it is that it decays gradually, beginning at the top, and, moreover, the whole being of a uniform height, a particular color in one plant corresponds exactly to the same in another, and so, though a single stalk would not attract attention, when seen in the mass they have this singular effect. I call it, therefore, the rainbow rush. When, moreover, you see it reflected in the water, the effect is very much increased.

We have a cool, white sunset, Novemberish, and no redness to warm our thoughts.

It is impossible to describe the infinite variety of hues, tints, and shades, for the language affords no names for them, and we must apply the same term monotonously to twenty different things. If I could exhibit so many different trees, or only leaves, the effect would be different. When the tints are the same they differ so much in purity and delicacy that language, to describe them truly, would have not only to be greatly enriched, but as it were dyed to the same colors herself, and speak to the eye as well as to the ear. And it is these subtle differences which especially attract and charm our eyes. To describe these colored leaves you must use colored words. Who will undertake to describe in words the difference in tint between two neighboring leaves on the same tree? or of two thousand?—for by so many the eye is addressed in a glance. In describing the richly spotted leaves, for instance, how often we find ourselves using ineffectually words which merely indicate faintly our good intentions, giving them in our despair a terminal twist toward our mark,—such as redd*ish*, yellow*ish*, purpl*ish*, etc. We cannot make a hue of words, for they are not to be compounded like colors, and hence we are obliged to use such ineffectual expressions as reddish brown, etc. They need to be ground together.

Oct. 29. Nature now, like an athlete, begins to strip herself in earnest for her contest with her great antagonist Winter. In the bare trees and twigs what a display of muscle!

Apple trees, though many are thick-leaved, are in the midst of their fall. Our English cherry has fallen. The silvery abele is still densely leaved, and green, or at most a yellowish green. The lilac still thickly leaved; a yellowish green or greenish yellow as the case may be. Privet thickly leaved, yellowish-green.

If these plants acquire brighter tints in Europe, then one would say that they did not fully ripen their leaves here before they were killed. The orchard trees are not for beauty, but use. English plants have English habits here: they are not yet acclimated; they are early or late as if ours were an English spring or autumn; and no doubt in course of time a change will be produced in their constitutions similar to that which is observed in the English man here.

Nov. 1. As the afternoons grow shorter, and the early evening drives us home to complete our chores, we are reminded of the shortness of life, and become more pensive, at least in this twilight of the year. We are prompted to make haste and finish our work before the night comes. I leaned over a rail in the twilight on the Walden road, waiting for the evening mail to be distributed, when such thoughts visited me. I seemed to recognize the November evening as a familiar thing come round again, and yet I could hardly tell whether I had ever known it or only divined it. The November twilights just begun! It appeared like a part of a panorama at which I sat spectator, a part with which I was perfectly familiar just coming into view, and I foresaw how it would look and roll along, and prepared to be pleased. We are independent on all that we see. The hangman whom I have *seen* cannot hang me. The earth which I have *seen* cannot bury me. Such doubleness and distance does sight prove. Only the rich and such as are troubled with ennui are implicated in the maze of phenomena. You cannot see anything until you are clear of it. The dark bank of clouds in the horizon long after sunset, the villagers crowding to the post-office, and the hastening home to supper by candle-light, had I not seen all this before! What new sweet was I to extract from it? Truly they mean that we shall learn our lesson well. Nature gets thumbed like an old spelling-book. I was no nearer, methinks, nor further off from my friends. Yet I sat the bench with perfect contentment, unwilling to exchange the familiar vision that was to be unrolled for any treasure or heaven that could be imagined. It was as if I was promised the greatest novelty the world has ever seen or shall see, though the utmost possible novelty would be the difference between me and myself a year ago. This alone encouraged me, and was my fuel for the approaching winter. That we may behold the panorama with this slight improvement or change, this is what we sustain life for with so much effort from year to year.

And yet there is no more tempting novelty than this new November. No going to Europe or another world is to be named with it. Give me the old familiar walk, post-office and all, with this ever new self, with this infinite expectation and faith, which does not know when it is beaten. We'll go nutting once more. We'll pluck the nut of the world, and crack it in the winter evenings. Theatres and all other sightseeing are puppet-shows in comparison. I will take another walk to the Cliff, another row on the river, another skate on the meadow, be out in the first snow, and associate with the winter birds. Here I am at home. In the bare and bleached crust of the earth I recognize my friend.

Pray, am I altogether a bachelor, or am I a widower, that I should go away and leave my bride? This Morrow that is ever knocking with irresistible force at our door, there is no such guest as that. I will stay at home and receive company.

Think of the consummate folly of attempting to go away from *here*! When the constant endeavor should be to get nearer and nearer *here*. Here are all the friends I ever had or shall have, and as friendly as ever. How many things can you go away from? They see the comet from the northwest coast just as plainly as we do, and the same stars through its tail. Take the shortest way round and stay at home. A man dwells in his native valley like a corolla in its calyx, like an acorn in its cup. *Here*, of course, is all that you love, all that you expect, all that you are. Here is your bride elect, as close to you as she can be got. Here is all the best and all the worst you can imagine. What more do you want? Foolish people imagine that what they imagine is somewhere else. That stuff is not made in any factory but their own.

Nov. 3. Colder weather, true November weather, comes again to-night, and I must rekindle my fire, which I had done without of late. I must walk briskly in order to keep warm in my thin coat.

By fall I mean literally the falling of the leaves, though some mean by it the changing or the acquisition of a brighter color. This I call the autumnal tint, the ripening to the fall.

Nothing makes me so dejected as to have met my friends, for they make me doubt if it is possible to have any friends. I feel what a fool I am. I cannot conceive of persons more strange to me than they actually are; not thinking, not believing, not doing as I do; interrupted by me. My only distinction must be that I am the greatest bore they ever had. Not in a single thought agreed; regularly balking one another. But when I get far away, my thoughts return to them. That is the way I *can* visit them. Thus I am taught that my friend is not an actual person. When I have withdrawn and am alone, I forget the actual person and remember only my ideal. Then I have a friend again. I am not so ready to perceive the illusion that is in Nature. I certainly come nearer, to say the least, to an actual and joyful intercourse with her. Every day I have more or less communion with her, *as I think*. At least, I do not feel as if I must withdraw out of nature. I feel like a welcome guest. Yet, strictly speaking, the same must be true of nature and of man; our ideal is the only real. It is not the finite and temporal that satisfies or concerns us in either case.

Nov. 4. A rainy day.

Called to C. from the outside of his house the other afternoon in the rain. At length he put his head out the attic window, and I inquired if he didn't want to take a walk, but he excused himself, saying that he had a cold. "But," added he, "you can take so much the longer walk. Double it."

If, about the last of October, you ascend any hill in the outskirts of the town and look over the forest, you will see, amid the brown of other oaks, which are now withered, and the green of the pines, the bright-red tops or crescents of the scarlet oaks, very equally and thickly distributed on all sides, even to the horizon. All this you will see, and much more, if you are prepared to see it,—if you *look* for it. Otherwise, regular and universal as this phenomenon is, you will think for threescore years and ten that all the wood is at this season sere and brown. Objects are concealed from our view not so much because they are out of the course of our visual ray as because there is no intention of the mind and eye toward them. We do not realize how far and widely, or how near and narrowly, we are to look. The greater part of the phenomena of nature are for this reason concealed to us all our lives. Here, too, as in political economy, the supply answers to the demand. Nature does not cast pearls before swine. There is just as much beauty visible to us in the landscape as we are prepared to appreciate,—not a grain more. The actual objects which one person will see from a particular hilltop are just as different from those which another will see as the persons are different. The scarlet oak must, in a sense, be in your eye when you go forth. We cannot see anything until we are possessed with the idea of it, and then we can hardly see anything else. In my botanical rambles I find that first the idea, or image, of a plant occupies my thoughts, though it may at first seem very foreign to this locality, and for some weeks or months I go thinking of it and expecting it unconsciously, and at length I surely see it, and it is henceforth an actual neighbor of mine. This is the history of my finding a score or more of rare plants which I could name.

Nov. 6. I guessed at Goodwin's age on the 1st. He is hale and stout and looks younger than he is, and I took care to set him high enough. I guessed he was fifty-five, and he said that if he lived two or three months longer he would be fifty-six. He then guessed at my age, thought I was forty. He thought that Emerson was a very young-looking man for his age, "But," said he, "he has not been out o'nights as much as you have."

Nov. 8. Goodwin, laying wall at Miss Ripley's, observed to me going by, "Well, it seems that Puffer thought that he had lived long enough." He committed suicide within a week, at his sister's house in Sudbury. A boy slept in the chamber with him, and, hearing a noise, got up and found P. on the floor with both his jugular veins cut, but his windpipe whole. He said to the boy, "Take the razor and cut deeper," but the boy ran, and P. died, and Garfield said it was about time, for P., in revenge for being sent to the house of correction, had set fire to a pile of wood of his, that long pile by the roadside beyond William Wheeler's, that I stood under in a rain once. P. probably burned Witherell's house too, and perhaps Boynton's stable.

The red osier at Mrs. Simmons's is quite bare; how long? Her hawthorn is still quite leafy and pretty, yellow-brown, dotted. A thorn at Hall's fence is dark scarlet and pretty.

Those trees and bushes which grow in dense masses and have many fine twigs, being bare, make an agreeable misty impression where there are a myriad retreating points to receive the eye, not a hard, abrupt wall; just as, in the sky, the visual ray is cushioned on clouds, unless it is launched into the illimitable ether. The eye is less worn and wearied, not to say wounded, by looking at these mazes where the seer is not often conscious of seeing anything. It is well that the eye is so rarely caught and detained by any object in one whole hemisphere of its range, *i.e.* the sky. It enjoys everlasting holiday on this side. Only the formless clouds and the objectless ether are presented to it. For they are nervous who see many faces in the clouds. Corresponding to the clouds in the sky are those mazes now on the earth. Nature disposes of her naked stems so softly as not to put our eyes out. She makes them a smoke, or stationary cloud, on this side or that, of whose objective existence we rarely take cognizance. She does not expect us to notice them.

Nature has many scenes to exhibit, and constantly draws a curtain over this part or that. She is constantly repainting the landscape and all surfaces, dressing up some scene for our entertainment. Lately we had a leafy wilderness, now bare twigs begin to prevail, and soon she will surprise us with a mantle of snow.[*] Some green she thinks so good for our eyes, like blue, that she never banishes it entirely, but has created evergreens.

It is remarkable how little any but a lichenist will observe on the bark of trees. The mass of men have but the vaguest and most indefinite notion of mosses, as a sort of shreds and fringes, and the world in which the lichenist dwells is much further from theirs than one side of this earth from the other. They see bark as if they saw it not. These objects which, though constantly visible, are rarely looked at are a sort of eye-brush.

Each phase of nature, while not invisible, is yet not too distinct and obtrusive. It is there to be found when we look for it, but not demanding our attention. It is like a silent but sympathizing companion in whose company we retain most of the advantages of solitude, with whom we can walk and talk, or be silent, naturally, without the necessity of talking in a strain foreign to the place.

Animals generally see things in the vacant way I have described. They rarely see anything but their food, or some real or imaginary foe. I never saw but one cow looking into the sky.

Lichens as they affect the scenery, as picturesque objects described by Gilpin or others, are one thing; as they concern the lichenist, quite another.

---

[*]I read that snow fell two or three inches deep in Bangor yesterday morning.

XXVIII.

Nov. 10. I look out westward across Fair Haven Pond. The warmer colors are now rare. A cool and silvery light is the prevailing one; dark-blue or slate-colored clouds in the west, and the sun going down in them. All the light of November may be called an after-glow.

Aphides on alder.

Sap still flows in scarlet oak.

Returned by Spanish Brook Path. Notice the glaucous white bloom on the thimble-berry of late, as there are fewer things to notice. So many objects are white or light, preparing us for winter.

Nov. 12. It is much the coldest day yet, and the ground is a little frozen and resounds under my tread. All people move the brisker for the cold, yet are braced and a little elated by it. They love to say, "Cold day, sir." Though the days are shorter, you get more work out of a hired man than before, for he must work to keep warm.

Now for a brisk and energetic walk, with a will and a purpose. Have done with sauntering, in the idle sense. You must rush to the assault of winter. Make haste into the outskirts, climb the ramparts of the town, be on the alert and let nothing escape your observation.

I think that the change to some higher color in a leaf is an evidence that it has arrived at a late and more perfect and final maturity, answering to the maturity of fruits, and not to that of green leaves, etc., etc., which merely serve a purpose. The word "ripe" is thought by some to be derived from the verb "to reap," according to which that is ripe which is ready to be reaped. The fall of the leaf is preceded by a ripe old age.

Nov. 14. It is very cold and windy; thermometer 26. I walk to Walden and Andromeda Ponds. This strong and cutting northwest wind makes the oak leaves rustle dryly enough to set your heart on edge.

Now, while the frosty air begins to nip your fingers and your nose, the frozen ground rapidly wears away the soles of your shoes, as sandpaper might; the old she wolf is nibbling at your very extremities. The frozen ground eating away the soles of your shoes is only typical of the vulture that gnaws your heart this month.

Nov. 17. Leaving my boat, I walk through the low wood west of Dove Rock, toward the scarlet oak. The very sunlight on the pale-brown bleached fields is an interesting object these cold days. I naturally look toward it as to a wood-fire. Not only different objects are presented to our attention at different seasons of the year, but we are in a frame of body and of mind to appreciate different objects at different seasons. I see one thing when it is cold and another when it is warm.

We are interested at this season by the manifold ways in which the light is reflected to us. Ascending a little knoll covered with sweet-fern, shortly after, the sun appearing but a point above the sweet-fern, its light was reflected from a dense mass of the bare downy twigs of this plant in a surprising manner which would not be believed if described. It was quite like the sunlight reflected from grass and weeds covered with hoar frost. A myriad of surfaces are now prepared to reflect the light. This is one of the hundred silvery lights of November. The setting sun, too, is reflected from windows more brightly than at any other season. "November Lights" would be a theme for me.

Nature is moderate and loves degrees. Winter is not all white and sere. Some trees are evergreen to cheer us, and on the forest floor our eyes do not fall on sere brown leaves alone, but some evergreen shrubs are placed there to relieve the eye. Mountain laurel, lambkill, checkerberry, wintergreen, etc., etc., etc., and a few evergreen ferns scattered about keep up the semblance of summer still.

Nov. 19. P.M.—Mocker-nutting, to Conantum.

Those long mocker-nuts appear not to have got well ripe this year. They do not shed their husks, and the meat is mostly skinny and soft and flabby. Perhaps the season has been too cold. I shook the trees. It is just the time to get them. How hard they rattle down, like stones! There is a harmony between this stony fruit and these hard, tough limbs which bear it. I did not think at first why these nuts had not been gathered, but I suspect it may be because Puffer, who probably used to get them, has committed suicide.

Nov. 24. Here is an author who contrasts love for "the beauties of the person" with that for "excellences of the mind," as if these were the alternatives. I must say that it is for neither of these that I should feel the strongest affection. I love that one with whom I sympathize, be she "beautiful" or otherwise, of excellent mind or not.

Nov. 25. While most keep close to their parlor fires this cold and blustering Thanksgiving afternoon, and think with compassion of those who are abroad, I find the sunny south side of this swamp as warm as their parlors, and warmer to my spirit. Aye, there is a serenity and warmth here which the parlor does not suggest, enhanced by the sound of the wind roaring on the northwest side of the swamp a dozen or so rods off. What a wholesome and inspiring warmth is this!

Nov. 26. Walden is very low, compared with itself for some years. There is a shore at least six feet wide inside the alders at my old shore, and what is remarkable, I find that not only Goose Pond also has fallen correspondingly within a month, but even the smaller pond-holes only four or five rods over, such as Little Goose Pond, shallow as they are. I begin to suspect, therefore, that this rise and fall extending through a long series of years is not peculiar to the

Walden system of ponds, but is true of ponds generally, and perhaps of rivers, though in their case it may be more difficult to detect. The Pout's Nest, also, has lost ten feet on all sides.

Those pouts' nests which I discovered in the spring are high and dry six feet from the water. I overhauled one, ripping up the frozen roof with my hands. The roof was only three inches thick, then a cavity and a bottom of wet mud. In this mud I found two small frogs. They were quite sluggish and had evidently gone into winter quarters there, but probably some mink would have got them.

Looking more attentively, I detected also a great many minnows about one inch long either floating dead there or frozen into the ice,—at least fifty of them. They were shaped like bream, but had the transverse bars of perch.

Examining those minnows by day, I find that they are one and one sixth inches long by two fifths of an inch wide (this my largest); in form like a bream; of a very pale golden like a perch, or more bluish. Have but one dorsal fin and, as near as I can count, rays, dorsal 19 (first, 9 stouter and stiff and more distinctly pointed, then 10 longer and flexible, whole fin about three times as long as average height), caudal 19, anal 13 or 14, ventral 6, pectoral 10 (?). They have about seven transverse dusky bars like a perch (!). Yet, from their form and single dorsal fin, I think they are breams. Are they not a new species? Have young breams transverse bars? A little narrower than this.[*]

Nov. 27. I got seventeen more of those little bream of yesterday. As I now count, the dorsal fin-rays are 9–10 (Girard says 9–11), caudal 17 (with apparently 4 short on each side), anal 3–11, pectoral 11, ventral 1–5. They have about seven transverse dark bars, a vertical dark mark under eye, and a dark spot on edge of operculum. They appear to be the young of the *Pomotis obesus*, described by Charles Girard to the Natural History Society in April, '54, obtained by Baird in fresh water about Hingham and in Charles River in Hol-

---

[*]*Vide* [next page].

liston. They are exceedingly pretty seen floating dead on their sides in a bowl of water, with all their fins spread out. From their size and form and position they cannot fail to remind you of coins in the basin.

[*Pasted-in newspaper clipping, from a report of the proceedings of the Boston Society of Natural History:* "Specimens of *Pomotis* and *Esox*, and of amphibians, were presented by Mr. H.D. Thoreau, from Concord, Mass. Mr. Putnam was of opinion that one of the *Pomotis* would prove a new species. There are with us two varieties of pickerel commonly known as the long or shovel-nosed, and the short or trout-nosed; these specimens were of the latter. Mr. Putnam was inclined to think these were distinct species, unless the differences should prove to be sexual. Drs. D.H. and H.R. Storer considered them varieties of the same species; Messrs. Baird and Girard think them (*Esox reticulatus* and *E. ornatus*) distinct."

Another clipping: "Mr. F.W. Putnam at a previous meeting stated that possibly the young Pomotis presented by Mr. Thoreau were the *P. obesus* of Girard. He had since then examined Girard's original specimens, and he finds that they are the same. The *P. guttatus* recently described in the Proceedings of the Academy of Natural Sciences at Philadelphia is identical with *P. obesus*. Having teeth on the palatines, and consequently belonging to the genus *Bryttus*, the proper name for the species is *B. obesus* (Putnam). He had also satisfied himself that the *Esox ornatus* of Girard is the same as the *E. fasciatus* of De Kay."]

How much more remote the newly discovered species seems to dwell than the old and familiar ones, though both inhabit the same pond! Where the *Pomotis obesus* swims must be a new country, unexplored by science. The seashore may be settled, but aborigines dwell unseen only thus far inland. This country is so new that species of fishes and birds and quadrupeds inhabit it which science has not yet detected. The water which such a fish swims in must still have a primitive forest decaying in it.

Nov. 28. A gray, overcast, still day, and more small birds—tree sparrows and chickadees—than usual about the house. There have been a very few fine snowflakes falling for many hours, and now, by 2 P.M., a regular snow-storm has commenced, fine flakes falling steadily, and rapidly whitening all the landscape. In half an hour the russet earth is painted white even to the horizon. Do we know of any other so silent and sudden a change?

And all the years that I have known Walden these striped breams have skulked in it without my knowledge! How many new thoughts, then, may I have?

Nov. 30. P.M.—To Walden with Channing, and Fair Haven Hill.

It is a pleasant day and the snow melting considerably.

I cannot but see still in my mind's eye those little striped breams poised in Walden's glaucous water. They balance all the rest of the world in my estimation at present, for this is the bream that I have just found, and for the time I neglect all its brethren and am ready to kill the fatted calf on its account. For more than two centuries have men fished here and have not distinguished this permanent settler of the township. When my eyes first rested on Walden the striped bream was poised in it, though I did not see it, and when Tahatawan paddled his canoe there. How wild it makes the pond and the township to find a new fish in it! America renews her youth here. But in my account of this bream I cannot go a hair's breadth beyond the mere statement that it exists,—the miracle of its existence, my contemporary and neighbor, yet so different from me! I can only poise my thought there by its side and try to think like a bream for a moment. I can only think of precious jewels, of music, poetry, beauty, and the mystery of life. I only see the bream in its orbit, as I see a star, but I care not to measure its distance or weight. The bream, appreciated, floats in the pond as the centre of the system, another image of God. Its life no man can explain more than he can his own. I want you to perceive the mystery of the bream. I have a contemporary in Walden. It has fins where I have legs and arms. I have a friend among the fishes, at least a new acquaintance. Its character will interest me, I trust, not its clothes and anatomy. I do not want it to eat. Acquaintance with it is to make my life more rich and eventful. It is as if a poet or an anchorite had moved into

the town, whom I can see from time to time and think of yet oftener. Perhaps there are a thousand of these striped bream which
no one had thought of in that pond,—not their mere impressions
in stone, but in the full tide of the bream life.

Though science may sometimes compare herself to a child picking up pebbles on the seashore, that is a rare mood with her; ordinarily her practical belief is that it is only a few pebbles which are
not known, weighed and measured. A new species of fish signifies
hardly more than a new name. See what is contributed in the scientific reports. One counts the fin-rays, another measures the in-
testines, a third daguerreotypes a scale, etc., etc.; otherwise there's
nothing to be said. As if all but this were done, and these were very
rich and generous contributions to science. Her votaries may be
seen wandering along the shore of the ocean of truth, with their
backs to that ocean, ready to seize on the shells which are cast up.
You would say that the scientific bodies were terribly put to it for
objects and subjects. A dead specimen of an animal, if it is only
well preserved in alcohol, is just as good for science as a living one
preserved in its native element.

What is the amount of my discovery to me? It is not that I have
got one in a bottle, that it has got a name in a book, but that I have
a little fishy friend in the pond. How was it when the youth first
discovered fishes? Was it the number of their fin-rays or their arrangement, or the place of the fish in some system that made the
boy dream of them? Is it these things that interest mankind in the
fish, the inhabitant of the water? No, but a faint recognition of a
living contemporary, a provoking mystery. One boy thinks of
fishes and goes a-fishing from the same motive that his brother
searches the poets for rare lines. It is the poetry of fishes which is
their chief use; their flesh is their lowest use. The beauty of the fish,
that is what it is best worth the while to measure. Its place in our
systems is of comparatively little importance. Generally the boy
loses some of his perception and his interest in the fish; he degener-
ates into a fisherman or an ichthyologist.[*]

---

[*] *Vide* Dec. 3.

Dec. 3. The largest of the four breams (*vide* November 26th) two and nine twentieths inches long, by one inch broad and nine twentieths thick. The back, sides forward, tail, and anal fin black or blackish or very dark; the transverse dark bars few and indistinct except in middle of fish; sides toward tail yellowish-olive. Rear of abdomen has violet reflections (and about base of anal fin). Operculums tinged, streaked, and spotted with golden, coppery, greenish, and violet reflections. A vertical dark mark or line, corresponding to the stripes, through the eye. Iris copper-color or darker. [*Etc.*]

Dec. 11. P.M.—To Walden. An overcast afternoon and rather warm. The snow on the ground in pastures brings out the warm red in leafy oak woodlands by contrast. These are what Thomson calls "the tawny copse." So that they suggest both shelter and warmth. All browns, indeed, are warmer now than a week ago. How much warmer our woodlands look and *are* for these withered leaves that still hang on! Without them the woods would be dreary, bleak, and wintry indeed.

A "swirl," applied to leaves suddenly caught up by a sort of whirlwind, is a good word enough, methinks.

Some, being offended, think sharp and satirical things, which yet they are not prepared consciously to utter. But in some unguarded moment these things escape from them, when they are as it were unconscious. They betray their thoughts, as it were by talking in their sleep, for the truth will out, under whatever veil of civility.

Dec. 12. P.M.—Up river on ice to Fair Haven Hill.

Crossing the fields, I see an immense flock of snow buntings, I think the largest that I ever saw. There must be a thousand or two at least. Flying from you, in some positions, you see only or chiefly the black part of their bodies, and then, as they wheel, the white comes into view, contrasted prettily with the former, and in all together at the same time. Seen flying higher against a cloudy sky they look like large snowflakes. When they rise all together their note is like the rattling of nuts in a bag, as if a whole binful were rolled from side to side. They also utter from time to time—*i.e.*, individuals do—a clear rippling note, perhaps of alarm, or a call. Suddenly the pioneers (or a part not foremost) will change their course when in full career, and when at length they know it, the rushing flock on the other side will be fetched about as it were with an undulating jerk, as in the boys' game of snap-the-whip, and those that occupy the place of the snapper are gradually off after their leaders on the new tack. As far as I observe, they confine themselves to upland, not alighting in the meadows. Like a snowstorm they come rushing down from the north.

I should like to know where all those snowbirds will roost tonight, for they will probably roost together. And what havoc an owl might make among them!*

Dec. 26. Call at a farmer's this Sunday afternoon, where I surprise the well-to-do masters of the house lounging in very ragged clothes (for which they think it necessary to apologize), and one of them is busy laying the supper-table (at which he invites me to sit down at last), bringing up cold meat from the cellar and a lump of butter on the end of his knife, and making the tea by the time his mother gets home from church. Thus sincere and homely, as I am glad to know, is the actual life of these New England men, wearing rags indoors there which would disgrace a beggar (and are not beggars and paupers they who *could be* disgraced so?) and doing the indispensable work, however humble. I am glad to find that our New England life has a genuine humane core to it; that inside, after all, there is so little pretense and brag.

Dec. 28. Aunt Jane says that she was born on Christmas Day, and they called her a Christmas gift, and she remembers hearing that her Aunt Hannah Orrock was so disconcerted by the event that she threw all the spoons outdoors, when she had washed them, or with the dishwater.

Father says that he and his sisters (except Elizabeth) were born

---

*Melvin tells me that he saw a thousand feeding a long time in the Great Meadows,—he thinks on the seeds of the wool-grass (!!),—about same time.

in Richmond Street, Boston, between Salem and Hanover Streets, on the spot where a bethel now stands, on the left hand going from Hanover Street. They had milk of a neighbor, who used to drive his cows to and from the Common every day.

Jan. 2. P.M.—To Cliffs and Walden.

Going up the hill through Stow's young oak woodland, I listen to the sharp, dry rustle of the withered oak leaves. This is the voice of the wood now. Just as the inhabitant of Cape Cod hears the surf ever breaking on its shores, so we countrymen hear this kindred surf on the leaves of the forest. Regarded as a voice,—though it is not articulate,—as our articulate sounds are divided into vowels (but this is nearer a consonant sound), labials, dentals, palatals, sibilants, mutes, aspirate, etc., so this may be called *folial* or *frondal*, produced by air driven against the leaves, and comes nearest to our sibilants or aspirate.

Why do young oaks retain their leaves while old ones shed them? Why do they die on the stem, having some life at the base in the one case, while they wither through at the base in the other case? Is it because in the former case they have more sap and vigor?

When I hear the hypercritical quarrelling about grammar and style, the position of the particles, etc., etc., stretching or contracting every speaker to certain rules of theirs,—Mr. Webster, perhaps, not having spoken according to Mr. Kirkham's rule,—I see that they forget that the first requisite and rule is that expression shall be vital and natural, as much as the voice of a brute or an interjection: first of all, mother tongue; and last of all, artificial or father tongue. Essentially your truest poetic sentence is as free and lawless as a lamb's bleat. The grammarian is often one who can neither cry nor laugh, yet thinks that he can express human emotions. So the posture-masters tell you how you shall walk,—turning your toes out, perhaps, excessively,—but so the beautiful walkers are not made.

Mediæval, or law, Latin seems to have invented the word "forest," not being satisfied with *silva, nemus,* etc. Webster makes it from the same root with "L. *foris*, Fr. *hors*, and the Saxon *faran*, to go, to depart." The allied words "all express distance from cities and civilization, and are from roots expressing departure or wandering,"—as if this newer term were needed to describe those strange, wild woods furthest from the centres of civilization.

Jan. 4. A northeast snow-storm, or rather a north snow-storm, very hard to face. P.M. to Walden in it. It snows very hard, driving along almost horizontally, falling but a foot or two in a rod. Nobody is in the street, or thinks of going out far except on important business. Most roads are trackless. The snow may be now fifteen to eighteen inches deep.

The pitch pines near Thrush Alley are the most interesting objects, for they hold much more snow. The snow lodges on their plumes, and, bending them down, it accumulates more and more on the angle generally at the base of the several plumes, in little conical heaps shaped somewhat like this:— differing according to the number and position of the plumes. They look as if a child had stuck up its elbow under a white sheet. Some small ones stand stiffly up-right like a soldier's plume. At the same time the lowermost small black and dead horizontal limbs near the ground, where there is least wind and jar,—these almost exclusively,—say for six or eight feet up, are covered with upright walls of snow five or six times their own height and zigzagging with them like the Wall of China; or like great white caterpillars they lie along them, these snowy sloths; or rather it is a labyrinth, a sort of cobweb, of broad white belts in the air. Only a dim twilight struggles through to this lower region, and the sight of these snowy walls or labyrinths suggests a rare stillness, freedom from wind and jar. If you try to stoop and wind your way there, you get your neck and ears full of snow. I can't draw it. That is, for each dead pine branch you have a thin flat branch of snow resting on it, an exaggeration of the former.

Your breath causes the snow to turn to ice in your beard; a shaggy mass of icicles it becomes, which makes you look like a man from the extreme north.

Jan. 13. The cold spell is over, and here this morning is a fog or mist; the wind, if there is any, I think, northerly; and there is built out horizontally on the north side of every twig and other surface a very remarkable sort of hoar frost, the crystallized fog, which is still increasing. It is quite rare here, at least on this scale. The mist lasts all this day, though it is far from warm (+11° at 8 A.M.), and till noon of the 14th, when it becomes rain, and all this time there is exceedingly little if any wind.

I go to the river this morning and walk up it to see the trees and bushes along it. As the frostwork (which is not thin and transparent like ice, but white and snow-like, or between the distinctly leaf with veins and a mere aggregation of snow, though you easily distinguish the distinct leaves) is built out northward from each surface, spreading at an angle of about forty-five degrees, *i.e.* some twenty-odd each side of the north, you must stand on the north side and look south at the trees, etc., when they appear, except the large limbs and trunk, wholly of snow or frostwork, mere ghosts of trees, seen softly against the mist for a background. It is mist on mist. The outline and character of each tree is more distinctly exhibited, being exaggerated, and you notice any peculiarity in the disposition of the twigs. Some elm twigs, thus enlarged into snowy fingers, are strikingly regular and handsome, thus: In the case of most evergreens, it amounts to a very rich sugaring, being so firmly attached. The weeping willow seems to weep with more remarkable and regular curve than ever, and stands still and white with thickened twigs, as if carved in white marble or alabaster. Those trees, like alders, which have not grown much the past year—which have short and angular twigs—are the richest in effect.

Jan. 14. The fog turns to a fine rain at noon, and in the evening and night it produces a glaze, which this morning,—

Jan. 15,—is quite handsome. Instead of that soft, white, faery-like mantle of down with which the trees were thickly powdered, they are now cased in a coat of mail, of icy mail, built out in many cases about as far from the twig with icy prominences. Birches, tree-tops, and especially slender-twigged willows or osiers are bent over by it, as they were not by the snow-white and light frost of yesterday and the day before, so that the character or expression of many trees and shrubs is wholly altered. I might not guess what the pollard willow row at Merrick's shore, with twigs one or two years old, was,—   instead of

Jan. 18. That wonderful frostwork of the 13th and 14th was too rare to be neglected,—succeeded as it was, also, by two days of glaze,—but, having company, I lost half the advantage of it. It was remarkable to have a fog for four days in midwinter without wind. Apparently as the fog was coarser and far more abundant, it was whiter, less delicate to examine, and of far greater depth than a frostwork formed of dew. We did not have an opportunity to see how it would look in the sun, but seen against the mist or fog it was too fair to be remembered. The trees were the ghosts of trees appearing in their winding-sheets, an intenser white against the comparatively dusky ground of the fog. I learn from the papers that this phenomenon prevailed all over this part of the country and attracted the admiration of all. The trees on Boston Common were clad in the same snow-white livery with our Musketaquid trees.

That glaze! I know what it was by my own experience; it was the frozen breath of the earth upon its beard.

Take the most rigid tree, the whole effect is peculiarly soft and spirit-like, for there is no marked edge or outline. How could you draw the outline of these snowy fingers seen against the fog, without exaggeration? There is no more a boundary-line or circumference that can be drawn, than a diameter. Hardly could the New England farmer drive to market under these trees without feeling that his sense of beauty was addressed. He would be aware that the phenomenon called beauty was become visible, if one were at leisure or had had the right culture to appreciate it. A miller with whom I rode actually remarked on the beauty of the trees; and a farmer told me in all sincerity that, having occasion to go into Walden Woods in his sleigh, he thought he never saw anything so beautiful in all his life, and if there had been men there who knew how to write about it, it would have been a great occasion for them.

Many times I thought that if the particular tree, commonly an elm, under which I was walking or riding were the only one like it in the country, it would be worth a journey across the continent to see it. Indeed, I have no doubt that such journeys would be undertaken on hearing a true account of it. But, instead of being confined to a single tree, this wonder was as cheap and common as the air itself. Every man's wood-lot was a miracle and surprise to him, and for those who could not go so far there were the trees in the street and the weeds in the yard.

In some moods you might suspect that it was the work of enchantment. Some magician had put your village into a crucible and it had crystallized thus.

Jan. 19. I noticed last night, just after sunset, a sheet of mackerel sky far in the west horizon, very finely imbricated and reflecting a coppery glow, and again I saw still more of it in the east this morning at sunrise, and now, at 3.30 P.M., looking up, I perceive that almost the entire heavens are covered with a very beautiful mackerel sky. This indicates a peculiar state of the atmosphere. The sky is most wonderfully and beautifully mottled with evenly distributed cloudlets, of indescribable variety yet regularity in their form, suggesting fishes' scales, with perhaps small fish-bones thrown in here and there. It is white in the midst, or most prominent part, of the scales, passing into blue in the crannies. Something like this blue and white mottling, methinks, is seen on a mackerel, and has suggested the name. Is not the peculiar propriety of this term lost sight of by the meteorologists? It is a luxury for the eye to rest on it. What curtains, what tapestry to our halls!

The form of these cloudlets is, by the way, like or akin to that of waves, of ripple-marks on sand, of small drifts, wave-like, on the surface of snow, and to the first small openings in the ice of the midstream.

Jan. 20. The green of the ice and water begins to be visible about half an hour before sunset. Is it produced by the reflected blue of the sky mingling with the yellow or pink of the setting sun?

Jan. 27. When you have been deprived of your usual quantity of sleep for several nights, you sleep much more soundly for it, and wake up suddenly like a bullet that strikes a wall.

FEB. 3. Five minutes before 3 P.M. Father died.

After a sickness of some two years, going down-town in pleasant weather, doing a little business from time to time, hoeing a little in the garden, etc., Father took to his chamber January 13th, and did not come down again. Most of the time previously he had coughed and expectorated a great deal. Latterly he did not cough, but continued to raise. He continued to sit up in his chamber till within a week before he died. He sat up for a little while on the Sunday four days before he died. Generally he was very silent for many months. He was quite conscious to the last, and his death was so easy that we should not have been aware that he was dying, though we were sitting around his bed, if we had not watched very closely.

I have touched a body which was flexible and warm, yet tenantless,—warmed by what fire? When the spirit that animated some matter has left it, who else, what else, can animate it?

How enduring are our bodies, after all! The forms of our brothers and sisters, our parents and children and wives, lie still in the hills and fields round about us, not to mention those of our remoter ancestors, and the matter which composed the body of our first human father still exists under another name.

When in sickness the body is emaciated, and the expression of the face in various ways is changed, you perceive unexpected resemblances to other members of the same family; as if within the same family there was a greater general similarity in the framework of the face than in its filling up and clothing.

Father first came to this town to live with his father about the end of the last century, when he was about twelve years old. (His father died in 1801.) Afterward he went to the Lexington Academy (Parker's?) a short time, perhaps a year, then into Deacon White's store as clerk; then learned the dry-goods business in a store in Salem. (Aunt J. shows me a letter from him directly after his going there, dated 1807.) Was with a Hathaway. When about twenty-one, opened a store for himself on the corner where the town house stands of late years, a yellow building, now moved and altered into John Keyes's house. He did so well there that Isaac Hurd went into partnership with him, to his injury. They soon dissolved, but could not settle without going to law, when my father gained the case, bringing his books into court. Then, I think, he went to Bangor and set up with Billings, selling to Indians (among others); married; lived in Boston; writes thence to aunts at Bangor in 1815 with John on his knee; moved to Concord (*where I was born*), then to Chelmsford, to Boston, to Concord again, and here remained. Mother first came to Concord about the same age that father did, but a little before him.

As far as I know, Father, when he died, was not only one of the oldest men in the middle of Concord, but the one perhaps best acquainted with the inhabitants, and the local, social, and street history of the middle of the town, for the last fifty years. He belonged in a peculiar sense to the village street; loved to sit in the shops or at the post-office and read the daily papers. I think that he remembered more about the worthies (and unworthies) of Concord village forty years ago, both from dealing as a trader and from familiar intercourse with them, than any one else. Our other neighbors, now living or very recently dead, have either come to the town more recently than he, or have lived more aloof from the mass of the inhabitants.

Some have spoken slightingly of the Indians, as a race possessing so little skill and wit, so low in the scale of humanity, and so brutish that they hardly deserved to be remembered,—using only the terms "miserable," "wretched," "pitiful," and the like. In writing their histories of this country they have so hastily disposed of this refuse of humanity (as they might have called it) which littered and defiled the shore and the interior. But even the indigenous animals are inexhaustibly interesting to us. How much more, then, the indigenous man of America! If wild men, so much more like ourselves than they are unlike, have inhabited these shores before us, we wish to know particularly what manner of men they were, how they lived here, their relation to nature, their arts and their customs, their fancies and superstitions. They paddled over these waters, they wandered in these woods, and they had their fancies and beliefs connected with the sea and the forest, which concern us quite as much as the fables of Oriental nations do. It frequently happens that the historian, though he professes more humanity than the trapper, mountain man, or gold-digger, who shoots one as a wild beast, really exhibits and practices a similar inhumanity to him, wielding a pen instead of a rifle.

One tells you with more contempt than pity that the Indian had no religion, holding up both hands, and this to all the shallow-brained and bigoted seems to mean something important, but it is commonly a distinction without a difference. Pray, how much more religion has the historian? If Henry Ward Beecher knows so much more about God than another, if he has made some discovery of truth in this direction, I would thank him to publish it in *Silliman's Journal*, with as few flourishes as possible.

It is the spirit of humanity, that which animates both so-called savages and civilized nations, working through a man, and not the man expressing himself, that interests us most. The thought of a so-called savage tribe is generally far more just than that of a single civilized man.

I perceive that we partially die ourselves through sympathy at the death of each of our friends or near relatives. Each such experience is an assault on our vital force. It becomes a source of wonder that they who have lost many friends still live. After long watching around the sick-bed of a friend, we, too, partially give up the ghost with him, and are the less to be identified with this state of things.

The writer must to some extent inspire himself. Most of his sentences may at first lie dead in his essay, but when all are arranged, some life and color will be reflected on them from the mature and successful lines; they will appear to pulsate with fresh life, and he will be enabled to eke out their slumbering sense, and make them worthy of their neighborhood. In his first essay on a given theme, he produces scarcely more than a frame and groundwork for his sentiment and poetry. Each clear thought that he attains to draws in its train many divided thoughts or perceptions. The writer has much to do even to create a theme for himself. Most that is first written on any subject is a mere groping after it, mere rubble-stone and foundation. It is only when many observations of different periods have been brought together that he begins to grasp his subject and can make one pertinent and just observation.

FEB. 5. When we have experienced many disappointments, such as the loss of friends, the notes of birds cease to affect us as they did.

I see another butcher-bird on the top of a young tree by the pond.

Feb. 7. Going along the Nut Meadow or Jimmy Miles road, when I see the sulphur lichens on the rails brightening with the moisture I feel like studying them again as a relisher or tonic, to make life go down and digest well, as we use pepper and vinegar and salads. They are a sort of winter greens which we gather and assimilate with our eyes. That's the true use of the study of lichens. I expect that the lichenist will have the keenest relish for Nature in her every-day mood and dress. To study lichens is to get a taste of earth and health, to go gnawing the rails and rocks. The lichenist extracts nutriment from the very crust of the earth. A taste for this study is an evidence of titanic health, a sane earthiness. It fits a man to deal with the barrenest and rockiest experience. A little moisture, a fog, or rain, or melted snow makes his wilderness to blossom like the rose. A lichenist fats where others starve. His provender never fails.

Feb. 13. The old ice is covered with a dry, powdery snow about one inch deep, from which, as I walk toward the sun, this perfectly clear, bright afternoon, at 3.30 o'clock, the colors of the rainbow are reflected from a myriad fine facets. It is as if the dust of diamonds and other precious stones were spread all around. The blue and red predominate. Though I distinguish these colors everywhere toward the sun, they are so much more abundantly reflected to me from two particular directions that I see two distant rays, or arms, so to call them, of this rainbow-like dust, one on each side of the sun, stretching away from me and about half a dozen feet wide, the two arms including an angle of about sixty degrees. When I look from the sun, I see merely dazzling white points. Yet I might easily, and commonly do, overlook all this.

Sometimes in our prosaic moods, life appears to us but a certain number more of days like those which we have lived, to be cheered not by more friends and friendship but probably fewer and less. As, perchance, we anticipate the end of this day before it is done, close the shutters, and with a cheerless resignation commence the barren evening whose fruitless end we clearly see, we despondingly think that all of life that is left is only this experience repeated a certain number of times. And so it would be, if it were not for the faculty of imagination.

A transient acquaintance with any phenomenon is not sufficient to make it completely the subject of your muse. You must be so conversant with it as to *remember* it and be reminded of it long afterward, while it lies remotely fair and elysian in the horizon, approachable only by the imagination.

Feb. 15. P.M.—Up river to Fair Haven Pond.

I thought, by the peculiar moaning sound of the wind about the dining-room at noon, that we should have a rain-storm. I heard only one blast through some crack, but no doubt that betrayed a *pluvious* breath.

Against Bittern Cliff I feel the first drop strike the right slope of my nose and run down the ravine there. Such is the origin of rivers. Not till half a mile further my doubting companion feels another on his nose also, and I get one in my eye, and soon after I see the countless dimples in the puddles on the ice. So measured and deliberate is Nature always. Then the gentle, spring-like rain begins, and we turn about.

The sound of it pattering on the dry oak leaves, where young oaks thickly cover a hillside, is just like that of wind stirring them, when first heard, but is steady and monotonous and so betrayed. We rejoice to be wetted, and the very smell of wet woollen clothes exhilarates us.

Feb. 20. In the composition it is the greatest art to find out as quickly as possible which are the best passages you have written, and tear the rest away to come at them. Even the poorest parts will be most effective when they serve these, as pediments to the column.

How much the writer lives and endures in coming before the public so often! A few years or books are with him equal to a long life of experience, suffering, etc. It is well if he does not become hardened. He learns how to bear contempt and to despise himself. He makes, as it were, *post-mortem* examinations of himself before he is dead. Such is art.

P.M.—The rain ceases, and it clears up at 5 P.M. It is a warm west wind and a remarkably soft sky, like plush; perhaps a lingering moisture there. What a revelation the blue and the bright tints in the west again, after the storm and darkness! It is the opening of the windows of heaven after the flood!

FEB. 22. Go to Worcester to lecture in a parlor.

Feb. 25. All the criticism which I got on my lecture on Autumnal Tints at Worcester on the 22d was that I assumed that my audience had not seen so much of them as they had. But after reading it I am more than ever convinced that they have not seen much of them,— that there are very few persons who do see much of nature.

March 2. As I go through the Cassandra Ponds, I look round on the young oak woods still clad with rustling leaves as in winter, with a feeling as if it were their last rustle before the spring, but then I reflect how far away still is the time when the new buds swelling will cause these leaves to fall. We thus commonly antedate the spring more than any other season, for we look forward to it with more longing. We talk about spring as at hand before the end of February, and yet it will be two good months, one sixth part of the whole year, before we can go a-maying. There may be a whole month of solid and uninterrupted winter yet, plenty of ice and good sleighing. We may not even see the bare ground, and hardly the water, and yet we sit down and warm our spirits annually with this distant prospect of spring. As if a man were to warm his hands by stretching them toward the rising sun and rubbing them.

March 3. Going by the solidago oak at Clamshell Hill bank, I heard a faint rippling note and, looking up, saw about fifteen snow buntings sitting in the top of the oak, all with their breasts toward me,—sitting so still and quite white, seen against the white cloudy sky, they did not look like birds but the ghosts of birds, and their boldness, allowing me to come quite near, enhanced this impression. These were almost as white as snowballs, and from time to time I heard a low, soft rippling note from them. I could see no features, but only the general outline of plump birds in white. It was a very spectral sight, and after I had watched them for several minutes, I can hardly say that I was prepared to see them fly away like ordinary buntings when I advanced further. At first they were almost concealed by being almost the same color with the cloudy sky.

Talk about reading!—a good reader! It depends on how he is heard. It takes two at least for this game, as for love, and they must coöperate. I saw some men unloading molasses-hogsheads from a truck at a depot the other day, rolling them up an inclined plane. The truckman stood behind and shoved, after putting a couple of ropes one round each end of the hogshead, while two men standing in the depot steadily pulled at the ropes. The first man was the lecturer, the last was the audience. It is the duty of the lecturer to team his hogshead of sweets to the depot, or Lyceum, place the horse, arrange the ropes, and shove; and it is the duty of the audience to take hold of the ropes and pull with all their might.

Read well! Did you ever suck cider through a straw? Did you ever know the cider to push out of the straw when you were not sucking,—unless it chanced to be in a complete ferment? An audience will draw out of a lecture, or enable a lecturer to read, only such parts of his lecture as they like. If it is pronounced good, it is partly to the credit of the hearers; if bad, it is partly their fault. Sometimes a lazy audience refuses to cooperate and pull on the ropes with a will, simply because the hogshead is full and therefore heavy, when if it were empty, or had only a little sugar adhering to it, they would whisk it up the slope in a jiffy.

March 7. The mystery of the life of plants is kindred with that of our own lives, and the physiologist must not presume to explain their growth according to mechanical laws, or as he might explain some machinery of his own making. We must not expect to probe with our fingers the sanctuary of any life, whether animal or vegetable. If we do, we shall discover nothing but surface still. The ultimate expression or fruit of any created thing is a fine effluence which only the most ingenuous worshipper perceives at a reverent distance from its surface even. Only that intellect makes any progress toward conceiving of the essence which at the same time perceives the effluence.

Accordingly, I reject Carpenter's explanation of the fact that a potato vine in a cellar grows toward the light, when he says, "The reason obviously is, that, in consequence of the loss of fluid from the tissue of the stem on the side on which the light falls, it is contracted, whilst that of the other side remains turgid with fluid; the stem makes a bend, therefore, until its growing point becomes opposite to the light, and then increases in that direction." (C.'s "Vegetable Physiology," page 174.)

There is no ripeness which is not, so to speak, something ultimate in itself, and not merely a perfected means to a higher end. In order to be ripe it must serve a transcendent use. The ripeness of a leaf, being perfected, leaves the tree at that point and never returns to it. It has nothing to do with any other fruit which the tree may bear, and only the genius of the poet can pluck it.

The fruit of a tree is neither in the seed nor the timber,—the full-grown tree,—but it is simply the highest use to which it can be put.

March 8. A rainy day.

P.M.—To Hill in rain.

To us snow and cold seem a mere delaying of the spring. How far we are from understanding the value of these things in the economy of Nature!

The earth is still mostly covered with ice and snow. As usual, I notice large pools of greenish water in the fields, on an icy bottom, which cannot owe their greenness to the reflected blue mingled with the yellowish light at sundown, as I supposed in the case of the green ice and water in clear winter days, for I see the former now at midday and in a rain-storm, when no sky is visible. I think that these green pools over an icy bottom must be produced by the yellow or common earth-stain in the water mingling with the blue which is reflected from the ice. Many pools have so large a proportion of this yellow tinge as not to look green but yellow. The stain, the tea, of withered vegetation—grass and leaves—and of the soil supplies the yellow tint.

But perhaps those patches of emerald sky, sky just tinged with green, which we sometimes see, far in the horizon or near it, are produced in the same way as I thought the green ice was,—some yellow glow reflected from a cloud mingled with the blue of the atmosphere.

One might say that the yellow of the earth mingled with the blue of the sky to make the green of vegetation.

Men of science, when they pause to contemplate "the power, wisdom, and goodness" of God, or, as they sometimes call him, "the Almighty Designer," speak of him as a total stranger whom it is necessary to treat with the highest consideration. They seem suddenly to have lost their wits.

March 11. P.M.—To Hunt house.

I go to get one more sight of the old house which Hosmer is pulling down, but I am too late to see much of it. The chimney is gone and little more than the oblong square frame stands. E. Hosmer and Nathan Hosmer are employed taking it down. The latter draws all the nails, however crooked, and puts them in his pockets, for, being wrought ones, he says it is worth the while.

On the chimney was the date 1703 (?),—I think that was it,— and if this was the date of the chimney, it would appear that the old part belonged to the Winthrops, and it may go back to near the settlement of the town. The timbers of the old part had been cased and the joists plastered over at some time, and, now that they were uncovered, you saw many old memorandums and scores in chalk on them, as "May ye 4th," "Ephraim Brown," "o—3s—4d," "oxen," ﬀﬀﬀﬀ —so they kept their score or tally,—such as the butcher and baker sometimes make. Perhaps the occupant had let his neighbor have the use of his oxen so many days. I asked if they had found any old coins. N. Hosmer answered, Yes, he had, and showed it me,—took it out of his pocket. It was about as big as a quarter of a dollar, with "Britain," etc., legible, "Geo II," and date "1742," but it was of lead. But there was no manuscript,— not a copy of verses, only these chalk records of butter and cheese, oxen and bacon, and a counterfeit coin, out of the smoky recesses.

My mother says that she has been to the charitable society there. One old jester of the town used to call it "the *chattable* society."

Mrs. A. takes on dolefully on account of the solitude in which she lives, but she gets little consolation. Mrs. B. says she envies her that retirement. Mrs. A. is aware that she does, and says it is as if a thirsty man should envy another the river in which he is drowning. So goes the world. It is either this extreme or that. Of solitude one gets too much and another not enough.

E. Hosmer says that a man told him that he had seen my uncle Charles take a twelve-foot ladder, set it up straight, and then run up and down the other side, kicking it from behind him as he went down. E. H. told of seeing him often at the tavern toss his hat to the ceiling, twirling it over, and catch it on his head every time.

Large flocks of blackbirds to-day in the elm-tops and other trees. These are the first conspicuous large flocks of birds. J. Farmer says he saw ducks this morning and has seen larks some days. Channing saw geese to-day.

Find out as soon as possible what are the best things in your composition, and then shape the rest to fit them. The former will be the midrib and veins of the leaf.

There is always some accident in the best things, whether thoughts or expressions or deeds. The memorable thought, the happy expression, the admirable deed are only partly ours. The thought came to us because we were in a fit mood; also we were unconscious and did not know that we had said or done a good thing. We must walk consciously only part way toward our goal, and then leap in the dark to our success. What we do best or most perfectly is what we have most thoroughly learned by the longest practice, and at length it falls from us without our notice, as a leaf from a tree. It is the *last* time we shall do it,—our unconscious leavings.

March 12. It is a regular spring rain, such as I remember walking in,—windy but warm. It alternately rains hard and then holds up a little. A similar alternation we see in the waves of water and all undulating surfaces,—in snow and sand and the clouds (the mackerel sky). Now you walk in a comparative lull, anticipating fair weather, with but a slight drizzling, and anon the wind blows and the rain drives down harder than ever. In one of these lulls, as I passed the Joe Hosmer (rough-cast) house, I thought I never saw any bank so handsome as the russet hillside behind it. It is a very barren, exhausted soil, where the cladonia lichens abound, and the lower side is a flowing sand, but this russet grass with its weeds, being saturated with moisture, was in this light the richest brown, methought, that I ever saw. A peculiar and unaccountable light seemed to fall on that bank or hillside, though it was thick storm all around. A sort of Newfoundland sun seemed to be shining on it. It was a prospect to excite a reindeer. These tints of brown were as softly and richly fair and sufficing as the most brilliant autumnal tints. This kind of light, the air being full of rain and all vegetation dripping with it, brings out the browns wonderfully.

March 13. I see a small flock of blackbirds flying over, some rising, others falling, yet all advancing together, one flock but many birds, some silent, others tchucking,—incessant alternation. This harmonious movement as in a dance, this agreeing to differ, makes the charm of the spectacle to me. One bird looks fractional, naked, like a single thread or ravelling from the web to which it belongs. Alternation! Alternation! Heaven and hell! Here again in the flight of a bird, its ricochet motion, is that undulation observed in so many materials, as in the mackerel sky.

I cannot easily forget the beauty of those terrestrial browns in the rain yesterday. The withered grass was not of that very pale hoary brown that it is to-day, now that it is dry and lifeless, but, being perfectly saturated and dripping with the rain, the whole hillside seemed to reflect a certain yellowish light, so that you looked around for the sun in the midst of the storm. All the yellow and red and leather-color in the fawn-colored weeds was more intense than at any other season. The withered ferns which fell last fall—pinweeds, sarothra, etc.—were actually a *glowing* brown for the same reason, being all dripping wet. The very bare sand slopes, with only here and there a thin crusting of mosses, was a richer color than ever it is.

In short, in these early spring rains, the withered herbage, thus saturated, and reflecting its brightest withered tint, seems in a certain degree to have revived, and sympathizes with the fresh greenish or yellowish or brownish lichens in its midst, which also seem to have withered. It seemed to me—and I think it may be the truth—that the abundant moisture, bringing out the highest color in the brown surface of the earth, generated a certain degree of light, which, when the rain held up a little, reminded you of the sun shining through a thick mist.

The barrenest surfaces, perhaps, are the most interesting in such weather as yesterday, when the most terrene colors are seen. The wet earth and sand, and especially subsoil, are very invigorating sights.

The Hunt house, to draw from memory,—though I have given its measures within two years in my Journal,—looked like this:—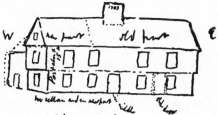

This is only generally correct, without a scale.

March 14. P.M.—To Hunt house.

I thought from the above drawing that the original door must have been in the middle of the old part and not at one end, and that I should detect it in the manner in which the studs were set in. I really did so and found some other traces of the old door (where I have dotted it) when I got there. Some of the chalkmarks which have been preserved under the casing of the timbers so long have been completely washed off in yesterday's rain, as the frame stood bare. Also read in chalk on a chamber floor joist (which had been plastered over beneath) "enfine Brown," so many s. and d., and what most read for "Feb 1666," but, being written over a rough knot, it is doubtful. "Hides 3."

March 16. I look down over Tarbell's Bay, just north of Ball's Hill. Not only meadows but potato and rye fields are buried deep, and you see there, sheltered by the hills on the northwest, a placid blue bay having the russet hills for shores. This kind of bay, or lake, made by the freshet—these deep and narrow "fiords"—can only be seen along such a stream as this, liable to an annual freshet. The water rests as gently as a dewdrop on a leaf, laving its tender temporary shores. It has no strand, leaves no permanent water-mark, but though you look at it a quarter of a mile off, you know that the rising flood is gently overflowing a myriad withered green blades there in succession. There is the magic of lakes that come and go. The lake or bay is not an institution, but a phenomenon. You plainly see that it is so much water poured into the hollows of the earth.

March 17. 6.30 A.M.—River risen still higher.

I realize how water predominates on the surface of the globe. I am surprised to see new and unexpected water-lines, drawn by the level edge of the flood about knolls in the meadows and in the woods,— waving lines, rarely if ever recognized or thought of by the walker or any, which mark the boundary of a possible or probable freshet any spring. Even if the highest water-mark were indicated at one point, the surveyor could not, with any labor short of infinite, draw these lines for us which wind about every elevation of earth or rock. Yet, though this slight difference of level which the water so simply and effectually points out, is so unobservable by us ordinarily, no doubt Nature never forgets it for a moment, but plants grow and insects, etc., breed in conformity to it. Many a kingdom of nature has its boundaries parallel with this waving line. By these freshets, the relation of some field, usually far from the stream, to future or past deluge is suggested. I am surprised and amused, at least, to walk in such a field and observe the nice distinctions which the great water-level makes there. So plants and animals and thoughts have their commonly unseen shores, and many portions of the earth are, with reference to them, islands or peninsulas or capes, shores or mountains.

We are stiff and set in our geography because the level of water is comparatively, or within short periods, unchangeable. We look only in the sea for islands and continents and their varieties. But there are more subtle and invisible and fluctuating floods which island this or that part of the earth whose geography has never been mapped. For instance, here is Mantatuket Rock, commonly a rocky peninsula with a low or swampy neck and all covered with wood. It is now a small rocky island, and not only the swampy neck but a considerable portion of the upland is blotted out by the flood, covered and concealed under water; and what surprises me is that the water should so instantly know and select its own shore on the upland, though I could not have told with my eye whether it would be thirty feet this way or as many that. A distinction is made for me by the water in this case which I had never thought of, revealing the relation of this surface to the flood ordinarily far from it, and which I now begin to perceive that every tree and shrub and herbaceous plant growing there knew, if I did not.

How different to-day from yesterday! Yesterday was a cool, bright day, the earth just washed bare by the rain, and a strong northwest wind raised respectable billows on our vernal seas and imparted remarkable life and spirit to the scene. To-day it is perfectly still and warm; but, seen through this air, though many might not notice the difference, the russet surface of the earth does not shine, is not bright. The air is comparatively dead when I attend to it, and it is as if there were the veil of a fine mist over all objects, dulling their edges. Yet this would be called a clear day. These aerial differences in the days are not commonly appreciated, though they affect our spirits.

As I float by the Rock, I hear rustling amid the oak leaves above that new water-line, and, there being no wind, I know it to be a striped squirrel, and soon see its long-unseen striped sides flirting about the instep of an oak. Its lateral stripes, alternate black and yellowish, are a type which I have not seen for a long time, or rather a punctuation-mark, the character to indicate where a new paragraph commences in the revolution of the seasons. Double lines.

March 18. Consider how I discovered where the Winthrop family in this town placed their front door some two hundred years ago, without any verbal or written or ocular evidence. I, with others, saw by the frame of the old Hunt house that an addition had been made to its west end in 1703. This brought the front door, which was in the middle of the present, near one end of the original or Winthrop house. I, sitting at home, said to myself, having an occult sympathy with the Winthrops of that date, "The front door must originally have been in the middle of the old house, for symmetry and convenience required it, and if it was, I shall find traces of it; I shall find there where studs have been set into the frame in a different manner from the rest." I went to the house and looked where the door should have been, and I found precisely the evidence I sought, and, beside, where the timber above had been cut out just the width of the door.

March 19. All sorts of lumber is afloat. Rails, planks, and timber, etc., which the unthrifty neglected to secure now change hands. Much railroad lumber is floated off. While one end rests on the land, it is the railroad's, but as soon as it is afloat it is made the property of him who saves it. I see some poor neighbors as earnest as the railroad employees are negligent, to secure it. It blows so hard that you walk aslant against the wind. Your very beard, if you wear a full one, is a serious cause of detention.

The meadows are all in commotion. The ducks are now concealed by the waves, if there are any floating there. The wind makes such a din about your ears that conversation is difficult; your words are blown away and do not strike the ear they were aimed at. If you walk by the water, the tumult of the waves confuses you. If you go by a tree or enter the woods, the din is yet greater. Nevertheless this universal commotion is very interesting and exciting.

We are interested in the phenomena of Nature mainly as children are, or as we are in games of chance. They are more or less exciting. Our appetite for novelty is insatiable. We do not attend to ordinary things, though they are most important, but to extraordinary ones. While it is only moderately hot or cold, or wet or dry, nobody attends to it, but when Nature goes to an extreme in any of these directions we are all on the alert with excitement. Not that we care about the philosophy or the effects of this phenomenon. *E.g.*, when I went to Boston in the early train the coldest morning of last winter, two topics mainly occupied the attention of the passengers, Morphy's chess victories and Nature's victorious cold that morning. The inhabitants of various towns were comparing notes, and that one whose door opened upon a greater degree of cold than any of his neighbors' doors chuckled not a little. Almost every one I met asked me almost before our salutations were over "how the glass stood" at my house or in my town,—the librarian of the college, the registrar of deeds at Cambridgeport,—a total stranger to me, whose form of inquiry made me think of another sort of glass,—and each rubbed his hands with pretended horror but real delight if I named a higher figure than he had yet heard. It was plain that one object which the cold was given us for was our amusement, a passing excitement. It would be perfectly consistent and American to bet on the coldness of our respective towns, of the morning that is to come. Thus a greater degree of cold may be said to warm us more than a less one. We hear with ill-concealed disgust the figures reported from some localities, where they never enjoy the luxury of severe cold. This is a perfectly legitimate amusement, only we should know that each day is peculiar and has its kindred excitements.

March 23. The qualities of the land that are most attractive to our eyes now are dryness and firmness. It is not the rich black soil, but warm and sandy hills and plains which tempt our steps. We love to sit on and walk over sandy tracts in the spring like cicindelas. These tongues of russet land tapering and sloping into the flood do almost speak to one. They are alternately in sun and shade. When the cloud is passed, and they reflect their pale-brown light to me, I am tempted to go to them.

The loud *peop* (?) of a pigeon woodpecker is heard in our sea, and anon the prolonged loud and shrill *cackle*, calling the thin-wooded hillsides and pastures to life. It is like the note of an alarm-clock set last fall so as to wake Nature up at exactly this date. *Up up up up up up up up up!*

It is suggested that the blue is darkest when reflected from the most agitated water, because of the shadow (occasioned by the inequalities) mingled with it.

Some Indians of the north have but one word for blue and black, and blue is with us considered the darkest color, though it is the color of the sky or air. Light, I should say, was white; the absence of it, black. Hold up to the light a perfectly opaque body and you get black, but hold up to it the least opaque body, such as air, and you get blue. Hence you may say that blue is light seen through a veil.

March 25. Again I walk in the rain and see the rich yellowish browns of the moist banks. Surely russet is not the name which describes the fields and hillsides now, whether wet or dry. There is not red enough in it. I do not know a better name for this (when wet) yellowish brown than "tawny." On the south side of these warm hills, it may perhaps be called one of the fawn-colors, *i.e.* brown inclining to green. Much of this peculiar yellowish color on the surface of the Clamshell plain is due to a little curled sedge or grass growing at short intervals, loosely covering the ground (with green mosses intermixed) in little tufts like curled hair.

Day before yesterday, in clear, dry weather, we had pale-brown or fawn-colored earth, *i.e.*, a dry, withered grass blade; to-day, a more yellow brown or tawny, the same being wet. The wet brings out an agreeable yellow light, as if the sun were shining through a mist on it. The earth is more truly russet in November, when there is more redness left in the withered and withering vegetation. Such is the change in the color of the bare portions of the earth (*i.e.* bare of trees and bushes) produced by rain. Also the oak leaves are much redder. In fair weather the light color of these objects was simply a light reflected from them, originating in the sun and sky; now it is a more proper and inward light, which attracts and confines our attention to moist sward itself.

A snipe flies away from the moist Clamshell shore, uttering its *cr-a-ack c-r-r-rack*.

I thought the other day, How we enjoy a warm and pleasant day at this season! We dance like gnats in the sun.

The color of spring hitherto,—I should say that in dry weather it was fawn-colored, in wet more yellowish or tawny. When wet, the green of the fawn is supplied by the lichens and the mosses.

March 28. P.M.—Paddle to the Bedford line.

It is now high time to look for arrowheads, etc. I spend many hours every spring gathering the crop which the melting snow and rain have washed bare. It is one of the regular pursuits of the spring.

I have not decided whether I had better publish my experience in searching for arrowheads in three volumes, with plates and an index, or try to compress it into one. These durable implements seem to have been suggested to the Indian mechanic with a view to my entertainment in a succeeding period. After all the labor expended on it, the bolt may have been shot but once perchance, and the shaft which was devoted to it decayed, and there lay the arrow-head, sinking into the ground, awaiting me. They lie all over the hills with like expectation, and in due time the husbandman is sent, and, tempted by the promise of corn or rye, he plows the land and turns them up to my view. Many as I have found, methinks the last one gives me about the same delight that the first did. Some time or other, you would say, it had rained arrowheads, for they lie all over the surface of America. You cannot tell the third-hand ones (for they are all second-hand) from the others, such is their persistent out-of-door durability; for they were chiefly made to be lost. They are sown, like a grain that is slow to germinate, broadcast over the earth. Like the dragon's teeth which bore a crop of soldiers, these bear crops of philosophers and poets, and the same seed is just as good to plant again. It is a stone fruit. Each one yields me a thought. I come nearer to the maker of it than if I found his bones. His bones would not prove any wit that wielded them, such as this work of his bones does. It is humanity inscribed on the face of the earth, patent to my eyes as soon as the snow goes off, not hidden away in some crypt or grave or under a pyramid. No disgusting mummy, but a clean stone, the best symbol or letter that could have been transmitted to me.

The Red Man, his mark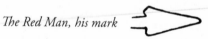

At every step I see it, and I can easily supply the "Tahatawan" or "Mantatuket" that might have been written if he had had a clerk. It is no single inscription on a particular rock, but a footprint—rather a mindprint—left everywhere, and altogether illegible.

Time will soon destroy the works of famous painters and sculptors, but the Indian arrowhead will balk his efforts and Eternity will have to come to his aid. They are not fossil bones, but, as it were, fossil thoughts, forever reminding me of the mind that shaped them. I would fain know that I am treading in the tracks of human game,—that I am on the trail of mind,—and these little reminders never fail to set me right.

It is a recommendation that they are so inobvious,—that they occur only to the eye and thought that chances to be directed toward them. When you pick up an arrowhead and put it in your pocket, it may say: "Eh, you think you have got me, do you? But I shall wear a hole in your pocket at last, or if you put me in your cabinet, your heir or great-grandson will forget me or throw me out the window directly, or when the house falls I shall drop into the cellar, and there I shall lie quite at home again. Ready to be *found* again, eh? Perhaps some new red man that is to come will fit me to a shaft and make me do his bidding for a bow-shot. What reck I?"

I suspect it will be found that there is really some advantage in large birds of passage flying in the wedge form and cleaving their way through the air,—that they really do overcome its resistance best in this way,—and perchance the direction and strength of the wind determine the comparative length of the two sides.

The great gulls fly generally up or down the river valley, cutting off the bends of the river, and so do these geese. These fly sympathizing with the river,—a stream in the air, soon lost in the distant sky.

We see these geese swimming and flying at midday and when it is perfectly fair.

If you scan the horizon at this season of the year you are very likely to detect a small flock of dark ducks moving with rapid wing athwart the sky, or see the undulating line of migrating geese against the sky.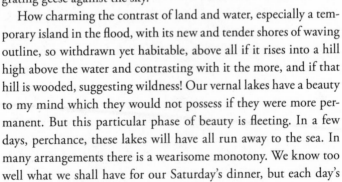

How charming the contrast of land and water, especially a temporary island in the flood, with its new and tender shores of waving outline, so withdrawn yet habitable, above all if it rises into a hill high above the water and contrasting with it the more, and if that hill is wooded, suggesting wildness! Our vernal lakes have a beauty to my mind which they would not possess if they were more permanent. But this particular phase of beauty is fleeting. In a few days, perchance, these lakes will have all run away to the sea. In many arrangements there is a wearisome monotony. We know too well what we shall have for our Saturday's dinner, but each day's feast in Nature's year is a surprise to us and adapted to our appetite and spirits. Her motive is not economy but satisfaction.

March 31. It will show how our prejudices interfere with our perception of color, to state that yesterday morning, after making a fire in the kitchen cooking-stove, as I sat over it I thought I saw a little bit of red or scarlet flannel on a chink near a bolt-head on the stove, and I tried to pick it out,—while I was a little surprised that I did not smell it burning. It was merely the reflection of the flame of the fire through a chink, on the dark stove. This showed me what the true color of the flame was, but when I knew what this was, it was not very easy to perceive it again. It appeared now more yellowish. I think that my senses made the truest report the first time.

It is a very windy afternoon, wind northwest, and at length a dark cloud rises on that side, evidently of a windy structure, a dusky mass with lighter intervals, like a parcel of brushes lying side by side,—a parcel of "mare's-tails" perhaps. It winds up with a flurry of rain.

April 3. Men's minds run so much on work and money that the mass instantly associate all literary labor with a pecuniary reward. They are mainly curious to know how much money the lecturer or author gets for his work. They think that the naturalist takes so much pains to collect plants or animals because he is paid for it. An Irishman who saw me in the fields making a minute in my notebook took it for granted that I was casting up my wages and actually inquired what they came to, as if he had never dreamed of any other use for writing. I might have quoted to him that the wages of sin is death, as the most pertinent answer. "What do you get for lecturing now?" I am occasionally asked. It is the more amusing since I only lecture about once a year out of my native town, often not at all; so that I might as well, if my objects were merely pecuniary, give up the business.

XXIX.

April 12. I look again at the meadow-crust carried off by the ice. There is one by the railroad bridge, say three rods by one, covered with button-bushes and willows. Another, some five rods by three, at the south end of Potter Swamp Meadow, also covered densely with button-bushes, etc. It is far from the river, by the edge of the wood. Another, and the most interesting one, lies up high some thirty rods north of this near the wood-side and fifteen rods from the river. I measure it with a tape. It is rudely triangular and about four rods on a side, though the sides are longer on the convex line. As well as the other, it is from one to three feet thick and very densely covered with button-bushes, with a few black and other willows and late roses from four to seven feet high. As dense and impassable as any kind of thicket that we have, and there are, besides, countless great yellow and white lily and pontederia roots in it. It is a large and densely bushy island in the meadow. It would surprise any one to behold it. Suppose that you were to find in the morning such a slice of the earth's crust with its vegetation dropped in your front yard, if it could contain it. I think we should not soon hear the last of it. It is an island such as might almost satisfy Sancho Panza's desires. It is a forest, in short, and not a very small one either. It is Birnam wood come to Dunsinane. It contained at least eight square rods.

Such revolutions can take place and none but the proprietor of the meadow notice it, for the traveller passing within sight does not begin to suspect that the bushy island which he sees in the meadow has floated from elsewhere, or if he saw it when on its voyage, he would not know it for a voyager. In one year all the raw edge is concealed, and the vegetation thus transplanted does not appear to find it out. These must have been carried off about the 16th of March or when the river broke up, perhaps in that strong southwest wind of the 19th. The ice, being eighteen or twenty inches thick and having ten thousand strong handles to take hold by, aided too often by the lightness of the frozen meadow, can easily lift these masses, and if there were rocks imbedded in them, would move them also.

The present islands, bushy or wooded, in the meadow have no doubt commonly had this origin. The soil is there doubled, and so elevated, and the plants set out at the same time. When the flood comes with icy hands you have got a mighty lifter at work. Black willows ten feet high and these four or five rods of button-bushes are all taken up together with their soil and carried upright and without jarring to a new locality half a mile or more distant.

April 15. The bay-wing now sings—the first I have been able to hear. It comes to revive with its song the dry uplands and pastures and grass-fields about the skirts of villages. If you yield for a moment to the impressions of sense, you hear some bird giving expression to its happiness in a pleasant strain. We are provided with singing birds and with ears to hear them. What an institution that!

Consider how much is annually spent on the farmer's life: the beauty of his abode, which has inspired poets since the world was made; the hundreds of delicate and beautiful flowers scattered profusely under his feet and all around him, as he walks or drives his team afield,—he cannot put his spade into uncultivated, nor into much cultivated, ground without disturbing some of them; a hundred or two of equally beautiful birds to sing to him morning and evening, and some at noonday, a good part of the year; a perfect sky arched over him, a perfect carpet spread under him, etc., etc.!

April 17. The air which was so lately void and silent begins to resound as it were with the breathing of a myriad fellow-creatures, and even the unhappy man, on the principle that misery loves company, is soothed by this infinite din of neighbors. I have listened for the notes of various birds, and now, in this faint hum of bees, I hear as it were the first twittering of the bird Summer.

A wood tortoise on bank; first seen, water so high.

April 21. Setting pines all day in R.W.E.'s Wyman lot. This makes two and a half days, with two men and a horse and cart to help me. We have set some four hundred trees at fifteen feet apart diamond-wise, covering some two acres. I set every one with my own hand, while another digs the holes where I indicate, and occasionally helps the other dig up the trees. We prefer bushy pines only one foot high which grow in open or pasture land, yellow-looking trees which are used to the sun, instead of the spindling dark-green ones from the shade of the woods. There are a great many more of these plants to be had along the edges and in the midst of any white pine wood than one would suppose.

Got about one hundred and twenty from George Heywood's land and the rest from the Brister lot and this Wyman lot itself.

R.W.E. has bought a quarter of a pound of white pine seed at $4.00 per pound.

We could not dig up pines on the north side of the wood on the Brister lot to-day on account of frost! Though we had quite forgotten it, and put the winter so far behind us.

April 22. When setting the pines at Walden the last three days, wandering thoughts visited me, which I have now forgotten. My senses were busily suggesting them, though I was unconscious of their origin. *E.g.*, I first *consciously* found myself entertaining the thought of a carriage on the road, and directly after I was aware that I heard it. No doubt I had heard it before, or rather my ears had, but I was quite unconscious of it,—it was not a fact of my then state of existence; yet such was the force of habit, it affected my thoughts nevertheless, so double, if not treble, even, are we. Sometimes the senses bring us information quicker than we can receive it. Perhaps these thoughts which run in ruts by themselves while we are engaged in some routine may be called automatic. I distinctly entertained the idea of a carriage, without the slightest suspicion how it had originated or been suggested to my mind. I have no doubt at all that my ears had heard it, but my mind, just then preoccupied, had refused to attend to it. This suggests that most, if not all, indeed, of our ideas may be due some sort of sensuous impression of which we may or may not be conscious.

April 24. There is a season for everything, and we do not notice a given phenomenon except at that season, if, indeed, it can be called the same phenomenon at any other season. There is a time to watch the ripples on Ripple Lake, to look for arrowheads, to study the rocks and lichens, a time to walk on sandy deserts; and the observer of nature must improve these seasons as much as the farmer his. So boys fly kites and play ball or hawkie at particular times all over the State. A wise man will know what game to play to-day, and play it. We must not be governed by rigid rules, as by the almanac, but let the season rule us. The moods and thoughts of man are revolving just as steadily and incessantly as nature's. Nothing must be postponed. Take time by the forelock. Now or never! You must live in the present, launch yourself on every wave, find your eternity in each moment. Take any other course, and life will be a succession of regrets. There is no world for the penitent and regretful.

Dr. B. asked me what I found that was new these days, if I was still looking after the beautiful. I told him yes, and that I wished to hire two or three good observers.

April 29. 7 A.M.—To Walden, and set one hundred larch trees from England, all two years from seed, about nine inches high, just begun to leaf.

May 1. We accuse savages of worshipping only the bad spirit, or devil, though they may distinguish both a good and a bad; but they regard only that one which they fear and worship the devil only. We too are savages in this, doing precisely the same thing. This occurred to me yesterday as I sat in the woods admiring the beauty of the blue butterfly. We are not chiefly interested in birds and insects, for example, as they are ornamental to the earth and cheering to man, but we spare the lives of the former only on condition that they eat more grubs than they do cherries, and the only account of the insects which the State encourages is of the "Insects *Injurious* to Vegetation." We too admit both a good and a bad spirit, but we worship chiefly the bad spirit, whom we fear. We do not think first of the good but of the harm things will do us.

The catechism says that the chief end of man is to glorify God and enjoy him forever, which of course is applicable mainly to God as seen in his works. Yet the only account of its beautiful insects— butterflies, etc.—which God has made and set before us which the State ever thinks of spending any money on is the account of those which are injurious to vegetation! This is the way we glorify God and enjoy him forever. Come out here and behold a thousand painted butterflies and other beautiful insects which people the air, then go to the libraries and see what kind of prayer and glorification of God is there recorded.

Science is inhuman. Things seen with a microscope begin to be insignificant. So described, they are as monstrous as if they should be magnified a thousand diameters. Suppose I should see and describe men and houses and trees and birds as if they were a thousand times larger than they are!

Very warm. See hundreds of turtles. All up and down our river meadows their backs are shining in the sun to-day. It is a turtle day.

As we sat on the steep hillside south of Nut Meadow Brook Crossing, we noticed a remarkable whirlwind on a small scale, which carried up the oak leaves from that Island copse in the meadow. The oak leaves now hang thinly and are very dry and light, and these small whirlwinds, which seem to be occasioned by the sudden hot and calm weather (like whirlpools or dimples in a smooth stream), wrench them off, and up they go, somewhat spirally, in countless flocks like birds, with a rustling sound; and higher and higher into the clear blue deeps they rise above our heads, till they are fairly lost to sight, looking, when last seen, mere light specks against the blue, like stars by day, in fact. I could distinguish some, I have no doubt, five or six hundred feet high at least, but if I looked aside a moment they were lost. The largest oak leaves looked not bigger than a five-cent-piece. These were drifting eastward,— to descend where? Methought that, instead of decaying on the earth or being consumed by fire, these were being translated and would soon be taken in at the windows of heaven. I had never observed this phenomenon so remarkable. The flight of the leaves. This was quite local, and it was comparatively still where we sat a few rods on one side. Thousands went up together in a rustling flock.

May 4. Wednesday. P.M.—To Lee's Cliff on foot.

This the fourth warm day. Looking up through this soft and warm southwest wind, I notice the conspicuous shadow of Middle Conantum Cliff, now at 3 P.M., and elsewhere the shade of a few apple trees,—their trunks and boughs. It is remarkable that shadow should only be noticed now when decidedly warm weather comes, though before the leaves have expanded, *i.e.*, when it begins to be grateful to our senses. This first shadow is as noticeable and memorable as a flower. I observe annually the first shadow of this cliff. When we begin to pass from sunshine into shade for our refreshment; when we look on shade with yearning as on a friend. That cliff and its shade suggests dark eyes and eyelashes and overhanging brows. Few things are more suggestive of heat than this first shade, though now we see only the tracery of tree-boughs on the greening grass and the sandy street. This I notice at the same time with the first bumblebee, when the *Rana palustris* purrs in the meadow generally, the white willow and aspen display their tender green full of yellow light, the parti-colored warbler is first heard over the swamp, the woodchuck, who loves warmth, is out on the hillsides in numbers, the jingle of the chip-bird is incessantly heard, the thrasher sings incessantly, the first cricket is heard in a warm rocky place, and that scent of vernal flowers is in the air.

Life out of doors begins.

May 5. Thursday. Red-wings fly in flocks yet. Near the oak beyond Jarvis land, a yellow butterfly,—how hot! this meteor dancing through the air. Also see a *scalloped*-edge dark-colored butterfly resting on the trunk of a tree, where, both by its form and color, its wings being closed, it resembles a bit of bark, or rather a lichen. Evidently their forms and colors, especially of the under sides of their wings, are designed to conceal them when at rest with their wings closed.

The wilderness, in the eyes of our forefathers, was a vast and howling place or *space*, where a man might roam naked of house and most other defense, exposed to wild beasts and wilder men. They who went to war with the Indians and French were said to have been "out," and the wounded and missing who at length returned after a fight were said to have "got in."

June 3. Friday. P.M.—Up Assabet.

A large yellow butterfly (somewhat Harris *Papilio Asterias* like but not *black*-winged) three and a half to four inches in expanse. Pale-yellow, the front wings crossed by three or four black bars; rear, or outer edge, of all wings widely bordered with black, and some yellow behind it; a short black tail to each hind one, with two blue spots in front of two red-brown ones on the tail.[*]

Nighthawk, two eggs, fresh. Quail heard.

June 24. The 22d, 23d, and 24th, I have been surveying the bridges and river from Heard's Bridge to the Billerica dam.

The testimony of the farmers, etc., is that the river thirty to fifty years ago was much lower in the summer than now. Deacon Richard Heard spoke of playing when a boy on the river side of the bushes where the pads are, and of wading with great ease at Heard's Bridge, and I hear that one Rice (of Wayland or Sudbury), an old man, remembers galloping his horse through the meadows to the edge of the river. The meadow just above the causeway on the Wayland side was spoken of as particularly valuable. Colonel David Heard, who accompanied me and is best acquainted of any with the details of the controversy,—has worked at clearing out the river (I think about 1820),—said that he did not know of a rock in the

---

[*] *P. Turnus?*

river from the falls near the Framingham line to perhaps the rear of Hubbard's in Concord.

July 4. P.M.—To Fair Haven Pond, measuring depth of river.

As you walk beside a ditch or brook, you see the frogs which you alarm launching themselves from a considerable distance into the brook. They spring considerably upward, so as to clear all intervening obstacles, and seem to know pretty well where the brook is. Yet no doubt they often strike, to their chagrin and perhaps sorrow, on a pebbly shore or rock. Their noses must be peculiarly organized to resist accidents of this kind, and allow them to cast themselves thus heedlessly into the air, trusting to fall into the water, for they come down nose foremost. A frog reckons that he knows where the brook is. I shudder for them when I see their soft, unshielded proboscis falling thus heedlessly on whatever may be beneath.

July 7. I learn from measuring on Baldwin's second map that the river (*i.e.* speaking of that part below Framingham) is much the straightest in the lower part of its course, or from Ball's Hill to the Dam.

It winds most in the broad meadows. The greatest meander is in the Sudbury meadows.

From upper end of Sudbury Canal to Sherman's Bridge direct is 558 rods (1 mile 238 rods); by thread of river, 1000 rods (3 miles 40 rods), or nearly twice as far.

But, though meandering, it is straighter in its general course than would be believed. These nearly twenty-three miles in length (or 16+ direct) are contained within a breadth of two miles twenty-six rods; *i.e.*, so much it takes to meander in. It can be plotted by the scale of one thousand feet to an inch on a sheet of paper seven feet one and one quarter inches long by eleven inches wide.

July 9. I see, at length, where the floated meadow (on Hubbard's meadow) came from last spring,—from opposite Bittern Cliff, and some below. There is a pond created in the meadow there, some five rods by four and three to three and a half feet deep, water being eleven and a half inches above summer level. So much of the meadow which has been mowed is thus converted into a pool.

We are accustomed to refer changes in the shore and the channel to the very gradual influence of the current washing away and depositing matter which was held in suspension, but certainly in many parts of our river the ice which moves these masses of bushes and meadow is a much more important agent. It will alter the map of the river in one year. The whole shore for forty rods on the east side below Bittern Cliff was stripped of its button-bushes and willows, etc., etc., last spring, and as I floated over the river there to-day, I could not at first account for the remarkable breadth of the river there, like a bay. I got a very novel impression of the size of the river, though it is now low water. In fact the width of the river has been increased fully three or four rods for more than forty rods in length, and is three to four feet deep on that side now. You cannot tell, of any clump or row of button-bushes, whether it grew up where it stands or was thus set out there.

July 11. The position of the button-bushes determines the width of the river, no less than the width or depth of the water determines the position of the button-bushes. We call that all river between the button-bushes, though sometimes they may have landed or sprung up in a regular brink fashion three or four rods further from, or nearer to, the channel.

That mass (described on the 9th, seen the 10th) in the Wayland meadows above Sherman's Bridge was, I think, the largest mass drifted or growing at all on that great meadow. So this transplantation is not on an insignificant scale when compared with the whole body that grows by our river.

I hear that Mr. and Mrs. Such-a-one are "going to the beach" for six weeks. What a failure and defeat this suggests their lives to be! Here they live, perchance, the rest of the year, trying to do as they would be done by and to exercise charity of all kinds, and now at last, the parents not having realized their aspirations in the married state, and the misses now begun to be old maids without having found any match at all, succumb and slope to the beach for six weeks. Yet, so far from being felt to be a proof of failure in the lives of these Christians, it is thought to be the culminating-point of their activity. At length their season of activity is arrived, and they go to the beach, they energetically keep cool. They bathe daily and are blown on by the sea-breeze. This keeps their courage up for the labors of the year. This recess which the Sabbath-school teachers take!

July 22. For the last mile above the Falls the river becomes rocky, the rocks gradually increasing in number, until at the Falls its bed is crowded with them. Some of the rocks are curiously water-worn. They are, as usual in our black river, almost as black as ink,— the parts much submerged,—and I notice that bricks and white crockery on the bottom acquire the same color from the water, as if painted black. The water of this river is a black paint-brush which coats all things with fast colors. Rocks half a dozen feet in diameter which were originally of the usual lumpish form are worn thus by the friction of the pebbles, etc., washed against them by the stream at high water. Several of them have this peculiar sheaf-like form; and black as ink. But, though evidently worn into this form by the rush of water, they are by no means worn smooth, but are as rough as a grater, such being their composition.

I was surprised to see on the rocks, densely covering them, though only in the midst of the fall, where was the swiftest water, a regular seaweed, growing just like rockweed and of the same olive-green color,—"*Podostemon Ceratophyllum*, River-weed,"—still in bloom, though chiefly gone to seed. Gray says it is "attached to loose stones," and Torrey says it "adheres to pebbles," but here it covered the rocks under water in the swiftest place only, and was partly uncovered by the fall of the water. I found, in what I gathered, a little pout which had taken refuge in it. Though the botanist, in obedience to his rules, puts it among phænogamous plants, I should not hesitate to associate it with the rockweed. It is the rockweed of our river. I have never seen it elsewhere in the river, though possibly it grows at the factory or other swift places. It seemed as if our river had there for a moment anticipated the sea, suffered a sea-change, mimicked the great ocean stream. I did not see it a few rods above or below, where the water is more sluggish. So far as I know, then, it grows only in the swiftest water, and there is only one place, and that the Falls, in Concord River where it can grow. A careless observer might confound it with the rockweed of the sea. It covers the rocks in exactly the same manner, and when I tore it off, it brought more or less of the thin, scaly surface of the rocks with it. It is a foretaste of the sea. It is very interesting and remarkable that at this one point we have in our river a plant which so perfectly represents the rockweed of the seashore. This is from four to eight or nine inches long. It has the peculiar strong fresh-water scent.

It is a question if the river has as much created the shoal places as found them.

The presence or absence of weeds at a given shallowness is a good gauge of the rapidity of the current. At the Fordway they do not grow where it is only two feet on an average, owing to the swiftness of the current (as well as stoniness), and in the very swiftest and narrowest part of the Falls occurs one species, the podostemon, which I have not found in any other part of the river.

It is remarkable how the river, even from its very source to its mouth, runs with great bends or zigzags regularly recurring and including many smaller ones, first northerly, then northeasterly, growing more and more simple and direct as it descends, like a tree; as if a mighty current had once filled the valley of the river, and meandered in it according to the same law that this small stream does in its own meadows.

A river of this character can hardly be said to fall at all: it rather runs over the extremity of its trough, being filled to overflowing. If, after flowing twenty miles, all the water has got to rise as high as it was when it started, or rather if it has got to pass over a bottom which is as high as that was where it started, it cannot be said to have gained anything or have fallen at all. It has not got down to a lower level. You do not produce a fall in the channel or bottom of a trough by cutting a notch in its edge. The bottom may lose as much as the surface gains.

If our river had been dry a thousand years, it would be difficult to *guess* even where its channel had been without a spirit level. I should expect to find waterworn stones and a few muddy pools and small swamps.

July 23. P.M.—To Walden.

Going through Thrush Alley and beyond, I am pestered by flies about my head,—*not till now* (though I may have said so before). They are perfect imps, for they gain nothing for their pains and only pester me. They do not for the most part attempt to settle on me, never sting me. Yet they seriously interfere with walking in the wood. Though I may keep a leafy twig constantly revolving about my head, they too constantly revolve, nevertheless, and appear to avoid it successfully. They seem to do it for deviltry and sport.

July 28. The black willows are the children of the river. They do not grow far from the water, not on the steep banks which the river is wearing into, not on the unconverted shore, but on the bars and banks which the river has made. A bank may soon get to be too high for it. It grows and thrives on the river-made shores and banks, and is a servant which the river uses to build up and defend its banks and isles. It is married to the river.

July 30. A.M.—On river to ascertain the rate of the current.

I see more moss(?)-covered rocks on the bottom and some rising quite near the surface, revealed in the sunny water, and little suspected before. They are so completely covered with moss-like weeds or tresses that you do not see them,—like the heads of mermaids. They sleep there concealed under these long tresses on the bottom, suggesting a new kind of antiquity. There is nothing to wear on and polish them there. They do not bear the paint rubbed off from any boat. Though unsuspected by the oldest fisher, they have eyed Concord for centuries through their watery veil without ever parting their tresses to look at her.

Trying the current there, there being a very faint, chiefly side, wind, commonly not enough to be felt on the cheek or to ripple the water,—what would be called by most a calm,—my bottle floats about seventy-five feet in forty minutes, and then, a very faint breeze beginning to drive it back, I cannot wait to see when it will go a hundred. It is, in short, an exceedingly feeble current, almost a complete standstill. My boat is altogether blown up-stream, even by this imperceptible breath. Indeed, you can in such a case feel the pulse of our river only in the shallowest places, where it preserves some slight passage between the weeds. It faints and gives up the ghost in deeper places on the least adverse wind, and you would presume it dead a thousand times, if you did not apply the nicest tests, such as a feather to the nostrils of a drowned man. It is a mere string of lakes which have not made up their minds to be rivers. As near as possible to a standstill.

Yet by sinking a strawberry box beneath the surface I found that there was a slight positive current there, that when a chip went pretty fast up-stream in this air, the same with the box sunk one foot and tied to it went slowly down, at three feet deep or more went faster than when the box was sunk only one foot. The water flowed faster down at three feet depth than at one, there where it was about seven feet deep, and though the surface for several inches deep may be flowing up in the wind, the weeds at bottom will all be slanted down. Indeed, I suspect that at four or five feet depth the weeds will be slanted downward in the strongest wind that blows up, in that the current is *always* creeping along downward underneath.

Yet the river in the middle of Concord is swifter than above or below, and if Concord people are slow in consequence of their river's influence, the people of Sudbury and Carlisle should be slower still.

Aug. 3. Since our river is so easily affected by wind, the fact that its general course is northeast and that the prevailing winds in summer are southwest is very favorable to its rapid drainage at that season.

If by fall you mean a swifter place occasioned by the bottom below for a considerable distance being lower than the bottom above for a considerable distance, I do not know of any such between Pelham Pond and the Falls. These swifter places are produced by a contraction of the stream,—chiefly by the elevation of the bottom at that point,—also by the narrowing of the stream.

The depths are very slight compared with the lengths. The average depth of this twenty-five miles is about one seventeen thousandth the length; so that if this portion of the river were laid down on a map four feet long the depth would be about equal to the thickness of ordinary letter paper, of which it takes three hundred and fifty to an inch. Double the thickness of the letter paper, and it will contain the deep holes which are so unfathomed and mysterious, not to say bottomless, to the swimmers and fishermen.

The haymakers are quite busy on the Great Meadows, it being drier than usual. It being remote from public view, some of them work in their shirts or half naked.

AUG. 5. See many yellowed peach leaves and butternut leaves, which have fallen in the wind yesterday and the rain to-day.

The lowest dark-colored rocks near the water at the stone bridge (*i.e.* part of the bridge) are prettily marked with (apparently) mosses, which have adhered to them at higher water and now withered and bleached on,—in fact are transferred,—and by their whitish color are seen very distinctly on the dark stone and have a very pretty effect. They are quite like sea-mosses in their delicacy, though not equally fine with many. These are very permanently and closely fastened to the rock. This is a phenomenon of low water. Also see them transferred to wood, as pieces of bridges.

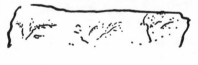

Aug. 9. Minott says that some used to wonder much at the windings of the Mill Brook and could not succeed in accounting for them, but his Uncle Ben Prescott settled the difficulty by saying that a great eel came out of Flint's Pond and rooted its way through to the river and so made the channel of the Mill Brook.

Aug. 14. When I reached the upper end of this weedy bar, at about 3 P.M., this warm day, I noticed some light-colored object in mid-river, near the other end of the bar. At first I thought of some large stake or board standing amid the weeds there, then of a fisherman in a brown holland sack, referring him to the shore beyond. Supposing it the last, I floated nearer and nearer till I saw plainly enough the motions of the person, whoever it was, and that it was no stake. Looking through my glass thirty or forty rods off, I thought certainly that I saw C., who had just bathed, making signals to me with his towel, for I referred the object to the shore twenty rods further. I saw his motions as he wiped himself,—the movements of his elbows and his towel. Then I saw that the person was nearer and therefore smaller, that it stood on the sand-bar in mid-stream in shallow water and must be some maiden in a bathing-dress,—for it was the color of brown holland web,—and a very peculiar kind of dress it seemed. But about this time I discovered with my naked eye that it was a blue heron standing in very shallow water amid the weeds of the bar and pluming itself. I had not noticed its legs at all, and its head, neck, and wings, being constantly moving, I had mistaken for arms, elbows, and towel of a bather, and when it stood stiller its shapely body looked like a peculiar bathing-dress.

Suddenly comes a second, flying low, and alights on the bar yet nearer to me, almost high and dry. Adjutant they were to my idea of the river, these two winged men.

You have not seen our weedy river, you do not know the significance of its weedy bars, until you have seen the blue heron wading and pluming itself on it. I see that it was made for these shallows, and they for it. Now the heron is gone from the weedy shoal, the scene appears incomplete. Of course, the heron has sounded the depth of the water on every bar of the river that is fordable to it. The water there is not so many feet deep, but so many heron's tibiæ. Instead of a foot rule you should use a heron's leg for a measure. If you would know the depth of the water on these few shoalest places of Musketaquid, ask the blue heron that wades and fishes there. In some places a heron can wade across.

How long we may have gazed on a particular scenery and think that we have seen and known it, when, at length, some bird or quadruped comes and takes possession of it before our eyes, and imparts to it a wholly new character. The heron uses these shallows as I cannot. I give them up to him.

By a gauge set in the river I can tell about what time the millers on the stream and its tributaries go to work in the morning and leave off at night, and also can distinguish the Sundays, since it is the day on which the river does not rise, but falls. If I had lost the day of the week, I could recover it by a careful examination of the river. It lies by in the various mill-ponds on Sunday and keeps the Sabbath. What its *persuasion* is, is another question.

Aug. 26. The first fall rain is a memorable occasion, when the river is raised and cooled, and the first crop of sere and yellow leaves falls. The air is cleared; the dogdays are over; sun-sparkles are seen on water; crickets sound more distinct; saw-grass reveals its spikes in the shorn fields; sparrows and bobolinks fly in flocks more and more. Farmers feel encouraged about their late potatoes and corn. Mill-wheels that have rested for want of water begin to revolve again. Meadow-haying is over.

The first significant event (for a long time) was the frost of the 17th. That was the beginning of winter, the first summons to summer. Some of her forces succumbed to it. The second event was the rain of yesterday.

Aug. 27. I was telling Jonas Potter of my lameness yesterday, whereat he says that he "broke" both his feet when he was young,—I imagined how they looked through his wrinkled cowhides,—and he did not get over it for four years, nay, even now he sometimes felt pains in them before a storm.

All our life, *i.e.* the living part of it, is a persistent dreaming awake. The boy does not camp in his father's yard. That would not be adventurous enough, there are too many sights and sounds to disturb the illusion; so he marches off twenty or thirty miles and there pitches his tent, where stranger inhabitants are tamely sleeping in their beds just like his father at home, and camps in *their* yard, perchance. But then he dreams uninterruptedly that he is anywhere but where he is.

I often see yarrow with a delicate pink tint, very distinct from the common pure-white ones.

The first notice I have that grapes are ripening is by the rich scent at evening from my own native vine against the house, when I go to the pump, though I thought there were none on it.

The children have done bringing huckleberries to sell for nearly a week.

Aug. 28. P.M.—To Walden.

A cool day; wind northwest. Need a half-thick coat. Thus gradually we withdraw into winter quarters. It is a clear, flashing air, and the shorn fields now look bright and yellowish and cool. You feel the less inclined to bathing this weather, and bathe from principle, when boys, who bathe for fun, omit it.

I saw a month or more ago where pine-needles which had fallen (old ones) stood erect on low leaves of the forest floor, having stuck in, or passed through, them. They stuck up as a fork which falls from the table. Yet you would not think that they fell with sufficient force.

Aug. 31. P.M.—To Fair Haven Hill.

Was caught in five successive showers, and took refuge in Hayden's barn, under the cliffs, and under a tree.

There was another shower in the night (at 9 P.M.), making the sixth after 1.30 P.M. It was evidently one cloud thus broken into six parts, with some broad intervals of clear sky and fair weather. It would have been convenient for us, if it had been printed on the first cloud, "Five more to come!" Such a shower has a history which has never been written. One would like to know how and where the cloud first gathered, what lands and water it passed over and watered, and where and when it ceased to rain and was finally dissipated.

Sept. 1. If you would study the birds now, go where their food is, *i.e.* the berries, especially to the wild black cherries, elder-berries, poke berries, mountain-ash berries, and ere long the barberries, and for pigeons the acorns. We sit near the tree and listen to the now unusual sounds of these birds, and from time to time one or two come dashing from out the sky toward this tree, till, seeing us, they whirl, disappointed, and perhaps alight on some neighboring twigs and wait till we are gone. The cherry-birds and robins seem to know the locality of every wild cherry in the town. You are as sure to find them on them now, as bees and butterflies on the thistles. If we stay long, they go off with a fling, to some other cherry tree, which they know of but we do not.

Bought a pair of shoes the other day, and, observing that as usual they were only wooden-pegged at the toes, I required the seller to put in an extra row of iron pegs there while I waited for them. So he called to his boy to bring those zinc pegs, but I insisted on iron pegs and no zinc ones. He gave me considerable advice on the subject of shoes, but I suggested that even the wearer of shoes, of whom I was one, had an opportunity to learn some of their qualities. I have learned to respect my own opinion in this matter. As I do not use blacking and the seller often throws in a box of blacking when I buy a pair of shoes, they accumulate on my hands.

You must be careful not to eat too many nuts. I one winter met a young man whose face was broken out into large pimples and sores, and when I inquired what was the matter, he answered that he and his wife were fond of shagbarks, and therefore he had bought a bushel of them, and they spent their winter evenings eating them, and this was the consequence.

SEPT. 3. A strong wind, which blows down much fruit. R.W.E. sits surrounded by choice windfall pears.

Sept. 8. The 7th, 8th, and 9th, the State muster is held here. The only observation I have to make is that Concord is fuller of dust and more uninhabitable than I ever knew it to be before. Not only the walls, fences, and houses are thickly covered with dust, but the fields and meadows and bushes; and the pads in the river for half a mile from the village are white with it. From a mile or two distant you see a cloud of dust over the town and extending thence to the muster-field. I went to the store the other day to buy a bolt for our front door, for, as I told the storekeeper, the Governor was coming here. "Aye," said he, "and the Legislature too." "Then I will take two bolts," said I. He said that there had been a steady demand for bolts and locks of late, for our protectors were coming.

Sept. 13. I remember my earliest going a-graping. (It was a wonder that we ever hit upon the ripe season.) There was more fun in finding and eying the big purple clusters high on the trees and climbing to them than in eating them. We used to take care not to chew the skins long lest they should make our mouths sore.

Some haws of the scarlet thorn are really a splendid fruit to look at now and far from inedible. They are not only large, but their beauty is enhanced by the persistent calyx relieving the clear scarlet of the fruit.

There are various degrees of living out-of-doors. You must be outdoors long, early and late, and travel far and earnestly, in order to perceive the phenomena of the day. Even then much will escape you. Few live so far outdoors as to hear the first geese go over.

Sept. 16. Grasshoppers have been very abundant in dry fields for two or three weeks. Sophia walked through the Depot Field a fortnight ago, and when she got home picked fifty or sixty from her skirts,—for she wore hoops and crinoline. Would not this be a good way to clear a field of them,—to send a bevy of fashionably dressed ladies across a field and leave them to clean their skirts when they get home? It would supplant anything at the patent office, and the motive power is cheap.

I am invited to take some party of ladies or gentlemen on an excursion,—to walk or sail, or the like,—but by all kinds of evasions I omit it, and am thought to be rude and unaccommodating therefore. They do not consider that the wood-path and the boat are my studio, where I maintain a sacred solitude and cannot admit promiscuous company. I will see them occasionally in an evening or at the table, however. They do not think of taking a child away from its school to go a-huckleberrying with them. Why should not I, then, have my school and school hours to be respected? Ask me for a certain number of dollars if you will, but do not ask me for my afternoons.

Sept. 18. Dr. Bartlett handed me a paper to-day, desiring me to subscribe for a statue to Horace Mann. I declined, and said that I thought a man ought not any more to take up room in the world after he was dead. We shall lose one advantage of a man's dying if we are to have a statue of him forthwith. This is probably meant to be an opposition statue to that of Webster. At this rate they will crowd the streets with them. A man will have to add a clause to his will, "No statue to be made of me." It is very offensive to my imagination to see the dying stiffen into statues at this rate. We should wait till their bones begin to crumble—and then avoid too near a likeness to the living.

Sept. 19. See many yellow butterflies in the road this very pleasant day after the rain of yesterday. One flutters across between the horse and the wagon safely enough, though it looks as if it would be run down.

XXX.

Sept. 24. I have many affairs to attend to, and feel hurried these days. Great works of art have endless leisure for a background, as the universe has space. Time stands still while they are created. The artist cannot be in hurry. The earth moves round the sun with inconceivable rapidity, and yet the surface of the lake is not ruffled by it. It is not by a compromise, it is not by a timid and feeble repentance, that a man will save his soul and *live*, at last. He has got to *conquer* a clear field, letting Repentance & Co. go. That's a well-meaning but weak firm that has assumed the debts of an old and worthless one. You are to fight in a field where no allowances will be made, no courteous bowing to one-handed knights. You are expected to do your duty, not in spite of every thing but *one*, but in spite of *everything*.

A man must attend to Nature closely for many years to know when, as well as where, to look for his objects, since he must always anticipate her a little. Young men have not learned the phases of Nature; they do not know what constitutes a year, or that one year is like another. I would know when in the year to expect certain thoughts and moods, as the sportsman knows when to look for plover.

Sept. 25. P.M.—To Emerson's Cliff.

Holding a white pine needle in my hand, and turning it in a favorable light, as I sit upon this cliff, I perceive that each of its three edges is notched or serrated with minute forward-pointing bristles. So much does Nature avoid an unbroken line that even this slender leaf is serrated; though, to my surprise, neither Gray nor Bigelow mention it. Loudon, however, says, "Scabrous and inconspicuously serrated on the margin; spreading in summer, but in winter contracted, and lying close to the branches." Fine and smooth as it looks, it is serrated after all. This is its concealed wildness, by which it connects itself with the wilder oaks.

Prinos berries are fairly ripe for a few days. Moles work in meadows.

Sept. 26. How feeble women, or rather ladies, are! They cannot bear to be shined on, but generally carry a parasol to *keep off* the sun.

Oct. 13. The swamp amelanchier is leafing again, as usual. What a pleasing phenomenon, perhaps an Indian-summer growth, an anticipation of the spring, like the notes of birds and frogs, etc., an evidence of warmth and genialness. Its buds are annually awakened by the October sun as if it were spring. The shad-bush is leafing again by the sunny swamp-side. It is like a youthful or poetic thought in old age. Several times I have been cheered by this sight when surveying in former years. In the fall I will take this for my coat-of-arms. It seems to detain the sun that expands it. These twigs are so full of life that they can hardly contain themselves. They ignore winter. They anticipate spring. What faith! In my latter years, let me have some *shad-bush* thoughts.

Oct. 14. I hear a man laughed at because he went to Europe twice in search of an imaginary wife who, he thought, was there, though he had never seen nor heard of her. But the majority have gone further while they stayed in America, have actually allied themselves to one whom they thought their wife and found out their mistake too late to mend it. It would be cruel to laugh at these.

Oct. 15. A cold northwest wind. I go along the east edge of Poplar Hill. This very cold and windy day, now that so many leaves have fallen, I begin to notice the silveriness of willows blown up in the wind,—a November sight.

This is a cold fall.

Oct. 16. Sunday. P.M.—Paddle to Puffer's and thence walk to Ledum Swamp and Conant's Wood.

A cold, clear, Novemberish day. The wind goes down and we do not sail. The button-bushes are just bare, and the black willows partly so, and the mikania all fairly gray now. I have not been on the river for some time, and it is the more novel to me this cool day.

When I get to Willow Bay I see the new musquash-houses erected, conspicuous on the now nearly leafless shores. To me this is an important and suggestive sight, as, perchance, in some countries new haystacks in the yards; as to the Esquimaux the erection of winter houses. I remember this phenomenon annually for thirty years. A more constant phenomenon here than the new haystacks in the yard, for they were erected here probably before man dwelt here and may still be erected here when man has departed. For thirty years I have annually observed, about this time or earlier, the freshly erected winter lodges of the musquash along the riverside, reminding us that, if we have no gypsies, we have a more indigenous race of furry, quadrupedal men maintaining their ground in our midst still. This may not be an annual phenomenon to you. It may not be in the Greenwich almanac or ephemeris, but it has an important place in my Kalendar. So surely as the sun appears to be in Libra or Scorpio, I see the conical winter lodges of the musquash rising above the withered pontederia and flags. There will be some reference to it, by way of parable or otherwise, in *my* New Testament. Surely, it is a defect in our Bible that it is not truly ours, but a Hebrew Bible. The most pertinent illustrations for us are to be drawn, not from Egypt or Babylonia, but from New England.

Talk about learning our *letters* and being *literate*! Why, the roots of *letters* are *things*. Natural objects and phenomena are the original symbols or types which express our thoughts and feelings, and yet American scholars, having little or no root in the soil, commonly strive with all their might to confine themselves to the imported symbols alone. All the true growth and experience, the living speech, they would fain reject as "Americanisms." It is the old error, which the church, the state, the school ever commit, choosing darkness rather than light, holding fast to the old and to tradition.

A more intimate knowledge, a deeper experience, will surely originate a word. When I really know that our river pursues a serpentine course to the Merrimack, shall I continue to describe it by referring to some other river no older than itself which is like it, and call it a *meander*? It is no more *meandering* than the Meander is *musketaquidding*. As well sing of the nightingale here as the Meander. What if there were a tariff on words, on language, for the encouragement of home manufactures? Have we not the genius to coin our own? Let the schoolmaster distinguish the true from the counterfeit.

They go on publishing the "chronological cycles" and "movable festivals of the Church" and the like from mere habit, but how insignificant are these compared with the annual phenomena of your life, which fall within your experience! The signs of the zodiac are not nearly of that significance to me that the sight of a dead sucker in the spring is. That is the occasion for an *im*movable festival in my church. Another kind of Lent then begins in my thoughts than you wot of. I am satisfied then to live on fish alone for a season.

The phenomena of our year are one thing, those of the almanac another. For October, for instance, instead of making the sun enter the sign of the scorpion, I would much sooner make him enter a musquash-house. Astronomy is a fashionable study, patronized by princes, but not fungi. "Royal Astronomer." The snapping turtle, too, must find a place among the constellations, though it may have to supplant some doubtful characters already there. If there is no place for him overhead, he can serve us bravely underneath, supporting the earth.

When we emerged from the pleasant footpath through the birches into Witherell Glade, looking along it toward the westering sun, the glittering white tufts of the *Andropogon scoparius*, lit up by the sun, were affectingly fair and cheering to behold. It was already a cheerful Novemberish scene. A thousand such tufts now catch up the sun and send to us its light but not heat. His heat is being steadily withdrawn from us. Light without heat is getting to be the prevailing phenomenon of the day now.

The ledum smells like a bee,—that peculiar scent they have.

I remark how still it is to-day, really Sabbath-like. This day, at least, we do not hear the rattle of cars nor the whistle. I cannot realize that the country was often as still as this twenty years ago.

The weeds are dressed in their frost jackets, naked down to their close-fitting downy or flannel shirts. Like athletes they challenge the winter, these bare twigs.

The cool, placid, silver-plated waters at even coolly await the frost. The musquash is steadily adding to his winter lodge. There is no need of supposing a peculiar instinct telling him how high to build his cabin. He has had a longer experience in this river-valley than we.

Your hands begin to be cool, rowing, now. At many a place in sprout-lands, where the sedge is peculiarly flat and white or hoary, I put down my hand to feel if there is frost on it. It must be the *trace* of frost.

Each ball of the button-bush reflected in the silvery water by the riverside appears to me as distinct and important as a star in the heavens viewed through "optic glass." This, too, deserves its Kepler and Galileo.

Oct. 19. It galls me to listen to the remarks of craven-hearted neighbors who speak disparagingly of John Brown because he resorted to violence, resisted the government, threw his life away!—what way have they thrown their lives, pray?—neighbors who would praise a man for attacking singly an ordinary band of thieves or murderers. Such minds are not equal to the occasion. They preserve the so-called peace of their community by deeds of petty violence every day.

The remarks of my neighbors upon Brown's death and supposed fate, with very few exceptions, are, "He is undoubtedly insane," "Died as the fool dieth," "Served him right;" and so they proceed to live their sane, and wise, and altogether admirable lives, reading their Plutarch a little.

A government that pretends to be Christian and crucifies a million Christs every day!

Our foes are in our midst and all about us. Hardly a house but is divided against itself. For our foe is the all but universal woodenness (both of head and heart).

Some eighteen hundred years ago Christ was crucified; this morning, perhaps, John Brown was hung. These are the two ends of a chain which I rejoice to know is not without its links.

Oct. 21. It is very cold and blustering to-day. It is the breath of winter, which is encamped not far off to the north.

A great many shrub oak acorns hold on, and are a darker brown than ever.

Insane! A father and seven sons, and several more men besides,—as many, at least, as twelve disciples,—all struck with insanity at once; while the sane tyrant holds with a firmer gripe than ever his four millions of slaves, and a thousand sane editors, his abettors, are saving their country and their bacon! Ask the tyrant who is his most dangerous foe, the sane man or the insane.

Oct. 22. I see now that it was necessary that the bravest and humanest man in all the country should be hung. Perhaps he saw it himself. If any leniency were shown him, any compromise made with him, any treating with him at all, by the government, he might be suspected.

I rejoice that I live in this age, that I was his contemporary.

I do not wish to kill or to be killed, but I can foresee circumstances in which both of these things would be by me unavoidable.

This event advertises me that there is such a fact as death,—the possibility of a man's dying. It seems as if no man had ever died in America; for in order to die you must first have lived.

It is the best news that America has ever heard.

It has already quickened the public pulse of the North; it has infused more, and more generous, blood into her veins and heart than any number of years of what is called commercial and political prosperity could. How many a man who was lately contemplating suicide has now something to live for!

NOV. 9. A fine Indian-summer day. Have had pleasant weather about a week.

NOV. 10. Rain; warm.

NOV. 12. The first sprinkling of snow, which for a short time whitens the ground in spots.

I do not know how to distinguish between our waking life and a dream. Are we not always living the life that we imagine we are? Fear creates danger, and courage dispels it.

There was a remarkable sunset, I think the 25th of October. The sunset sky reached quite from west to east, and it was the most varied in its forms and colors of any that I remember to have seen. At one time the clouds were most softly and delicately rippled, like the ripple-marks on sand. But it was hard for me to see its beauty then, when my mind was filled with Captain Brown. So great a wrong as his fate implied overshadowed all beauty in the world.

Dec. 5. Rather hard walking in the snow. There is a slight mist in the air and accordingly some glaze on the twigs and leaves, and thus suddenly we have passed from Indian summer to winter. It is as if you had stepped from a withered garden into the yard of a sculptor or worker in marble, crowded with delicate works, rich and rare.

Dec. 6. Came upon a round bed of tansy, half a dozen feet in diameter, which was withered quite black, as seen above the snow,— blacker than any plant I remember. This reminded me that its name was by some thought to be from ἀθανασία, or immortality, from its not withering early, but in this case it suggested its funereal reputation.

The death of Irving, which at any other time would have attracted universal attention, having occurred while these things were transpiring, goes almost unobserved. Literary gentlemen, editors, and critics think that they know how to write because they have studied grammar and rhetoric; but the art of composition is as simple as the discharge of a bullet from a rifle, and its masterpieces imply an infinitely greater force behind it. This unlettered man's speaking and writing is standard English. Some words and phrases deemed vulgarisms and Americanisms before, he has made standard American. *"It will pay."* It suggests that the one great rule of composition—and if I were a professor of rhetoric I should insist on this—is to *speak the truth*. This first, this second, this third.

Dec. 8. Two hundred years ago is about as great an antiquity as we can comprehend or often have to deal with. It is nearly as good as two thousand to our imaginations. It carries us back to the days of aborigines and the Pilgrims; beyond the limits of oral testimony, to history which begins already to be enamelled with a gloss of fable, and we do not quite believe what we read; to a strange style of writing and spelling and of expression; to those ancestors whose names we do not know, and to whom we are related only as we are to the race generally. It is the age of our very oldest houses and cultivated trees. Nor is New England very peculiar in this. In England also, a house two hundred years old, especially if it be a wooden one, is pointed out as an interesting relic of the past.

When we read the history of the world, centuries look cheap to us and we find that we had doubted if the hundred years preceding the life of Herodotus seemed as great an antiquity to him as a hundred years does to us. We are inclined to think of all Romans who lived within five hundred years b.c. as *contemporaries* to each other. Yet Time moved at the same deliberate pace then as now. Pliny the Elder, who died in the 79th year of the Christian era, speaking of the paper made of papyrus which was then used,—how carefully it was made,—says, *just as we might say*, as if it were something remarkable: "There are, thus, ancient memorials in the handwriting of Caius and Tiberius Gracchus, almost two hundred years old, which I have seen in the possession of Pomponius Secundus the poet, a very illustrious citizen. As for the handwriting of Cicero, Augustus, and Virgil, we very often meet with it still."

How is it that what is actually present and transpiring is commonly perceived by the common sense and understanding only, is bare and bald, without halo or the blue enamel of intervening air?

But let it be past or to come, and it is at once idealized. It is not simply the understanding now, but the imagination, that takes cognizance of it. The imagination requires a long range. It is the faculty of the poet to see present things as if, in this sense, also past and future, as if distant or universally significant.

Dec. 13. P.M.—On river to Fair Haven Pond.

My first true winter walk is perhaps that which I take on the river, or where I cannot go in the summer. It is the walk peculiar to winter, and now first I take it.

What a spectacle the subtle vapors that have their habitation in the sky present these winter days! You have not only ever-varying forms of a given type of cloud, but various types at different heights or hours. It is a scene, for variety, for beauty and grandeur, out of all proportion to the attention it gets. Who watched the forms of the clouds over this part of the earth a thousand years ago? Who watches them to-day?

Now that the river is frozen we have a sky under our feet also. Going over black ice three or four inches thick, only reassured by seeing the thickness at the cracks, I see it richly marked internally with large whitish figures suggesting rosettes of ostrich-feathers or coral. These at first appear to be a dust on the surface, but, looking closely, are found to be at various angles with it internally, in the grain. The work of crystallization.

DEC. 14. At 2 P.M. begins to snow again. I walk to Walden.

Snow-storms might be classified. This is a fine, dry snow, drifting nearly horizontally from the north, so that it is quite blinding to face, almost as much so as sand. It is cold also. It is drifting but not accumulating fast. I can see the woods about a quarter of a mile distant through it. That of the 11th was a still storm, of large flakes falling gently in the quiet air, like so many white feathers descending in different directions when seen against a wood-side,—the regular snow-storm such as is painted. A myriad falling flakes weaving a coarse garment by which the eye is amused. The snow was a little moist and the weather rather mild. Also I remember the perfectly crystalline or *star* snows, when each flake is a perfect six(?)-rayed wheel. This must be the *chef-d'œuvre* of the Genius of the storm. Also there is the pellet or shot snow, which consists of little dry spherical pellets the size of robin-shot. This, I think, belongs to cold weather. Probably never have much of it. Also there is sleet, which is half snow, half rain.

The *Juncus tenuis*, with its conspicuous acheniums, is very noticeable now, rising above the snow in the wood-paths, commonly aslant.

Dec. 15. Philosophy is a Greek word by good rights, and it stands almost for a Greek thing. Yet some rumor of it has reached the commonest mind. M. Miles, who came to collect his wood bill to-day, said, when I objected to the small size of his wood, that it was necessary to split wood fine in order to cure it well, that he had found that wood that was more than four inches in diameter would not dry, and moreover a good deal depended on the manner in which it was corded up in the woods. He piled his high and tightly. If this were not well done the stakes would spread and the wood lie loosely, and so the rain and snow find their way into it. And he added, "I have handled a good deal of wood, and I think that I understand the *philosophy* of it."

DEC. 16. A.M.—To Cambridge, where I read in Gerard's Herbal.* His admirable though quaint descriptions are, to my mind, greatly superior to the modern more scientific ones. He describes not according to rule but to his natural delight in the plants. He brings them vividly before you, as one who has seen and delighted in them. It is almost as good as to see the plants themselves. It suggests that we cannot too often get rid of the barren assumption that is in our science. His leaves are leaves; his flowers, flowers; his fruit, fruit. They are green and colored and fragrant. It is a man's knowledge added to a child's delight. Modern botanical descriptions approach ever nearer to the dryness of an algebraic formula, as if $x + y$ were = to a love-letter. It is the keen joy and discrimination of the

---

Vide extracts from preface made in October, 1859.

child who has just seen a flower for the first time and comes running in with it to its friends. How much better to describe your object in fresh English words rather than in these conventional Latinisms! He has really seen, and smelt, and tasted, and reports his sensations.

Bought a book at Little & Brown's, paying a nine-pence more on a volume than it was offered me for elsewhere. The customer thus pays for the more elegant style of the store.

Dec. 17. Under the hill, on the southeast side of R. W. E.'s lot, where the hemlock stands, I see many tracks of squirrels (I am not sure whether they are red or gray or both, for I see none) leading straight from the base of one tree to that of another, thus leaving untrodden triangles, squares, and polygons of every form, bounded by much trodden highways. One, two, three, and the track is lost on the upright bole of a pine,—as if they had played at base-running from goal to goal, while pine cones were thrown at them on the way. You come thus on the tracks of these frisky and volatile (semivolitant) creatures in the midst of perfect stillness and solitude, as you might stand in a hall half an hour after the dancers had departed.

Dec. 22. Another fine winter day.

P.M.—To Flint's Pond.

We pause and gaze into the Mill Brook on the Turnpike bridge. C. says that in Persia they call the ripple-marks on sandy bottoms "chains" or "chain-work." I see a good deal of cress there, on the bottom, for a rod or two, the only green thing to be seen. No more slimy than it usually is beneath the water in summer. Is not this the plant which most, or most conspicuously, preserves its greenness in the winter? Is it not now most completely in its summer state of any plant? So far as the water and the mud and the cress go, it is a summer scene. It is green as ever, and waving in the stream as in summer.

How nicely is Nature adjusted! The least disturbance of her equilibrium is betrayed and corrects itself. As I looked down on the surface of the brook, I was surprised to see a leaf floating, as I thought, up the stream, but I was mistaken. The motion of a particle of dust on the surface of any brook far inland shows which way the earth declines toward the sea, which way lies the constantly descending route, and the only one.

The fisherman stands erect and still on the ice, awaiting our approach, as usual forward to say that he has had no luck. He has been here since early morning, and for some reason or other the fishes won't bite. You won't catch him here again in a hurry. They all tell the same story. The amount of it is he has had "fisherman's luck," and if you walk that way you may find him at his old post to-morrow. It is hard, to be sure,—four little fishes to be divided between three men, and two and a half miles to walk; and you have only got a more ravenous appetite for the supper which you have not earned. However, the pond floor is not a bad place to spend a winter day.

Dec. 25. You may think that you need take no care to preserve your woodland, but every tree comes either from the stump of another tree or from a seed. With the present management, will there always be a fresh stump, or a nut in the soil, think you? Will not the nobler kinds of trees, which bear comparatively few seeds, grow more and more scarce? What is become of our chestnut wood? There are but few stumps for sprouts to spring from, and, as for the chestnuts, there are not enough for the squirrels, and nobody is planting them.

How different are men and women, *e.g.* in respect to the adornment of their heads! Do you ever see an old or jammed bonnet on the head of a woman at a public meeting? But look at any assembly of men with their hats on; how large a proportion of the hats will be old, weather-beaten, and indented, but I think so much the more picturesque and interesting! One farmer rides by my door in a hat which it does me good to see, there is so much character in it,—so much independence to begin with, and then affection for his old friends, etc., etc. I should not wonder if there were lichens on it. Think of painting a hero in a bran-new hat! But go to a lyceum and look at the bonnets and various other headgear of the women and girls,—who, by the way, keep their hats on, it being too dangerous and expensive to take them off!! Why, every one looks as fragile as a butterfly's wings, having just come out of a bandbox,—as it will go into a bandbox again when the lyceum is over. Men wear their hats for use; women theirs for ornament.

Again, what an ado women make about trifles! Here is one tells me that she cannot possibly wear india-rubber boots in sloshy weather, because they have heels. Men have been wearing boots with heels from time immemorial; little boys soon learn the art, and are eager to try the experiment. The woodchoppers and teamsters, and the merchants and lawyers, go and come quietly the livelong day, and though they may meet with many accidents, I do not remember any that originated in the heels of their boots. But not so with women; they bolt at once, recklessly as runaway horses, the moment they get the boots on, before they have learned the wonderful art of wearing them. My informant tells me of a friend who has got a white swelling from coming down-stairs imprudently in boots, and of another seriously injured on the meeting-house steps,—for when you deal with steps, then comes the rub,—and of a third who involuntarily dashed down the front stairs, knocked a hat-tree through the side-lights, and broke I do not know how many ribs. Indeed, that quarter-inch obstruction about the heels seems to be an insuperable one to the women.

Dec. 29. When I went to walk it was about 10° above zero, and when I returned, 1°. I did not notice any vapor rising from the open places, as I did in the morning, when it was −16° and also −6°. Therefore the cold must be between +1° and −6° in order that vapor may rise from these places. It takes a greater degree of cold to show the breath of the river than that of man. Apparently, the river is not enough warmer than the air to permit of its rising into it, *i.e.,* evaporating, unless the air is of a very low temperature. When the air is say four or five degrees below, the water being +32°, then there is a visible evaporation. Is there the same difference, or some 40°, between the heat of the human breath and that air in which the moisture in the breath becomes visible in vapor? This has to do with the dew-point. Next, what makes the water of those open places thus warm? and is it any warmer than elsewhere? There is considerable heat reflected from a sandy bottom where the water is shallow, and at these places it is always sandy and shallow, but I doubt if this actually makes the water warmer, though it may melt the more opaque ice which absorbs it. The fact that Holt Bend, which is deep, is late to freeze, being narrow, seems to prove it to be the swiftness of the water and not reflected heat that prevents freezing.

Taking the river in Concord in its present condition, it is, with one exception, only the shallowest places that are open; and the shallowest place in all in Concord is the latest of all to freeze, *e.g.* at the junction. So, if you get into the river at this season, it is most likely to be at the shallowest places, they being either open or most thinly frozen over. That is one consolation for you.

Dec. 30. Those who depend on skylights found theirs but a dim, religious light this forenoon and hitherto, owing to the thickness of snow resting on them. Also cellar windows are covered, and cellars are accordingly darkened.

Jan. 4. See that long meandering track where a deer mouse hopped over the soft snow last night, scarcely making any impression. What if you could witness with owls' eyes the revelry of the wood mice some night, frisking about the wood like so many little kangaroos? Here is such populousness as commonly only the imagination dreams of.

A man receives only what he is ready to receive, whether physically or intellectually or morally, as animals conceive at certain seasons their kind only. We hear and apprehend only what we already half know. If there is something which does not concern me, which is out of my line, which by experience or by genius my attention is not drawn to, however novel and remarkable it may be, if it is spoken, we hear it not, if it is written, we read it not, or if we read it, it does not detain us. Every man thus *tracks himself* through life, in all his hearing and reading and observation and travelling. His observations make a chain. The phenomenon or fact that cannot in any wise be linked with the rest which he has observed, he does not observe. By and by we may be ready to receive what we cannot receive now. I find, for example, in Aristotle something about the spawning, etc., of the pout and perch, because I know something about it already and have my attention aroused; but I do not discover till very late that he has made other equally important observations on the spawning of other fishes, because I am not interested in those fishes.

Jan. 18. 2 P.M.—To Fair Haven Pond, on river. Thermometer 46; sky mostly overcast.

The temperature of the air and the clearness or serenity of the sky are indispensable to a knowledge of a day, so entirely do we sympathize with the moods of nature. It is important to know of a day that is past whether it was warm or cold, clear or cloudy, calm or windy, etc.

They are very different seasons in the winter when the ice of the river and meadows and ponds is bare,—blue or green, a vast glittering crystal,—and when it is all covered with snow or slosh; and our moods correspond. The former may be called a crystalline winter.

Jan. 25. In keeping a journal of one's walks and thoughts it seems to be worth the while to record those phenomena which are most interesting to us at the time. Such is the weather. It makes a material difference whether it is foul or fair, affecting surely our mood and thoughts. Then there are various degrees and kinds of foulness and fairness. It may be cloudless, or there may be sailing clouds which threaten no storm, or it may be partially overcast. On the other hand it may rain, or snow, or hail, with various degrees of intensity. It may be a transient thunder-storm, or a shower, or a flurry of snow, or it may be a prolonged storm of rain or snow. Or the sky may be overcast or rain-threatening. So with regard to temperature. It may be warm or cold. Above 40° is warm for winter. One day, at 38 even, I walk dry and it is good sleighing; the next day it may have risen to 48, and the snow is rapidly changed to slosh. It may be calm or windy. The finest winter day is a cold but clear and glittering one. There is a remarkable life in the air then, and birds and other creatures appear to feel it, to be excited and invigorated by it. Also warm and melting days in winter are inspiring, though less characteristic.

I will call the weather fair, if it does not threaten rain or snow or hail; foul, if it rains or snows or hails, or is so overcast that we expect one or the other from hour to hour. To-day it is fair, though the sky is slightly overcast, but there are *sailing* clouds in the south-west.

Jan. 27. Fair and hardly a cloud to be seen. Thermometer 28. (But it is overcast from the northwest before sunset.)

Now I see, as I am on the ice by Hubbard's meadow, some wisps of vapor in the west and southwest advancing. They are of a fine, white, thready grain, curved like skates at the end. Have we not more finely divided clouds in winter than in summer? flame-shaped, asbestos-like? I doubt if the clouds show as fine a grain in warm weather. They are wrung dry now. They are not expanded but contracted, like spiculæ. What hieroglyphics in the winter sky!

As I go along the edge of Hubbard's Wood, on the ice, it is very warm in the sun—and calm there. There are certain spots I could name, by hill and wood sides, which are always thus sunny and warm in fair weather, and have been, for aught I know, since the world was made. What a distinction they enjoy!

How many memorable localities in a river walk! Here is the warm wood-side; next, the good fishing bay; and next, where the old settler was drowned when crossing on the ice a hundred years ago. It is all storied.

When you think that your walk is profitless and a failure, and you can hardly persuade yourself not to return, it is on the point of being a success, for then you are in that subdued and knocking mood to which Nature never fails to open.

Feb. 2. 6° below at about 8 A.M.

Clock has stopped. Teams squeak.

2 P.M.—To Fair Haven Pond.

The river, which was breaking up, is frozen over again. The new ice over the channel is of a yellow tinge, and is covered with handsome rosettes two or three inches in diameter where the vapor which rose through froze and crystallized. This new ice for forty rods together is thickly covered with these rosettes, often as thick as snow, an inch deep, and sometimes in ridges like frozen froth three inches high. Sometimes they are in a straight line along a crack. The frozen breath of the river at a myriad breathing-holes.

It blowed considerably yesterday, though it is very still to-day, and the light, dry snow, especially on the meadow ice and the river, was remarkably plowed and drifted by it, and now presents a very wild and arctic scene. Indeed, no part of our scenery is ever more arctic than the river and its meadows now, though the snow was only some three inches deep on a level. It is cold and perfectly still, and you walk over a level snowy tract. It is a sea of white waves of nearly uniform shape and size. Each drift is a low, sharp promontory directed toward the northwest, and showing which way the wind blowed with occasional small patches of bare ice amid them. It is exactly as if you walked over a solid sea where the waves rose about two feet high. These promontories have a general resemblance to one another. Many of them are perfect tongues of snow more or less curving and sharp.

One hour you have bare ice; the next, a level counterpane of snow; and the next, the wind has tossed and sculptured it into these endless and varied forms. I go sliding over the few bare spots, getting a foothold for my run on the very thin sloping and ridged snow.

I frequently see where oak leaves, absorbing the heat of the sun, have sunk into the ice an inch in depth and afterward been blown out, leaving a perfect type of the leaf with its petiole and lobes sharply cut, with perfectly upright sides, so that I can easily tell the species of oak that made it. Sometimes these moulds have been evenly filled with snow while the ice is dark, and you have the figure of the leaf in white.

Feb. 5. Coming home last night in the twilight, I recognized a neighbor a dozen rods off by his walk or carriage, though it was so dark that I could not see a single feature of his person. Indeed, his person was all covered up excepting his face and hands, and I could not possibly have distinguished these at this distance from another man's. Nor was it owing to any peculiarity in his dress, for I should have known him though he had had on a perfectly new suit. It was because the man within the clothes moved them in a peculiar manner that I knew him thus at once at a distance and in the twilight. He made a certain figure in any clothes he might wear, and moved in it in a peculiar manner. Indeed, we have a very intimate knowledge of one another; we see through thick and thin; spirit meets spirit. A man hangs out innumerable signs by which we may know him. So, last summer, I knew another neighbor half a mile off up the river, though I did not see him, by the manner in which the breath from his lungs and mouth, *i.e.* his voice, made the air strike my ear. In that manner he communicated himself to all his acquaintance within a diameter of one mile (if it were all up and down the river). So I remember to have been sure once in a very dark night who was preceding me on the sidewalk,—though I could not see him,—by the sound of his tread. I was surprised to find that I knew it.

And to-day, seeing a peculiar very long track of a man in the snow, who has been along up the river this morning, I guessed that it was George Melvin, because it was accompanied by a hound's track. There was a thin snow on the ice, and I observed that he not only furrowed the snow for a foot before he completed his step, but that the (toe) of his track was always indefinite, as if his boot had been worn out and prolonged at the toe. I noticed that I and my companion made a clear and distinct track at the toe, but when I experimented, and tried to make a track like this by not lifting my feet but gliding and partly scuffing along, I found myself walking just like Melvin, and that perfectly convinced me that it was he.*

We have no occasion to wonder at the instinct of a dog. In these last two instances I surpassed the instinct of the dog.

It may always be a question how much or how little of a man goes to any particular act. It is not merely by taking time and by a conscious effort that he betrays himself. A man is revealed, and a man is concealed, in a myriad unexpected ways; *e. g.,* I can hardly think of a more effectual way of disguising neighbors to one another than by stripping them naked.

Feb. 8. 2 P.M.—Up river to Fair Haven Hill.

Thermometer 43. 40° and upward may be called a *warm* day in the winter.

We have had much of this weather for a month past, reminding us of spring. February may be called *earine* (springlike). There is a peculiarity in the air when the temperature is thus high and the weather fair, at this season, which makes sounds more clear and pervading, as if they trusted themselves abroad further in this genial state of the air. A different sound comes to my ear now from iron rails which are struck, as from the cawing crows, etc. Sound is not abrupt, piercing, or rending, but softly sweet and musical. It will take a yet more genial and milder air before the bluebird's warble can be heard.

Walking over Hubbard's broad meadow on the softened ice, I admire the markings in it. The more interesting and prevailing ones now appearing ingrained and giving it a more or less marbled look,—one, what you may call *checkered* marbling (?), consisting of small polygonal figures three quarters in diameter, bounded by whitish lines more or less curved within the ice, and apparently covered with an entire thin surface ice, and so on for rods (these when five or six inches wide make a mackerel-sky ice); the other apparently passing from this into a sort of fibrous structure of wav-

---

*I told him of it afterward, and he gave a corresponding account of himself.

ing lines, hair-like or rather flame-like,—call it *phlogistic*:—only far more regular and beautiful than I can draw. Sometimes like perhaps a cassowary's feathers, the branches being very long and fine. This fibrous or phlogistic structure is evidently connected with the flow of the surface water, for I see some old holes, now smoothly frozen over, where these rays have flowed from all sides into the hole in the midst of the checked ice, making a circular figure which reminded me of a jellyfish: only far more beautiful than this. The whitish lines which bound these figures and form the parallel fibres are apparently lines of fine bubbles more dense than elsewhere. I am not sure that these markings always imply a double or triple ice, *i.e.* a thinner surface ice, which contains them.

The ice is thus marked under my feet somewhat as the heavens overhead; there is both the mackerel sky and the fibrous flame or asbestos-like form in both. The mackerel spotted or marked ice is very common, and also reminds me of the reticulations of the pickerel.

Then there is occasionally, where puddles on the ice have frozen, that triangular rib-work of crystals,—a beautiful casting in alto-relievo of low crystal prisms with one edge up,—so meeting and crossing as to form triangular and other figures. Shining splinters in the sun. Giving a rough hold to the feet. One would think that the forms of ice-crystals must include all others.

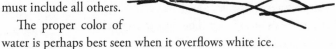

The proper color of water is perhaps best seen when it overflows white ice.

Feb. 12. I walk over a smooth green sea, or *aequor*, amid thousands of these flat isles as purple as the petals of a flower. It would not be more enchanting to walk amid the purple clouds of the sunset sky.

And, by the way, this is but a sunset sky under our feet, produced by the same law, the same slanting rays and twilight. Here the clouds are these patches of snow or frozen vapor, and the ice is the greenish sky between them. Thus all of heaven is realized on earth. You have seen those purple fortunate isles in the sunset heavens, and that green and amber sky between them. Would you believe that you could ever walk amid those isles? You can on many a winter evening. I have done so a hundred times. The ice is a solid crystalline sky under our feet.

Whatever aid is to be derived from the use of a scientific term, we can never begin to see anything as it is so long as we remember the scientific term which always our ignorance has imposed on it. Natural objects and phenomena are in this sense forever wild and unnamed by us.

Thus the sky and the earth sympathize, and are subject to the same laws, and in the horizon they, as it were, meet and are seen to be one.

I have walked in such a place and found it hard as marble.

Not only the earth but the heavens are made our footstool. That is what the phenomenon of ice means. The earth is annually inverted and we walk upon the sky. The ice reflects the blue of the sky. The waters become solid and make a sky below. The clouds grow heavy and fall to earth, and we walk on them. We live and walk on solidified fluids.

We have such a habit of looking away that we see not what is around us. These snow-clad hills answer to the rosy isles in the west. The winter is coming when I shall walk the sky. The ice is a solid sky on which we walk. It is the inverted year. There is an annual light in the darkness of the winter night. The shadows are blue, as the sky is forever blue. In winter we are purified and translated. The earth does not absorb our thoughts. It becomes a Valhalla.

FEB. 13. 2 P.M.—Down river.

Thermometer 38°. Warm; a cloud just appearing in the west.

That hard meadow just below the boys' bathing-place below the North Bridge is another elfin burial-ground. It would be a bad place to walk in a dark night. The mounds are often in ridges, even as if turned up by the plow.

Water overflowing the ice at an opening in the river, and mixing with thin snow, saturating it, seen now on one side at right angles with the sun's direction, is as black as black cloth. It is surprising what a variety of distinct colors the winter can show us, using but few pigments, so to call them. The principal charm of a winter walk over ice is perhaps the peculiar and pure colors exhibited.

There is the *red* of the sunset sky, and of the snow at evening, and in rainbow flocks during the day, and in sun-dogs.

The *blue* of the sky, and of the ice and water reflected, and of shadows on snow.

The *yellow* of the sun and the morning and evening sky, and of the sedge (or straw-color, bright when lit on edge of ice at evening), and *all three* in hoar frost crystals.

Then, for the secondary, there is the *purple* of the snow in drifts or on hills, of the mountains, and clouds at evening.

The *green* of evergreen woods, of the sky, and of the ice and water toward evening.

The *orange* of the sky at evening.

The *white* of snow and clouds, and the *black* of clouds, of water agitated, and water saturating thin snow on ice.

The *russet* and *brown* and *gray*, etc., of deciduous woods.

The *tawny* of the bare earth.

I suspect that the green and rose (or purple) are not noticed on ice and snow unless it is pretty cold, and perhaps there is less greenness of the ice now than in December, when the days were shorter. The ice may now be too old and white.

Those horn, knob, and rake icicles on the southeast sides of all open places—or that were open on the 10th near enough to the bushes—are suddenly softening and turning white on one side to-day, so that they remind me of the alabaster (?) or plaster images on an Italian's board. All along the ice belt or shelf—for the river has fallen more than a foot—countless white figures stand crowded, their minute cores of sedge or twigs being concealed. Some are like beaks of birds,—cranes or herons. Having seen this phenomenon in one place, I know with certainty in just how many places and where, throughout the town,—four or five,—I shall find these icicles, on the southeast sides of the larger open places which approached near enough to a bushy or reedy shore.

The grass comes very nearly being completely encrusted in some places, but commonly rounded knobs stand up.

The ground being bare, I pick up two or three arrowheads in Tarbell's field near Ball's Hill.

There is nothing more affecting and beautiful to man, a child of the earth, than the sight of the naked soil in the spring. I feel a kindredship with it.

The sun being in a cloud, partly obscured, I see a very dark purple tinge on the flat drifts on the ice earlier than usual, and when afterward the sun comes out below the cloud, I see no purple nor rose. Hence it seems that the twilight has as much or more to do with this phenomenon, supposing the sun to be low, than the slight angle of its rays with the horizon.

Always you have to contend with the stupidity of men. It is like a stiff soil, a hard-pan. If you go deeper than usual, you are sure to meet with a pan made harder even by the superficial cultivation. The stupid you have always with you. Men are more obedient at first to words than ideas. They mind names more than things. Read to them a lecture on "Education," naming that subject, and they will think that they have heard something important, but call it "Transcendentalism," and they will think it moonshine. Or halve your lecture, and put a psalm at the beginning and a prayer at the end of it and read it from a pulpit, and they will pronounce it good without thinking.

The Scripture rule, "Unto him that hath shall be given," is true of composition. The more you have thought and written on a given theme, the more you can still write. Thought breeds thought. It grows under your hands.

XXXI.

THE EARLY SPRING

Feb. 15. As in the expression of moral truths we admire any close-ness to the physical fact which in all language is the symbol of the spiritual, so, finally, when natural objects are described, it is an advantage if words derived originally from nature, it is true, but which have been turned (*tropes*) from their primary signification to a moral sense, are used, *i.e.*, if the object is personified. The one who loves and understands a thing the best will incline to use the personal pronouns in speaking of it. To him there is no *neuter* gender. Many of the words of the old naturalists were in this sense doubly tropes.

P.M.—About 30° at 2 P.M. Skated to Bound Rock.

Feb. 17. We cannot spare the very lively and lifelike descriptions of some of the old naturalists. They sympathize with the creatures which they describe. Edward Topsell in his translation of Conrad Gesner, in 1607, called "The History of Four-footed Beasts," says of the antelopes that "they are bred in India and Syria, near the river Euphrates," and then—which enables you to realize the living creature and its habitat—he adds, "and delight much to drink of the cold water thereof." The beasts which most modern naturalists describe do not *delight* in anything, and their water is neither hot nor cold. Reading the above makes you want to go and drink of the Euphrates yourself, if it is warm weather. I do not know how much of his spirit he owes to Gesner, but he proceeds in his translation to say that "they have horns growing forth of the crown of their head, which are very long and sharp; so that Alexander affirmed they pierced through the shields of his soldiers, and fought with them very irefully: at which time his company slew as he travelled to India, eight thousand five hundred and fifty, which great slaughter may be the occasion why they are so rare and seldom seen to this day."

Now here *something* is described at any rate; it is a real account, whether of a real animal or not. You can plainly see the horns which "grew forth" from their crowns, and how well that word "irefully" describes a beast's fighting! And then for the number which Alexander's men slew "as he travelled to India,"—and what a travelling was that, my hearers!—eight thousand five hundred and fifty, just the number you would have guessed after the thousands were given, and an easy one to remember too. He goes on to say that "their horns are great and made like a saw, and they with them can cut asunder the branches of osier or small trees, whereby it cometh to pass that many times their necks are taken in the twists of the falling boughs, whereat the beast with repining cry, bewrayeth himself to the hunters, and so is taken." The artist too has done his part equally well, for you are presented with a drawing of the beast with serrated horns, the tail of a lion, a cheek tooth (canine?) as big as a boar's, a stout front, and an exceedingly "ireful" look, as if he were facing all Alexander's army.

Though some beasts are described in this book which have no existence as I can learn but in the imagination of the writers, they really have an existence there, which is saying not a little, for most of our modern authors have not imagined the actual beasts which they presume to describe. The very frontispiece is a figure of "the gorgon," which looks sufficiently like a hungry beast covered with scales, which you may have dreamed of, apparently just fallen on the track of you, the reader, and snuffing the odor with greediness.

These men had an adequate idea of a beast, or what a beast should be, a very *bellua* (the translator makes the word *bestia* to be "*a vastando*"); and they will describe and will draw you a cat with four strokes, more beastly or beast-like to look at than Mr. Ruskin's favorite artist draws a tiger. They had an adequate idea of the wildness of beasts and of men, and in their descriptions and drawings they did not always fail when they *surpassed* nature.

Gesner says of apes that "they are held for a subtil, ironical, ridiculous and unprofitable beast, whose flesh is not good for meat as a sheep, neither his back for burthen as an asses, nor yet commodious to keep a house like a dog, but of the Grecians termed gelotopoios, made for laughter."

Feb. 18. A snow-storm, falling all day; wind northeast.

The snow is fine and drives low; is composed of granulated masses one sixteenth to one twentieth of an inch in diameter. Not in flakes at all. I think it is not those large-flaked snow-storms that are the worst for the traveller, or the deepest.

Gesner (unless we owe it to the translator) has a livelier conception of an animal which has no existence, or of an action which was never performed, than most naturalists have of what passes before their eyes. The ability to report a thing *as if it had occurred*, whether it did or not, is surely important to a describer. They do not half tell a thing because you might expect them to but half believe it. I feel, of course, very ignorant in a museum. I know nothing about the things which they have there,—no more than I should know my friends in the tomb. I walk amid those jars of bloated creatures which they label frogs, a total stranger, without the least froggy thought being suggested. Not one of them can croak. They leave behind all life they that enter there, both frogs and men.

Sometimes, when I go forth at 2 P.M., there is searcely a cloud in the sky, but soon one will appear in the west and steadily advance and expand itself, and so change the whole character of the afternoon and of my thoughts. The history of the sky for that afternoon will be but the development of that cloud.

I think that the most important requisite in describing an animal, is to be sure and give its character and spirit, for in that you have, without error, the sum and effect of all its parts, known and unknown. You must tell what it is to man. Surely the most important part of an animal is its *anima*, its vital spirit, on which is based its character and all the peculiarities by which it most concerns us. Yet most scientific books which treat of animals leave this out altogether, and what they describe are as it were phenomena of dead matter. What is most interesting in a dog, for example, is his attachment to his master, his intelligence, courage, and the like, and not his anatomical structure or even many habits which affect us less.

If you have undertaken to write the biography of an animal, you will have to present to us the living creature, *i.e.*, a result which no man can understand, but only in his degree report the impression made on him.

Science in many departments of natural history does not pretend to go beyond the shell; *i.e.*, it does not get to animated nature at all. A history of animated nature must itself be animated.

The ancients, one would say, with their gorgons, sphinxes, satyrs, mantichora, etc., could imagine more than existed, while the moderns cannot imagine so much as exists.

In describing brutes, as in describing men, we shall naturally dwell most on those particulars in which they are most like ourselves,—in which we have most sympathy with them.

We are as often injured as benefited by our systems, for, to speak the truth, no human system is a true one, and a name is at most a mere convenience and carries no information with it. As soon as I begin to be aware of the life of any creature, I at once forget its name. To know the names of creatures is only a convenience to us at first, but so soon as we have learned to distinguish them, the sooner we forget their names the better, so far as any true appreciation of them is concerned. I think, therefore, that the best and most harmless names are those which are an imitation of the voice or note of an animal, or the most poetic ones. But the name adheres only to the accepted and conventional bird or quadruped, never an instant to the real one. There is always something ridiculous in the name of a great man,—as if he were named John Smith. The name is convenient in communicating with others, but it is not to be remembered when I communicate with myself.

If you look over a list of medicinal recipes in vogue in the last century, how foolish and useless they are seen to be! And yet we use equally absurd ones with faith to-day.

When the ancients had not found an animal wild and strange enough to suit them, they created one by the mingled traits of the most savage already known,—as hyenas, lionesses, pards, panthers, etc., etc.,—one with another. Their beasts were thus of wildness and savageness all compact, and more *ferine* and *terrible* than any of an unmixed breed could be. They allowed nature great license in these directions. The most strange and fearful beasts were by them supposed to be the off-spring of two different savage kinds. So fertile were their imaginations, and such fertility did they assign to nature. In the modern account the fabulous part will be omitted, it is true, but the portrait of the real and living creature also.

The old writers have left a more lively and lifelike account of the gorgon than modern writers give us of real animals.

Feb. 20. P.M.—I see directly in front of the Depot Ice house, on the only piece of bare ground I see hereabouts, a large flock of lesser redpolls feeding. They must be picking up earth, sand, or the withered grass. They are so intent on it that they allow me to come quite near. This, then, is one use for the drifting of snow which lays bare some spots, however deep it may be elsewhere,—so that the birds, etc., can come at the earth.

Feb. 21. It was their very admiration of nature that made the ancients attribute those magnanimous qualities which are rarely to be found in man to the lion as her masterpiece, and it is only by a readiness, or rather preparedness, to see more than appears in a creature that one can appreciate what is manifest.

It is remarkable how many berries are the food of birds, mice, etc. Perhaps I may say that all are, however hard or bitter. This I am inclined to say, judging of what I do not know from what I do.

Feb. 23. 2 P.M.—Thermometer 56°. Wind south.

3 P.M.—Thermometer 58° and snow almost gone. River rising.

We have not had such a warm day since the beginning of December (which was remarkably warm).

The words "pardall" and "libbard," applied by Gesner to the same animal, express as much of the wild beast as any.

I read in Brand's "Popular Antiquities" that "Bishop Stillingfleet observes, that among the Saxons of the northern nations, the Feast of the New Year was observed with more than ordinary jollity: thence, as Olaus Wormius and Scheffer observe, they reckoned their age by so many Iolas." (*Iola*, to make merry.—Gothic.) So may we measure our lives by our joys. We have lived, not in proportion to the number of years that we have spent on the earth, but in proportion as we have enjoyed.

A fact stated barely is dry. It must be the vehicle of some humanity in order to interest us. It is like giving a man a stone when he asks you for bread. Ultimately the moral is all in all, and we do not mind it if inferior truth is sacrificed to superior, as when the moralist fables and makes animals speak and act like men. It must be warm, moist, incarnated,—have been breathed on at least. A man has not seen a thing who has not felt it.

Feb. 24. 2 P.M.—Thermometer 42. A very spring-like day, so much sparkling light in the air.

The clouds reflecting a dazzling brightness from their edges, and though it is rather warm (the wind raw) there are many, finely divided, in a stream southwest to northeast all the afternoon, and some most brilliant mother-o'-pearl. I never saw the green in it more distinct.

Feb. 28. Looking from Hubbard's Bridge, I see a great water-bug even on the river, so forward is the season.

I take up a handsomely spread (or blossomed) pitch pine cone, but I find that a squirrel has begun to strip it first, having gnawed off a few of the scales at the base. The squirrel always begins to gnaw a cone thus at the base, as if it were a stringent law among the squirrel people,—as if the old squirrels taught the young ones a few simple rules like this.

C. saw a dozen robins to-day on the ground on Ebby Hubbard's hill by the Yellow Birch Swamp.

March 2. Notice the brightness of a row of osiers this morning. This phenomenon, whether referable to a change in the condition of the twig or to the spring air and light, or even to our imaginations, is not the less a real phenomenon, affecting us annually at this season. This is one compensation for having them lopped so often along the causeways, that it is only these new and vigorous growths which shine thus.

March 8. 2.30 P.M.—50°. To Cliffs and Walden.

See a small flock of grackles on the willow-row above railroad bridge. How they sit and make a business of chattering! for it cannot be called singing, and no improvement from age to age perhaps. Yet, as *nature* is a *becoming*, their notes may become melodious at last. At length, on my very near approach, they flit suspiciously away, uttering a few subdued notes as they hurry off.

March 9. Snows this forenoon, whitening the ground again.

I have seen three or four pieces of coral in the fields of Concord, and Mr. Pratt has found three or four on his farm. How shall they be accounted for? Who brought them here? and when?

March 14. 2 P.M.—Thermometer 39. Overcast, with a flurry of snow and a little rain, till 4.30 P.M. To Walden and Cliffs.

I am surprised to find Walden almost entirely open. I have not observed it to open before before the 23d of March.* However, it is clear enough why Walden has broken up thus early this year. It does not ordinarily freeze till near the end of December (average of twelve observations, December 25th), while Fair Haven Pond freezes about December 2d. But this past winter our cold weather was mostly confined to December, which was remarkable for its uniform cold, while January and February were very open and pleasant. So that

---

*March 19, 1856, it was twenty-six inches thick!!

Fair Haven Pond, having more than three weeks the start, and that being almost all the cold weather that we had, froze much the thickest. Walden did not freeze so thick as usual. If we have an average winter up to January, but a particularly warm one afterward, Walden will break up early, not having had any chance to freeze thick.

As I stand there, I see some dark ripples already drop and sweep over the surface of the pond, as they will ere long over Ripple Lake and other pools in the wood. No sooner has the ice of Walden melted than the wind begins to play in dark ripples over the surface of the virgin water. It is affecting to see Nature so tender, however old, and wearing none of the wrinkles of age. Ice dissolved is the next moment as perfect water as if it had been melted a million years. To see that which was lately so hard and immovable now so soft and impressible! What if our moods could dissolve thus completely? It seems as if it must rejoice in its own newly acquired fluidity, as it affects the beholder with joy. Often the March winds have no chance to ripple its face at all.

I see on the peak several young English cherry trees six or eight feet high, evidently planted by birds and growing well. These grew nearly a foot last year and look quite healthy. The bird must have brought the stone far to this locality.

Every craftsman looks at his own objects with peculiar eyes. I thought of this on seeing these young cherry trees and remembering how I used to distinguish the erect and lusty shoots when I cultivated a small nursery, for budding. One eye will mark how much the twigs grew last year, another the lichens on the trunk.

March 15. A hen-hawk sails away from the wood southward. I get a very fair sight of it sailing overhead. What a perfectly regular and neat outline it presents! an easily recognized figure anywhere. Yet I never see it represented in any books. The exact correspondence of the marks on one side to those on the other, as the black or dark tip of one wing to the other, and the dark line midway the wing. I have no idea that one can get as correct an idea of the form and color of the under sides of a hen-hawk's wings by spreading those of a dead specimen in his study as by looking up at a free and living hawk soaring above him in the fields. The penalty for obtaining a petty knowledge thus dishonestly is that it is less interesting to men generally, as it is less significant. What is an eagle in captivity!—screaming in a courtyard! I am not the wiser respecting eagles for having seen one there. I do not wish to know the length of its entrails.

March 18. Sunday. 2 P.M.—Thermometer 56. Wind south, but soon changes to southeast, making the air fresh and hazy and rippling the before smooth water.

All along under that bank I heard the hum of honey-bees in the air, attracted by this flower. What a remarkable instinct it is that leads them to this flower! This bee is said to have been introduced by the white man, but how much it has learned!

You see a fly come forth from its hibernaculum in your yard, stretch its wings in the sun, and set forth on its flowery journey. You little think that it knows the locality of early flowers better than you. You have not dreamed of them yet. It knows a spot a mile off under a warm bank-side where the skunk-cabbage is in bloom. No doubt this flower, too, has learned to expect its winged visitor knocking at its door in the spring.

Pratt says that his bees come out in a pleasant day at any time in the winter; that of late they have come out and eased themselves, the ground being covered around the hives with their yellow droppings. Were not these the little yellow pellets I saw in a skunk-cabbage flower some years ago?* He says they come home now all yellow. I tell him it is skunk-cabbage pollen. I think there would be no surer way to tell when this flower had bloomed than to keep bees and watch when they first returned laden with pollen. Let them search for you,—a swarm of bees. Probably with a microscope you could tell exactly when each of the bee-frequented flowers began to bloom throughout the year.

March 22. The phenomena of an average March are increasing warmth, melting the snow and ice and, gradually, the frost in the

---

*No, for Farmer says the former are liquid.

ground; cold and blustering weather, with high, commonly north-west winds for many days together; misty and other rains taking out frost, and whitenings of snow, and winter often back again, both its cold and snow; bare ground and open waters, and more or less of a freshet; some calm and pleasant days reminding us of summer, with a blue haze or a thicker mist wreathing the woods at last, in which, perchance, we take off our coats awhile and sit without a fire a day; ways getting settled, and some greenness appearing on south bank; April-like rains, after the frost is chiefly out; plowing and planting of peas, etc., just beginning, and the old leaves getting dry in the woods.

Vegetation fairly begins,—conferva and mosses, grass and carex, etc.,—and gradually many early herbaceous plants start, and noticed radical leaves; *Stellaria media* and shepherd's-purse bloom; maple and buttonwood sap (6th) flow; spiræas start, cladonias flush, and bæomyces handsome; willow catkins become silvery, aspens downy; osiers, etc., look bright, white maple and elm buds expand and open, oak woods thin-leaved; alder and hazel catkins become relaxed and elongated. First perceptible greenness on south banks, 22d. The skunk-cabbage begins to bloom (23d); plant peas, etc., 26th; spring rye, wheat, lettuce; maple swamps red-tinged (?) 28th, and lake grass; and perchance the gooseberry and lilac begin to show a little green. That is, *one indigenous native flower* blooms. (*Vide* if the early sedge does.)

About twenty-nine migratory birds arrive (including hawks and crows), and two or three more utter their spring notes and sounds, as nuthatch and chickadee, turkeys, and woodpecker tapping, while apparently the snow bunting, lesser redpoll, shrike, and doubtless several more—as owls, crossbills (?)—leave us, and woodcocks and hawks begin to lay.

Many insects and worms come forth and are active,—and the perla insects still about ice and water,—as tipula, grubs, and fuzzy caterpillars, minute hoppers on grass at springs; gnats, large and small, dance in air; the common and the green fly buzz outdoors; the gyrinus, large and small, on brooks, etc., and skaters; spiders shoot their webs, and at last gossamer floats; the honey-bee visits the skunk-cabbage; fishworms come up, sow-bugs, wireworms, etc.; various larvæ are seen in pools; small green and also brown grasshoppers begin to hop, small ants to stir (25th); *Vanessa Antiopa* out 29th; cicindelas run on sand; and small reddish butterflies are seen in wood-paths, etc., etc., etc.

Skunks are active and frolic; woodchucks and ground squirrels come forth; moles root; musquash are commonly drowned out and shot, and sometimes erect a new house, and at length are smelled; and foxes have young (?).

As for fishes, etc., trout glance in the brooks, brook minnows are seen; see furrows on sandy bottoms, and small shell snails copulate; dead suckers, etc., are seen floating on meadows; pickerel and perch are running up brooks, and suckers (24th) and pickerel begin to dart in shallows.

And for reptiles, not only salamanders and pollywogs are more commonly seen, and also those little frogs (*sylvatica* males?) at spring-holes and ditches, the yellow-spot turtle and wood turtle, *Rana fontinalis*, and painted tortoise come forth, and the *Rana sylvatica* croaks.

Our river opened in 1851, much before February 25; 1852, March 14 at least; 1853, say March 8 at least; 1854, say March 9; average March 5. Hudson River opened, according to Patent Office Reports, 1854, page 435: 1851, February 25; 1852, March 28; 1853, March 23; 1854, March 17; average March 16. According to which our river opens some eleven days the soonest. Perhaps this is owing partly to the fact that our river is nearer the ocean and that it rises southward instead of northward.

March 23. It will be seen by the annexed scrap* that March is the fourth coldest month, or about midway between December and November. The same appears from the fifteen years' observation at Mendon. ("American Almanac," page 86.) The descent to extreme cold occupies seven months and is therefore more gradual (though a part of it is more rapid) than the ascent to extreme heat, which

---

*[Tables from the Patent Office Reports, 1853, p. 332; 1854, p. 427; 1855, p. 375.]

takes only five months. The mean average temperature of the coldest month (February) being 23.25, and of the warmest (July) being 72.35, the whole ascent from extreme cold to extreme heat is 49.10°, and in March (32.73) we have accomplished 8.48°, or a little less than one sixth the ascent. (According to the Mendon fifteen years' average the whole ascent is 47.5, and in March we have advanced 9.2, a little more than one fifth.) It appears (from the scrap) that December, January, and February, the three winter months, differ very little in temperature, and the three summer months and September are next most alike, though they differ considerably more. (Same from Mendon tables.) The greatest or abruptest change is from November to December (in Mendon tables from September to October), the next most abrupt from April to May (in Mendon tables from March to April). The least change (according to the above tables) is from December to January. (According to Mendon tables, the same from December to January as from January to February.) The three spring months, and also October and November, are transition months, in which the temperature rapidly changes.

March 24. According to a table in the "American Almanac" for '49, page 84, made at Cambridge, from May, '47, to May, '48, the monthly mean force of the wind for March, April, and May were equal, and were inferior to July and June; for quantity of clouds March and May were equal, and were preceded by December, November, September, January, June, and August. For depth of rain, [*etc.*].

March 25. To speak of the general phenomena of March: When March arrives, a tolerably calm, clear, sunny, spring-like day, the snow is so far gone that sleighing ends and our compassion is excited by the sight of horses laboriously dragging wheeled vehicles through mud and water and slosh. We shall no longer hear the jingling of sleigh-bells. The sleigh is housed, or, perchance, converted into a wheeled vehicle by the travelling peddler caught far from home. The wood-sled is perhaps abandoned by the roadside,

where the snow ended, with two sticks put under its runners,—
there to rest, it may be, while the grass springs up green around it,
till another winter comes round. Even the boy's sled gets put away
by degrees, or when it is found to be in the way, and his thoughts
are directed gradually to more earthy games. There are now water
privileges for him by every roadside.

The boy's sled gets put away in the barn or shed or garret, and
there lies dormant all summer, like a woodchuck in the winter. It
goes into its burrow just before woodchucks come out, so that you
may say a woodchuck never sees a sled, nor a sled a woodchuck,—
unless it were a prematurely risen woodchuck or a belated and un-
seasonable sled. Before the woodchuck comes out the sled goes in.
They dwell at the antipodes of each other. Before sleds rise woodchucks have set. The ground squirrel too shares the privileges and
misfortunes of the woodchuck. The sun now passes from the con-
stellation of the sled into that of the woodchuck.

The sleighing, the sledding, or sliding, is gone. We now begin to
wheel or roll ourselves and commodities along, which requires
more tractile power. The high-set chaise, the lumbering coach like
wasps and gnats and bees come humming forth.

The traveller, when he returns the hired horse to his stable, concludes at last that it is worse sleighing than wheeling. To be sure,
there was one reach where he slid along pretty well under the north
side of a wood, but for the most part he cut through, as when the
cook cuts edgings of dough for her pies, and the grating on the
gravel set his teeth on edge.

To proceed with March: Frost comes out of warm sand-banks
exposed to the sun, and the sand flows down in the form of foliage.
But I see still adhering to the bridges the great chandelier icicles
formed in yesterday's cold and windy weather.

By the 2d, ice suddenly softens and skating ends. This warmer
and springlike day, the inexperienced eagerly revisit the pond
where yesterday they found hard and glassy ice, and are surprised
and disappointed to find it soft and rotten. Skates, then, have become useless tools and follow sleds to their winter quarters. They

are ungratefully parted with, not like old friends surely. They and the thoughts of them are shuffled out of the way, and you will probably have to hunt long before you find them next December.

The air is springlike. The milkman closes his ice-house doors against the milder air.

By the 3d, [*etc., day by day through March 31*].

March 26. Tried by various tests, this season fluctuates more or less. For example, we may have absolutely no sleighing during the year. There was none in the winter months of '58 (only from March 4 to 14). '52–'53 was an open winter. Or it may continue uninterrupted from the beginning of winter to the 3d of April, as in '56, and the dependent phenomena be equally late. The river may be either only transiently closed, as in '52–'53 and '57–'58, or it may not be open entirely (up *to* pond) till April 4th.

As for cold, some years we may have as cold days in March as in any winter month. March 4, 1858, it was –14, and on the 29th, 1854, the pump froze so as to require thawing.

The river may be quite high in March or at summer level.

Fair Haven Pond may be open by the 20th of March, as this year, or not till April 13 as in '56, or twenty-three days later.

Tried by the skunk-cabbage, this may flower March 2 ('60) or April 6 or 8 (as in '55 and '54), or some five weeks later,—say thirty-six days.

The bluebird may be seen February 24, as in '50, '57, and '60, or not till March 24, as in '56,—say twenty-eight days.

The yellow-spotted tortoise may be seen February 23, as in '57, or not till March 28, as in '55,—thirty-three days.

The wood frog may be heard March 15, as this year, or not till April 13, as in '56,—twenty-nine days.

That is, tried by the last four phenomena, there may be about a month's fluctuation, so that March may be said to have receded half-way into February or advanced half-way into April, *i.e.*, it borrows half of February or half of April.

April 1. Warm, with the thick haze still concealing the sun.

Our gooseberry begins to show a little green, but not our currant.

The fruit a thinker bears is *sentences*,—statements or opinions. He seeks to affirm something as true. I am surprised that my affirmations or utterances come to me ready-made,—not forethought,—so that I occasionally awake in the night simply to let fall ripe a statement which I had never consciously considered before, and as surprising and novel and agreeable to me as anything can be. As if we only thought by sympathy with the universal mind, which thought while we were asleep. There is such a necessity to make a definite statement that our minds at length do it without our consciousness, just as we carry our food to our mouths. This occurred to me last night, but I was so surprised by the fact which I have just endeavored to report that I have entirely forgotten what the particular observation was.

April 20. Moore tells me that last fall his men, digging sand in that hollow just up the hill, dug up a parcel of snakes half torpid. They were both striped and black together. The men killed them, and laid them all in a line on the ground, and they measured several hundred feet. This seems to be the common practice when such collections are found; they are at once killed and stretched out in a line, and the sum of their lengths measured and related.

May 3. To Cambridge and Boston.

I see at the Aquarium many of my little striped or barred breams, now labelled *Bryttus obesus*. Compared with the common, they have rounded tails, larger dorsal and anal fins, and are fuller or heavier forward. I observe that they incline to stand on their heads more.

May 12. Celandine. Very hot.

2.30 P.M.—81°.

We seek the shade to sit in for a day or two.

The sugar maple blossoms on the Common resound with bees.

First bathe in the river. Quite warm enough.

May 17. Standing in the meadow near the early aspen at the island, I hear the first fluttering of leaves,—a peculiar sound, at first unaccountable to me. The breeze causes the now fully expanded aspen leaves there to rustle with a pattering sound, striking on one another. It is much like a gentle surge breaking on a shore, or the rippling of waves. This is the first softer music which the wind draws from the forest, the woods generally being comparatively bare and just bursting into leaf. It was delicious to behold that dark mass and hear that soft rippling sound.

Hear of a hummingbird on the 12th.

Hear the first bullfrog's *trump.*

May 23. Critchicrotches some two or three days; now tender to eat.

How agreeable and surprising the peculiar fragrance of the sweet flag when bruised! That this plant alone should have extracted this odor surely for so many ages each summer from the moist earth!

The quarter-grown red oak leaves between you and the sun, how yellow-green!

June 4. The clear brightness of June was well represented yesterday by the buttercups (*Ranunculus bulbosus*) along the roadside. Their yellow so glossy and varnished within; but not without. Surely there is no reason why the new butter should not be yellow now.

One asks me to-day when it is that the leaves are fully expanded, so that the trees and woods look dark and heavy with leaves. I answered that there were leaves on many if not on most trees already fully expanded, but that there were not many on a tree, the shoots having grown only some three inches, but by and by they will have grown a foot or two and there will be ten times as many leaves. Each tree (or most trees) now holds out many little twigs, some three inches long, with two or three fully expanded leaves on it, between us and the sun, making already a grateful but thin shade, like a coarse sieve, so open that we see the fluttering of each leaf in its shadow; but in a week or more the twigs will have so extended themselves, and the number of fully expanded leaves be so increased, that the trees will look heavy and dark with foliage and the shadow be dark and opaque,—a gelid shade.

You may say that now, when most trees have fully expanded leaves and the black ash fairly shows green, the leafy season has fairly commenced. (I see that I so called it May 31 and 27, 1853.)

June 7. The peculiarities of the new leaves, or young ones, are to be observed. *As I now remember,* there is the whitish shoot of the white pine; the reddish brown of the pitch pine, giving a new tinge to its tops; the bead-work of the hemlock; the now just conspicuous bursting lighter glaucous-green buds of the black spruce in cold swamps; the frizzly-looking glaucous-green shoots and leafets of the fir (and fragrant now or soon); the thin and delicate foliage of the larch; the inconspicuous and fragrant arbor-vitæ; the bead-work of the *Juniperus repens* (red cedar inconspicuous); [*etc.—24 more*].

June 8. 2 P.M.—To Well Meadow *via* Walden.

Within a day or two has begun that season of summer when you see afternoon showers, maybe with thunder, or the threat of them, dark in the horizon, and are uncertain whether to venture far away or without an umbrella. I noticed the very first such cloud on the 25th of May,—the dark iris of June.

As I look at the mountains in the horizon, I am struck by the fact that they are all pyramidal—
pyramids, more or less low—
and have a peak. Why have the mountains usually a peak? This is not the common form of hills. They do not so impress us at least.

June 16. It appears to me that these phenomena occur simultaneously, say June 12th, *viz.*:—

Heat about 85° at 2 P.M. True summer.

Hylodes cease to peep.

Purring frogs (*Rana palustris*) cease.

Lightning-bugs first seen.

Bullfrogs trump *generally.*

Mosquitoes begin to be really troublesome.

Afternoon thunder-showers almost regular.[*]

Sleep with open window (10th), and wear thin coat and ribbon on neck.

Turtles fairly and generally begun to lay.

June 21. Having noticed the pine pollen washed up on the shore of three or four ponds in the woods lately and at Ripple Lake, a dozen rods from the nearest pine, also having seen the pollen carried off visibly half a dozen rods from a pitch pine which I had jarred, and rising all the while when there was very little wind, it suggested to me that the air must be full of this fine dust at this season, that it must be carried to great distances, when dry, and falling at night perhaps, or with a change in the atmosphere, its presence might be detected remote from pines by examining the edges of pretty large bodies of water, where it would be collected to one side by the wind and waves from a large area.

So I thought over all the small ponds in the township in order to select one or more most remote from the woods or pines, whose shores I might examine and so test my theory. I could think of none more favorable than this little pond only four rods in diameter, a watering-place in John Brown's pasture, which has but few pads in it. It is a small round pond at the bottom of a hollow in the midst of a perfectly bare, dry pasture. The nearest wood of any kind is just thirty-nine rods distant northward, and across a road from the edge of the pond. Any other wood in other directions is five or six times as far. I knew it was a bad time to try my experiment,—just after such heavy rains and when the pines are effete,— a little too late. The wind was now blowing quite strong from the northeast, whereas all the pollen that I had seen hitherto had been collected on the northeast sides of ponds by a southwest wind. I approached the pond from the northeast and, looking over it and carefully along the shore there, could detect no pollen. I then proceeded to walk round it, but still could detect none. I then said to

---

[*]15th, 16th, 17th.

myself, If there was any here before the rain and northeast wind, it must have been on the northeast side and then have been washed over and now up high quite at or on the shore. I looked there carefully, stooping down, and was gratified to find, after all, a distinct yellow line of pollen dust about half an inch in width—or washing off to two or three times that width—quite on the edge, and some dead twigs which I took up from the wet shore were completely coated with it, as with sulphur. This yellow line reached half a rod along the southwest side, and I then detected a little of the dust slightly graying the surface for two or three feet out there.

When I thought I had failed, I was much pleased to detect, after all, this distinct yellow line, revealing unmistakably the presence of pines in the neighborhood and thus confirming my theory. As chemists detect the presence of ozone in the atmosphere by exposing to it a delicately prepared paper, so the lakes detect for us thus the presence of the pine pollen in the atmosphere. They are our *pollinometers*. How much of this invisible dust must be floating in the atmosphere, and be inhaled and drunk by us at this season!! Who knows but the pollen of some plants may be unwholesome to inhale, and produce the diseases of the season?*

Of course a large pond will collect the most, and you will find most at the bottom of long deep bays into which the wind blows.

I did not expect to find any pollen, the pond was so small and distant from any wood, but I thought that I would examine. Who knows but the pollen of various kinds floating through the air at this season may be the source of some of the peculiar perfumes which are not traceable to their sources?

June 27. Farmer says that he found on the 24th a black snake laying her eggs on the side of the hill between his peach-orchard and the ledge in the woods. Was close by where his uncle (?) tried to dig through to the other side of the world. Dug more or less for three years. Used to dig nights, as long as one candle lasted. Left a stone

---

Vide June 20 and 22, 1858.

just between him and the other side, not to be removed till he was ready to marry Washington's sister. The foxes now occupy his hole.

June 28. This month, it must be 85° at 2 P.M. and *still* to make hot weather. 80° with wind is quite comfortable. June-grass is now generally browned atop, its spikes being out of bloom and old. Herd's-grass out, two or three days.

Farmer said yesterday that he thought foxes did not live so much in the depth of the woods as on open hillsides, where they lay out and overlooked the operations of men,—studied their ways,—which made them so cunning.

JUNE 29. Dogdayish and showery, with thunder.

At 6 P.M. 91°, the hottest yet, though a thunder-shower has passed northeast and grazed us, and, in consequence, at 6.30 or 7, another thunder-shower comes up from the southwest and there is a sudden burst from it with a remarkably strong, gusty wind, and the rain for fifteen minutes falls in a blinding deluge. I think I never saw it rain so hard. The roof of the depot shed is taken off, many trees torn to pieces, the garden flooded at once, corn and potatoes, etc., beaten flat.* You could not see distinctly many rods through the rain. It was the very strong gusts added to the weight of the rain that did the mischief. There was little or no wind before the shower; it belonged wholly to it. Thus our most violent thunder-shower followed the hottest hour of the month.

July 3. Looked for the marsh hawk's nest in the Great Meadows. We had much difficulty in finding it again, but at last nearly stumbled on to a young hawk with a great head, staring eyes, and open gaping or panting mouth, yet mere down, grayish-white down, as yet; but I detected another which had crawled a foot one side amid

---

*There was the same sudden and remarkably violent storm about two hours earlier all up and down the Hudson, and it struck the Great Eastern at her moorings in New York and caused some damage.

the bushes for shade or safety, more than half as large again, with small feathers and a yet more angry, hawk-like look. How naturally anger sits on the young hawk's head! June is an up-country month, when our air and landscape is most like that of a more mountainous region, full of freshness.

July 7. June 30th, July 3d, 4th, 6th, and 7th, I carried round a thermometer in the afternoon and ascertained the temperature of the springs, brooks, etc. [*Eight pages of data, averaged and analyzed, on 18 springs, 11 brooks, 15 river temperatures, and 6 other local bodies of water.*]

I should say, then, that a spring colder than 48° was remarkably cold; 48° to 50°, inclusive, quite cold, a very good cold spring; above 50° and not above 54°, cold; above that and not above 58°, *tolerable* merely. Or, I should rather say that only 50° and below was *cold* for a *spring*; say below 48°, remarkably cold; between that and 50°, inclusive, cold; 50° to 54°, inclusive, *pretty* cold; thence to 58°, inclusive, merely tolerable to drink.

It appears that in a cold day at present the water of the river at 6 A.M. will be ten to fourteen degrees warmer than the air, and accordingly feels warm to the touch. In the translation into English of Cranz's "Greenland" from High Dutch (1767) I find "an elve or mountain spring," and again "Salmon elves, or the little streams from the hills."

July 13. 2 P.M.—To Little Truro.

You now especially notice some very red fields where the red-top grass grows luxuriantly and is now in full bloom,—a red purple, passing into brown, looking at a distance like a red-sandstone soil. The different cultivated fields are thus like so many different-colored checkers on a checker-board. First we had the June-grass reddish-brown, and the sorrel red, of June; now the red-top red of July. For a week—and if you look very closely, for a fortnight or more—past, the season has had a more advanced look, from the reddening, imbrowning, or yellowing, and ripening of many grasses, as the sweet-scented vernal (for some time generally withered) and the June-grass, and some grain,—rye, wheat, etc.,—so that the fields and hillsides present a less liquid green than they did. The vernal freshness of June is passed.

July 17. 2 P.M.—To Walden.

The soft sand on the bottom of Walden, as deep as I can wade, feels very warm to my feet, while the water feels cold. This may be partly a mere sensation, but I suspect that the sand is really much warmer than the water and that some creatures take refuge in it accordingly, that much heat passes through the water and is absorbed in the sand. Yet when I let a thermometer lie on the bottom and draw it up quickly I detect no difference between the temperature of the bottom and of the water at the surface. Probably it would have been different if the thermometer had been buried in the sand.

July 19. The rich crimson under sides (with their regularly branching veins) of some white lily pads surpasses the color of most flowers. No wonder the spiders are red that swim beneath; and think of the fishes that swim beneath this crimson canopy,—beneath a crimson sky. I can frequently trace the passage of a boat, a pickerel-fisher, perhaps, by the crimson under sides of the pads upturned.

The pads crowd and overlap each other in most amicable fashion. Sometimes one lobe of a yellow lily pad is above its neighbor, while the other is beneath. The pads are rapidly consumed, but fresh ones are all the while pushing up and unrolling. They push up and spread out in the least crevice that offers.

July 22. Yesterday having been a rainy day, the air is now remarkably clear and cool and you rarely see the horizon so distinct. The surface of the earth, especially looking westward,—grass grounds, pastures, and meadows,—is remarkably beautiful. I stand in Heywood's pasture west of the leek and, leaning over the wall, look westward. All things—grass, etc.—are peculiarly fresh this season on account of the copious rains.

The next field on the west slopes gently from both east and west to a meadow in the middle. So, as I look over the wall, it is first dark-green, where white clover has been cut (still showing a myriad low white heads which resound with the hum of bees); next, along the edge of the bottom or meadow, is a strip or belt three or four rods wide of red-top, uncut, perfectly distinct; then the cheerful bright-yellow sedge of the meadow, yellow almost as gamboge; then a corresponding belt of red-top on its upper edge, quite straight and rectilinear like the first; then a glaucous-green field of grain still quite low; and, in the further corner of the field, a much darker square of green than any yet, all brilliant in this wonderful light. You thus have a sort of terrestrial rainbow, thus:—

The farmer accustomed to look at his crops from a mercenary point of view is not aware how beautiful they are. This prospect was really exciting, even as a rainbow is.

XXXII.

July 23. I saw the other day where the lightning on the 12th or 13th had struck the telegraph-posts at Walden Pond. It had shattered five posts in succession, they being a dozen rods apart, spoiling them entirely; though all of them *stood* but one, yet they were a mere wrack of splinters through which you could look. It had omitted a great many more posts and struck half a dozen more at a great distance from these on each side. And at the same time there was a smart shock, an explosion, at the operating office at the depot, two miles off from the furthest point. I should think, speaking from memory, that the posts struck were the oldest and dampest, or most rotten. At one or two posts it had plainly entered the ground and plowed toward the railroad-track, slightly injuring it. It struck a pitch pine standing within four or five feet of the wire, leaving a white seam down one side of it, also two large oaks a little further off. This was where the telegraph ran parallel to, and a few feet only from, a wood. It also struck a small oak on the opposite side of the track. The lightning struck for two miles (!!) at least.

So far as leaves are concerned, one of the most noticeable phenomena of this green-leaf season is the conspicuous reflection of light in clear breezy days from the silvery under sides of some.

All trees and shrubs which have light-colored or silvery under sides to their leaves, but especially the swamp white oak and the red maple, are now very bright and conspicuous in the strong wind after the rain of the morning. To be sure, most, if not all leaves, not to mention grasses, are a paler green beneath, and hence the oaks and other trees behind show various shades of green, which would be more observed if it were not for these stronger contrasts. Though the wind may not be very strong nor incessant, you appear to see *only* the under sides of those first named, and they make a uniform impression, as if their leaves, having been turned up, were permanently held so. Before the wind arose, the wooded shore and hillsides were an almost uniform green, but now the whole outline of the swamp white oaks and maples is revealed by the wind—a sort of magic, a "presto change"—distinctly against trees whose leaves are nearly of the same color with the upper sides of these.

In a maple swamp every maple-top stands now distinguished thus from the birches in their midst. Before they were confounded, but a wind comes and lifts their leaves, showing their lighter under sides, and suddenly, as by magic, the maple stands out from the birch. There is a great deal of life in this landscape. What an airing the leaves get! Perchance it is necessary that their under sides be thus exposed to the light and air in order that they may be hardened and darkened by it.

I read of the Amazon that its current, indeed, is strong, but the wind always blows up the stream. This sounds too good to be true.

July 31. Before it rained hardest I could see in the midst of the dark and smoother water a lighter-colored and rougher surface, generally in oblong patches, which moved steadily down the stream, and this, I think, was the new water from above welling up and making its way downward amid the old. The water or currents of a river are thus not homogeneous, but the surface is seen to be of two shades, the smoother and darker water which already fills its bed and the fresh influx of lighter-colored and rougher, probably more rapid, currents which spot it here and there; *i.e.*, some water seems to occupy it as a lake to some extent, other is passing through it as a stream,—the lacustrine and the fluviatile water. These lighter reaches without reflections (?) are, as it were, water wrong side up. But do I ever see these except when it rains? And are they not the rain-water which has not yet mingled with the water of the river?

Aug. 1. I stand at the wall-end on the Cliffs and look over the Miles meadow on Conantum. It is an unusually clear day after yesterday's rain.

How much of beauty—of color, as well as form—on which our eyes daily rest goes unperceived by us! No one but a botanist is likely to distinguish nicely the different shades of green with which the open surface of the earth is clothed,—not even a landscape-painter if he does not know the species of sedges and grasses which paint it. With respect to the color of grass, most of those even who attend peculiarly to the aspects of Nature only observe that it is more or less dark or light, green or brown, or velvety, fresh or parched, etc. But if you are studying grasses you look for another and different beauty, and you find it, in the wonderful variety of color, etc., presented by the various species.

The immediate and raised edge of the river, with its willows and button-bushes and polygonums, is a light green, but the immediately adjacent low meadows, where the sedge prevails, is a brilliant and cheerful yellow, intensely, incredibly bright, such color as you never see in pictures; yellow of various tints, in the lowest and sedgiest parts deepening to so much color as if gamboge had been rubbed into the meadow there; the most cheering color in all the landscape; shaded with little darker isles of green in the midst of this yellow sea of sedge. Yet it is the bright and cheerful yellow, as of spring, and with nothing in the least autumnal in it. How this contrasts with the adjacent fields of red-top, now fast falling before the scythe!

When your attention has been drawn to them, nothing is more charming than the common colors of the earth's surface. See yonder flashing field of corn through the *shimmering* air. (This was said day before yesterday.)

Aug. 4. 8.30 A.M.—Start for Monadnock.

We crossed the immense rocky and springy pastures, containing at first raspberries, but much more hard-hack in flower, reddening them afar, where cattle and horses collected about us, sometimes came running to us, as we thought for society, but probably not. I told Bent of it,—how they gathered about us, they were so glad to see a human being,—but he said I might put it in my book so, it would do no harm, but then the fact was they came about me for salt. "Well," said I, "it was probably because I had so much salt in my constitution." Said he, "If you had had a little salt with you you could hardly have got away from them." "Well," said I, "I had some salt in my pocket." "That's what they smelt," said he. They gathered around us while we took shelter under a black spruce from the rain.

Aug. 24. P.M.—To Walden to get its temperature. The air is only 66 (in the mizzling rain the 23d it was 78); the water at top, 75° (the 23d also 75). What I had sunk to the bottom in the middle, where a hundred feet deep by my line, left there half an hour, then pulled up and poured into a quart dipper, stood at 53°. I tried the same experiment yesterday, but then in my haste was uncertain whether it was not 51°; certain that a little later it was 54°. So 53° it must be for the present. I may have been two or more minutes pulling up the line so as to prevent its snarling. Therefore I think the water must have acquired a temperature two or three degrees higher than it had at the bottom by the time I tried it. So it appears that the bottom of Walden has, in fact, the temperature of a genuine and cold spring, or probably is of the same temperature with the average mean temperature of the earth, and, I *suspect*, the same all the year. This shows that springs need not come from a very great depth in order to be cold. What various temperatures, then, the fishes of this pond can enjoy! They require no other refrigerator than their deeps afford. They can in a few moments sink to winter or rise to summer. Walden, then, must be included among the springs, but it is one which has no outlet,—is a well rather. It reaches down to where the temperature of the earth is unchanging. It is not a superficial pond,—not in the mere skin of the earth. It goes deeper. How much this varied temperature must have to do with the distribution of the fishes in it! The few trout must oftenest go down below in summer.

Aug. 26. We are amused with foam, a hybrid between two elements. A breeze comes and gradually mingles some of the water with the air. It is, as it were, the aspiration of the pond to soar into the air. The debatable ground between two oceans, the earth, or shore, being only the point of resistance, where they are held to mingle.

It is remarkable how commonly you see the thistle-down sailing just over water (as I do after this—the 2d of September—at Walden). I see there, *i.e.* at Walden, at 5 P.M., September 2d, many seedless thistle-downs sailing about a foot above the water, and some in it, as if there was a current just above the surface which prevented their falling or rising. They are probably wafted to the water because there is more air over water.

Aug. 30. Surveying Minott's land.

Am surprised to find on his hard land, where he once raised potatoes, the hairy huckleberry, which before I had seen in swamps only. Here, too, they are more edible, not so insipid, yet not quite edible generally. They are improved, you would say, by the firmer ground.

The hairy huckleberry and muhlenbergia, I think, grow here still because Minott is an old-fashioned man and has not scrubbed up and improved his land as many, or most, have. It is in a wilder and more primitive condition. The very huckleberries are shaggy there. There was only one straight side to his land, and that I cut through a dense swamp. The fences are all meandering just as they were at least in 1746, when it was described.

Sept. 4. It is cooler these days and nights, and I move into an eastern chamber in the morning, that I may sit in the sun. The water, too, is cooler when I bathe in it, and I am reminded that this recreation has its period. I feel like a melon or other fruit laid in the sun to ripen. I grow, not gray, but yellow.

Sept. 5. Having walked through a quantity of desmodium under Ball's Hill, by the shore there, we found our pants covered with its seeds to a remarkable and amusing degree. It amounted to a kind of coat of mail. It was the event of our walk, and we were proud to wear this badge, as if he were the most distinguished who had the most on his clothes. My companion expressed a certain superstitious feeling about it, for he said he thought it would not be right to walk intentionally amid the desmodium so as to get more of the ticks on us, nor yet to pick them off, but they must be carried about till they are rubbed off accidentally. I saw that Nature's design was furthered even by his superstition.

Sept. 10. Leaving Lowell at 7 A.M. in the cars, I observed and admired the dew on a fine grass in the meadows, which was almost as white and silvery as frost when the rays of the newly risen sun fell on it. Some of it *was* probably the frost of the morning melted. I saw that this phenomenon was confined to one species of grass, which grew in narrow curving lines and small patches along the edges of the meadows or lowest ground,—a grass with very fine stems and branches, which held the dew like a cobweb,—a clear drop at the end and lesser drops or beads all along the fine branches and stems. It grows on the higher parts of the meadows, where other herbage is thin, and is the less apt to be cut; and, seen toward the sun not long after sunrise, it is very conspicuous and bright a quarter of a mile off, like frostwork. Call it dew-grass. I find its *hyaline* seed.

Almost every plant, however humble, has thus its day, and sooner or later becomes the characteristic feature of some part of the landscape or other.

Sept. 11. George Melvin came to tell me this forenoon that a strange animal was killed on Sunday, the 9th, near the north line of the town, and it was not known certainly what it was. From his description I judged it to be a Canada lynx. In the afternoon I went to see it.

Some weeks ago a little girl named Buttrick, who was huckleberrying near where the lynx was killed, was frightened by a wild animal leaping out of the bushes near her—*over* her, as she said—and bounding off. But no one then regarded her story. Also a Mr. Grimes, who lives in Concord just on the line, tells me that some month ago he heard from his house the loud cry of an animal in the woods northward, and told his wife that if he were in Canada he should say it was a bob-tailed cat. He had lived seven years in Canada and seen a number of this kind of animal. Also a neighbor of his, riding home in the night, had heard a similar cry. Jacob Farmer saw a strange animal at Bateman's Pond a year ago, which he thinks was this.

It was now skinned and the skin stuffed with hay, and the skull had been boiled, in order to be put into the head.

I measured the stuffed skin carefully. From the forehead (the nose pointing down) to end of tail, 3 feet 4½. [*Etc. for 3 pages.*]

Sept. 12. Very heavy rain to-day (equinoctial), raising the river suddenly. I have said, within a week, that the river would rise this fall because it did not at all in the spring, and now it rises. A very dark and stormy night (after it); shops but half open. Where the fence is not painted white I can see nothing, and go whistling for fear I run against some one, though there is little danger that any one will be out. I come against a stone post and bruise my knees; then stumble over a bridge,—being in the gutter. You walk with your hands out to feel the fences and trees.

Sept. 13. It is remarkable how slow people are to believe that there are any wild animals in their neighborhood. They who have seen this generally suppose that it got out of a menagerie; others that it strayed down from far north. At most they call it *Canada* lynx. In Willey's White Mountain book the same animal is spoken of as a terror to the hunter and called the "Siberian Lynx." What they call it I know not.

I do not think it necessary even to suppose it a straggler, but only very rare hereabouts. I have seen two lynxes that were killed between here and Salem since '27. Have heard of another killed in or near Andover.

Sept. 18. This is a beautiful day, warm but not too warm, a harvest day (I am going down the railroad causeway), the first unquestionable and conspicuous autumnal day, when the willows and button-bushes are a yellowed bower in parallel lines along the swollen and shining stream. The first autumnal tints (of red maples) are now generally noticed. The shrilling of the alder locust fills the air. A brightness as of spring is reflected from the green shorn fields. Both sky and earth are bright. The first clear blue and shining white (of clouds). Cornstalk-tops are stacked about the fields; potatoes are being dug; smokes are seen in the horizon. It is the season of agricultural fairs. If you are not happy to-day you will hardly be so to-morrow.

Sept. 23. I see on the top of the Cliffs to-day the dung of a fox, consisting of fur, with part of the jaw and one of the long rodent teeth of a woodchuck in it, and the rest of it huckleberry seeds with some whole berries. It is evident, then, that the fox eats huckleberries and so contributes very much to the dispersion of this shrub. To spread these seeds, Nature employs not only a great many birds but this restless ranger the fox. Like ourselves, he likes two courses, rabbit and huckleberries.

SEPT. 29. Another hard frost and a very cold day.

SEPT. 30. Frost and ice.

Oct. 1. Remarkable frost and ice this morning; quite a wintry prospect. The leaves of trees stiff and white at 7 A.M. I hear it was 21° this morning early. I do not remember such cold at this season. This is about the full of the moon (it fulled at 9 P.M. the 29th) in clear, bright moonlight nights. We have fine and bright but cold days after it.

Oct. 7. Probably the blueberry and huckleberry, amelanchier, and other bushes which spring up immediately when the woods are cut have been already planted and started annually, as the little oaks have. Nature thus keeps a supply of these plants in her nursery (*i.e.* under the larger wood), always ready for casualties, as fires, windfalls, and clearings by man. Birds and foxes, etc., are annually conveying the seed into the woods.

Rice reminds me that when the maples in a blueberry swamp have got up high, the blueberries die, and you have at length a maple wood clear of underwood.

Remarking to old Mr. Brabrook the other day on the abundance of the apples, "Yes," says he, "and fair as dollars too." That's the kind of beauty they see in apples.

If we have not attended to the subject, we may think that the activity of the animals is not enough to account for the annual planting of such extensive tracts; just as we wonder where all the flies and other insects come from in the spring, because we have not followed them into their winter quarters and counted them there. Yet nature does preserve and multiply the race of flies while we are inattentive and sleeping.

Many people have a foolish way of talking about small things, and apologize for themselves or another having attended to a small thing, having neglected their ordinary business and amused or instructed themselves by attending to a small thing; when, if the truth were known, their ordinary business was the small thing, and almost their whole lives were misspent, but they were such fools as not to know it.

Oct. 9. Though the red maples have not their common brilliancy on account of the very severe frost about the end of September, some are very interesting. I now see one small red maple which is all a pure yellow within and a bright red scarlet on its outer surface and prominences. It is a remarkably distinct painting of scarlet on a yellow ground. It is an indescribably beautiful contrast of scarlet and yellow. Another is yellow and green where this was scarlet and yellow, and in this case the bright and liquid green, now getting to be rare, is by contrast as charming a color as the scarlet.

I met in the street afterward a young lady who rowed up the river after me, and I could tell exactly where she plucked the maple twig which she held in her hand. It was the one so conspicuous for a quarter of a mile in one reach of the river.

I wonder that the very cows and the dogs in the street do not manifest a recognition of the bright tints about and above them. I saw a terrier dog glance up and down the painted street before he turned in at his master's gate, and I wondered what he thought of those lit trees,—if they did not touch his philosophy or spirits,— but I fear he had only his common doggish thoughts after all. He trotted down the yard as if it were a matter of course after all, or else as if he deserved it all.

Oct. 10. Went to a fire—or smoke—at Mrs. Hoar's. There is a slight blaze and more smoke. Two or three hundred men rush to the house, cut large holes in the roof, throw many hogsheads of water into it,—when a few pails full well directed would suffice,—and then they run off again, leaving your attic three inches deep with water, which is rapidly descending through the ceiling to the basement and spoiling all that can be spoiled, while a torrent is running down the stairways. They were very forward to put out the fire, but they take no pains to put out the water, which does far more damage. The first was amusement; the last would be mere work and utility. Why is there not a little machine invented to throw the water out of a house?

They are hopelessly cockneys everywhere who learn to swim with a machine. They take neither disease nor health, nay, nor life itself, the natural way. I see dumb-bells in the minister's study, and some of their dumbness gets into his sermons. Some travellers carry them round the world in their carpetbags. Can he be said to travel who requires still this exercise? A party of school-children had a picnic at the Easterbrooks Country the other day, and they carried bags of beans from their gymnasium to exercise with there. I cannot be interested in these extremely artificial amusements.

Oct. 13. I rejoice when the white oaks bear an abundant crop. I speak of it to many whom I meet, but I find few to sympathize with me. They seem to care much more for potatoes. The Indians say that many acorns are a sign of a cold winter. It is a cold fall at any rate.

The scientific differs from the poetic or lively description some-what as the photographs, which we so weary of viewing, from paintings and sketches, though this comparison is too favorable to science. After all, the truest description, and that by which another living man can most readily recognize a flower, is the unmeasured and eloquent one which the sight of it inspires. No scientific description will supply the want of this, though you should count and measure and analyze every atom that seems to compose it.

But unconsidered expressions of our delight which any natural object draws from us are something complete and final in themselves, since all nature is to be regarded as it concerns man; and who knows how near to absolute truth such unconscious affirmations may come? Which are the truest, the sublime conceptions of Hebrew poets and *seers*, or the guarded statements of modern geologists, which we must modify or unlearn so fast?

As they who were present early at the discovery of gold in California, and observed the sudden fall in its value, have most truly described that state of things, so it is commonly the old naturalists who first received American plants that describe them best. A scientific description is such as you would get if you should send out the scholars of the polytechnic school with all sorts of metres made and patented to take the measures for you of any natural object. In a sense you have got nothing new thus, for every object that we see mechanically is mechanically daguerreotyped on our eyes, but a true description growing out of the perception and appreciation of it is itself a new fact, never to be daguerreotyped, indicating the highest quality of the plant,—its relation to man,—of far more importance than any merely medicinal quality that it may possess, or be thought to-day to possess. There is a certainty and permanence about this kind of observation, too, that does not belong to the other, for every flower and weed has its day in the medical pharmacopœia, but the beauty of flowers is perennial in the taste of men.

Truly this is a world of vain delights. We think that men have a substratum of common sense but sometimes are peculiarly frivolous. But consider what a value is seriously and permanently attached to gold and so-called precious stones almost universally. Day and night, summer and winter, sick or well, in war and in peace, men speak of and believe in gold as a great treasure. By a thousand comparisons they prove their devotion to it. If wise men or true philosophers bore any considerable proportion to the whole number of men, gold would be treated with no such distinction. Men seriously and, if possible, religiously believe in and worship gold. They hope to earn golden opinions, to celebrate their golden wedding. They dream of the golden age. Now it is not its intrinsic beauty or value, but its rarity and arbitrarily attached value, that distinguishes gold. You would think it was the reign of shams.

The one description interests those chiefly who have not seen the thing; the other chiefly interests those who have seen it and are most familiar with it, and brings it home to the reader. We like to read a good description of no thing so well as of that which we already know the best, as our friend, or ourselves even. In proportion as we get and are near to our object, we do without the measured or scientific account, which is like the measure they take, or the description they write, of a man when he leaves his country, and insert in his passport for the use of the detective police of other countries. The men of science merely look at the object with sinister eye, to see if it corresponds with the passport, and merely make some trifling additional mark on its passport and let it go; but the real acquaintances and friends which it may have in foreign parts do not ask to see nor think of its passport.

Gerard has not only heard of and seen and raised a plant, but felt and smelled and tasted it, applying all his senses to it. You are not distracted from the thing to the system or arrangement. In the true natural order the order or system is not insisted on. Each is first, and each last. That which presents itself to us this moment occupies the whole of the present and rests on the very topmost point of the sphere, under the zenith. The species and individuals of all the natural kingdoms ask our attention and admiration in a round robin. We make straight lines, putting a captain at their head and a lieutenant at their tails, with sergeants and corporals all along the line and a flourish of trumpets near the beginning, insisting on a particular uniformity where Nature has made curves to which belongs their own sphere-music. It is indispensable for us to square her circles, and we offer our rewards to him who will do it.

Who describes the most familiar object with a zest and vividness of imagery as if he saw it for the first time, the novelty consisting not in the strangeness of the object, but in the new and clearer perception of it.

Oct. 16. P.M.—To White Pond and neighborhood.

As a consequence of the different manner in which trees which have winged seeds and those which have not are planted,—the former being blown together in one direction by the wind, the latter being dispersed irregularly by animals,—I observe that the former, as pines (which (the white) are said in the primitive wood to grow in communities), white birches, red maples, alders, etc., often grow in more or less regular rounded or oval or conical patches, as the seeds fell, while oaks, chestnuts, hickories, etc., simply form woods of greater or less extent whether by themselves or mixed; *i.e.*, they do not naturally spring up in an oval form (or elliptical) unless they derive it from the pines under which they were planted.

For example, take this young white pine wood half a dozen years old, which has sprung up in a pasture adjacent to a wood of oaks and pines mixed. It has the form of a broad crescent, or half-moon, with its diameter resting on the old wood near where a large white pine stood. It is true most such groves are early squared by our plows and fences, for we square these circles every day in our rude practice. And in the same manner often they fall in a sprout-land amid oaks, and I, looking from a hilltop, can distinguish in distant old woods still, of pine and oak mixed, these more exclusive and regular communities of pine, a dozen or more rods wide, while it is the oak commonly that fills up the irregular crevices, beside occupying extensive spaces itself. So it happens that, as the pines themselves and their fruit have a more regularly conical outline than deciduous trees, the groves they form also have.

Our wood-lots, of course, have a history, and we may often recover it for a hundred years back, though we *do* not. A small pine lot may be a side of such an oval, or a half, or a square in the inside with all the curving sides cut off by fences. Yet if we attended more to the history of our lots we should manage them more wisely.

I have come up here this afternoon to see Wheeler's dense white pine lot beyond the pond, that was cut off last winter, to know how the little oaks look in it. To my surprise and chagrin, I find that the fellow who calls himself its owner has burned it all over and sowed winter-rye here. He, no doubt, means to let it grow up again in a year or two, but he thought it would be clear gain if he could extract a little rye from it in the mean-while. What a fool! Here nature had got everything ready for this emergency, and kept them ready for many years,—oaks half a dozen years old or more, with fusiform roots full charged and tops already pointing sky-ward, only waiting to be touched off by the sun,—and he thought he knew better, and would get a little rye out of it first, which he could feel at once between his fingers, and so he burned it, and dragged his harrow over it. As if oaks would bide *his* time or come at his bidding. Or as if he preferred to have a pine or a birch wood here possibly half a century hence—for the land is "pine sick"—rather than an oak wood at once. So he trifles with nature. I am chagrined for him. That he should call himself an agriculturalist! He needs to have a guardian placed over him. A forest-warden should be appointed by the town. Overseers of poor husband-men.

Let us purchase a mass for his soul. A greediness that defeats its own ends.

As time elapses, and the resources from which our forests have been supplied fail, we shall of necessity be more and more convinced of the significance of the seed.

I see in a thick pitch pine wood half a dozen stout pine twigs five eighths of an inch thick that have been gnawed off with their plumes. Why?

The history of a wood-lot is often, if not commonly, *here*, a history of cross-purposes,—of steady and consistent endeavor on the part of Nature, of interference and blundering with a glimmering of intelligence at the eleventh hour on the part of the proprietor. The proprietor of wood-lots commonly treats Nature as an Irishman drives a horse,—by standing before him and beating him in the face all the way across a field.

Oct. 17. Hereabouts a pine wood, or even a birch wood, is no sooner established than the squirrels and birds begin to plant acorns in it. First the pines, then the oaks; and coniferous trees, geologists tell us, are older, as they are lower in the order of development,—were created before oaks.

I observe to-day a great many pitch pine plumes cut off by squirrels and strewn under the trees, as I did yesterday.*

While the man that killed my lynx (and many others) thinks it came out of a menagerie, and the naturalists call it the Canada lynx, and at the White Mountains they call it the Siberian lynx,—in each case forgetting, or ignoring, that it belongs here,—I call it the Concord lynx.

Oct. 18. I see spatter-dock pads and pontederia in that little pool at south end of Beck Stow's. How did they get there? There is no stream in this case? It was perhaps rather reptiles and birds than fishes, then. Indeed we might as well ask how they got anywhere, for all the pools and fields have been stocked thus, and we are not to suppose as many new creations as pools. This suggests to inquire how any plant came where it is,—how, for instance, the pools which were stocked with lilies before we were born or this town was settled, and ages ago, were so stocked, as well as those which we dug. I think that we are warranted only in supposing that the former was stocked in the same way as the latter, and that there was not a sudden new creation,—at least since the first; yet I have no doubt that peculiarities more or less considerable have thus been gradually produced in the lilies thus planted in various pools, in consequence of their various conditions, though they all came originally from one seed.

We find ourselves in a world that is already planted, but is also still being planted as at first. We say of some plants that they grow

---

*The next day (18th) I see twenty pine twigs, some three-plumed, at Beck Stow's, recently gnawed off and lying under one tree. This is to be seen now on all sides of the town. Why so? Saw the same last fall and before.

in wet places and of others that they grow in desert places. The truth is that their seeds are scattered almost everywhere, but here only do they succeed. Unless you can show me the pool where the lily was created, I shall believe that the oldest fossil lilies which the geologist has detected (if this is found fossil) originated in that locality in a similar manner to these of Beck Stow's. We see thus how the fossil lilies which the geologist has detected are dispersed, as well as these which we carry in our hands to church.

The development theory [*i.e., Darwin's, not Agassiz's*] implies a greater vital force in nature, because it is more flexible and accommodating, and equivalent to a sort of constant *new* creation.

Oct. 20. Edmund Hosmer tells me of a gray squirrel which he kept in his old (Everett) house; that he would go off to the woods every summer, and in the winter come back and into his cage, where he whirled the wire cylinder. He would be surprised to see it take a whole and large ear of corn and run out a broken window and up over the roof of the corn-barn with it, and also up the elms.

We have a kitten a third grown which often carries its tail almost flat on its back like a squirrel.

Oct. 22. Yet what is the character of our gratitude to these squirrels, these planters of forests? We regard them as vermin, and annually shoot and destroy them in great numbers, because—if we have any excuse—they sometimes devour a little of our Indian corn, while, perhaps, they are planting the nobler oak-corn (acorn) in its place. In various parts of the country an army of grown-up boys assembles for a squirrel hunt. They choose sides, and the side that kills the greatest number of thousands enjoys a supper at the expense of the other side, and the whole neighborhood rejoices. Would it not be far more civilized and humane, not to say godlike, to recognize once in the year by some significant symbolical ceremony the part which the squirrel plays, the great service it performs, in the economy of the universe?

Oct. 25. The thistles which I now see have their heads recurved, which at least saves their down from so great a soaking. But when I pull out the down, the seed is for the most part left in the receptacle (?), in regular order there, like the pricks in a thimble. The perfectly dry and bristly involucre which hedges them round, so repulsive externally, is very neat and attractive within,—as smooth and tender toward its charge as it is rough and prickly externally toward the foes that might do it injury. It is a hedge of imbricated thin and narrow leafets of a light-brown color, beautifully glossy like silk, a most fit receptacle for the delicate downy parachutes of the seed, a cradle lined with silk or satin. I know of no object more unsightly to a careless glance than an empty thistle-head, yet, if you examine it closely, it may remind you of the silk-lined cradle in which a prince was rocked. Thus that which seemed a mere brown and worn-out relic of the summer, sinking into the earth by the roadside, turns out to be a precious casket.

Oct. 30. Having seen this fall a great many pitch pine twigs which had been cut off and dropped under the trees by squirrels, I tried the other night while in bed to account for it. I began by referring it to their necessities, and, remembering my own experience, I said then it was done either for food, shelter, clothing, or fuel, but throwing out the last two, which they do not use, it was either for food or shelter. But I never see these twigs used in their nests. Hence I presume it was for food, and as all that I know them to eat on the pitch pine is its seeds, my swift conclusion was that they cut off these twigs in order to come at the cones and also to make them more portable. I am to-day convinced of this,—for I have been looking after it for a day or two. As usual, the ground under this grove is quite strewn with the twigs, but here is one eleven inches long and nearly half an inch thick cut off close below two closed cones, one cone-stem also being partly cut. Also, three or four rods west from this grove, in open land, I see three twigs which have been dropped close together. One is just two feet long and cut off where half an inch thick and more than one foot below three cones (two on one branch and one on another), and the cones are left. Another is still larger, and the other smaller, but their cones are gone. The greater part of the twigs have been cut off above the cones,—mere plumes.

So even the squirrels carry and spread the pine seed far over the fields. I suspect that they bury these cones like nuts. I have seen the cones collected ready to be carried off, where they did not live. It is remarkable to consider how rudely they strip and spoil the trees. It is remarkable how they carried some of these great twigs with their burden of cones.[*]

The fact that the lower limbs of pines growing within a wood always die shows how much they depend on light and air. They are only a green spiring top.

Oct. 31. Yes, these dense and stretching oak forests, whose withered leaves now redden and rustle on the hills for many a New England mile, were all planted by the labor of animals. For after some weeks of close scrutiny I cannot avoid the conclusion that our modern oak woods sooner or later spring up from an acorn, not where it has fallen from its tree, for that is the exception, but where it has been dropped or placed by an animal. Consider what a vast work these forest-planters are doing!

So far as our noblest hardwood forests are concerned, the animals, especially squirrels and jays, are our greatest and almost only benefactors. It is to them that we owe this gift. It is not in vain that the squirrels live in or about every forest tree, or hollow log, and every wall and heap of stones.

I first noticed the pitch pine twigs cut off by squirrels the 16th. Think how busy they were about that time in every pitch pine grove all over the State, cutting off the twigs and collecting the cones! While the farmer is digging his potatoes and gathering his corn he little thinks of this harvest of pine cones which the squirrel is gathering in the neighboring woods still more sedulously than himself.

I hear the sound of the flail in M. Miles's barn, and gradually draw near to it from the woods, thinking many things. I find that

---

[*]*Vide* Hosmer's gray squirrel.

the thresher is a Haynes of Sudbury, and he complains of the hard work and a lame back. Indeed, he cannot stand up straight. So all is not gold that glitters. This sound is not so musical after I have withdrawn. It was as well to have heard this music afar off. The floor, too, is uneven, and he pointed out one board more prominent on which he had broken two or three swingles.

Nov. 1. 2 P.M.—To Tommy Wheeler wood-lot.

A perfect Indian-summer day, and wonderfully warm. 72+ at 1 P.M. and probably warmer at two.

The butterflies are out again,—probably some new broods. I see the common yellow and two *Vanessa Antiopa*, and yellow-winged grasshoppers with blackish edges.

A striped snake basks in the sun amid dry leaves. Very much gossamer on the withered grass is shimmering in the fields, and flocks of it are sailing in the air.

Measure some pine stumps on Tommy Wheeler's land, about that now frosty hollow, cut as I judge from sprouts four years ago.

First the pitch pine:—

1	is	18½	inches	diameter	and has	145 (?)rings	
2		18	"	"	"	137	"
3		20	"	"	"	128	"
4		21	"	"	"	148	"
5		21	"	"	"	140	"
6		22¾	"	"	"	160+4	(Counted the last 64 at home)
7		20	"	"	"	167 or 168 (?)	
7		)141¼				7)1026 + 4	
Average	20					Average 147 + 1, or 148	

[*Very many such details and large tables of calculations fill the 80 pages of Thoreau's November 1860 Journal.*]

Nov. 5. I am struck by the fact that the more slowly trees grow at first, the sounder they are at the core, and I think that the same is true of human beings. We do not wish to see children precocious, making great strides in their early years like sprouts, producing a soft and perishable timber, but better if they expand slowly at first, as if contending with difficulties, and so are solidified and perfected. Such trees continue to expand with nearly equal rapidity to an extreme old age.

Nov. 10. How little there is on an ordinary map! How little, I mean, that concerns the walker and the lover of nature. Between those lines indicating roads is a plain blank space in the form of a square or triangle or polygon or segment of a circle, and there is naught to distinguish this from another area of similar size and form. Yet the one may be covered, in fact, with a primitive oak wood, like that of Boxboro, waving and creaking in the wind, such as may make the reputation of a county, while the other is a stretching plain with scarcely a tree on it. The waving woods, the dells and glades and green banks and smiling fields, the huge boulders, etc., etc., are not on the map, nor to be inferred from the map.

That grand old oak wood is just the most remarkable and memorable thing in Boxboro, and yet if there is a history of this town written anywhere, the history or even mention of this is probably altogether omitted, while that of the first (and may be last) parish is enlarged on.

What sort of cultivation, or civilization and improvement, is ours to boast of, if it turns out that, as in this instance, unhandselled nature is worth more even by our modes of valuation than our improvements are,—if we leave the land poorer than we found it? Is it good economy, to try it by the lowest standards, to cut down all our forests, if a forest will pay into the town treasury a greater tax than the farms which may supplant it,—if the oaks by steadily growing according to their nature leave our improvements in the rear?

How little we insist on truly grand and beautiful natural features! How many have ever heard of the Boxboro oak woods? How many have ever explored them? I have lived so long in this neighborhood and but just heard of this noble forest,—probably as fine an oak wood as there is in New England, only eight miles west of me.

A peculiarity of this, as compared with much younger woods, is that there is little or no underwood and you walk freely in every direction, though in the midst of a dense wood. You walk, in fact, *under* the wood.

Seeing this, I can realize how this country appeared when it was discovered. Such were the oak woods which the Indian threaded hereabouts.

Nov. 17. How they do things in West Acton. As we were walking through West Acton the other afternoon, on the main road, we saw a rock larger than a man could lift, lying in the road, exactly in the wheel-track, and were puzzled to tell how it came there, but supposed it had slipped off a drag,—yet we noticed that it was peculiarly black. Returning the same way in the twilight, when we had got within four or five rods of this very spot, looking up, we saw a man in the field, three or four rods on one side of that spot, running off as fast as he could. By the time he had got out of sight over the hill it occurred to us that he was blasting rocks and had just touched one off; so, at the eleventh hour, we turned about and ran the other way, and when we had gone a few rods, off went two blasts, but fortunately none of the rocks struck us. Some time after we had passed we saw the men returning. They looked out for themselves, but for nobody else. This is the way they do things in West Acton.

Nov. 21. Another finger-cold evening, which I improve in pulling my turnips—the usual amusement of such weather—before they shall be frozen in. It is worth the while to see how green and lusty they are yet, still adding to their stock of nutriment for another year; and between the green and also withering leaves it does me good to see their great crimson round or scalloped tops, sometimes quite above ground, they are so bold. They remind you of rosy cheeks in cool weather, and indeed there is a relationship. All kinds of harvestry, even pulling turnips when the first cold weather numbs your fingers, are interesting, if you have been the sower, and have not sown too many.

Got a section to-day of a white cedar railroad sleeper which I am told came from the eastward and was brought up from Charlestown. First count gives 254 rings; second, on opposite side, where the centre is less plain, 246 rings; average, 250. Its diameter is 16¼ inches, or nearly 31 rings to an inch. This is the oldest, as well as slowest-growing, tree that I have counted the rings of. I see other sleepers nearly as old. It may not have been the butt end of the log, or at any rate it must have been several years old before it reached the height at which it was cut, so that it must have begun to exist before the settlement of Jamestown. It was a flourishing young cedar of at least some fifteen summers when the Pilgrims came over. Thus the cars on our railroad, and all their passengers, roll over the trunks of trees *sleeping* beneath them which were planted years before the first white man settled in New England.

Nov. 22. This is a very beautiful November day,—a cool but clear, crystalline air, through which even the white pines with their silvery sheen are an affecting sight. It is a day to behold and to ramble over the hard (stiffening) and withered surface of the tawny earth. I rejoice in the bare, bleak, hard, and barren-looking surface of the tawny pastures, the firm outline of the hills, so convenient to walk over, and the air so bracing and wholesome. Though you are finger-cold toward night, and you cast a stone on to your first ice, and see the unmelted crystals under every bank, it is glorious November weather, and only November fruits are out. On some hickories you see a thousand black nuts against the sky.

You walk fast and far, and every apple left out is grateful to your invigorated taste. You enjoy not only the bracing coolness, but all the heat and sunlight that there is, reflected back to you from the earth. The sandy road itself, lit by the November sun, is beautiful.

Simply to see to a distant horizon through a clear air,—the fine outline of a distant hill or a blue mountain-top through some new vista,—this is wealth enough for one afternoon.

XXXIII.

Nov. 24. The first spitting of snow—a flurry or squall—from out a gray or slate-colored cloud that came up from the west. Though a slight touch, this was the first wintry scene of the season. The hands seek the warmth of the pockets, and fingers are so benumbed that you cannot open your jack-knife. The rabbits in the swamps enjoy it, as well as you. Methinks the winter gives them more liberty, like a night.

Nov. 25. Last night and to-day are very cold and blustering. Winter weather has come suddenly this year. The house was shaken by wind last night, and there was a general deficiency of bedclothes. This morning some windows were as handsomely covered with frost as ever in winter. I wear mittens or gloves and my greatcoat. There is much ice on the meadows now, the broken edges shining in the sun. Now for the phenomena of winter,—the red buds of the high blueberry and the purple berries of the smilax.

How is any scientific discovery made? Why, the discoverer takes it into his head first. He must all but see it.

How commonly you see pitch pines, white pines, and birches filling up a pasture, and, when they are a dozen or fifteen years old, shrub and other oaks beginning to show themselves, inclosing apple trees and walls and fences gradually and so changing the whole aspect of the region. These trees do not cover the whole surface equally at present, but are grouped very agreeably after natural laws which they obey. You remember, perhaps, that fifteen years ago there was not a single tree in this pasture,—not a germinating seed of one,—and now it is a pretty dense forest ten feet high. I confess that I love to be convinced of this inextinguishable vitality in Nature. I would rather that my body should be buried in a soil thus wide-awake than in a mere inert and dead earth.

Nov. 26. Of course it is the spirit in which you do a thing which makes it interesting, whether it is sweeping a room or pulling turnips. Peaches are unquestionably a very beautiful and palatable fruit, but the gathering of them for the market is not nearly so interesting as the gathering of huckleberries for your own use.

I anticipated the other day that if anybody should write the history of Boxboro, once a part of Stow, he would be pretty sure to omit to notice the most interesting thing in it—its forest—and lay all the stress on the history of its parish; and I find that I had conjectured rightly, for Mr. Gardner, after telling us who was his predecessor in the ministry and where he himself was settled, goes on to say: "As for any remarkables, I am of the mind there have been the fewest of any town of our standing in the Province.... I can't call to mind above one thing worthy of publick notice, and that is the grave of Mr. John Green," who, it appears, "was made . . . clerk of the exchequer" by Cromwell. "Whether he was excluded the Act of Oblivion or not I cannot tell," says Mr. Gardner. At any rate he tells us that he returned to New England, "lived and died, and lies buried in this place." I can assure Mr. Gardner that he was not excluded from the act of oblivion.

However, Boxboro was less peculiar for its woods a hundred years ago.

Nov. 29. You would say that some men had been tempted to live in this world at all only by the offer of a bounty by the general government—a bounty on living—the object of the governors being to create a nursery for their navy. I told such a man the other day that I had got a Canada lynx here in Concord, and his instant question was, "Have you got the reward for him?" What reward? Why, the ten dollars which the State offers. As long as I saw him he neither said nor thought anything about the lynx, but only about this reward. "Yes," said he, "this State offers ten dollars reward." You might have inferred that ten dollars was something rarer in his neighborhood than a lynx even, and he was anxious to see it on that account. I have thought that a lynx was a bright-eyed, four-legged, furry beast of the cat kind, very *current*, indeed, though its natural gait is by leaps. But he knew it to be a draught drawn by the cashier of the wildcat bank on the State treasury, payable at sight. Then I reflected that the first money was of leather, or a whole creature (whence *pecunia*, from *pecus*, a herd), and, since leather was at first furry, I easily understood the connection between a lynx and ten dollars, and found that all money was traceable right back to the original wildcat bank. But the fact was that, instead of receiving ten dollars for the lynx which I had got, I had paid away some dollars in order to get him. So, you see, I was away back in a gray antiquity behind the institution of money,—further than history goes.

So you will see that all prosaic people who possess only the commonest sense, who believe strictly in this kind of wealth, are speculators in fancy stocks and continually cheat themselves, but poets and all discerning people, who have an object in life and know what they want, speculate in real values. The mean and low values of anything depend on its convertibility into something else—*i.e.* have nothing to do with its intrinsic value.

We hear a good deal said about moonshine by so-called practical people, and the next day, perchance, we hear of their failure, they having been dealing in fancy stocks; but there really never is any moonshine of this kind in the practice of poets and philosophers; there never are any hard times or failures with them, for they deal with permanent values.

Dec. 3. Talking with Walcott and Staples to-day, they declared that John Brown did wrong. When I said that I thought he was right, they agreed in asserting that he did wrong because he threw his life away, and that no man had a right to undertake anything which he knew would cost him his life. I inquired if Christ did not foresee that he would be crucified if he preached such doctrines as he did, but they both, though as if it was their only escape, asserted that they did not believe that he did. Upon which a third party threw in, "You do not think that he had so much foresight as Brown." Of course, they as good as said that, if Christ *had* foreseen that he would be crucified, he would have "backed out." Such are the principles and the logic of the mass of men.

It is to be remembered that by good deeds or words you encourage yourself, who always have need to witness or hear them.

Dec. 4. The first snow, four or five inches, this evening.

Talk about slavery! It is not the peculiar institution of the South. It exists wherever men are bought and sold, wherever a man allows himself to be made a mere thing or a tool, and surrenders his inalienable rights of reason and conscience. It exists in the Northern States, and I am reminded by what I find in the newspapers that it exists in Canada. I never yet met with, or heard of, a judge who was not a slave of this kind, and so the finest and most unfailing weapon of injustice. He fetches a slightly higher price than the black man only because he is a more valuable slave.

It appears that a colored man killed his would-be kidnapper in Missouri and fled to Canada. The blood-hounds have tracked him to Toronto and now demand him of her judges. From all that I can learn, they are playing their parts like judges. They are servile, while the poor fugitive in their jail is free in spirit at least.

This is what a Canadian writes to the *New York Tribune*: "Our judges may be compelled to render a judgment adverse to the prisoner. Depend upon it, they will not do it unless *compelled* [his italics]. And then the poor fellow will be taken back, and probably burned to death by the brutes of the South." Compelled! By whom? Does God compel them? or is it some other master whom they serve? Can't they hold out a little longer against the *tremendous pressure*? Will this excuse avail them when the real day of judgment comes? They have not to fear the slightest bodily harm: no one stands over them with a stick or a knife even. They have at the worst only to resign their places and not a mouse will squeak about it. And yet they are likely to assist in tying this victim to the stake!

C. says that Walden was first frozen over on the 16th December.

Part Three

THE CONSTANTLY
DESCENDING ROUTE

On March 22, 1861, Thoreau wrote to his friend Daniel Ricketson: "I took a severe cold about the 3d of December, which at length resulted in a kind of bronchitis, so that I have been confined to the house ever since." There was an eighteen-day gap in his Journal after December 4, resuming with the first pair of entries which follow, and he was never able to return to his usual walking and writing practice. His illness continued to worsen; he traveled to Minnesota in the summer of 1861 in a last attempt to improve his health, and all ten of his Journal entries from after he returned are included here. His final months were spent cross-referencing the Journal, compiling lists and charts, and writing and revising his last essays, the books The Maine Woods *and* Cape Cod, *and the work that would eventually be published as* Faith in a Seed *and* Wild Fruits. *He died on May 6, 1862.*

XXXIII, CONTINUED

DEC. 22. This evening and night, the second important snow, there having been sleighing since the 4th, and now,—

DEC. 23.—there is seven or eight inches of snow at least. Larks were about our house the middle of this month.

Dec. 30. Sunday. I saw the crows a week ago perched on the swamp white oaks over the road just beyond Wood's Bridge, and many acorns and bits of bark and moss, evidently dropped or knocked off by them, lay on the snow beneath. One sat within twenty feet over my head with what looked like a piece of acorn in his bill. To-day I see that they have carried these same white oak acorns, cups and all, to the ash tree by the riverside, some thirty rods southeast, and dropped them there.

I find that in Bomare's "Dictionnaire Raisonné" the *Vitis Idæa* (of many kinds) is called "raisin des bois." Our word "berry," according to lexicographers, is from the Saxon *beria*, a grape or cluster of grapes; but it must acquire a new significance here, if a new word is not substituted for it.

According to Father Rasles' Dictionary, the Abenaki word for bluets was, fresh, *satar* (in another place *saté, tar*); dry, *sakisatar.*

Jan. 3. What are the natural features which make a township handsome? A river, with its waterfalls and meadows, a lake, a hill, a cliff or individual rocks, a forest, and ancient trees standing singly. Such things are beautiful; they have a high use which dollars and cents never represent. If the inhabitants of a town were wise, they would seek to preserve these things, though at a considerable expense; for such things educate far more than any hired teachers or preachers, or any at present recognized system of school education. I do not think him fit to be the founder of a state or even of a town who does not foresee the use of these things, but legislates chiefly for oxen, as it were.

Thank God, men cannot as yet fly, and lay waste the sky as well as the earth! We are safe on that side for the present.

We cut down the few old oaks which witnessed the transfer of the township from the Indian to the white man, and commence our museum with a cartridge-box taken from a British soldier in 1775!

He pauses at the end of his four or five thousand dollars, and then only fears that he has not got enough to carry him through,— that is, merely to pay for what he will eat and wear and burn and for his lodging for the rest of his life. But, pray, what does he stay here for? Suicide would be cheaper. Indeed, it would be nobler to found some good institution with the money and then cut your throat.

As boys are sometimes required to show an excuse for being absent from school, so it seems to me that men should show some excuse for being here.

I noticed a week or two ago that one of my white pines, some six feet high with a thick top, was bent under a great burden of very moist snow, almost to the point of breaking, so that an ounce more of weight would surely have broken it. As I was confined to the house by sickness, and the tree had already been four or five days in that position, I despaired of its ever recovering itself; but, greatly to my surprise, when, a few days after, the snow had melted off, I saw the tree almost perfectly upright again.

It is evident that trees will bear to be bent by this cause and at this season much more than by the hand of man. Probably the less harm is done in the first place by the weight being so gradually applied, and perhaps the tree is better able to bear it at this season of the year.

Jan. 14. Thus we should say that oak forests are produced by a kind of accident, *i.e.* by the failure of animals to reap the fruit of their labors. Yet who shall say that they have not a fair knowledge of the value of their labors—that the squirrel when it plants an acorn, or the jay when it lets one slip from under its foot, has not a transient thought for its posterity?

Possibly here, a thousand years hence, every oak will know the human hand that planted it.

How many of the botanist's *arts* and inventions are thus but the rediscovery of a lost art, *i.e.* lost to him here or elsewhere!

FEB. 8. Coldest day yet; −22° at least (all we can read), at 8 A.M., and, as I can learn, not above −6° all day.

Feb. 15. A little thunder and lightning late in the afternoon. I see two flashes and hear two claps.

A kitten is so flexible that she is almost double; the hind parts are equivalent to another kitten with which the fore part plays. She does not discover that her tail belongs to her till you tread upon it.

How eloquent she can be with her tail! Its sudden swellings and vibrations! Then what a delicate hint she can give! passing perhaps underneath, as you sit at table, and letting the tip of her tail just touch your legs, as much as to say, I am here and ready for that milk or meat, though she may not be so forward as to look round at you when she emerges.

Only skin-deep lies the feral nature of the cat, unchanged still. I just had the misfortune to rock on to our cat's leg, as she was lying playfully spread out under my chair. Imagine the sound that arose, and which was excusable; but what will you say to the fierce growls and flashing eyes with which she met me for a quarter of an hour thereafter? No tiger in its jungle could have been savager.

March 11. C. says that Walden is almost entirely open to-day, so that the lines on my map would not strike any ice, but that there is ice in the deep cove. It will be open then the 12th or 13th. This is earlier than I ever knew it to open. Why, then, should Walden have broken up thus early? for it froze over early and the winter was steadily cold up to February at least. I think it must have been because the ice was uncommonly covered with snow, just as the earth was, and so, as there was little or no frost in the earth, the ice also was thin, and it did not increase upward with snow ice as much as usual because there was no thaw or rain at all till February 2d, and then very little. According to all accounts there has been no skating on Walden the past winter on account of the snow. It was unusually covered with snow. This shows how many things are to be taken into account in judging of such a pond. I have not been able to go to the pond the past winter.

March 18. You can't read any genuine history—as that of Herodotus or the Venerable Bede—without perceiving that our interest depends not on the subject but on the man,—on the manner in which he treats the subject and the importance he gives it. A feeble writer and without genius must have what he thinks a great theme, which we are already interested in through the accounts of others, but a genius—a Shakespeare, for instance—would make the history of his parish more interesting than another's history of the world.

Wherever men have lived there is a story to be told, and it depends chiefly on the story-teller or historian whether that is interesting or not. You are simply a witness on the stand to tell what you know about your neighbors and neighborhood.

March 22. Botanists talk about the possibility and impossibility of plants being naturalized here or there. But what plants have not been naturalized? Of course only those which grow to-day exactly where the original plant of the species was created. It is true we do not know whether one or many plants of a given kind were originally created, but I think it is the most reasonable and simple to suppose that only one was,—to suppose as little departure as possible from the existing order of things. They commenced to spread themselves at once and by whatever means they possessed as far as they could, and they are still doing so. Many were common to Europe and America at the period of the discovery of the latter country, and I have no doubt that they had naturalized themselves in one or the other country. This is more philosophical than to suppose that they were independently created in each.

I suppose that most have seen—at any rate I can show them—English cherry trees, so called, coming up not uncommonly in our woods and under favorable circumstances becoming full-grown trees. Now I think that they will not pretend that they came up there in the same manner before this country was discovered by the whites. But, if cherry trees come up by spontaneous generation, why should they not have sprung up there in that way a thousand years ago as well as now?

If the pine seed is spontaneously generated, why is it not so produced in the Old World as well as in America?

APRIL 23. Think I hear bay-wings. Toads ring.

May 12. SET OUT FOR MINNESOTA *via* Worcester.

May 13. Worcester to Albany.
The leafing is decidedly more advanced in western Massachusetts than in eastern. Apple trees are greenish. Red elder-berry is apparently just beginning to bloom.

Put up at the Delavan House. Not so good as costly.

May 15. To Niagara Falls. Sight of the Rapids from the Bridge like the sea off Cape Cod,—most imposing sight as yet. The great apparent height of the waves tumbling over the immense ledges—at a distance; while the water view is broad and boundless in that direction, as if you were looking out to sea, you are so low. Yet the distances are very deceptive; the most distant billow was scarcely more than a quarter of a mile off, though it appeared two miles or more.

This is quite a town, with numerous hotels and stores, and with paved streets; and I imagine the Falls will soon be surrounded by a city. I pay a dollar a day here. The population of Niagara Falls village is about five thousand.

May 21. Detroit to Chicago. Very level to Ypsilanti, then hilly to Ann Arbor, then less hilly to Lake Michigan. All hard wood, or no evergreen, except some white pine when we struck Lake Michigan, on the sands from the Lake, and some larch before. Phlox, varying from white to bluish, and painted cup deep scarlet, and also yellow (?) or was this wallflower (?) all very common through Michigan, and the former, at least, earlier. The prevailing shade-tree in Chicago is the cottonwood.

May 23. From Chicago to Dunleith ?? very level the first twenty miles; then considerably more undulating; the greatest rolling prairie without trees is just beyond Winnebago. The last forty miles in the northwest of Illinois quite hilly. The Mississippi causes backwater in the Galena River for eight miles back. The water is high now; the thin woods flooded, with open water behind. See the marsh pink and apples on a flowered, apple-like tree (thorn-like) through Illinois, which may be the Pyrus coronaria. The distances on the prairie are deceptive; a stack of wheat-straw looks like a hill in the horizon, a quarter or half-mile off,—it stands out so bold and high.

May 24. Up river,—the river, say sixty rods wide, or three-quarters of a mile between the bluffs. Broad, flooded, low intervale covered with the willow in bloom (twenty feet high, rather slender), and probably other kinds—elms and white maple and cottonwood. The bluffs are (say) one hundred and fifty to two hundred feet high. Rarely is there room for a village at the base of the cliffs. The birds are kingfishers, small ducks, swallows, jays, etc. Passengers land on the shore oftentimes with a plank. Occasionally a little lonely house stands on a flat or slope, often deserted. The river banks are in their primitive condition between the towns,—which is almost everywhere.

May 26. Sunday. Breakfast at the "American House" in St. Paul, and come on by stage in the rain nine miles to St. Anthony, over the prairie,—the road muddy and sandy. At St. Paul they dig their building stone out of the cellar; but it is apparently poor stuff.

St. Anthony was settled about 1847; Minneapolis in 1851. Its main streets are the unaltered prairie, with bur and other oaks left standing. The roads on the prairie are a mere trail, more or less broad and distinct.

Going over a low hill which had its wood cut off a year or two since (and the fire had run over it afterward), I stooped to pluck a flower, and smelled the spring fragrance I have so often perceived here, but stronger and nearer than ever. So, going on and breaking off plants that were freshly leafed and vigorously growing, and smelling at them, I found at last a square-stemmed one which yielded the strong anise scent that I had noticed, especially when bruised. But then it was far from being so agreeable as when perceived floating in the air. This seems to be the *Lophanthus anisatus* or *scrophulariafolius*, which must yield the fragrance mentioned. Parry calls it "a characteristic northwestern species."

June 17, six P.M. Start up the Minnesota River in the *Frank Steele.* River valley till nine P.M., very broad between the bluffs and hills; banks some six feet high, with much handsome but weedy grass, mixed with roses; but soon sloping to low, wet, and reedy meadows or shallow lagoons behind the river, which is some ten rods wide, fringed with willows (black). The large trees occasionally were cottonwood and elm. The cottonwood is shaped somewhat like an ash. At nine P.M. we are near Stanhope. At five A.M. we are said to be in the big woods; the wood all alive with pigeons, and they flying across our course. The river is often only eight rods wide, and quite snaggy. About 7.30 we pass a beautiful open intervale of native grass on the right. Many large turtle-tracks on shore; many erigerons in the grass. The black willows are often quite tall (thirty-five feet) and slender, and straight too. The small Salix longifolia beneath it. Very crooked river; acres of roses in the intervale. Swallows, kingfishers, blue jays, and warbling vireos along the shores. Grapevines in blossom climbing on a cottonwood. We often strike the shore with our stern, or stop and back to get round snags and bars. Muddy-looking water, with soft-shelled and snapping turtles in it. See a turkey-buzzard and blue herons, and in the river some young ducks. The long-leaved willow is common, and there is a dense growth of upright weeds.

A regular council was held at Redwood with the Indians, who had come in on their ponies; and speeches were made on both sides through an interpreter, quite in the described mode; the Indians, as usual, having the advantage in point of truth and earnestness, and therefore of eloquence. The most prominent chief was named Little Crow. They were quite dissatisfied with the white man's treatment of them, and probably have reason to be so. This council was to be continued for two or three days,—the payments to be made the second day; and another payment, to other bands a little higher up, on the Yellow Medicine, a tributary of the Minnesota, a few days thereafter. In the afternoon the half-naked Indians performed a dance at the request of the Governor, for our amusement and their own benefit. Then we took leave of them, and of the officials who had come to treat with them. In the dance were thirty men dancing and twelve musicians with drums, while others struck their arrows against their bows. The dancers blew some flutes, and kept good time, moving their feet or their shoulders, sometimes one, sometimes both. They wear no shirts. Five bands of Indians came in, and were feasted on an ox cut into five parts, one for each band.

Indian strike-fire. Take a little punk,—the Illinois man says from the white maple, and hold it flat against a flint; then strike across the edge with a steel ring, and put the ignited punk on or in the pipe.

[*June 23*, Red Wing.] What is the upright, alternate, entire, elliptic-leaved, and sessile-leaved plant, considerably hairy, with six petals (?) white, no sepals, six stamens and six styles, about one-third of an inch in diameter, on Barn Bluff? What the orobanche-like plant, *Aphyllon fasciculatum*, on the edge of the bluff? the same six-sepalled, grassy-leaved plant (Zygadenus) as at the Redwood prairie. Colchicum and mints; Melanthium, in the next wet place, on the prairie, and the dry top of the bluff. On this top a small, pale pur-plish or pale violet lobelia, with toothed leaves. On the bluff top, perhaps the green milkweed; the wild red cherry, with fruit partly in a raceme: the pulsatilla still in bloom. Probably the same lark-spur as up in Minnesota. Lepidium one of the commonest weeds about in the towns and on the hills.

Milwaukee, of all the settled places, has the best harbor on Lake Michigan. There are shoals and rocks up the lake, but good harbors at Traverse Bay and behind islands on the northeast side. The lake is ninety miles wide and we cannot see across it; but we see the land loom sometimes on each side, from our steamer in the middle. At ten in the morning of the 29th we enter the Carp River. We had passed the Manitou Islands in the morning, on the left, and saw the Fox Island in the offing. Ran out of Carp River and left there at noon, steering N. by W. to Beaver or Mormon Island, with its fishing huts and Mormon homes, and leaving there at evening we reached Mackinaw at two A.M. on June 30.

According to Parker's History of Minnesota, there were but three white families in St. Paul in 1847; in the spring of 1857 there were ten thousand inhabitants. A St. Paul writer calls the Redwood In-dian wigwams, "tepees," and thinks there were five hundred Indi-ans there at the time of our visit; they danced the "Monkey Dance." Waconta was there, but the principal speaker was Red Owl.

On June 1, I copied from the Annals of the Minnesota Histori-cal Society for 1853, at St. Paul, the following (No. 4.): "Previous to the year 1695, the canoe laden with trinkets, tobacco, and knives had entered the Minnesota, or 'sky-tinted' River; and in 1700 trading houses were erected on the banks of the Mankato or 'Blue Earth.'" Professor Keating was the historian of Long's Expedition to the Minnesota and Red Rivers in 1823, and is said to have written an interesting account of the Dakota Indians in it. Their principal chief was or "Sky-man"; another chief of this band was called, "My Head Aches." John W. Bond says that the Mississippi generally closes in December early, and opens the latter part of March. The latter part of May and early in June is the usual seeding-time. They are thus considerably later than we are in Concord. "The summer here is very cool and pleasant, with a fine breeze at all times, blowing mostly from the west, southwest and south." In the Annals of the same Society for 1856, Professor Neill of Minnesota says: "The discoverer of the stream of this name (Minnesota) was Le Sueur, and in the first map that delineates the stream, which was issued in France more than a century ago, it is marked as the 'Minisota.' This is a Dakota word, and means as above indicated, 'sky-colored.' All waterfalls in the Dakota tongue are called 'Ha-ha'—never 'Minne-ha-ha' (as Longfellow has it). The 'h' has a strong guttural sound. The word is applied because of the curling of the waters. The verb 'I-ha-ha' primarily means to curl,—secondarily, to laugh, because of the curling motion of the mouth in laughter."

This (October 5) is a rainy or drizzling day at last, and the robins and sparrows are more numerous in the yard and about the house than ever. They swarm on the ground where stood the heap of weeds which was burned yesterday, picking up the seeds which rattled from it. Why should these birds be so much more numerous about the house such a day as this? I think of no other reason than because it is darker and fewer people are moving about to frighten them. Our little mountain-ash is all alive with them. A dozen robins on it at once, busily reaching after and plucking the berries, actually make the whole tree shake. There are also some little birds (I think purple finches) with them. A robin will swallow half a dozen berries, at least, in rapid succession before it goes off, and apparently it soon comes back for more.

The reason why naturalists make so little account of color is because it is so insignificant to them; they do not understand it. But the lover of flowers or animals makes very much of color. To a fancier of cats it is not indifferent whether one be black or gray, for the color expresses *character*.

Prescott is not inclined to go to the wars again (October, '61), and so Concord has no company to represent her at present. Cyrus Warren thinks that Derby, the first lieutenant (and butcher that was), would do for captain as well as Prescott, and adds, as his principal qualification, "There is n't one in the company can cut up a crittur like him."

Henry Mitchell of the Coast Survey (page 317) has invented a new kind of pile, to be made of some heavy and strong wood and "so cut that the lower portion of it, for a space of six or eight feet, presents the appearance of a number of inverted frustums of cones, placed one above another." When this is swayed to and fro by the waves, instead of being loosened and washed out, it sinks deeper and deeper. This, as Professor Bache (in Coast Survey Report for 1859, page 30) says, "is a device borrowed from nature, he [Mitchell] having observed that certain seed vessels, by virtue of their forms, bury themselves in the earth when agitated by wind or water." No seeds are named, but they must be similar to the seed of the porcupine grass of the West.

Young Macey, who has been camping on Monadnock this summer, tells me that he found one of my spruce huts made last year in August, and that as many as eighteen, reshingling it, had camped in it while he was there.

See a large hornets' nest on a maple (September 29), the *half immersed* leaves turned scarlet.

Four little kittens just born; lay like stuffed skins of kittens in a heap, with pink feet; so flimsy and helpless they lie, yet blind, without any stiffness or ability to stand.

Edward Lord Herbert says in his autobiography, "It is well known to those that wait in my chamber, that the shirts, waistcoats, and other garments I wear next my body, are sweet, beyond what either easily can be believed, or hath been observed in any else, which sweetness also was found to be in my breath above others, before I used to take tobacco."

The kitten can already spit at a fortnight old, and it can mew from the first, though it often makes the motion of mewing without uttering any sound.

The cat about to bring forth seeks out some dark and secret place for the purpose, not frequented by other cats.

The kittens' ears are at first nearly concealed in the fur, and at a fortnight old they are mere broad-based triangles with a side foremost. But the old cat is ears for them at present, and comes running hastily to their aid when she hears them mew and licks them into contentment again. Even at three weeks the kitten cannot fairly walk, but only creeps feebly with outspread legs. But thenceforth its ears visibly though gradually lift and sharpen themselves.

At three weeks old the kitten begins to walk in a staggering and creeping manner and even to play a little with its mother, and, if you put your ear close, you may hear it purr. It is remarkable that it will not wander far from the dark corner where the cat has left it, but will instinctively find its way back to it, probably by the sense of touch, and will rest nowhere else. Also it is careful not to venture too near the edge of a precipice, and its claws are ever extended to save itself in such places. It washes itself somewhat, and assumes many of the attitudes of an old cat at this age. By the disproportionate size of its feet and head and legs now it reminds you of a lion.

I saw it scratch its ear to-day, probably for the first time; yet it lifted one of its hind legs and scratched its ear as effectually as an old cat does. So this is instinctive, and you may say that, when a kitten's ear first itches, Providence comes to the rescue and lifts its hind leg for it. You would say that this little creature was as perfectly protected by its instinct in its infancy as an old man can be by his wisdom. I observed when she first noticed the figures on the carpet, and also put up her paws to touch or play with surfaces a foot off. By the same instinct that they find the mother's teat before they can see they scratch their ears and guard against falling.

After a violent easterly storm in the night, which clears up at noon (November 3, 1861), I notice that the surface of the railroad causeway, composed of gravel, is singularly marked, as if stratified like some slate rocks, on their edges, so that I can tell within a small fraction of a degree from what quarter the rain came. These lines, as it were of stratification, are perfectly parallel, and straight as a ruler, diagonally across the flat surface of the causeway for its whole length. Behind each little pebble, as a protecting boulder, an eighth or a tenth of an inch in diameter, extends northwest a ridge of sand an inch or more, which it has protected from being washed away, while the heavy drops driven almost horizontally have washed out a furrow on each side, and on all sides are these ridges, half an inch apart and perfectly parallel.

All this is perfectly distinct to an observant eye, and yet could easily pass unnoticed by most. Thus each wind is self-registering.

TITLES IN SERIES

*For a complete list of titles, visit www.nyrb.com or write to:
Catalog Requests, NYRB, 435 Hudson Street, New York, NY 10014*